ADVANCES
OLD FRISIAN PH

AMSTERDAMER BEITRÄGE ZUR ÄLTEREN GERMANISTIK

Begründet von
Cola Minis†

In Verbindung mit
A.D. Kylstra, A.H. Touber

herausgegeben von
Erika Langbroek, Arend Quak
und Annelies Roeleveld

Band 64 — 2007

Estrikken / Ålstråke 80

Amsterdam - New York, NY 2007

ADVANCES IN OLD FRISIAN PHILOLOGY

Edited by
Rolf H. Bremmer Jr.
Stephen Laker
Oebele Vries

Anschrift der Redaktion:

Prof. Dr. Arend Quak
Instituut voor Oudgermanistiek
Scandinavisch Seminarium
Spuistraat 134
1012 VB Amsterdam

The reproduction on p.72 appears by kind permission of the Universiteitsbibliotheek, Rijksuniversiteit Groningen

Estrikken / Ålstråke
Teksten en stúdzjes op it mêd fan de Fryske taal en skriftekennisse, foar it Frysk Ynstitút RU Grins útjûn fan 'e Stifting FFYRUG / Takste än unersäkinge awt fälj foon e Frasch späke- än literatuurwaasenschap, ütdänj foont Feek Frasch Filologii foon e CAU önj Kil

The paper on which this book is printed meets the requirements of "ISO 9706: 1994, Information and documentation - Paper for documents - Requirements for permanence".

ISSN: 0165-7305
ISBN-13: 978-90-420-2181-5

Printed in The Netherlands

Contents

Abbreviations of frequently used publications

ABäG	*Amsterdamer Beiträge zur älteren Germanistik*
AR	Altfriesische Rechtsquellen
Approaches	*Approaches to Old Frisian Philology*, ed. R. H. Bremmer Jr, T. S. B. Johnston and O. Vries (Amsterdam, Atlanta, GA, and Groningen, 1998) [= *ABäG* 49, *Estrikken* 72]
Aspects	*Aspects of Old Frisian Philology*, ed. R. H. Bremmer Jr, G. van der Meer and O. Vries (Amsterdam, Atlanta, GA, and Groningen, 1990) [= *ABäG* 31/32, *Estrikken* 69]
BGdSL	*Beiträge zur Geschichte der deutschen Sprache und Literatur*
Handbuch / Handbook	*Handbuch des Friesischen / Handbook of Frisian Studies*, ed. H. H. Munske (Tübingen, 2001)
IB	*It Beaken. Tydskrift fan de Fryske Akademy*
IF	*Indogermanische Forschungen*
MGH	Monumenta Germaniae Historica
NW	*Niederdeutsches Wort*
OTR	Oudfries(ch)e Taal- en Rechtsbronnen
PL	Patrologia Latina
QF	Quellen und Forschungen zur Sprach- und Kulturgeschichte der germanischen Völker
Reallexikon	*Reallexikon der Germanischen Altertumkunde*, ed. J. Hoops *et al.*, 2nd edn, 34 vols. (Berlin, 1968–2007)
TNTL	*Tijdschrift voor Nederlands(ch)e Taal en Letterkunde*
TRG	*Tijdschrift voor Rechtsgeschiedenis* (*Revue d'histoire du droit / Legal History Review*)
UW	*Us Wurk. Tydskrift foar Frisistyk*
ZfdA	*Zeitschrift für deutsches Altertum und deutsche Literatur*
ZfdP	*Zeitschrift für deutsche Philologie*

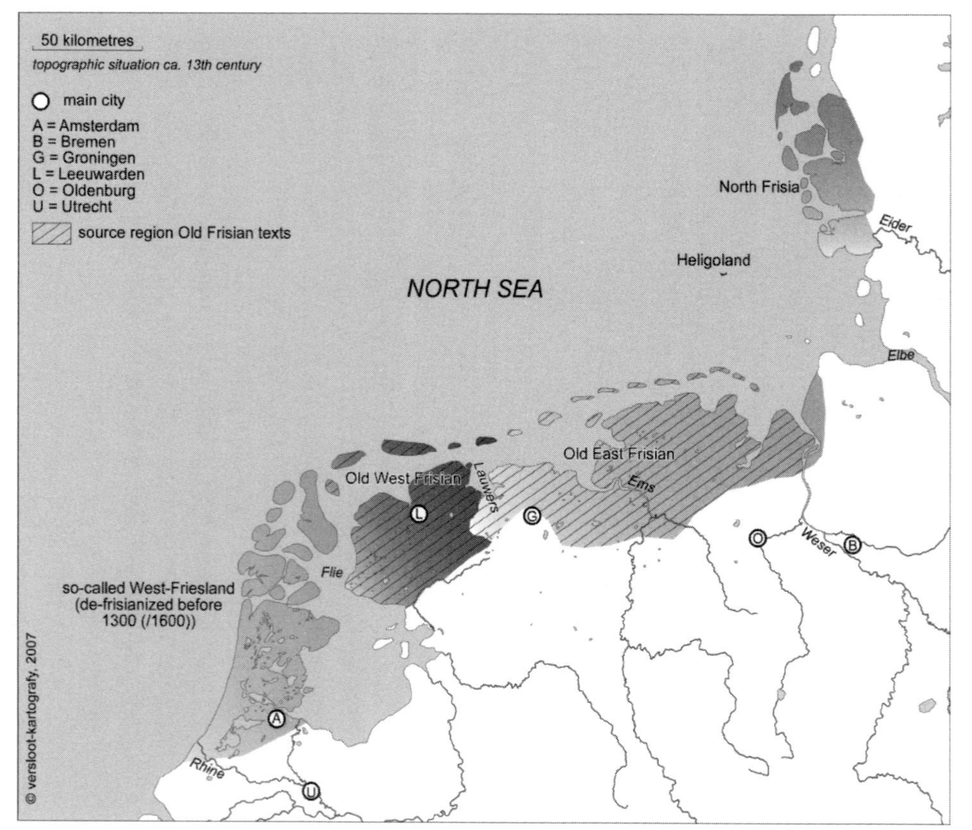

50 kilometres
topographic situation ca. 13th century
main city
A = Amsterdam
B = Bremen
G = Groningen
L = Leeuwarden
O = Oldenburg
U = Utrecht
source region Old Frisian texts
NORTH SEA
North Frisia
Eider
Heligoland
Elbe
Old East Frisian
Old West Frisian
Lauwers
Ems
Weser
Flie
so-called West-Friesland
(de-frisianized before
1300 (/1600))
Rhine
© versloot-kartografy, 2007

Old Frisian Philology: Along the Road

This volume is the third in a series of studies devoted to Old Frisian language, literature and (cultural) history, the sum of which is encapsulated in the time-honoured term 'philology'.[1] What makes these volumes special is that they bring together between their covers a group of beginning as well as established scholars who are either specialized (or going to be) in the discipline of Old Frisian philology or in disciplines adjacent to it. Such an unexpected company creates an opportunity for a great deal of dialogue from which Old Frisian studies will certainly profit, but which may also have its effects in the neighbouring disciplines. Indeed, references in the present volume to the previous two illustrate that the potential for a fruitful discussion has been explored. In what follows, a brief overview of the most important monograph publications in the field since 1998 will be presented.[2]

One of the most outstanding feats in the study of Frisian during the last decade has been the publication of the *Handbuch des Friesischen / Handbook of Frisian Studies* (Tübingen, 2001).[3] The first steps to realize this important handbook were taken by Horst H. Munske in 1994, and under his guidance, with the support of an editorial board, the length and breadth of Frisian studies were treated in seventy-nine encyclopaedic articles by forty-five authors from the United Kingdom, the Netherlands, Germany and Denmark. To be sure, the handbook is not confined to Old Frisian, but the significant role which this phase of the Frisian language has played in scholarly explorations is brought out by the fact that almost half of the

---

1 The previous ones are: *Aspects of Old Frisian Philology*, ed. R. H. Bremmer, G. Van der Meer and O. Vries, *ABäG* 31–32 / Estrikken 69 (Amsterdam, Atlanta, GA, and Groningen, 2000; repr. 2007) and *Approaches to Old Frisian Philology*, ed. R. H. Bremmer, T. S. B. Johnston and O. Vries, *ABäG* 49 / Estrikken 72 (Amsterdam and Atlanta, GA, 1998).

2 This overview is intended as a sequel to my 'Old Frisian Philology: The Way Ahead', *Approaches*, vii–xv. For a regular stock-taking of all the publications pertaining to Old Frisian, see the sources mentioned in footnote 1 of that article.

3 I know of the following reviews: A. Petersen, *Nordfriesisches Jahrbuch* 38 (2002), 217–19; S. Dyk, *UW* 52 (2003), 77–87, with a rejoinder by H. H. Munske, *UW* 53 (2004), 55–58; M. Görlach, *Sociolinguistica* 17 (2003), 182–84; A. Liberman, *NOWELE* 45 (2004), 101–08; M. Heida, *Neerlandica extra muros* 26 (2004), 199–201; G. Köbler, *Zeitschrift der Savigny-Stiftung für Rechtsgeschichte, Germanistische Abteilung* 121 (2004), 558–59; A. Popkema, *ABäG* 60 (2005), 261–70; E. H. Bary, *IB* 67 (2005), 33–39; S. Krogh, *Beiträge zur Namenforschung* 40 (2005), 230–37; D. Stellmacher, *Zeitschrift für Dialektologie und Linguistik* 73 (2006), 364–65.

book's 800 pages are devoted to it. It is thus a worthy successor to the one-man treatment of Frisian which Theodor Siebs contributed to Herman Paul's *Grundriss der germanischen Philologie* more than one hundred years ago (and still consulted with profit today, witness also the present volume). And besides taking stock of what has been achieved in the various fields of Frisian studies, the handbook also signals what still has to be done, or, to put it more realistically, what still can be done.

For Old Frisian, there is, for example, still a need to publish manuscripts. Codex Unia, unfortunately lost but surviving in collations and transcripts made by Francis Junius in the 1660s and now resting in the Bodleian Library, Oxford, is the last of the major Old West Frisian legal miscellanies to await an integral edition. Several attempts to achieve this have been made since Theodor Siebs announced its discovery in 1895, but all have floundered so far. The text of the incunable of the *Freeska Landriucht*, printed 1484–1486, was included by Karl von Richthofen in his collective edition, *Friesische Rechtsquellen* (1840). However, his edition was based on an earlier, eighteenth-century edition and not the result of his own philological acuity. A first, important step towards a modern edition was made when Tresoar, the well-stocked library of Fryslân in Leeuwarden, decided to digitize one of three copies kept in its holdings. Together with an explanatory text and a bibliography, written by Anne Tjerk Popkema, its pages can now be viewed from anywhere in the world.[4] Finally, another long-term project is the edition of the texts in Codex Roorda, copied ca. 1500, the bulk of which consists of the *Jurisprudentia Frisica*, a long discussion in Frisian of Roman and canon law, related with some frequency to native Frisian legal traditions and extensively provided with Latin commentary. The Old Frisian text had been published, with a Dutch translation, in 1836, but this edition is far from reliable and moreover omits the Latin commentary. Fortunately, Bram Jagersma has well advanced in his preparation of an electronic edition which will in due time be made accessible to a wider group of users through the services of the Fryske Akademy in Leeuwarden.[5]

The lexicography of Old Frisian is another field that is awaiting better times. We still have to make do with von Richthofen's *Altfriesisches Wörterbuch* (1840), which, however incomplete it is, presents words helpfully in context sentences. On a more modest scale, but with extensive exemplification, is Wybren Jan Buma's *Vollständiges Wörterbuch zum westerlauwersschen Jus Municipale Frisonum* (1996), which covers the vocabulary of the largest of the Old West Frisian legal manuscripts. Furthermore,

4 <http://schatkamer.tresoar.nl/landriucht/index.html> with explanatory text in Dutch, and <http://skatkeamer.tresoar.nl/landriucht/index-fr.html> for the Frisian version.

5 <http://www.fa.knaw.nl/fa>.

we have Ferdinand Holthausen's *Altfriesisches Wörterbuch* (1927) in a somewhat clumsily improved revision by Dietrich Hofmann, published in 1984. Hofmann's own completely new concise dictionary of Old Frisian remained unfinished at his death in 1998. Fortunately, with the financial support of the Deutsche Forschungsgemeinschaft, a four-year project at the Frisian Department of the University of Kiel has seen to it that this dictionary will be published in Heidelberg, perhaps still in 2008, as *Altfriesisches Handwörterbuch*. Responsible for the edition and completion of Hofmann's dictionary is Anne Tjerk Popkema.

Apart from the etymological cues which Holthausen presented at the end of the entries in his *Altfriesisches Wörterbuch*, there is still no etymological dictionary of Old Frisian. With the publication of Dirk Boutkan's *Old Frisian Etymological Dictionary* in 2005, much incomplete at his untimely death in 2002, but finalized and edited by Sjoerd Siebinga, at least some headway has been made. Despite its physical size, this book is based on the vocabulary of the First Riustring Manuscript only, covering perhaps only 10% of the Old Frisian vocabulary, so that its title does not fulfil what it promises to the innocent user by far.[6]

The grammars and textbooks of Old Frisian were all written long ago and must usually be purchased second-hand. With my *Introduction to Old Frisian*, to be published in 2008, an urgent need will hopefully be alleviated.

Beside such primary studies of the medieval Frisian language, there is a related world to be found in the Latin texts that were produced in Frisia at the time. A very important source publication comprises a dual-language edition of the lives of five thirteenth-century Frisian abbots of Mariengaarde Abbey, some thirty kilometres north-west of Leeuwarden.[7] These lives give access to a spiritual side of life in medieval Frisia that is not immediately perceivable through the legal texts (even though it is visible there too, sometimes). At the same time, such *vitae* allow us narrative glimpses of abbots who also fulfilled a role in the world outside their monastic walls as arbiters in quarrels between secular factions. As sons, usually of Frisian aristocratic families, such monastic princes were often equally well steeped in regional law as they were in canon law.

6 Reviews: E. Seebold, *UW* 54 (2005), 202–05; A. Liberman, *Trefwoord* 2006 <http://www.fa.knaw.nl/fa/uitgaven/trefwoord/jaargang-2006/old-frisian-etymological-dictionary>, with a rejoinder by R. Beekes; A.T. Popkema, in *ABäG* 63 (2007), 291–96.

7 *Vitae abbatum Orti Sancte Marie. Vijf abtenlevens van het klooster Mariëngaarde in Friesland*, ed. and trans. H. Th. M. Lambooij and J. A. Mol with the assistance of M. Gumbert-Hepp and P. N. Noomen (Hilversum and Leeuwarden, 2001). Reviews: U. Leinsle, *Analecta Praemonstratensia* 8 (2002), 291–94; I. van 't Spijker, *IB* 65 (2003), 64–67; B. Meijns, *Ons Geestelijk Erf* 77 (2003), 128–30; R. Nip, *Bijdragen en Mededelingen betreffende de Geschiedenis der Nederlanden* 118 (2003), 84–86.W. S. van Egmond, *Deutsches Archiv für die Erforschung des Mittelkalters* 58 (2004), 650.

Two major exhibitions on the material side of the Frisian Middle Ages can still be seen even though the objects have long since been packed and shipped to their original museums thanks to two beautiful catalogues. The one concerns 'Hel en hemel. De Middeleeuwen in het Noorden' ('Hell and Heaven. The Middle Ages in the North [i.e. of the Netherlands]'), staged in the Groningen Museum in 2001 and impressively, sometimes even provocatively, arranged by the British filmmaker Peter Greenaway. The catalogue contains an abundant selection of the exposed objects with beautiful photographs, and is complemented by a number of relevant essays on various aspects of medieval Frisia.[8] The other exhibition was 'Die Friesische Freiheit des Mittelalters. Leben und Legende', organized by the Ostfriesische Landschaft and distributed over two locations, Emden and Aurich, in 2003. For this event, the scholarly companion was kept separate from the catalogue of exhibited objects. Tastefully designed, the companion contains eighteen well-illustrated articles on the theme of 'Frisian Freedom', discussing a variety of topics such as the archeology, geology, demography, economy, politics and religion of medieval Frisia, with an emphasis on the part of Frisia which is now Ostfriesland in Germany.[9]

Since most of the Old Frisian texts concerns law and legal treatises, some knowledge of the legal customs at the time is indispensable. In a way, the study of medieval Frisian law suffers from the fact that it was enthusiastically practised in the nineteenth and early twentieth centuries, but that methods and theories have drastically changed since then. These changes have not or only rarely so been brought to the laws in the present time. For example, the only monograph on crime and punishment, anachronistically called 'The penal law of the Frisians in the Middle Ages', appeared more than a century ago.[10] Precisely because many of the legal texts are not immediately understandable to scholars who are not trained jurists, Nicolaas Algra has written a lengthy study on Medieval Frisian law in which he directed himself first of all to the philologist rather than to the legal historian. The result is an insightful exploration (in Dutch) of legal institutions and customs, provided with an extensive and hence a very useful subject index.[11] A problem in many legal texts is the diversity of means of payment and the measure of values. This problem is tackled by Dirk Jan Henstra in a lengthy study which

---

[8] *Hel en hemel. De Middeleeuwen in het Noorden*, ed. E. Knol, J. M. M. Hermans and M. Driebergen (Groningen, 2001).

[9] *Die Friesische Freiheit des Mittelalters – Leben und Legende*, ed. H. van Lengen (Aurich, 2003).

[10] R. His, *Das Strafrecht der Friesen im Mittelalter* (Leipzig, 1901).

[11] N. E. Algra, *Oudfries recht 800–1256* (Leeuwarden, 2000). Reviews: D. Lambrecht, *Pro Memorie* 4 (2002), 202–04; H. Schmidt, *UW* 51 (2002), 153–58; B. S. Hempenius-van Dijk, *IB* 65 (2003), 181–88.

pairs historical economy with the implications of the feuding society that Frisia was at the time.[12]

The cultural and intellectual context in which the skills of reading and writing arrived in Frisia and started to thrive there in the thirteenth century is the subject of *'Hir is eskriven'* ('Here is written') . Based on a variety of written sources but also on material evidence such as inscriptions and murals, this purposefully illustrated book constitutes a first attempt at establishing the change which literacy, both in Latin and in the vernacular, brought to the Frisians and which for one thing dramatically changed their outlook on the traditional laws that continued many a custom from pre-Christian times, particularly the right for compensations for breaches of the law. Owing to the new skills, these laws were written down but paradoxically reading and writing also contributed to their eventual demise.[13]

Finally, Oebele Vries has seen to it that a rich anthology of Old Frisian texts is now available to a wider reading public in a triple-language edition, in Old Frisian, Modern Frisian and in Modern Dutch. The anthology not only presents short and helpful introductions to each text but also addresses important aspects of medieval Frisian society. An extra bonus that comes with this *de-luxe* production is the fact that it features professional colour photographs of all of the medieval Old Frisian manuscripts as well as of the early modern transcripts of medieval codices now lost.[14]

*

---

12 D. J. Henstra, *The Evolution of the Money Standard in Medieval Frisia. A Treatise of the Systems of Account in the Former Frisia (c.600–c.1500),* PhD-dissertation Groningen ([Groningen, 2000]). Reviews: R. Timmer, *Pro Memorie* 3 (2001), 334–39; A. Janse, *Millennium. Tijdschrift voor Middeleeuwse Studies* 15 (2001), 69–70; N. J. Mayhew, *English Historical Review* 117 (2002), 941–42; B. Kluge, *Deutsches Archiv für Erforschung des Mittelalters* 58 (2002), 313–14; J. A. Mol, *Nederlandsch Historisch-Economisch Archief* 16 (2002), 94–96.

13 R. H. Bremmer Jr, *'Hir is eskriven'. Lezen en schrijven in de Friese landen rond 1300* (Hilversum, 2004). Reviews: M. Aaij, *The Heroic Age. A Journal of Early Medieval Northwestern Europe*, Issue 9 (2006) <http://www.heroicage.org>; W. van Egmond, *Madoc. Tijdschrift over de Middeleeuwen* 19 (2005), 105–07; T. S. B. Johnston, *Tijdschrift voor Geschiedenis* 119 (2006), 410–11; E. Langbroek, *ABäG* 62 (2006), 262–67; H. D. Meijering, *UW* 54 (2005), 196–201; A. B. Mulder-Bakker, *Bijdragen en Mededelingen betreffende de Geschiedenis der Nederlanden* 121 (2006), 131–32; B. Murdoch, *Speculum. Journal of Medieval Studies* 84 (2005), 1165–66; A. T. Popkema, *IB* 67 (2005), 102–17; W. Scheepsma, *TNTL* 121 (2005), 186–87. Furthermore on this book, see also the special issue of *UW* 56 (2007), 1–87, with contributions by M. Mostert, H. D. Meijering, A. T. Popkema and the author himself.

14 O. Vries, *Asega, is het dingtijd? De hoogtepunten van de Oudfriese tekstoverlevering*, in collaboration with D. Hempenius-van Dijk (Leeuwarden, 2007).

The articles in *Advances in Old Frisian Philology* are presented following the alphabetical order of the authors' names, although order could also have been imposed differently. The contents of the present volume show a bias towards the linguistic side of Old Frisian philology. Several contributions are devoted to the study of the smallest constituents of language: phonology. Siebren Dyk reveals to us the key to understanding what underlies one of the major sound changes that gave Old West Frisian (and hence Modern West Frisian) its peculiar fabric: 'Jorwert Breaking'. Stephen Laker reviews old and new data with respect to the Old Frisian and Old English palatalization of velar stops and fricatives and discusses the effect of this sound change in these two closely related languages in the light of explanations given by previous scholars. Joseph Salmons considers the effects of *i*-mutation in Old Frisian and what it can tell us about this major change in the other North-West Germanic dialects. Laura Smith subjects the most conspicuous features of the Riustring dialect of Old Frisian – Vowel Balance and Vowel Harmony – to a new theoretical approach and views its workings, like Salmons, in a wider, West Germanic context.

Closely related in their approach are three contributions devoted to disclosing the presence of different scribal layers in Old Frisian manuscripts. Two of these concern a mid-fifteenth-century manuscript compiled by Bernard Rordahusim, a West Frisian clergyman of indefinite rank and position, whose literate horizon interests stretched from Latin to Frisian and from Dutch to Low German, witness his miscellany now preserved in the library of Basel University. Alderik Blom seeks to establish to what extent the Frisian wedding speeches in this manuscript exhibit interference from Dutch, while Erika Langbroek subjects a Low German poem on the Apocalypse in the same manuscript to a close scrutiny in order to establish how much Bernard's Frisian interfered with the Low German of the exemplar which he copied. Rolf Bremmer, finally, queries the archaicness and purity that has always been assumed for the Old Frisian language of the Riustring manuscripts.

In an innovative approach to a morphological aspect of Old Frisian, Irmengard Rauch discusses the consequences of incongruity between natural gender and grammatical gender. Syntactic studies are represented by the contributions of Rosemarie Lühr and of Eric Hoekstra with Sjoerd Siebinga. Lühr focuses her attention to the syntactic properties of conditional clauses, a type of clause that is abundantly present in the Old Frisian legal discourse. Hoekstra and Siebinga weigh the syntactic properties of the Old Frisian pronoun *aeng* 'any'.

Word studies have always taken up a prominent position within the discipline, and it is therefore no surprise that they are also present in this volume. The vast semantic field of the Old Frisian words for 'oath' is for the first time carefully mapped by Anne Popkema, while Oebele Vries investigates the terminology that was used in legal procedures between two private parties, especially with relation to disputes concerning property. Whereas Popkema and Vries have taken a synchronic approach, David Yeandle's approach is diachronic, as he fathoms the origin of four loan words that were adopted by the Frisians upon their conversion to Christianity, thus bridging the distance between cultural history and linguistics. Another such bridge, bringing us back to the era just preceding the conversion, is Robert Nedoma's exacting analysis of two runic inscriptions with personal names.

Justice and religion often go hand in hand. Concetta Giliberto presents an in-depth analysis of the Old Frisian version of the Fifteen Signs of Doomsday while Ineke van 't Spijker draws our attention to the Latin side of medieval Frisian literature which lodges a spirituality that never surfaced in the vernacular in as far as we know. Justice in its ultimate consequence is visualized by the gallows-and-wheel constructions, a once-familiar sight in the Frisian landscape, as Johannes Mol points out to us in a detailed investigation. Henk Meijering demonstrates that Old Frisian law was not static but underwent innovations which paradoxically did not surface in the Frisian language but in the Low German that had replaced it in the erstwhile Frisian districts north of the city of Groningen from 1400 onwards. In their attempt to keep distance between that city and their lands, its aristocratic leaders clung to Frisian law as an important expression of their identity. In a different way and beyond the Middle Ages, as Kees Dekker demonstrates, the Frisian humanist Sibrandus Siccama, too, used the earliest first written Frisian law text, the Carolingian *Lex Frisionum*, as a means to demonstrate a Frisian identity under new circumstances, namely as his Frisia became part of the young Dutch Republic.

*

The first steps towards the realization of this volume were taken almost two years ago when I found Oebele Vries and Stephen Laker willing to embark on a sequel to *Approaches to Old Frisian Philology*. Arend Quak magnanimously gave the green light to devote yet another volume of 'his' *Amsterdamer Beiträge zur älteren Germanistik* to only Old Frisian. I would like to thank him, and also Fred van der Zee of Rodopi, for their guidance and advice. The invitations went out to potential contributors who without exception responded enthusiastically, although several of them had never published on Old Frisian before. The result is a volume whose contents can rightfully make a claim to advance the discipline of Old Frisian philology. For technical support and advice, my gratitude is due to Kees Dekker, Sandor Chardonnens and Daniel O'Donnell. Arjen Versloot and Sander

Strating signed for the cartography. Financial and material support was given by the 'Stifting Freonen Frysk Ynstitút Ryksunversiteit Grins' and the Department of English, University of Leiden. To conclude on a proverbial note: three makes a crowd; yet, it is my wish that this volume may find a sequel once more in the future. After all, the more the merrier.

Alra selena dei 2007 *Rolf H. Bremmer Jr*

Language Admixture in the Old West Frisian *Basle Wedding Speeches*?

Alderik H. Blom

1. Introduction[1]

Basle, Universitätsbibliothek, F. VII. 12 is a composite manuscript which consists of four originally separate units that were joined together around 1500 and have later received a consecutive page numbering.[2] The fourth unit (fols 93–219) contains a plethora of texts of various genres, ranging from computational texts, exempla, and extracts from patristic writings to recipes for medicines and even short instructions on how to make paint.[3] Most of these items are in Latin, Middle Dutch, and Middle Low German, with the exception of three wedding speeches which are written in Old (West) Frisian and are hence known as the Old Frisian *Basle Wedding Speeches*. Two of these (Texts I and II) occur on fols 147v to 148v of the manuscript. The third text is written on a loose sheet, now fols 148ar–148av, which was later inserted into the manuscript between fols 147 and 148. Text III is executed in a different, notably smaller hand, and the extensive use of non-standard abbreviated forms suggests it to be an autograph that was intended for private purposes. Text III must also have been penned in some haste, for it contains several mistakes and omissions. Indeed, Text III appears to have been drafted for a specific occasion, since it mentions the names of the persons to be married – Tiark and Thyka – whereas in Texts I and II the scribe left room for names which he indicated by 'N'.[4]

1 I am indebted to H. Nijdam (Fryske Akademy, Leeuwarden) and Dr P. Russell (Department of Anglo-Saxon, Norse, and Celtic, University of Cambridge) for reading several drafts of this article and making many helpful comments. Furthermore I owe thanks to the Fryske Akademy for providing me with texts from the electronic corpus of Old Frisian, and to Dr O. Vries (Frysk Institút, University of Groningen) for providing me with the electronic edition of the Old Frisian charters.

2 The manuscript originally belonged to the Carthusian House in Basle, see W. J. Buma, *Aldfryske Houlikstaspraken. Mei ynlieding, oantekeningen, nammelist, wurdboek en in Ingelske gearfetting* (Assen, 1957), 4–6.

3 For a detailed description of the context of the manuscript's fourth unit by Gerbenzon, see Buma, *Aldfryske Houlikstaspraken*, 6–15; cf. R. Jansen-Sieben, *Repertorium van de Middelnederlandse Artes-literatuur* (Utrecht, 1989), 232.

4 Buma, *Aldfryske Houlikstaspraken*, 21.

The three speeches were first edited and annotated extensively by Buma in 1957.[5] He remarked that the language of the three speeches shows a curious admixture of Middle Dutch and Middle Low German forms. According to Buma the base language of all three texts is a late form of Old West Frisian, even though it shows strong interference: 'Frisian undoubtedly underlies the writings mentioned, but with respect to sound-system, spelling and vocabulary many foreign, especially Low German forms were absorbed in it'.[6] This admixture of forms was described in detail by Buma in his 1957 edition, but in fact he mainly listed the deviant forms without interpreting the phenomena.[7]

Therefore, in what follows I aim to come to a better understanding of this alleged admixture in the Basle wedding speeches. I start with a discussion of previous scholarship. In the section that follows I present a new analysis of the deviant forms in the three separate texts. Subsequently, I discuss the possible Middle Low German and Middle Dutch provenance of a number of forms. I then consider whether the admixture should be seen in sociolinguistic terms or, alternatively, in the light of the particularities of written language. Finally, I offer a comparison of the language of the speeches with a similar admixture of forms in the fifteenth-century verse chronicle *Thet Freske Riim*. Such a comparison may bring to light whether this type of admixture was idiosyncratic for the authors of the wedding speeches or, as I shall argue, characteristic for a common literary register in Old West Frisian, by which I mean a shared written form of the language which may have a more or less close connection to the spoken variety.

2. Previous scholarship

Despite its many excellencies, Buma's pioneering work failed to raise two important issues. First, it did not seem to have realised that the phonological status of the spelling in the speeches is problematic. As I will show, many deviant forms differ from the current Old Frisian norm only in the alternation of a vowel or an initial consonant. In these cases we may wonder

---

5 For discussions of the non-linguistic background of the Basle speeches, see K. Heeroma, 'Auteurschap en structuur der "Aldfryske Houlikstaspraken"', *Archief voor de Geschiedenis van de Katholieke Kerk in Nederland* 1 (1959), 344–59, at 344–50; K. Heeroma, 'Bernardus Rordahusim in Munster', *UW* 9 (1960), 67–69; M. van Gelderen and A. Orbán, 'Ein lateinisches Ehetraktat in einer baseler Handschrift aus dem 15. Jahrhundert und dessen Beziehung zu der drei altfriesischen Traureden in dem Manuskript', *Aspects*, 102–24; W. Scheepsma, 'Aldfryske preken?', *Philologia Frisica anno 2002* (Leeuwarden, 2003), 183–99.

6 Buma, *Houlikstaspraken*, 41: 'It Frysk makket sûnder mis de grounslach fan'e neamde skriften út, mar wat lûding, stavering en wurdfoarrie oangiet, binne der in bulte útlânske, binammen Nederdútske foarmen opnommen'.

7 *Ibid.* 37–41.

whether we are dealing with actual language choice (that is between Old Frisian and Middle Dutch/Middle Low German forms) or merely with spelling choices (that is between different spellings, which to the scribe satisfactorily represented the same sound). I will discuss the matter further in section 5. Secondly, Buma did not take the question of authorship into account when he described the admixture in the speeches. Accordingly, he analysed them as one integral system. However, subsequent studies of the Basle speeches suggest that the three texts in all likelihood have a different authorship.

Establishing the authorship of the speeches is hampered by the fact that the entire fourth unit of the Basle manuscript is written in the same hand.[8] This scribe identifies himself on fol. 208r:

> Explicit computus sacerdotalis scriptum per manus bernardi rordahusim qui temporis tunc uisitans hildensim sub anno domini 1445.[9]

Rordahusim (Modern Frisian *Reduzum*) today is a small village near the north-west coast of West Frisia. Since the Lüchtenhof in Hildesheim, a house of the Brethren of the Common Life, had strong links with the *Devotio Moderna*, it has been tentatively concluded that Bernard was connected to this religious reform movement.[10] On the basis of other texts in the manuscript Van Buijtenen suggested that Bernard may also have had strong connections with the house at Münster, where he probably stayed around the year 1442.[11]

There has been some scholarly disagreement about the role of Bernard in the genesis of the three speeches. Buma's initial understanding was that Bernard Rordahuizum should be regarded as the author of Texts I and II, but that he could not have composed Text III as well.[12] However, Heeroma has demonstrated on certain stylistic, orthographic, and linguistic grounds that Texts I and II must have had different authors. He also suggested that it is highly unlikely that the scribe of the codex, probably Bernard, was one of

---

8 *Ibid.* 16.

9 '(Here) ends the *computus sacerdotalis* written by the hand of Bernard Rordahusim, who (was) at that point in time visiting Hildesheim in the year of our Lord 1445'. Elsewhere, on fol. 180r, Bernard writes: *Deo gracias Finitus et completus per me bernardum studentem temporis tunc hildensim Anno domini M^o cccc^o XLV°*. 'Thanks be to God. Finished and completed by me, Bernard, at that time a student at Hildesheim in the year of our Lord 1445.'

10 M. P. van Buijtenen, 'Bernardus Rordahusim en zijn kring', *Archief voor de Geschiedenis van de Katholieke Kerk in Nederland* 1 (1959), 294–334, at 318–34; Scheepsma, 'Aldfryske preken?', 188.

11 Heeroma, 'Bernardus', 67.

12 Buma, *Houlikstaspraken*, 16–17.

their authors.[13] Indeed, Texts I and II have very little in common with regards to style and content.[14] Moreover, it appears that the author of Text III used both Texts I and II for composing his own speech.[15] Hence, Heeroma claimed that Bernard should be regarded as the scribe of the codex as well as the author of Text III,[16] and this claim has been accepted by subsequent scholarship.[17] Van Gelderen and Orbán suggested further that Bernard must have copied the first two texts to serve as models. He then composed his own speech on a loose sheet, which he inserted into the manuscript at a later point in time.[18] Bernard may have brought the originals of Texts I and II from Frisia and copied them during his stay in Hildesheim.[19] In the light of this scholarship, I shall treat the three speeches separately in the following analysis.

Various approaches to the language of the Basle speeches have been taken. Bremmer, for example, analysed a somewhat similar admixture in the Middle Low German *Life of St Hubert*, also found in the Basle manuscript, according to orthographical and phonological, morphological, lexicological, and syntactic criteria, explaining the admixture in sociolinguistic terms.[20] Sociolinguistic concepts, techniques, and findings have recently been applied to corpus languages, with various results.[21] However, since these

---

13 Heeroma, 'Auteurschap en structuur', 345–50.

14 For a comparison of the three texts, see van Gelderen and Orbán, 'Ehetraktat', 113–20.

15 The Latin tract on matrimony following the speeches on fol. 149r has been identified as an excerpt from Raymundus de Pennaforte's *Summa legum* . Text III seems partly to rely on it. See van Gelderen and Orbán, 'Ehetraktat', 117–18.

16 Heeroma, 'Auteurschap en structuur', 344, 348, and 354.

17 Van Gelderen and Orbán, 'Ehetraktat', 121–22; Scheepsma, 'Aldfryske preken?', 191–92.

18 Van Gelderen and Orbán, 'Ehetraktat', 122.

19 Heeroma, 'Bernardus', 67–68.

20 R. H. Bremmer Jr, 'Bad Frisian and Bad Low German: Interference in the Writings of a Medieval West Frisian', *Multilingua* 16 (1997), 375–88, at 383.

21 For recent studies into language contact between Middle Low German and the Scandinavian languages, see e.g. E. H. Jahr, 'Nedertysk og nordisk: språksamfunn og språkkontakt i Hansa-tida', *Nordisk og nedertysk: språkkontakt og språkutvikling i Norden i seinmellomalderen*, ed. E. H. Jahr (Oslo, 1995), 9–28; revised as 'Sociolinguistics in Historical Language Contact. The Scandinavian Languages and Low German during the Hanseatic Period', *Language Change. Advances in Historical Sociolinguistics*, ed. E. H. Jahr (Berlin and New York, 1999), 119–139. Other contributions to this volume deal with North-Western Europe in general. On Latin in contact with other languages of the Roman Empire, see *Bilingualism in Ancient Society. Language Contact and the Written Text*, ed. J. N. Adams, M. Janse, and S. Swain (Oxford, 2002); J. N. Adams, *Bilingualism and the Latin Language* (Cambridge, 2003). On Ancient Mesopotamia, see M. Worthington, 'Dialect Admixture of Babylonian and Assyrian in *SAA* VIII, X, XII, XVII, and XVIII', *Iraq* 68 (2006) 59–84.

concepts and techniques are derived from the study of spoken language in contemporary speech communities, their application to earlier, written stages of a language can be problematic, as I hope to demonstrate for the *Basle Wedding Speeches*. Nonetheless, Bremmer concludes that the author of the *Life of St Hubert* had:

> [...] a full command neither of Frisian nor Low German, certainly not in his writing, nor in all likelihood in his spoken usage. As a result he is an interesting representative of the (erudite) Frisian who no longer has/does not yet have a good command of these two languages. He thus represents a case of what has been called a 'semilingual' or 'balanced' bilingual, that is, someone 'who has an equal, though not necessarily full knowledge of two languages.[22]

For this reason Bremmer wants to see in the language of the *Life* 'an early witness of language mixing that has resulted in the Frisian substratum underlying the present-day Low German dialects of the former Frisian speaking areas of Groningen and Ostfriesland', and he sees in the language of the *Life* and the speeches a process of language shift.[23] Thus it seems as if Bremmer regards this language as partly reflecting a spoken idiolect (although he does not use this term himself) from which he then generalises about the language situation in East Frisia.

Nevertheless, there are other possible explanations for the admixture in the Basle speeches. In a review of Buma's edition, which to the best of my knowledge has not been referred to in subsequent scholarship, Campbell pointed out that a similar admixture of 'Dutch (or Low German)' forms occurs in the aforementioned verse chronicle *Thet Freske Riim* and that apparently 'such a mixture was normal in Frisian at the time.' He expressed the hope 'that the appearance [...] of editions of the speeches and the *Riim* will focus attention to *the curious mixed Frisian of the fifteenth century* (my emphasis).'[24] If the language of the *Basle Wedding Speeches* and *Thet Freske Riim* is indeed comparable, as Campbell suggests, the language of

---

22 Bremmer, 'Interference', 383, referring to S. Romaine, *Bilingualism* (Oxford, 1989), 235.

23 Bremmer, 'Interference', 383. On the topic of language contact and language shift in the various (historically) Frisian-speaking areas, see H. D. Meijering, 'De tael fan de Ommelanner rjochtshânskriften', *Philologia Frisica anno 1975* (Leeuwarden, 1977), 14–31; H. Niebaum, 'Der Niedergang des Friesischen zwischen Lauwers und Weser', *Handbuch / Handbook*, 430–42; U. Scheuermann, 'Friesische Relikte im Ostfriesischen Niederdeutsch', *ibid.* 443–48; E. Hoekstra, 'Frisian Relics in the Dutch Dialects', *ibid.* 138–42; M. Fort, 'Sprachkontakt im dreisprachigen Saterland', *Deutsch im Kontakt mit germanischen Sprachen*, ed. H. H. Munske (Tübingen, 2004), 77–98.

24 A. Campbell, Review of Buma, *Houlikstaspraken*, *IB* 21 (1959), 207–08, at 208.

the speeches should no longer be regarded as an idiolect. The similarity then rather points towards the existence of a specific literary register in Frisian which allowed such admixture.

3. Deviant forms in the *Basle Wedding Speeches*

Taking Old West Frisian as my starting point, I have identified and listed all the deviant, i.e. non-Frisian forms found in each text separately, indicating the word categories – noun, adjective, etc. – to which these deviant forms belong. Empty slots denote that there is no evidence available for the feature in question.

1. *ā* ⟨ae⟩ and ⟨a⟩ instead of OFris *ē* (of various origin)
Text I: *daer* av., rel. (cp. OFris *thēr*) and its derivations: *aldaer*, *aldaerwm*, *aldaerafter*, *aldaarney*, *daer meed*, *darum*, *darma* (N.B. the element *-ma* is OFris); *waer* 'true' aj. (cp. OFris *wēr*); *openbarlike* 'manifestly' av. (cp. OFris suffix *-bēr*); *laten* 'to let, have' inf. (cp. OFris *lēta*).
Text II: *daer* av., rel. and its derivations: *aldaervp, aldaer*; *gaet* 'goes' pres.3sg. (cp. OFris *g(h)ēt, giet*); *slap* 'sleep' n. (cp. OFris *slēp*); *vnderdanich* 'obedient' aj. (cp. OFris *underdēnoch*); *aldusdan* 'such' aj. (cp. OFris *aldusdēn*).
Text III: *dar* rel.; *saelich* 'righteous' aj. (cp. OFris *sēlich*, *sillich*); *un⟨der⟩-danich* aj.

2. *a* ⟨a⟩ instead of *e* (< WGmc *a*; 'Anglo-Frisian fronting')
Text I: *dat* 'that' dem., rel., conj. (cp. OFris *thet*); *wat* 'what' indef.pron. (cp. OFris *hwet*, OWFris *hot*); *ghescapen* 'created' pp. (cp. OFris *eskepin, eskipin*); *starckheyt* 'strength' n. (possibly OFris, cp. *sterk, stark*).
Text II: *dat* dem., conj.; *stad* 'place, spot, town' n. (cp. OFris *sted(e)*).
Text III: *dat* dem., conj.; vast 'firm' aj. (cp. OFris *fest*); *ma⟨er⟩*[25] 'but' av. (cp. OFris *mer*); *stark* 'firm, strong' aj. (possibly OFris, cp. *sterk, stark*).

3. *ō* ⟨oe⟩ and ⟨o⟩ instead of OFris *ā* (of various origin)
Text I: *soe, zoe* 'then, so, as, if' av.; conj. (cp. OFris *sā*); *alzo* 'thus' av. (cp. OFris *alsā*); *tho/doe* 'then' av., conj. (cp. OFris *thā*); *oec* 'also, too' av. (cp. OFris *āc*); *groet* 'big, large' aj. (cp. OFris *grāt*).
Text II: *zoe, soe* av., conj., *alzo, also* av.; *tho, doe* av., conj.; *troest* 'help, support' n. (cp. OFris *trāst*); *troeste* 'to help, support' inf.
Text III: *so(e)* av., conj., *alzo, also* av.; *tho* av.; *t⟨roest⟩* n.; *oech* av.; *grote* aj.

4. *ē* instead of OFris *ā* (< Gmc *ai*)
Text I: *twe* 'two' num. (cp. OFris *twā*).

---

[25] Reading uncertain.

Text II: *twe* num.; *emmermer* 'evermore' av. (cp. OFris *emmermār*).
Text III: *eers* 'first' av. (cp. OFris *ār(i)st, aerst*);[26] *mēr* 'more' av. (cp. OFris *mār*).

5. *e* and *i* before /χ/, /χt/, /χs/ instead of OFris *iu* or *io* (breaking)
Text I: *richt* 'just, right(ful)' aj. (cp. OFris *riucht, riocht*).
Text II: --
Text III: --

6. *-n-* before original voiceless fricatives *-s-*, *-þ-*
Text I: *vns, ons* 'us' pers.pron. (cp. OFris *ūs*); *onze* 'our' poss. (cp. OFris *ūse*); *anders* 'otherwise' av. (cp. OFris *ōther*).[27]
Text II: *ons* pers.pron.; *onse, onze* poss.pron.; *malcander* 'each other' pron.
Text III: --

7. Absence of *i*-mutation
Text I: *konnighen* 'kings' n. (cp. OFris *kening*); *lutiik* 'little' aj. (cp. OFris *litik, littech*); *zunde* 'sin' n. (cp. OFris *sende*); *ghehoert* 'heard' pp.; *thoe behoert* 'belongs' pres.3sg. (cp. OFris *hēra*); *noet* 'danger, hardship' n. (cp. OFris *nēd*); *ghesproghen* 'spoken' pp. (cp. OFris *spritzen*).
Text II: *nutte* 'useful' aj. (cp. OFris *nette*); *hoer(d)t (tho)* 'listens' pres.3sg.; *scone* 'beautiful' aj. (cp. OFris *skēne*).
Text III: *beh⟨oeret⟩* 'belong' pl.pres.

8. Plain infinitives in *-n*
Text I: *gheuen* 'to give'; *laten* 'to let'; *uertellen* 'to tell, relate'.
Text II: --
Text III: *hanghen* 'to hang'; *merken* 'to observe'; *habben* 'to have'.

9. Prefix *ghe-* in verbal and nominal forms
Text I: *ghehoert* 'heard'; *ghesproghen* 'spoken'; *ghewiist* 'shown'; *gheseet* 'seen'; *gheheten* 'called'; *ghescapen* 'created'; *gheheylighet* 'sanctified'; *ghesecht* 'said'; *ghemaket* 'made'; *ghescreuen* 'written' pp.; *escoep* 'created' pret.3sg. (cp. OFris *skōp*).
Text II: *ghemaket* 'made' pp.
Text III: *ghescreuen* 'written' pp.

10. Occurrence of *mach* 'can, be able' 1/3sg.pres. (cp. OFris *mei*)
Text I : *mach.*
Text II: --
Text III: --

11. Occurrence of *sal* 'shall, must' pres.3sg. (cp. OFris *skel*, *skil*)
Text I: --

[26] Subsequently corrected by the scribe into *aers*.
[27] Also deviant is *stond* 'stood' pret.3sg. (cp. OFris *stōd*).

Text II: *sal.*
Text III: *sall.*

12. Occurrence of *heft/heeft* 'to have' pres.3sg. (cp. OFris *hat(h)*)
Text I: *heft, heeft.*
Text II: *heft, heeft.*
Text III: --

13 Occurrence of *vare* 'to be' pl.pret.subj. (cp. OFris *wēre*)
Text I : *vare.*
Text II: --
Text III: --

14. Occurrence of *wert* 'to become' pret.3sg. (cp. OFris *wart*)
Text I: --
Text II: *wert.*
Text III: *wert.*

15. Occurrence of *sprac* 'to speak' pret.3sg. (cp. OFris *sprec*)
Text I: --
Text II: --
Text III: *sprac.*

16. Occurrence of *quam* 'to come' pret.3sg. (cp. OFris *cōm*, *cām*)
Text I: --
Text II: --
Text III: *quam.*

17. Occurrence of *die* dem.pron.acc.pl. (cp. OFris *thâ, dâ*)
Text I: *die.*
Text II: --
Text III: --

18. Occurrence of *ghy* pers.pron.nom.2pl. (cp. OFris *ī, hī, hī*)
Text I: *ghy*, *ghiis* (ghi + es).
Text II: --
Text III: *ghiit* (ghi + it).

19. Occurrence of *ū* ⟨w⟩ pers.pron.dat./acc.2pl. (cp. OFris *jū, jō*)
Text I: *u.*
Text II: *w.*
Text III: *w.*

20. Occurrence of *hoer* 'them' pers.pron.dat.3pl. (cp. OFris *hemmen*, *hyaren*)
Text I: *hoer*, *horen.*
Text II: --
Text III: --

21. Occurrence of *hoer(e)* 'their' poss.3pl. (cp. OFris *hi(a)re*)
Text I: *hoer*, *hoere*.
Text II: --
Text III: --

22. Occurrence of *ghemen* 'no one' indef.pron. (cp. OWFris *nemmen*, *nimmen*)
Text I: *ghemen.*
Text II: --
Text III: --

23. Occurrence of *gheen* 'nobody' indef.pron. (cp. OFris *nēn*)
Text I : *gheen.*
Text II: *gheen.*
Text III: --

24. Occurrence of *bouen* 'above' prep. (cp. OFris *bova*)
Text I: *bouen.*
Text II: --
Text III: --

25. Occurrence of *yeghens* 'against' prep. (cp. OFris *iens*)
Text I: --
Text II: --
Text III: *yeghens.*

26. Occurrence of *ende* 'and' conj. (cp. OFris *and(e)*)
Text I: *ende.*
Text II: *ende.*
Text III: *ende.*

27. Occurrence of *wo* 'how, why' pron./conj. (cp. OFris *hō, hū*)
Text I: --
Text II: --
Text III: *wo.*

28. Occurrence of *gherne* 'gladly, eagerly' av. (cp. OFris *ierne*)
Text I: *gherne, fol gherne.*
Text II: --
Text III: --

29. Occurrence of *werelt* 'world' n. (cp. OFris *wrald*)
Text I: --
Text II: --
Text III: *werelt.*

30. Occurrence of *leuen* 'life' n. (cp. OFris *lif*)
Text I: --
Text II: --
Text III: *leuen.*

31. Occurrence of *eyghen* 'own' aj. (cp. OFris *ein, ain*)
Text I: *eyghen.*
Text II: --
Text III: ---

32. Occurrence of *niet* 'not' av. (cp. OFris *nāt*, *naut*)
Text I: --
Text II: --
Text III: *nyet.*

We can make the following observations about the nature of the admixture in the three speeches. The above survey demonstrates that in all three texts the admixture occurs in all the major word categories. Furthermore, some of the deviant forms occur alongside Old Frisian forms, indicating that in some cases the loan-form had not replaced the original one, for example the use of the past participle *ghesproghen* beside *spritzen* (with *i*-mutation and assibilation), or the use of the indefinite pronoun *gheen* beside *neen* in Text I. For a list of all deviant forms that occur alongside corresponding regular Old Frisian form(s) in the same text, see Appendix I.

Finally, we observe that sometimes the three speeches exhibit different deviant forms. Buma's analysis has overlooked this fact because it treated the three speeches as one integral system. We note the following examples: Text I only has the Old Frisian pres. 3sg. 'will, shall' *schel* (with /sk/), whereas Texts II and III have both *sc(h)el, schil* and the deviant form *sal*. Furthermore, whereas Texts I and II only use Old Frisian *wrald* 'world', Text III has both deviant *werelt* and regular *wrald*, and where Texts I and II use both *gheen* 'nobody' and *ne(e)n*, III only has *ne(e)n*. Finally, we note the various plurals for the noun 'child': *kiinden* in Text I; *kiinderen* (a form not otherwise known in Old Frisian; *bern* is the common word) and *kiinder* in II; *kinden* and *kinder* in III. The distribution of these different forms per speech can be explained in various ways. They may reflect the different authorship of the speeches, but they may also have been inserted during the genesis of the separate texts – it is not known how often Texts I and II had been copied before they were written down in the extant form.

4. Middle Dutch or Middle Low German?

With regard to the provenance of the deviant forms, Buma thought that in most cases it was impossible to determine whether these deviant forms are of Middle Dutch or Middle Low German derivation.[28] Still, he ascribed most of the deviant forms to Middle Low German.[29] Over the last decades, however, scholars have studied the transitional zone between the Middle Dutch and Middle Low German-speaking areas and the increasing influence of written (Middle) Dutch in the eastern Netherlands during the fifteenth and sixteenth centuries. Their investigations allow us to compile sets of contrasting variables which indicate whether a given form is of either Middle Dutch or Middle Low German derivation.[30] Since the three speeches contain a limited number of loan-forms only, most of these variables are not relevant for my purpose, but the following criteria appear to be useful:[31]

1. The lowering of *u* > *o* before nasal + consonant is a distinguishing mark of Middle Dutch, but it also occurs on the western border of the Middle Low German area, as well as in the transitional zone between Middle Dutch and Middle Low German: *ons* (I and II), and *onse/onze* (I and II) as opposed to *vns/wns* (I and II).[32]

2. The lowering of *e* > *a* before r + consonant is a distinguishing feature of Middle Low German (with the exception of the Westphalian variety); Middle Dutch generally retains *-er* (note that *e* > *a* before r + velar occurs in Middle Dutch also, albeit in fifteenth-century (East) Flemish and other southern dialects).[33] In the speeches we find *starkheyt* (I), *stark* (III).

3. From the fifteenth century, starting in the northern Middle Low German area, we find the spelling ⟨a⟩ for *ō* (from older *o* and *u* in open syllables), for

---

[28] Buma, *Houlikstapraken*, 37.

[29] *Ibid.* 41 and 125.

[30] H. Niebaum, 'Noordoostmiddelnederlands–Noordwestmiddelnederduits– (West)-middelnedersaksisch. Vorbemerkungen zur Schreibsprachenlandschaft der heutigen östlichen Niederlande im späten Mittelalter und in der frühen Neuzeit', *Driemaandelijkse Bladen* 38 (1986), 153–77; H. Niebaum, 'Zwischen Niederländisch und Niederdeutsch: Sprachvariation in den östlichen Niederlanden im 17. Jahrhundert', *Verhandlungen des internationalen Dialektologenkongresses, Bamberg 29.7–4.8. 1990*, ed. W. Viereck (Stuttgart, 1993) II, 209–26; H. Niebaum, '*brot vnde beer ijs hijr ser goet kop...* Zur Sprache der Briefe eines in Löwen studierenden Groningers aus dem Jahre 1552', *Lingua Theodisca. Beiträge zur Sprach- und Literaturwissenschaft Jan Goossens zum 65. Geburtstag*, ed. J. Cajot, L. Kremer, and H. Niebaum (Münster, 1995), 223–31.

[31] Nos. 1–3: phonological; no. 4: morphological; nos. 5–10: lexical.

[32] Already described by Buma, *Houlikstaspraken*, 38.

[33] A. Van Loey, *Middelnederlandse spraakkunst*, 2 vols (Antwerp, 1948) II, §2.

example in the preposition *bauen* 'above'.[34] In Westphalian Middle Low German, however, ⟨a⟩ never completely replaced the older ⟨o⟩ spelling,[35] as in Middle Dutch, where the common form of the preposition is *bouen*. This is also the form that occurs in Text I.

4. pres.3sg. 'to have' in Middle Dutch and in the western Middle Low German area is *heeft*, whereas Middle Low German generally has *hef(f)t*:[36] in the speeches we find *heft* (I: 1x and II: 1x) and *heeft* (I: 3x and II: 2x). These forms are only diagnostic, of course, when we assume that the spelling is distinctive – a problem which is acute in our texts. Niebaum comments on the form *heft*: 'letztere Form ist schwer zu interpretieren. Sie könnte Kurzvokal aufweisen und damit den nd. Befund verstärken. Es wäre aber auch denkbar, daß in diesen Schreibungen Langvokal vorliegt; dann hätten wir es bei diesen Beispiel mit variablen Befund zu tun.'[37]

5. The most common Middle Low German variant for 'friend' is *vrunt*, whereas the form *vri(e)nt* can be considered as the usual Middle Dutch form.[38] In the speeches we find *wrinden* (I and III), *vrinden* (I), and *frynden* (III).

6. The indefinite pronoun *gheen* is exclusively Middle Dutch, whereas Middle Low German (and Old Frisian) have *neen*.[39] In the speeches we find *gheen* (I and II). Note that *neen* occurs in all three texts.

7. The interrogative pronoun *wō* (once in III) is to be regarded as northern Middle Low German; the Middle Dutch form, which was also current on the western border of Middle Low German, is *hō*.[40] Still, the corresponding form *hoe*, which also occurs in our texts, can also be regarded as Old Frisian, which has both *hō* and *hū*.

8. The loan-form of the adverb *nyet* 'not' (once in III) is exclusively Middle Dutch. The most common Middle Low Geman form is *nicht*, with *neet*

---

34 For examples, see A. Lasch, *Mittelniederdeutsche Grammatik* (Tübingen, 1974 [1914]), §89.

35 *Ibid.* §88.

36 *Ibid.* §§217 and 439.1; Van Loey, *Middelnederlandse spraakkunst* I, §62; R. Peters, 'Katalog sprachlicher Merkmale zur variabelenlinguistischen Erforschung des Mittelniederdeutschen. Teil I', *NW* 27 (1987), 61–93, at 78.

37 Niebaum, 'Zur Sprache', 227.

38 Lasch, *Mittelniederdeutsche Grammatik*, §101; Van Loey, *Middelnederlandse spraakkunst* II, §§20 and 71; R. Peters, 'Katalog sprachlicher Merkmale zur variabelenlinguistischen Erforschung des Mittelniederdeutschen. Teil II', *NW* 28 (1988), 75–106, at 80.

39 Lasch, *Mittelniederdeutsche Grammatik*, §411; Peters, 'Katalog II', 103.

40 Lasch, *Mittelniederdeutsche Grammatik*, §§163 and 299 no. 2; R. Peters, 'Katalog sprachlicher Merkmale zur variabelenlinguistischen Erforschung des Mittelniederdeutschen. Teil III', *NW* 30 (1990), 1–17, at 1.

found in the transitional zone between Middle Dutch and Middle Low German.[41]

9. The conjunction *ende* is generally found in the Middle Dutch area as well as on the western border of the Middle Low German area (especially Westphalia). The forms *unde, ande*, and *inde* are to be regarded as more typically Middle Low German.[42]

10. According to Niebaum we must assign the possessive 3sg./pl.fem. *hoer(e)* to Middle Dutch (more common: *hare*) because of the presence of initial *h*-;[43] moreover, Van Loey took the spelling ⟨oe⟩ as typical for Gelre,[44] whereas the common Middle Low German form is *ere*.[45]

This analysis brings out the alternation between Middle Dutch and Middle Low German forms in the speeches, possibly revealing a preference for Middle Dutch in Texts I and II. With the spelling in the Basle speeches being as inconsistent as it is, it may be hazardous to put too much weight on these variables. Even so, the variation between Middle Dutch and Middle Low German spelling conventions in the Basle speeches is regarded as typical for the Eastern Netherlands.[46] This geographical area was also the centre of the *Devotio Moderna*, the religious reform movement to which Bernard of Rordahusim is supposed to have been connected.[47] It is certainly possible, therefore, that the choice of spelling and forms in the three speeches was influenced by the writings of the *Devotio Moderna*, even though further comparative research is required in order to establish this for certain. Commenting on the fact that the chancery of the Frisian town of Bolsward used Middle Dutch to communicate with Hanseatic cities such as Hamburg, Vries suggested: 'Zwar war die Hansesprache nicht das Niederländische, sondern das Niederdeutsche, aber weil diese Sprachen einem Schreibsprachenkontinuum angehörten, wurden sie nicht als prinzipiell verschieden empfunden.'[48] Although the contents of the speeches and much of the manuscript suggest a clerical rather than a chancery-like environment, it is possible that for the authors/scribe of the Basle speeches the two written

41 Lasch, *Mittelniederdeutsche Grammatik*, §357; Peters, 'Katalog II', 99; Peters, 'Katalog III', 15.

42 Lasch, *Mittelniederdeutsche Grammatik*, §§38, 60, and 139.

43 Niebaum, 'Noordoostmiddelnederlands', 171 note 34.

44 Van Loey, *Middelnederlandse spraakkunst* I, §43.

45 Lasch, *Mittelniederdeutsche Grammatik*, §404.

46 Niebaum, 'Noordoostmiddelnederlands', 153–77.

47 E. Iserloh, 'Devotio Moderna', *Lexikon des Mittelalters*, ed. G. Avella-Wildhalm, L. Lutz, R. Mattejiet and U. Mattejiet, 10 vols. (Munich and Zürich, 1980–99) III, 928–30.

48 O. Vries, 'Die Verdrängung des Altfriesischen als Schreibsprache', *Handbuch / Handbook*, 606–13, at 609.

languages were not necessarily regarded as distinctive either. In such an environment they/he may well have become familiar with a similar admixture of written varieties.

5. Spoken or written language?

The question remains how we can explain the alleged admixture in the three speeches. First of all, it has to be borne in mind that a substantial part of the deviant forms concerns forms which are practically homonymous with contemporary Old Frisian forms, for example *richt, waer, wert, twe, emmermer*. In these cases it is merely the stem vowel that deviates from the current Old Frisian form, or, in the case of *ghy*, a difference in (initial) consonant as compared to Old Frisian *hy*. As I mentioned before, the phonological status of such written forms is often problematic – in many such cases it is debatable whether the spelling can be regarded as diagnostic of a particular language, and also whether these spellings were considered as such by the scribe himself (the more so since the texts were apparently intended for private use). Especially in the cases of vowel alternation we could well ask how significant the spelling is; while consonants are phonetically distinguished by the stopping of the air-flow, distinctions between vowels are more fluid, dependent as they are on tongue-position without any interruption of the air-flow and vulnerable to reduction in unstressed positions.[49] Consequently, we might expect more fluidity in the spelling of vowels than consonants. In addition, the author/scribe of the speeches was probably first and foremost influenced by the language in which he had been trained to write (and in which he perhaps wrote most often) – as Bischof observed: 'im allgemeinen schreibt man nicht, wie man spricht, sondern wie man zu schreiben gelernt hat'.[50] Therefore, in many such cases of near homonymy the deviant forms should be regarded as spelling choices influenced by the language in the author/scribe was trained to write rather than as loan-forms borrowed into the author/scribe's Frisian. Hence, the deviant forms may have much more to do with the way in which closely related languages were written down rather than with the speech patterns of the author/scribe. An interesting parallel may be found in the problematic interpretation of several Brittonic (Celtic) glosses preserved in a late ninth-century manuscript now in Angers. One stratum of glosses is recognisably Old Breton, but we can also discern a layer of Old Welsh influence. At the time of composition these two closely related languages differed only slightly in their written

---

[49] For example, see D. B. Fry, *The Physics of Speech* (Cambridge, 1979), *passim*.

[50] K. Bischof, 'Reflexe gesprochener Sprache in Mittelniederdeutschen', *Sprachgeschichte. Ein Handbuch zur Geschichte der deutschen Sprache und ihre Erforschung*, ed. W. Besch, O. Reichmann and S. Sonderegger, 2 vols. (Berlin and New York, 1984–85) II, 1263–68, at 1263.

form. Here we may be dealing with a Breton scribe who had been trained to write and spell in Wales.[51]

However, not just all the deviant forms can be explained by spelling variation. Some differ considerably from current Old Frisian, for example alternating forms such as *ghesproghen* and *spritzen*, *mach* and *mey*. The question is then how these deviant forms were inserted into the texts. It should be realised that this may have happened gradually, and possibly increased or decreased during copying. Assuming that Text III was composed in its extant form and therefore is an original composition, we can at least conclude that here the admixture was present from the start, though some of its forms may originate in the mixed language of Texts I and II.

It is difficult to establish whether the admixture was present in Texts I and II before they were copied into the Basle manuscript. However, I would like to point out the possibility that the author(s) of Texts I and II used Middle Low German and/or Middle Dutch written sources while composing their texts, and that deviant forms thus entered the language of the speeches. In fact, in several cases the author(s) of Texts I, and especially II and III, are known to have used written sources. In the first place there are quotations from the Bible (especially in II and III), mostly in Latin but sometimes followed by an Old Frisian translation.[52] Furthermore, in Texts II and III reference is made to St Gregory, St Augustine, St Ambrose, and (Pseudo-) Boethius, sometimes in Latin, sometimes in translation. Not all of these references have yet been identified. One such written source seems to underlie II, 50–52, a citation claimed to be from St Augustine, but unidentified as such:

> dye man ende dyo vrouwe in alla falschlika [*sic*] werkin schellat zee al een wesa ende hy sal anders gheen spise hebbe dan zee.
> ['husband and wife shall be completely one in all carnal deeds and he shall have no other food than her'.]

In this sentence we find a number of deviant elements: the conjunction *ende* (though this may not be diagnostic and regular Old Frisian by this time); the auxiliary *sal*; adverb *anders*; the indefinite pronoun *gheen*. It is certainly possible that the author(s) of Text II paraphrased (and thereby 'Frisianised') a Middle Dutch or Middle Low German source. If this is the case, then at least a part of the admixture can be explained as interference springing from

---

51 Angers, Bibliothèque d'Angers, MS 476. See L. Fleuriot, *A Dictionary of Old Breton. Dictionnaire du vieux breton*, 2 vols. (Toronto, 1985) I, 9 and 18–31.

52 For a discussion of the quotations in the three speeches, see Buma, *Houlikstaspraken*, 45–48.

'imperfect Frisianisation' of written Middle Dutch and/or Middle Low German exemplars.

Such a case of interference also appears to have happened in Text III, and this time the source can be identified. While Buma pointed out that the author of III had used Pseudo-Boethius' *De disciplina scholarium*,[53] and Orbán and Van Gelderen established that Text III relies heavily on Raymundus Pennaforte's *Summa legum*,[54] Heeroma argued that Text III shows not only an overlap in theme, but in several instances also an almost word-for-word correspondence with Pseudo-Veghe's *Lectulus noster floridus* – a Low German tract by an anonymous author from the house of Münster, which Bernard may well have used.[55] For example, both authors suggested that marriage should bring forth children in order, among other things, to replace the fallen angels in heaven. In Text III, 85–87 (the corresponding passages are printed in bold):

> [...] om den koer der engelen **to foerfullen der lucifer myt al siner gheselcip is wt werpen inder aff gront der hellen.**
> ['... to fill the choir of angels, where Lucifer with all his followers has been cast into the abyss of Hell'.]

and compare the *Lectulus*:

> [...] **unde vervullen de stede des eersten engels lucifers, de daer uth gheworpen is** um syn hoveerdicheit **myt alle synen gheselschop** ut den oversten jherusalem **int nederste der hellen**.[56]
> ['... and fill the place of the first angel Lucifer, who has been cast from there because of his pride together with all his followers from the highest Jerusalem into the deepest of Hell'.]

The paraphrasing of a Middle Low German example in Frisian led to the transfer of Middle Low German features (i.e. the prefix *ghe-*) into Text III. It is worth noting several mistakes and corrections made by the scribe, because they also suggest the (imperfect) 'Frisianisation' of Middle Dutch or

---

53 Buma, *Houlikstapsraken*, 46 and 48.

54 Van Gelderen and Orbán, 'Ehetraktat'.

55 Heeroma, 'Bernardus', 68–69; D. Schmidtke, 'Johannes Veghe und Pseudo-Veghe', *Die deutsche Literatur des Mittelalters. Verfasserlexikon*, ed. B. Wachinger, K. Ruh, W. Schröder, F. Z. Worstbrock, 10 vols. (Berlin and New York, 1978–99) X, 190–99, at 196–97. Edition: *Lectulus Noster Floridus, Unser Blumenbettchen. Eine devot-mystische Schrift des 15. Jh.s. Niederdeutsch von Johannes Veghe*, ed. H. Rademacher (Münster, 1938).

56 Heeroma, 'Bernardus', 68.

Middle Low German forms.[57] Text I, in particular, shows some telling corrections: in line 103 the scribe corrected the form *misdaen* into *misdeen* with the correct Old Frisian vocalism. Furthermore, the deviant form *mach* in line 93 was corrected into the cognate OFris *mey*, although we have seen that the form *mach* was allowed to remain elsewhere in Text I. Finally, in line 99 the form *abuten* 'inside', with deviant *-en*, was corrected into regular OFris *abuta*. Hence it is likely that some of these deviant and subsequently 'Frisianised' forms originate in (Middle Dutch or Middle Low German) written sources used by the author(s). This suggests that the admixture takes place at a written level rather than reflecting the language spoken by the author/scribe. In fact, we do not know anything about the sociolinguistic status of the three speeches. Most probably they formed the basis for an oral performance, but the relationship between the written text and the hypothetical oral sermon is problematic. It may be possible that the preacher performed a Frisian (as well as Dutch/Low German?) speech from a 'mixed' text such as Text III.

In fact, the admixture in the three texts may not be idiosyncratic for the authors of the speeches, but rather characteristic for a shared literary register that was current in late mediaeval Frisia. In order to illustrate this possibility, I shall present in the following section a brief comparison of the language of the Basle speeches with the alleged 'mixed' language of another fifteenth-century text: *Thet Freske Riim*.

6. Deviant forms in *Thet Freske Riim*

The narrative poem *Thet Freske Riim* is preserved in Leeuwarden, Tresoar, Friesch Genootschap, MS II, b, 28. This copy is entirely in the hand of the antiquary Simon Abbes Gabbema (1628–1688), but various earlier summaries show this work to have been in existence in a similar form shortly before 1500.[58] Siebs described the text in 1901 as 'eine Chronik, die in einem von Widersprüchen strotzenden Mischdialekt verfasst ist, wie er nie und nimmer geredet sein kann', and he thought that it must have been 'eine Übertragung niederdeutscher Verse'.[59] Campbell, on the other hand, noticed the poet's indebtedness to Middle Dutch poetic conventions, especially in his use of specific compounds and expressions.[60] However, because of the absence of comparable works in Old Frisian, Campbell remarked that 'it is naturally difficult to decide how much of this material had become an established part of Frisian diction, and how much is peculiar to the author

57 Discussed in Buma, *Houlikstaspraken*, 20–24.

58 *Thet Freske Riim. Tractatus Aluini*, ed. A. Campbell (The Hague, 1952), 1.

59 T. Siebs, 'Friesische Literatur', *Grundriss der germanischen Philologie*, ed. H. Paul (Strassbourg, 1893) II.2, 494–509, at 498.

60 Campbell, *Freske Riim*, 30.

of the *Riim*.' According to Campbell, the author of the *Riim* was 'by no means even concerned to use even Frisian phonological forms consistently', and he observed the remarkable freedom with which Dutch and Frisian forms interchange in the poem.[61]

The spelling of the *Riim* is very inconsistent and at times demonstrably heavily influenced by Dutch. In fact, some of the archaic spellings that also occur in the text may well have been inserted by Gabbema, who is known to have been familiar with other Old Frisian texts.[62] Nonetheless, the admixture of Dutch and Frisian forms which the text of the *Riim* exhibits is thought to go back in large measure to the poet, who frequently used both distinctively Frisian and distinctively Dutch forms in order to obtain rhymes.[63] Campbell concluded therefore that this admixture of forms was not the result of successive scribes copying the text.[64] Furthermore, observing the similarities between the language of the *Riim* and that of the Basle speeches, Campbell suggested that perhaps 'such a mixture of forms was normal in Frisian writing at the time', even though he did not pursue this matter any further. In order to assess whether such an admixture of forms was really current at the time I have made an inventory of the deviant forms in the *Riim* and compared them to the Basle speeches. In doing so, I have followed the same methodology as above.[65]

1. *ā* ⟨ae⟩ and ⟨a⟩ instead of OFris *ē* (of various origin): *rad*, *raed*, *raet*, *rade* 'council' n. (cp. OFris *rēd*); *daer* 'there' av.; *daer* 'where' conj. (cp. OFris *thēr*); *jare*, *jaer* 'year' n. (cp. OFris *iēr*); *nade* 'mercy' n. (cp. OFris *nēthe*); *slapa* 'to sleep' inf. (cp. OFris *slēpa*); *slaep*, *slape* 'sleep' n.; *openbaer*, *openbare* 'clear, public, manifest' aj. (cp. OFris *-bēr*, suffix); *waerheid* 'truth' n. (cp. OFris *wēr*); *waerelyke*, *waerelijke* 'truly' av.; *for ware*, *for war* 'truly' av.; *da(e)n(e)*, *edan* 'done' pp. (cp. OFris *(e)dēn*, *dien*); *salicheid* 'blessed condition' n. (cp. OFris *sēlich* 'pious, righteous').
2. *a* ⟨a⟩ instead of OFris *e* (< WGmc *a*; 'Anglo-Frisian Fronting')]: *dat*, *that* conj. (cp. OFris *thet*); *dat* 'that' pron. acc.sg.neut. (cp. OFris *thet*); *water* 'water' n. (cp. OFris *weter*).

---

61 *Ibid.* 31–32 and 36, respectively.

62 *Ibid.* 39–40.

63 *Ibid.* 37; especially the monosyllabic verbs (*dwan, gan, stan, jan,* etc.) and their derivations are made to rhyme with deviant words in final *-n*, mostly infinitives and the past participle *(e)dan*, but also nouns such as *underdan* and the verbal form *quam*. The word *openbaere* generates the use of many deviant rhymes, such as *ware*, *jare*, but note the regular rhymes *openbere* : *were*, and even *openbare* : *were*.

64 Campbell, Review of Buma, *Houlikstaspraken*, 208.

65 Note that all forms after ':' have been taken from the text.

3. *ō* ⟨oe⟩ and ⟨o⟩ instead of OFris *ā* (of various origin): *also* 'thus' av.; *so* 'then, so, as, if' av., conj. (cp. OFris *sā*); *tho, do* 'then' av. (cp. OFris *thā*); *also* 'thus, so, when' conj.; *doet* 'dead' aj. (cp. OFris *dād, dāth*); *grote, groet* 'great, big, large' aj. (cp. OFris *grāt*); *hoge, hoghe, hogesta* 'high' aj. (cp. OFris *hāch*); hoge 'earnestly' av. (cp. OFris *hāge*); *hoft* 'head' n. (cp. OFris *hāved, haud, hāwid*).

4. *ē* instead of OFris *ā* (< Gmc *ai*): *meer* 'more' av. (cp. OFris *mār*).

5. Retention of *-n-* before original voiceless fricatives *-s-*, *-þ-*: *unse, onser* 'our' poss. (cp. OFris *ūse(r)*); *ander* 'other' aj. (cp. OFris *ōther*, *ōr*); *cund* 'known' aj. (cp. OFris *kūth*).

6. Absence of *i*-mutation: *koning* 'king' n. (cp. OFris *kening*); *sonde* 'sin' n. (cp. OFris *sende*); *forhorde* 'to hear' pret.3sg. (cp. OFris *hēra*); *horad, hored* 'to hear' imp.pl; *noet* 'fear, danger, hardship' n. (cp. OFris *nēd*); *scone, scoen* 'beautiful' aj. (cp. OFris *skēne, skiene*).

7. Retention of final *-n* in infinitives and prepositions, a feature not known in Old Frisian: *binden* 'to bind'; *bodian* 'to summon'; *far(r)an* 'to go'; *feran* 'to carry'; *fiochten* 'to fight'; *flian* 'to fly'; *hlopen* 'to run';[66] *keran, keren* 'to turn'; *comman* 'to come'; *leran, leren* 'to teach'; *letten* 'to prevent'; *prediken* 'to preach'; *rijden* 'to ride'; *segan, seg(g)en* 'to say'; *springan* 'to leap' inf.; and the prepostions *binnan* 'within' (OFris*binna*) and *bowen, bouen* 'above' (OFris *bova*).

8. Use of the prefix *ghe-* in verbal and nominal forms, a feature not known in Old Frisian: *ghebonden* 'bound'; *ghecomen* 'come' *gheleid* 'lead' pp.; *welgheboren* 'nobly born' aj.

9. Occurrence of pres.1sg. 'can, able, be allowed': *mach* (cp. OFris *mey, mei*).

10. Occurrence of pres.2/3sg. 'shall': *sal(tu), ?scal* (cp. OFris *skel, skil*).

11. Occurrence of pres.sg. 'to have': *hevet* (cp. OFris *hat*).

12. Occurrence of pret.pl. 'to be': *waren* (cp. OFris *wēren*).

13. Occurrence of pret.pl.subj 'to be': *ware* (cp. OFris *wēre*).

14. Occurrence of pret.3sg. 'to become': *wert* (cp. OFris *wart*).

15. Occurrence of pret.3sg. 'to speak': *sprac(k)* (cp. OFris *sprec*).

16. Occurrence of pret.3sg. 'to come': *(to) quam* (cp. OFris *cōm*).

---

66 The form *hlopen* is interesting, because initial *h-* in *hl-* was lost in Low German around 1000 A.D., whereas it was retained in Old Frisian much longer, i.e. *hlapa*. I owe this observation to H. Nijdam.

17. Occurrence of pers.pron.nom.2pl. 'you': *ghi* (cp. OFris *ī, hī, hy*).
18. Occurrence of conjunction 'and': *end(e)* (cp. OFris *and(e)*).
19. Occurrence of adverb 'gladly, eagerly': *gerne* (cp. OFris *ierne*).
20. Occurrence of noun '(age of) the world': *werrild, werald, werreld* (cp. OFris *wrald*).
21. Occurrence of adverb 'not': *niet* (cp. OFris *nāt, naut*).

As in the three *Basle Wedding Speeches*, the admixture occurs in all the major word categories. We also observe the same alternation between deviant and 'proper' forms – for a list of all deviant forms that occur alongside the corresponding regular Old Frisian form(s) in the *Riim*, see Appendix II.[67] As in the speeches, the spelling in the *Riim* is problematic. First, we have to take into account that the extant text of the *Riim* is a seventeenth-century transcript made by Gabbema. It is not known how much he altered the spelling and the forms in the text. Additionally, as in the speeches the deviant forms are often practically homonymous with the current Old Frisian forms, for example *slaep/sleep, waarheid/weerheid, gerne/ierne,* and again we should wonder whether we are not dealing with spelling choices rather than with language choice. The spelling is generally inconsistent, for example *rad*, *raed*, and *raet* for the same lexeme, but this is the rule for any mediaeval vernacular. Nonetheless, in the *Riim* we encounter spelling varieties that seem to fall somewhere in between an acceptable Old Frisian form and the recognisably Middle Dutch form, for example the infinitive ending *-an*, but also *scal*, *cam*, and *that.* Still, as in the Basle speeches, there are also deviant forms which are too dissimilar from Old Frisian to be explained away as spelling choices, such as *hoft, ander, werreld, onser/unse.* We have seen that the alleged admixture in the Basle speeches may partly arise from the transfer of Middle Low German or Middle Dutch elements into the language of the speeches due to the use of specific written examples. To the best of my knowledge nothing comparable has been suggested for the *Riim*, even though Campbell has suggested instead that in the *Riim* part of the

67 The following function words which occur in (some of) the Basle speeches are absent from the *Riim*: the personal pronoun dat./acc.2pl. *u* 'you'; *io/jo* is used throughout; the indefinite pronouns *ghemen* 'no one' and *gheen* 'nobody'; *nin* and *ne(e)n* are used throughout; the pronoun/conjunction *wo* 'how, why'; *ho*, *hu*, and *hoe* is used throughout; the adjective *eyghen* 'own'; *ain* is used throughout. The following 'current' Old Frisian forms are used which are deviant in (some of) the Basle speeches: *aeck* 'also', *buta* 'outside', *dath*, *dad* 'death', *trast* 'help, support', *altheer / alder* 'there', *twa* 'two', *kinden* 'children' with current plural in *-en*; *stoed* pret.3sg., *hemmen* pers.dat./acc.3pl., *h(i)ara* poss. 3pl. Infinitives in *-an* do not occur in the Basle speeches. In many cases such infinitives appear to be a hybrid form between the Old Frisian ending *-a* and MDu/MLG *-en*.

transfer of Dutch elements may have been caused by the use of fixed expressions known from Middle Dutch verse.

7. Conclusion

We have to conclude that the *Riim* does indeed exhibit features very similar to those encountered in the three *Basle Wedding Speeches*. As I have shown, deviant elements are also found in the *Riim* in all the major word categories. Indeed, among the function words in the *Riim*, we often encounter the same deviant forms as in (some of) the speeches. Furthermore, the *Riim* shows an alternation of 'borrowed' and 'regular' forms similar to that observed in the speeches. In fact, this feature seems to be even more widespread in the *Riim*.

The admixture in all four texts is therefore certainly comparable, and the suggestion made by Campbell that we are dealing here with an admixture that was normal in written Frisian in the fifteenth century is a likely explanation – a specific register of fifteenth-century West Frisian which allowed the use of forms from the neighbouring languages, because 'literary activity had been more normal in Dutch and Low German than in Frisian, and hence the non-Frisian forms had a certain literary flavour.'[68] Indeed, in all likelihood literate mediaeval Frisians were multilingual. It is significant that of all literary (historical, devotional) works written in fifteenth-century Frisia a substantial number was written in Dutch. Literate Frisians were certainly familiar with chronicles and religious texts in Middle Dutch and Middle Low German. Furthermore, exactly those genres that flourished in the Low German area did not really develop in Frisia. Vries suggested that the Frisian-speaking area must to a certain extent have been dependent on the culture of the surrounding areas.[69] Since literate Frisians such as the authors of the speeches and the *Riim* were certainly familiar with these texts and their languages, it is very likely that these will have influenced their written Frisian considerably.

The possibility that all texts discussed here partly spring from the same literary tradition may also be supported by the occurrence of the same Frisian phraseology in both the *Riim* and Basle Text I (and III, though this may derive from I), for example:

> *Riim* 231: *Thit willa wi nu leta staen*
> *Riim* 306–07: *Thet wille wi nu lete stan / and en other rijm ontfaen*
> *Riim* 432–33: *Thet wil ic leta stan / it Camme wil icket ontfaen*
> *Riim*, 529–30: *Thit willa wi nu leta stan / een other willa wi onfan*

---

[68] Campbell, Review of Buma, *Houlikstaspraken*, 208.

[69] O. Vries, *'Naar ploeg en koestal vluchtte uw taal'. De verdringing van het Fries als schrijftaal door het Nederlands (tot 1580)* (Leeuwarden, 1993), 65.

Basle I, 40–41: *Dyt ville vy nv laten stan / ende vollet nv tho kerle faen*
Basle III, 15–17: *Want da twa lesta da wil ik leta stan / ende ik wil da eersta an faen etc.*
Basle III, 157: *Dyt will wy leta stan etc.*

Further research needs to be done in order to assess the nature of such a 'mixed' Old Frisian register in existence during the later fifteenth century. The language of other (contemporary) texts such as the corpus of charters (the greater part of which was written between 1450–1525) or the texts in *Jus*, *Unia*, and especially the contemporary *Druk* will also need to be searched for Middle Dutch or Middle Low German features.

A preliminary survey of the language of the charters yields several deviant forms which also occur in the Basle speeches and the *Riim*.[70] They are generally cases of morphological and lexical deviance. Even so, past participles like *ghescreuen* do occur, but are outnumbered by forms without prefix *ghe-*. Furthermore, forms like *vns(e)/ons(e)* are frequent, but certainly less so than the regular Old Frisian forms *ws(e)/us(e)*; we find both *ander* and *other*; also *sal*, but Old Frisian forms *sc(h)el* and *sc(h)il* are more common; *g(h)een* occurs, but *ne(e)n* is more dominant. On the other hand, the forms *dat* and *so(e)/zo(e)* are clearly more widely used than corresponding *thet* and *sa*. The forms that deviate in their vocalism or initial consonants seem to be considerably less common in the charters. A few examples: *da(e)r* occurs regularly, but *the(e)r* clearly dominates; we find both *oeck* and *ack*; also *jaer*, but *je(e)r* is more common. The form *jaer* often occurs in the dating formula *int jaer ons/ws Heren* 'in the year of our Lord'. This further supports my suggestion that some deviant elements entered the language through the influence of Dutch and Low German exempalrs and their spelling conventions. Needless to say that further research is required. Nevertheless, the preliminary picture that emerges is that of a stratification of Middle Dutch/Middle Low German influence in Old Frisian texts. The more literary the register (the register with the least native tradition) the higher the frequency of deviant forms.

Finally, I have argued that the alleged admixture in the four texts under scrutiny was principally a feature of written language. Regarding the Basle speeches, I have suggested that it sprang partly from spelling choices and the overlap between the spelling of Frisian and that of Middle Dutch and Middle Low German; partly from the use of specific texts in these languages, whose features sometimes ended up in the extant texts of the speeches. Additionally, it may have been perfectly acceptable in certain Old Frisian genres freely to borrow from neighbouring languages with which most literate Frisians

70 For an introductory survey of the language of the charters, see O. Vries, 'Die altfriesischen Urkunden', *Handbuch / Handbook*, 594–601, at 597–600.

would have been familiar, perhaps in order to add to the stock of rhymes or because of the literary flavour of these languages. Therefore, whether the extant texts can tell us anything about the contemporary spoken language situation remains problematic. It seems hazardous to draw firm conclusions about the language spoken by their authors, let alone to regard these texts as an indication of language shift. Texts such as the *Basle Wedding Speeches* may serve as an example of how difficult it is to make statements about spoken language on the basis of these kinds of written texts, with their own particular and often problematic origins and traditions.[71]

[71] As I have also shown for Late Gaulish (Celtic) in A. Blom, '*Lingua Gallica*: Studies in the Languages of Late Antique Gaul' (Unpublished Ph.D. Thesis, Cambridge).

Appendix I

Alternation between deviant and regular forms in the three *Basle Wedding Speeches*. Numbers between brackets denote the frequency with which the forms occur in the text.

I	II	III
		werelt (1) n. *wrald* (1) n.
		leuen (2) n. *lib⟨ba⟩* (2) inf.
		aldus dan aj. (1) *aldus den* aj. (1)
heft (1), *heeft* (3) pres.3sg.	*hat* (1) pres.3sg.	*heft* (1) *heeft* (2) pres.3sg. *hat* (3) pres.3sg.
mach (1) pres.1sg.	*mey* (2) pres.3sg.	
		sal (1) pres.3sg. *sc(h)el* (7), *schil* (1) pres.3sg.
		wert (1) pret.3sg. *wart* (1) pret.3sg. *wert* (4) pret.3sg. *wart* (1) pret.3sg.
		quam (1) pret.3sg. *kom, com* (4) pret.3sg.
ghescoep (1) pret.3sg.	*scop* (1) pret.3sg.	
ghemaket (1) pp.	*maket* (2), *makat* (1) pp.	*ghemaket* (1) pp. *maghet* (1), *maket* (2) pp.
ghescreuen (1) pp.	*screuen* (1) pp.	*ghescreuen* (2) pp.[1] *screuen* (2) pp.
ghesproghen (1) pp.	*spritzen* (1) pp.	
gheheylighet (2) pp.	*heylighat* (1) pp.	
gheuen (1) inf.	*iuwe* (1), *jowe* (4) pres.subj.3sg.	
laten (1) inf.	*lete* (1) inf.	
		merken (1) inf. *merka* (1) inf.
		nyet (1) av. *na(e)t* (7) av.
		ma⟨er⟩ (1) av.[2] *mer* (4) conj.
		wo (1) av. *ho(e)* (2) av. *hoe* (1) conj.

I	II	III
		daer (1) av. *ther* (3) av. *dar* (2) rel. *der* (16) rel.
		tho/do (5) av. *tho/doe* (3) conj. *da* (1) av. *tha/da* (3) conj. *tho* (1) av. *da* (5) av.
		dat/that (8) conj. *dat/that* (9) pron. *thet* (4) conj. *thet* (6) pron.
		ende (27) conj. *and* (7) conj.
		twe (1) num. *twa woerd* (1) n.
bouen (1) prep.	*buppa* (3) prep.	
gheen (1) pron.	*ne(e)n(e)* (3) pron.	*gheen* (4) pron. *nen(e)* (3) pron.
ons (1), *vns* (1) 1pers.pl. dat./acc.	*ws* (2), *hws* (3) 1pers.pl. dat./acc.	
ghy (2) 2pers.pl. nom.	*hy* (1) 2pers.pl. nom	
		w (1) 2pers.pl. dat. *yo* (1) 2pers.pl. dat.
sye (1) 3pers.pl.nom.	*hya* (5) 3pers.pl. nom.	
hoer (2), *horen* (2) 3pers.pl. dat.	*hyaren* (2) 3pers.pl. dat.	
hoer(e) (2) poss. 3pl.	*hyare* (1) poss. 3pl.	

1 Note that both have been abbreviated in the manuscript.

2 Reading uncertain.

Appendix II

Alternation between deviant and regular forms in *Thet Freske Riim*

Deviant	Regular
rad(e) (11), *raed* (4), *raet* (1) 'council'	*reed* (1), *rede* (4)
jare (3), *jaer* (1) 'year' n.	*je(e)r* (4)
nade (2) 'mercy' n.	*nede* (5), *nethe* (2)
slaep (1), *slape* (1) 'sleep' n.	*sleep* (3), *slepe* (3)
waerheid (1) 'truth' n.	*weerheid* (2)
water (1) 'water' n.	*weter* (3)
hoft (1) 'head' n.	*haud* (15), *hawet* (1), *haved* (1)
hemelrijke (1)[1] 'heavenly kingdom' n.	*himelrijke* (5), *himelryk(e)* (3)
werreld (2), *werrild* (1), *werald* (1) 'world' n.	*wrald(e)* (18)
doet (3) 'dead' aj.	*dad* (6)
gro(e)t(e) (2) 'great, big, large' aj.	*gra(e)t(e)* (15)
hogesta (1) 'highest' aj.	*hagesta* (1)
scone (11) 'beautiful' aj.	*scene* (2)
welgheboren (1) 'nobly born' aj.	*wel boren* (1)
ander (2) 'other' aj.	*other(e)*, *or(a)* (18)
bodian (1) 'to summon' inf.	*bodia* (2)
far(r)ran (7) 'to go' inf.	*far(r)a* (4), *vare* (2)
feran (1) 'to carry' inf.	*fera* (2)
keran (1), *keren* (2) 'to turn' inf.	*kera* (1), *kere* (1)
comman (1) 'to come' inf.	*coma* (1)[2]
leran (1), *leren* (1) 'to teach' inf.	*lera* (2)
rijden (1) 'to ride' inf.	*ride* (1)
segan (1), *seg(g)en* (2) 'to say' inf.	*sega* (3)
mach (2) 'can, be able' pres 1sg	*mei* pres.3sg. (1)
sal(tu) (1) 'shall' pres 2sg	*scil tu* (14) pres.2sg., *scil* (17) pres.3sg.[3]
hevet (1) 'to have' pres.3sg.	*hat* (1), *hath* (1)
wert (1) 'to become' pret.3sg.	*ward* (1), *wart* (4)
forhorde (1) 'to hear' pret.3sg. *horad* (15), *hored* (2) 'to hear' imp.pl.	*hera* (1) inf.
quam (13) 'to come' pret.3sg.	*com* (37), *coem* (2)[4]
waren (4) 'to be' pret.3pl.	*weren* (26), *were* (8)
ware (2) 'to be' pret.3pl.subj.	*were* (1)
ghebonden (1) 'to bind' pp.	*bonden* (1)
ghecomen (1) 'to come' pp.	*comen* (9), *komen* (4)
daer (1)[5] 'there'	*ther* (19), *theer* (1)
openbaer (2), *openbare* (13) 'clear, public, manifest' av.	*openber(e)* (14), *oppenbere* (1)
for war(e) (2) 'truly' av.	*wer(e)* 'true' aj. (throughout the text)[6]
hoge (1) 'earnestly' av.	*hage* (1)
gerne (3) 'gladly, eagerly' av.	*ierne* (2)

Deviant	Regular
niet (1) 'not' av.	*na(e)t* (35), *naut* (7)
neder (11) *nether* (1) 'down' av.	*nitha* (1)
daer (1) 'where' conj.	*ther* (4)
dat (1), *that* (5) 'that, so that' conj.[7] *dat* (1), *that* (1) conj.[8]	*thet* (114) *thet* (23)
tho (9), *do* (3) 'then' av.	*tha* (44)
tho (32), *do* (1) 'when' conj.	*tha* (70), *da* (2)[9]
ende (13), *en* (10), *end* (124), *ent* (1) 'and' conj.	*and* (231), *ande* (3), *an* (7)
binnan (2) 'within, inside' prep.	*binna* (11)
bowen (1), *bouen* (1) 'above, over' prep.	*boppe* (1)
wat (3) 'what' inter[10]	*hot* (14)
dat (15), *that* (2) 'the, that' dem.acc.sg.neut.	*thet* (129)
ghi (18) 'you' pers.nom.2pl.	*i* (10), *j* (29)
si (1), *se* (3) 'they' pers.nom.3pl.; as first word of clause	*hia* (77), *hja* (4), *hio* (1)
unse (1), *onsen* (1) 'our' poss.1pl.	*ws* (1), *wsa* (2), *usa* (1), *wse* (6), *user* (1), *wser* (2), *use* (1)

1 Note that *himel* 'heaven' and *himelsch* 'heavenly' always have (Frisian) *-i-* in the *Riim.*

2 Note the curious form *comnia* (2). It probably arose as a copying error through confusing ⟨m⟩ with ⟨ni⟩: ⟨m⟩ renders 'correct' Old Frisian *comma.*

3 Note the hybrid(?) form *scal* (1).

4 Note the hybrid(?) form *cam* (8).

5 As the equivalent of a pronoun referring to a thing, anticipating a noun clause, or of general reference governed by a following proposition, see Campbell, *Freske Riim*, 229.

6 Note the form *verwere* (1) 'truly' av., which is 'miswritten' according to Campbell.

7 Introducing nominal clauses.

8 Introduced pleonastically into clauses in which some element other than the subject is emphasised by the addition of *thet.*

9 N.B. Several erroneous forms.

10 In indirect questions.

Language and Contents of the Old Frisian Manuscripts from Rüstringen (*c.*1300): A 'Veritable *Mixtum Compositum*'

Rolf H. Bremmer Jr

0. Introduction

The Old Frisian that has come down to us in medieval manuscripts written in the *terra Rustringa / Rustringorum* or *Riostringalond* differs in some remarkable ways from the Old Frisian as we know it from contemporary or near-contemporary sources originating from other Frisian regions. The difference is most exceptional in its vocalism – a brief glance is sufficient to establish whether or not a text is written in Riustring Old Frisian. Most of the sound changes which gave this Old Frisian dialect its peculiar shape have been described long ago. In the present study, I shall first treat of the various medieval and post-medieval sources that together allow us to establish the rules that applied to Riustring Old Frisian. Next I shall draw attention to a number of problematic forms in the Riustring manuscripts that do not follow these rules. I conclude with a discussion of these deviant forms which, I shall argue, are relicts of exemplars written in a non-Riustring Frisian dialect. Their presence has unexpected implications for our understanding of the genesis of the manuscripts in which they have been recorded.

1. Weser Old Frisian – the Background

At least since Karl Freiherr von Richthofen's dictionary of 1840, Old Frisian has been divided into two main dialects, West and East Frisian.[1] The border line dividing these two branches is the river Lauwers, only a small stream today but in the Middle Ages an important watercourse which discharged the water of vast inland marshes to the North Sea. Even in Carolingian times, as the *Lex Frisionum* (*c.*802) tells us, the Lauwers constituted an important territorial barrier. Later, Theodor Siebs subdivided East Frisian into a western branch which he called 'Ems Frisian', because it was spoken on

1 K. von Richthofen, *Altfriesisches Wörterbuch* (Göttingen, 1840; repr. Aalen 1961, 1970), [581–82].

either side of the Ems estuary, and an eastern branch which he termed 'Weser Frisian', spoken on either side of the Weser estuary.[2] Basically, the three main dialect branches of West, Ems and Weser Frisian concur – not entirely fortuitously it would seem – with the late-eighth- and early-ninth-century diocesan division of medieval Frisia: the bishoprics of Utrecht, Münster and Bremen, respectively.

Weser Old Frisian survives in a number of sources of varying quantity and quality, but they have in common that all of them were produced in Rüstringen, the most important *terra* of the Frisian part of the Bremen diocese. We have no Old Frisian documents from the other Frisian *terrae* in this bishopric, Astringen, Wangerland, Harlingerland, Norderland and the eastern half of Brokmerland to the west, and the small trans-Weser 'colonies', Würden and Wursten, to the east of Rüstringen (see map on p. viii). Economically, socially and politically, these lands did not differ much from the other Frisian lands in the thirteenth century. Agriculture was one cornerstone of their prosperity, trade in agricultural products another. Their merchants plied the 'water streets' to Bremen and Hamburg, the coastal waters to Holland, Zealand, and the open sea to as far as England, France, Scandinavia and the Baltic shores. They were an adventurous people for whom no horizon seemed too distant. Adam of Bremen, author of the *Gesta Hammaburgensis ecclesiae pontificum* (*c.* 1075), relates how Frisian sailors living on the Weser estuary ventured beyond the North Cape into the Arctic Ocean. In the late 1270s, the joint judges and diet of Astringen and Wangerland wrote a request to King Philip III of France in which they asked for certain privileges for their merchants. Quite diplomatically, they also reminded Philip of their participation in the crusade which his late father (St.) Louis had undertaken to Tunis not long before.[3] By this time, the Weser Frisians had been free from feudal overlordship for more than a century. Instead it was their local aristocracy, consisting of allodial peasants, who steered public life. From their midst they chose judges in rotation to regulate communal and political matters. It was their duty, amongst other things, to conclude treaties with external parties, to send delegations to the inter-Frisian assembly at Upstalsbam in Brokmerland, to draw up statutes for its

---

[2] T. Siebs, 'Geschichte der friesischen Sprache', *Grundriss der germanischen Philologie*, ed. H. Paul, 2nd edn (Strassbourg, 1901), §§4–5.

[3] Adam of Bremen, *Gesta Hammaburgensis ecclesiae pontificum*, ed. B. Schmeidler, MGH SS in usu scholarum (Hanover and Leipzig, 1917), IV.42–43; Astringen request: P. J. Blok, 'Oorkonden betrekkelijk Friesland en zijne verhouding tot Frankrijk in de 13e en 14e eeuw', *De Vrije Fries* 19 (1900), 317–34, at 324; Louis had been actively recruiting support throughout Frisia for this (eighth) crusade, see *Kroniek van het klooster Bloemhof te Wittewierum*, ed. H. P. H. Jansen and A. Janse (Hilversum, 1991), 422–23.

inhabitants to live by, and to negotiate with neighbouring Frisian lands – more than once with Astringen – for the compensations of casualties and injuries after violent clashes.

The Christian faith had been preached to the Weser Frisians by the Northumbrian St Willehad at the behest of Charlemagne in the 780s, after he had subjected all of Frisia Magna to his rule. It was in Blexen, Rüstringen, that Willehad died in 789. Around 1100, an anonymous annotator of Adam of Bremen's *History of the Archbishops of the Hamburg Church* boasted in a *scholion* that the Frisian lands in the Bremen diocese counted no fewer than fifty churches. The first monastery, a Benedictine foundation in all likelihood, had been established in Reepsholt (Astringen) in 986, but it would take more than two centuries before the next ones followed. First, around 1200, a Benedictine double monastery in Meerhusen was established by Hathebrand, the first abbot of Feldwerd Monastery in Fivelgo. After a reform in 1228, Meerhusen became a nunnery, while its monks joined the Cistercians and founded a new monastery, Schola Dei, in Ihlow, a few miles south of Meerhusen. Both houses were situated in the vast and as yet unreclaimed moors of the Bremen part of Brokmerland. Rüstringen had to make do without monasteries except for a house of the Hospitallers of St. John which was founded near Varel before 1319. All in all, in the thirteenth century there was a considerable clerical potential in and around Rüstringen. We have no information on the presence of schools there, but some kind of instruction must have been available; for advanced education the Bremen cathedral school seemed to be a good first option. Most evidence of Riustring literacy lies in the Latin charters; the formulas with which they were written and the seals attached to them bear witness to their participating in the international conventions of written diplomacy, but by whom they were written and where in Rüstringen, again, is unknown. Much the same applies to the vernacular documents.

2. The Riustring Manuscripts and their language – archaic?

The most important of the vernacular sources is the First Riustring Manuscript (R1), a well-produced parchment codex provided with a number of ornamental initials of various size to signal the beginning of individual texts. One of its two scribes reveals himself in the colophon rhyme as Ricmarus. On paleographical grounds this codex can be dated to the close of the thirteenth century.[4] R1 is followed in size by the Second Riustring Manu

4 Oldenburg, Niedersächsisches Staatsarchiv, Bestand 24-I, An. Nr. 1; cf. I. Stahl, *Handschriften in Nordwestdeutschland. Aurich-Emden-Oldenburg* (Wiesbaden, 1993), 217: 'um 1300'. Diplomatic edition: *De Eerste Riustringer Codex*, ed. W. J. Buma, OTR 11 (The Hague, 1961); critical edition with facing German translation: *Das Rüstringer*

script (R2), which has not survived as a medieval manuscript, but in one complete and two partial transcripts made by the Bremen syndic and historian Gerhard Oelrichs (1727–1787). According to the medieval scribe's colophon, R2 was finished in 1327.[5] Our third source concerns four short Frisian passages which were copied in the late fifteenth century from a manuscript (R3), now lost, onto two facing leaves (fols. 15v and 16r) of an octavo paper document recording lists of rents paid to the lord of Rüstringen, Astringen and Wangerland, who resided in Jever.[6] The first of these passages gives the compensation to be paid for cutting off somebody's hair while simultaneously bloodily removing the scalp in the action. The other three passages concern instructions on how to convert older Riustring types of money into more recent ones. Apart from the regulation for compensation, the Frisian of these passages is highly coloured by Low German spelling conventions.[7] Finally, a third early-fourteenth-century Riustring manuscript (R4) lamentably survives only as five fragmentary strips of one leaf of unknown provenance.[8] In addition to these manuscript sources, we also have a few stray vernacular words and names in Weser Old Frisian interspersed in Latin charters and chronicles.

The Old Frisian language as found in R1 has long attracted the attention of scholars, including Jacob Grimm and Rasmus Rask, because its texts with a detailed commentary had already been published by Tiedeman Wiarda in the early years of the nineteenth century.[9] In the introductory matter to his edition, Buma remarked: 'The Riustring Codex R1 has been held in high

---

Recht, ed. W. J. Buma and W. Ebel, AR 1 (Göttingen, 1961), part A. My quotations from R1 in this article are from Buma 1961.

5 Diplomatic edition: *Het Tweede Rüstringer Handschrift*, ed. W. J. Buma, OTR 8 (The Hague, 1954). Critical edition: *Das Rüstringer Recht*, ed. Buma and Ebel, part B. My quotations from R2 are from Buma's OTR edition.

6 By then, one Frisian aristocratic family had assumed the role of supreme ruler of these lands.

7 The present whereabouts are unknown of this manuscript that should have been in Oldenburg, Niedersächsisches Landesarchiv-Staatsarchiv, Mscr. Abt. Jeverland (kind information Dr Matthias Nistal, 16 January 2006). Diplomatic editions: A. Lübben (1874), 'Altfriesisches', *ZfdP* 5, 201–03; G. Sello, *Sudien zur Geschichte von Oestringen und Rüstringen* (Varel, 1898), 78–79; critical edition: F. Holthausen, 'Altfriesische Münzwerte und Bußsätze', *BGdSL* 60 (1936), 458–60. The provision for compensation is almost verbatim the same as found in the *Riustring Register of Compensations* in R1 VI 1c.

8 The Hague, Koninklijke Bibliotheek, Hs. 135 C 81; discussed and edited in P. Gerbenzon, 'Oudfriese handschriftfragmenten in de Koninklijke Bibliotheek te 's-Gravenhage', *TRG* 50 (1982), 263–77. My quotations from R4 refer to Gerbenzon's edition.

9 T. D. Wiarda, *Asega-Buch. Ein altfriesisches Gesetzbuch der Rüstringer* (Berlin and Stettin, 1805).

esteem since the rise of Germanic studies, not only on account of its contents and style, but also because of the form of its language. On account of its age, this manuscript considerably differs in linguistic respect from the sources which have come down to us from other Old Frisian districts'. And: 'The old-fashioned Riustring legal language with its clear orthography and full inflexional endings is hence a delight for the eye and the ear'.[10] A greater advocate for the merits of the Riustring language than Buma is hard to find. It would seem that Dirk Boutkan tried to emulate Buma: 'The First Riustring Manuscript is a precious, perhaps the most precious artifact of Old Frisian literature. … [I]ts style is of an unexpected literary colouring. It has been the subject of intensive study because of its archaic language'.[11] Boutkan also echoes Buma's words quoted above in his justification of the selection of only R1 as the basis for an etymological dictionary of Old Frisian, 'because linguistically, [R1] is the most archaic Old Frisian manuscript'.[12]

Neither Buma nor Boutkan madke any attempt at justifying their claims with regard to the alleged age of the language of R1. As such, they are representatives of a long line of scholars who implicitly expressed a desire of reading a receding Germanic past into many Old Frisian texts rather than valuing these records as reflections of the period in which they had been written. In fact, their opinions appear to be a kind of commonplace which stretches back all the way to the mid-eighteenth century when it was formulated by Matthias von Wicht (1694–1778). This legal historian was the first scholar to have consulted the First Riustring Manuscript which for a long time had been gathering dust in the library of the Counts of Oldenburg. Von Wicht, who owned a number of less sumptuously produced Old Frisian manuscripts himself, was surprised when he took notice of the language of what he called the 'Asega Book' and opined that it was written 'in der ächten uralten Friesischen Sprache' and considered it to be 'ein theures Kleinod des Alterthums'.[13] The common-place notwithstanding, only a brief glance at the language as found in both R2 (finished in 1327) and R4 (*c.*1300–1330; Buma did not yet know the latter in 1961) should have made Buma and Boutkan aware of the fact that it looks just as 'archaic' as it does

---

[10] *De Eerste Riustringer Codex*, ed. Buma, 47 (all translations from Dutch are mine). Buma does not give references to earlier scholarship in support of his claims, but he may have been thinking of, e.g. W. Heuser, *Altfriesisches Lesebuch mit Grammatik und Glossar* (Heidelberg, 1903), 36, who contended that the Riustring dialect showed Frisian 'in seiner altertümlichsten, edelsten Form'.

[11] D. Boutkan, *A Concise Grammar of the Old Frisian Dialect of the First Riustring Manuscript*, NOWELE Suppl. 10 (Odense, 1996), 1.

[12] D. Boutkan and S. M. Siebinga, *Old Frisian Etymological Dictionary*, Leiden Indo-European Etymological Dictionary Series I (Leiden and Boston, 2005), xi.

[13] M. von Wicht, *Das Ostfriesische Land-recht, nebst dem Deich- und Syhl-rechte* (Aurich, 1746), 171 and 172, respectively.

in R1. Surely, the great linguistic similarity between R1, R2, and R4 cannot be accounted for by the age of the respective manuscripts, because they are all three (near-)contemporary. If the Old Frisian of R1 is archaic, then it follows that the same qualification applies to the language that we find in R2 and R4.

There are further philological reasons for questioning the alleged archaicness of Riustring Old Frisian. As we have seen, R1 is dated to *c.*1300 on paleographical grounds. This date makes R1 roughly coeval with at least one Ems Old Frisian manuscript, the First Brokmer Manuscript (B1), dated to *c.*1300, but certainly after 1276.[14] Moreover, R1, R2 and R4 are all three quite later than the fragment of a Latin psalter with interverbal Frisian glosses, which should be dated on paleographical grounds to the first quarter of the thirteenth century and localized on linguistic indications to an area west of the Ems, most probably to Fivelgo.[15] Neither the Frisian of B1 nor that of the psalter fragment exhibits any of the features that have given Riustring Old Frisian its idiosyncratic shape. Consequently, it is only reasonable to assign no older status or date to Riustring Old Frisian than that it faithfully reflects the language as it was around 1300. Van Helten's commonsensical yardstick for the age of the language of the various Old Frisian manuscripts still holds true: 'Für das alter dieser mundarten ist wohl das alter der mss. als ungefährer massstab anzunehmen'. Certain manuscripts, according to van Helten, might exhibit signs of conservatism in their orthography, but sometimes it is hard to decide whether particular features are indicative of a given time or, alternatively, characteristic of a dialect. In this respect, van Helten singled out the language of Rüstringen which would show some archaisms ('manche altertümlichkeit') in its vocalism, but its dative plural ending in *-n*, against *-m* in non-Riustring manuscripts, would be dialectal.[16]

---

[14] B1: Oldenburg, Niederdeutsches Staatsarchiv, Bestand 24-I, Ab. Nr. 3. On the date, see *Die Brokmer Rechtshandschriften*, ed. W. J. Buma, OTR 5 (The Hague, 1949), 18*; cf. Stahl, *Handschriften in Nordwestdeutschland*, 218: '13. Jh. Ende'. The point was also briefly made by D. Hofmann, 'Die Sprache der Fivelgoer Handschrift', *Studia Neophilologica* 43 (1971), 352–74, at 367; repr. in his *Gesammelte Schriften II*, 299. In 1971 Hofmann pointed out that the vocalism is dialectal rather than archaic; ten years earlier he still was of the opinion that Riustring Old Frisian was 'konservativer' than the other Old Frisian dialects, see his '*Snuh* "Sohn". – Akzentverschiebung und Stammsilbenreduktion im Wurster Friesisch', 304–05; repr. in his *Gesammelte Schriften II*, 140–41.

[15] Groningen, Universiteitsbibliotheek, Hs. 404; edition and commentary by E. Langbroek, '*Condensa atque tenebrosa*; die altfriesischen Psalmen: Neulesung und Rekonstruktion (UB Groningen Hs 404)', *Aspects*, 255–84; R. H. Bremmer, 'Footprints of Monastic Instruction: A Latin Psalter with Interverbal Old Frisian Glosses', *Signs on the Edge. Space, Text and Margin in Medieval Manuscripts*, ed. S. L. Keefer and R. H. Bremmer Jr (Paris, Leuven and Dudley, MA, 2007), 203–34.

[16] W. L. van Helten, *Altostfriesische Grammatik* (Leeuwarden, 1890), xii.

In his edition of the Second Riustring Manuscript (R2) which preceded that of R1 by some seven years, Buma had also addressed the subject of the language of this manuscript. However, he did not discuss such matters as phonology and morphology, but confined himself to the author's style, which according to him 'from beginning to end has something personal about it'.[17] What it is precisely that constitutes this 'something personal' Buma left to the reader to discover. It can hardly be the paraphrase of a statute or the many alliterative phrases and other 'archaic' elements which Buma claims to have noticed particularly in the *Commentary on the Seventeen Statutes* (R2 II) and the *Riustring Register of Compensations* (R2 I). Such stylistic features abound in all of the early Old Frisian legal texts and can barely be said to reveal a personal style. Moreover, there is no ground for us to equate the scribe(s) of the manuscript with the author(s) of its texts.[18] Such an assumption is extremely unlikely if only because the *Riustring Register of Compensations* was included not only in R2, but also in R1 and R4, while one of its provisions was copied into R3. We do not even know whether R2 was produced by only one scribe or several. The latter, for example, is the case with R1, in which scribe two continues the task of scribe one from fol. 19 onwards. Nonetheless, with Oelrichs's transcripts of R2 we are fortunate to have a small corpus which lends us a useful tool with which to compare the language of R1.

Luckily, the evidence of the Old Riustring texts is supplemented by three modern Weser Frisian dialects: those of Harlingerland (recorded in the late seventeenth century), Wursten (two early-eighteenth-century glossaries) and the island of Wangerooge (rather extensively documented in the nineteenth and early twentieth centuries). Of these three, Wangeroogish preserved the Riustring Old Frisian features best, followed by the Wursten dialects, situated in the eastern bank of the Weser, whereas that of Harlingerland participated only very moderately in the Riustring innovations or, alternatively, gave up some of them.[19] The evidence of these modern dialects, in particular

---

[17] *Het Tweede Rüstringer Handschrift*, ed. Buma, 37.

[18] Buma uses the ambiguous Dutch word *schrijver* which can mean both 'author' and 'scribe'.

[19] Harlingerland: Johannes Cadovius Müller, *Memoriale linguae Frisicae. Nach der Jeverschen Originalhandschrift*, ed. E. König (Norden and Leipzig, 1911); Wursten: R. Möllencamp, *Die friesischen Sprachdenkmale des Landes Wursten* (Bremerhaven, 1968); Wangerooge: H. G. Ehrentraut, 'Mittheilungen aus der Sprache der Wangeroger', *Friesisches Archiv* I (1849; repr. Wiesbaden, 1968), 3–109; 338–406; H. G. Ehrentraut, *Mittheilungen aus der Sprache der Wangeroger*, ed. A. Versloot (Leeuwarden, 1996). The latter is a much extended edition of the former, based on Ehrentraut's archives. Unless otherwise noted, all my Wangeroogish forms are taken from this edition. See also the survey in Versloot, 'Grundzüge ostfriesischer Sprachgeschichte'.

the one best recorded, that of Wangerooge, provide a check on what constituted Weser Frisian features.

3. Were the texts in R1 and R2 composed in Rüstringen?

Although the Old Frisian in the Riustring manuscripts may look archaic, this appearance is in fact misleading and is the result of a series of linguistic innovations which it does not share with the other Old Frisian dialects. Especially the effects of vowel balance and vowel harmony have helped give Riustring Old Frisian its peculiar physiognomy which is characterized by full vowels in unstressed final syllables.[20] In the introductory matter to his edition of R1, Buma carefully enumerates, amply discusses and extensively illustrates sixteen characteristics which make Riustring Old Frisian different from the Ems Old Frisian dialect and he points out their regular appearance throughout the manuscript.[21] Fifteen of these characteristics concern innovations, although Buma does not use this term. Buma remained silent on a number of forms in R1 that do not conform to the Riustring rules.

Just as van Helten and Siebs took a bird's eye view of Old Frisian – van Helten of Old East Frisian and Siebs of both Old East and West Frisian – Buma and Boutkan can be said to have taken a holistic approach in their respective analyses of the language of R1. They have treated R1 as if it were not a compilation of twenty separate items but as if the manuscript contained one long, uniform text. By contrast, I have chosen to investigate the language of R1 in relation to its individual texts which are of varying length and genre, most of them of a juridical nature.[22] Some of R1's texts also appear in other, non-Riustring Old Frisian manuscripts, notably the *Seventeen Statutes* (III), the *Twenty-four Landlaws* (IV) – together with a version of the historiographical *Prologue* that precedes this legal tandem in two versions in R1 (items I and II). Next, there is the *General Register of Compensations* (V and XIV) – of which the second part, one third of the entire text, follows only after eight other text items. We know that the *General Register* is split in R1, because it is also known to us from integral recensions in Ems Old Frisian manuscripts. Such texts that feature in all the major manuscripts are also known as 'pan-Frisian' law texts and were intended to

20 On Riustring vowel balance and vowel harmony, see Laura C. Smith's contribution to this volume, and N. Smith and K. van Leyden, 'The Unusual Outcome of a Level-Stress Situation: the Case of Wursten Frisian', *NOWELE* 52 (2007), 31–66.

21 *Eerste Riustringer Codex*, ed. Buma, 47–52 (§10); summarized in Boutkan, *Concise Grammar*, 9–11.

22 Following Buma's edition, I indicate their numbering with roman numerals in my running text, but for practical reasons with arabic numerals in my tables.

contribute to shaping a common ethnic, cultural and political consciousness throughout the conglomerate of the individual Frisian lands.[23]

The pan-Frisian texts in R1 show some signs of having been adapted for a Riustring audience. The 'later' version of the *Prologue*,[24] for example, uniquely adds how during the days of King Charles the younger (i.e. Charlemagne), son of Pippin: '... warth Brema emakad and Frisa wrdon kersten fon tha fiuwer biscopon' (R1 I 115–16: '... [the church of] Bremen was built and Frisians were converted to Christianity by the four bishops'). The missionaries' names are also given: Boniface and Willibrord, Willehad, and Liudger. These four evangelizing pioneers are representative, as it were, of the three bishoprics into which medieval Frisia was divided: Boniface and Willibrord for Utrecht, Willehad for Bremen and Liudger for Münster. Since only the foundation of the church of Bremen is mentioned and since Riustringen belonged to that diocese, it follows that the addition about Bremen in the 'later' *Prologue* in R1 was made to serve local purposes. A similar strategy appears from the tenth of the *Seventeenth Statutes*. Whereas other redactions grant the Frisians exemption from military service further west than the Flie and further east than the Weser, the Riustring recension adds: '[or] further south than the *Wepilinge* and further north than the sea shore' (R1 III 80–81). The Wapel, as it called today, is a small river which marked the southern border of Rüstringen with Ammerland in Saxon territory. Again, such an addition can have been relevant only for a readership/ audience in Rüstringen.

Other texts in R1 seem to be intended for a Riustring audience only, because they explicitly regulate matters for the inhabitants of Riustringen, especially the *Riustring Statutes* (VIII), the *New Riustring Statutes* (IX) and the *Riustring Synodal Law* (XX). Still other ones give no clue as to their regional origin. Such texts are so to speak 'neutral' when it comes to localization on account of their contents, such as *The Fifteen Signs before Doomsday* (XI). Nonetheless, some of these texts have been given modern editorial titles to suggest a Riustring origin, for example: the *Riustring Register of Compensations* (VI) or the *Riustring Compensations for Priests* (XII and XVIII). The only grounds for assuming a Rüstring origin for such 'neutral' texts are that they are included in a manuscript that also contains

---

[23] As extensively argued by T. S. B. Johnston, 'Old Frisian Law and the Frisian Freedom: Text and Manuscript Composition as a Marketing Device', *Approaches*, 179–214. The *General Register* was known west of the Lauwers, even if it has survived only in manuscripts with an East Frisian provenance.

[24] The chronological distinction between the two versions of the *Prologue* in R1 was made by Buma without any arguments. One might just as well call them the 'longer' and the 'shorter' *Prologue*; cf. B. Murdoch, 'Authority and Authenticity: Comments on the Prologues to the Old Frisian Laws', *Approaches*, 215–43, esp. 219 and n. 9.

texts with an explicit Rüstring localization and that their language shows the same features as those that make themselves explicitly known as Riustring.[25]

The spatial 'neutrality' of a text may turn out to be deceptive, however. Let us consider the item *Thet is Ac Frisesk Riucht* (items X and XV), a ragbag of shorter and longer legal provisions with no apparent cohesion and split into two by four intervening unconnected text items. All but one of these provisions begin with the phrase that has led modern editors to give the entire collection its present title. Where the collector had found the disparate items is not clear, except for one, but he surely wanted to highlight their being typically Frisian 'right', thus reaching out to a (western) horizon that stretched out far beyond Rüstringen. According to Buma, part 1 (item X) would be older than part 2 (item XV), because the former is more 'archaistic and poetic' with respect to style than the latter (item XV). As to their relative temporal origin, the two parts would 'definitely' follow one another in chronological order and part two would be 'apparently' later and should be kept separate from the former.[26] In this respect, Buma dissented from von Richthofen's editorial decision to join the two parts to form one running text in his edition of 1840.

I have my doubts whether the collection of legal provisions assembled in *Thet is Ac Frisesk Riucht* allows us to establish such nice chronological distinctions in this particular case. Rather, several indications suggest to me that the two scribes of R1 have been working somewhat chaotically: first, scribe one copied, one after the other, two quite different versions of the *Prologue* (items I and II), a presentation unparalleled in any other of the seven manuscripts which contain the *Prologue*. Next, when he began to write the ninth Statute in text III, scribe two erroneously copied a passage from the seventh Statute from a different exemplar. Finally, like he did with *Thet is Ac Frisesk Riucht*, scribe two, for no obvious reason, copied the *General Register of Compensations* in two parts (items V and XIV), separated from each other by no fewer than eight texts, a procedure he also seems to have followed with the *Riustring Compensations for Priests* (items XII and XVIII). Probably, because the *General Register* is also known to us from other manuscripts, Buma refrained from distinguishing its two parts in

---

25 On the problem of identifying the various Old Frisian manuscripts and their contents with particular Frisian lands, see the seminal study by B. Sjölin, 'Zur Gliederung des Altfriesischen', *UW* 15 (1966), 25–38, esp. 25–29, in which he challenged the traditional regional nomenclature of these manuscripts, such as the First Riustring Manuscript. However, Sjölin's far-reaching conclusion that we cannot distinguish Old Frisian on account of dialects is unwarranted. For counterarguments, see, e.g. Hofmann, 'Die Sprache der Fivelgoer Handschrift', 297–306; H. D. Meijering, 'Die altfriesischen monosyllabischen Infinitive auf *-n* und die Gliederung des Altfriesischen', *Aspects*, 336–48.

26 *De Eerste Riustringer Codex*, ed. Buma, 39 and 42, respectively.

R1 chronologically. On the other hand, I wonder whether Buma was right in giving the same title to the two items that now go under the title *Riustring Compensations for Priests*. We are dealing here with two independent documents although Richthofen edited them, again, as one coherent text. Item XII opens with a short, ideologically charged proem which claims that Charlemagne and Pope Leo together with St Liudger granted a peace (i.e. wergeld) for all priests. Item XVIII, on the other hand, is cast in the shape of a catechism and begins: 'If a *papa* is maimed by a lay man, how much in pounds must he [the lay man] pay in compensation for the seven consecrations?' Moreover, item XVIII borrows almost verbatim an entire passage from item XII, something which would have been redundant if the two items had originally constituted one document.[27] Finally, there is no indication whatsoever to locate these two complementary texts in Rüstringen. On the contrary, the 'Matter of Frisia' in the proem to item XII lifts its contents emphatically above the regional level, and the mention of St Liudger rather than of St. Willehad suggests an origin from that part of Frisia that fell under Münster. Item XVIII, on the wergeld for priests in relation to the number of consecrations they had received, is a topic that is also addressed in other Old Frisian manuscripts.

Thet is Ac Frisesk Riucht in R1 is paralleled by a similar collection in R2 (item V) that has been given the same title for the same reason. The text of this piece in R2 even shares a number of paragraphs with part 2 of R1 (item XV) in a somewhat different recension, suggesting that this text had at least a Riustring circulation. The final clause of *Thet is Ac Frisesk Riucht* in R2, however, deals with 'all the markets in *Hriostringa lond*'. This is another clear indication in view of their overlaps that not only the two collections of *Thet is Ac Frisesk Riucht* but also the two manuscripts themselves in which they appear were produced in Rüstringen for a Rüstring audience.

The unavoidable conclusion that the manuscripts R1 and R2 were produced in Rüstringen does not mean that all the texts they contain were local compositions. The presence of the first five, pan-Frisian items makes such a conclusion abundantly clear and there are further arguments to underpin it. Thomas Johnston has pointed out that the only paragraph of *Thet is ac Frisesk Riucht* in R1 that does not begin with the phrase 'Thet is ac Fresisk riucht', but instead with 'Thet is ac landriucht' ('This is also landlaw'; X.10), was also current in the Frisian districts between the Lauwers and the Ems in the thirteenth century. Johnston demonstrated that the text, which in almost lyrical terms regulates the maintenance of the sea dike (called a 'golden hoop'), indeed originated from that area.[28] Somehow or other, this

27 As pointed out by Buma, *De Eerste Riustringer Codex,* 45.

28 T. S. B. Johnston, '"*Ene zie borch tho bouwenn ...*". A New Look at the *Pan-Frisian Dike Law* in Light of a Low German Ommeland Version', *UW* 44 (1995), 1–37.

dike law had also been received and copied in Rüstringen. We must therefore be aware of the possibility that Rüstringen participated more actively in a much wider circulation of texts written within a wider Frisian space than has hitherto been realized.

4. Analysis and discussion of exceptional forms

As I have briefly indicated, there are a number of forms in Riustring Old Frisian textsthat do not follow the expected rules. For my analysis of these exceptional forms I have taken R1 as my starting point. The discussion of each problematic item is concluded by the plotting of such items in a table in which the texts of R1 are numbered from 1 to 20, in the order that they appear in the manuscript. A key to the respective titles can be found at the end of this paper. In order to gain a clearer picture of Riustring Old Frisian, I have also taken R2 and R4 into consideration for my analysis. Like R1, R2 is a juridical miscellany, if much smaller with its eight texts and, in as far as we know, none of these with precise parallels in non-Riustring Old Frisian manuscripts. The fragments of R4 include a passage from a recension of the *Riustring Register of Compensations*, a list of compositions for injuries which also appears in various degrees of completeness in R1, R2 and R3, as mentioned before. Because the Old Frisian of R3 to a greater or lesser extent is impaired by Middle Low German spelling conventions, I have excluded it from my analysis.

Before I proceed, however, I should first like to express my linguistic creed: I believe, with the Neogrammarians, that each rule concerning phonological and/or morphological changes should in principle be without exception. Likewise, each exception should be explained, preferably according to a rule or at least not with the aid of an *ad hoc* solution. On the other hand, I do not believe with the Neogrammarians that each exception requires a phonological, analogical or intra-paradigmatic levelling explanation. After all, even though we may assume that the scribes who compiled the manuscripts R1, R2 and R4 were native speakers of Riustring Frisian of around 1300, we are dealing not with spoken language but with 'text language'. This language confronts us with the results of multiple copying during an often intricate process of transmission and may not therefore always give a precise reflection of the spoken variety of Riustring Frisian.[29] To be sure, we are dealing with the various scribes' individual realizations of their dialect. However, when the scribes consistently share a significant number of peculiarities which cannot reasonably be interpreted as idiosyncratic spel-

[29] Cf. M. Laing, 'Multidimensionality: Time, Space and Stratigraphy in Historical Dialectology', *Methods and Data in English Historical Dialectology*, ed. M. Dossena and R. Lass (Bern, 2004), 49–96, at 50.

lings and therefore must represent features of their spoken languages – as is also testified by reflexes in the modern dialects – and if, moreover, these peculiarities do not occur in more or less contemporary Old Frisian manuscripts produced outside Rüstringen, we may safely regard these peculiarities as features of the Riustring Old Frisian dialect. My explanation for the exceptional forms will come below in section 6, after I have presented an inventory of nine Riustring dialect features with the forms that deviate from their pattern.[30] Where relevant, each item begins with a reference to the number under which Buma discussed the feature in question.

4.1 Despite my conclusion in the previous section that the language systems of R1, R2 and R4 are more or less coeval and hence broadly similar, in its spelling system R2 sometimes turns out to be slightly different from R1.

In R1, for example, the spelling ⟨ck⟩ for /k/ is found only once, in *Blackeson* (item XX; 'Blexen', a place name), it is encountered five times in R2: *smecka* 'taste', *bithancka* 'to think for oneself', *alreck* 'each of all' (the last one twice; all of them in text I) and *dick-* 'dike' (VI).

The difference in spelling habits between R1 and R2 is borne out even more by the usage of ⟨gh⟩, whether alone to represent /ɣ/:[31] *claghia* 'to raise a complaint', *enighere* 'any' (gen.sg.fem.'), *Walburghe di* 'St Walburga day', or in combinations to represent /ŋg/: *dusinghe* 'dizziness', *lunghene* 'lung(s), *kininghes* 'king' (gen.sg.),*forifonghera* 'bailsman', *longhe* 'long', *thinghe* 'court', or /ɣ:/: *wigghe* 'horse'.[32] In other words, in R2 ⟨gh⟩ serves to represent both [ɣ] and [g] in the cluster [ŋg], but not [g] on its own. R1 has no ⟨gh⟩ spellings.

Whereas the usage of ⟨gh⟩ is confined to R2, and that of ⟨ck⟩ too (with one exception, ⟨ey⟩ as a variant of ⟨ei⟩, on the other hand, is a not unfamiliar spelling both in R1 and R2. For example, in R1 ⟨keiser⟩ occurs once in text I against ⟨keyser⟩- eight times (and 1x in II, 2x in III). The other instances of ⟨ey⟩ in R1 are: *Beyeron* 'Bavaria', *eyder* 'either' (1x against *eider* 12x), *leyd* 'laid', *eyn-* 'own' (3x against *ein-* 13x), *heya-* 'to inaugurate', *leya*

---

[30] The evidence for Riustring Old Frisian is so massive that it seems presumptuous to me to dismiss the existence of this dialect merely as the result of 'vereinzelte graphische Eigentümlichkeiten einer bestimmten Hs.', which have been 'umfunktioniert' by dogmatic Neogrammarians 'zu Merkmale einer gesprochenen Mundart: so entsteht quasi aus dem Nichts eine altfriesische Dialektlandschaft', as claimed by B. Sjölin, '",. . . die aus den friesischen handschriften hervortauchenden dialecte"', *Vulpis Adolatio. Festschrift für Hubertus Menke*, ed. R. Peters, H. P. Pütz and U. Weber (Heidelberg, 2001), 801–08, at 803.

[31] Cf. A. Lasch, *Mittelniederdeutsche Grammatik* (Halle/S., 1914), §341.

[32] With an occasional exception, I have refrained from burdening my argument with the endless mention of precise references to text and line number. The forms in question are easy to track with the inclusive glossaries in Buma's editions.

‘layman’ (2x), *neyl-* ‘nail’. The spelling ⟨ei⟩, however, is dominant in R1 by far. R2, which is less than half the size of R1, nevertheless exhibits a slightly greater number of such spellings: *eyder* (1x against *eider* 7x), *eyn-* (3x), *heya* ‘to inaugurate’ (2x), *heyde* ‘inaugurated’ (3x), *leynd* ‘lying, false’ (1x), *leynmark* ‘mark of a certain value’, *wey* ‘way’ (2x), as well as *wayn-* ‘wain’ (1x) and *ayn-* ‘own’ (3x).[33] R4, a very small portion of text, turns up a single instance of *eyder* against *eider* four times.

Maybe the spelling of R1 is not as ‘clear’ as Buma once thought and as archaic as he implied with the qualification of ‘clear’. For example, Boutkan remarks that ‘[s]poradically we find variation with single *h* in absolute final position or in combination with *-t* to represent [xt]’.[34] He is right, but further analysis tells us that the distribution of absolute final *-h* is confined to text I: *fiuwertih* (1x) against *-tich* (2x) in this text and numerous more instances of *-tich* in the rest of R1;[35] also limited to text I are instances of *-ht*: *riuht* (2x) and *rivht* (3x), and once *londruiht*, a scribal error for *londriuht*, against *riucht* (1x) and *rivcht* (3x). The spelling variant *rivcht* itself makes a limited appearance in R1, and is not found beyond text IV. In the remaining text items, *riucht* is the only form. The spelling of the first syllable in ‘king’, to give another example, turns out to have two possibilities: *kin-* and *kyn-*. Their distribution can hardly be random, *kyn-* being restricted only to items II and III. Even ‘cross’ shows a small, but distinctive distribution pattern: *crioce* appears twice in text I, while *criose* turns up three times elsewhere in R1, and once in R2. The distribution pattern of these non-dialectal but graphologically marked differences is as follows:

R1	*1*	*2*	*3*	*4*	*5*	*6*	*7*	*8*	*9*	*10*	*11*	*12*	*13*	*14*	*15*	*16*	*17*	*18*	*19*	*20*
⟨ey⟩	+	+	+								+				+			+	+	+
⟨ei⟩	+		+	+	+	+	+	+	+	+			+	+	+	+	+	+	+	+
-tih	1																			
riuht	2																			
rivht	3																			
rivcht	3	6	3	4																
riucht	1	0	14	45																
kin-	27	1	20	6			1	1				4								5
kyn-		8	5																	

[33] I take ⟨ay⟩ and ⟨ai⟩ to be allographs for ⟨ei⟩ and ⟨ey⟩, cf. R2 spellings: *aider* ‘either’ (3x), *slaitotha* ‘canine tooth’, and *eslain* ‘struck’ (3x; past ptc.); R4: *slain* ‘id.’.

[34] Boutkan, *Concise Grammar*, 13.

[35] Actually, the form *fiuwertih* was first written as ⟨fiuwerth⟩ after which the scribe, or a corrector, placed an ⟨i⟩ halfway in the space over the ⟨t⟩ and ⟨h⟩ with an insertion mark underneath these two letters.

R1	*1*	*2*	*3*	*4*	*5*	*6*	*7*	*8*	*9*	*10*	*11*	*12*	*13*	*14*	*15*	*16*	*17*	*18*	*19*	*20*
crioce	2																			
criose											2									1

R2	*1*	*2*	*3*	*4*	*5*	*6*	*7*	*8*
⟨ey⟩	1	5		1	1		1	3
⟨gh⟩	3	1			5			3
⟨ck⟩	4					1		

While in this section I have discussed some remarkable differences on a graphematical level, in the following sections I shall treat a number of phonological and morphological forms that call for further attention.

4.2 An indication that the language of R1 is up to the date of its production rather than archaicizing is visible from the way in which the initial cluster Gmc **hr*- is represented in the manuscript.[36] The name of the land and of its inhabitants appears consistently as *Riostring*- (9x). The name is recorded for the first time in Latin narratives as 'Hriustri' in the ninth century (*Annales Francorum*, *Annales Einhardi*) and as 'Riustri' in the *Vita Willehadi* (ca. 861). The latter form may indicate a development from /hr/ > /r/, but need not because ⟨hr⟩ is not an initial cluster in Latin. However, we may assume that the second scribe of R1 – no forms of the name are found in the portion copied by scribe one – knew how to render (and pronounce) the name of the land and the people he was writing for. Apparently, the aspirated nature of the initial cluster /hr/ had become a thing of the past in this scribe's pronunciation. By contrast, the two times that the name occurs in R2 (items V and VI) it appears as *Hriostring*-, as if the scribe was still conscious of its 'good old' spelling. Whether he still realized the aspirated character of /hr/ cannot be stated with any certainty; place-names often retain conservative spellings that do not represent their actual pronunciation.

The *h*-less forms in R1 are: *reilmerk* (9x), *mid-rede* 'midriff' (3x), *in-rif* 'midriff' (2x), *reglemithe* 'back injury' (1x), *rither* 'cattle, neat', *-roft* 'clamour, outcry' (2x), *biropth* 'calls at', and in R2 *rena* 'to smell' (1x) and again *midrede* (4x). The form *midrede* is also encountered once in R4 – the only word in these fragments where *hr*- could have been expected. The forms in R1 with *hr* are: *hrena* 'to smell', *hrene* '(sense of) smell', *bihrepen* 'called at' (past ptc.), all three of them once in the *General Register* (items V and XIV) and *hropath* 'they call', once in the *Fifteen Signs* (XI). Beside

36 On this issue in general, see H. Nijdam, 'The Loss of Old Frisian *H* in Initial Consonant Clusters', *ABäG* 51 (1999), 81–104. In his analysis, Nijdam considers entire manuscripts, not individual texts.

Hriostring, no *hr-* spellings are found in R2. In other words, the scribe of R2 must have been consciously archaising the written form of the name. The absence of *hr-* in R4 and especially in R2, other than in *Hriostring*, suggests to me once more that *r-* < *hr-* had become the rule in Rüstringen by 1300 and that *hr-* was the exception. The distribution is as follows:

R1	*1-3*	*4*	*5*	*6*	*7*	*8*	*9-10*	*11*	*12*	*13*	*14*	*15*	*17*	*18*	*19*	*20*
r < *hr*		+	+	+		+				+		+		+		+
hr			+					+			+					

4.3 (Buma, no. 15) Whereas the dative plural of *hiā* 'they' is *him* in the other Old Frisian dialects, R1 and R2 consistently show *hiam*. At least, that is what van Helten claims[37] and Buma suggests, although the text and Buma's glossary clearly include one occurrence of *him* in R1 (IV 121).

4.4 (Buma, no. 12). In Riustring texts the Old Frisian verb *āga* 'to own; to have to' appears as *hāga* with a prothetic *h*, although not exclusively. In R1, the verb occurs twice without *h* and four times in R2, against numerous times with *h* in both manuscripts. No forms of this verb occur in R4. What the origin is of this *h* is not clear, according to van Helten; it would have been influenced by the *h* of *hebba* 'to have'.[38] The verb has no reflex in Wangeroogish and will have disappeared from the language, as it has done from the other modern Frisian dialects (as well as from Dutch and German). The distribution is as follows:

R1	*1-2*	*3*	*4*	*5*	*6*	*7-8*	*9*	*10*	*11*	*12*	*13*	*14*	*15*	*16-7*	*18*	*19*	*20*
aga		1		1													
haga		12	14	4	1		1	2		1	1	2	14		14	1	11

R2	*1*	*2*	*3*	*4*	*5*	*6*	*7*	*8*
aga		2			1		3	
haga	2	9			2		1	

4.5 Old Frisian displays a wide variety of endings for the nom./acc. plural of strong masculine nouns, the most exceptional of which is *-ar*, *-er*. By the close of the Middle Ages, however, the masc.pl. ending *-ar* had given way in all Old Frisian dialects to other endings, first to *-a* and *-e*, and later to *-an/ -en*.[39]

37 Van Helten, *Altostfriesische Grammatik*, §242.

38 *Ibid.* §307α; so, too, Siebs, 'Geschichte der friesischen Sprache', §132.2.

39 Wangeroogish did not continue the Riustring system of pluralization of the masculine *a*-stems, viz. in *-a*, but played a medley of plural endings instead: *-e*, *-(e)n*, *-s*, and *-er*.

Meijering has made a detailed study of the appearance and distribution of the ending *-ar/-er*.[40] From his survey it appears that this ending can be found in the First Riustring Manuscript and in the Brokmer, Emsingo and Hunsingo manuscripts, all of them of East Frisian provenance. The only other major East Frisian manuscript, the Fivelgo codex, turns up just one such plural form in *letar* 'half-free men', which Meijering takes to be a petrified form. Meijering also calculated how many strong masculine nouns in R1 show the plural ending *-ar*: 25%. They are: text I: *biskopar* 'bishops' (1x), *kiningar* 'kings' (12x) against *kininga* (1x); II: *kyningar* (2x) against *kyninga* (2x); III: *hirigongar* 'inimical raids' (1x); IV: *hirigongar* (1x), *knilingar* 'blood-relations, relatives' (1x), *letar* (1x); VI: *beilar* 'lumps, bruises'; XI: *fiskar* 'fishes', *bamar* 'trees'; XIV: *neilar* 'nails' against *nila* (1x).[41] According to Meijering, the local texts in this manuscript only use *-a* to mark the nom./acc. plural. However, Meijering does not further specify which texts in R1 are local and which not. I assume therefore that those texts which have no counterpart in non-Riustring manuscripts were taken by him to be local. At least that is was his tabulation suggests, but from his listing the form *beilar* is missing so that Meijering must have overlooked it. Quite surprisingly, this form occurs in the *Riustring Register of Compensations*, a text that has always been assumed to be of Rüstring origin. Apart from this, Meijering's survey also clearly demonstrates that by 1300 *-a* had become the productive plural marker. It is quite unlikely for the two scribes of R1 to have used in their daily language the *-ar* and *-a* endings side by side, also because instances of such a free choice are absent from R2 or R4. The following table can be confined to R1:

R1	*1*	*2*	*3*	*4*	*5*	*6*	*7*	*8*	*9*	*10*	*11*	*12*	*13*	*14*	*15*	*16*	*17-9*	*20*
bamar											+							
beilar						+												
biscopar	+																	
hirigongar			+	+														
kiningar	+	+																
fiskar											+							
knilingar				+														
letar				+														

40 H. D. Meijering, 'Het Oudfriese *ar*-meervoud. Feiten en interpretaties', *ABäG* 28 (1989), 21–41.

41 In two successive paragraphs, XIV 9a and 9b, we find first *her and nila* 'hair and nails' and then *her and neilar*. On this fixed phrase, see M. Elsakkers, '*Her anda neylar*': An Intriguing Criterion for Abortion in Old Frisian Law', *Scientiarum Historica* 30 (2004), 107–54.

R1	*1*	*2*	*3*	*4*	*5*	*6*	*7*	*8*	*9*	*10*	*11*	*12*	*13*	*14*	*15*	*16*	*17-9*	*20*
neilar														+				
-*ar* plural	+	+	+	+		+					+			+				
-*a* plural	+	+	+	+	+	+		+		+	+	+	+	+	+	+		+

4.6 (Buma, nos. 5 and 6) An exceptional development for Frisian was (a) Gmc **ag* > **eg* (by way of Fronting) > *ei* (by way of Palatalization), and (b) Gmc **eg* > *ei* (Palatalization). In Riustring Old Frisian the outcome of both these changes was taken one step further and developed to *ī*. For each item in the following exhaustive list I first give the non-Riustring Old Frisian form, followed by its Riustring counterpart:

(a) non-R *dei* ~ R *dī* 'day', non-R *mei* ~ R *mī* 'may', non-R *neil* ~ R *nīl* 'nail', non-R *brein* ~ R *brīn* 'brain', non-R *seininge* ~ R *sīninge* 'blessing (with the sign of the cross)' and non-R *leith* ~ R *līth* 'he lies'
(b) non-R *breida* ~ R *brīda* 'to pull', non-R *wei* ~ R *wī* 'way'

There are nonetheless in R1 a number of exceptions to the rule which Buma does not draw into his discussion of this feature. They are first of all *(-)neil* (5x) / *neyl-* (1x) against the expected form *nīl* (1x, R2 2x).[42] One of these forms is *neilar*, which is exceptional also because of its plural ending (see **4.5**). Moreover, the form *wey* 'way', found twice in R2, is suspect, too; it should have been *wī*, in which form we indeed find it six times in R1 and once in R2. Wangeroogish, too, has *niil* and *wii*, regular reflexes of the Riustring rule.[43] Apparently, *neylon* in R1 and *wey* in R2 call for an explanation, because they run counter to the rule.

Another group of words with *ei* calls for attention, viz. a number of 3.sg.pres. verb forms. They are *sleith* 'he strikes' (< **slagiþ*, 6x, R2 1x), *leith* 'he lies' (< **lagiþ*, 3x), and *dreith* 'he carries' (< **dragiþ*, R2 1x).[44] Only once do we find *lith* 'he lies' conforming to the rule, which in this particular case makes it suspect. When tabulated, we get the following distribution:

---

[42] R2 I 10f reads 'Hiles': either Oelrichs or the scribe erroneously wrote capital 'H' instead of 'N'.

[43] Compare Wang. *dii* 'day', *hiil* 'hail', *mii* 'may', *wii* 'way', *kiil* (< **keil* < **kagil-*) 'cone; skittle', *siil* (< *seil*) 'sail'; *briin* 'brain', *riin* 'rain'; Harlingen *dy* 'day', *nihel* 'nail', *riehn* 'rain'; Wursten *die* 'day', *rin* 'rain', but note Harl. and Wursten *wey* 'way'.

[44] Only *sleith* has a regular reflex in Wang. *slait*; otherwise we have Wang. *licht* and *drächt*. R1 also has *wreith* 'he accuses' form *wrēia* < **wrōgjan-* (cf. OE *wrēgan*) and should therefore be excluded from the discussion here.

R1	*1-4*	*5*	*6*	*7-9*	*10*	*11*	*12-3*	*14*	*15-20*
neil		+	3			+		+	
lith					+				

R2	*1*	*2*	*3*	*4*	*5*	*6*	*7*	*8*
wey		2						

Excursus

In addition to the forms tabulated above, there are a number of problematic forms with ⟨ei⟩, the first of which is *reilmerk* '"cloth"-mark, a certain value for a quantity of cloth', equivalent to four shillings and found *passim* in R1 and R2. In his glossary, Buma (with reference to van Helten) identifies the first element in *reilmark* (usually found as *hreilmerk* in Ems Old Frisian) with OE *hrægl* and OHG *hregil*, *hrecil* 'dress'. Possibly, the word *reilmerk* as a term of value was introduced in Rüstringen from the Ems Frisian area after the rule of *ei* > *ī* had lost its virulence.

The same element *reil-* seems to be present in *reilbende* 'certain kind of fetter', but this lexeme, still according to van Helten, would be cognate to OHG *rigel* (G *Riegel*), MLG, MDu *regel* 'bar, bolt, rail'.[45] Unlike *reilmerk*, which is attested numerous times as *(h)reilmerk* in Ems Old Frisian, *reilbende* is hapax in Old Frisian. The word occurs in R1 in the *General Register of Compensations* in a string of regulations concerning various ways of unlawful fettering. In similar contexts in non-Riustring manuscripts we find *(h)ring-*, *rim-*, *rin-* and *reyngbende* 'ring-shaped fetter, cuffs', often further qualified as 'cold iron'.[46] The form *hrembende* also occurs in this context, albeit once. It could make sense if we take the first element to be related to e.g OE *hremman* 'to hinder, impede' and that is how the word is recorded in current Old Frisian dictionaries.[47] This notwithstanding, I think that we are dealing with originally one lexeme, *hringbende*, which either through phonetic changes or through scribal error has yielded this plethora of forms.

Remarkably, a number of forms seemed to have resisted the rule when they ended in /n/. First of all, there is *wein* (R1 4x) and *wayn* (R2 1x) 'wain', which survived as Wang. *wain*. I have been unable to discover what factor(s) impeded its change to **wīn*, because after all we do have Riustring *brin* 'brain' and *sininge* 'blessing. Then we have *leinmerk* 'a mark worth twelve shillings' (1x), the first element of which is obscure. It has been interpreted as a form of *līn* 'linen', which in view of *reilmerk* makes good sense but is problematic for the ⟨ei⟩. Alternatively,

---

[45] W. L. van Helten, *Zur Lexicologie des Altostfriesischen* (Amsterdam, 1907; repr. Vaduz, Liechtenstein, 1984), 184–85.

[46] Apparently, a *hringbende* consisted of several components, perhaps two cuffs linked with a rope or chain, as indicated by the plural from *send* 'are', e.g.: 'Tha midleste bende, huasa inna thet calde irsen slein werth thet send ena rinbende' ('The middle [manner of] fettering, if anyone is put in cold iron, those are a "ring fetter"'), *De Eerste Emsinger Codex*, ed. P. Sipma, OTR 4 (The Hague, 1941), VII 233–34; cf. *Die 'Fivelgoer' Handschrift*, ed. B. Sjölin, OTR 12 (The Hague, 1970), 197–98, s.v. *hreyngbende*.

[47] F. Holthausen, *Altfriesisches Wörterbuch*, rev. D. Hofmann (Heidelberg, 1985), s.v. *hrembend*.

it has been derived from **lagina* 'what is laid (down)' which formally seems correct, but semantically less convincing. Another problematic hapax is *havedleine* '?head-line, ?noose' in the phrase 'whenever a man is innocently tied around with a *haved-leina*' (R1 IV 15), clearly as a case of unlawful fettering. Van Helten suggested to read *havedsleine* 'head bight (of rope)', Buma preferred the emendation to *havedline* 'head line', Holthausen, followed by Boutkan, also derived this element from **lagina*.[48] This solution is questionable, because *lein* < **lagina* is the past participle of the intransitive verb 'to lie' where semantically we would expect *leid* '(what is) laid' (< **lagid-*). This past participle is indeed once encountered as *leid* in R1, and once as *leyd*, both of them without expected development of *ei* to *ī*.

In R2, a perjurous *asega* ('law speaker') is called a *leynd asyga*. On the face of it, we have a present participle here, but according to van Helten we would be dealing with an adjectival past participle derived from **gi-lugina-id* 'lie, falsehood', with regular dropping of the prefix **gi-* and syncopation of the vowels *-a-i-*. The word would literally mean 'lied'; indeed, *leine* 'lie' is well attested for Old Frisian as is this type of word formation.[49]

A number of past participles likewise failed to obey to the rule, especially those belonging to the strong verbs classes II, VI and VII. For Old Frisian, such past participles were not formed with the Germanic suffix *-*anaz* but with *-*inaz*.[50] The latter suffix brought about *i*-mutation of the stem vowel and palatalization of stem-final -*g*. Thus, **slegina-* > *slein* 'struck, slain' of *slā* – or in compounds such as *thruchslā* 'to strike through (sth.)' – is present with the amply attested forms: *(e-) slein* in R1 (13x) and R2 (3x), and *(e-)slain* in R2 (3x) and R4 (1x). The past participle *tein* of *tiā* 'to pull' is found once (R1). Of these forms, only the former survives in Wangeroogish as *slain*. Remarkably, a derivation of the verb *slā* also fails to conform to the rule: *sleitoth* 'canine tooth, eye-tooth' (< **slege-*), 3x in R1, and once as *slaitoth* in R2.[51] The Wangeroogish reflex of the past participle of *tiā*, on the other hand, shows the rule of monophthongization: *tiinen* (*tiin* + secondary suffix -*en* < *tein*). Monophthongization is also evident in Wang. *fliin* 'flein' of *fliuug* (OFris *fliā/ga*) 'to fly' and Wang. *driin* of *driggë* 'to carry' (R *drega*), but for these last three verbs, no past participles are recorded for R.

In conclusion, then, most exceptions to the rule *ei* > *ī* concern forms where an -*n* immediately follows: *wein/wayn*, *lein-*, *-leine*, *leynd*, *slein/slain* and *tein*; *reilmerk* could be a later loan, *hreilbende* a corrupted from. The only form that remains inexplicable to me is *leid/leyd*.

---

[48] Boutkan and Siebinga, *Old Frisian Etymological Dictionary*, s.v. *leinmerk* and *-leine*, with references.

[49] V. F. Faltings, 'Zur Bildung desubstantivischer Adjektiva mit dem Derivationssuffix *-ed/-et* im Friesischen und in verwandten Sprachen', *UW* 45 (1996), 79–113.

[50] N. Århammar, 'Friesisch und Sächsisch. Zur Problematik ihrer gegenseitigen Ab-grenzung im Früh- und Hochmittelalter', *Aspects*, 1–25, at 22.

[51] Actually, one of the attestations in R1 appears in the manuscript as *slein totha*, the first element of which van Helten, *Zur Lexicogologie des Altostfriesischen*, 307, assumes to be the Frisian cognate of MHG *slagen* 'hammer', but which I think might just as well be a scribal error.

4.7 A phenomenon to which Buma paid no attention in his list of Riustring features is the occurrence of competing stem vowels in such forms as *bitigath* ~ *bitegath* 'he accuses', *kuma* ~ *koma* 'to come', *nima* ~ *nema* 'to take', *wita* ~ *weta* 'to know', and *durun* 'doors' (dat.pl.) ~ *dora* 'doors' (acc.pl.). We are dealing here with Riustring *a*-mutation, a sound change formulated by Ernst Löfstedt in 1932.[52] 'Löfstedt's Law' is clear and simple: in open syllables *i* was lowered to *e*, and *u* to *o*, when they were followed by *a*. For example, non-R *wita* 'to know'~ R *weta,* non-R *binitha* 'beneath' ~ R *binetha*, non-R *kuma* 'to come' ~ R *koma*, non-R *dura* 'doors (acc.pl.)' ~ R *dora*. The rule also shows its effect in Wangeroogish and it was actually through an incisive study of this dialect that Löfstedt established the rule.[53] Although the Riustring change resembles the much earlier West Germanic *a*-mutation, it should not be confused with it. Löfstedt repeatedly emphasized its later operation and regional limitation.

Buma seems not to have been aware of Löfstedt's article – in any case, he did not list it in his bibliography. Hence we find separate entries for such words in the glossary to his edition of R1, verbs with their two infinitival forms, e.g. *weta* and *wita*, and nouns with two nominative forms, e.g. *dore* and *dure*.[54] Boutkan, on the other hand, took notice of Löfstedt's article, but seems not to have grasped its essence and hence the importance of Löfstedt's law. Instead, he has given preference to van Helten's explanations or, alternatively, offered his own *ad hoc* solutions for seemingly mysterious forms.[55]

Occasionally it would seem that the rule was not strictly carried through in Riustring Old Frisian, since we find forms in R1 in which *i* and *u* were allowed to remain unchanged despite a following *a*. They are the following forms: *bitigath* (1x) against *bitegath* (5x) 'he accuses', *litha* 'bodily parts (gen.pl.)' (1x) against *letha(na)* (2x), *to witande* 'to know (infl.inf.) (1x)

[52] Löfstedt, 'Zur Lautgeschichte der Mundart von Wangeroog', in *idem*, *Zwei Beiträge zur friesischen Sprachgeschichte*, Lunds Universitets Årskrift, NF Avd. 1, Bd. 28, nr. 2 (Lund, 1932), 3–33, at 14–21 and 29–31.

[53] Löfstedt, 'Zur Lautgeschichte', tried to explain away some of the non-*a*-mutated forms with *i* as scribal errors (p. 16) and others as the result of *Systemzwang* (p. 19). He also applied the latter solution to the two occurrences of *-kuma* (p. 26).

[54] Boutkan and Siebinga, *Old Frisian Etymological Dictionary*, follow Buma in giving the same double entries, but *dore* runs counter to Löfstedt's Law.

[55] Van Helten, *Altostfriesische Grammatik*, §§10α, 157* for *i* > *e*. Van Helten later postulated *wētande* with a long stem vowel, as influenced by singular *wēt* in his *Zur Lexicologie des Altostfriesischen*, 381. The lowering of *u* > *o* in *kuma*, according to Boutkan, *Concise Grammar*, 24–25, might be ascribed to the following nasal, following a suggestion made by van Helten, *Grammatik*, §13γ. In the case of *dora*, Boutkan, *ibid.*, muses that we would be dealing with either 'old *a*-mutation' or 'phonetic lowering of **u* > [o]/__r', while *nima* 'may have introduced the vowel of the present 2/3s forms **nimis*, **nimiþ* ('PGmc.' i-umlaut of **e*) or show an incidental raising of *e* before a nasal'.

against *to wetande* (5x), *-nima(nde)* 'to take' (2x) against *(-)nema-* (3x), *koma-* 'to come'(3x) against *(-)kuma* (3x). R2 does not show any deviations from the rule. Besides the regular Riustring forms *binetha* 'beneath' and *boua* 'above', R4 would display one instance where the rule seems to have failed: instead of regular *opa* 'upon' we find *upa*. At least, this is how Gerbenzon read the word on a bad spot in the fragment. Examination of the manuscript shows that we might just as well read *opa*. The distribution of the exceptional forms is as follows:

R1	*1*	*2*	*3*	*4*	*5*	*6-20*
bitigath				+		
litha					+	
wita-			+			
nima-				+	+	
kuma			+	+		

4.8 There is a tendency – not a rule – in Old Frisian for *ē*, whether originally long or lengthened before a lengthening cluster (e.g. *-nC*), to diphthongize to *ei* before alveolars and dentals. Thus we find in Ems Old Frisian and/or Old West Frisian *breid* (< *brēd* 'bride'), *heilich* 'holy' (< *hēlich*), *beil* 'bruise, lump' (< *bēl*), *neyn* 'not one'(< *nēn*), *weind* 'matter; exception' (< *wend*). Do we also meet this tendency in Riustring Old Frisian?

In R1 we find the compound *ābēl* 'raised scar (permanent lump)' three times beside *beilar* 'bruises, lumps' (1x), while R2 features *bēla* 'bruises, lumps' with a different plural ending; both stems reflect Gmc **būli-* (cognate with ModE *boil* 'pus-filled swelling'). The regular outcome of all mutated vowels in Old Frisian is *e*, both long and short. Consequently, the form *beilar* can only be explained as an instance of diphthongization of *ē* > *ei* before dentals and alveolars. It is the sole instance of this change that I have found in Riustring Old Frisian. Evidence for this change from the Modern Weser Frisian dialects is ambiguous Wang. *breid* 'bride' (< OFris *brēd* < **brūdi-*). According to Siebs, nothing certain can be said of the stem vowel of Wang. *breid* because it can reflect both Old Wang. *ē* and *ei*.[56] For similar examples, compare Wang. *heil* < R *hēl* 'whole' and Wang. *leith* < R *lēth* 'harm'. If OFris *ē* of whatever origin had become *ei* in Riustring, it should have followed the rule of OFris *ei* > *ī* (see **4.4** above). In other words, just as we find Wang. *hiill* 'heel' < *heila*, we should expect to find Wang. +*biill* < *beil-*. Unfortunately, we do not, because the word appears to be *buull* which cannot possibly have developed from *beil*. In all likelihood, the

56 Siebs, 'Geschichte der friesischen Sprache', §53, Anm. 1.

Wangeroogish form will have been borrowed from Low German (*būl*), because Wang. /u:/ is the result of either Riustring *ū* or the result of lengthening of *u* in open syllable.[57] Moreover, the form *beilar* is suspect not only because of its stem vowel, but also on account of its plural ending *-ar* (on which see **4.5**). The regular form is *bēla*, as found in R2.[58]

4.9 There is, again, a strong tendency in Old Frisian for **aN* in closed syllables plus an *i*-mutation factor to turn out as *a* and not as *e* as might have been expected. According to van Helten, the mutated stem vowel never developed further than /æ/ and it was this sound which was represented by the spelling ⟨a⟩.[59] However, it would appear that what was a tendency elsewhere was a rule for Riustring Old Frisian. I have noted the following forms (R1 unless indicated otherwise): *angel* 'angel' (1x), *Angelond* 'England' (1x), *bikanna* 'to confess guilty, admit' (4x; R2 1x), *bithanka* 'to take care of oneself' (1x), *branga* 'to bring' (8x; R2 2x) and the compounds *foribranga* 'to adduce, declare' (1x) and *fulbranga* 'to complete (payment)' (1x), *fang* 'a grasp' (3x), *framde* 'strange, not related' (1x), *ganse* 'current, valid' (1x), *hanzoch* 'dependent, subject' (1x), *kampa* 'champion, duelist' (6x, R2 3x), *langor* 'longer' (1x, R2 1x), *manne/isk-* 'human', *man* pl. 'men' (*passim*) (also *passim* in R2), *panni(n)g* 'penny' (*passim*) (also *passim* in R2 and R4), *sprangel* 'holy water sprinkler, aspersory' (1x), *swang* 'blow, stroke' (2x), *thampene* 'suffocation' (1x; also once in R2 and R4), *-thanka* 'to think' (1x; R2 1x as *-thancka*). The rule did not apply when the syllable ended in *-nd*, as is evidenced by *-bende* 'bond, fetter' and its compounds (6x), *blendinge* '(act of) blinding' (1x), *ende* 'end' (4x; R2 4x), *ililende* 'exile' (1x; R2 1x), *sende(bodon)* 'messengers (dat.pl.)' (1x), *(bi-)wend* 'change; turn; case' (7x; R2 9x), *(sprek-)wendene* '(speech) impediment' (R2 2x), *wenda* 'to change' (1x).

Again, we find exceptions to the situation outlined above. First, beside one instance of regular *hanzoch* we also find *heinzoch* and *heinzioch*. The lexeme is found in all recensions of in the seventh of the *Seventeen Statutes*, either used on its own or, more often, in a fixed alliterative formula, in R1 III 52 as *hanzoch and heroch* 'dependent on and subject to' the king in a feudal relationship. When working on the ninth Statute, the scribe of R1 erroneously took over some lines from the seventh Statute, but this time

57 *Ibid.* §1381; Löfstedt, 'Zur Lautgeschichte der Mundart von Wangeroog', 21–22.

58 The consequence of taking *bēla* to be the regular Riustring plural form of *bēl* (< **būli-*, masc.) is that we need no longer interpret this form as a feminine noun < **būljō-*.

59 Siebs, 'Geschichte der friesischen Sprache', §14; W. L. van Helten, 'Zum altfriesischen Vokalismus', *IF* 19 (1906), 171–201, esp. 'II. Zum Umlaut des *a* im Vorfriesischen', 175–85. So too, Hofmann, 'Zur Entwicklung von germ. **fanja* 'Sumpf, Moor' im niederdeutsch-niederländisch-friesischen Nordwesten', *NW* 10 (1970), 95–108, at 101; repr. in his *Gesammelte Schriften*, 234.

from a different manuscript with a different recension as appears, amongst other variants, from his writing *heinzoch and heroch* (R1 III 73).[60] The former member of the phrase is a derivation of **hang-* plus the adjectival suffix **-ig*. The stem vowel underwent *i*-mutation (cf. ModG *abhängig*) and the velar was palatalized and subsequently assibilated, all neatly according to the rule. In the Old Ems Frisian versions, the word appears in the seventh Statute as *hendsegch* (E1), *henzech* (F), *henzech* (H), *hensich* (Fragm.),[61] and in Old West Frisian as *hensich* (D, J). Moreover, the alliterative phrase is also encountered several times in Old West Frisian charters as *hensich (hinsich) and herich*.[62] From all these examples, I conclude that *hanzoch* is the form to be expected in Riustring Old Frisian, and that *heinz(i)och* is the exceptional one, also because it shows *-ei-*, which must be explained as the reflex of lengthening before *-nC* (**4.8**).

Another apparent exception to the rule of lowering of *i*-mutated *e* > *a* before nasal in closed syllables is *fennon* 'pastures' (dat.pl.) instead of **fannon*. Both its feminine gender and its meaning are typically a Frisian development.[63] The distribution of these two exceptional forms is as follows:

R1	*1-2*	*3*	*4-9*	*10*	*11-9*	*20*
heinz(i)och		+				+
fennon				+		

5. Textual History and Layers of Transmission

We can draw several conclusions from my analysis of the exceptional forms in R1, R2 and R4 in section 4. Let us take a look at the accumulative table, in which I have included the results of all the individual tables. At a glance, it is evident that especially the *Seventeen Statutes* (no. 3), the *Twenty-four Landlaws* (no. 4) and the *General Register of Compensations* (nos. 5 and

60 See *De Eerste Riustringer Codex*, ed. Buma, 97, note on line 73; J. Hoekstra, *Die gemeinfriesischen Siebzehn Küren* (Assen, 1940), 65–66. The error is felicitous, because it reveals that the scribe was working with more than one version of the *Seventeen Statutes* on his desk. Incidentally, the recension from which he copied is most closely related to those we find in the Old West Frisian manuscripts.

61 A fifteenth-century parchment fragment with portions of the seventh and ninth of the *Seventeenth Statutes*, found in the binding of a late seventeenth-century book. For an edition of this text, see my 'Old Frisian Dialectology and the Position of the Ommelanden', in *A Frisian and Germanic Miscellany Published in Honour of Nils Århammar*, ed. H. F. Nielsen *et al.*, NOWELE 28–29 (1996), 1–18, at 1.

62 For example, *Oudfriesche Oorkonden*; ed. P. Sipma, OTR 1–3 (The Hague, 1927–1941), *hinsich*: II 50, line 43 (1462); *hensich*: II 107/6 (1482), II 110/19 (1482), II 111/8 (1483).

63 Hofmann, 'Zur Entwicklung von germ. **fanja* "Sumpf, Moor"', 228–29.

14) contain a high number of exceptional forms. Perhaps this prominence might be attributed to the length of these three texts. With their 156, 240 and 203 lines in Buma's edition, they are relatively long in comparison with most other texts and they thus provide more scope for exceptional forms to occur. On the other hand, we also run across exceptions in shorter texts, so that length is not necessarily a condition that should be taken into account.

I can see two further possibilities for explaining the presence of non-Riustring Old Frisian forms in the three texts mentioned in the previous paragraph. Scenario one is that such forms exhibit traces of an older phase of the language in which the various changes discussed had not yet been in operation or had not yet been finished. While copying these texts word by word from his rather old exemplar, the scribe must have carried over some of these older forms while in general he updated the spelling. Such an explanation, however, presents us with the problem concerning the date when the *Seventeen Statutes*, the *Twenty-four Landlaws* and the *General Register of Compensations* were composed in Old Frisian. I have argued elsewhere that rather than attributing the vernacular versions to the twelfth or even eleventh century, as previous generations of scholars have done, the written form of these important texts must be dated to somewhere between 1225 and 1250, that is some fifty to seventy-five years before the production of R1.[64] I do not think that this stretch of time would have sufficed for all the linguistic innovations in Riustring Old Frisian to have taken place on such a dramatic scale.[65] Although we have no means, in as far as I know, to assign a particular century to the respective Riustring sound changes nor to date them relatively other than that they are post Proto-Frisian (i.e. post 600), yet I assume these changes to have taken place a century or more before 1200. The absence of exceptional forms in quite a number of texts in R1 and in practically all of R2 seems to support this assumption. Nonetheless, the

64 R. H. Bremmer Jr, '*Hir is eskriven'. Lezen en schrijven in de Friese landen rond 1300* (Hilversum and Leeuwarden, 2004), chap. 8. Cf. Johnston, 'Old Frisian Law and the Frisian Freedom', 191–92, who also advocates an early thirteenth-century date for the vernacular Frisian law texts: 'Particularly in the wake of the Fourth Lateran Council (1215), the general rule that a legal question which had not been addressed with Gratian's [*Decretum*] was to be decided upon according to the secular customs of the land concerned triggered a rush throughout Europe to register the legal customs of a particular territory or people in writing'.

65 A. Kock, 'Vocalbalance im Altfriesischen', *BGdSL* 29 (1904), 174–93, at 191–92, surmised that at least vowel balance was operative in 'einer sprachperiode, die nur wenig hinter der von uns überkommenen Rüstringer texten repräsentierten zeit zurücklegt', and that vowel harmony, if only 'in geringem masse', became current afterwards. However, Kock made no pronouncements concerning the period when vowel balance began to take place. Understandably, he made no guesses with respect to virulence of other sound changes of which he was not yet aware, such as Rüstring *a*-umlaut.

Seventeen Statutes, *Twenty-four Landlaws* and the *General Register of Compensations* are commonly reckoned among the oldest vernacular Frisian texts. The *Prologue* to the *Statutes* and *Landlaws*, like the other three a pan-Frisian text, must be slightly later. It appears to have been written – most likely in Latin first – during the reign of Emperor Frederick II who ruled from 1210 to 1250. Still, the problem remains that a number of exceptional forms are also encountered in texts in R1 that are generally taken to be later and which, moreover, are not counted among the pan-Frisian texts, such as the *Riustring Register of Compensations* and the *Riustring Synodal Law*. This observation therefore requires another conclusion than that these traces bear witness to an older phase of the language. We must therefore look for another scenario.

In1996, I demonstrated that the Emsingo recension of *Processus Judicii*, a handbook in Frisian on how to proceed in law courts, displays a significant number of forms that cannot possibly be reconciled with the Ems Old Frisian dialect of the scribe (who identifies himself with name, place and year).[66] They can only be accounted for as 'relicts' of an Old West Frisian exemplar from which the scribe copied and adapted his text.[67] This conclusion is also warranted on external evidence: the three other versions of this legal handbook are all found in manuscripts originating from west of the Lauwers. We see a similar situation in the poem *Fon Alra Fresena Fridome*, as it is recorded in the two East Frisian Hunsingo Manuscripts, because it exhibits a dozen or more forms and words that are otherwise found only in Old West Frisian.[68] The corollary is that these two texts cannot have been composed in the East Frisian dialect of Emsingo and Hunsingo, respectively, but were (ultimately) copied from exemplars from west of the Lauwers. Admittedly, the scribes – or, in the case of the poem, his predecessor – had tried to adapt the Old West Frisian to their own Ems Frisian dialect, but obviously, the Old West Frisian 'sediments' make clear that they did not entirely succeed. The

66 Bremmer, 'Old Frisian Dialectology and the Position of the "Ommelanden"', 7–8.

67 On the term 'relict', see M. Benskin and M. Laing, 'Translations and *Mischsprachen* in Middle English Manuscripts', *So Meny People Longages and Tonges. Philological Essays in Scots and Mediaeval English Presented to Angus McIntosh*, ed. M. Benskin and M. L. Samuels (Edinburgh, 1981), 55–107, at 58.

68 Old West Frisian forms and words in *Fon Alra Fresena Fridome* include: OWFris *iowa* (70) 'to give', also in 76, as opposed to OEFris *ieva*; similarly, *iof* 'gave' (73) vs. OEFris *ief* (114). Other West Frisian forms include (-)*stān* (14, 78, 115) vs. OEFris *stonda* 'to stand' and other infinitives ending in *-n*: *dwān* (7, 13) vs. OEFris *dwā* 'to do', *tiān* (8) vs. *tiā* 'to draw', *siān* (97) vs. *siā* 'to see'. Furthermore: *hodir* (14) vs. OEFris *hwether* 'whether', *toiōnis* 'towards'(20; otherwise only in OWFris), *tōsamene* 'together' (45; otherwise only in OWFris; OEFris *(tō-)semine* [R1]). Line numbers refer to *Das Hunsingoer Recht*, ed. W. J. Buma and W. Ebel, AR 4 (Göttingen, 1969), text XVIII.

language of these two texts therefore does not represent an idiom that was ever spoken by their scribes in reality.[69]

More recently, Margaret Laing has elaborated on her 1981 article with Michael Benskin. Based on especially the ground-breaking work of Angus McIntosh and her own examination and analysis of the work of no fewer than 150 scribes of early Middle English manuscripts (1150–1350), she is able to distinguish three types of scribes: the 'Literatim', the 'Translator', and the 'Mixer'. The Literatim accurately copies whatever text he has in front of him, indifferent to whether its dialect agrees with the variety of English (in our case: Frisian) that he himself prefers. The Translator changes whatever does not agree with or cannot in his opinion be tolerated in his own preferred usage. The Mixer, finally, takes up the middle position. He sometimes copies faithfully but at other times follows the strategy of the Translator.[70] One of the disadvantages for Old Frisian studies is that we possess only some eighteen manuscripts or parts thereof, ranging from *c.*1300 to *c.*1535. Four of these, moreover, are seventeenth- and eighteenth-century transcripts of manuscripts that have since disappeared.[71] Unlike Middle English dialectologists, scholars of Old Frisian – a rare breed in themselves – are rarely in the favourable position of being able to trace the work of one scribe in two or more manuscripts or, what is more, of studying an abundance of more or less identical texts in a variety of contemporary manuscripts. However, as Fortune will have it, there is at least one case that allows us to test Laing's threefold category of scribes: the First and the Second Hunsingo Manuscripts.[72] These two early-fourteenth-century legal miscellanies were copied by one and the same scribe from the same exemplar. The only real distinction between the two manuscripts is that the individual items do not appear in precisely the same order. As has been established a long time ago, the textual differences between the two manuscripts are minimal and can all of them be accounted for as scribal errors.[73] The scribe of these two manuscripts can therefore be classified as a fine representative of the Literatim.

There are several reasons, then, for us to assume that the majority of exceptional forms in R1 that I have signalled and discussed in **4** should be

69 A famous case for Germany is the unique copy of the Old High German *Hildebrandslied*, which contains a number of forms that betray it to have been translated from Old Saxon. I would like to thank David Yeandle for reminding me of this.

70 Laing, 'Multidimensionality: Time, Space and Stratigraphy', 51–52.

71 The four transcripts are: the Second Rüstring Manuscript, the Emsingo *Processus Judicii*, Codex Unia and Codex Furmerius.

72 *De Eerste en de Tweede Hunsinger Codex*, ed. J. Hoekstra, OTR 6 (The Hague, 1950).

73 P. Gerbenzon, 'De forhâlding fan it earste en twade Hunsinger hânskrift', *UW* 3 (1951), 58–64.

explained as relicts of a non-Riustring dialect, testament to the complicated process that was involved in textual transmission. These forms are not loan-words in the usual sense, words in this case from Ems Frisian that had become part of the Riustring vocabulary; they are 'extra-terrestrials', incidental aliens from outside the *terra Rustringorum* which somehow or other escaped the conscious screening of the scribe(s) when they were translating and adapting the dialect of their exemplar(s) to that of their own. I have expressly written 'scribe(s)' and 'exemplar(s)', because we are ignorant of whether one or more items were copied for the first time from non-Riustring exemplars into R1 or whether these relicts were already present in the document(s) from which they compiled what is now known as the First Riustring Manuscript. What we have is the work of one or more Mixers. In any case, not only is the language of R1 not 'archaic' or the 'altertümlichste' representation of Old Frisian, neither is it, in Heuser's words, the 'edelste'.[74] Nobility after all, even from a medieval Frisian legal point of view, excludes the presence of 'bastards' in the line of descent.

6. Sampling the layers in R1 and R2

Let us now take a closer look at the evidence. There is little need for arguing the presence of relicts in texts that are generally accepted as 'pan-Frisian', such as the *Prologue*, the *Seventeen Statutes*, the *Twenty-four Landlaws* and the *General Register of Compensations*. Especially the results for the last three of these texts leap to the eye because of a variety of relicts: one or more of them exhibits instances of initial *hr-* (**4.2**), of *him* (**4.3**), of *aga* (**4.4**), of *-ar* plurals (**4.5**), of *ei* instead of *ī* (**4.6**), of absence of *a*-mutation (**4.7**), of *ē* > *ei* (**4.8**), and of absence of lowering of *e* > *a* before nasals plus *i*-mutation factor (**4.9**). An origin for these texts from east of the Lauwers has been demonstrated on word-geographical evidence.[75] The presence of non-Riustring relicts now makes sure that at least the recensions that we have in R1 are not ultimately original to Rüstringen but, especially on account of the *-ar* plural, to the Ems Frisian region. This conclusion suggests that the reception in Rüstringen of these three texts must have taken place with some delay. Although the two versions of the *Prologue* display only one significant alien, the *-ar* plural, yet this is sufficient to assume that also these two prefaces hailed from Ems Frisian territory. For similar reasons, we can justify the presence of *neilar* in the *General Register* as an Ems Frisian relict.

---

74 For Heuser, see note 10.

75 H. H. Munske, *Der germanische Rechtswortschatz im Bereich der Missetaten. Philologische und sprachgeographische Untersuchungen. I. Die Terminologie der älteren westgermanischen Rechtsquellen* (Berlin and New York, 1973), §294.

More surprising perhaps is the inevitable conclusion that other than pan-Frisian texts in R1 also show traces of an Ems Frisian origin. First of all, as we have seen in section **3**, there is the dike-law, tucked away in that bran-tub of legal provisions, *Thet is Ac Frisesk Riucht*. Because this regulation demonstrably originates from outside Rüstringen, we may safely expect the presence of relicts in it, and indeed there are: *fennon* instead of the form to be expected, *fannon* (**4.9**). Yet another form in this law looks suspect: *lith* 'he lies'. It would seem to follow the Riustring rule of *ei* > *ī*, but, as we have seen, it is the only 3rd sg.pres. to have obeyed it (**4.6**). My suspicion is that the copying scribe overreacted to the form **leith* in his exemplar and hyper-correctly wrote down *lith*. In this particular case it would then be a typically Riustring form that betrayed a non-Riustring origin for the passage.

The greatest surprises that my analysis has brought to light are the relicts in texts that had hitherto remained unquestioned for their Rüstring origin. I shall begin with *The Fifteen Signs of Doomsday* (XI). Strictly speaking, there is nothing against taking this text as non-Riustring in origin; on the contrary, it has an international background, because it is an almost literal translation from Pseudo-Bede's *De quindecim signis dii iudicii* (early ninth century) and partly inspired by Peter Comestor's *Historia scolastica* (*c*.1170).[76] Four deviant forms betray the translation to have originally been made in Old Ems Frisian: two occurrences of the plural ending *-ar* in *bamar* and *fiskar* (**4.5**), the diphthong *ei* instead of *ī* in *neylon* (**4.6**), and the retention of the cluster *hr-* in *hropath* 'they call' (**4.2**).

Another unexpected outcome is the presence of *beilar* 'lumps' (**4.8**) in the *Riustring Register of Compensations* (item VI). This form is found in the tail-end of the register, in the last of a handful of regulations that fall outside the structure of this register of compensations. They were added as a kind of appendix after the main text, perhaps because the scribe/compiler thought they might come in useful, but certainly, on account of the *-ar* plural (**4.5**), from an Ems Frisian source.

One form remains to be explained for R1: *heinzioch* in the *Riustring Synodal Law*, a lengthy document that was obviously written to regulate ecclesiastical life in Rüstringen. Be that as it may, in the process of its transmission – it may at one point have been translated from Latin into Frisian – somebody has consciously tampered with its beginning and its end. What is exceptional is that this document lacks any authorization of an ecclesiastical dignitary, such as the dean of Rüstringen or perhaps even the bishop of Bremen, who must have promulgated these regulations. Nor does it provide any indication of the place where and the *annus Domini* when it was issued. The effect of what must have been a conscious 'editorial' intervention is that

76 See Concetta Giliberto's contribution to this volume.

this important document has become timeless and placeless in its opening and conclusion. By way of compensation, however, the regulations proper were sandwiched between a new preamble and epilogue. The former briefly summarizes how the Frisians came to the support of Charlemagne during a siege of Rome after its inhabitants had blinded Pope Leo. The Frisians were the first to break into the town. With the grace of God, the Frisians worked great slaughter amongst the Romans so that people in St Peter's had to wade through the blood up to their ankles. In gratitude for this feat, the Frisians – and not the people of Rüstringen – received their secular and spiritual rights from Charlemagne and Pope Leo. The postamble reiterates that these regulations were granted by Charlemagne and Pope Leo, and, significantly for Rüstringen, adds 'in the days of St Willehad under whom we became Christians'. It ends with a threat and a promise: whoever will rob 'us, Frisians' from these rights will be robbed from God and all saints and sentenced to the bottom of hell. Those, however, who keep these rights should have no fear for Judgment Day, because God will lead them to the heavenly kingdom. With these two prospects, the epilogue harks back almost word for word to a passage in the two versions of the *Prologue* to the *Seventeen Statutes* and the *Twenty-four Landlaws*.[77] The presence of the word *heinzioch* occurs in the heavily ideological preamble, together with its alliterative companion *heroch*. It can only be explained, I think, if we assume that its author copied the phrase together with the narrative matter from an extra-Rüstring source.

Johnston has grouped R1 among the manuscripts which were designed not just for practical legal purposes but for propagating the claim that the Frisians occupied a special place within the Holy Roman Empire in that they were obedient to no other superior, be they count or duke, but to the Emperor himself and that this privileged position was granted to them by Charlemagne.[78] Clearly, the compiler(s) of R1 or the person who commissioned it wanted to produce a manuscript that expressly positioned Rüstringen within the larger cultural and political Frisian space. Chronologically, this Rüstring desire to join the pan-Frisian ideological bandwagon must have been fairly recent. The other two large areas of Frisia, even though they belonged to two different bishoprics, Utrecht and Münster, had already entertained quite intensive mutual ties, noticeable for one thing from the fact that daughter monasteries had been founded, shortly before and after 1200, in a wave that began in Frisia west of the Lauwers and moved in an easterly direction to come to a standstill in the vast moors that separated the Münster diocese from that of Bremen.[79] Therefore, the compiler(s) took

77 Cf. *Eerste Riustringer Codex*, ed. Buma, items I.11 and II.3.

78 Johnston, 'Old Frisian Law and the Frisian Freedom Ideology', 197–98.

79 Bremmer, *'Hir is eskriven'*, 86.

recourse to the example set in the more western parts of Frisia, most notably in the Frisian part of the Münster bishopric, and hence they made use of extra-Riustring exemplars.

A similar solution must be given for the exceptional forms in R2. The function of the Second Riustring Manuscript has been explained by Buma to be some kind of supplement, a 'juridical compendium', to R1 or to a compilation similar in nature.[80] The reason for this assumption is the absence of such major items as the *Seventeen Statutes*, the *Twenty-four Landlaws* and the *General Register of Compensations*. However, the presence of the long, if somewhat different redaction of the *Riustring Register of Compensations* (item I) does not really belong in a supplement, it seems to me. On the other hand, the presence in R2 of commentaries on the first of these two texts (items II and III) would underline its supplementary nature. While this is a likely explanation of its *raison d'être*, it is true that there are not enough vernacular manuscripts from Rüstringen to allow us to gain a clear idea of what its purpose may have been. The two commentaries point to the extent that the pan-Frisian texts were appreciated in Rüstringen. Several other passages in R2 confirm the desire on behalf of the Rüstring law-issuing *élite* to regard themselves as fully participating in the construct of a Frisia independent of feudal overlords but directly subject to the king/emperor. Johnston has pointed out that the author of the *Commentary on the Seventeen Statutes* (item II) surpassed the *Statutes* themselves in the use of elements from the 'Matter of Frisia'.[81] This appears, for example, in his comment on the seventh Statute, which contains a brief summary of how Charlemagne granted free jurisdiction to the Frisians after he had liberated them from Redbad 'the Danish king', to whom they had been obliged to pay Danegeld and who had forced them to wear an oak collar as a token of their servitude to the Danes. In his comment on the eighth Statute, the author defines the term *ethelinga* as 'all free Frisians' to whom Charlemagne and Pope Leo and St Liudger had given *etheldom*, that is those who had been born free and were not bastards. As in R1 – but not in any other of the Frisian manuscripts with this text – the shared ethnic identity is expressed in his comment on the ninth Statute with such terms as 'we Frisians' and 'we Frisian merchants'. None of this sentiment is to be found so emphatically expressed in the *Seventeen Statutes* of non-Riustring redactions. In *Thet is Ac Frisesk Riucht* (V), three of its eighteen provisions refer to 'Frisian right', one such claim is made in the *Miscellaneous 'Riustring' Regulations*, while in the *Miscellaneous Procedural Regulations* the term is used twice (VIII.8).

80 *Het Tweede Rüstringer Handschrift*, ed. Buma, 25.

81 Johnston, 'Old Frisian Law and the Frisian Freedom Ideology', 198.

It would appear that at least some of the items in R2 were imported from somewhere in Frisia outside Rüstringen, but whence the forms do not allow us to say with any precision. The occurrence, for example, of *aga* instead of regular *haga* (**4.4**) in the commentary on the *Seventeen Statutes* (item II) suggests that the commentator was using a non-Riustring recension of this text. This conclusion is further borne out by his writing *wey* twice instead of *wi* (**4.6**). The other occurrences of *aga* in R2 are found in *Thet is Ac Frisesk Riucht* (item V). We have seen that a similar collection with this title in R1 also contained relicts of a non-Riustring exemplar, so that it need not surprise us here. Finally, *ach*, a form of *aga*, occurs three times in *Miscellaneous 'Riustring' Regulations* (item VII). As its modern title suggests, this collection, too, is a ragbag, or, in Buma's more academic terminology, 'a veritable *mixtum compositum*'.[82] The *h*-less forms do not appear randomly in these regulations, but only in paragraph VII.3a-b, an independent set of instructions on how to proceed when a poor man has killed somebody else.[83] There are no immediate parallels for this particular regulation, but its purport is parallelled in non-Rüstring sources, according to Buma.[84] The linguistic evidence presented by the three forms of *aga* in this passage therefore clinches Buma's observation. At the same time, this conclusion would also once more disprove Buma's claim that all the texts in R2 were authored by the same person (**2**). Moreover, it removes the conventional tradition of attributing a Rüstring localization to this batch of regulations. We might just as well call this group *Thet is Ac Frisesk Riucht*, part 2, on account of the phrase 'Hwante thet is Frisesk riucht thet …' ('For this is Frisian law, that …'),[85] were it not for the fact that it proves hard to change firmly established titles of texts. Interestingly, the texts in R2 which feature these non-Riustring forms are also promoting the place of the intended audience within the larger Frisian community.

7. Scribal layers

Still there is more to be inferred from my survey, such as the beginning of an answer to the following question: how many people in Rüstringen around 1300 were able to write in the vernacular tongue and had they learnt to do so at the same 'school'? We have three more or less contemporary manu-

---

[82] *Tweede Rüstringer Handschrift*, ed. Buma, 31.

[83] Buma also takes R2 VII.c to belong to the regulation concerning the poor man, but unjustly so, I think. No mention is made in it of a poor man.

[84] *Ibid.* 33.

[85] R2 VII c. Oelrich's transcript reads 'frisik' which Buma emends to 'frisisk', an emendation which, however understandable, seems unwarranted to me; it runs counter to the rule of Vowel Balance and would hence be the only such spelling against 30x *frisesk* in R1 and R2.

scripts, one of which is an eighteenth-century transcript. As pointed out, R1 was executed by two scribes; the fragment R4 is in one hand which is not the same as either of the two hands of R1, and at least one scribe was involved in the production of R2. Yet, a closer look at the diverging spelling habits displayed in R2 can bring us a little further.

No study has yet been made of the principles with which Frisian literates developed their vernacular writing system(s) in the thirteenth century, but I take it that all of them, at least in the period of our three Riustring manuscripts, had begun their education in the shadow of a church or a monastery. As boys – I assume the scribes all to have been adult males – they will have received many years of instruction in reading of Latin first and writing it later before they ever set a word of Frisian on parchment. In other words, their vernacular writing system was firmly grounded in the conventions of contemporary Latin orthography. Only where Latin did not cater for the representation of a certain sound did they have to be inventive. This appears, for example, in the various strategies that were developed to represent initial /ts/, the result of palatalized /k/. Scribe two of R1 – scribe one did not have the opportunity to show how he would have spelled it – has chosen for *sth-* (*sthereke* 'church', *sthiake* 'cheek', *sthetil* 'kettle'), a spelling that is not encountered anywhere else in the entire Old Frisian corpus. The scribe(s) of R2, on the other hand, seem(s) to have opted for *sz-* (*szereke*, in items V and VIII), a solution we also find in the two Brokmer manuscripts and in the Hunsingo manuscripts. However, in the first text in R2, the *Riustring Register of Compensations*, 'cheek' appears as *ziake*. The spelling ⟨z⟩ for initial /ts/ is otherwise found only in the First Emsingo Manuscript (*ziurk-* 'church'). The spelling ⟨ziake⟩ in R2 could be an indication, therefore, however small, that the *Riustring Register* was copied from an exemplar that featured a slightly different spelling convention. Further evidence to support this suggestion can be found in the combined occurrence of the spellings ⟨gh⟩ and ⟨ck⟩ in the *Riustring Register* (see final table R2).

The answer to the first question raised at the beginning of this section is that we have evidence of at least five different scribes who were able to write Frisian. One might even want to argue for a sixth one because the distributions observed in **4.1** of ⟨ei⟩ versus ⟨ey⟩ or ⟨kin⟩- versus ⟨kyn⟩- (in the word for 'king') betrays a pattern that is suggestive of a usage that is not attributable to the two scribes who wrote R1, as is the tiny variation in the spelling of 'cross'. The difference between R1 and R2 in spelling initial /ts/ as ⟨sth⟩ and ⟨z⟩, respectively, might point to different traditions and hence to different centres of instruction. Further than this I dare not go. There is certainly room for further study in the spellings of the Riustring manuscripts.

8. Conclusion

The results of my investigation can be summed up as followed: First of all, we must abandon the notion that the language of R1 (and R2 and R4) is 'archaic' with respect to its phonological system. Nor is its Frisian older than that contained in contemporary non-Riustring manuscripts – it only is different, that is all. Furthermore, Old Frisian manuscripts that are compilations should be approached not as a whole, but text by text – a variation on the dictum 'chaque mot a son histoire'. In a number of cases I have argued that the transmission of individual texts in these two manuscripts reveals a multi-layered history that takes us from Rüstringen into the Ems Frisian area. While we still have the Riustring translations, the loss of their exemplars makes us realize once more that the production of Old Frisian texts in presumably the Ems Frisian area must have been larger and, in the case of the *Fifteen Signs*, wider in genre than merely legal compared to what we possess today. In the case of R1 and R2, it has been demonstrated that their text language is not as pure as has hitherto been assumed. Nor is the Riustring spelling system as 'clear' as Buma once thought. With respect to the contents of R1 and R2, my analysis has brought to light that Rüstringen eagerly participated in the reception of vernacular texts, a reception that seems to point to an intense desire on behalf of those who commissioned these manuscripts to be part and parcel of the larger Frisian community. To me, these conclusions do not diminish my interest in the language of Riustring Old Frisian. On the contrary, they make it even more exciting than my respected teacher Wybren Jan Buma may ever have thought possible, because they have allowed us a glimpse into the genesis and the *raison d'être* of the First and Second Riustring Manuscripts. It is a glimpse which was granted to us because we were allowed to stand on Buma's shoulders.

General survey of distribution of exceptional forms in R1

Please note that text 14 is a continuation of text 5.

R1	*1*	*2*	*3*	*4*	*5*	*6*	*7-9*	*10*	*11*	*12-3*	*14*	*15-9*	*20*
4.2 *hr-*					+				+		+		
4.3 *him*				+									
4.4 *aga*			+		+								
4.5 *-ar* plural	+	+	+	+		+			+				
4.6 *ei* not > *i*					+	+			+		+		
lith								+					
4.7 no *a*-mutation			+	+	+								
4.8 *ē* > *ei*			+		+								+
4.9 no lowering			+					+					+

Key to the numbers in the top row of the table. The titles are followed by their length in lines in *De Eerste Riustringer Codex*, ed. Buma. The number in italics indicates a text's relative size. NB. The spelling variations that are not indicative of dialectal variance (**4.1**) have not been included.

1. 'Later' Prologue (135 lines) (*4*)
2. 'Elder' Prologue (36 lines) (*13*)
3. Seventeen Statutes (156 lines) (*2*)
   (Scribe 2 begins on p. 19 with III.7)
4. Twenty Landlaws (240 lines) (*1*)
5. General Register of Compensations, part 1 (148 lines) (*3*)
6. Riustring Register of Compensations (116 lines) (*5*)
7. Five Exceptions to the Seventeen Statutes (20 lines) (*14*)
8. Riustring Statutes (78 lines) (*7*)
9. New Riustring Statutes (63 lines) (*8*)
10. 'Thet is ac Frisesk riucht', part 1 I (61 lines) (*9*)
11. Fifteen Signs before Doomsday (40 lines) (*11*)
12. Riustring Compensations for Priests A (37 lines) (*12*)
13. Permission to Break into a Church (12 lines) (*17*)
14. General Register of Compensations, part 2 (53 lines) (*10*)
15. 'Thet is Ac Frisesk riucht', part 2 (83 lines) (*6*)
16. Currency Values (6 lines) (*19*)
17. On Killing a Relative (8 lines) (*18*)
18. Riustring Compensations for Priests, part 2 (29 lines) (*15*)
19. On Desecrating the Church (Yard) (19 lines) (*16*)
20. Riustring Synodal Law (116 lines) (*5*)

General survey of distribution of exceptional forms in R2

R2	*1*	*2*	*3*	*4*	*5*	*6*	*7*	*8*
4.4 aga		+			+		+	
4.6 *ei* not > *i*		+						
ziake	1							
⟨gh⟩	3	1			5			4
⟨ck⟩	4					1		

Key to the texts in the Second Riustring Manuscript

1. Riustring Register of Compensations (129 lines) (*1*)
2. Comments on the Seventeen Statutes (77 lines) (*3*)
3. Comments on the Twenty-four Landlaws (8 lines) (*7*)
4. Monetary equivalents (5 lines) (*8*)
5. 'Thet is Ac Frisesk Riucht' (70 lines) (*4*)
6. Riustring Proclamations for Special Cases of Peace (24 lines) (*6*)
7. Miscellaneous 'Riustring' Regulations (90 lines) (*2*)
8. Miscellaneous Procedural Regulations (61 lines) (*5*)

Sibrandus Siccama on the *Lex Frisionum* (1617): Frisian Identity as a Philological Construct

Kees Dekker

The history of Old Frisian studies is marked by two highly remarkable printed editions of early law texts: the incunable of the Old Frisian land laws, printed in the late fifteenth century (c. 1485) and Sibrandus Siccama's edition of the *Lex Frisionum*, published in Franeker, in 1617.[1] The former has won acclaim for being the earliest printed edition of a text in an Old Germanic language.[2] Its role in the study of Old Frisian began when seventeenth-century philologists such as Johannes de Laet, Francis Junius, Jan van Vliet and Thomas Marshall used their copies of this book to compare Old Frisian with Old English.[3] Siccama's edition of the *Lex Frisionum*, published with an extensive commentary including passages from vernacular Old Frisian laws, is less well-known, partly because the book is of a less spectacular antiquity, and partly because the quantity of Old Frisian text it includes is much smaller. It, too, played a role in the onset of Old Frisian studies, but in spite of that, this edition of the *Lex Frisionum* has received little scholarly attention, and the same can be said for its author, Sibrandus Siccama.[4] Meinte Oosterhout has traced the sources of the Old Frisian text

---

1 Sibrandus Siccama, *Lex Frisionum sive antiquæ Frisiorum leges, a reliquis veterum Germanorum legibus separatim editæ et notis illustratæ* (Franeker: Johannes Lamrinck, 1617). It was reprinted in a new improved edition by Karl Wilhelm Gärtner as *Lex Frisionum sive antiquae Frisiorum leges a reliquis veterum Germanorum legibus, separatim editae et notis illustratae a Sibrando Siccama; accedunt statuta Opstalbomica anno 1323 rogata* (Leipzig, 1730); sometimes added to Gärtner's *Saxonum leges tres, quæ extant antiquissimæ ætate Caroli M. confectæ* (Leipzig, 1730). On the incunable edition of the Frisian land laws, see T. S. B. Johnston, 'The Old Frisian Law Manuscripts and Law Texts', *Handbuch / Handbook*, 571–87, at 572.

2 Printed editions of texts in Old English and Old High German did not appear until after the middle of the sixteenth century. There is, of course, a difference between the antiquarian nature of earliest Old English and Old High German publications and the utilitarian reason for printing the Old Frisian land laws in a period when these laws were, at least partly, still in use.

3 K. Dekker, 'Sibrandus Siccama's editie van de *Lex Frisionum*: actie en reactie', *Speculum Frisicum: Stúdzjes oanbean oan Philippus H. Breuker*, ed. R. H. Bremmer Jr, L. G. Jansma and P. Visser (Leeuwarden and Leiden, 2001), 95–116.

4 Although the *Lex Frisionum* proper has received ample scholarly attention, the historiographical and philological significance of Siccama's edition has not. Positive exceptions are: E. H. Waterbolk, *Twee eeuwen Friese geschiedsschrijving: Opkomst,*

fragments in the *Lex Frisionum*, showing that Siccama used not only the incunable edition of the Frisian land laws, but also the manuscript *Jus Municipale Frisionum* and the now lost manuscript Unia (or a closely related manuscript): in fact, he consulted most known renderings of the West Frisian laws.[5] However, the questions of why Siccama included these Old Frisian fragments, what was his motivation behind his edition and behind his way of presenting the material, have, so far, remained undiscussed. As I will show, the method and structure of Siccama's book suggest a clear purpose on the part of the author: to demonstrate a continuous legal, historical, and – by implication – linguistic Frisian tradition from the Augustan age to later medieval Frisia. In the process, the book offered a revaluation of Frisian identity and placed the study of Old Frisian firmly on the map.

1. Sibrandus Siccama

The author of the book, Sibrandus Siccama, was born in Bolsward in 1571. As son of the town secretary, Tjaerd Claessen Siccama and his wife Auck Gerlofs, Sibrandus grew up in an upper middle-class environment closely involved with civic government.[6] His father, a protestant convert and a legal scholar, sent him to the local Latin School, after which he matriculated at Franeker University in 1590, ultimately to read Law.[7] In 1595 he became the town secretary of Hasselt, in Overijssel, but three years later, in 1598, he was registered as a lawyer and *Doctor utriusque iuris* in Bolsward, where he succeeded his father as town secretary in 1602. His publications and

bloei en verval van de Friese historiografie in de zestiende en zeventiende eeuw (Groningen and Djakarta, 1952), 231–34, who acknowledges Siccama's original approach to ancient laws; and M. Oosterhout, 'Sibrandus Siccama en it hânskrift Jus', *Flecht op 'e koai: Stúdzjes oanbean oan Prof. Dr. W. J. Buma ta syn sechstichste jierdei*, ed. T. Hoekema, Y. Poortinga and J. Spahr van der Hoek (Groningen, 1970), 95–110, who has compared 23 passages of Old Frisian cited by Siccama with the extant sources. It is, however, at least remarkable that the index to *De Vrije Fries*, a scholarly journal on Frisian history and language published since 1839, does not list Siccama at all. See *De Vrije Fries: Inhoudsopgave en Register 1839–2000* (Leeuwarden, 2000).

5 See Oosterhout, 'Sibrandus Siccama', 108–10.

6 See Ph. H. Breuker, *It wurk fan Gysbert Japix*, 3 vols. (Leeuwarden, 1989), II-1, 232–33; A. C. Fokkema-Siccama, *De Siccama's*, ([Kortenhoef, 1973]), 390–01. G. A. Wumkes, *Bodders yn de Fryske striid* (Bolsward, 1926), 198–208, also presents a very interesting account of Siccama's life. Genealogical information from, presumably, the eighteenth century can be found in a copy of Siccama's *Lex Frisionum*, now Leeuwarden, Tresoar 1070 R bis, on the verso of a fly-leaf and on the title page.

7 Wumkes, *Bodders*, 203, writes that Sibrandus matriculated as a law student at the age of 20 in the summer of 1590. In view of the often early age of matriculation at the time, and the conventional course of academic education, it is highly likely that he had already completed one or two years of 'humanities' studies at Franeker. He was awarded a doctorate in 1596.

writings are indicative of his humanist upbringing and education. He composed Greek and Latin verse,[8] and, while living in Franeker and Hasselt, wrote three books: one on legal history and two about the Roman calendar.[9] One of these, the *Antitheses*, contains in a dedication his proud account of a visit to the Leiden arch-philologist Joseph Justus Scaliger in 1597. Apparently Siccama took an interest in Scaliger's favourite topics: antiquities and chronology. His admiration of Scaliger testifies to Siccama's predilection for the historical-philological method of scholarship on a humanist basis for which Leiden, and in its wake other universities in the United Provinces such as Franeker, had become renowned, and of which Scaliger was the prime exponent.[10] Siccama's scholarly network included, besides Scaliger, the Heidelberg humanist and librarian Janus Gruterus, the Harderwijk professor Johannes Isaacus Pontanus, the Leiden historian Petrus Scriverius, the Franeker University rector Johannes Saeckma, and the Frisian State historian Bernardus Furmerius – an indication of his high scholarly status and international reknown.[11]

Siccama's interest in Frisian history became known to a wider public when he published the *Lex Frisionum* in 1617. His concern for Frisia's past must have grown out of a combination of paternal influence and professional occupation. His father kept a chronicle of contemporary history,[12] and, like

---

[8] For example, *Oratio panegyrica in illvstrissimi comitis VVilhelmi Lvdovici [...] in provinciam reditum* (Leeuwarden, 1610; rpt. 1619). See also M. H. H. Engels, *Hekeldichten van Thomas Herbaius en Sibrandus Siccama, uit 1604 en 1608, bewaard door Johannes Saeckma* (Leeuwarden, 1994), and A. J. van der Aa *et al.*, *Biografisch woordenboek der Nederlanden*, 21 vols. (Haarlem, 1878) XVII, 645–46.

[9] *De judicio centumvirali libri II* (Franeker, 1596; rpt. Halle/S., 1725); again reprinted in an improved edition by Karl Friedrich Zepernick (Halle/S., 1776). *De veteri anno Romano Romuli et Numae Pompilii antitheses* (Kampen, 1599); *In fastos kalendares Romanos praecidanea* (Kampen, 1599), published again with a new title page as *Fastorvm kalendarivm lib. II, ex veterum monimentis, marmoribus, numismatibus aliisque antiquitatum fragmentis, aucti et emendati* (Amsterdam, 1600).

[10] See also *Brieven aan de curator van de Universiteit van Franeker Johannes Saeckma (1572–1636): Uitgave van de Codex Saeckma en de brieven van 12 overeenkomstige correspondenten uit de verzameling Gabbema*, ed. M. H. H. Engels, 2 vols. (Leeuwarden, 1995) I, 107–08. In a letter from Janus Gruterus to Johannes Saeckma, dating from September 1624, the former calls Siccama an eminent philologist.

[11] Much remains to be investigated about Siccama's scholarly network and activities. Scriverius, Gruterus, Pontanus and Saeckma received copies of the *Lex Frisionum*. A picture of the front page of Scriverius's copy with Siccama's dedication is printed in Wumkes, *Bodders*, 207; Saeckma's copy is in Leeuwarden, Historisch Centrum, B 1775. See also the informative website of M. H. H. Engels, whose work includes many references to Siccama: <http://home.wanadoo.nl/mpaginae/> (19 Sept. 2007).

[12] Van der Aa *et al.*, *Biografisch woordenboek*, XVII, 647. In 1604 Siccama lent the chronicle to Bernardus Furmerius, from whom he borrowed a manuscript containing the Life of St Liudger; see D. W. Kok and O. Hellinga, *Diarium Furmerii: Dagboek van*

his father, Siccama was town secretary of Bolsward for many years, an office which often forced to consult the ancient records of the town, including many documents in Old Frisian.[13] Other types of Frisian texts also interested him. In 1615 he promised to send Janus Gruterus a collection of Frisian proverbs, conveniently furnished with Latin translations, for Gruterus's comparative study of proverbs.[14] In the same letter he announced to Gruterus that he would send him a copy of the *Lex Frisionum*.[15] No doubt, Siccama shared his contemporaries' admiration of Frisia's ancient history and privileges, and, in all probability, had read works from the 'official' but rather apocryphal historiographies by Suffridus Petrus and Bernardus Furmerius. These two historians, officially appointed by the States ('government') of Friesland, frequently relied on forged chronicles, far-fetched mythologies and mythical ancestors to provide Frisia with a glorious past which would fit into the pseudo-historical framework of nations deriving their ancestry from legendary Scythians, Trojans and the sons of Noah.[16]

Bernardus Gerbrandi Furmerius 1603–1615. Landgeschiedschrijver van Friesland (Leeuwarden, 2006), 32–33. Siccama used the Life of St Liudger in the *Lex Frisionum* (p. 139).

13 *Oudfriese oorkonden* IV, ed. O. Vries, OTR 14 (The Hague, 1977), has edited Old Frisian charters from the Bolsward orphanage, but also points out in his *'Naar ploeg en koestal vluchtte uw taal': De verdringing van het Fries als schrijftaal door het Nederlands (tot 1580)* (Leeuwarden, 1993), 34–35, that during the second half of the fifteenth century the Bolsward town chancery used Dutch for its official documents; there are, however, indications that Frisian was used in documents that have not survived.

14 See F. J. van der Kuip, *De Burmania-sprekwurden: santjinde-ieuske Fryske sprekwurden ferklearre en yn har tiid besjoen* (Leeuwarden, 2003), 45. Ph. H. Breuker, 'Literatuur als liefhebberij: Van 1540 tot 1822', *'Zolang de wind van de wolken waait'. Geschiedenis van de Friese literatuur*, ed. T. Oppewal, B. Gezelle Meerburg, J. Krol and T. Steenmeijer-Wielenga (Amsterdam, 2006), 31–54, at 32, refers to Siccama's collection of Frisian proverbs, now lost, but does not exclude the possibility that he was actually the collector of the proverbs that are now known as the Burmania collection. These proverbs occur in a manuscript from 1614 attributed on the basis of the initials 'C.G.*V*B.' to Carel Georg van Burmania. According to M. H. H. Engels, 'Friese Spreekwoorden, Verzameling 1614', <http:// home.wanadoo.nl/m.bourgonjen/CGVB/Frsprw.htm> (19 Sept. 2007), the manuscript with these proverbs belonged to the Dordrecht mayor and humanist Cornelis van Beveren, who had studied in Franeker. This keeps open the possibility that Siccama was the actual collector, especially since Van Beveren was not a Frisian (Philippus Breuker, p.c.).

15 Vatican City, Biblioteca Apostolica Vaticana, Codex Palatinus Latinus 1907, fol. 351 (xerox copy sent to me by Philippus Breuker).

16 See the second chapter of Waterbolk, *Twee eeuwen Friese geschiedschrijving*, 59–92, which deals with the 'fantastical or apocryphal historiography', and also his 'Hoe is de fantastische geschiedschrijving in Friesland ontvangen', *Mythe en geschiedschrijving in Nederland en Friesland*, *IB* 56 (1994), 124–45. See, in the same volume of *It Beaken*, W. Bergsma, 'Suffridus Petrus als landshistorieschrijver', 80–123, and P. N. Noomen, 'Suffridus Petrus en de Friese Identiteit', 146–87.

However, Siccama's access to ancient records must have inspired and enabled him to adopt a more factual, humanist approach to history, more in line with the critical historiographical method of the Groningen professor Ubbo Emmius.[17] Siccama's selection of the *Lex Frisionum* testifies to this approach in that he considered it to be among the oldest sources describing the Frisians, and he was the first to make substantial use of this particular text.[18]

2. THE *LEX FRISIONUM*

Together with the laws of the Visigoths, the Burgundians, the Langobards, the Bavarians and the Salic Franks, the *Lex Frisionum* belonged to the so-named *Leges Barbarorum* – a legal corpus consisting of either tribal laws codified in the fifth or sixth centuries in areas in which Roman domination had introduced the Latin language, or of legislation compiled as a result of Frankish rule in areas inhabited by speakers of a Germanic language.[19] The *Lex Frisionum* was drawn up presumably between 785 and 794, with the help of Frankish scholars, and is regarded not as a finished work but as a collection of materials from which a definitive '*Lex Frisionum*' was to be distilled.[20] It consists of the *Lex* proper plus the *Additio sapientum*, additional articles attributed to the *sapientes Vulemar* and *Saxmund*. Like the other *Leges Barbarorum*, the *Lex Frisionum* was written in Latin, but with vernacular terminology found throughout, interspersed with the Latin text, and in a Latinised form. Many of the vernacular terms in the *Lex Frisionum*, however, are not Frisian but Frankish and were presumably added by Carolingian compilers.

In 1557 the *Lex Frisionum* was published by the German humanist Johannes Herold as part of a collection of laws, the codification of which is commonly associated with the Carolingian court at the time of Emperor

---

17 See Waterbolk, *Twee eeuwen Friese geschiedschijving*, 192, who ranks Siccama with such historians as Ubbo Emmius and Christianus Schotanus.

18 Waterbolk, *ibid.*, 232, mentions Ubbo Emmius, Suffridus Petrus and Bernardus Furmerius as scholars who made limited use of the *Lex Frisionum* before Siccama.

19 This division was first proposed by H. Nehlsen, *Sklavenrecht zwischen Antike und Mittelalter. Germanisches und römisches Recht in den germanischen Rechtsaufzeichnungen [...]*, Göttinger Studien zur Rechtsgeschichte 7 (Göttingen, 1972), 61, and maintained in U. Lade, *Flur und Feld: Volkssprachige Bezeichnungen in den frühmittelalterlichen Leges*, Diss. Universität Münster (1986), 26, who also provides a concise overview of the two categories of *Leges Barbarorum*, 26–55.

20 See N. E. Algra, *Oudfries Recht 800–1256* (Leeuwarden, 2000), 91–100, and, with special regard to numismatic matters, D. J. Henstra, *The Evolution of the Money Standard in Medieval Frisia* (Groningen,1999).

Charlemagne.[21] His printed text is the archetype of all later renderings because no manuscripts have survived.[22] In 1613 the Hamburg polymath Friedrich Lindenbrog used Herold's edition to publish the *Lex Frisionum* again, as part of his monumental *Codex Legum Antiquarum*, a comprehensive edition of the *leges barbarorum*.[23] In a substantial glossary at the end of the book, Lindenbrog tried to elucidate the many latinized vernacular terms that obscured the meaning of the ancient laws. Siccama's edition also presents the *Lex Frisionum* from Herold's text (1–51), with some minor omissions, inaccuracies and alterations to bring the Latin in line with humanist conventions.[24] The *Lex* is followed by a Latin text of the 'statutes of *Upstalbam*' (52–62), a corpus of statutes drawn up for the whole of Frisia, at Opstalsbam near Aurich in 1323, and named by Siccama the *Leges opstalbomicae*.[25]

In a wider European perspective, Siccama's interest in the *Leges barbarorum* was part of a tradition that had existed for almost a century. The German antiquarian scholars Johannes Sichard and Johannes Herold had both published a collection of ancient Germanic law texts after they found manuscripts in the libraries of South German abbeys.[26] Other scholars

---

[21] Johannes Herold, *Originum ac Germanicarum Antiquitatum libri ...* (Basel, 1557). A facsimile of Herold's edition is appended to H. Siems, *Studien zur Lex Frisionum* (Ebelsbach, 1980).

[22] From the *editio princeps* by the German humanist Johannes Herold in 1557 to the latest edition in conventional print in 1982, the *Lex Frisionum* appeared in print 18 times, and is now also available on the internet: <http://www.keesn.nl/lex/index.html>. A list has been published by Wumkes, *Bodders*, 206. See also R. H Bremmer Jr, *A Bibliographical Guide to Old Frisian Studies*, NOWELE suppl. vol. 6 (Odense, 1992), who mentions: K.-A. Eckhardt and A. Eckhardt, *Lex Frisionum*, MGH. Fontes iuris germanici antiqui in usum scholarum separatim editi 12 (Hanover, 1982); G. Franz, *Lex Frisionum* (Weimar, 1935); P. Heck, *Die Entstehung der Lex Frisionum* (Stuttgart, 1927).

[23] Friedrich Lindenbrog, *Codex legum antiquarum, in quo continentur, leges Wisigothorum, edictum Theodoric regis. Lex Burgundionum. Lex Salica. Lex Alamannorum. Lex Bavvaiorum. Decretum Tassilinis Duci. Lex Ripuariorum. Lex Saxonum. Anglorum et Werinorum. Frisionum Langobardorum constitutiones Siculae sive Neapolitanae capitulare Karoli M. et Hludowici Impp. &C. Quibus accedunt formulae solennes prisca publicorum privatorumque negotium, nunc primum editae: Et glossarium sive interpretatio rerum vocumque difficilum et obscuriorum.* (Frankfurt, 1613).

[24] Siems, *Studien*, 44–45.

[25] H. D. Meijering, *De willekeuren van de Opstalsboom (1323): Een filologisch-historische monografie* (Groningen, 1974), 82–85, 124, presents the complete tradition of the Latin rendering, and explains that Siccama was responsible for the title *leges Upstalbomicae*, which is not found in medieval sources.

[26] Johannes Sichard, *Leges Ribuariorum, Baiuvariorum et Alamannorum* (Basel, 1530); Johannes Herold, *Originum ac Germanicarum Antiquitatum libri, leges videlicet Salicæ, Allemannorum, Saxonum, Angliorum, Thuringorum, Burgundionum, Francorum, Ripuariæ, Boioariorum, Vuestphalorum, Vuerinorum, Frisionum, Langobardorum, Theutonum*

published individual law texts which pertained to one particular ancient tribe or one area or nation. Thus, in 1537, an edition of the *Leges Longobardorum* had been published in Venice, in a monumental edition with marginal glosses, emendations and a commentary by several scholars.[27] In 1602 the laws of the Salic Franks were published for the first time with a glossary explaining the many difficult and obscure terms, often of vernacular Germanic origin.[28] The publication of these laws emanated from an antiquarian interest: in the words of Herold's extended title, they contained the exploits, words and customs of the Germanic ancestors.[29] Although it is impossible to state exactly how many of these publications were circulating in Friesland in the early seventeenth century, the libraries of the University of Franeker and its resident professors, as well as a flourishing intellectual climate, suggest broad access to scholarly publications.[30]

(Basel, 1557). On Herold, see A. Burckhardt, *Johannes Basilius Herold: Kaiser und Reich im protestantischen Schrifttum des Basler Buchdrucks um die Mitte des 16. Jahrhunderts* (Basel, 1967).

27 *Leges Longobardorum, cum argutissimis glosis Caroli de Tocco: multis marginalibus postillis decorate; una cum Capitulari Caroli Magni, regis Francorum; addita fuere insuper in easdem leges luculentissima commentaria Andreę de Barulo; necnon annotationes Nicolai Boctij; preterea triplex alphabeticum repertorium ...; que omnia nuper in lucem sunt edita, cunctisque mendis et erroribus dilligenter expurgata per Joannem Baptistam Nennam* (Venice, 1537).

28 François Pithou, *Liber Legis Salicae: Glossarium sive interpretatio rerum et verborum obscuriorum quae in ea lege habentur* (Paris, 1602).

29 'In quo non solum Rerum ac Vocum, nostrarum proprietas cernitur, sed maiorum quoque nostrorum Imperium, eorundem q⟨uam⟩ ..., sese exhibet imitanda⟨m⟩'.

30 R. Feenstra, 'De Libri juridici van de Franeker universiteitsbibliotheek in de zeventiende eeuw', *De Franeker universiteitsbibliotheek in de zeventiende eeuw: Beleid en belang van een academiebibliotheek*, ed. J. M. M. Hermans, G. Jensma, J. van der Sluis and L. Wierda (Hilversum, 2007), 29–62, at 43, points out that humanist and antiquarian books, including editions of the *Leges barbarorum*, were scarce, in comparison to the rich holdings of Leiden. However, a copy of Lindenbrog's *Codex legum antiquarum* was sold at the auction of the library of Johannes Saeckma and his son Theodore in 1666; see M. H. H. Engels, *Bibliografische aanvullingen en registers op de catalogus van de bibliotheek van de friese juristen en humanisten Johannes (1572–1636) en Theodorus (1610–1666) Saeckma* (Leeuwarden, 1995), no. Hf 026. On Franeker book culture, see also M. H. H. Engels, *Franeker folianten: Frieslands Universiteitsbibliotheek, 1585–1713* (Franeker, 1985); R. Stein, 'Hoe Fries was de Franeker Akademie?', *Speculum Frisicum*, ed. Bremmer *et al.*, 157–71, at 164–67; Ph. H. Breuker, 'Learboeken op de akademy en de Latynske skoallen yn Fryslân', *Universiteit te Franeker 1585–1811: Bijdragen tot de geschiedenis van de Friese hogeschool*, ed. G. T. Jensma, F. R. H. Smit en F. Westra (Leeuwarden, 1985), 438–51.

LEX
FRISIONVM
SIVE
ANTIQVÆ
FRISIORVM
LEGES,
A reliquis Veterum Germanorum Legibus separatim æditæ & NOTIS Illustratæ
A
SIBRANDO SICCAMA
ICTO,

FRANEKERÆ
Apud
IOANNEM LAMRINCK,
ORDINVM FRISIAE TYPOGR.
ANNO MDCXVII.

3. DEDICATION AND *AD LECTOREM*

Siccama's book consists of the standard elements of a text edition on humanist principles and gives evidence of the author's competence in this field: in addition to the text of the *Lex Frisionum* there are a dedication, an epistle *ad lectorem*, a table of contents (*2–**4), a commentary to the text, or *notae* (63–151) and indices (V1r–V4v). Whereas the dedication and *Ad* *lectorem* are short, the commentary is substantial. It is divided into the same twenty-two chapters as the *Lex Frisionum*, with a single additional section for the *Additio sapientum*, followed by separate sections for the paragraphs on *Qui alteram viam contradixerit*, *De rebus fugitivis*, *De re praestitia* and *De honore templi*. At the end Siccama provided no less than three indices: one *verborum & rerum*, one *vocabulorum Germanicorum et Frisicorum*, and one *Auctorum & instrumentorum, quorum Testimoniis usi sumus*. Nonetheless, he felt that more remained to be said about the *Lex Frisionum*, and mentions in a letter from 1621 to Johannes Isaacus Pontanus that a second edition is in print and that Pontanus will be able to inspect it before the end of the year. This new version – which never appeared – was to be expanded with a commentary on the privilege to the Frisians issued in 1417 by the Holy Roman Emperor Sigismund.[31] It suggests that the 1617 edition might have been only a precursor to a larger work,[32] not an uncommon course of action in those times.

Siccama dedicated his *Lex Frisionum* to the States of Friesland, the provincial governing body, consisting of representatives from the towns and the landed gentry. In accordance with the generic conventions of dedications, the virtues of the dedicatees are broadly meted out: the members of the States are the buttresses of the state and rule with the same bravery and wisdom as their ancestors; similarly, Siccama also included a request for protection from slanderers. He received twenty guilders from the States, a high amount when compared to other publications;[33] whether he was also thinking of compensation in the form of a position is not known, but it is perhaps significant that Siccama mentions the bestowal of offices as one of the tasks of the States.[34] With the help of capital letters it is made to stand out from the text that the States rule 'MORE MAIORVM', in a period of 'AVREAM LIBERTATEM', and preserve 'RELIGIONEM & CONCORDIAM'. Siccama's book is meant to teach what these *mores maiorum* are, and he therefore describes it as a *pugillus* 'a little fistful' of important knowledge for those who are interested in shedding more light on the fatherland.

---

[31] For the text of this privilege, referred to by Siccama as *pragmatica sanctio*, see the edition in O. Vries, *Het Heilige Roomse Rijk en de Friese vrijheid* (Leeuwarden, 1986), 251–55.

[32] Antonius Matthaeus, *Andreae Alciati tractatus contra vitam monasticam ad collegam olim suum, qui transierat Franciscanos Bernardum Mattium epistola: accedit sylloge epistolarum Giphanii, Vulcanii ... aliorumque virorum clarissimorum, quae variam doctrinam continent ...* (Leiden, 1695; rpt. 1708; The Hague, 1740), letter no. 83 (p. 152 in the edition of 1740).

[33] As Philippus Breuker informed me. See Leeuwarden, Tresoar, Statenarchief 1580–1795, Gf 50 (21–05–1617).

[34] Siccama, *Lex Frisionum*, *4v: 'dignitates tribuistis'.

The dedication explains in a nutshell the principles of Siccama's methodology: he will focus on the *name* of the country, its *place or situation*, the *civil status and liberty* of its people, and, finally its *laws*. In the humanist historical tradition, these four aspects featured regularly in the study of antiquities or *antiquitates*: the name of a country, people or tribe was determined and etymologised, so as to determine its place in a particular demographic constellation; the place of a country or region was demonstrated as either having been stationary from times immemorial, or the result of migration and just conquest; the civil status of the people showed whether they were independent or serfs; and the presence and nature of a country's laws and customs were deemed to be indicative of its civilisation. Fundamental to this antiquarian method is its dependence on ancient sources and documents.[35] The central claim in the dedication is that the Frisians were an ancient nation of that very name, who had lived in Frisia since the times of Emperor Augustus, whence they had spread out along the North Sea coasts, who had maintained since that time an independent social structure, and whose ancient laws could be seen to echo the customs of the Germanic tribes described by Tacitus in his *Germania*. The Frisians were, in Siccama's words: 'inter veteres Germanos noti', and 'Romanis formidabiles [...] propter fortitudinem, & acre libertatis studium'.[36]

In order for the *Lex Frisionum* to qualify as appropriate evidence for Siccama's claims about Frisian antiquity it had to be dated and contextualised fittingly; something Siccama does in the *Ad lectorem*, in which he states that the *Lex* proper – that is, up to the *additio sapientum* – dates back to Roman times:

> First about these laws, which are divided into two lists: the first contains *those laws of the Frisians which were already there in the times of the Romans*, as evidenced by the [laws] about drawing lots, about fines concerning cattle, about hostility among relations, about duelling, about the *liti* [half free], about the sharing of fines, and others which Tacitus clearly

---

35 E. Cochrane, *Historians and Historiography in the Italian Renaissance* (Chicago and London, 1981), 423–44, discusses the role, characteristics and limitations of the study of *antiquitates* within the context of Humanist historiography. Antiquarians wrote about the distant past with the help of a wide variety of ancient sources; historiographers wrote about the recent past or the present, according to the literary model of their ancient forebears. According to Cochrane's definition Siccama is definitely an antiquarian scholar and not a historiographer. Cochrane's assumption that 'antiquarians seldom claimed for their own discipline what the historians unanimously claimed for theirs: practical utility; and when occasionally they did so, they did not take the claims seriously' (443), does not hold for Siccama, whose dedication to the States of Friesland expresses the value of a knowledge of the *Lex Frisionum* for Frisian society.

36 Siccama, *Lex Frisionum*, *2r.

> attributes to the Germans, of whom we were part. However, those very [laws] also prove that much was added by Frankish kings, and adapted to Christian rituals.[37]

In establishing the circumstances surrounding the codification of the *Lex Frisionum*, the *Lex Salica* provided a convenient parallel for Siccama, who records that in the prologue to the *Lex Salica* as printed by Herold there is an account of how the Frankish King Theodoric selected wise legislators to record the customs of the various tribes in a codex, and how subsequently, through the efforts of later kings, the often pagan customs were adapted and improved to fit in with Christian *mores*. Siccama believed that a similar process had taken place in Frisia: as the ancient Franks had their laws codified through the efforts of Wisogast, Salogast, Bosogast and Vindogast, so the Frisians had it done by Saxmund and Vulemar.[38] In other words, the codification of the *Lex Frisionum* was thought to have run parallel to that of the *Lex Salica*, and was, by implication, just as old. Siccama complains of a lack of reverence among the Frisians for their ancient past, and it is this disregard of their glorious antiquity which incited him to write his book.[39]

The 'Notae'

The 86 pages of *notae* are not only the bulk of the book, but also, from a historiographical point of view, its most important part, because they provided the evidence to back up the assertions made in the dedication. Siccama's historical positioning of the Frisians is incorporated in his overall method of commenting on the laws, which involves the explanation of words and phrases from the text that are obscure in a legal or historical sense, or because they are words of Germanic/Frisian origin. In his comments, ranging in length from a few lines to more than nine pages per *lemma*, Siccama shows himself to be an adherent to the philological approach to the study of law: words or passages are illustrated with the help of a range of historical, chorographical and lexicographical sources in relatively brief comments, in which words, their context and meaning, receive

---

37 Siccama, *Lex Frisionum*, **2r: 'Primum de ipsis legibus, quæ in duas tabulas divisæ. Prior ipsas leges Frisionu⟨m⟩ co⟨n⟩tinet, quales etiam Romanis Temporibus fuêre, cui argumento esse possunt illæ, de Sortibus, de pœnis pecuarijs, de inimicitia propinquoru⟨m⟩, de duello, de litis, de mulctarum partitione, aliæque, quas Tacitus Germanis, quorum portio eramus, clarè tribuit. Multa tamen esse addita à Francorum Regibus, et ad Christianos ritus mutata, ipsa per se probant'.

38 Siccama, *Lex Frisionum*, 134; see *Pactus legis Salicae*, ed. K. A. Eckhardt, MGH, Legum I, iv, part II 'Lex Salica' (Hanover, 1969), 4–5.

39 Siccama, *Lex Frisionum*, *4r–v.

a great deal of attention.[40] This style of legal commentary can be associated with the *Mos Gallicus*, after France, the country where it originated, in the school of Andrea Alciato (1492–1550). In his discussion of the 'Lawyer as a Renaissance Man', Donald R. Kelley explains how Alciato added 'the eloquence and erudition of humanism to the profession of civil science' and sums up the essence of how a lawyer like Siccama may have seen himself:

> The 'perfect jurist' was thus the product and the beneficiary of a rich heritage of history, legend and eponymous heroes (or villains), linking classical and modern times and celebrated reverently in Renaissance history, philosophy, literature and, in a large variety of iconographic forms, art'.[41]

Siccama's philological methodology is thus part of the more universal style of humanist textual criticism, visible in annotated editions of classical literary texts, in legal scholarship – significantly, Alciato's seminal work was called *De verborum significatione* (Lyon, 1530) – and in biblical commentaries current in the seventeenth century.[42]

In the *notae*, the four thematic spear-heads listed in the dedication return as important focal points in the discussion. The *nomen Frisionum* is the first word that receives an explanation (65–66), but although Siccama disapproves of those who derive *frisian* from *vrij* 'free', he does not provide a new etymology.[43] The location of Frisia receives much broader attention (136–45). Siccama discusses three subsequent divisions of Frisia: first the division between *Frisii Maiores* and *Minores*, as found in Tacitus; then the triple division in the areas between the rivers Weser and Lauwers, Lauwers and Vlie, and Vlie and *Sincval* (explained as the *Zwin* in Flanders), respectively; and finally the extent of the Seven Sealands, between the rivers Weser and *Kinhem,*[44] which Siccama regards as present-day Friesland. The discussion about the status of the people and their degrees of freedom and

---

40 See N. W. Gilbert, *Renaissance Concepts of Method* (New York, 1960), 92–98.

41 D. R. Kelley, 'Jurisconsultus perfectus: The Lawyer as Renaissance Man', *Journal of the Warburg and Courtauld Institutes* 51 (1988), 84–102, at 88.

42 See H. J. de Jonge, 'The Study of the New Testament in the Dutch Universities 1575–1700', *History of Universities* 2 (1981), 113–29.

43 W. Krogmann, 'Der Name der Friesen', I, II, *UW* 13 (1964), 18–41, discusses a range of opinions about the etymology of 'Fries', both historical and modern, but leaves Siccama unmentioned. For a more recent survey of opinions since the time of Jacob Grimm, see G. Neumann, 'Friesen', *Reallexikon*, X, 2–5. See also E. Seebold, 'Die Friesen im Zeugnis antiker und spätantiker Autoren', *Handbuch / Handbook*, 479–87, at 485–86.

44 Siccama, *Lex Frisionum*, 144, wrongly explains the name of Kennemerland as that of a river: 'fluviumque Kinhemum'.

servitude (66–75) develops into a diachronic outline of the structures of Frisian society: the ancient binary division between nobles and non-nobles developed, under Frankish influence, into the three-pronged structure of nobles, free men and unfree. The subject is of great interest to Siccama, whose conclusion to the discussion – *Nunc manus de tabula, & ad reliqua pergamus* – suggests that he was caught in its web. The laws are the final topic in Siccama's list and are, of course, the continuous thread running through the commentary. Their discussion is a comparative one, in which the point of reference is the *Lex Frisionum*, and the points of comparison sources which are either older than, or contemporaneous with, or younger than the *Lex Frisionum*. The resulting image is, as we will see, one of a continued cultural and legal tradition, from the days of the Romans to the end of the Middle Ages.

Most conspicuous among the many sources used by Siccama to substantiate his claims about the Frisians are the works of Tacitus: the *Annales*, the *Historiae*, but especially the *Germania*. The rediscovery of Tacitus's works in the fifteenth century had made an enormous impact on Humanist historiography, and had fostered the search for regional and national identity in Germany and the Low Countries especially.[45] Tacitus, whose works date from the end of the first century, must have been a godsend for Siccama. In the *Germania* (ch. 34) the *Frisii*, both *maiores* and *minores*, were localised as one of the Germanic tribes, while both in the *Historiae* and in the *Annales* the *Frisii* returned as a tribe that was in contact with the ancient Romans.[46] All Siccama had to do was to trace the correspondences between aspects from the *Lex Frisionum* and the information from Tacitus's works, and these would allow him to make a very strong case for the assertion that, in their original form, the rules and customs described in the *Lex Frisionum* had existed in Roman times. The uneven distribution of references to Tacitus's *Germania* – eleven citations in 67–82 (the section on *De homicidiis)*, and only seven in the entire remainder of the book – suggests that Siccama started off his commentary with this preconceived notion in mind.

A closer inspection of the evidence gathered from Tacitus shows how Siccama tried to project onto Frisia certain social customs and structures which Tacitus mentioned as pertaining to *Germania* as a whole. Thus, the

---

45 See, e.g., E.-L. Etter, *Tacitus in der Geistesgeschichte des 16. und 17. Jahrhunderts*, Basler Beiträge zur Geschichtswissenschaft 103 (Stuttgart, 1966); K. C. Schellhase, *Tacitus in Renaissance Political Thought* (Chicago, 1976), and for the influence of Tacitus on Historiography in Holland at the beginning of the seventeenth century, J. Waszink, 'Tacitisme in Holland: de *Annales et historiae de rebus Belgicis* van Hugo de Groot', *De Zeventiende Eeuw* 20 (2004), 240–63.

46 See Tacitus, *Germania*, ed. and trans. J. B. Rives (Oxford, 1999). All my citations are from Rives's translation.

first section of notes on *De homicidiis* (65–82) contains Siccama's discussion of the structure of Frisian society, divided into noblemen, freemen, half free and slaves, in accordance with the *wergild* or 'man price' which was to be paid in compensation for killing a member of a particular class. However, since the Frisians had prided themselves in their medieval status of freedom directly under the Holy Roman Emperor, without intercession of hereditary nobility, the distinction made in the *Lex Frisionum* between nobleman and freeman required a proper political explanation. In what is effectively a humanist redefinition of gentility, Siccama explains that 'of the free men among the ancient Germans and Frisians, some were nobles, but others commoners' (67).[47] His citations from Tacitus's *Germania* show how all peoples of Germania were to be divided into only two classes: nobles and commoners, and how nobility was the result of merit and military valour.

> Kings they choose for their birth, generals for their valour [VI.1]. Then, according to his age, birth, military distinction, and eloquence, the king or leading man is given a hearing, more through his influence in persuasion than his power in command [XI.2]. Distinction of birth or great deeds done by their fathers confer on mere lads the rank of chief [XIII.2]. If their native state grows sluggish from prolonged peace and leisure, many well-born youths actively seek tribes that are then involved in a war [XIV.2].

Siccama's view of ancient Frisian society shines through from this and other selections of quotes from Tacitus. The free men in society had consisted of two basic groups, nobles and commoners, but the latter could, through their actions, be regarded as equal, if not by ancestry, then in status: not only a noble parentage but also a father's heroic deeds could bestow a high rank on a young man, and persuasion is more important than power.

Subsequently, Tacitus's *Germania* was cited to define other strata in Frisian society: priests and those who were not free. The former enjoyed a special status in Germanic society:

> But no one is allowed to punish or bind or even flog the soldiers except the priest: and not as a penalty on the general's orders, but as though by command of the god who, as they believe, supports them in war [VII.1]. At the command of the priests there is silence, since at this time they too have the right of enforcement [XI.2].

---

[47] 'Liberorum hominum apud veteres Germanos, Frisiosque alij Nobiles, alij plebei fuere'.

In his commentary, Siccama emphasises that the role of a priest was that of a moral guide, not that of a judge or secular lord. Priests were allowed special rights *only* in times of war – not because of their secular rights but out of religious fervour – and he hastens to add that 'nowhere do we read in Tacitus or other authors of Germanic history that among the Germanic people priests formed a sacred order'.[48] His promise to discuss this matter further in the comments on the '*statuta opstalsbomica*' remains unsubstantiated because no commentary on the Upstalsboom laws were included in the book.

Slaves – other than debt slaves – were described by Tacitus as being bond tenants rather than domestic slaves at their masters' beck and call:

> The other slaves they do not use as we do, with designated duties throughout the household; each controls his own holding and his home. The master requires from him, as from a tenant, some amount of grain or livestock or clothing, and only so far must the slave submit [XXV.1].

While presenting the social situation in a positive light, Siccama cosmetically leaves out Tacitus's remarks that slaves were apt to be killed by their masters in a fit of rage, nor does he mention the fact that, among the Germanic tribes, manumission hardly ever led to an improved status, as Tacitus stated. In Siccama's opinion, the slaves as described by Tacitus resembled the *liti* 'half free' in the *Lex Frisionum*, while proper slaves were a Frankish innovation. Although essentially, the *Lex Frisionum* starts from a system of three estates, noblemen, free men and half free, in Siccama's perspective the main distinction was between the free and the unfree.[49]

Other evidence from Tacitus's *Germania* which Siccama deemed important enough to list pertains to the system of providing reparation for crimes through financial compensation according to rank and status (XII.2, XXI.1), which he mentioned with respect to homicide (75–76) and feuds among kinsmen (85). The abhorrence of adultery by women among the Germanic tribes is illustrated through *Germania* XIX.1 (98), as are other customs mentioned in the *Lex Frisionum*, such as the drawing of lots (109), the significance of the *sagum* 'military cloak' (112) and the fact that the Germanic tribes worshipped not in temples but in groves (149–50).

[48] Siccama, *Lex Frisionum*, 70: 'nec uspiam apud Tacitum, aliosque scriptores de rebus Germaniæ legimus, Sacerdotes apud Germanos constituisse sacrum ordinem'.

[49] The three estates in the *Lex Frisionum* are discussed by Algra, *Oudfries recht*, 129–38, who explains that the slaves did not count as an estate. Siccama, however, combines *nobiles* and free men, on the one side, and half free and slaves, on the other.

At times, there seems to be room for a political and religious agenda in Siccama's commentaries, which reveals the Protestant republican spirit that was characteristic of the period of the twelve-year truce in the Dutch Provinces' war with Spain.[50] On the whole, however, Siccama adduces the passages from Tacitus to demonstrate that the Frisians were indisputably and inextricably a part of the noble Germanic nation, and that they stand out among neighbours as the nation which has best preserved the noble traits of their Germanic ancestors. The Frisians were not so much different from the other Germans as 'noted among them' for their courage and valour – the very reasons why they terrified the Romans.

The attempt to link the Frisians to other Germanic nations also appears from the frequent collations of the *Lex Frisionum* with the other *Leges barbarorum* – as a cluster, the only other Latin source besides Tacitus that was used consistently and rather frequently throughout the book.[51] The comparisons serve mostly to explain and complement information from the *Lex Frisionum*. Thus, in relation to the seven oath helpers with which a nobleman could deny the accusation of having killed a free man, Siccama adds that:

> the manner of exculpating and vindicating through taking oaths was extremely old among the ancient Franks and Frisians, even before they had accepted the Christian faith, when they were still pagans. This is established from chapters 50, 51, 55, 59 of the Salic laws, of which it is certain that they were widespread before Christianity, and where those who swore were not called *sacramentales* [i.e. those swearing on relics, ed.] because they had not yet accepted the holy rites and ceremonies of Christianity.[52]

---

[50] W. Bergsma, 'Kerk en staat in Friesland na 1580', *Fryslân, staat en macht 1450–1650*, ed. J. Frieswijk, A. H. Huussen Jr, Y. B. Kuiper and J. A. Mol (Hilversum and Leeuwarden, 1999), 158–72, describes the on-going power struggle in Friesland between the Reformed Church and more secularly minded patricians. It is possible, I think, to read between the lines Siccama's preference for secularism.

[51] The spelling of *Lex Bojoariorum* and his use of the *Capitula Caroli Magni* suggest that Siccama used both Herold's edition and that of Friedrich Lindenbrog, which had come out only in 1613 – four years before Siccama's book. Lindenbrog spelled Herold's *Bojoariorum* as *Baivvariorvm*, while the *Capitvlare Karoli Magni* does not occur in Herold's edition.

[52] Siccama, *Lex Frisionum*, 77: 'Antiquissimus purgandi, & defendendi per Iuramentum modus fuit apud veteres Francos, & Frisios etiam ante Christi fidem susceptam, cum adhuc Pagani essent, quod ex tit. L, LI, LV, LXI. Legum Salicarum, quæ ante Christianismum latas esse certum est, constat, ubi juratores non Sacramentales dicuntur, quod sacra & ceremonias Christianorum adhucdum non suscepissent'.

In this case, the Frisians are compared with the Franks rather than set against them. There are, admittedly, also cases in which Siccama shows that the picture varied in the different *leges*: for example, whereas Frisians, Franks, Salic Franks, Bavarians and Longobards treated theft as an offence reparable by fines, with the Saxons and Ripuarian Franks it was a capital offence (88–89).

The Vernacular

Where the works of Tacitus – and some other Classical texts[53] – functioned as a connection between the *Lex Frisionum* and the Roman/Germanic past, the *Leges Barbarorum* and a substantial number of other historical sources dating back to the Carolingian period firmly embedded the Frisians and their laws within the Germanic culture of the early Middle Ages. The next step in this time-line construction of Frisian history is Siccama's comparison of the *Lex Frisionum* with later medieval Frisian laws: the Latin laws of Upstalsboom from 1323 and – what his book has become famous for – passages from the vernacular Frisian laws: the land-laws of *Westerlauwers Friesland*. In twenty-three quotations, varying in length from a single line to complete paragraphs, Siccama illustrated his commentary with evidence from the *Seventeen Statutes* and *Twenty-four Land Laws*, the *Bolsward Synodal Law*, the *Wymbritseradeel Statutes*, the *Synodal Law of Frisia West of the Lauwers*, the *Elder Magistrate's Law*, and the *Fine Registers from West of the Lauwers*.[54] This wide variety of texts is indicative of Siccama's expertise in the field of Old Frisian legal sources – something he must have acquired through his study of charters and other legal documents. He selected passages where they showed correspondence with the *Lex Frisionum* and thus attempted to demonstrate the continuity of the Frisian legal tradition. For example, the use of oath helpers (77–81) is first presented as an ancient custom that originates in pagan times and is then shown to occur frequently in the vernacular laws by means of no less than four citations. Even though the passages in Old Frisian were only there as illustrations of how Frisian law had remained unchanged, they made Siccama the first early modern editor of substantial fragments from the Frisian Land-laws and indeed the earliest humanist scholar to demonstrate some knowledge of the corpus.

---

[53] For example, Julius Caesar's *De bello Gallico* (p. 70), Pliny's *Historia naturalis* (pp. 137, 141), Seneca's *De beneficiis* (p. 145).

[54] See Oosterhout, 'Sibrandus Siccama'. The English titles of the Old Frisian law texts are based on T. S. B. Johnston, 'The Old Frisian Law Manuscripts and Law Texts', *Handbuch / Handbook*, 571–87.

Siccama's treatment of the vernacular is puzzling, but his interest in Frisian is beyond doubt.[55] In line with humanist conventions, Siccama made emendations and alterations in his excerpts from the Frisian laws, which makes it sometimes difficult to assign them to a certain source.[56] This practice of silent emendation suggests that he may have had ideas about what was right and wrong in Old Frisian, but these ideas are never made explicit. His Latin translations of the Old Frisian passages were accurate, but not flawless, and enabled a large scholarly audience, within Frisia and without, to read and understand the passages.[57]

There is little or no methodological streamlining in his explanations of words: in some cases the etymogical approach is almost entirely historical; in other ones it is a type of etymology characterised by a mixture of linguistic and historical information. Thus, he begins his commentary with a discussion of *Frisiones*. The attestation of this form found with Roman writers, including Tacitus, as well as in the *Leges Barbarorum*, led him to claim that 'the Roman writers and those who imitate the Romans call us *Frisii*'.[58] However, in medieval vernacular sources Siccama had encountered mostly forms spelled with *e*. To explain this discrepancy he resorted to Greek forms, and explained that *φρεισίους* and *φίρησιους* had resulted in *φρησίους* through *synaeresis* (contraction), a concept he adopted from classical grammar.[59] With this linguistic development he could explain the forms with long *ē* (*fresos*, *fresones*) encountered in medieval sources, and decided that 'the true and authentic pronunciation could be said to be *e*'.[60] Immediately afterwards he argues against the etymology of 'Frisian' coming from *vrij* 'free', because in Roman times 'we were not freer than our neigh-

55 Rolf Bremmer has even named him as the potential author of an anonymous Latin fragment describing Frisian grammar, published by Simon Abbes Gabbema in 1681, see R. H. Bremmer Jr, 'Oer datearring, funksje en auteurskip fan de earste Fryske grammatika (1681)', *Philologia Frisica anno 1990* (Leeuwarden, 1992), 9–32, at 23.

56 Oosterhout, 'Sibrandus Siccama', 108–10.

57 The first vernacular passage on page 80 seems to be paraphrased rather than translated: 'Jeffma in man bitygat dat hy in famna aen nede nijmen haet Jeff hijt jecht so jelde hyse tweda/ Jeff hijt biseckr so ontswarra hysa/ achtarsium an da wytede' is rendered as 'Si aliquem accusamus quod virginem aliquam vi. rapuit, ipse cum septem Sacramentalibus iuret', with the middle of the article left untranslated.

58 Siccama, *Lex Frisionum*, 65: 'Romani scriptores, & qui Romanos imitantur, Frisios nos appellant'.

59 Siccama attributes his Greek forms to 'Dion' and 'Ptolemaeus'. The former refers to Cassius Dio, *Historiae Romanae* 54. 32, 2 and 3, who wrote *Φρείσιοι*; the latter to Ptolemaeus, *Geograpia* II.11, 7, who wrote *Φρισσοι*. See W. Pape and G. E. Benseler, *Wörterbuch der griechischen Eigennamen*, 2 vols. (Braunschweig, 1863–70), 1647–48. I am grateful to Professor Stefan Radt for this information. Siccama's concept of *synaeresis* presumably derives from Quintilian, *Institutiones Oratoriae* 1.5.17.

60 Siccama, *Lex Frisionum*, 65: 'ut vera & genuina pronunciatio per è dici possit'.

bours'.[61] Characteristically, the discussion concludes with an historic statement connecting the Frisians with the neighbouring Germanic tribes, rather than with a solution to the linguistic problem.

As far as the origin of the Frisian language is concerned, Siccama must have been acquainted with the kind of ethno-linguistics *avant la lettre* found, for example, in the form of Suffridus Petrus's exposition on the exotic nature of Frisian, of Ubbo Emmius's traditional connection between Frisian and English, and of Bonaventura Vulcanius's claim that Frisian was closely related to Gothic.[62] Siccama abstains from such speculations, and also chose not to comment in any way on opinions of his contemporaries and predecessors. Instead, his views have to be deduced from his commentary, and the overreaching statement that can be gauged from these notes is simply that Frisian is a Germanic language – even though the claim is made implicitly anyway. The sources used to explain Frisian words contribute to this Germanic image. In his discussion of *dolg*, 'wound' (127), he cites and translates a line from Otfrid von Weissenburg's *Evangelienbuch*, the 1571 edition of which he must have known or possessed.[63] After translating article 50 of the *Synodal Law of Frisia West of the Lauwers*, on adultery, Siccama explained *filla*, 'to whip', with the help of *fillunga*, from Justus Lipsius's Wachtendonk Psalter glosses (99),[64] and the same glossary was used for his explanation of *litus* 'half free'(105), which he linked to Old Franconian *letiston* 'most recent' and to the form *litici* 'small ones', which he recon-

61 Siccama, *Lex Frisionum*, 66: 'cum non magis liberi essemus quam vicini nostri'.

62 In Suffridus Petrus, *De Frisiorum antiquitate et origine* (Cologne, 1578), 5–8; Ubbo Emmius, *Rerum Frisicarum historiae* (Franeker, 1596), 33; Bonaventura Vulcanius, *De literis et lingua Getarum sive Gothorum* (Leiden, 1597), *8r; see R. H. Bremmer Jr, 'Late Medieval and Early Modern Opinions on the Affinity between English and Frisian: The Growth of a Commonplace', *Folia Linguistica Historica* 9 (1990), 167–91, at 175–76; K. Dekker, *The Origin of Old Germanic Studies in the Low Countries*, Brill's Studies in Intellectual History 92 (Leiden, Boston, Cologne, 1999), 27–28; A. Feitsma, *Tussen volkstaal en schrijftaal: Meningen van filologen over het Fries* (Leeuwarden, 1978), 6–8.

63 Matthias Flacius Illyricus, *Otfridi evangeliorum liber veterum Germanorum grammaticae, poesos, theologiae, praeclarum munimentum. Evanglienbuch in alt frenkischen Reimen/ durch Otfrid von Weissenburg/ münch zu S. Gallen/ vor sibenhundert Jahren beschriben* (Basel, 1571).

64 Old Low Franconian psalter glosses discovered by the humanist scholar Justus Lipsius and published in *Iusti Lipsii epistolarum selectarum centuria tertia ad Belgas* (Antwerp, 1602). Siccama's reference to page 44 of the edition is wrong; the entry is on page 46, where Lipsius wrote: '*Fillunga*, Flagellum. an quia cutem radit, quasi *villen*?'. Siccama then reconstructs the form *filun*, translated as 'flagellare'. On *fillunga*, see A. Quak, *Wortkonkordanz zu den altmittel- und altniederfränkischen Psalmen und Glossen*, Amsterdamer Publikationen zur Sprache und Literatur 22 (Amsterdam, 1975), 54; for a facsimile of Lipsius's edition, *idem*, *Studien zu den altmittel- und altniederfränkischen Psalmen und Glossen*, Amsterdamer Publikationen zur Sprache und Literatur 12 (Amsterdam, 1973), 42.

structed.[65] For the meaning of *granones* 'hairs of a moustache', Siccama resorts to Cornelis Kiliaan's *Etymologicum Teutonico-Latinum*, a prime source of etymological knowledge for seventeenth-century philologists.[66]

Other vernacular terms are clarified without overt references to sources; such as *wergildo* (114), which Siccama himself connected with '*werra*, meaning fight or manslaughter, and *gild* meaning value or estimate, as if it is the estimate of the fight or manslaughter'.[67] *Faxfang* was explained as deriving from *fax* 'hair' or *vachs*, a cognate supposedly from Dutch (131). The place-name *sincval* (141–42) was thought to be a corrupted form of *sindval*, because *sind* or *sund* meaning 'sound' or 'sea' combined with the second element, 'a fall', could be interpreted as a narrow stretch of water falling into the sea. Its analogy with *zondvloed* (Dutch for Noah's flood), and the occurrence of *Sindval* with Adam of Bremen caused Siccama to pose the rhetorical question 'whether there was anything clearer that could be adduced'.[68] On the whole, Siccama gives evidence of some familiarity with various important sources of Old Germanic material, although his restricted use of these sources show that comparative philology was not his main aim.

In the cases where Siccama does resort to a comparison between Frisian and other languages a similar emphasis on the Germanic nature of Frisian appears. Such an attempt at comparative philology is the explanation of *thiubda* 'theft', a latinization of Old High German *diob*, which he takes to be corrupted Frisian, because the form *thiafta* occurs regularly in the vernacular laws. The initial consonant ⟨th⟩, he thought, resulted from the fact that 'the old Francs, Frisians and Saxons always used ⟨th⟩ for ⟨d⟩ [erroneously printed as '*t* pro *b*'], to which the Frisians and the English now still adhere'.[69] He supports this claim by a list of Dutch and Frisian examples, adding that he had found two or three hundred-year-old documents in which

---

65 See Quak, *Wortkonkordanz*, 105; *idem*, *Studien*, 45. Here, too, Siccama's form *litici* was reconstructed on the basis of Lipsius's entry: '*Luzzilon*, Paruulis: & *Luticon*, idem'.

66 Cornelis Kiliaan, *Etymologicum Teutonicae Linguae sive Dictionarium Teutonico-Latinum, praecipuas Teutonicae linguae dictiones et phrases Latine interpretatas, et cum aliis nonnullis linguis obiter collatas complectens* ... (Antwerp, 1599); rpt. in facsimile with an introduction by F. Claes, Oude Nederlandse woordenboeken 3 (reeks 2) (The Hague, 1972); cf. K. Dekker, '"Vide Kilian ...": The Role of Kiliaan's *Etymologicum* in Old English Studies Between 1650 and 1665', *Anglia* 114 (1996), 514–43. On *granones*, see C. DuFresne DuCange *et al.*, *Glossarium mediæ at infimæ latinitatis*, 7 vols. (Paris, 1840–50) III, 554–55, s.v. *grani*.

67 Siccama, *Lex Frisionum*, 114: 'Dictum vero *Wergildum* à Werra, quod pugnam, & cædem, & gild, quod valorem, & æstimationem significat, quasi cædis, & pugnæ æstimatio'.

68 Siccama, *Lex Frisionum*, 142: 'Quid clarius, quid manifestius adferri potest?'

69 Siccama, *Lex Frisionum*, 88: 'nam veteres *Franci*, *Frisij*, *Saxones* semper *t* pro *b* usurpabant, quod etiam nunc *Frisij* & *Angli* observant'.

these words were nearly always found with ⟨th⟩, which reflected not only the pronunciation then, but also that of present-day 'pure and clear southern Frisian'[70] – a very early value judgement on a dialect of Frisian. The dialect referred to may well be that of Hindeloopen and Molkwerum, which had a special renown among seventeenth-century philologists and commentators, and, if so, helps to confirm the assumption that the reputation of this dialect existed already at the beginning of the seventeenth century, and may well go back to the sixteenth century.[71] For Siccama this reputedly ancient dialect contributed to his objective of demonstrating a tradition of the Frisian language from Roman times – when he believed the *Lex Frisionum* to have been written – to the language of his own days.

The attention to the vernacular was the most important reason for the interest in Siccama's *Lex Frisionum* later in the seventeenth century, when the study of Old Frisian took off. The Leiden entrepreneur and polymath Johannes de Laet who compiled a dictionary of Old English in the 1640s and had been engaged in the study of Anglo-Saxon laws possessed a copy of Siccama's *Lex Frisionum*.[72] De Laet's friend, the English antiquarian John Morris was also interested in Frisian and asked de Laet for a copy of the *Lex Frisionum* in 1634.[73] Five years later Morris repeated his request, lamenting that the book was very hard to find, not only in English bookshops, but also in the Netherlands. The fact that Frisians and Saxons are almost the same people was, according to Morris, the reason why the prospect of Old Frisian laws with a Latin translation seemed very attractive to him, for such a bilingual edition would enable him to read the Old Frisian.[74] The Dutch

---

[70] *Ibid.* 88: 'Habeo vetera instrumenta ante annos CC. & CCC. scripta, ubi omnia per th. raro per b. [*recte d.*] efferi invenies, nec aliter pronunciabant, hodie pronunciant, puri puti australes Frisij'. C. D. van Strien and Ph. H. Breuker, 'Friesland in de reisverslagen van Britse reizigers omstreeks 1700. Mei in útjefte fan it part oer Fryslân út Farrington (1710)', *IB* 52 (1990), 194–216, provide an outline of this tradition in the seventeenth century, but find very little before the 1640s.

[71] Earlier than the ideas about the dialects of Hindeloopen and Molkwerum; see R. H. Bremmer Jr, 'Old English–Old Frisian: the Relationship Reviewed', *Philologia Frisica anno 1981* (Leeuwarden, 1981), 79–91, at 86; *idem*, 'Late Medieval and Early Modern Opinions', 180–81.

[72] De Laet's dictionary was lost in the Copenhagen fire in 1728. His annotations to the laws of King Hlothere and King Eadric (London, Lambeth Palace Library MS 1742, fols. 137–49) contain references to the *Lex Frisionum* but leaves Siccama unmentioned. See J. A. F. Bekkers, *The Correspondence of John Morris with Johannes de Laet (1634–1649)* (Assen, 1970), XVIII–XXVII; R. H. Bremmer Jr, 'The Correspondence of Johannes de Laet', *Lias* 25 (1998), 139–64.

[73] See Bekkers, *The Correspondence*, 2 (Morris to de Laet; 12–04–1634).

[74] *Ibid.* 26 (Morris to de Laet; 01–01–1639). Another Englishman who made use of Siccama's *Lex Frisionum* was the antiquarian and lexicographer William Somner (1598–1669), in his *Glossarium* to Roger Twysden's *Historiae Anglicanae Scriptores X*

philologist Francis Junius possessed a copy of Siccama's *Lex Frisionum* (now Oxford, Bodleian Library, MS Junius 111),[75] in which he collated the *Leges Opstalsbomicae* with the vernacular rendering of this text in MS Unia (Junius's *apographa* in Oxford, Bodleian Library, MS Junius 49, fols. 76–99). Conversely, references to Siccama's *Leges Upstalbomicae* and excerpts of vernacular law were noted by Junius in his copy of the Frisian incunable (MS Junius 109).[76] Similarly, the Old Frisian studies of Junius's friend, the Breda lawyer Jan van Vliet,[77] contain references to Siccama – in van Vliet's own copy of the incunable edition of the Land-laws (Oxford, Bodleian Library, Marshall 60) and in a glossary of Old Frisian words.[78] Next to the incunable, the *Lex Frisionum* was *the* book to have for the study of Old Frisian.

Siccama's Friesland

The contents and method of the *dedicatio* and *notae* show that Siccama's edition of the *Lex Frisionum* fulfils a dual purpose. On the one hand, it provides the first text edition of the *Lex Frisionum* printed in Friesland, with comments and vernacular analogues, presented according to proper humanist conventions. On the other hand, however, the book constitutes a

---

(London, 1652). See M. S. Hetherington, *The Beginnings of Old English Lexicography*. Private publication (Spicewood Texas, 1980), 135–41, 199; Bremmer, 'Late Medieval and Early Modern Opinions', 176–79.

75 P. H. Breuker, "On the Course of Francis Junius' Germanic Studies, with Special Reference to Frisian", *Aspects*, 42–68; rpt. with additions in *Franciscus Junius F. F. and His Circle*, ed. R. H. Bremmer Jr (Amsterdam and Atlanta, 1997), 129–57.

76 Pp. 17, 19, 24, 55, 59, 101, 126, 129, 131, 132, 144, 169, 171. That Junius not only collated the passages but also appreciated Siccama's explanatory comments appears from the marginal comment: *Citat hæc diverse et interp⟨retatur⟩ Siccama*. See MS Junius 109, p. 17. Junius's comment relates to fragment no. 14 in Oosterhout, who recognizes elements from various sources in Siccama's rendering. More instances of Junius's using Siccama as a lexicographical source can be found in London, Lambeth Palace Library MS 783. In a glossary of both Latin and vernacular legal terms Junius refers to Siccama's explanations of *Freda*, *heribannum*, *liduna*/*malina*, *lidwagi*, *jechtwird*/*seckwird*, *aelwird* [*recte aeftswird*], all of which are broadly discussed in the notes to the *Lex Frisionum*. See Lambeth MS 783, fols. 342v (Sicc., pp. 120, 124), 344r (Sicc., pp. 122–23), 345r (Sicc., p. 150), 345v (Sicc., p. 130), 350v (Sicc., p. 109), 369v (Sicc., p. 100).

77 See Breuker (in Bremmer, ed. 1998), 152; K. Dekker, 'The Old Frisian Studies of Jan van Vliet (1622–1666) and Thomas Marshall (1621–1685), *Approaches*, 113–38, at 130–32.

78 Lambeth MS 783, fols. 91v–126v. References to Siccama also occur in van Vliet's annotated copy of William Somner's *Dictionarium Saxonico-Latino-Anglicum*, a dictionary of Old English which van Vliet purchased in 1659/60. Leiden, Universiteitsbibliotheek 766 A6; see Dekker, *The Origins*, 125–28.

discourse of Frisian cultural identity in which it is shown – particularly to the Frisian States – what the Frisian nation and being Frisian is all about:

> In order, Noble Councillors, that it [= the book?] may also straighten the pillars of the Republic, I pray and beg the Almighty God on my knees that He may direct your transactions and deliberations to public welfare, and preserve for you the ancient courage and perseverance, with which our ancestors, through so many centuries, so many cruelties of war, have handed down to us unscathed *golden liberty* [my italics], nothing greater than which, nothing holier than which, can appear to peoples and nations.[79]

This conclusion to the *dedicatio* connects the virtues of the ancient Frisians, as described in the *Lex Frisionum*, with the central theme of 'golden liberty'.

For any contemporary Frisian reader this reference to 'golden liberty' could only refer to the 'legend of Frisian liberty', which relates how the Frisians received exceptional privileges from Charlemagne in exchange for helping him conquer Rome. Emperor and Pope had rewarded the Frisians – and most notably their legendary leader, Magnus – with the right of self-rule under the Emperor's *aegis*, without interference of noble overlords.[80] This legend featured most extensively in the late medieval *Freske Riim*, 'The Frisian Rhyme' (before 1500) and its Middle Dutch adaptation, the *Tractatus Alvini*, which trace back the Frisians to Asia as the descendants of Japhet, the son of Noah. They arrived in seven ships on the banks of the river Ems, where they lived in freedom until they became subservient to the king of Denmark. Subsequently, they regained their freedom by nobly serving Charlemagne in his conquest of Rome, in exchange for which he rewarded them with eternal freedom.[81] Such accounts of the (mythical) origin of a nation or tribe are found in what Bernard Lewis described as 'remembered history', 'the collective memory of a community or nation or

---

79 Siccama, *Lex Frisionum*, x4v–xx1r: 'Quod rectat, Inclyti Proceres, et publicæ rei statumina, Deum Opt. Max. supplex precor, venerorque, ut acta, et consilia vestra ad salutem publicam diriget, servetque vobis veterem fortitudinem & constantiam, quâ Maiores nostri AVREAM LIBERTATEM, quâ populis gentibusque nihil majus, nihil sanctius præstari potest, per tot secula, tot aspera bellorum nobis incolumem tradidêre'.

80 On aspects of the 'Frisian liberty', see *Die Friesische Freiheit des Mittelalters: Leben und Legende*, ed. H. van Lengen, R. Driever and W. Kuppers (Aurich, 2003); its political aspects in medieval history are discussed in Vries, *Het Heilige Roomse Rijk en de Friese Vrijheid*.

81 The legend of Frisian liberty is the subject of the Old Frisian 'Thet Freske Riim' and the Middle Dutch 'Tractatus Alvini'. Both texts have been edited by A. Campbell, *Thet Freske Riim; Tractatus Alvini* (The Hague, 1952), in which Campbell provides an extensive literary and historical introduction to the story.

other entity – what it, or its rulers, poets and sages choose to remember as significant, both as reality and symbol', and are referred to as 'cultural myths'.[82] Without a doubt, Siccama knew this legend of Frisian liberty, from the incunable edition of the Frisian Land Laws and other manuscripts, from a summary of the *Tractatus Alvini* in Suffridus Petrus's *De scriptoribus Frisiae*, and possibly even from a manuscript of the *Freske Riim* or the *Tractatus Alvini.*[83]

Nevertheless, however attractive the traditional legend of Frisian liberty might have been, for Siccama – as for some of his contemporaries – it cannot have sufficed any longer as an acceptable 'cultural myth'.[84] Such a myth has to meet certain generic precepts, in that, for example, it anchors on 'the assumption that there is a vital connection running through the stages of a people's history' and 'testifies to the belief that the past can shape the present, and, by extension, the future'.[85] The traditional legend of Frisian liberty completely disregarded Tacitus's account of Frisian antiquity during the time of the early Roman Empire and therefore no longer met the requirements of the genre. By incorporating not only the humanist (re-)discovery of the writings of Tacitus, but also the *Leges Barbarorum*, and, last but not

---

82 See B. Lewis, *History Remembered, Recovered, Invented* (Princeton, 1975), 11–12; N. Howe, *Migration and Mythmaking in Anglo-Saxon England*, 2nd ed. (Notre Dame, 2001) uses Lewis's ideas to contextualise the migration myth of the Anglo-Saxons in Old English literature. On pp. 3 and 4 of his 'Introduction', Howe lists a number of essential characteristics of cultural myths.

83 Suffridus Petrus, *De scriptoribus Frisiae* (Cologne, 1593), 41; see Campbell, *Thet Freske Riim*, 2–3. Siccama mentions Suffridus's book explicitly on pages 134–35 of his *Lex Frisionum*.

84 Siccama was not alone in his negative attitude to remembered history. Ubbo Emmius criticised Suffridus Petrus's claim that the story of Friso as the ancestor of the Frisians was based on written sources now lost – a classical device for historical forgers, as A. Grafton, *Forgers and Critics: Creativity and Duplicity in Western Scholarship* (Princeton, 1990), 121–22, explains. Siccama also found a staunch supporter in Johannes Isaacus Pontanus. In his letter to Siccama of 10 August 1621 he thanks the latter for the *Lex Frisionum* and voices in very strong terms his full support for Siccama's argument, partly in relation to a forthcoming book on Frisia and its origin that Siccama was reportedly working on: 'Away with this rabble, nothing but mud, who are seeking the name of 'Frisians' among the Indians or Persians' (Valeant ergo sordes istae et lutum merum, qui nomen Frisiorum inter Indos aut Persas quaerunt). Pontanus sees no ground whatsoever for the assumption that the Frisians come from the other side of the earth, nor does he see any indication that trustworthy ancient authors provided information to support this. Moreover he states that Furmerius contradicted himself and disapproves of Johannes Trithemius's forged history from the mouth of the spurious monk Hunibald. The letter is a unique example of the scholarly reception of Siccama's *Lex Frisionum*, from a historical point of view. See Matthaeus, *Andreae Alciati Tractatus*, 204–07 (letter 107).

85 Howe, *Migration and Mythmaking*, 4.

least, the incipient interest in the vernacular, in a new reconstruction of the past, Siccama attempted to change the broadly accepted Frisian past – and as the past underwent a reconstruction, so, by implication, did the present.

Frisian identity was an important aspect of this reconstruction. The traditional legend of Frisian liberty made no mention of the Frisians as a Germanic tribe; instead, by directly linking the Frisians with Noah's progeny, the legend set them apart from their Germanic neighbours. This separateness had given rise to daring mythologies advanced by, among others, Siccama's contemporary Suffridus Petrus, who linked the Frisians to as far a place as India.[86] In Siccama's edition of the *Lex Frisionum* one central theme pervades: the revaluation and recontextualisation of Frisian history within a strictly Germanic context. Instead of providing an exclusive history, such as a Frisian ancestry from the Trojans, Greeks, or some biblical tribe, Siccama, heavily influenced by Tacitus, opts for an inclusive history, in which he embeds the Frisian nation, together with its neighbours, within a Germanic ancestry. As a result, the main distinguishing feature of the Frisian nation changes from ethnicity (the Frisians as a separate ethnic group) to identity (the Frisians as the most genuine, unadulterated Germanic tribe). Moreover, the historical paradigm shifts from 'remembered history' to 'recovered history': 'history ... recovered by academic scholarship ... and the consequent reconstruction of a forgotten past'.[87] The resulting construct is a philological one, based on ancient written sources and humanist textual criticism.

The emphasis on texts entailed that in Siccama's *Lex Frisionum* the discourse of cultural myth for the first time involved the Old Frisian language in a realistic and fact-based setting, i.e. based on citations rather than assumptions grounded on fantasy. The presence of the vernacular fragments was, in the first place, an indispensable aspect of Siccama's purpose and methodology, in that they formed an essential link in the chain of events that had to demonstrate the ancient Frisian legal tradition. However, the implications of the inclusion of Old Frisian and the attention Siccama paid to language and philology proceeded far beyond the historical, in that it presented the Old Frisian language to an international scholarly audience in

[86] See fn. 17, above. Two sixteenth-century chronicles, Ocko Scarlensis, *Croniick, ende warachtige beschryvinghe van Vrieslant ...* (Leeuwarden, 1597) and Worp of Thabor, *Chronicon Frisiae libri tres*, ed. J. G. Ottema (Leeuwarden, 1847), located the original Frisians in Asia. Even though Worp's *Chronicon* existed only in manuscript, it is very likely that Siccama knew both works; the fact that neither of the two chronicles are mentioned in Siccama's *Lex Frisionum* can only be interpreted as an expression of his disapproval. On these chronicles, see Ph. H. Breuker and A. Janse, 'Beelden', *Negen Eeuwen Friesland – Holland: Geschiedenis van een haat–liefde verhouding*, ed. Breuker and Janse (Zutphen, 1997), 9–66.

[87] Lewis, *History*, 12–13.

a context which emphasised and vindicated its importance as an Old Germanic language. The positive reception of Siccama's *Lex Frisionum* among the first generation of Germanic philologists is indicative of the importance they attached to the book and of the position of Frisian within their work. The Germanic identity which Siccama constructed for the Frisians reflected positively on their language and positioned it, for the first time, among the Old Germanic tongues.[88]

[88] I should like to express my warm-hearted gratitude to Philippus Breuker for his many suggestions and corrections and for generously sharing his unpublished material on Siccama with me. Special thanks are also due to Rolf Bremmer, Oebele Vries and Christine Rauer for their many valuable suggestions.

Jorwert Breaking: A Late Old West Frisian Sound Change

Siebren Dyk

1. Introduction [1]

More than twenty-five years ago, Henk Meijering called for further investigation in the area of Old Frisian phonology: 'It might be a good idea to take up the study of other linguistic changes which begin to show in the late Old Frisian period [...] like e.g. the *h*-deletion in initial position before a consonant, the so-called younger palatalization of /k/, the development of *(-)ewe(-)* to *(-)iowe(-)*'.[2] I suspect that Frisian linguistics is not known for its rapid developments but, nevertheless, the first of the three phenomena mentioned by Meijering did subsequently become the subject of one study,[3] and here I want to take up the third.

It is certainly not the case that the phenomenon in question has never been granted any attention; however, the longest treatment, by Willem van Helten, is now over a century old.[4] The field of phonology has made some progress since that time, and although van Helten had a good knowledge of Old Frisian, he was handicapped in that he was not well aware of developments in later stages of Frisian. Moreover, neither in van Helten's nor in

---

[1] This article is an abridged and slightly updated version of a paper written in Frisian, 'Jorwertbrekking', *IB* 64 (2002), 272–314. The most important difference is that I have dropped a complete section on the historiography of the phenomenon which would be of limited importance outside the inner circle of Frisian studies. Furthermore, I have removed a few questionable cases from my analysis that are not essential for the point I am trying to make. – Preparing a new version of an older paper has offered me the pleasant opportunity to express a few words of gratitude again. So, for the second time I may thank Jarich Hoekstra, Arjen Versloot and Willem Visser for commenting on a draft version. I also would like to thank Karel Gildemacher, Henk Meijering and Jenny Visser for each providing me with fresh examples.

[2] H. D. Meijering, '*d(e)*-Deletion in the Past Tense of the Class II Weak Verbs in Old Frisian', *Linguistic Studies Offered to Berthe Siertsema*, ed. D.J. van Alkemade *et al.* (Amsterdam, 1980), 277–86, at 285.

[3] H. Nijdam, 'The Loss of Old Frisian *h* in Initial Consonant Clusters', *ABäG* 51 (1999), 81–104.

[4] W. L. van Helten, 'Zur Lexicologie und Grammatik des Altwestfriesischen', *BGdSL* 19 (1894), 345–440; 560.

later studies has the phenomenon been studied in its own right. At most, it has been mentioned in passing in accounts detailing the possible developments of individual vowels, like /i:/ or /e:/.[5] In etymological studies it was used as an argument to point to the source of the word in question; a good example is Hoekstra's recent study, which connects Modern West Frisian *jamk* with OFris **evenlik*.[6] Other examples of this genre will come to pass in section 4. In summary, it is fair to say that although the phenomenon is not unknown among Frisian linguists and philologists, it has never been subject to an in depth treatment.

As Meijering has noted, the Old Frisian sequence *ew* can change into *jow*; but it is my contention that this is not the only relevant change in this respect. I hope to show that combinations of *w* and vowels at other heights underwent a similar change, and in my opinion this change can be analysed as a direct one, in that the phonological height remains constant. Putting length distinctions aside, this holds for /i(:)/ + /w/, which changes to /ju.w/, and possibly also for /ɛ(:)/ + /w/, resulting in /jɔ.w/; this idea will be elaborated in section 2. Section 3 provides some phonological evidence in favour of the position taken here. The bulk of the evidence, however, is to be found in section 4, where an attempt is made to catalogue all the Frisian words which have undergone the process. In section 5, something will be said about the historical implementation of the change. The story ends in section 6 with a short conclusion.

It should be emphasized that the process under discussion is a feature of (Old) West Frisian only.[7] In North Frisian and East Frisian it is unknown, possibly, with the exception of a few place-names such as *Jukwerd*, *Joeswerd* and *Sjuxum* in the province of Groningen, i.e. in a formerly East Frisian area.[8]

As can be deduced from the title, I dub the process with the term Jorwert Breaking. 'Breaking' is a well-known phenomenon within the field of Frisian historical phonology. Most commonly, it refers to the change of a

---

[5] See, for instance, the overviews by T. Siebs, *Zur Geschichte der englisch-friesischen Sprache* (Halle/S., 1889); J. Jacobs, *Vormleer van het Oudfriesch werkwoord* (Gent, 1899); P. Kloosterman, *Het vocalisme der beklemtoonde lettergrepen van den Metslawierschen tongval, historisch uiteengezet. Een bijdrage tot de kennis der historische grammatica van het Nieuwwestfriesch* (Groningen, 1907); J. S. H. Boersma, *De Friesche oorkonden uit het archief van het St. Anthony-gasthuis te Leeuwarden*, II (Amsterdam, 1939).

[6] J. Hoekstra, '*Iampck ist en iamcker wirtet mecke*: Jitris oer it komôf fan Nijfrysk *jamk*', *IB* 60 (1998), 1–14.

[7] The change is seen as a characteristic of Old West Frisian by W. J. Buma, *Aldfryske houlikstaspraken* (Assen, 1957), 35–36.

[8] H. T. J. Miedema, *Van York naar Jorwerd. Enkele problemen uit de Friese taalgeschiedenis* (Groningen, 1966), 11.

falling (central) diphthong into a rising one, for example in /stjɪnən/, the plural of /sti.ən/ 'stone'. This change can be traced back to the Middle Frisian period, around the year 1700. Although the process is traditionally referred to as 'Modern Frisian Breaking', one cannot say that a monophthong is literally broken into a diphthong here; maybe this change is better described as a shift of accent within the diphthong itself. To be sure, the term 'breaking' is already used for two types of changes in the Old Frisian period. First, there is the breaking of short *e* into *iu* or *io* before the consonant clusters /xt/ or /xs/ which produces Old Frisian forms such as *fiuchta* 'to fight' and *riucht* 'right'. And, secondly, there is a breaking process before *l* + consonant clusters, also traceable to the late Old Frisian period, which yields Modern West Frisian forms like *fjild* 'field', *jelmisse* 'alms' and *jelne* 'ell' (measure of length).[9]

In light of the above examples, the term 'breaking' for the process under review does not seem inappropriate. As we will see in the next section, it can be analysed as a shift of accent within the diphthong, a process quite similar to Modern Frisian Breaking. However, judging by the transition e.g. *ew* > *jow*, the approximant *w* seems to be a constant factor, so one could also claim that *e* polarizes into a rising diphthong *jo*. Let us therefore assume that it is justified to characterize the process as a form of breaking, especially when the Frisian linguistic tradition is taken into account.

Although this type of breaking does not solely occur in Frisian, I have not been able to come across a special term for it, other than 'stress shift'. But stresses can be shifted in many ways and places, so this term does not seem very fitting, and a new term to refer to the process might be in order. I have therefore decided to refer to the process as 'Jorwert Breaking', after the village of Jorwert, some 15 kilometres south-west of Ljouwert (Dutch: Leeuwarden), the capital of the province of Fryslân. This is done for three reasons. First, the first part of its name, *Jor-*, is a clear example of the process, the name of the village was formerly *Everwerd*. Second, using the name of this village in reference to the process has a certain tradition: witness Miedema's inaugural lecture *Van York naar Jorwerd* ('From York to Jorwerd'). And last but not least, it so happens that I became an inhabitant of the village. Had I not moved to Jorwert, I am sure this article would never have been written.

---

9 For these two types of 'breaking' process, see, respectively, D. Boutkan, 'On Labial Mutation and Breaking in Old Frisian', *Approaches*, 77–88, and H. T. J. Miedema, 'Friese plaatsnamen, tweetaligheid, brekingen en andere problemen', *Naamkunde* 19 (1987), 104–41.

2. Analysis

The existence of Jorwert Breaking in Frisian, especially on such a large scale, is unthinkable without the weakening, i.e. vocalization of /v/ in Old Frisian.[10] The weakening could result in a deletion of /v/ after *r* and *l*, cf. MoFris *stjerre* 'to die' from /stɛrva/ and *keal* 'calf' from /kalv/. In intervocalic position, *v* could vocalize to the approximant *w*, e.g. OFris *skriva* /skri:va/ 'to write' changed to /skri:wa/.

As a second point of departure for my analysis, I assume that Old Frisian had four vowel heights. Although some scholars are undecided on this point,[11] this position is already alluded to by Theodor Siebs, and defended by Pieter Sipma, Henricus Miedema and Dietrich Hofmann; furthermore, on the basis of later developments in West Frisian dialects, Arjen Versloot has also concluded that there were two *ē*'s in Old West Frisian.[12] In this paper I also take the position that there were two *ē*'s, but as we will see later, it may be useful to keep an eye on this as yet unresolved question. As to both *ē*'s, the open one, here symbolized by [ɛ:], developed from a former long **ai* and **œy* (from Germanic *ai* and *au* plus *i*-umlaut, respectively), while closed [e:] derived from PGmc *ē*, *ō* and *ū* by *i*-umlaut. One difficulty lies in the fact that both *ē*'s were not differentiated in Old Frisian orthography. However, thanks to the notation in Holthausen's *Altfriesisches Wörterbuch* the two are easily identified, as this dictionary registers the reflexes from the long monophthongs as *ē* and the reflexes from the old diphthongs as *ê*. Arne Spenter assumes even five vowel heights for the long vowels in Old West Frisian,[13] but it is unlikely that such a constellation would have formed a stable system. Therefore, I prefer a four-height system as in (1):[14]

---

[10] In this sense G. Gosses ('Snjeon', *De Pompebledden* 13 [1940], 39–43, at 40) was completely right in characterizing 'de V as moater' ['V (functions) as a motor'].

[11] E.g. T. L. Markey, *Frisian* (The Hague, 1981), 109, and J. Hoekstra, 'An Outline History of West Frisian', *Handbuch / Handbook*, 722–34, at 725; D. Boutkan, 'Phonology and Orthographic System of Old Frisian', *ibid.* 613–20, at 618.

[12] T. Siebs, *Der Vocalismus der Stammsilben in der altfriesischen Sprache* (Halle/S., 1885), 22; P. Sipma, *Fon Alra Fresena Fridome. In ynlieding yn it Aldfrysk* (Sneek, 1947), 55–56; H. T. J. Miedema, 'Oer de fokaelsystemen fan Reyner Bogerman en Gysbert Japiks as oergongssstadia tusken Ald- en Nijfrysk', *Fryske stúdzjes oanbean oan Prof. dr. J. H. Brouwer op syn sechstichste jierdei 23 augustus 1960*, ed. K. Dykstra *et al.* (Assen, 1960), 153–60; D. Hofmann, '"Germanisch" $\bar{e}^2$ im Friesischen', in D. Hofmann, *Gesammelte Schriften*, 2 vols. (Hamburg, 1988–1989) II, 165–90; A. Versloot, 'Aldwesterlauwersk Fryske /e:/ yn it Nijwesterlauwersk Frysk', *IB* 53 (1991), 71–96.

[13] A. Spenter, *Der Vokalismus der akzentuierten Silben in der Schiermonnikooger Mundart. Eine geschichtliche Studie des autochthonen westfriesischen Inseldialekts* (Copenhagen, 1968), 150.

[14] I present the vowels here as long, but Old Frisian also had short vowels before /v/.

(1)

i: u:
e: o:
ɛ: ɔ:
a:

As long as *v* was a fricative, it belonged to the onset of a following syllable, e.g. OFris *skri-va*. However, as a glide *w*, it became an ambisyllabic transition sound between two syllables. Hence, *w* became the last element of the preceding syllable and merged with the preceding vowel.[15] This kind of contraction caused Modern West Frisian to differ somewhat more from neighbouring languages. It resulted in such forms as *nâle* 'navel', *hauk* 'hawk' (Du *havik*), *Aldehou* 'church tower in Leeuwarden' (Du *Oldehove*), *do* 'pigeon' (Du *duif*), and *ûne* 'oven' (Du *oven*).

Applied to the schema in (1), the contraction of *w* yields the following combinations:

(2)

i.w u.w
e.w o.w
ɛ.w ɔ.w
a.w

In the contraction process, the original long vowel was undoubtedly shortened somewhat, and the original short vowels will have been lengthened. The net result is indicated here by a single dot. For ease of reference I will use the term 'diphthong' for this result, although I leave open the question whether this is correct, i.e. whether *w* is part of the nucleus of the syllable or should be situated outside of it.

After contraction, a further process of diphthongization took place. And this is what I call 'Jorwert Breaking'. The front vowel becomes a back vowel which itself is preceded by the palatal glide /j/. Since /a.w/ cannot be retracted, this combination is not involved in the process. As to *a(:)* and vocalized *v*, there was only contraction to /a.w/, which later merged with /ɔ.w/.[16]

---

15 See D. Hofmann, 'Die "spätgermanische" Silbenquantitätsverschiebung und die Doppelschreibung alter kurzer Konsonanten in den altwestfriesischen Quellen', *Gesammelte Schriften*, II, 206–14, at 210.

16 Hoekstra, 'An Outline History of West Frisian', 727.

Nature, according to a sound basic assumption, is organized in a simple way. Therefore, it would be most natural to assume that vowel height in this operation remains constant, hence the following schema:

(3)
i.w > ju.w
e.w > jo.w
ɛ.w > jɔ.w

Now, I would like to claim that this is what did actually take place, and I shall provide evidence for this stance in the next sections. At this point, it can already be detected from the schema that in Jorwert Breaking three falling diphthongs are involved. Two of these diphthongs result from two distinct varieties of *e* – such a differentiation has never been suggested in the literature on Jorwert Breaking until now. This notion of vowel height retention is new, as will emerge in the discussion of some earlier proposals later on in this section.

Superficially, 'Jorwert Breaking' is reminiscent of back-mutation, in the literature also referred to as *u*- or *w-Umlaut*, labial mutation, etc.[17] A few Modern Frisian examples which once underwent that change follow below:[18]

(4)
njoggen 'nine', compare OE *nigun*
sjonge 'to sing', compare Go *siggwan*
tsjok 'thick' < Gmc **thekw(i)a-*

An important difference is that the *w*-element is positioned in the next syllable, so *w* and the preceding vowel can never form a unity. But I will not dwell upon back-mutation any longer; for Old Frisian, the subject was taken up again by Dirk Boutkan.[19] Nor will I pay attention here to the Old Frisian diphthong *io*, from Gmc **eu*.[20] I just mention these points to make the reader aware that Old Frisian rising diphthongs can have several origins.

---

17 For an overview of the terminology, see M. L. A. I. Philippa, 'Verwarring rond de velaarumlaut: een kwestie van terminologie', *ABäG* 17 (1982), 113–28.

18 These examples are taken from G. Gosses, 'Stijgende diphtongen en accentverschuiving in het Friesch', *Accentwisseling in de diphtongen*. Bijdragen en mededelingen der Dialecten-Commissie van de Nederlandse Akademie van Wetenschappen te Amsterdam 5 (1944), 9–17, at 12.

19 Boutkan, 'On Labial Mutation and Breaking in Old Frisian'.

20 For relevant Frisian examples of that change I refer to Spenter, *Vokalismus der Schiermonnikooger Mundart*, ch. 3. For a broader perspective, see also K. Heeroma, 'De Gm. *eu* in het Nederlands (II)', *TNTL* 65 (1947), 7–17.

For Jorwert Breaking, it will be clear that the change is instigated by the glide *w*. However, what influence can be attributed to *w*? It has two features that may be of moment: it is back and it is round. These two features are related, in that [+ back] implicates [+ round]. In (3), the vocal nucleus of the resulting sound is a back vowel, which suggests that it has been the feature [+ back] of the glide *w* that has caused the change. The feature [+ back] would have spread then to the left. Something like this appears to have been the idea of Damaris Nübling in her discussion of MoWFris *jouwe* 'give (pl.)' in the paradigm of the verb *jaan* 'to give' (OFris *ieva*), since she analyses such a form as 'eine nichtlautgesetzliche regressiv-assimilatorische Velarisierung und Labialisierung des vorangehenden *e* > *o(u)*'.[21] For a verb like *ieva* such a regressive assimilation might hold water, since it happens to possess /j/ in *anlaut*. But the problem is that an initial /j/ pops up in front of the new back vowel in other cases of Jorwert Breaking. Why should this be? If it were really the case that *w* would pass its feature [+ back] to the preceding vowel, why should that not be enough? Why does Jorwert Breaking not result in /u.w/ instead of /ju.w/, /o.w/ instead of /jo.w/, and /ɔ.w/ instead of /jɔ.w/?

The answer, I suspect, is to be found in the phonetics of the process. To get an idea of what is going on, it is instructive to pronounce the original falling diphthong very slowly. Then it will appear that the outcome is already found in the input. Let us take /i.w/ as an example. On careful listening it will appear that, in the transition of *i* to *w*, a light *u* can be heard. The transition is not abrupt, but rather, as in all connected speech, the one sound smoothly runs over into the following one. After *i*, the mouth is preparing for *w*, there is lip-rounding and the tongue is moving backwards. The result is something like *u*, which changes into *w* in the course of speech. When we apply the same experiment to /e.w/, then we can hear a sound resembling *o*, between *e* and *w*. No wonder, since by rounding an /e:/, and at the same time moving the tongue backwards, we end up with an /o:/. And with respect to /ɛ.w/, this transitory sound is even more open, and hence it can be identified with /ɔ:/.

As such, these transitory sounds are of minor importance. The ordinary speaker/listener will not notice them, at most he will be aware of both parts of the diphthong, and not what subtleties are going on in the transition between the two parts. These only have a phonetic role. For the medium level, we might assign the following notation for this state of affairs: **E**oW. The lower-case letter only has phonetic value, and both capital letters have also phonological value. The one in boldface represents the head of the

[21] D. Nübling, *Prinzipien der Irregularisierung. Eine kontrastive Analyse von zehn Verben in zehn germanischen Sprachen* (Tübingen, 2000), 112–15.

cluster. However, let us imagine that things are beginning to shift, and that within the combination the prominence does not rest on the first element any longer. In that case, the transitory element would become more stressed and might take over the prominence, producing an intermediate stage symbolized here as E**O**W. As a result, the first element has no other choice but to weaken and become a glide, possibly as a consequence of the Glide Parameter: 'a non-head vowel is [+ high]'.[22] The end result, then, is J**O**W.

Perhaps, we can make the emergence of *j* plausible even without appealing to such a formal principle. It is a striking fact that one of the features of /j/ is that of a hiatus filler, i.e. a transitional element when a front vowel and a back vowel come together, the more so when the latter has more stress. This is nicely illustrated in the Dutch acronym *EO* (for *Evangelische Omroep* 'Evangelical Broadcast') or the name *Theo*. In concatenated speech these two are pronounced as [e.jo:] and [te.jo:], respectively. Now, recall that we have found that the transition of [e:] to [w] raises an *o*. In turn, we now see that the transition from [e:] to [o] can evoke a *j*. All in all, phonetically we get something like [e:jow], of course pronounced in concatenation.

Now, if [e:jow] is indeed formed, then the following scenario is conceivable. We take as a point of departure that the stress shifted to the second part, so to *o*, and hence that the first part lost its stress, at least to a large extent. Schematically, this gives EJ**O**W. In this sequence, we can perceive two pure vocalic elements: E and **O**. However, the existence of two full vowels in one syllable is precluded. Hence, the logical outcome is that the stronger of the two, which is now [o:], survives and that the weaker one, now [e.], is lost. What is left, then, is the sequence [jo:w], or, as we assumed before, phonetically possibly more correct: [jo.w]. And thus, this remnant opens with *j*.

A crucial assumption for the analysis is that the accent within the diphthong must have shifted backwards. Such a development is probably not coincidental. In Frisian there appears to exist a tendency to change falling diphthongs into rising ones. In the introductory section, I already mentioned the phenomenon of Modern Frisian Breaking. But also in the Old Frisian period the same tendency can be observed. Take for instance OFris *dua* 'to do', which, after shifting stress, became MoFris *dwaan*.[23] Or, to turn to another category and at the same time to the front glide, take OFris *liaf* (cf. Du *lief*, G *lieb*, E *lief*), which after a shift of stress changed to *ljaaf*, eventually becoming MFris *ljeaf* and MoFris *leaf*. There are more examples like these; however, the effects of such instances of accent shift are less far-reaching

---

[22] W. Visser, *The Syllable in Frisian* (Ljouwert, 1997), 221.

[23] For comparable verbs, see H. D. Meijering, 'Die altfriesischen monosyllabischen Infinitive auf -*N* und die Gliederung des Altfriesischen', *Aspects*, 336–45.

than of Jorwert Breaking. One of the differences is that the first part of the original diphthong was already represented by a high vowel (*i* or *u*), and therefore it could rather easily change into a glide. A more serious difference is to be found in the second part of the original diphthong. That was not formed by a glide, but rather by a full vowel, though this vowel did not bear the main stress. It received main stress after the shift, however, and afterwards it underwent all the historical changes that affected comparable full vowels.

All in all, for Jorwert Breaking we can conclude that *w* was the instigator of the process, but that it was not involved any further. The element was there before the process and remained afterwards. This *w* is real, and is more than just a phonetic termination inherent to every round vowel. For instance, for those speakers of southern or eastern West Frisian dialects which have the word *bedriuw* 'company' as [bədrju.w], this word surely does not rhyme with *doe* [du] 'then', containing a short monophthong, or with the interjection *boeh* [bu:] 'boo!', with a long vowel.

The analysis, as applied to the mediate level /e.w/, can be transferred to the other levels /i.w/ and /ɛ.w/ as well. Nevertheless, some slight differences may possibly exist. Realization of a transitional *j* seems easiest within *i.w*. The reason is, of course, that *i* is phonetically closest to *j*. But the situation with respect to *ɛ.w* is different, as in the transition of *ɛ* to intermediate *ɔ* an intermediate *j* is far from conspicuous. Naturally, this can be related to the greater degree of opening of /ɛ/ and /ɔ/, in which environment the formation of *j* is far more difficult. No doubt, the situation with respect to *e.w* can be situated between these two extremes. That *j* is easier to be formed after /e:/ than after /ɛ:/ can also be heard from these monophthongs themselves, at least in Modern West Frisian. After /e:/, a *j*-like ending always shows up; for this reason the sound may be characterized as a kind of diphthong in the phonetic sense. In contrast, the pronunciation of /ɛ:/ is far closer to that of a real monophthong.

It is possible that differences in the emergence of *j* have repercussions for the emergence of Jorwert Breaking itself. The phenomenon of Jorwert Breaking does not occur very frequently, it seems, but, as we will see in the next section, when it does, then mostly at the highest level, i.e. *i.w* > *ju.w*. Outside Frisian, I have not come across the transition *e.w* > *jo.w*, nor *ɛ.w* > *jɔ.w*. However, to the best of my knowledge, the occurrence of the phenomenon across the world's languages has never been investigated, so it is conceivable that there are other languages that exhibit the process at the lower levels too. It would be interesting if my idea turns out to be true, namely that the phenomenon is more frequent at the higher levels, and that the hierarchy manifests itself in such a way that if a language features the phenomenon at a lower level, then it will also exhibit it at higher level(s). Of course, this hypothesis can only be tested if the language in question has the relevant vowels in its phonological system. This hierarchy also predicts that the breaking of *ɛ.w* > *jɔ.w* is the most difficult to realize. It will become clear in section 4 that Frisian itself may provide a direct illustration for this hypothesis.

As noted at the outset, the phenomenon of Jorwert Breaking has not gone unnoticed in Frisian linguistics, and there have been attempts of an analysis before. Already in the first publication which mentions the phenomenon, Buitenrust Hettema suggested that a shift of stress was involved; he also assumed an insertion of *u* before *w*.[24] However, this insertion is not motivated phonetically, but mainly for reasons of orthography, it seems. The insertion of *u*, regardless of the quality of the preceding sound, is repeated by many authors.[25] Problematic is also the emergence of initial /j/. Buitenrust Hettema simply assumed a development *e* > *i* > *j*, and Siebs suggests a 'spaltung des *ê* und vocalisierung des *b*,- zu *iou*?', both without motivation.[26] A more plausible explanation for the emergence of /j/ is offered by Van Helten.[27] If I interpret him well, van Helten suggests that the transition of a falling into a rising diphthong is performed at the highest level, so in /iu/. The change *i* > *j* is indeed a small one. This analysis has found general acceptance in the literature, also for the transition at the lower level(s).[28] The effect is that in order to perform the change, the falling diphthong first has to be raised to /iu/. Then, at that level, the shift to a rising diphthong has to take place, which subsequently lowers again. This analysis has some obvious disadvantages. First, in contrast to my analysis, the change is not a direct one. Second, the raising (and lowering) is unmotivated. At best, it is connected to the general Frisian raising of /eː/ > /i.ə/; but for /ɛː/ such a raising to the highest level is problematic.[29] However, the most serious objection that can be raised against such an analysis is that what once went up must also come down again. Assuming that all transitions of a falling diphthong into a rising one were performed within /iu/, how could a speaker

---

24 F. Buitenrust Hettema, *Bijdragen tot het Oudfriesch Woordenboek* (Leiden, 1888), 64. Likewise, van Helten, 'Zur Lexicologie und Grammatik des Altwestfriesischen', *passim*.

25 E.g. D. Boutkan, 'Phonology and Orthographic System of Old Frisian', *Handbuch / Handbook*, 613–20, at 617.

26 Siebs, *Zur Geschichte der englisch-friesischen Sprache*, 262.

27 Van Helten, 'Zur Lexicologie und Grammatik des Altwestfriesischen', *passim*.

28 See, most recently, Hoekstra, 'An Outline History of West Frisian'.

29 Explicitly in M. J. van der Meer, *Fryske ôfliedkinde mei foarbylden. Foardracht hâlden for de Fryske Fakânsje-Kursus to Ljouwert de 3de fen Rispmoanne 1929* (Snits, 1929), and W. J. Buma, 'Wurdsneuperijen. 54. Nijfrysk *greauwen* en *grevel*', *UW* 24 (1975), 55–59.

of Old Frisian know that in the one case he had to keep the output at the highest level, and in the other case he had to lower it to /jo.w/, or even further to /jɔ.w/? In sum, the bad motivation for the emergence of intitial /j/ and the arbitrariness between input and output of the process are serious flaws of this and previous analyses. Other details could be criticized as well, but reasons of space prevent me from discussing them here.[30]

3. EVIDENCE (I): THE SOUNDS

Up till now, the analysis has been a fairly theoretical construct, so the time has come to provide some tangible evidence. Firstly, I will give some direct evidence, and then turn to earlier stages in the language.

The most striking element in my analysis is that it predicts that in Jorwert Breaking vowel height is constant, compare the schema in (3). The first indication for a constant vowel height can be destilled from a simple phonetic experiment. If one slowly tries to accomplish Jorwert Breaking orally, then it will appear that the simplest way to realize this is by remaining at the same height. So, the change of /i.w/ to /ju.w/ is the easiest one. A potential conversion from /i.w/ to /jo.w/ requires much more effort, and even more so the change from /i.w/ to /jɔ.w/. The reverse is also true. So, /ɛ.w/ is most easily transformed into /jɔ.w/, whilst a change into /ju.w/ would feel quite unnatural.

An example of how easy the transition can be accomplished is the word *sleau* 'lethargic'. I think I picked up the pronunciation [sle.w] from my home language, but I guess that nowadays it is more often [sljo.w]. However, potential varieties such as [sli.w], [slɛ.w], [slju.w] or [sljɔ.w] are absolutely out of order. But within the same vowel height there is an easy and smooth transition. This makes it also possible that within the falling diphthong, on its way to its final goal, the first element can already prepare for rounding.[31]

To a certain extent, it can also be perceived in other languages that Jorwert Breaking occurs in one and the same vowel height. One source is the dialect of the Frisian island of Schiermonnikoog. Although definitely Frisian, this dialect differs considerably from varieties of Frisian spoken on the mainland. In the first printed texts of the Schiermonnikoog dialect, we see the spellings *jieoewer* for modern *ieuwr* [i.wr] 'over', *Bjuer* for modern *bieuwr* [bi.wr] 'farmer' and *djuesen* for modern *dieuwzen* [di.wzən] 'thousand'.[32] At the beginning of the twentieth century, the pronunciation of

[30] For a comprehensive account, see my, 'Jorwertbrekking', section 4.

[31] For instance, a notation /yu/ is offered for words such as *liuw* 'lion' and *bliuwe* 'to stay' in Hoekstra, 'Standard West Frisian', 84.

[32] See J. H. Halbertsma, 'Vertaling van een paar plaatsen uit het nieuwe testament in de tongval van Schiermonnikoog', J. H. Halbertsma, *Hulde aan Gysbert Japiks, tweede stuk* (Leeuwarden, 1827), 165–68.

present-day *hieuwn* [hi.wn] 'dog' was *hju.n.*[33] Fokkema observes for /i.w/: 'Deze tweeklank is soms stijgend en klinkt dan als *ju*'.[34] From a recent inquiry, I learned that today the diphthong /i.w/ is only falling, but this material teaches us nevertheless that once it could easily be converted into a rising /ju.w/. However, in the Schiermonnikoog dialect I did not come across a conversion at lower levels, i.e. into /jo.w/ or /jɔ.w/. It is also worth noting that the Schiermonnikoog examples are pronounced with a high back vowel in their mainland Frisian counterparts, and thus do not constitute a possible input for Jorwert Breaking there.

In English, we can observe something similar. Words such as *new* or *ewe* are pronounced as [nju:] and [ju:]. Roger Lass dates this 'Jorwert Breaking' back to the seventeenth century, so at a time when the former diphthong /eu/ (in Lass's notation) was already raised to /iu/.[35] The fact that we particularly observe Jorwert Breaking of /i.w/ in the Schiermonnikoog dialect and in English might not be a coincidence, as I have argued in the preceding section.

If Jorwert Breaking can be pursued so easily as argued above, and if it is sometimes not easy either to obtain a clear perceptual difference between input and outcome, then it may not come as a surprise that there can be a great deal of variation. In the Old Frisian sources, forms with and without Jorwert Breaking sometimes act together. It also occurs that words that exhibited Jorwert Breaking in Old Frisian lost the feature in later times. Miedema draws attention to the co-occurrence of forms with a rising and a falling diphthong in Old Frisian, but this phenomenon can be observed in later times too.[36] His explanation that spelling conventions have a role to play may well be true, but at the same time it should not necessarily be the whole truth in light of the phonetic uncertainty just sketched.

The fact that Jorwert Breaking could easily come but also easily go makes one somewhat suspicious about the central message of Miedema's inaugural lecture *Van York naar Jorwerd* of 1966. Miedema observes that in the early Middle Ages maritime Frisians and Vikings entertained intensive contacts. Furthermore, he claims that Old Norse also exhibited Jorwert Breaking and concludes that the Vikings must have exported the phenomenon to Frisia. He mentions the place-name *York* (from *Ever-vik*)

---

[33] According to L. P. H. Eijkman, *Phonetische beschrijving van de klanken der Schiermonnikoogsche taal* (Amsterdam, 1925), 30.

[34] 'Sometimes, this diphthong is rising, and then it sounds as *ju*', D. Fokkema, *Beknopte spraakkunst van het Schiermonnikoogs* (Leeuwarden, 1969), 10.

[35] R. Lass, 'Phonology and Morphology', *The Cambridge History of the English Language*, vol. III: *1476–1776*, ed. R. Lass (Cambridge, 1999) 56–186, at 99.

[36] See Miedema, *Van York naar Jorwerd*, 12, and H. T. J. Miedema, 'Problemen met het Friese credo', *Taal en Tongval* 25 (1973), 33–47, at 36–38.

and the name of the Frisian village *Jorwert* (from *Ever-werd*) as typical examples. However, the problem with such a theory, especially when the phenomena are situated in pre-history, is that its validity is hard to prove. At best, one can assume a certain plausibility, but nevertheless doubts can be raised against Miedema's position. It can always be questioned how serious and frequent such contacts with speakers of Norse actually were – according to Dirk Blok they should not be estimated too highly.[37] This notwithstanding, from the kind of language contact involved, it can be predicted that this must have resulted in borrowing of lexical material rather than in the imposition of grammatical features. However, even the quantity of shared words exhibiting Jorwert Breaking provided by Miedema is not very impressive. Miedema overlooked the obvious possibility that the change could emerge within the Frisian language itself. As we have seen above, Jorwert Breaking fell on fertile soil, since as a result of the weakening of *v* it can be predicted so many words could act as possible input. I am not alone in my doubts about Old Norse as a cause of Frisian Jorwert Breaking: neither Dietrich Hofmann nor Karel Gildemacher believe the thesis, nor does Blok, who observes the extended lapse between the time when the shift manifested itself in *York* (ninth century) and *Jorwerd* (fourteenth century).[38]

4. Evidence (II): the words

4.1 Introduction

I would now like to turn to the historical evidence in Frisian. It is my aim to present all the words that have undergone Jorwert Breaking. Of course it is important to present as much evidence concerning the phenomenon as possible, especially as these data can support the analysis presented in section 2.

The compilation of the list has not been without difficulties. Our reconstructions of former forms and situations cannot be more than theoretical concepts; they need not necessarily correspond with the reality of the past. A typical example is the uncertainty about both long *e*'s as discussed in section 2. Furthermore, it cannot be assumed in advance that Jorwert Breaking took place at one point in history. Furthermore, a complicating factor is that there have been all kinds of sound changes which may have disturbed the input and also the output of the process. For instance, in Frisian, lengthening of short /a/ instigated a series of raisings: original long /a:/ raised to /ɛ:/, original long /ɛ:/ raised to /e:/ or even /i.ə/, and finally former /e:/

[37] D. P. Blok, 'De Wikingen in Friesland', *Naamkunde* 10 (1978), 25–47.

[38] D. Hofmann, '*Thor*, "Donnerstag" und "Donner" in Friesland', D. Hofmann, *Gesammelte Schriften* II, 366–75, at 371; K. F. Gildemacher, 'West Frisian Place Names', *Handbuch / Handbook*, 155–70, at 167; Blok, 'De Wikingen in Friesland', 45.

changed to /i.ə/.[39] Moreover, there can be dialectical differences, and those of former centuries are often unknown to us. Most additional changes come up in the course of the following discussion. One feature I already want to mention here is the deletion of initial /j/ of the broken cluster. For one thing, this is part of a much broader tendency, especially in the south-western regions of the province, and then especially after *r* and *l*.[40] So, the preterite form *bleau* /bljɔ.w/ of the verb *bliuwe* 'to remain' became /blɔ.w/. However, this *j* was sometimes not written also in Old Frisian times, for example in *op grouwa* 'to dig up' in Codex Aysma.[41] This observation brings us to the issue of unreliable spellings.

It has been noted that both open and closed *e* are not kept apart in Old Frisian orthography. As for the digraph <ou>, it could represent /ɔ.w/, but also /o:/ or its diphthongized product (/o.w/), and maybe even /u(:)/.[42] And what about a spelling like *joegh* 'eternal'? Miedema supposes a pronunciation [ju(:)x] but, in my opinion, [jo:x] is equally plausible.[43] To give one more example: in the Old Frisian spelling *iuw* the initial *i* may indicate /j/, and in this case we are concerned with a broken sound. But it could just as well stand for /i/, and then it represents the first part of a falling diphthong.

As mentioned previously, the primary purpose of the present account of Jorwert Breaking in Frisian is to give support to the hypothesis of constant vowel height, and its arrangement follows from this perspective. Of the words involved, I just offer the basic forms – compounds and derivations are implicated. The list is not restricted to Old Frisian *per se*; for a proper view at the phenomenon it seems appropriate to take a wider perspective. In fact, the picture is quite diverse. Some instances of Jorwert Breaking only seem to show up for the relevant word in the Old Frisian period, e.g. forms like *op grouwa* and *nouwa*. Since Old Frisian sources are rather scarce, there are also younger forms that have not come to us from medieval sources, but many of them have probably existed for a longer time. And of course, many forms show Jorwert Breaking in the whole period from Old to Modern Frisian.

---

39 See A. Versloot, 'Aldwesterlauwersk Frysk /e:/', *IB* 53 (1991), 71–96.

40 See, for instance, G. van der Meer, 'Toppenhúster konsonantyske bigjingroepen', *UW* 19 (1970), 39–43.

41 W. L. van Helten, 'Zur Lexicologie und Grammatik des Altwestfriesischen', 360, offers the writings *nowa* and *nouwa* 'nephew', where some letter *j* or *i* was to be expected.

42 A nice indication of possible uncertainty in this respect is indicated in the overview in A. Feitsma, *De autografemen in het werk van Gysbert Japicx. Een verkennend grafematisch onderzoek naar de taal van Gysbert Japicx en een bijdrage tot de friese spellinggeschiedenis* (Leeuwarden, 1974), 448–51 and 482–90.

43 H. T. J. Miedema, 'Iets over A. Spenter (1926–1977) en de etymologie van Fries *slûch* "slaperich" en *stjûch* "koppig"', *Taal en Tongval* 32 (1982), 212–24, at 219.

Although it has been my intention to be exhaustive, I am not under the illusion that the collection is complete. Especially in the rather heterogeneous field of personal names and place-names, I may well have overlooked some candidates. But also the fact that especially Old West Frisian is poorly investigated lexicographically poses a hindrance. For these reasons, I have restricted myself to those words that represent relatively clear cases.

4.2 The highest level: /i.w/ > /ju.w/

For the most closed vowel, i.e. /i(:)/, I have assumed a change from /i.w/ into /ju.w/. This change can easily be recognized:

(5)

liuw(es). According to van Helten such spellings of OFris *līf* 'body', found in MS Jus and in the charters, have undergone Jorwert Breaking, resulting in the pronunciation /ju.w/.[44]

liuwath, *liuwade*, *liuwet*. Forms from the paradigm of the verb *libba* 'to live', in MS Jus.[45] Compare also the adjective *liuwech* 'lively'; Buma reinterpreted this word from the form *luweth* in MS Jus, on the basis of comparable *lijuich* in MS Roorda.[46] In my opinion, both forms indicate Jorwert Breaking.

skiūd. According to Boersma, occurring in the Old Frisian charters; he makes the following remark (translated from Dutch): 'Of the verb **skīvia* (OIce. *skífa*) "to satisfy; to divide" we find the following forms of the past participle: *schiwet*, *schiiwet*, *schywd*, *schiud*, *schioed* in the expression *schiwet ende schat* "decided by arbitration".'[47] The latter two spellings indicate Jorwert Breaking. Hofmann, in the supplement to his revision of Holthausen's dictionary, comments on *skīvia* 'teilen; befriedigen': 'nur Part.Prät. *skīved* (*skived*?), *skēw(e)d*, *skiowet*, *skiūd* (*skūd*, *skōd*) u.a. Formen "entschieden".'[48] To me, *skiūd* appears to be the broken form of *skīved*; in view of the form *skūd* the product of breaking could easily disappear, owing to the complex initial cluster *skj*-. From Hofmann's examples one might conclude that among the variants there should also have been Jorwert Breaking of /e.w/ > /jo.w/. For this question, I refer to *skiūd* in (12) below. See also *sjudden* in (8).

---

44 Van Helten, 'Zur Lexicologie und Grammatik des Altwestfriesischen', 355.

45 Signalled by van Helten, 'Zur Lexicologie und Grammatik des Altwestfriesischen', 359; see also W. J. Buma, *Vollständiges Wörterbuch zum westerlauwersschen Jus Municipale Frisonum* (Leeuwarden, 1996), s.v. *libba*.

46 Buma, *Vollständiges Wörterbuch*, s.v. *lîvich*.

47 Boersma, *De Friesche oorkonden*, 96.

48 F. Holthausen, *Altfriesisches Wörterbuch*, rev. D. Hofmann (Heidelberg, 1985), 173, at 'S. 98. - 5'.

These are the cases of a direct change of /i.w/ > /ju.w/. At best, they might be supplemented by two other words from Middle and Modern Frisian, namely *njoer* 'angry; frightening' and *slûch* 'sleepy', but their derivation is problematic; moreover, plausible alternative etymologies have been offered elsewhere.[49]

As already noted, the regularity of Jorwert Breaking is disturbed by other phonological changes. One of these is Lowering, which caused OFris /u:/ to change to /o:/. Examples are OFris *kū* 'cow', compared to MoFris *ko*, and OFris *skūva* 'to shift, shove', which is now *skowe*. Jarich Hoekstra gives as a condition that the relevant sound should be in 'word-final position and hiatus',[50] and this seems to be fulfilled by the relevant words involved in Jorwert Breaking. The result, then, is that the breaking product /ju.w/ changed into /jo.w/. It is tempting to assume that the heartland of this change is to be situated in the north-west, in particular since in the region north-east of the town of Harns (Dutch: Harlingen) the vowels in words like *ko* and *skowe* lowered even further to *kou* [kɔ.w] and *skouwe*, respectively. This further lowering seldom took place in words which were involved in Jorwert Breaking, but here it is striking that this one-stage lowering of /ju.w/ > /jo.w/ indeed covered the northern, western and central language area, and that only a small strip in the south and in the east was left unaffected, in addition to isolated places such as the Frisian islands and the fishing villages of Peazens and Moddergat in the north-east.

The awkward effect of this lowering is that its results interfere with the outcome of Jorwert Breaking one level lower, i.e. /e.w/ > /jo.w/. Nevertheless, there are some ways of distinguishing the two. This can be done on the basis of etymology, and dialectal varieties can often be found where the old /ju.w/-outcome is still alive. Here follow the words in which Lowering has been active:

(6)

bliuwe etc. This Modern Frisian verb, 'to remain', was OFris *b(i)līva*. According to Hof it has become /bljuwə/ in the south and along the eastern border of the language area.[51] Hof is of the opinion – and I wholeheartedly agree – that the form /bljowə/ is a later development. Indeed, none of the Old Frisian forms of this verb assembled in Vries' study exhibits an ⟨o⟩.[52] Nor is this to be observed in the writings of the

---

49 For further discussion, see my 'Jorwertbrekking', 288–89.

50 Hoekstra, 'An Outline History of West Frisian', 725.

51 J. J. Hof, *Friesche dialectgeographie* (The Hague, 1933), 58-60.

52 O. Vries, 'Zu einem Wörterbuch der altfriesischen Urkundensprache?', *Aspects*, 483–94.

seventeenth-century poet Gysbert Japicx.[53] The Frisian islands, together with Peazens and Moddergat on the mainland, still have /ju.w/. This sound is not only observed in the infinitive but also in the forms of the present tense. There are several verbs which behaves exactly like *bliuwe*: *driuwe*, *riuwe*, *skriuwe*, *triuwe*, *wiuwe*, *wriuwe* and, in all probability, also *kliuwe*.

Diuwke. Female form of the personal name *Dieuwe* from *Diet* + *war(d)*.[54] Variants of this name abound. *Diuwke* itself is pronounced as [djukə], but also as [djo:kə].

driuwe, OFris *drīva* 'to drive'. For further information, cf. *bliuwe* above.

Juw. According to Winkler 'from the common Germanic [personal] name *Ivo*, which in Friesland also occurs as *Ive*, *Iwe*' (my translation).[55] This name occurs in a great many varieties, not only in spelling but also in pronunciation. The vowel /u./ could lower to /o./, but sometimes even further to /ɔ.w/, at least in the opinion of Winkler, who relates present-day names such as *Jouke*, *Joute*, *Jouwsma*, *Joustra*, *Jouta* or *Joukema* to this etymon. However, for this last series a different interpretation is available, see under Jouke in (11).

kliuwe, OFris *klīva* 'to climb'. For further information, cf. *bliuwe* above.

liuweria (OFris) 'to deliver'. Van Helten suggests Jorwert Breaking in this case.[56] *WFT*,[57] s.v. *leverje*, has a secondary entry *lieuwerje* and offers – albeit with a question mark – a broken pronunciation for this variant. The same holds for the secondary entry *leauwerje*, but then with pronunciation [ljo.]. However, it cannot be ruled out that this last form is a direct result of the Jorwert Breaking of /e.w/. See also *leauwerje* in (12), in section 4.4.

riuwe '(hay) rake'. MoDu *rijf* points to an earlier /i:/, so that we can posit OFris **hriva* and **hrīve*.[58] According to Hof's dialect survey, the word occurs only in the east, as a result of lexical pressure from the synonym *harke*. The south-east has /rju.wə/, the north-east /rjo.wə/.[59]

---

53 See W. L. Brandsma, *Het werkwoord bij Gysbert Japicx* (Assen, 1936).

54 J. van der Schaar, *Prisma voornamen*, rev. D. Gerritzen (Utrecht, 2002), 109.

55 J. Winkler, *Friesche Naamlijst (Onomasticon Frisicum)* (Leeuwarden, 1898), 204.

56 Van Helten, 'Zur Lexicologie und Grammatik des Altwestfriesischen', 362.

57 *Wurdboek fan de Fryske Taal*, ed. K. Van der Veen *et al.* (Leeuwarden, 1984–..). Henceforth *WFT*.

58 See, respectively, van Helten, 'Zur Lexicologie und Grammatik des Altwestfriesischen', 355, and N. Århammar, 'Zur Rekonstruktion des altfriesischen Lexikons mit Hilfe der neufriesischen Dialekte', *Philologia Frisica anno 1988* (Leeuwarden, 1989) 94–128, at 98. Kloosterman, *Het vocalisme der beklemtoonde lettergrepen van den Metslawierschen tongval*, 60, points to ON *hrífa* 'rake' which makes a reconstruction with *ī more likely.

59 Hof, *Friesche dialectgeographie*, 191.

Sieuwke. According to Van der Schaar and Gerritzen, this personal name has the same origin as *Sjoerd*,[60] see below under (9). It is broken to [sjukə], but also lowered to [sjo:kə].
skriuwe, OFris *skrīva* 'to write'. For further information, cf. *bliuwe* above.
triuwe 'to throw'. Miedema relates this verb to ON *þrífa* 'to take, catch' and reconstructs an Old Frisian form **thrīva*.[61] For more information, cf. *bliuwe* above.
wiuwe 'to wave'. Middle Dutch knew a form *wiven*.[62] The Old Frisian cognate will have been **wīva*. For more information, cf. *bliuwe* above.
Wiuwert. For this place-name, van Berkel and Samplonius mention an early form *Wywerth* (1370).[63] Today the pronunciation is [vju.wət], which is also lowered to [vjo.wət].
wriuwe 'to rub'. In view of MDu *wriven*, the Old Frisian form will have been **wrīva*, a form also assumed by Kloosterman.[64] For more information, cf. *bliuwe* above.

The verb *priuwe* 'to taste' constitutes a small problem. Van Helten assumed an older form **prêva*,[65] which is in accordance with the northern form 'prɪ.əuwə', mentioned by Hof,[66] hence with *v*-vocalization, but without Jorwert Breaking. However, according to Hof, the word acts like *bliuwe* etc. in the other regions. Analogy could be at play here, and then the word does not fit well in the category discussed here. But it may also be the case that former /e:/ took part in the raising to /i:/ before it entered Jorwert Breaking.

Lowering of the broken product is one possibility for a later development. Another is palatalization. The nuclear vowel of the broken diphthong is then fronted, thereby keeping its rounded character.[67] Without doubt, the instigator of this fronting is the initial /j/, it being a front element, too. Note also that /j/ often deleted after fronting the vowel. As was the case with Lowering, this fronting is part of a wider process in which the products of

---

60 Van der Schaar, *Prisma voornamen*, 354.

61 H. T. J. Miedema, 'Fries *triuwe* (Oudnoord *thrifa*) en *trytza*, twee woorden voor "duwen, drukken"', *Taal en Tongval* 31 (1979), 56–61, at 56–57.

62 J. Verdam, *Middelnederlandsch Handwoordenboek*, rev. C. H. Ebbinge Wubben (The Hague, 1932), s.v. *weiven*.

63 G. van Berkel and K. Samplonius, *Nederlandse plaatsnamen. De herkomst en betekenis van onze plaatsnamen* (Utrecht, 1995), 259.

64 Kloosterman, *Het vocalisme der beklemtoonde lettergrepen van den Metslawierschen tongval*, 60.

65 Van Helten, 'Zur Lexicologie und Grammatik des Altwestfriesischen', 356. Likewise, Spenter, *Vokalismus der Schiermonnikooger Mundart*, 305.

66 Hof, *Friesche dialectgeographie*, 58.

67 Within the scope of Jorwert Breaking, particular attention to this feature was called by Gosses, 'Snjeon'.

Jorwert Breaking were simply absorbed. Hof provides beautiful data, and he already points to *j* as the instigator.[68] From this data one can conclude that such fronting only took place after complex initial clusters, i.e. if there is at least one more consonant before *j*. Apparently, as a consequence of this complexity, there was a need for simplification which was accomplished by way of adjusting the following back vowel to *j*. So, this condition might explain why no palatalization took place in MoFris *jûn* 'evening', with its simple onset, in contrast to *sneon* 'Saturday', with its complex initial cluster *snj-*, although both possessed the same element *joon* (< *evend*). However, this is an example of fronting of /o(:)/, which will be discussed in more detail below.

Palatalization at a higher level, i.e. fronting of /u(:)/, is not to be excluded out of hand, either. With constant vowel height, something like /(j)ü(:)/ is to be expected. Indeed, Hoekstra observes [skr(j)ü.wə] as a possible present-day pronunciation of *skriuwe* 'to write'.[69] And if it were a solid example of Jorwert Breaking, Gysbert Japix's spelling *njuer* (17th c.) might be another case, but we have already questioned whether the word *njoer* underwent Jorwert Breaking at all. So, a better historical example might be:

(7)

Ruerd. Personal name, from *Rieuwert*.[70] This form must have undergone Jorwert Breaking, fronting and *j*-deletion.

However, it is striking that in most of the relevant cases, especially in environments where shortening may occur, it is not the expected /ü/ that emerges, but rather short /ö/. This lower outcome may be explained by assuming that these words were first involved in the lowering of /ju.w/ to /jo.w/. Hence, these words also came into the reach of a different level of Jorwert Breaking, and so added to the complicated picture:

(8)

rju 'much'. Compare MDu/MLG *rive* 'abundant' and MoE *rife*. Hof reports to have heard the word spoken at two different vowel heights: /rjö/ and /rü.ə/.

sjudden 'flax waste'. According to Hoekema from OFris *skiv-*, from the verb *skivia* 'to divide' or from the adjective *skif* 'parted' plus a suffix *-(i)the*.[71] Compare MoDu *vlasscheef* 'piece of the bark of flax'. After Jorwert

68 Hof, *Friesche dialectgeographie*, 238–42.

69 Hoekstra, 'An Outline History of West Frisian', 727.

70 Van der Schaar and Gerritzen, *Prisma voornamen*, 340.

71 T. Hoekema, 'It Skylger wurd *sjudden* "bern"', *UW* 17 (1968), 71–72.

Breaking, the word must have been lowered, before undergoing palatalization. See also *skiūd* in (5) and *skiōd* in (12).

stjurje 'to congeal, clot'. According to Miedema from *stiverje* 'to become stiff'.[72] After Jorwert Breaking, one would expect this to change to /stju.ərjə/. This form must later have undergone Lowering and Fronting.

Words having two variants, one with palatalization and one without, are also found:

(9)

Sjoerd, male personal name, according to Miedema from *Sieuwerd* (< (*)*Sigiward*).[73] The name has a female counterpart in *Sjoerdsje*. For the female form, Winkler also mentions the palatalized variants *Sjutsje* and *Sjuurdtje*, *Sjuutje* (the last two in Dutch spelling).[74]

stjûch 'headstrong, stubborn'. This adjective is now obsolete, but was still current before 1800. Only in the conservative dialect of Hylpen (Dutch: Hindeloopen) does the non-broken form *stiuwch* 'stiff' still exist. Although there have been other etymological suggestions, a derivation of *stivich* from *stiif* 'stiff' plus suffix *-ich* is most plausible. Miedema mentions the palatalized form *stjuch* /stjöx/ found in the writings of the early twentieth-century dialectologist J. J. Hof.[75] Another variant, *steuch* /stö:x/, could possibly be interpreted as a result of fronting (plus *j*-deletion) as well.[76]

In conclusion, it appears that Jorwert Breaking at the highest level holds up to the expectation that /i.w/ changes to /ju.w/, so retaining its vowel height. However, the outcome of the process is disturbed in many places, due to secondary processes such as Lowering and Fronting.

4.3 The lowest level: ɛ.w > jɔ.w

As discussed in section 2, we may assume, albeit with some provisos, that there existed two *ē*'s, a closed one and an open one. It has been my contention that Jorwert Breaking of the open variety results in /jɔ.w/. As stated before, complicating is the fact that the late Old Frisian period saw a series of raisings, so that words with previous long /a:/ also came into the

---

72 Miedema, *Van York naar Jorwerd*, 12.

73 *Ibid.*

74 Winkler, *Friesche Naamlijst*, 349.

75 Miedema, 'Iets over A. Spenter (1926–1977)', 212–24.

76 This word has various intricacies; for a more detailed discussion, see Dyk, 'Jorwert-brekking', 292–93.

scope of the rule. Be that as it may, I think that the following words are candidates to have undergone Jorwert Breaking at the lowest level:

(10)

jouwe (OFris), from *ēwa* 'law'.[77] The *Old Frisian Wedding Speeches* have the form *jowe*.[78]

liouwen (OFris) 'scale, dish'. In MS Jus, it is also spelled as *liowen* and, without Jorwert Breaking, as *lewen*. Middle Dutch and Middle Low German have *loven*. Holthausen, in his *Friesisches Wörterbuch*, gives the notation *lêven*, which points to /ɛ:/.

liôwa (OFris), Buma gives the meaning 'hinterlassen',[79] compare MoE *to leave*. Old Frisian also knows *lêva*. MS Jus has forms with *louw-* and *liow-*. Van Helten offers the derivation *bilyowa* 'gewähren; einen oder etwas bleiben lassen, von einem oder etwas scheiden'.[80]

However, not only words with original long /ɛ:/ are qualified for Jorwert Breaking at the lowest level. Short /ɛ/ occurred before original *v* as well. When *v* vocalized, then without doubt short /ɛ/ will have lenghtened in the subsequent diphthongization process, resulting in /ɛ.w/. The next words are representative:

(11)

hjouwer 'oat', not recorded for Old Frisian. According to Spenter from Gmc **a* with 'Tonerhöhung' ('Fronting'), so presumably resulting in /ɛ/.[81] Hoekstra reconstructs OFris **hevere*.[82]

Jorwert, place-name, from *Ever-werd*. After Jorwert Breaking had taken place, Miedema assumes a form *Jouwer-*.[83] Then, contraction resulted in /jɔr/-. According to Winkler, the element *Ever-* was also prone to breaking in other name types.[84] De Vries mentions that the *ev*-cluster was retained in the former Frisian areas east of the river Lauwers.[85]

---

77 Holthausen, *Altfriesisches Wörterbuch*, ed. Hofmann, 23 and 156.

78 W. J. Buma, *Aldfryske houlikstaspraken. Mei ynlieding, oantekeningen, nammelist, wurdboek en in Ingelske gearfetting* (Assen, 1957), 61.

79 Buma, *Vollständiges Wörterbuch*, 183.

80 Van Helten, 'Zur Lexicologie und Grammatik des Altwestfriesischen', 256–57.

81 Spenter, *Vokalismus der Schiermonnikooger Mundart*, 313.

82 Hoekstra, '*Iampck ist en iamcker wirtet mecke*', 7.

83 H. T. J. Miedema, 'Van Dublin naar Dokkum. Oudnoord *Jarl* "dux", Oudfries *Jarla* en de mogelijkheid van oudnoorse relicten in het Oudfries', *Naamkunde* 10 (1978), 48–80, at 55.

84 Winkler, *Friesche Naamlijst*, 55.

85 W. de Vries, *Friese persoonsnamen* (Assen, 1952), 66.

Jouke, personal name, according to Miedema and Hoekstra from *Gĕveke*, without breaking still current in the personal name *Geveke*.[86] For a different opinion on the derivation of the name *Jouke*, see *Juw* in (6) (section 4.2).

Jouswert, place-name, from **Geves-würði* according to Miedema, who also claims that the first element is found in the place-names *Jousterp* and *Jouswier*, and in *Joeswerd* in the neighbouring province of Groningen.[87]

jouel (OFris). Holthausen lists *evel* 'herd', but according to Hofmann the word occurs only in the expression *en jouel gān* '(jmdm.) sein Eigentum gegen lebenslänglichen Unterhalt übertragen' and in the compound *jouel-bref* 'Eigentumsübertragungsurkunde' ['charter recording transfer of property'].[88] Breaking to *jou-* may occur directly on the basis of the combination /ɛ/ + /w/.

jout, *jouwe*, present tense forms of MoFris *jaan* 'to give', in Old Frisian with a stem *jev-*, from *jeva*. Jorwert Breaking of short /ɛ/ + /w/ directly results in *jou-*.

jouwe (OFris) 'gift', from *jewe*, so from /ɛ/ + /w/. In MS Jus mostly spelled as *jouw-*, once as *jow-*. The broken form also occurs in an East Old Frisian document, but Bremmer has demonstrated that the text must be of Old West Frisian descent.[89]

De Jouwer, Gysseling mentions the form *ter Heuwera* for this place name, and assumes an older **Gevarō*.[90] If the latter has short /ɛ/, then Jorwert Breaking to /jɔ.w/- is plausible. Arjen Versloot (personal communication) draws my attention to the non-broken place name *Jever* in Rüstringen, formerly Frisian, in Germany.

jouwinge (OFris) noun, interpreted as 'Ausübung, gewohntes Verfahren/ Handeln',[91] either from **evinge* (Hofmann) or from *jevinge* (Holthausen's original entry). It is Hofmann who mentions the broken form *jouwinge*. Both spellings suggest short /ɛ/ in the stem, and therefore Jorwert Breaking yields *jouw-*. Ahlsson has a long stem in his entry

---

86 Miedema, *Van York naar Jorwerd*, 11; Hoekstra, '*Iampck ist en iamcker wirtet mecke*', 7.

87 Miedema, *Van York naar Jorwerd*, 11.

88 Holthausen, *Altfriesisches Wörterbuch*, ed. Hofmann, 155.

89 *Das Emsinger Recht*, ed. W. J. Buma and W. Ebel, AR 3 (Göttingen, 1967), 252; R. H. Bremmer Jr., 'Old Frisian Dialectology and the Position of the "Ommelanden"', *A Frisian and Germanic Miscellany. Published in Honour of Nils Århammar on his Sixty-fifth Birthday, 7 August 1996*, ed. A. Petersen and H. F. Nielsen (Odense and Bredstedt, 1996), 1–18, at 7.

90 M. Gysseling, 'De oudste Friese toponimie', *Philologia Frisica anno 1969* (Groningen, 1970), 41–51, at 41.

91 Holthausen, *Altfriesisches Wörterbuch*, ed. Hofmann, 186.

êwinge, and a broken form *jōwinge*.[92] The broken form also occurs in an Old East Frisian text, but see *jouwe* 'gift' above.

niouwa (OFris) 'nephew'. Holthausen lists *neva*, and from this short /ɛ/ + *w* the rising diphthong *jou* should have emerged. This is confirmed by forms like *niawen/nyawen* in Jus, while Hofmann reports *niawa* for the codexes Aysma and Unia, and *nowa* for Codex Roorda.[93] After the Old Frisian period the broken form disappeared (under Dutch influence?); Modern Frisian has *neef*.

It appears that my prediction that vowel height is constant in breaking at the lowest level, i.e. /ɛ.w/ > /jɔ.w/, was right. Unfortunately, things are not always quite as straightforward as one expects and hopes. However, in order to come to grips with this problem, first it is necessary to have a look at the middle level.

4.4 The middle level: e.w > jo.w

With respect to the diphthong /e.w/, I predicted that it would change to /jo.w/. This seems to be borne out by the following data:

(12)

dreauwert 'loss of working hours due to rain'. *WFT* gives the pronunciation /drjo.wət/, and at the same time it mentions another, unbroken, form *drevert*.

Gjoo, personal name. According to Jenny Visser (personal communication) used in her family as a variant of *Geeuwke* /ge.wkə/.

griowa (OFris) 'count', in Holthausen's dictionary entered as *grēva*. In Old Frisian also often spelled with *ou*. The variety with Jorwert Breaking did not succeed to Modern Frisian.

joegh, *jōwelik* (OFris) 'eternal'. Sipma assumed that the form *ewelike* had /e:/, on the ground of MoFris /i:vəx/; Boersma appears to have reached the same conclusion and also noted the forms *jogha*, *joegha*, *joegh* and *yowich*.[94]

Joo, hydronym in the south-west of Fryslân. According to Gildemacher, it derives from OFris **ēw*.[95]

---

[92] L.-E. Ahlsson, *Die altfriesischen Abstraktbildungen* (Uppsala, 1960), 48.

[93] Buma, *Vollständiges Wörterbuch*, 218; Hofmann, 'Die "spätgermanische" Silbenquantitätsverschiebung', 210.

[94] Sipma, *Fon Alra Fresena Fridome*, 241; Boersma, *De Friesche oorkonden*, 98.

[95] K. F. Gildemacher, *Waternamen in Friesland* (Leeuwarden, 1993), 229.

jowel '(house)front, façade'.[96] A non-broken variant *geuel* appears in the *Snitser Recesboeken*,[97] with cognates in MDu *ghevel* (MoDu *gevel*) and MLG *gēvel*.

kreauwe (MoFris) 'to quarrel'. *WFT* only gives the pronunciation /krjo.wə/, but an unbroken /e.w/ occurs as well, especially in the south. Possibly there is an older form *creva* in *Fragmentum de Literis Frisicis*, an incomplete grammatical treatise published in the 1681 edition of Gysbert Japix' *Rymlerije*.[98] Perhaps something of the older form, and without *v*-lenition, is retained in *krevelje* 'to play around' in the Schiermonnikoog dialect. Van Helten assumes the older forms **kreuwia* < **krevia*.[99]

leauwerje /ljo.wərjə/ 'to deliver', a variant of MoFris *leverje*. See also *liuweria* in (6), section 4.2.

liuw 'lion'. Spenter reconstructs the form /le.w/ for Old Frisian;[100] according to an unpublished dialect survey of the Fryske Akademy (1993, question 12a), this pronunciation still exists today, but in the very north-east it is broken to /ljo.w/. Most of the province has /li.w/, however, presumably with regular raising from former /le.w/, compare also modern *ieu* 'century' and early MoFris *eeuw(e)* (cf. *joegh* above).

reau 'tools, equipment'; according to *WFT* generally pronounced as /rjo:/. For its etymology this dictionary points to Du *gerei*, *gereed(schap)* and G *Gerät*, a suggestion which on formal grounds must be seriously questioned. Alternatively, Buitenrust Hettema's assumption of OFris **rêwe* is much more plausible.[101] Presumably, the latter word is incorporated in the derivation *birêvia* in MS Jus, interpreted by Buma as '[Dutch] laden, beladen' (to load, burden').[102] It is interesting to notice that this Old Frisian verb also seems to have undergone Jorwert Breaking. At least, Jus also has a variant *birouwia*.

skiōd (OFris), probably from earlier *skewed*. For more details, cf. *skiūd* under (5) in section 4.2 above and *sjudden* in (8).

---

[96] See P. Sipma, *Oudfriesche Oorkonden*, OTR 2 (The Hague, 1933) II, no. 221/13 (p. 241), an original charter from the town of Workum (1485).

[97] See M. Oosterhout, *Snitser Recesboeken 1490–1517* (Assen, 1960), 467. I thank Henk Meijering and Oebele Vries for bringing these attestations to my attention.

[98] See P. H. Breuker, *It wurk fan Gysbert Japix. I. Tekst yn facsimilee* (Leeuwarden, 1989), 299. However, the Old Frisian words in this treatise are not always reliable, see R. H. Bremmer Jr., 'Oer datearring, funksje en auteurskip fan de earste Fryske grammatika (1681)', *Philologia Frisica anno 1990* (Leeuwarden, 1992), 9–32, at 22.

[99] Van Helten, 'Zur Lexicologie und Grammatik des Altwestfriesischen', 362.

[100] Spenter, *Vokalismus der Schiermonnikooger Mundart*, 298.

[101] Buitenrust Hettema, *Bijdragen tot het Oudfriesch Woordenboek*, 17.

[102] Buma, *Vollständiges Wörterbuch*, 42.

skreauwe (MoFris) 'to shout', perhaps a loan from MoDu *schreeuwen*. *WFT* only mentions the pronunciation /skrjo.wə/, but according to my own observations /skre.wə/ occurs as well.
sleau 'lethargic', from OFris **slēw(e)*. Both the pronunciations /sle.w/ and /sljo.w/ are found. It is cognate with, e.g., Du *sleeuw* and E *slow*.

As in the highest level, fronting occurs here too, mostly in its long form, as /ö.ə/, but also shortened to /ö/. Among other forms, this palatalization can be observed in the past tense and past participle forms *bleau* /blö.ə/ and *bleaun* /blö.ən/ from the verb *bliuwe* 'to remain' and similar verbs. However, the situation in this instance is rather complex and will be discussed later. The same applies to *kleaune* in (16), which also has its particular complications. Consequently, for direct cases of fronting we are left with:

(13)
ljurk 'lark'. Århammar has argued that this word was borrowed from Middle Dutch as *lêwerik*.[103] Next, Jorwert Breaking and some further contraction would have given **ljoork*, whence modern *ljurk* /ljörk/ as the result of subsequent palatalization and shortening. Van Helten postulated a form with *iou*,[104] a form which Århammar thinks is confirmed in the early seventeenth-century spelling *liourck* (*Burmania Proverbs*). But as argued above, it is not possible to draw reliable conclusions on the basis of the spelling ⟨ou⟩.
sneon [snö.ən], from OFris *sunna-evend* 'Saturday'. Holthausen presents *ēvend*, which points to /e.w/. Spenter, too, gives /e:/ as the input, which therefore yields an expected Jorwert Breaking to /jo.w/.[105] Of the first element, only *sn-* survived. After palatalization, *j* was also deleted.

In section 4.2, in our account of Jorwert Breaking at the level of /i.w/ > /ju.w/, we saw that its product could undergo a lowering to /jo.w/. A similar lowering seems to be possible for the products of Jorwert Breaking of original /e.w/, in this case lowering resulting in /jɔ.w/. Again, the criterion seems to be the position in open syllable. We have already encountered an example in our account of *ljurk* in (13) and perhaps also in some other spellings with ⟨ou⟩. And as before, this lowering has a wider range than

103 N. Århammar, 'Die Lerche (*Alauda*) im Friesischen: ein Beitrag zum *Atlas Linguarum Europae*. Über Inlautassibilierung, unregelmäßige Lautentwicklung und "Lehnlautungen"', *Miscellanea Frisica. In nije bondel Fryske stúdzjes*, ed. N. Århammar *et al.* (Assen 1984), 137–52, at 146.
104 Van Helten, 'Zur Lexicologie und Grammatik des Altwestfriesischen', 379.
105 Holthausen, *Altfriesisches Wörterbuch*, ed. Hofmann, 23; Spenter, *Vokalismus der Schiermonnikooger Mundart*, 314.

solely the products of Jorwert Breaking. Already Hofmann pointed out this fact, as did Hoekstra in a subsequent article. Hoekstra mentions cases such as MoFris *(Alde)hou* '(old) churchyard' < *howe*, *rouwe* 'scab' < **rowe* and *douk* 'bung' < **dowik*.[106] And, as we have seen before, an inconvenient consequence of this lowering process is that its results match the direct results of Jorwert Breaking at one level lower. Two relevant cases are worth mentioning:

(14)

hjouw(e) (MoFris) 'dip net', cf. Du *haaf*, *have*; in Scandinavian languages also with long *a*. This vowel could have been closed /e:/ in Old Frisian; Buma assumes OFris **hêve*. The breaking product /jo.w/ will have been lowered to /jɔ.w/.[107]

Ljouwert, the name of the capital of Fryslân. According to Buma from *Lêwert*. In Old Frisian, spellings with *-ow-* as well as *-ouw-* are found.[108]

However, at the mid level, a movement to a lower position is not the only possibility. Theoretically, the opposite direction is also available. And indeed, this is what has happened, at least in some instances. The condition seems to have been that the stem vowel was followed by *l* or *n*. Again, this is part of a more general process. Examples are MoFris *stoel* /stu.əl/ < OFris *stōl* or ModFris *sûn* < OFris *sond*. Relevant for our purposes are:

(15)

jûn (MoFris) 'evening'. For Old Frisian, Holthausen lists *ēvend*, which points to /e.w/, and also Spenter has /e:/ as input with subsequent Jorwert Breaking to /jo.w/. In the Old West Frisian manuscript Jus we find (case endings included), spellings such as *iounde*, *ioendes*, *jond*, *iond*, *jonde*. In Modern Frisian the form *joon* /jo.n/ is still found in a small area in the south-east, in the other areas it was raised to /jun/.

sjoel(-). This stem can be found in nouns and verbs designating 'to slide' or 'to drag'. According to Hoekema it should be related to an Old Frisian verb 'to slide'.[109] The ordinary Old Frisian form for this meaning is *skūva*, but Hoekema argues that a variant *skiāva* must have existed, too. Later, that form must have raised to *skiēva*. To make things complete we have to assume that a suffix *-el* is also involved (Hoekema does not mention this). Then, a combination of verbal stem plus suffix would manifest itself in such Modern Frisian compounds as *skevelbûgel*, *skevel-*

---

106 Hofmann, '*Thor*, "Donnerstag" und "Donner" in Friesland'; Hoekstra, '*Iampck ist en iamcker wirtet mecke*'.

107 W. J. Buma, 'Wurdsneuperijen. 11. *Hjouwe* en *peasjou*', *UW* 7 (1958), 71–72.

108 *Ibid.*; see also Miedema, *Van York naar Jorwerd*, 9–10.

109 T. Hoekema, '*Sjoel(j)e*; *sjouwe*', *UW* 34 (1985), 102–05, at 102.

keatting and *skevelplaat* (all parts of an old-fashioned plough) and in the verb *skeuvelje* 'to shuffle'. Since *-k-* can delete in the consonant cluster *skj-* (MoFris *sjitte* 'to shoot' from OFris *skiāta* is a case in point), application of Jorwert Breaking would result in **sjool*. After raising, this form would have ended in *sjoel*.

Although some secondary changes were witnessed, the picture that has emerged up till now is pretty clear: Jorwert Breaking can change /e.w/ into /jo.w/. However, there are also words which distort the picture somewhat. First, some came up with original long /a:/ which in Frisian raised to /ɛ:/; here it looks as if Jorwert Breaking took place only at the higher level of /e:/:

(16)

greauwen (MoFris) 'dripping', but more relevant is E *greaves*, G *Grieben*. In the south-east this word is still without *v*-weakening (*greven*), but the south-west has it; moreover, most of the language area also shows Jorwert Breaking, resulting in /grjo.wən/. Spenter suggests that the word should have shown *iā*, with subsequent deletion of its first part 'Gemäß der Regel vor Resorption der ersten Komponente des Diphthongs *iā* unter Verengung der zweiten Komponente zu afries. *ē*'.[110] If Spenter is right, then this word belongs to this sample, and not to regular (12).

kleaune (MoFris) 'ball (of wool, etc)'. According to Spenter, this word had /e.w/ in Old Frisian from Gmc **eu*.[111] This reconstruction is confirmed by the dialect map in Van der Veen, Versloot and Rypma.[112] In the north, the west and the middle of the language area fronting and deletion of *j* changed a broken form into /klö.ən(ə)/. However, a pure, broken variety still shows up: *kl(j)owen*. Some places in the south-east have /kli.uwən/, which form may result from analogy under influence of the *bliuwe* verbs, but Dutch interference from *klieuwen* cannot be ruled out either. Alternatively, another course of events is also conceivable: Gmc **eu* showed up in Old Frisian as *iā*, which would yield **kliāwen*;[113] with deletion of *j* and raising of the stem vowel one would also arrive at /kle.wən/, and again with the same contemporary manifestations.

reaf (MoFris) 'skein'. According to Hof, in the north this word is still found without *v*-weakening: *reaf* /rɪ.əf/.[114] In the south it shows *v*-weakening, /re.w/, as well as variants with Jorwert Breaking: /rjo.w/. The northern

---

110 Spenter, *Vokalismus der Schiermonnikooger Mundart*, 296.

111 *Ibid.* 297.

112 K. F. van der Veen, A. Versloot and W. Rypma, *Dialektgeografyske oantekens fan J. J. Hof* (Leeuwarden, 2001), 91.

113 W. J. Buma 'Nijfrysk *greauwen* en *grevel*', *UW* 24 (1975), 57–58.

114 Hof, *Friesche Dialectgeographie*, 55–56.

form points to a late Old Frisian stem vowel /ɛ:/, from OFris *ā*, cf. Du *roof*. Indeed, the *Woordenboek der Nederlandsche Taal* offers an Old Frisian counterpart *rāf*.[115] Hof also observed a lowered variety /rɔ.w/, but this may be a remnant of the Old Frisian form after *v*-weakening and contraction.

It appears that the cases above are rather unclear; this is even more the case in the following words:

(17)

kleau 'split, crevice', *kleauwe* 'to split'. Du *kloof* and ON *klauf* suggest a Germanic etymon **klauf* for the noun. This would have resulted in **klāf* for Old Frisian. Indeed, we find *klâve* in Holthausen or, in Hofmanns improved edition, *kla(u)wa*. For the verb, van Helten assumed an early Old Frisian **kleuwa* ('aus *klêva(n)'). Maybe, it is better to depart from Gmc **klaubjan*, which would yield /ɛ:/ in Old Frisian. The modern pronunciation for both categories is /kljo.w/, which should have a source /kle.w/, and which still is the form in the Hylpen dialect.[116]

leauwe (MoFris), both noun 'belief' and verb 'to believe'. According to Miedema, the verb is the reflex of OFris *lêva*.[117] He points to Gothic *galaubjan* for the umlaut factor that brought about *ê*. One would therefore expect Jorwert Breaking to have resulted in *ljouwe*, and indeed this form does exist, albeit in the margins of the language area.[118] Nevertheless, in the larger part of the province the pronunciation is /ljo.wə/, at first sight corresponding to the area where *bliuwe* etc. is pronounced as /bljo.wə/, so that analogy may have played a role here. However, modern *leauwe* is not only a verb, but also a noun. In Old Frisian the two were kept apart, the noun having the form *lâva*. It is possible therefore that /a:/ in this noun was raised as in similar cases, that it was accompanied by the corresponding verb in the /ɛ:/-stage, and that Jorwert Breaking was applied not earlier than the /e:/-stage – a scenario comparable with what was assumed for *kleauw*, *kleauwe* above, which would explain the form /ljo.wə/ in a direct manner. The dialect variant *ljouwe* can be seen as the result of further lowering in open syllable, and as a form to which the other forms of the verbal paradigm adapted later.

---

115 *Woordenboek der Nederlandsche Taal*, ed. M. de Vries *et al.*, 29 vols. (Leiden, 1882–1998), s.v. *roof* (II).

116 Holthausen, *Altfriesisches Wörterbuch*, ed. Hofmann, 58; van Helten, 'Zur Lexicologie und Grammatik des Altwestfriesischen', 361

117 H. T. J. Miedema, 'Problemen met het Friese credo', 34.

118 This can be destilled from a map in Miedema, *ibid.* 41, which is based on data from K. Boelens and G. van der Woude, *Dialect-atlas van Friesland*, Reeks Nederlandse Dialect-atlassen 15 (Antwerp, 1955).

4.5 The two *e*'s revisited

If the analysis of the last sample of words in the preceding subsection holds water, this would imply that words with original /a:/, in the course of raising, did not use the potential possibility to apply Jorwert Breaking in the stage of /ɛ:/. This might indicate that there was an aversion towards Jorwert Breaking at the lowest level, i.e. the change /ɛ.w/ > /jɔ.w/. Such an aversion seems to be confirmed by the following sample of words, all of which had short *e* in their stem originally. They underwent Jorwert Breaking, but with such a result that one is compelled to conclude that they were involved in the transition /e.w/ > /jo.w/. Some of them show /o(:)/, which is difficult to explain by other means, while others show /u(.ə)/ in Modern Frisian, which must be raised from an *o*-sound. Moreover, in one case we even encounter fronting to /ö.ə/ or /ö:/, which is not conceivable on the basis of /jɔ.w/. The following words are relevant:

(18)

gjoele, probably Middle Frisian or Late Old Frisian. Postma reports that in old inventories he had found the following words for Dutch *gaffel* 'gaff, fork': *gyoele*, *guel* or *guele*, *joele*, *juile* and *jole*.[119] The etymological dictionaries mention *gafala* for Old Saxon and *gafol*, *geafel* for Old English. With fronting of short **a*, we may assume **gevle* for Old Frisian. In three of Postma's six forms *g* is deleted before *j*, which is not uncommon in Frisian.[120] I suppose that *jole* is the form after Jorwert Breaking, possibly also *gyoele* and *joele*, but these forms might also show raising to *u* before *l*. Presumably, *guel*, *guele* and *juil* show influences of palatalization.

griowa, *griowe* (Old Frisian) 'to dig'. In his 'Berichtigungen und Nachträge', Holthausen, gives the notation *greva*, which points to a short stem vowel (the lemma in the original dictionary had *grêva*). Addition of the suffix *-inge* resulted in **grevinge*, the base for a number of water names.[121] In *Grûns* (< *Grons*) we find raising to *u*. Palatalization of the cluster /jo.w/ has resulted in *Greuns*. The compound *Greventerp* stands at the basis of the palatalized place-name *Greonterp* (/grö.əntɛrp/).[122]

jowen (Old Frisian) 'even', also in *jowncristen* 'fellow-Christian'. Van Helten also mentions the derivations *onjown* 'ungleich' and *jowns* 'gleichfalls', and Hoekstra adds two further attestations of this form in

---

119 O. Postma, 'Noch eat oer it wurd "tsjoele"', *Fryske Plaknammen* 8 (1956), 5–6.

120 H. T. J. Miedema, 'De friese voornamen *Gjalt* en *Jelte* naast fries *gjalt*, *geld* "onbevrucht"', *Feestbundel aangeboden aan prof.dr. D. P. Blok*, ed. J. B. Berns *et al.* (Hilversum, 1990), 254–60.

121 Gildemacher, *Waternamen in Friesland*, 271–73.

122 Gosses, 'Snjeon', 43; Miedema, *Van York naar Jorwerd*, 12.

the compound *allijons* < **alevens* 'likewise'.[123] The variants with Jorwert Breaking appear most frequently in Codex Roorda and in the Old Frisian charters. The problem here is MoFris *jamk*, which Hoekstra claimes to be derived from **evenlik*. Compared to the other forms, this should have been **jomk* /jomk/. To arrive at *jamk*, Hoekstra assumes an intermediate **jowen* which in the process of lowering, thanks to its open syllable, resulted in **jɔ.wen*. Then, contraction would produce **jɔmk*. However, since in Frisian ɔ is not allowed before *m*, the vowel is lowered further to *jamk*. Incorporation of Jorwert Breaking of this stem into this sample is mainly based on interpreting the spellings to represent /jo.w/. If, on the other hand, this were /jɔ.w/, this complex could be subsumed under (11)

jûn (MoFris), past participle of *jaan* 'to give'. The south-east still has the older form *joon*, so without raising. Old Frisian has *ieven*, with short *e*.[124]

njonken (MoFris) preposition 'beside, next to'. From **nevenlik*;[125] the sound [o] in the modern word points at Jorwert Breaking of /e.w/.

sjoen (MoFris), past participle of *sjen* 'to see'. From a root **sewVn-*.[126] Apparently, Jorwert Breaking resulted in a stem with /jo.w/, and afterwards the vowel was raised before final *-n*.

stjûne (MoFris) 'stem (of a ship)' For Old Frisian, Holthausen lists *stevene*.[127] Jorwert Breaking must have changed this to /stjo.w(ə)nə/, which raised before *n* to /stjunə/.

tiole (OFris) 'table'. Holthausen presents *tefle* and *tevle*, in addition to *tiōle*.[128] In MS Jus, the form with Jorwert Breaking occurs most frequently, whereas *teula* is attested only once. According to Hoekstra, *tsjoele* 'square fishing net' is a modern remnant of the Old Frisian broken form; the word *tsjoele* also survives in field-names.[129]

---

123 Van Helten, 'Zur Lexicologie und Grammatik des Altwestfriesischen', 358; J. Hoekstra, 'In nijwesterlauwerskfryske wjergader fan Aldfrysk *(hona) etsel* '(hoanne)-spoar', *UW* 48 (1999), 3–9, at 8.

124 W. Steller, *Abriss der altfriesischen Grammatik* (Halle/S., 1928), 62.

125 T. Hoekema, 'Njonken nêst neffens', *De Pompeblêdden* 22 (1951), 69–70; 104; T. Hoekema, 'Njonken, tusken', *De Pompeblêdden* 24 (1953), 47–48; also W. J. Buma in J. L. A. Heestermans, *'Naar', 'naast', 'langs' en 'in'. Een onomasiologisch-semasiologische studie over enige voorzetsels met een locaal betekeniskenmerk in de Nederlandse dialecten en het Fries* (The Hague, 1979), 74.

126 Reconstruced variously as **sewan*, **gisewin*, **sewun*, **sewen*, respectively, by van Helten, 'Zur Lexicologie und Grammatik des Altwestfriesischen', 379; J. Jacobs, 'Geschilpunten in de Oudfriesche klank- en vormleer', *Leuvensche Bijdragen* 4 (1900–1902), 125–37, at 136; Boersma, *De Friesche oorkonden*, 98; Gosses, 'Snjeon', 42.

127 Holthausen, *Altfriesisches Wörterbuch*, ed. Hofmann, 104.

128 *Ibid.* 109 and 176.

129 Hoekstra, '*Iampck ist en iamcker wirtet mecke*', 7. See also O. Postma, 'Tyole, tyolle, tsjoele, ensfh.', *Fryske Plaknammen* 7 (1955), 3–4; Postma, 'Noch eat oer it wurd "tsjoele"'; P. B. Winsemius, 'Tsjoele - tyole', *Fryske Plaknammen* 7 (1955), 4–8; P. B.

If the words listed above have in fact undergone the transition /e.w/ > /jo.w/, then one wonders how this is possible. In section 4.3, we assumed that in lengthening short *e* + *w* would change in quality as little as possible, and hence would result in the diphtong /ɛ.w/. The segment /ɛ./ could have been part in the general tendency towards raising, which would have resulted in /e.w/. But (18) seems to contain very early examples of Jorwert Breaking, and it can be questioned whether raising had made enough progress at the time. Another possibility is that the result of lenghtening of /ɛw/ was not /ɛ.w/, as we assumed thus far, but /e.w/. Lengthening of /ɛ/ > /e:/ was not uncommon in West Germanic languages, cf. Dutch *gebed* and its plural *gebeden* as a clear example. In discussing lengthening in *anlaut*, Hoekstra also assumes a pattern /ɛ/ > /e:/ for Old Frisian.[130] In his view, these sounds build a natural pair for the older stages of Old Frisian. In a subsequent article, Hoekstra still assumes a three level system, both for the short and the long vowels, and the middle levels are occupied by /ɛ/ and /e:/, respectively.[131]

If it could be taken for granted that the cases in (18), with original short ɛ, as a result of lengthening were involved in the Jorwert Breaking /e.w/ > /jo.w/, then one might wonder how other cases of short *ɛ* plus *w* fared. For the relevant words in (11) in section 4.3 we assumed that they obeyed the rule of /ɛ.w/ > /jɔ.w/, but actually this might occur one level higher without any problem, so at the level of /e.w/ > /jo.w/, since its result, thanks to the position in open syllable, is a possible input for the lowering rule, eventually ending in /jɔ.w/ again. By the very existence of this lowering process, it remains indecisive whether we are dealing with Jorwert Breaking at the lowest or at the middle level.

So, if in principle it is possible for words with short *e* as a stem vowel to be eliminated in Jorwert Breaking of the lowest level, how about stems with original /ɛ:/? In principle, these could be eliminated, too. The cases of Jorwert Breaking in (10) all show an output /jɔ.w/ in open syllable, so again the route via /jo.w/ is not to be excluded out of hand. Therefore, it is to be expected that those people who doubt the existence of two kinds of *e* in Old Frisian (cf. section 2) will not readily change their minds on the basis of the facts of Jorwert Breaking. The existence of Jorwert Breaking /ɛ.w/ > /jɔ.w/ cannot be proved on the basis of solid evidence.

Winsemius, 'Jitris "tyole, tsjoele"', *Fryske Plaknammen* 8 (1956), 7–10; J. J. Spahr van der Hoek, 'Tsjoele', *Fryske Plaknammen* 7 (1955), 9–16.

130 Hoekstra, 'In nijwesterlauwerskfryske wjergader', 5–6.

131 Hoekstra, 'An Outline History of West Frisian', 722. Similarly, in Boutkan, 'Phonology and Orthographic System of Old Frisian', 617, where the existence of a long /ɛ:/ is doubted, i.e. as a consequence /e:/ would be the natural lenghtening product of /ɛ/.

If it indeed were the case that the lowest level of Jorwert Breaking was never there – and perhaps its 'skipping' in the admittedly rather unclear samples (16) and (17) is perhaps the strongest indication for this position – then such an outcome is not totally unexpected. The prediction should be remembered from section 2 that of the three levels the lowest is the most difficult to perform. If it turned out that the transition /ɛ.w/ > /jɔ.w/ never took place, this might be a confirmation for the hypothesis.

It will have become clear by now that it is far from easy to make an unequivocal reconstruction for Jorwert Breaking. As an additional illustration, I shall now discuss one form, or rather a group of forms. It concerns the preterite and past participle of *bliuwe* 'to remain', and with it the corresponding forms of *driuwe* 'to drive', *riuwe* 'to lace', *skriuwe* 'to write', *triuwe* 'to push', *wriuwe* 'to rub', and also *priuwe* 'to taste':

(19)

bleau(wen), *bleaun*, etc. These preterite and participle forms of the verb *bliuwe* 'to remain' are pronounced as *bljou* [bljɔ.w], *bljoun* (also *bljound* or *bloun*) in the south, but also in the north-west. The Germanic stem vowel of the preterite singular *ai* should have shown up as /ɛ:/ in Old Frisian;[132] we can still observe this in the writings of the poet Gysbert Japicx (1603–1666).[133] The present-day pronunciation /blɪ.əf/ in a small area in the north-west is compatible with that open quality. So, the southern dialectical varieties receive an explanation if we assume that the quality of the stem vowel of the preterite singular spread towards the preterite plural and the participle. However, in the major part of the province the pronuciation is /blö.ə(n)/ nowadays. This palatalized form points to /jo.w/ as input, not /jɔ.w/, which would have fronted to /jɔ̈.w/ or something similar. However, in Frisian such a sound does not exist, which might explain why it was raised to the sound which is closest, i.e. /ö.e/. On the other hand, it is equally possible that the difference should be traced in a change in the input. However, in this case the problem is how to arrive at alleged /e.w/. Analogy on the preterite plural or even past participle is not obvious, as originally this was /i/.[134] Hence, it is tempting to recall the discussion about the two *e*'s. For one thing, if the breaking product is /jo.w/, then the form /jɔ.w/ at the fringes of the language area could easily be accounted for by taking recourse to the lowering rule. But then we are nevertheless left with the *bleaf*-area in the north-west, and maybe also for a small area in the east, where Hof

[132] Steller, *Abriss der altfriesischen Grammatik*, 59.

[133] Gysbert Japicx always spelled <eau> for the pronunciation just mentioned, according to Feitsma, *De autografemen in het werk van Gysbert Japicx*, 577.

[134] Steller, *Abriss der altfriesischen Grammatik*, 59.

records the pronunciation *blɪ.ewen*. In short, with the one *e* the form *bleaf* is left unexplained, and with the other the derivation of the fronted form is difficult. On the basis of these facts one is inclined to assume a dialectical existence of two different '*e*'s already in the Old Frisian period, but it will be hard to find independent evidence for such a position.

4.6 Summary

In the introduction to this section, I expressed some provisos with respect to the ability to give a reconstruction of Jorwert Breaking in separate words. As to the exact interpretation of spellings as well as in the area of pronunciation one comes across lots of uncertainties that can disturb a clear view of the real course of events. In this light, it is nevertheless striking how well the hypothesized system, as it is sketched in section 2, is corroborated. In addition, it is especially important to keep an eye on subsequent processes. For instance, in some cases palatalization yields a different result than expected; in particular, the later raisings (*o: > u(:)*) and especially the lowerings (*u: > o:* and *o: > ɔ.w*) considerably disturb the outcome of Jorwert Breaking.

When we take these later processes into account, then Jorwert Breaking, as it is sketched in section 2, can be recognized quite well in the material which has passed down to us. This is most clearly the case with regard to the transition /i.w/ > /ju.w/, but it can be upheld for the transition one level lower, i.e. /e.w/ > /jo.w/ as well. However, much more problematic is the hypothetically presupposed transition /ɛ.w/ > /jɔ.w/. The very availability of the independent lowering process /jo.w/ > /jɔ.w/ prevents us from proving the existence of Jorwert Breaking at the lowest level, but neither can its non-existence be proven either. However this may be, from this overview of Frisian word material the point made in section 2 still stands, namely that in Jorwert Breaking vowel height is constant.

5. Implementation

In the preceding section, an overview was given of those words in West Frisian that underwent Jorwert Breaking. Although we may assume that this list is fairly complete, it nevertheless gives a one-sided picture in that only the outcome of the process is presented. It offers no information about how the change was performed, how fast, at which time, and how many of the potential words were involved. In this section, I would like to address some of these questions.

To be sure, these questions are more readily put than answered. We are dealing here with a historical process; we have no contemporary witnesses.

And the sources, as will be well known, are scarce. Frisian has a modest written tradition, and the diversity of text sorts is equally modest. Some words can hardly, if at all, be found in historical texts. Especially after *c.*1550 the stream almost runs dry, and this situation continues for a century or so. At the very beginning of the written tradition, the Old West Frisian legal codexes provide a fair amount of linguistic material, but the repertoire is limited, and such a codex remains a relatively instantaneous exposure in itself. In comparison, the Old Frisian charters present a much more useful source for our purposes. They constitute an ongoing stream of texts, roughly from the end of the fourteenth until de middle of the sixteenth century. Moreover, all these texts are dated. Since they are bound to a certain place and are written by a certain writer, they are also important for dialectical research, although it must be admitted that the database of the charters in the Frisian institute at the University in Groningen is not equipped well enough at the present time for such special purposes. So, I leave the dialectical aspect for what it is. To be sure, research into the emergence and further development is a time consuming affair; I have left it with some random checks, which nevertheless provided enough useful data to get the beginning of a picture.[135]

When looking into these historical sources, it is hard to make up a consistent picture from the data. A well known example of Jorwert Breaking is MoFris *jûn* 'evening'. In the medieval charters, this is mostly *jond*. Codex Unia, generally considered to be the most conservative Old West Frisian manuscript, still has *ewend*, which is consistent. However, it would be too hasty to conclude that Jorwert Breaking as a whole had settled before charters were compiled in Old Frisian.

Take the past participle of modern *bliuwe* 'to remain', for example. In the charters, this form does not show completed application of Jorwert Breaking – the figures never exceed two-thirds of the potential instances. Nor is it true that the cases of Jorwert Breaking typically show up at the end of the period. For instance, in the years 1503, 1519 and 1543 we still find the spelling *bleven*. Moreover, according to Feitsma, the seventeenth-century poet Gysbert Japix had no Jorwert Breaking in this form.[136] To be sure, the preterite in an area in the north-west of Fryslân today still has the form *bleaf*, so also without *v*-vocalization.

[135] For these random checks, I skipped the transition *i.w* > *ju.w*. The reason is the unreliability of the orthography. For instance, a historical spelling like *iu* can be interpreted in two ways, broken or unbroken. The sign ⟨i⟩ can represent both *i* or *j*, and the same can be said of the sign ⟨u⟩: both /u/ or the semivowel *w* come into mind. Therefore, I confine myself to Jorwert Breaking of both '*e*'s.

[136] Feitsma, *De autografemen in het werk van Gysbert Japicx*, 468.

Could it be that *jûn* 'evening' underwent Jorwert Breaking so early and so completely because the breaking product /jo.w/ was reanalyzed in such a way that *j* was no longer considered to be part of the thriphthong, but rather as the onset of the complete syllable, which would create a more common syllable structure according to a CV pattern?[137] This might seem to be a plausible explanation but appears not to be supported by the facts. Take the Old Frisian etymon for MoFris *ivich* 'eternal', which occurs relatively frequently in the charters. Only in about 30% of the cases does it show signs of having undergone Jorwert Breaking, and its adverbial derivative with suffix *-lik* (*jowelika*, *iouwelike*, *joulike*) scores even lower. In this instance, Jorwert Breaking manifests itself most frequently in the second half of the fifteenth century, but after 1500 the relative number rapidly diminishes. This pattern matches with the modern form *ivich*, which shows neither Jorwert Breaking nor even *v*-weakening. Furthermore, in the charters, a loanword like *eventure* 'unforseen event' never shows Jorwert Breaking, but the same applies to such native words as *ewen wol* 'however' and *ewa* 'law', although, again, the relevant material is minimal.

That a word displays Jorwert Breaking in the Old Frisian period, but later stops doing so, is not an accident. Of course, I do not refer to words that vanished from the lexicon, such as *jouel* 'property', *jouwe* 'law' or *jouwinge* 'custom'. Also words like MoFris *graaf* 'count' and *grave* 'to dig' do not count in this respect. At least, it seems that these forms are loans from Dutch rather than continuations of their Old Frisian ancestors, whether broken or not. A word like *neef* 'cousin', not broken nowadays, must also be a Dutch loan, since Frisian short /e/ is not lengthened in open syllables, and the same applies to a word like *even* 'even, equal'.

There are even some words that never betrayed a sign of Jorwert Breaking. They include the following:

(20)

tsjeaf	'thief'	pl. *tsjeaven*
skeaf	'sheaf'	pl. *skeaven*
sleef	'ladle'	pl. *sleven*
reef	'reef'	pl. *reven*
stêf	'staff'	pl. *stêven*
stiif	'stiff'	infl. *stive*

One might object that these words end in voiceless *f*, and hence cannot undergo *v*-vocalization. However, the right-hand column show that these

[137] For example, see G. N. Clements and S. J. Keyser, *CV Phonology. A Generative Theory of the Syllable* (Cambridge, MA, 1985).

words exhibit a *v* in inflected forms; moreover, Fokkema demonstrated that final devoicing in Frisian must be of relatively recent date.[138] What is more, there are also words with intervocalic *v* which never turned into voiceless *f*, and nevertheless they show the same aberrant behaviour of not having undergone Jorwert Breaking:

(21)

lever	'liver'
jenever	'gin'
iver	'diligence'
fiver	'pond'
grevel	'a little bit'
skevel	'fellow'
swevel	'sulphur'
leven	'noise'

Without doubt, this sample contains a great many loanwords. If *v*-vocalization ceased after the Old Frisian period – and it looks as if this was the case – then their present-day form is unremarkable. Nonetheless, in these Modern Frisian examples *v* is not vocalized, and hence a crucial condition for Jorwert Breaking is absent. As such, these words present no clue for the grade of application of the sound change.

As regards Jorwert Breaking, we have just seen that within the Old Frisian period some words were affected completely, some were not affected at all, and there were some which were only partly affected. The files of the lexical database of Old Frisian charters in Groningen show us that after 1500 the heyday of Jorwert Breaking was over. On the basis of some modern dialectical varieties, such as the verbs *bliuwe*, etc., it can be concluded that Jorwert Breaking has not been applied across the board.

Did Jorwert Breaking cease to be active in the Middle and Modern Frisian periods? It looks like it, although it is hard to verify, since few words are eligible to test the hypothesis. In addition, in many cases it is hard to tell when a particular word found acceptance in Frisian. Be that as it may, I must confess that I have never heard the words *ieu* 'century' or *Sieu* 'inhabitant of the province of Zeeland' being pronounced in a broken way. On the other hand, it is probably going too far to conjecture that the tendency towards Jorwert Breaking completely disappeared. It may well be that a pronunciation /ljo.w/ for *liuw* 'lion' need not necessarily be traced back to the

---

[138] K. Fokkema, 'De verzachting van enkele slotconsonanten na lange klinker of tweeklank in het Fries', K. Fokkema, *Nei wider kimen. Kar út syn forsprate skriften* (Groningen, 1969), 185–90.

Middle Ages. And, on the basis of *WFT*, when would the broken variety of the words in (22) have gained acceptance?

(22)

geau / geauwe	'(to) yawn'	[gjo.w]/[gjo.wə]
kiuw	'gill'	[kju.w], [kjo.w], also [ki.w]
miuw (meau)	'mew, seagull'	[mjo.w], but also [mi.w]
piuwe	'to dawdle'	[pju.ə], [pjo.wə]

Uncertainty will – inevitably, I am afraid – remain concerning the exact commencement and extent of the broken pronunciations. As such, I would like to refer again to section 3, to the discussion of the easy transition between the various pronunciations of the word *sleau*. Nevertheless, without exaggeration, it can be maintained that the heyday of Jorwert Breaking must have been in the late Old Frisian period.

6. Conclusion

In Old West Frisian a falling diphthong, consisting of a front vowel and the glide *w*, may convert into a rising diphthong, or rather a triphthong, with a back vowel as a nucleus and with an initial glide *j*. This change, which for want of a better term I have dubbed 'Jorwert Breaking' here, can be characterized as natural, if we assume that the stress within the diphthong moved backwards. Only then can the process have followed in a direct way. In this derivation, vowel height remains constant. Thus, assuming a system of four vowel heights, the change was threefold: *i.w > ju.w*, *e.w > jo.w* and *ɛ.w > jɔ.w*. This analysis clearly differs from the idea that was upheld until now, which assumed that for each vowel height the core of the change be performed at the highest level *i.w > ju.w*.

Evidence for my analysis can be found in the phonetics of the process itself, and is supported by data from English and the dialect of the Frisian island of Schiermonnikoog. The main source of evidence, however, is provided by the Frisian words that underwent the change, although it turned out that tracing their precise development is far from easy. This is due to several factors, such as a lack of data and uncertainty about older spellings. A disturbing factor is the fact that in the relevant period other changes were taking place as well. At the input side we see raising of front vowels, and, more seriously, at the output of Jorwert Breaking, processes were active such as lowering in open syllables, raising before *l* and *n*, and fronting and sometimes subsequent shortening of back vowels under the influence of preceding *j*. However, putting these influences aside, we see that the inventory of Frisian words offers clear support for the hypothesis that the change was a direct one. One point remains unresolved, however: it cannot be proven – nor disproven, for that matter – that the transition *ε.w>jɔ.w* actually did occur. This is in line with the long-standing question of whether Old Frisian had one or two long *e*'s.

Finally, among the three main branches of Frisian, Jorwert Breaking can only be observed in West Frisian. Its heyday must have been in the late Middle Ages, although it cannot be fully excluded that the transition also occurred at later periods. From the Old West Frisian data, a rather diffuse picture emerges. It is certainly not the case that all potential input words underwent the change, and sometimes only a part of the tokens that have come down to us show the case.

The Fifteen Signs of Doomsday of the First Riustring Manuscript

Concetta Giliberto

Introduction

The belief in the destruction of the world and of mankind has an ancient origin;[1] it has a place in the great monotheistic religions. Christian eschatology also includes the second advent of Christ, or *parousia*, the resurrection of the dead and the Last Judgment.

In early medieval Europe, the growth of millennialist movements and chiliastic expectations fostered the rise of a literary tradition in which the interest in eschatological motifs found a large and fertile field of development.[2] This particular cultural framework represents the background which gave origin – along with other literary expressions about the Final Judgment – to the legend of the Fifteen Signs before Doomsday, concerning wonders and fatal events, which are said to occur in the two weeks preceding the end of the world.[3] The legend enjoyed a large circulation throughout the Middle

---

1 See D. Gowan, *Eschatology in the Old Testament* (Edinburgh, 2000); *Eschatology and the New Testament. Essays in Honor of George Raymond Beasley-Murray*, ed. W. H. Gloer (Peabody, MA, 1988); P. C. Phan, *Eternity in Time* (Selinsgrove, 1988); R. H. Charles, *Eschatology: The Doctrine of the Future Life in Israel, Judaism and Christianity* (New York, 1963); R. K. Bultmann, *The Presence of Eternity: History and Eschatology* (New York, 1957); M. Eliade, *Le mythe de l'éternel retour. Archétypes et répétition* (Paris, 1949).

2 *L'attente des temps nouveaux: Eschatologie, millénarisme et visions du futur du Moyen Age au XXème siècle*, ed. A. Vauchez (Turnhout, 2002); *Ende und Vollendung. Eschatologische Perspektiven im Mittelalter*, ed. A. Aertsen and M. Pickavé (Berlin and New York, 2001); *Last Things: Death and the Apocalypse in the Middle Ages*, ed. C. W. Bynum and P. Freedman (Philadelphia, 2000); *The Apocalypse in the Middle Ages*, ed. R. K. Emmerson and B. McGinn (Ithaca, 1993); *The Use and Abuse of Eschatology in the Middle Ages*, ed. W. Verbeke, D. Verhelst and A. Welkenhuysen (Louvain, 1988).

3 The scholarly attention to the eschatological themes and particularly to the legend of the Signs before Doomsday began in the nineteenth century, when a number of significant essays were published. Among others: E. Sommer, 'Die fünfzehn Zeichen des jüngsten Gerichtes', *ZfdA* 3 (1843), 523–30, C. Michaelis, 'Quindecim Signa ante Judicium', *Herrigs Archiv* 46 (1870), 33–60, and, above all, G. Nölle, 'Die Legende von den fünfzehn Zeichen vor dem jüngsten Gerichte', *BGdSL* 6 (1879), 413–76, which offers the first systematic investigation of the legend and of its sources. G. Grau, *Quellen*

Ages, especially from the eleventh century onwards. Many versions are single, independent works and deal just with the Signs of Judgment; others are incorporated into longer eschatological works, in which – together with the Signs of Judgment – other events, such as the coming of the Antichrist, Christ's return to the earth and the Last Judgment, are also described.

The Old Frisian version of the Fifteen Signs before Doomsday is preserved in Oldenburg, Niedersächsisches Staatsarchiv, Bestand 24-1, Ab. Nr. 2, the so-called First Riustring Manuscript, also known as the 'Asega Book', and compiled around 1300.[4] The Old Frisian list of the Fifteen Signs was edited in 1840 by Karl von Richthofen with the title 'Vom jüngsten Gerichte'.[5] A century later, this text was examined by Buma in an article in which the Old Frisian version is accompanied by a Modern Dutch translation;[6] later it was also included in Buma's edition of the First Riustring Manuscript.[7]

In his article,[8] Buma offers a brief excursus on the origin of the legend, with a short list of the vernacular versions. He points out that the Old Frisian text is based on the Pseudo-Bede version of the list, but follows the reversed order of signs twelve and thirteen as found in a version written by Petrus Comestor. The conclusion, written in 'glowing words' were added by the anonymous Frisian author. Buma refers to the known sources of the list, stressing the importance of IV Ezra, chapters 5 and 6. According to his description, the Old Frisian text is but a patchwork of several writers. On the other hand, the Old Frisian text, although based on a number of sources, is mostly indebted to one of them, but at the same time features a well contrived version of the list, with personal touches and a peculiar style in line with the Old Frisian tradition.

---

und Verwandtschaften der älteren germanischen Darstellungen des Jüngsten Gerichtes (Halle/S., 1908) presents a detailed treatment of the eschatological tradition in the ancient and medieval Germanic world, taking into account a number of Anglo-Saxon as well as of Old High German works (such as *Christ II* and *Christ III*, *Judgment Day II* and *Muspilli*), and devoting to the legend of the Signs before Doomsday a section in the appendix. The monumental work by W. W. Heist, *The Fifteen Signs before Doomsday* (East Lansing, MI, 1952), analyses a large number of lists of the Fifteen Signs written in the vernacular languages of Western Europe. It aims at demonstrating that this legend could have been derived from the *Apocalypse of Thomas* and that an Irish poem, *Saltair na Rann*, represents an intermediate step in this evolution.

4 *De Eerste Riustringer Codex*, ed. W. J. Buma, OTR 11 (The Hague, 1961); *Das Rüstringer Recht*, ed. W. J. Buma and W. Ebel, AR 1 (Göttingen, 1963).

5 K. von Richthofen, *Friesische Rechtsquellen* (Göttingen, 1840), 130–31.

6 W. J. Buma, 'Geestelijke literatuur in Oud-Friesland', *Trijeresom. Ynliedingen hâlden yn de Fryske seksje fan it Nederlânsk Philologekongres 1950* (Grins [Groningen] and Djakarta, 1950), 5–50, at 9–18.

7 *De Eerste Riustringer Codex*, ed. Buma, 122–23.

8 Buma, 'Geestelijke literatuur in Oud-Friesland', 9–18.

Bremmer, who has taken the text into examination in his *Hir is eskriven*,[9] points out the attribution to Jerome, which is not original but already there in the source, the so-called Pseudo-Bedan version of the list. At the same time, according to Bremmer, the mention of Jerome will have given dignity to the text and fostered its preservation and diffusion. Moreover, Bremmer highlights that the conclusion attached to the Frisian Fifteen Signs, containing the description of Jesus's coming, follows Comestor's *Historia scholastica*, which features an analogous passage. The observation that the concluding passage is drawn from Comestor (who died around 1178), Bremmer argues, suggests that the Frisian text cannot be earlier than 1200.

The present study deals with the Old Frisian version of the legend of the Signs before Doomsday, trying to place it within the tradition and to identify its possible sources and analogues; the investigation of its peculiar elements will help to find a connection between the eschatological motifs which characterize it and the legal context of the manuscript in which it occurs.

Origin and Propagation of the Legend

References to a number of signs heralding the *parousia* and the Last Judgment are to be found in various passages of the Bible, both in the Old and in the New Testament. The prediction of a universal cataclysm is attested in Isa. 2.18–21, 24, 25.2, 26.19–20, 27.8–13, 34.4, 40.4; Ezek. 32.6–8, 38.19–22; Joel 1.15; Amos 8.9; Mic. 5.10,12; Zech. 12–14. In Ez. 38.20, a sequence of catastrophic phenomena is described: the fishes of the sea, the birds of the heaven, the beasts of the field and all the men will shake at the Lord's presence, the mountains will be thrown down, the steep places will collapse, and every wall will fall to the ground. General prophecies occur in the Gospels, the Acts of the Apostles, the Epistles, and the Apocalypse of St John. Among the most recurrent signs there are the darkening of the sun and moon (Matt. 24.29; Mark 13.24), the change of the moon to blood (Apoc. 6.12) and the falling of heavenly bodies (Matt. 24.29, Luke 21.25, Mark 13.25, Apoc. 6.13). Thunder and lighting and earthquakes are also predicted (Apoc. 8.5), as well as a general feeling of terror overwhelming all human beings (Matt. 8.12, 13.42), who desperately try to hide themselves from the Lord's wrath (Apoc. 6.15–17). A formidable sign is the resurrection of the dead (Acts 17.32; I Cor. 15.52), as well as the destruction of all the elements through fire, which is the predominant event in the eschatological tradition (2 Pet. 3.12).

A number of apocalyptical signs are also to be found in the apocrypha, from which medieval authors of eschatological works drew on for many

[9] R. H. Bremmer Jr, *'Hir is eskriven'. Lezen en schrijven in de Friese landen rond 1300* (Hilversum, 2004), 66–67.

details. Among them, IV Esdras (chs. 5–7 and 15–16) offers a description of the events occurring before the Last Judgment which is particularly rich in fearsome images.[10]

The works of the Church Fathers contained a good deal of material which was used and reshaped in the later representations of the Signs of Judgment. The earliest patristic work in which some signs are described is *Liber de consummatione mundi* (ch. 37), formerly attributed to Hippolytus, bishop of Ostia (third century).[11] A series of eschatological allusions is recorded in Lactantius' *Divinae institutiones* (Book VII, chs. 16, 17 and 19),[12] which provide the description of several portents that later turn up in Fifteen-Signs lists, such as the destruction of cities through fire and sword, earthquakes, floods, diseases, famines, barrenness of earth, the desiccation of fountains and rivers; the alteration of waters to blood; the death of birds, beasts and fishes; signs in comets, sun, moon and stars; the fall of mountains and their levelling; the alteration of the sea which becomes unnavigable; a trumpet from heaven. Lactantius quotes some verses of a famous Greek acrostic poem (drawn from the apocryphal *Oracula Sibyllina*, Book VIII), known from the Latin translation included in Augustine's *De civitate Dei* (Book XVIII, ch. 23).[13] However, the influence of this acrostic poem upon the shaping of the legend of the Fifteen Signs before Doomsday – even though undeniable – can be considered neither immediate, nor significant, because of the absence in it of some distinctive signs of the legend, such as the rising up and sinking down of the sea waters, the meeting (and the fighting) of the animals, and the battle of the stones.

A number of these portents and phenomena, derived from biblical and patristic sources, were remolded and arranged in a list of fifteen signs distributed over the last fifteen days preceding Doomsday. The genesis of the legend is obscure, as well as the reason why the number of the signs became

10 *Der lateinische Text der Apokalypse des Esra*, ed. A. F. J. Klijn (Berlin, 1983).

11 Patrologia Graeca 10, col. 939.

12 Ed. S. Brandt, Corpus Scriptorum Ecclesiasticorum Latinorum 19 (Prague, Vienna and Leipzig, 1890).

13 Ed. B. Dombart and A. Kalb, Corpus Christianorum, Series Latina 48 (Turnhout, 1955), 613–14. For a survey of the *Oracula Sibyllina* tradition and of the relationship between the acrostic and the Signs of Judgment, see P. Lendinara, 'The *Versus Sibyllae de die iudicii* in Anglo-Saxon England', *Apocryphal Texts and Traditions in Anglo-Saxon England*, ed. K. Powell and D. G. Scragg (Cambridge, 2003), 85–101; F. Alcamesi, 'The Sibylline Acrostic in Anglo-Saxon Manuscripts: the Augustinian Text and the other Versions', *Foundations of Learning. The Transfer of Encyclopaedic Knowledge in the Early Middle Ages*, ed. R. H. Bremmer Jr. and K. Dekker (Leuven, Paris and Dudley, MA, 2007), 147–73.

fixed at fifteen.[14] The earliest datable version of the legend with fifteen signs in as many days is the catalogue contained in the *Epistola de die iudicii* of Peter Damian, composed around 1062.[15] Afterwards, the work was translated into many languages and enjoyed wide popularity. The first known vernacular version is an Old English homily, preserved in London, British Library, Cotton Vespasian, D. xiv, fols. 102r–103v (s. xii).[16] A great variety of vernacular versions of the list of the Fifteen Signs were also in circulation, both in prose and in verse.[17] These versions of the list have been separated into various groups, or types, according to the sources used by their authors, on the basis of the different kinds of signs described, and on account of their features and sequence.[18] This grouping has resulted in the following five types:

---

14 There are some lists of signs whose number is unspecified and which are not apportioned to any particular day. Moreover, a series of versions with seven signs in the last seven days before Doomsday must also have circulated, see Heist, *The Fifteen Signs*, 32, and Nölle, 'Die Legende von den fünfzehn Zeichen', 414. The ultimate source of the legend of the seven days can be traced to the apocryphal Apocalypse of Thomas, see C. D. Wright, '*The Apocalypse of Thomas*: Some New Latin Texts and their Significance for the Old English Versions', *Apocryphal Texts and Traditions*, ed. Powell and Scragg, 27–64; M. Swan, '*The Apocalypse of Thomas* in Old English', *Leeds Studies in English* 29 (1998), 333–46; M. Förster, 'A New Version of the Apocalypse of Thomas in Old English', *Anglia* 73 (1955), 6–35; M. R. James, *The Apocryphal New Testament* (Oxford, 1924), 555–56; F. Wilhelm, *Deutsche Legenden und Legendare* (Leipzig, 1907), 40*–42*. The relationship between the legend of the Fifteen Signs and that of the seven days is unclear. According to Grau, *Quellen und Verwandtschaften*, 269, the distribution of the signs into fifteen days resulted from a misunderstanding of IV Esdras VII, 30–31: 'Et convertetur saeculum in antiquum silentium diebus septem sicut in prioribus initiis, … . Et erit post dies septem, et excitabitur qui nondum vigilat saeculum et morietur corruptum'. This suggestion never met with unanimous scholarly approval.

15 *Die Briefe des Petrus Damiani*, ed. K. Reindel, vol. 3, MGH. Die Briefe der deutschen Kaiserzeit IV (Munich 1989), 20–23.

16 *Early Homilies from the Twelfth-Century MS. Vespasian D. XIV*, ed. R. D.-N. Warner (London, 1917), 89–91.

17 Heist, *The Fifteen Signs*, 204–14, lists 23 Latin, 30 German, 1 Middle Dutch, 1 Old Frisian, 17 Celtic, 19 English, 1 Anglo-Norman, 14 French, 4 Provençal, 7 Italian, 2 Spanish and 1 Basque versions.

18 The first proposal for a taxonomy of the versions of the legend into families was offered in Nölle, 'Die Legende von den fünfzehn Zeichen', 413–76. Further classifications are then provided in Heist, *The Fifteen Signs*; H. Eggers, 'Fünfzehn Vorzeichen des Jüngsten Gerichts', *Die deutsche Literatur des Mittelalters. Verfasserlexikon*, ed. K. Ruh *et al.*, 12 vols. (Berlin and New York, 1977–..) II, 1014–20; C. Gerhardt and N. F. Palmer, *Das Münchner Gedicht von den fünfzehn Zeichen vor dem Jüngsten Gericht* (Berlin, 2002), 59–67. Such grouping of the versions of the Fifteen-Signs list into different families is not intended as a strict and rigid classification, but rather as a systematization of the material of the Fifteen Signs, in order to identify analogies and differences among the lists, and to shed light on the possible relationships among them.

'Damian': it comprises versions derived from the list of the Fifteen Signs contained in the *Epistola de die iudicii* of Peter Damian (composed around 1062);[19]

'Pseudo-Bede': it embraces all the lists descending from the so-called version of Pseudo-Bede, a text of doubtful origin, formerly ascribed to Bede and published in 1563 by J. Herwagen in his *Opera Bedae Venerabilis presbyteri Anglosaxonis*; however, this text dates to a period much later than the age of the famous Anglo-Latin writer.[20]

'Comestor': it gathers versions developed from the *Historia scholastica* by Peter Comestor, ch. 141 (1169–73);[21]

'Anglo-Norman': it includes the lists developed from a long passage on the Fifteen Signs inserted in the concluding section of a play dated to the mid-twelfth-century, the *Jeu d'Adam*, preserved in Tours, Bibliothèque municipale, 927;[22]

'Voragine': it comprises the versions deriving from a list included in the first chapter of the *Legenda aurea sanctorum, sive Lombardica historia*, or simply *Legenda Aurea*, by Jacob of Voragine (1270).[23]

---

[19] See note 15.

[20] The codex used by Herwagen is now lost. The most recent edition is *Collectanea Pseudo-Bedae*, ed. M. Bayless and M. Lapidge (Dublin, 1998), 178. Pseudo-Bede's list of the Fifteen Signs also occurs as a single item (separated from the *Collectanea*) in a great deal of later insular and continental manuscripts, dating from the twelfth century onwards. A preliminary list of the manuscripts preserving Pseudo-Bede's version is offered in G. Grau, *Quellen und Verwandtschaften*, 274–75; a number of bibliographical references concerning the manuscript tradition of Pseudo-Bede's list is also contained in Heist, *The Fifteen Signs*, 96, and in Gerhardt and Palmer, *Das Münchner Gedicht von den fünfzehn Zeichen*, 60. H. Schenkl, *Bibliotheca patrologia Britannica* (published from time to time in the *Sitzungsberichte der kaiserlichen Österreichischen Akademie der Wissenschaften*, phil.-hist. Klasse, 1890–1904) listed a number of texts of the Fifteen Signs, all of which he ascribed to Bede. According to Schenkl, the earliest manuscripts containing this list are Eton, Eton College Library, k. 2. 8. (s. xii) and Cambridge, Trinity College, O.1.59 (s. xii). Purpose of a current research of mine is a complete and deep investigation into the manuscript tradition of Pseudo-Bede's list of the Fifteen Signs (as a single piece, separate from the *Collectanea*), which is still wanting to this day.

[21] PL 198, col. 1611.

[22] *Le Mystère d'Adam (Ordo representacionis Ade)*, ed. P. Aebischer (Geneva and Paris, 1963), lines 945–1305. The passage with the Fifteen Signs was first included in the editions of the *Jeu d'Adam: Adam, Drame anglo-normand du XIIe siècle*, ed. V. Luzarche (Tours, 1854) and *Adam, mystère du XIIe siècle*, ed. L. Palustre (Paris, 1877); this excerpt was published in the first edition of *Das Adamsspiel, Anglonormannisches Gedicht des XII. Jahrhunderts*, ed. K. Grass (Halle/S., 1891), but omitted from later editions.

[23] Iacopo da Varazze, *Legenda Aurea*, ed. G. P. Maggioni, 2 vols. (Florence, 1998). The catalogue of the Fifteen Signs in the *Legenda Aurea* conflates the versions of Comestor and Peter Damian, see H. Sandison, 'Quindecim signa ante iudicium', *Archiv für das Studium der neueren Sprachen und Literaturen* 124 (1910), 73–82, at 73–75.

The archetypes 'Damian', 'Pseudo-Bede', 'Comestor' and 'Voragine' differ in the kinds of signs listed and in their arrangement, yet share the attribution of the legend's (spurious) authorship to Jerome, who is said to have found it in certain Hebrew records. Nevertheless, the works which are assigned to this Church Father with certainty, contain no explicit reference to the Signs before Doomsday, even though it cannot be excluded that a work of Jerome's dealing with such a subject is now lost. Furthermore, in the versions of Pseudo-Bede, Comestor and Voragine some Hebrew records are quoted, vaguely identified as, for example, *Annales Hebraeorum*, from which Jerome is said to have derived the material for the Fifteen Signs legend. Nonetheless, of this alleged source there is no trace in the Jewish manuscript tradition. Doubtlessly, the attribution of the Fifteen Signs to the holy Jerome – which is present also in the Old Frisian version – contributed to the dissemination and to the immense popularity of the legend in Western Europe.

The List of the Fifteen Signs of the First Riustring Manuscript

It is common knowledge that Old Frisian has come down to us chiefly in legal documents clustered in miscellaneous manuscripts. The most recorded genres in the Frisian written tradition include law texts, charters, letters and official documents. Therefore, the occurrence in the First Riustring Manuscript of a non-legal item, such as the Fifteen Signs of Doomsday, is particularly striking and noteworthy.

The text which is here presented diplomatically is drawn from Buma's edition of the First Riustring Manuscript,[24] while the translation is mine:

Thit send tha fiftine tekna ther er domes di koma skilun . ther sancte iero [ms. p. 76(78)] nimus fand escriuin an thera iothana bokon .

Thes erosta dis sa stigath alle wetir fiuwertich fethma boua alle bergon . and stondath to likere wis and thiu mure ther fon stene ewrocht is.

Thes otheres dis . sa werthath se lik there selua skipnese . ther se bi fara weron .

Thes thredda dis fallath se alsa side . thet se nen age bi sia ne mi .

Thes fiarda dis sa somniat se alle fiskar ther send an tha wetiron to semine . and hropath al to godi . and tha stifne net nen manniska buta god al ena .

Thes fifta dis burnath alle wetir . fon asta there wralde . to westa there wralde .

[24] *De Eerste Riustringer Codex*, ed. Buma, 122–23. From an inspection of the manuscript, I can affirm that Buma's edition does not need any improvements.

Thes sexta dis . sa send alle bamar . and alle gerso . mith ena blodiga dawe bi fangen .

Thes siugunda dis . sa fallath alle tha timber fon asta there wralde to westa there wralde . and werthat al gadur to breken .

Thes achtunda dis . sa [ms. 77(79)] falt thi sten . withir thene sten . and to brekth al semin . and tha berga werthath e ifnad .

Thes niugunda dis . sa werth alsa grat irth biuinge . sa ther fon on bi iennene there wralde er nen sa den nas .

Thes tianda dis . werth thiu wrald e iuenad an there selua skipnese . ther se was . er se use drochten se skepen hede .

Thes andlofta dis . sa gunth thi manniska with thene otherne . and ne mi nen mon otheron ondwardia . fon there nede . and fon tha ongosta . hwande thenne is ia hwelik mon thes sinnes bi rauad .

Thes twilifta dis . sa werth egadurad . alle thet benete efter there wralde anna ene stidi .

Thes thredtinda dis . sa fallath alle tha stera fon tha himule .

Thes fiuwertinda dis sa steruath alle tha liode . and skilun ther efter up stonda mith othera dathon .

Thes fiftinda dis . sa burnt alle thiu wrald . fon asta there [ms. p. 78(80)] wralde . to westa there wralde . al to there hille porta . Ther efter werth domes di . Sa cumth use hera mith alle sine anglon . and mith alle sine heligon . sa beuath alle thiu wrald alsa thet espene laf . alsa se hini siath mith tha criose . and mith tha spiri . and mith tha neylon . and mith there thornena crona . and mith tha fif wndon . ther hi an tha criose tholade fori us . and fori al mansesklik slachte .

['These are the fifteen signs that will come before Doomsday, which Jerome found written in the books of the Jews.

On the first day, all waters will rise forty fathoms above all mountains and will stand like a wall which is made of stone.

On the second day, they will take the same shape which they had before.

On the third day, they will fall so deep that no eye can see them.

On the fourth day, all the fishes which live in the waters will gather together and will all call to God and their voice will not be noticed by anybody, except by God alone.

On the fifth day, all the waters will burn, from the east of the world to the west of the world.

On the sixth day, all the trees and all the herbs will be covered with a bloody dew.

On the seventh day, all the buildings will fall down, from the east of the world to the west of the world and they will altogether be destroyed.

On the eighth day, each stone will fall onto the other stone and they will all be destroyed and the mountains will be flattened.

On the ninth day, such a great earthquake will take place, as never was on earth since the beginning of times.

On the tenth day, the earth will be levelled to the same shape it had before our Lord created it.

On the eleventh day, one human being will turn against the other, and nobody will be able to answer the other, because of distress and terror, since every man will then be deprived of his mind.

On the twelfth day, all the bones of the world will be gathered in one place.

On the thirteenth day, all the stars will fall from the sky.

On the fourteenth day, all the people will die and afterwards they will rise with the other dead.

On the fifteenth day, all the world will burn, from the east of the world to the west of the world, until the gate of hell. Afterwards, Doomsday will come. Then our Lord will come with all His angels and with all His saints. Then all the world will tremble like an aspen leaf, when they will see Him with the cross and with the spear and with the nails and with the thorny crown and with the five wounds which He suffered on the cross for us and for all human kind.']

Commentary on the Fifteen Signs of Doomsday of the First Riustring Manuscript

In the same way as the Latin source from which it stems, the Old Frisian text opens with the attribution to Jerome, an element which guarantees to this version the necessary dignity to be included among the works of theology and of learned literature circulating in medieval Europe. Moreover, as far as the Frisian corpus is concerned, the association to Jerome has probably rendered the legend acceptable even inside such a peculiar context like that of the First Riustring Manuscript, which is otherwise a compilation of a strictly legal nature.

The signs predicted for the first three days refer to the waters and to the creatures which live in water. On the first day all the waters of the world will rise up forty fathoms and will stand like a stone wall. The description of this sign in the Old Frisian legend is absolutely identical to the conventional sources, beginning with Pseudo-Bede, even in the detail of the measurement of the forty fathoms. The comparison of the waters to a stone wall is also recorded in other sources, such as in the versions of Comestor and of Peter Damian. On the second day, the waters will come back to their original level, while on the third day they will fall so deep that no eye will be able to see them. At this point, the Frisian text inverts the order of these two signs in contrast to Pseudo-Bede's and Peter Damian's versions, which instead present on the second day the sinking of the waters and on the third day the return to their original level.[25]

The Old Frisian version shows an alteration of the sequence of signs – with respect to the Pseudo-Bede text – also in describing the gathering of the bones and the falling of all stars from the sky. In the list of the First Riustring Manuscript, the gathering of bones is foreseen on the twelfth day, differently from its direct Latin source, which assigns this event to the thirteenth day; the stellar disaster is placed on the thirteenth day, while in Pseudo-Bede it appears on the twelfth day. The inversion of the twelfth and thirteenth signs could be considered as a piece of evidence testifying to the influence exerted upon the Old Frisian version by chapter 141 of Peter Comestor's *Historia scholastica*, in which, indeed, the assembling of the bones precedes the falling of stars.[26]

As far as the fourth sign (the gathering of the fishes), the fifth (the burning of the waters), the sixth (the bloody dew covering trees and plants), the ninth (the greatest earthquake ever) and the fourteenth (the death and resurrection of all human beings) are concerned, the Old Frisian text is absolutely identical to Pseudo-Bede's version:[27]

> Quarta die pisces et omnes beluae marinae, et congregabuntur super aquas, et dabunt uoces et gemitus, quarum significationem nemo scit nisi Deus.
> Quinta die ardebunt ipsae aquae ab ortu suo usque ad occasum.
> Sexta die omnes herbae et arbores sanguineum rorem dabunt.
> Septima die omnia aedificia destruentur.
> (…)
> Nona die erit teraemotus, qualis non fuit ab initio mundi.
> (…)
> Decimaquarta die omnes homines morientur, ut simul resurgant cum mortuis.
> [On the fourth day the fish and all the monsters of the sea will gather on the surface of the water and will utter cries and groans whose meaning is known only to God.
> On the fifth day, the waters themselves will burn from the rising to the setting of the sun.
> On the sixth day all herbs and trees will give forth a bloody dew.

[25] The sign of the waters coming back to their preceding position – which in the versions of Pseudo-Bede and Peter Damian is allocated the third day – is omitted in the version of the Fifteen Signs contained in Peter Comestor's *Historia scholastica*. Consequently, all the subsequent signs move back one day and a newly invented sign is attached to the fifteenth day.

[26] See also Buma, 'Geestelijke literatuur in Oud-Friesland', 11.

[27] Bayless and Lapidge, *Collectanea Pseudo-Bedae*, 178–79.

On the seventh day all buildings will be destroyed.
(…)
On the ninth day there will be an earthquake unlike any since the beginning of the world.
(…)
On the fourteenth day all men will die, so that they can rise again with the dead.']

By contrast, the Frisian text, while describing the other signs, introduces a number of innovations which distinguish it from the literary tradition of the Fifteen Signs before Doomsday to which it belongs.

The fifth sign includes the phrase 'fon asta there wralde to westa there wralde' (lines 12–13), which clearly renders the Latin expression 'ab ortu suo usque ad occasum' occurring in the fifth sign of Pseudo-Bede's list. Nonetheless, the Frisian text adds this sentence also in the seventh sign (lines 16–17), which foresees the collapse of all buildings in the world, as well as in the fifteenth sign (lines 32–33), which is that of the universal conflagration preceding the divine Judgment, which is without any parallel in the corresponding signs of Pseudo-Bede's version. This phrase seems to be shaped according to the stereotyped structure of a formula and could be an interpolation introduced by the Frisian author to adapt the language and style of this text to the rest of the documents preserved in the First Riustring Manuscript and clearly pertaining to the juridical tradition, which is so peculiar to the Old Frisian literary corpus.

As far as the struggle of the stones is concerned (the sign predicted for the eighth day), in the Frisian version the stones are said to fall one onto the other, until they break into pieces completely; there is no mention of their splitting up into three parts[28] and of their subsequent battle, as described in Pseudo-Bede's version. Moreover, in this sign, the Frisian legend anticipates the levelling of the mountains, a motif which is fully developed in the tenth sign.

A parallel can be identified in the tenth sign of a continental version of the legend of the Fifteen Signs before Doomsday, the Middle High German poem in Munich, Bayerische Staatsbibliothek, Cgm 717,[29] written in 1348,

---

28 All stones will break into three parts in Pseudo-Bede's version, whereas in Peter Damian's and in Jacob of Voragine's lists they will break into four parts.

29 This Middle High German version is edited by Gerhardt and Palmer, *Das Münchner Gedicht von den fünfzehn Zeichen*; see also C. Giliberto, 'I segni del Giudizio della famiglia "Ava" e gli aspetti innovativi del poemetto del ms. München, Bayerische Staatsbibliothek, Cgm 717', *Le lingue e le letterature germaniche fra il XII e il XVI secolo. Atti del XXIX Convegno dell'Associazione Italiana di Filologia Germanica – Trento 5–7 giugno 2002*, ed. F. Ferrari and M. Bampi (Trento, 2004), 253–94; H. Eggers, 'Von den fünfzehenn Zaichen vor dem iungsten Tag', *BGdSL* 74 (1952), 355–409 and *idem*,

where the portent of the destruction of the stones is associated with the flattening of mountains and valleys:[30]

An dem zehenden tag,
als wir div bůch hören sagen,
(…)
so ist vf der vert
kain stain so groz noch so hert,
†wa er in der wält si gelegen,
er můss erstieben als ain mel†.
die hohen berg überal
müssent nider in div tal.
['On the tenth day,
as we hear the scriptures say,
(…)
Then is suddenly
no stone so big or so hard,
wherever in the world it may lie,
it must be blown away like flour.
The high mountains everywhere
must (go) down into the valleys.]

Another detail in which the Frisian text differs from Pseudo-Bede's list is that by its levelling the earth takes the same shape it had before it was created by God.

In the representation of the eleventh sign, the Frisian legend varies significantly from its Latin sources, Pseudo-Bede and Comestor. In the Frisian version, human beings will turn to each other, yet nobody will be able to give any answer to the other because of distress and terror, and all people will be deprived of their minds; their coming out from the caverns – which is prophesied in Pseudo-Bede's and Comestor's versions – is here left out. The reference to the widespread panic preventing people from communicating with each other and causing a general state of insanity resembles the situation narrated in the Old English homily on the Fifteen Signs before Doomsday, preserved in London, British Library, Cotton Vespasian, D. xiv, fols. 102r–103v. In this version, it reads:[31]

'Fünfzehn Vorzeichen des Jüngsten Gerichts'; M. Haupt, 'Die Zeichen des jüngsten Tages', *ZfdA* 1 (1841), 117–26.

30 Gerhardt and Palmer, *Das Münchner Gedicht von den fünfzehn Zeichen*, 19. The translation is mine.

31 Warner, *Early Homilies from the Twelfth-Century*, 91. The translation is mine.

> *On þan twelften dæige* eorneð mænn geon(d) eall middeneard byfigende 7 drædende Cristes tocyme to demene cwican 7 deaden, swa *þæt* se were ne gret his wif, ne þæt wif hire were, þeh heo heom gemeten, ac byð swa swa wittlease 7 unspecende.
> ['On the twelfth day, men will run all over the earth, trembling and fearing the coming of Christ to judge the quick and the dead, so that the husband does not greet his wife, nor the wife her husband, though they were measured to each other, but they will be like mad and unable to speak.']

This passage highlights the state of mental disorder of each human being on the day of the Last Judgment, when, in front of the supreme Lord and overwhelmed by the dark terror of the Doom, nobody will be able to speak a word, nor to recognize his/her lifetime partner.[32]

Inside the tradition of the signs before Doomsday, this theme appears in two stanzas of a thirteenth-century Irish poem on the Fifteen Signs,[33] ascribed to the poet Donnchadh Mór Ó Dálaigh:[34]

> Ni urmhais neach ní do rádh
> Acht bheith ar sraon 's ar seachrán
> Gé deach ar aghaidh gach fhir
> ní labhair neah ré naoidhin.
>
> Sgarfar gach fear ré mhnaoi a muigh
> Sgarfar gach mae ré mháthair
> Nocha mbia dias ar domhan
> Bhias ó Dhia gan dealoghadh.
>
> ['No man can speak
> but overwhelmed and distraught;
> no man says a word to his child
> though it dies before his eyes.

[32] The motif can be compared to a similar theme, viz. the one of the loneliness of each human being on Judgment Day, when nobody can count on the support of any relative or friend, who previously in their earthly existence had always helped them in every moment of sorrow and trouble. For a survey of this motif, used in various forms in Anglo-Saxon homilies, see P. Lendinara, '"frater non redimit, redimet homo…": a Homiletic Motif and its Variants in Old English', *Early Medieval English Texts and Interpretations: Studies Presented to Donald G. Scragg*, ed. E. Treharne and S. Rosser (Tempe, AZ, 2002), 67–80.

[33] See Heist, *The Fifteen Signs before Doomsday*, 126 and 205. This poem is edited by E. C. Quiggin, *Poems from the Book of the Dean of Lismore* (Cambridge, 1937), 11, and in L. S. J. McKenna, 'The Signs of the Judgment', *The Irish Monthly* 55 (1927), 260–64.

[34] *Ibid.* 262. English translation from Heist, *The Fifteen Signs before Doomsday*, 126.

Every man shall be torn from his wife
every son from his mother
so that no couple on earth
but shall be separated by God.']

Finally, the conclusion attached to the Frisian catalogue of the Fifteen Signs, containing the description of Jesus's coming with the angels and the saints and with the attributes of his crucifixion (cross, spear, nails, thorny crown and five wounds), which seems to parahrase Mark XIII. 26–27,[35] could have been derived from Comestor's *Historia scholastica*,[36] which in fact, after the enumeration of the Fifteen Signs of Doomsday, features an analogous passage:[37]

> Et addidit Jesus: Sicut fulgur exit ab oriente et paret usque in occidentem, sic erit adventus Filii hominis, subitus scilicet, et coruscus, et tunc apparebit signum Filii hominis in coelo, id est in aere, supra locum unde ascendit, et ante eum erunt instrumenta mortis suae, quasi vexilla triumphi, crux, clavi, lancea, et in carne ejus videbuntur cicatrices, ut videant in quem pupugerunt, et in valle Josaphat judicabitur omnis homo, angelis congregantibus eos.
> ['And Jesus added: just as the the ligthning comes out from the east and flashes as far as the west, so will be the coming of the Son of man, namely all of a sudden, and flashing, and then the sign of the son of man will appear in the sky, that is in the air, above the place whence he ascended, and the tools of his death will be before him, just as standards of triumph, the cross, the nails, the spear, and the scars will be seen in his body, so that they can see where they stabbed, and every man will be judged in the valley of Josaphat, when the angels will have gathered them together.']

The image of Christ portrayed on the day of his second coming as surrounded by angels and saints and with the most significant attributes of his martyrdom is a powerful allegory of the Final Doom, quite common in medieval religious culture. There is a connection between the *parousia* and the crucifixion, which is manifest both in literary and artistic monuments.[38]

---

35 *Biblia Sacra. Iuxta vulgatam versionem*, ed. R. Weber, 3rd edn (Stuttgart, 1983): 'Et tunc videbunt Filium hominis venientem in nubibus cum virtute multa et gloria. Et tunc mittet angelos et congregabit electos suos a quattuor ventis, a summo terrae usque ad summum caeli'.

36 See Bremmer, *Hir is eskriven*, 66–67.

37 PL 198, col. 1611.

38 In the course of the Middle Ages the representation of Christ showing at Doomsday the signs of his crucifixion, such as the cross and the wounds, was widely diffused and found even in early medieval art and architecture, see B. C. Raw, *Anglo-Saxon Cruci-*

In the Anglo-Saxon poem *Christ III*,[39] preserved in the Exeter Book, for example, Jesus appears at Doom, showing the wounds inflicted at the crucifixion:

Ond eac þa ealdan wunde ond þa openan dolg
on hyra dryhtne geseoð dreorigferðe,
swa him mid næglum þurhdrifan niðhycgende
þa hwitan honda ond þa halgan fet,
ond of his sidan swa some swat forletan,
þær blod ond wæter bu tu ætsomne
ut bicwoman fore eagna gesyhð,
rinnan fore rincum, þa he on rode wæs. (1107–14)
['And also the ancient wounds and the gaping gash upon their Lord they will behold, desolate in spirit, according as men of malicious purpose pierced with nails those white hands and those holy feet and likewise set flowing the blood from his side, whence blood and water both came running out together in front of the men and in the sight of their eyes, when he was on the Cross.']

Comparable is the image in the Old High German poem *Muspilli*, lines 102–05:[40]

uuirdit denne furi kitragan daz frono chruci,
dar der heligo Christ ana arhangan uuard.
denne augit er dio masun, dio er in deru menniski anfenc,
dio er duruh desse mancunnes minna fardoleta. 102–05
['Then the Lord's Cross will be brought forth,

---

fixion Iconography and the Art of the Monastic Revival (Cambridge, 1990).

39 *The Exeter Book*, ed. G. P. Krapp and E. V. K. Dobbie, Anglo-Saxon Poetic Records 3 (New York, 1936). Translation taken from *Anglo-Saxon Poetry*, ed. S. A. J. Bradley (London, 1998), 232.

40 The bibliography on *Muspilli* is immense and continually increasing. See *Frühe deutsche Literatur und lateinische Literatur in Deutschland 800– 50*, ed. W. Haug and B. K. Vollmann (Frankfurt/M., 1991), n. III.2; *Die kleineren althochdeutschen Sprachdenkmäler*, ed. E. von Steinmeyer, 3rd edn (Berlin and Zurich, 1963), no. XIV; C. Händl, 'Muspilli', *Literatur Lexikon: Autoren und Werke deutscher Sprache*, ed. W. Killy, 15 vols. (Munich, 1988–1993) VIII (1990), 316–17; H. H. Steinhoff, 'Muspilli', *Die deutsche Literatur des Mittelalters. Verfasserlexikon*, ed. Ruh *et al.*, VI (1987), 821–28; A. M. Luiselli Fadda, 'Il Muspilli e l'escatologia cristiana', *Romanobarbarica* 4 (1979), 107–30; W. Mohr and W. Haug, *Zweimal Muspilli* (Tübingen, 1977); H. Finger, *Untersuchungen zum Muspilli* (Göppingen, 1977); C. Minis, *Handschrift, Form und Sprache des Muspilli* (Berlin, 1966); G. Manganella, 'Muspilli. Problemi e Interpretazioni', *Annali dell'Istituto Orientale di Napoli, Sezione Germanica* 3 (1960), 17–49. The quotation above is from W. Braune and E. A. Ebbinghaus, *Althochdeutsches Lesebuch* (Tübingen, 1962), 169–71, at 171.

On which Holy Christ was hanged.
Then He will show the wounds which He in His humanity received,
Which He suffered for love of the human race.']

On the other hand, elsewhere, on Judgement Day, Christ is presented as a victorious hero, with the cross and the crown, in the glory of the saints and angels. A description of the triumphant Christ on Doomsday is offered by the list of Fifteen Signs included in Frau Ava's poem on the Last Judgment:[41]

die engel vuorent scone
daz criuce unde die corone
vor Christe an daz tagedinch,
daz werdent sorgichlichiu dinch.

So chumet Christ der riche
vil gewaltichlichen,
der e tougen in die werlt quam:
da sihet in wip unde man.
im ist sin scare vil breit,
wa er die versmacheit leit
von sinen vianden,
da wil er iz anden.
['Beautifully, the angels carry
The cross and the crown
before Christ to the Judgment.
That becomes a worrisome thing.

Then comes Christ, the mighty,
full powerful,
who previously came into the world secretely.
Woman and man see him now.
His army is great.
Where he suffers the scorn,
of his enemies,
there he will punish it.']

---

[41] The most recent edition (with an English translation) of Frau Ava's poems is by J. A. Rushing Jr., *Ava's New Testament Narratives: 'When the Old Law Passed Away'* (Kalamazoo, MI, 2003), the quotation here given at 218–19; see also K. Schacks, *Die Dichtungen der Frau Ava* (Graz, 1986); F. Maurer, *Die Dichtungen der Frau Ava* (Tübingen, 1966); P. Piper, 'Die Gedichte der Ava', *ZfdP* 19 (1887), 129–96 and 275–318.

In the final passage of the Old Frisian version of the Fifteen Signs, the Lord is shown as coming with his host of angels and saints and displaying the attributes and marks of his Passion while the whole world will shake at his sight.

As far as the language and style are concerned, one should take into account that this work inevitably shows the influence exerted by the linguistic structures of its Latin source (Pseudo-Bede), of which it is for the most part a faithful translation. The syntactical construction is quite terse, because the text is mainly composed of short and simple sentences connected chiefly through paratactic relationships. The following examples, in which the coordination between the clauses is realized through the use of conjunctions such as *and* and *sa*, will make this clear:

> Thes achtunda dis . **sa** falt thi sten . withir thene
> sten . **and** to brekth al semin . **and** tha berga werthath e ifnad
> (…)
> Ther efter werth domes di . **Sa** cumth use hera mith alle sine anglon .
> **and** mith alle sine heligon . **sa** beuath alle thiu wrald alsa thet
> espene laf . al**sa** se hini siath mith tha criose . **and** mith tha spiri .
> **and** mith tha neylon . **and** mith there thornena crona . **and** mith tha
> fif wndon . ther hi an tha criose tholade fori us . **and** fori al mansesk
> lik slachte .

The employment of paratactic constructions is sometimes modelled on the Latin pattern, as in the case of the eighth sign, for which the Pseudo-Bedan version reads:[42]

> Octaua die debellabunt petrae adinuicem, et unaquaeque in tres partes se diuidet, et unaquaeque pars collidet aduersus alteram.
> ['On the eighth day the rocks will fight one another, and each one will divide into three parts, and each part will dash against another.']

But generally it seems more plausible to interpret this syntactical organization as a relic of an oral tradition. As it has been stated by Walter Ong,[43]

---

[42] Bayless and Lapidge, *Collectanea Pseudo-Bedae*, 178–79.

[43] W. J. Ong, *Orality and Literacy: The Technologizing of the Word* (London and New York, 1982), 37. In the study of the transitions from orality to literacy, Ong was strongly influenced by E. Havelock's theories, expressed in his *Preface to Plato* (Cambridge, Mass., 1963) and in *Origins of Western Literacy* (Toronto, 1976). On the relationship between orality and literacy, see also, among others, J. Goody, *The Domestication of the Savage Mind* (Cambridge, 1977); H. J. Chaytor, *From Script to Print: an Introduction to Medieval Literature* (Cambridge, 1945); W. L. Chafe, 'Integration and Involvement

paratactic constructions, or – according to his terminology – ‘additive’, are identified as one of the characteristics of orality. The additive structure leads the listener gradually from one concept to the next, fastening the images together, one after the other. Ong’s principle that thought and expression in oral cultures are ‘additive rather than subordinative’ can be applied in the style of the Frisian text of the Fifteen Signs.[44]

The text displays a number of linguistic patterns which resemble the stylistic techniques used in the drafting of Old Frisian legal texts. This version of the Fifteen Signs is interspersed with fomulaic expressions of various kind. I have already mentioned the case of the formula in the fifth sign (lines 12–13) ‘fon asta there wralde to westa there wralde’, which translates the Latin ‘ab ortu suo usque ad occasum’, yet interpolated also in the seventh sign (lines 16–17) and in the fifteenth sign (lines 32–33).

Noteworthy are also the expressions ‘alle bamar and alle gerso’ (line 15), and ‘mith alle sine anglon and mith alle sine heligon’ (lines 34–35), both based on the combination of two nouns connected by the conjunction ‘and’ and comparable to analogous phrases recorded in other items preserved in the First Riustring Manuscript, such as ‘mit bote and mith urbote’,[45] ‘mith fiuwer moder megum . and mith achta feder megon’,[46] ‘mith afta gode . and mith hiara fria erue’,[47] ‘mit skrichta and mith tianut rofte’,[48] ‘mith ur ielde . and mith ielde’.[49]

The figure of *hendiadys* is applied in the phrase ‘fon there nede and fon tha ongosta’ (line 25). Here the idea of the intense horror felt by the human beings before the Last Judgment is emphasized by means of two nouns connected by a conjunction, instead of expressing it by means of an adjective-plus-noun.

Word-pairs, or double expressions, are found in many languages of the world, and their use vary widely from time to time and according to the different styles of language.[50] These linguistic patterns, which were em

in Speaking, Writing and Oral Literature’, *Spoken and Written Language: Exploring Orality and Literacy*, ed. D. Tannen (Norwood, NJ, 1982), 35–53.

44 To illustrate this basic tenet, Ong uses as an example the passage from Gen. I.1–5 (in the Douay version of 1610), pointing out the repeated use there of the conjunction ‘and’.

45 *Seventeen Statutes*, *De Eerste Riustringer Codex*, ed. ed. Buma, III.99: ‘with compensation and extra compensation’.

46 *Twenty-four Land-laws*, *ibid.* IV.57: ‘with four maternal kinsmen and eight paternal kinsmen’.

47 *Ibid.* IV.34: ‘with lawful (movable) property and her free, inherited landed property’.

48 *This is also Frisian Law*, *ibid.* XV.72: ‘with hue and cry’.

49 *Twenty-four Land-laws*, *ibid.* IV.209: ‘with extra wergeld and with wergeld’.

50 A number of such double formulas are recorded in several Indo-European traditions, see W. Krause, ‘Die Wortstellung in den zweigliedrigen Wortverbindungen, untersucht für das Altindische, Awestische, Litauische und Altnordische’, *Zeitschrift für ver-*

ployed as strategy of amplification of the speech stream, had also a parallel in the Old Germanic poetry.[51]

In the Frisian Fifteen Signs text the double expression 'alle bamar and alle gerso' has been modelled on the corresponding Latin combination 'omnes herbae et arbores' in the Pseudo-Bedan version. This formula has a parallel in the Old English 'ealle wyrte 7 ealle treowwes', recorded in the homily on the Fifteen Signs of Cotton Vespasian D xiv.

Instead, as far the double formulas 'mith alle sine anglon and mith alle sine heligon' and 'fon there nede and fon tha ongosta' are concerned, they were not introduced by the Frisian author to translate a passage of the Latin source. Again, we can refer to another principle of Ong, according to which the oral style is 'aggregative rather than analytic'.[52] These two phrases are referable to a penchant for the use of formulas, which, because of their 'aggregative weight', represent another feature of the oral expression.

An interesting figure of speech is the simile, which is present in the concluding section, when it is said that, at the fearsome sight of the victorious Christ in the day of his second coming, surrounded by angels and saints and with the tools of the crucifixion, all the universe will tremble 'alsa thet espene laf' (line 35). The motif of the shivering of the aspen leaves must be an original addition of the Frisian author, since it occurs neither in ch. 141 of Comestor's *Historia Scholastica*, from which the concluding section of the Frisian Fifteen Sign text has been derived, nor (to my knowledge), in any other source of the legend.

---

gleichende Sprachforschung 50 (1922), 74–129; for the Germanic languages, see R. H. Bremmer Jr., 'Old English *feoh and feorh*, Old Norse *fé ok fjọr*, ergo: Old Frisian *fiā and ferech* 'Money and Life', *UW* 32 (1983), 55–62. On Old English word-pairs, see I. Koskenniemi, *Repetitive Word Pairs in Old and Early Middle English Prose* (Turku, 1968); A. M. Guerrieri, 'La congiunzione *ond* nel Beowulf: problemi di dizione, di sintassi e di stile', *Annali dell'Istituto Universitario Orientale di Napoli, Sezione Germanica* 25 (1982), 7–55; J. Kail, 'Über die Parallelstellen in der ags. Poesie', *Anglia* 12 (1889), 17–47.

[51] For example, the Old Frisian word-pair 'dega and nachta' (in the *First Prologue*, *De Eerste Riustringer Codex*, ed. Buma, I,10) is comparable with Old English 'dæges ond nihtes' (*Beowulf*, line 2269a.); Old Frisian 'thes wintres and thes sumures' (in *This is also Frisian Law*, *De Eerste Riustringer Codex*, ed. Buma, X.46) has a parallel in Old English 'wintres ond sumeres' (*Phoenix*, line 37a). A number of lexical choices and stylistic elements are common both to some poems and to law texts in the Old English corpus, see P. Lendinara, 'La battaglia contro il diavolo nel Salomone e Saturno I', *Annali dell'Istituto Universitario Orientale di Napoli, Sezione Germanica*, n. s. IV, 1–2 (1994), 23–32; a number of parallels are also found in the Old Frisian legal corpus, see P. Lendinara, 'The Kentish Laws', *The Anglo-Saxons from the Migration Period to the Eighth Century. An Ethnographic Perspective*, ed. J. Hines (Woodbridge, 1997), 211–43.

[52] Ong, *Orality and Literacy*, 38.

The aspen is a deciduous tree of the poplar family, also known as *Populus tremula*, 'trembling poplar'. It is a very hardy species and tolerates long, cold winters and short summers, and grows naturally inside the Arctic Circle and in Scandinavia. Its leaves are attached by flattened leafstalks, so that they twist and flutter even in the lightest wind; hence the reason for its botanical name. The name of this tree occurs in the Germanic languages already in medieval times: OE *æspe*, OHG *aspa*, MHG *aspe*, ON *ösp*, OFris *espe*. The habit of the poplar leaves to quiver in the wind has given origin to the popular expression 'trembling like an aspenleaf', which has parallels, for example, in German ('zittern wie Espenlaub') and in Dutch ('beven als een espenblad').[53] The image of the trembling aspen leaves inspired the growth of folk legends in the world. In Christian folklore, a belief arose that the poplar was condemned forever to tremble, because its wood had been used for the cross upon which Christ was crucified.[54]

Still, the poetic motif of the aspen leaves trembling in the wind, which seems to evoke the enchanting atmosphere of the landscape in Northern Europe (to which the poplar tree is native), reveals a further link with the oral tradition. According to Ong,[55] oral cultures are anchored to the manifold aspects of human lifeworld and tend to use concepts in concrete situations, rather than abstract. The use of this simile, based on the tangible idea of the trembling poplar, once more contributes to connect the Frisian text of the Fifteen Signs to a dimension of orality.

In conclusion, it can be surmised that, although the Frisian version of the Fifteen Signs appears to be strongly influenced by its Latin sources, it nonetheless exhibits a number of innovations and original elements. It displays some double expressions, which sometimes find a parallel in the Latin source, but which in other instances are comparable to analogous formulas occurring in the corpus of Frisian laws. Such traits, together with the usage of paratactic structures, are to be interpreted as residual traces of an oral tradition. Similar stylistic means are also found in the legal items preserved in the First Riustring Manuscript. Most of the Old Frisian law texts were originally destined for oral recitation in the public law-assembly to be performed by the *asega*, the law-speaker. Therefore, the necessity to remember a great deal of regulations led to the development of a number of linguistic

---

[53] The simile was also used by Geoffrey Chaucer: 'Lyk an aspen leef he quok for ire' (*Somn. Prol.* 3).

[54] For an overview of the mythology and folklore concerning plants and trees, see J. E. Milner, *The Tree Book: the Indispensable Guide to Tree Facts, Crafts and Lore* (London, 1992).

[55] Ong, *Orality and Literacy*, 49.

patterns based on mnemonic techniques, such as the use of word-pairs or formulas.[56]

Moving on from these assertions, it is possible to affirm that both the international, 'learned' text of the Fifteen Signs and the local, legal documents of the First Riustring Manuscript share some of the most conspicuous aspects of an oral tradition; it is evident that these written texts were produced and transmitted in a period of Frisian literacy, which still preserves evidence of orality, an orality which is recognizable in the linguistic patterns, in the stylistic figures and in the syntactical arrangement of the argument.

The role of the Fifteen Signs in the First Riustring Manuscript

This version of the Fifteen Signs before Doomsday is one of the few non-legal documents surviving in Old Frisian literature, which for the greater part is represented by works belonging to the juridical tradition. The prevalence of this legal dimension reflects the peculiar political and social background from which the Old Frisian literature springs. It is a fact that the actual power of the Frankish Empire over the conquered tribes declined rapidly after the death of Charlemagne; and that in Frisia, during the Middle Ages, a number of small republics developed, which gradually acquired a considerable degree of political and legal autonomy by which they remained, on the whole, free from the feudal system. Although these Frisian communities were formally included within the Holy Roman Empire, they enjoyed a certain independence from its sphere of influence and governed themselves according to the traditional principles and regulations of the customary law of Germanic origin. This crucial aspect of autonomy and freedom represents the ideological core expressed in the Old Frisian legal codices and is fundamental in the history of the Frisian culture and civilization.[57]

The collections of legal texts, which represent the bulk of the Old Frisian literary corpus, bear witness to this particular situation of sovereignty of the Frisian territories inside the German Holy Roman Empire. The First Riust-

[56] *De Eerste Riustringer Codex*, ed. Buma, 52–53. Such stylistic means and mnemonic devices are also employed in the poetry, which – in every culture of the world – for a long time were circulating orally before being set down in writing. This is the field of research in which the oral-formulaic theory developed, see *The Making of Homeric Verse: The Collected Papers of Milman Parry*, ed. A. Parry (Oxford, 1971); for an updated and stimulating overview of the application of the oral-formulaic theory to Germanic literatures, see M. C. Amodio, *Writing the Oral Tradition: Oral Poetics and Literate Culture in Medieval England* (Notre Dame, IN, 2004).

[57] T. S. B. Johnston, 'Old Frisian Law and the Frisian Freedom Ideology: Text and Manuscript Composition as a Marketing Device', *Approaches*, 179–214.

ring Manuscript makes no exception in this respect. An anthology of mainly legal documents, it is the earliest complete Frisian manuscript to have come down to us. The exact date of its compilation, as well as its geographical provenance are still a matter of some debate among scholars. The use of the vernacular, instead of Latin – the traditional language of administration – implies a time in which the legal system had become a local affair in Frisia, immune from interference by foreign rulers, perhaps not long after 1225.[58]

Like other Frisian legal collections, the First Riustring Manuscript also contains a heterogeneous cluster of regulations and decrees, which are not apparently linked to each other for a coherent purpose. Alongside the most important 'Pan-Frisian' legal documents, such as the *Seventeen Statutes*, the *Twenty-four Land-laws*, the *General Register of Compensations*, or the *Five Exceptions to the Seventeenth Statute*, this manuscript also contains a number of regulations which specifically concern the Riustring district: the *Riustring Statutes*, the *Younger Riustring Statutes*, the *Riustring Compensation Tariffs*, the *Riustring Fines Concerning Crimes against Clergymen* and the *Riustring Synodal Laws*.

It is likely that the original core of the collection – which may have been intended for practical use in law-courts – was composed by the *Seventeen Statutes*, the *Twenty-Four Land-laws* and the *General Register of Compensations*, and that later other items were gradually added, until the corpus achieved its current structure. The fact that it opens with two different but similar prologues to the *Seventeen Statutes* and to the *Twenty-Four Land-laws* indicates that the compiler of the codex had more than one source available for use. It is evident that – along with the legal matter – the underlying theme, which unites all the items assembled in this miscellany (the list of the Fifteen Signs included), betrays a strong interest in numerology and its application in the sphere of jurisprudence. Numerology, that is the mystical interpretation of numbers, is a feature of many literary traditions and circulated intensively in certain medieval intellectual circles; inspirations and sources are to be found in the Bible (especially in the Old Testament) and in some patristic writings.[59]

The text of the Fifteen Signs of Doomsday must be one of the items that was inserted at a later stage in the original miscellany of regulations. This

58 Bremmer, *Hir is eskriven*.

59 On this subject, see, e.g., R. L. Surles, *Medieval Numerology: A Book of Essays* (New York and London, 1993); V. Hopper, *Medieval Number Symbolism* (New York, 1938, repr. 1969); J. J. Davies, *Biblical Numerology* (Grand Rapids, MI, 1968, repr. 1971); C. D. Wright, 'The Irish "Enumerative Style" in Old English Homiletic Literature, Especially Vercelli Homily IX', *Cambridge Medieval Celtic Studies* 18 (1989), 27–74; C. D. Wright, 'The "Enumerative Style" in Ireland and Anglo-Saxon England', in his *The Irish Tradition in Old English Literature* (Cambridge, 1993), 49–105.

is not the only case of a non-legal text being embedded in a juridical context in the Frisian literature. Apart from a set of interverbal Frisian glosses to a Latin psalter fragment,[60] the list of non-legal texts scattered among the Frisian law collections includes a number of items, such as *The Five Keys to Wisdom* and *The Ten Commandments*, as well as an account of the growth of a foetus,[61] and a description of Adam's creation.[62] These examples of different literary genres are usually linked with legal matters or deal with events and legends connected with the history of Frisia.

In addition to the enumerative style by which it organized the eschatological material, the *Fifteen Signs of Doomsday* shows another aspect which makes it fit within the miscellany of the First Riustring Manuscript. In this text it is possible to recognize some implications of a legal nature, such as the occurrence and the use of the word 'dom' or the reference to the role of Christ as supreme judge, who administers the law and conducts a court, determining the final destiny of humanity. The presence of the *Fifteen Signs of Doomsday* in the First Riustring Manuscript might be compared to that of the Old Frisian version of the *Ten Commandments* included in the *Preface to the Seventeen Statutes and Twenty-four Land-laws* in which all law is said to derive, through the mediation of the Roman kings and Moses, from God Himself.[63] The *Ten Commandments*, which are considered the sacred laws of mankind, are included in the First Riustring Manuscript to legitimate the freedom of the Frisians, as well as to lend solemnity to the codification of their laws.

Likewise, it can be argued that the text of the *Fifteen Signs of Doomsday* has the function of legitimizing authority to the secular courts of law in Frisia, in which justice is administered by human magistrates, according to the divine pattern of the Supreme Lord. The Last Judgment, which will take place at the end of the world, represents a kind of divine counterpart to the verdicts delivered by the earthly tribunals.

The idea of the celebration of a solemn trial followed by the righteous judgment of God (which represents the keynote of the entire text), as well as the external structure and the insistence in numerological *topoi* (like many of the other items surviving in the First Riustring Manuscript), are all ele-

[60] R. H. Bremmer Jr, 'Footprints of Monastic Instruction: a Latin Psalter with Interverbal Old Frisian Glosses', *Signs on the Edge. Space, Text and Margin in Medieval Manuscripts*, ed. S. L. Keefer and R. H. Bremmer Jr (Paris, Leuven and Dudley, MA, 2007), 203–34; E. Langbroek, '*Condensa atque tenebrosa*. Die altfriesischen Psalmen: Neulesung und Rekonstruktion (UB Groningen Hs 404)', *Aspects*, 255–84.

[61] M. Elsakkers, '*Her anda neylar*: an Intriguing Criterion for Abortion in Old Frisian law', *Scientiarum Historia* 30 (2004), 107–54.

[62] B. Murdoch, 'The Old Frisian *Adam Octopartitus*', *ABäG* 40 (1994), 131–38.

[63] B. Murdoch, 'Authority and Authenticity: Comments on the Prologues to the Old Frisian Laws', *Approaches*, 215–44.

ments which allow for the integration of the text of the Fifteen Signs of Doomsday within a collection of laws and decrees like the one of this Riustring codex. Particularly remarkable is the parallelism with the text of the *Ten Commandments*. With the latter it shares – through a numerological approach – the treatment of legal knowledge in a biblical and theological perspective.

Exploring the Distribution of *aeng*, the Old Frisian Counterpart of Modern English *any*, Modern Dutch *enig*

Eric Hoekstra and Sjoerd M. Siebinga

1. Introduction[1]

This article explores the distribution of the word *aeng* in Old Frisian. To this end, we utilized the text archive available on the *Deutsches Rechtswörterbuch* website.[2] This text archive is the largest Old Frisian corpus currently accessible through the internet and contains Old Frisian texts as they appear in the dual-language editions of Buma and Ebel.[3]

Actually, the word *aeng* appears in various spellings: *aeng, eng, enig, enich*; for practical reasons, we subsume all the variant spellings under the (arbitrarily chosen) form *aeng*. Of course, these forms may be inflected depending on their specification for the morphosyntactic features of case, number and gender, e.g. *aenge, aegne* and *engne*. Forms like *enich* are related to Modern English *any*, Modern West Frisian *iennich* and Modern Dutch *enig*. The Old Frisian forms in which the vowel of the second syllable has been elided, *aeng, eng,* are not easily accounted for. It is not clear what process was responsible for the elision of the vowel *i*, nor even how the resulting consonant cluster 'ng' was to be pronounced. However, these phonological issues do not interfere with the purpose of our article.

In section 2, a set of syntactic contexts will be presented in which the word *aeng* (and its spelling variants) may occur. After explaining the phenomenon of negative polarity, we proceed to show that OFris *aeng*

---

1 The authors' names appear in alphabetical order. An earlier version of this paper was presented at the Oudgermanistendag, Ghent, 22 April 2006. We would like to thank the audience for their questions.

2 See: < http://www.rzuser.uni-heidelberg.de/~cd2/drw/frameset.htm>. The other text archive that we know to contain some Old Frisian material is the TITUS-project (Thesaurus Indogermanischer Text- und Sprachmaterialien); for further information., see <http://titus.uni-frankfurt.de/indexe.htm>.

3 Ed. W. J. Buma and W. Ebel, AR, vol. 1: *Das Rüstringer Recht*; vol. 2: *Das Brokmer Recht*; vol. 3: *Das Emsiger Recht*; vol. 4: *Das Hunsingoer Recht*; vol. 5: *Das Fivelgoer Recht*; vol. 6/1–2: *Westerlauwerssches Recht. I. Jus municipale Frisonum* (Göttingen, 1963–1977).

behaves like a negative polarity item (= NPI), as it does so in Modern English. Finally, with reference to the theory of negative polarity put forth by Ladusaw and Zwarts,[4] we suggest that the environments featuring *aeng* can be characterised partially by the feature of NPI.

2. Contexts featuring Old-Frisian *aeng*

2.1 Verb-first contexts

The word *aeng* is most commonly found in verb-first clauses, that is clauses introduced by a tensed verb. An example is given below:

> And deth thi talemon aenge monne **eng** vnriuth, sa riuchte thet sine sithar bi tha brewe, and thene thictega vprivchte hi, and achta merc retze hi, and sin hus ne berne ma naut. (BrokmerR. 026 § 9 g)
> ['Und tut der Talemann jemandem ein Unrecht, so sollen seine Amtsgenossen darüber nach dem (Rechts)brief richten, und für die Bezichtigung leiste er Schadenersatz und zahle acht Mark, und sein Haus verbrenne man nicht'.]

The tensed verbs can be preceded at most by a sentence connective such as *ac* 'also'. A number of such such examples has been given in Appendix I. The examples have been put into alphabetical order according to the word immediately following *aeng*, which is usually a noun. Particularly interesting are the examples involving *thing* 'thing' under (l), of which two have been given. They are interesting, because this combination has developed into a fixed collocation 'anything' which behaves as a negative polarity item. The negative polar character of *anything* in Modern English is illustrated by the following pair of sentences:

(1a) * I saw anything
(1b) Nobody saw anything

The NPI *anything* cannot be used in a simple affirmative sentence like (1a). Instead, it needs something 'negative in some sense' in its syntactic environment. Later on we shall provide a more exact characterisation of what is meant by the notion 'negative in some sense'. Verb-first sentences

---

4 W. Ladusaw, *Polarity Sensitivity as Inherent Scope Relations*. Indiana University Linguistics Club (Bloomington, 1984); F. Zwarts, *Categoriale grammatica en algebraïsche semantiek: Een onderzoek naar negatie en polariteit in het Nederlands*. PhD thesis, Rijksuniversiteit Groningen 1986; *idem*, 'Negatief polaire uitdrukkingen', *Glot. Tijdschrift voor Taalwetenschap* 4 (1981), 35–132.

will also turn out to also be subsumed under this characterisation of 'negative in some sense'.

2.2. Clauses introduced by '*if*'

Clauses introduced by *if* regularly feature the word *aeng*, as is shown in Appendix II. An example is given below:

> Jef **aeng** mon **eng** bethera wiste, theth mathet lichtere lette and ma theth bethere helde. (EmsigerR. 096)
> ['Wenn irgend jemand ein besseres (Recht) wüßte, sollte man das weniger richtige aufgeben und das bessere befolgen'.]

This feature is not surprising since the two clause types, verb-first clauses and clauses introduced by *if*, have the semantics of conditionals. Unlike the verb-first clauses that we examined, the collection of *if*-clauses in Appendix II feature two examples of *aeng* used independently, that is *aeng*, not as an adjective but as a nominalised adjective that was followed by a genitive phrase. Two such examples have been given in Appendix II under (a). Furthermore, we have found examples of *aeng* followed by nouns such as *mon*, instances of which we had also found in verb-first clauses.

2.3. Clauses introduced by 'whenever'

The word *aeng* is also repeatedly found in clauses introduced by *hwersa* or *hwersar* (= *hwersa* + *ther*). They can roughly be translated as 'whenever'. An example is given below:

> Hwersa mon bernt fon sijn aijne fiur ant him bitigie ma, thet hi hebbe binna waghen heud clather iefta gold iefta **eng** thing, sa ne thur hi mith nanene onzere agenstonda bihala tham, ther him lend is. (EmsigerR. 158 [33])
> ['Wenn jemand durch sein eigenes Feuer abbrennt, und man ihn damit belastet, daß er in seinem Hause Kleider oder Gold oder irgendeine (andere) Sache (eines anderen) gehabt habe, so braucht er dafür keine Verantwortung zu übernehmen, außer für das, was ihm geliehen ist'.]

The meaning of *hwersa(r)*-clauses is very similar to that of *if*-clauses and verb-first clauses. Indeed, the question is whether they can be distinguished semantically at all. In fact, Appendix VI presents an example of a co-ordination of Verb-first and *hwersa(r)*-clauses, apparently used indiscriminately, indicating that the two types are semantically very similar. Both types can be subsumed under the semantic label of involving conditional semantics.[5] One of the *hwersa(r)*-clauses also involves independent use of *aeng* followed by a genitive. The other examples concern adjectival usage of *aeng* followed by such nouns as *erwa* 'heir', *mon* 'man' and *thing* 'thing'. See Appendix III for more examples.

2.4. Relative clauses

The word *aeng* can also be encountered in relative clauses following the combination of the quantifier *alle* + noun. We have found only one example for this pattern (see Appendix IV):

> Thervmbe vnhante wi se alsa, thet wij in **alle tichtighen, ther eng** tsiwe iefta kase fon ewesen hede, weta weke fon there werde thes gastlike riuhtes and wij metlike hnige tore seftechhed there nethe. (EmsigerR. 144 [8])
> ['Deshalb nahmen wir sie so an, daß wir in allen Klagen, über die irgendwelche Streitigkeit oder Schlägerei stattgefunden hatte, ein wenig von den Satzungen des geistlichen Rechtes abweichen und mit Maßen zur Milde der Gnade neigen sollten.']

2.5. Comparatives

The word *aeng* also occurs in comparative sentences of inequality, as is shown by the two instances from our corpus (see Appendix V), of which we presnt one here:

> Thet fereste lith thes thuma thrimene diurra tha thera othera fingra **eng**. (EmsigerR. 58 [81])
> ['Das vorderste Glied des Daumens (ist) um die Hälfte teurer als eines der anderen Finger'.]

In both cases, the comparative item is *diurra* 'more expensive'.

2.6. Summary and problem

We have seen that the word *aeng* is to be found in Old Frisian in three types of contexts:

* in conditional clauses (subsuming verb-first, *if* and *hwersa(r)*-clauses)
* in relative clauses following the word *alle*
* after a comparative element

[5] On conditional clauses, see also the contribution by Rosemary Lühr to this volume.

In section 3. we shall explain what these three types of clauses have in common.

3. Downwards entailing contexts

The environments listed in the previous section have much in common according to a semantic theory proposed by Ladusaw and Zwart. Contrary to simple affirmative sentences, these environments under discussion are all downwards entailing (also referred to as 'monotone decreasing'), whereas simple affirmative sentences are upwards entailing or monotone increasing. Consider first the concept of 'upwards entailment'. A sentence is upwards entailing, if it is closed under supersets; an example will illustrate this concept.[6] The VP *dreams restlessly* is part of the superset *dreams*. The truth of the sentence *John dreams restlessly* is preserved under supersets: if it is true that *John dreams restlessly*, then it is also true that *John dreams*. Thus, the simple affirmative sentence *John dreams restlessly* is upwards entailing. Conversely, it is not the case that simple affirmative sentences are downwards entailing. Take the sentence *John dreams*. Even if it is true that *John dreams*, it is not necessarily true that *John dreams restlessly*. Truth is not preserved under VP-subsets; hence *John dreams* is not downwards entailing.

The reverse state of affairs obtains if we take as subject the NP quantifier *nobody*. The sentence *Nobody dreams* entails the sentence *Nobody dreams restlessly*. Consequently, this sentence passes the test for downwards entailment: truth is preserved under subsets, with 'restlessly dreaming' being a subset of 'dreaming'. However, *Nobody dreams restlessly* fails the test for upwards entailment, as *Nobody dreams restlessly* does not entail *Nobody dreams*.

Why is this observation relevant? In present-day English, words like *anything* characteristically occur in downwards entailing environments. The concept of downward entailment explains the contrast in (1), which we repeat for the sake of convenience:

(1a) * I saw anything
(1b) Nobody saw anything

Words like *anything* require an environment which is 'negative in some sense'. Work in generalised quantifier theory has shown that such an environment can be partially characterised by the notion of downwards entailment (or monotone decrease). Words like *anything*, which require a

---

6 We speak of sentences being upwards entailing or being closed under supersets. This is a simplification for expository reasons, as we should say that the semantic denotation of the sentences is monotone increasing, and so on.

downwards entailing context, are therefore commonly referred to as 'negative polarity items'.

Modern Dutch also features several negative polarity items. One of them is *ook maar iets* 'anything'.[7] Like its English counterpart, the string can occur only in environments which are downwards entailing, as is shown by the following sentences:

(2a) *Ik heb ook maar iets gezien
I have anything seen
(2b) Niemand heeft ook maar iets gezien
Nobody has anything seen

The environments in which we found Old Frisian *aeng* all seem to be downwards entailing. To show that they are actually doing so, we shall inspect both upwards and downwards entailments in the contexts which feature *aeng* in Old Frisian, that is: conditional clauses, comparative clauses and relative clauses following the universal quantifier *alle*.

(3) Entailments conditional clauses
(3a) If John dreams restlessly, he will be bad-humoured in the morning.
(3b) If John dreams, he will be bad-humoured in the morning.

Suppose (3a) is true. Then it does not follow that (3b) is true. Thus (3a), notably the *if*-clause, fails the test for upwards entailment. Suppose (3b) is true. It follows from (3b) that (3a) is also true. Thus, (3b), notably the *if*-clause, passes the test for downwards entailment. Furthermore, if the *if*-clause is downwards entailing, then a negative polarity item should be acceptable in it. This turns out to be correct for both Dutch and English:

(4) If anything happens, phone the police.
(5) Als er ook maar iets gebeurt, moet je de politie bellen.
If there anything happens, you must phone the police
'If anything happens, you must phone the police'

In view of the above, we hypothesize that conditional clauses, which characteristically feature *aeng* in Old Frisian, will also be downwards entailing.

Relative clauses following the universal quantifier *all* can similarly be shown to be downwards entailing.[8] Consider the following pair of sentences:

---

[7] See footnote 4.

[8] Because of some complications involving so-called free-choice *any*, see L. Horn, *On the Semantic Properties of Logical Operators in English*. UCLA dissertation 1972, repr. Indiana U. Linguistics Club, 1976. We take our facts from Dutch.

(6a) Alle jongens die rusteloos dromen moeten zich melden bij de psycholoog
All boys who restlessly dream must themselves report at the psychologist
'All boys who dream restlessly must report to the psychologist'
(6b) Alle jongens die dromen moeten zich melden bij de psycholoog
All boys who dream must themselves report at the psychologist
'All boys who dream must report to the psychologist'

The inference to supersets, from (6a) to (6b), does not hold. Thus the relative clause in (6a) is not upwards entailing. However, the inference from (6b) to (6a) holds. Therefore, the relative clause in (6b) is downwards entailing. Hence we expect that a negative polarity item may show up there, and this expectation is correct:

(7) Alle jongens die ook maar iets gezien hebben moeten zich melden.
All boys who anything seen have must themselves report
'Anybody who saw anything must report himself'

Thus relative clauses governed by the quantifier *alle,* which also have *aeng* in Old Frisian, are likewise downwards entailing (or downward entailing) as well.

Finally, consider the comparative construction, as illustrated in (8):

(8a) Coffee is more expensive than black tea
(8b) Coffee is more expensive than tea

If (8a) is true, (8b) need not be; perhaps green tea is very expensive, for example. Hence, what follows the word *than* is not upwards entailing. Conversely, if (8b) is true, then (8a) must also be true. Hence, what follows *than* appears to be downwards entailing. We therefore expect that the negative polarity item *anything* can occur after *than*:

(9) I love you more than anything

As the song line in (9) shows, this expectation is correct.

4. Conclusion

An exploratory investigation of the Old Frisian word *aeng* has yielded the result that it is found in three contexts: (a) in conditional clauses; (b) in relative clauses following the universal quantifier *alle*; (c) in comparative contexts. These contexts are all three of them downwards entailing. This observation strongly suggests that *aeng* was a negative polarity item in Old Frisian, like the Modern English cognate form *anything* and its Modern Dutch counterpart *ook maar iets*.

Some odd facts are possibly related to the problem discussed above. In English, *any* can be used with a following noun, but it also occurs in fixed combinations like *anybody* and *anything*, analogous to *everybody* and *everything*. Modern Frisian has one phenomenon which is remotely reminiscent of this: the universal quantifier *alle*, which normally takes only plural antecedents if they are countable, can be used in the singular when it is follows *ding*, the Frisian cognate of English *thing*:

(10a) Countable: *alle famkes* 'all girls', **alle famke* '*all girl"
(10b) Not countable: *alle bûter* 'all butter'
(10c) Exceptional behaviour of *ding*: *alle ding* 'all thing => everything'

It is unclear why Frisian exceptionally allows *alle* to be followed by the singular count noun *ding* 'thing' to the exclusion of other singular count nouns. Another pertinent observation is that Modern Frisian lacks the negative polarity item 'ook maar iets', which Dutch features. Although Frisian possesses the equivalents of the three Dutch words 'ook', *ek*, 'maar', *mar*, and 'iets', *eat*, the combination *ek mar eat* is decidedly 'non-Frisian'.

Appendixes

The Old Frisian examples in the appendixes below are followed by Buma and Ebels' German translations. References follow the method of the digitized corpus of the *Deutsche Rechtswörterbuch.*[9]

Appendix I. Verb-first clauses

a) and naut lessa; and skether **eng** brond inare wic ettere missa fon enre iechtegere case and thi redieua thet onlet, sa ielde mane mith thrim ieldum, and thet ingod beswere thi hana and wite selwa thene hauding. (BrokmerR[echt] 054 § 65 [= Rq. § 74, 75])
['und nicht weniger; und bricht da in der Wik während der Handelsmesse infolge einer offenkundigen Schlägerei ein Brand aus, und bestätigt das (die Tatumstände) der Redjeve, so büße man den (Brand) mit dreifachem Gelde, und der Kläger beschwöre den (Wert des verbrannten) Hausrats und nenne selbst unter Eid den Haupttäter.']

b) and sketh ther **aeng** daddel, sa nime tha redieua ene hageste merc. (BrokmerR. 036 § 29 [= Rq. § 42])
['und geschieht da irgendein Totschlag, so sollen die Redjeven eine höchste Mark dafür nehmen']

c) Sprecth teth **aeng** fach and frethelas mon, thet him thiu faijthe vriewen se, and sine fiund spreke na, sa meij hi tha vrieft biprowia and wer makia mith sine prestere and mith [sine] rediewa, mith tuam fogethem and mith triuwe burem and sa skel thi vrieft elle festa stonde. (EmsigerR. 140)
['Sagt irgendein befehdeter und friedloser Mann, daß ihm die Fehde erlassen sei, und sagen seine Feinde "nein", so darf er die Vergebung mit seinem Priester und mit seinem Redjeven, mit zwei Kirchenvögten und mit glaubwürdigen Dorfgenossen beweisen und dartun, und dann soll die Vergebung unverbrüchlich Bestand haben'.]

d) Ac sterft hir **eng** Fresa oppa Saxlonde, ther fon seken fri se, sa agen tha erwa sin god to fagiane vmberawad. (EmsigerR. 150 [32])
['Und stirbt da im Sachsenland irgendein Friese, der von Ansprüchen frei ist, so sollen seine Erben sein Gut unangefochten in Besitz nehmen'.]

e) wel hir **aeng** liudamon thene prestere halda inna lene, sa geie hi mith achta mercum. (BrokmerR. 098 § 168 [= Rq. § 177])
['will hier(zulande) irgendein Volksgenosse den Priester in seinen Diensten halten, so büße er mit acht Mark'.]

f) Vrwaxt hir **aenge** monne sin hei, thet hine rediewa berne er tha riuchta dei, sa resze hi achta merc. (BrokmerR. 030 § 16 b [= Rq. § 27])
['Überwältigt hier einen Mann sein Zorn, so daß er (das Haus des) Redjeven vor dem gerichtlich bestimmten Tage niederbrennt, so zahle er acht Mark'.]

g) Skether **aeng** raf, sa skel thi redieua thet wita, and efter skel thi huswerda thet biswera. (BrokmerR. 040 § 36 [= Rq. § 47])

[9] See footnote 2.

['Wird etwas geraubt, so soll der Redjeve das bezeugen, und danach soll der Hauswirt das beschwören'.]

h) Slitter **aeng** rediewa er tha riuchta dei auder wach ioftha rhoof, sa resze hi achta merc. (BrokmerR. 030 § 16 a [= Rq. § 26])

['Trägt da ein Redjeve vor dem gerichtlich bestimmten Tage (der Wüstung) entweder Wand oder Dach ab, so zahle er acht Mark'.]

i) and dether **aeng** liudamon tha rediewa engne skatha, sa felle hit a tuira wegena. (BrokmerR. 022 § 6 b [= Rq. § 5])

['und fügt ein Volksgenosse dem Redjeven irgendwelchen Schaden zu, so büße er es doppelt'.]

j) werther **eng** sogenath and hir ne se nen thing eketh, hwet sa ther sketh, sa se hit enfaldech. (BrokmerR. 038 § 30 [= Rq. § 43])

['findet irgendeine Versammlung statt und ist da kein Gericht angesagt worden, so sei die Buße einfach, was immer da geschieht']

k) Hwerther **aeng** stenhus hagra rvocht sa tuelf ierdfota hach andre thivcke and szelner vr tua feke andre thiuchke, sa geie mith achta mercum thi, thert ach. (BrokmerR. 090 § 150 [= Rq. § 159 a])

['Wird irgendein Steinhaus höher gebaut als zwölf Rutenfuß hoch im Geviert, und ein Keller über zwei Hausfächer im Geviert reichend, so büße der, dem es gehört, mit acht Mark'.]

l) vrliust hi clathar ieftha **eng** thing, and thi redieua alsa rede, sa ielde math mith thrium ieldum. (BrokmerR. 040 § 37 [= Rq. § 157])

['büßt er (dabei) Kleider ein oder irgendwelche (anderen) Sachen, und bestätigt dies der Redjeve, so bezahle man das mit dreifachem Betrage'.]

m) Jst thet mar **eng** ting on achte, sa ach thi fiarde panneng of te fallane. (EmsigerR. 152 [5])

['Falls man dafür (doch) irgendwelche Ware nach Abschätzung in Zahlung gibt, so soll der vierte Teil (des Wertes) abgezogen werden'.]

n) And deth thi talemon aenge monne **eng** vnriuth, sa riuchte thet sine sithar bi tha brewe, and thene thictega vprivchte hi, and achta merc retze hi, and sin hus ne berne ma naut. (BrokmerR. 026 § 9 g [= Rq. § 16])

['Und tut der Talemann jemandem ein Unrecht, so sollen seine Amtsgenossen darüber nach dem (Rechts)brief richten, und für die Bezichtigung leiste er Schadenersatz und zahle acht Mark, und sein Haus verbrenne man nicht'.]

Appendix II. Clauses introduced by *if*

a) Thiu othere kere: ief there soghen selonda **aeng** vrherath vrde auder fon tha suther sareda ridderum jeftha fon northeska wigandum, thet tha sex tha soghenda hulpe, theth hit alsa wel machte sa there sexa hoc. (EmsigerR. 096)

['Die zweite Küre: Wenn irgendeines der sieben Seelande entweder von den im Süden gerüsteten Rittern oder von nordischen Kriegern verheert würde, so sollten die sechs dem siebenten helfen, damit es ebenso stark bliebe wie jedes der sechs'.]

b) Thiu thredde kera: ief thera soghen selonda **aeng** welde liude raweia ieftha morth sla, [thet] tha sex thet soghenda bithunghe, theth hit elle riuchte fore. (EmsigerR. 096)
['Die dritte Küre: Wenn irgendeines der sieben Seelande Leute berauben oder umbringen wollte, so sollten die sechs das siebente dazu zwingen, völlig gerecht zu verfahren'.]

c) Hwersa thi redieua of tha werve gengt and tha ofledene withseith, iof tha fiund thenna **aenge** case makiath, sa felle thit, ther tha dede deth. (BrokmerR. 040 § 34 [= Rq. § 46a])
['Wenn der Redjeve von der Warf geht und den Fehdezug untersagt, so soll, falls die Feinde dann irgendwelche Schlägerei anfangen, derjenige die Buße zahlen, der die Wunde schlägt'.]

d) Alle keddar se en ier weldech, buta talemonnum; iof hir **aeng** mon wel weldech wesa leng sa ier, sa geie hi mith achta mercum. (BrokmerR. 026 § 10a [= Rq. § 17])
['Alle Kedden sollen ein Jahr Amtsgewalt haben, außer den Talemannen; wenn hier jemand länger als ein Jahr Amtsgewalt ausüben will, so büße er mit acht Mark'.]

e) Jef **aeng** mon **eng** bethera wiste, theth mathet lichtere lette and ma theth bethere helde. (EmsigerR. 096)
['Wenn irgend jemand ein besseres (Recht) wüßte, sollte man das weniger richtige aufgeben und das bessere befolgen'.]

Appendix III. Clauses introduced by *hwersar*

a) Hwersa thi mon wergat sin wif, ieftha thi hera ieftha thiu frowe ieftha thi sviaring ieftha thiu snore, **aeng** thira wirgat thene otherne, and hira sziwe se burkuth, and tha redia se thria clagad, sa ielde ma se mith thrim ieldum (BrokmerR. 102 § 173 [= Rq. § 181])
['Wenn der Mann seine Frau umbringt, oder der Schwiegervater oder die Schwiegermutter oder der Schwiegersohn oder die Schwiegertochter einer den andern umbringt, und ihr Streit dorfkundig ist, und beim Redjeven dreimal Klage erhoben ist, so büße man sie mit dreifachem Wergeld']

b) Hwersar send tuene tamar teijn, and thetter fon there thama other eng erwa sterwe, and thetter bira othere sida knape and fonna se, sa mughen tha knapa mitha fonnem kniaija witha halfsibbe (EmsigerR. 164 [54])
['Wenn da zweierlei Nachkommen gezeugt sind, und von der einen Nachkommenschaft irgendein Erbe stirbt, und auf der anderen Seite Jungen und Mädchen sind, so dürfen diese Jungen mit den Mädchen gemäß der Halbsippe ihre Verwandtschaft geltend machen']

c) Hwersa thi broder slaijt ene orne jefta thi sune thene fether ieftha **aeng** mon anne mon slaijt, ther lawa lewe skele, sa ne skel nanen bona nena lawa fagia, wara thi, ther olra nest knia is. (EmsigerR. 162 I)
['Wenn ein Bruder den anderen erschlägt, oder der Sohn den Vater, oder wenn irgend jemand einen Mann erschlägt, der eine Erbschaft hinterlassen wird, so soll kein Totschläger eine Erbschaft erhalten, sondern derjenige, der (nach dem Totschläger) der nächste Verwandte (des Erschlagenen) ist'.]

d) Hwersa thi mon bernt fon owene ieftha fon herthe ieftha fon thera, and him bitigie ma, thet hi binna wagum hebbe clathar hewed ieftha gold ieftha **aeng** thing, sa ne thur hi ther mith nanene onszere aienstonda, bihalwa tham alena, ther beden is ieftha lened; (BrokmerR. 088 § 145 [= Rq. § 153])
['Wenn jemand durch (Entzündung von) Ofen oder Herd oder Darre abbrennt, und man ihn damit belastet, daß er Kleider oder Gold oder irgendeine (andere) Sache (eines anderen) im Hause gehabt habe, so braucht er dafür keine Verantwortung zu übernehmen, außer für das, was er bitt- oder leihweise erhalten hat'.]

e) Hwersa mon bernt fon sijn aijne fiur ant him bitigie ma, thet hi hebbe binna waghen heud clather iefta gold iefta **eng** thing, sa ne thur hi mith nanene onzere agenstonda bihala tham, ther him lend is. (EmsigerR. 158 [33])
['Wenn jemand durch sein eigenes Feuer abbrennt, und man ihn damit belastet, daß er in seinem Hause Kleider oder Gold oder irgendeine (andere) Sache (eines anderen) gehabt habe, so braucht er dafür keine Verantwortung zu übernehmen, außer für das, was ihm geliehen ist'.]

Appendix IV. Relative clause accompanied by *alle* + noun

Thervmbe vnhante wi se alsa, thet wij in alle tichtighen, ther **eng** tsiwe iefta kase fon ewesen hede, weta weke fon there werde thes gastlike riuchtes and wij metlike hnige tnre seftechhed there nethe. (EmsigerR. 144 [8])
['Deshalb nahmen wir sie so an, daß wir in allen Klagen, über die irgendwelche Streitigkeit oder Schlägerei stattgefunden hatte, ein wenig von den Satzungen des geistlichen Rechtes abweichen und mit Maßen zur Milde der Gnade neigen sollten'.]

Appendix V. Comparative clauses

a) Thet fereste lith thes thuma thrimene diurra tha thera othera fingra **eng**. (EmsigerR. 58 [81])
['Das vorderste Glied des Daumens (ist) um die Hälfte teurer als eines der anderen Finger'.]

b) Thera thrira finghera andera ferra hond trimene diurra tha thera othera **eng** umbe tha seinenga, ther ma ther [mithe] dua scel withene diuuel. (EmsigerR. 58 [85])
['(Das Abschlagen) der drei Finger der rechten Hand (ist) wegen der Kreuze, die man damit gegen den Teufel schlagen soll, um die Hälfte höher als einer der anderen (Finger zu büßen)']

Appendix VI. Mix of *hwersar* and Verb-first clauses

Hwersar is en alderlas erwa and hi se mitha werandstewe and thet god se naut edeled, sprech ther **aeng** mon fon there federsida ieftha fon there modersida binna tha thredda, and hia clagie fore thene alderlasa erwa, sa skel thi, ther tha lawa heth, en riuth del dela witthene alderlasa erwa. (BrokmerR. 064 § 91 [= Rq. § 101])
['Wenn da ein elternloser Erbe ist und er unter einem Vormund steht und das Gut (noch) nicht geteilt ist, und da jemand von der Vaterseite oder von der Mutterseite (des Erben) innerhalb des dritten (Verwandtschaftsgrades) sich beschwert und sie für den elternlosen Erben Klage erheben, so soll derjenige, der den Nachlaß (in Besitz) hat, eine rechtmäßige Teilung mit dem elternlosen Erben treffen'.]

Palatalization of Velars: A Major Link of Old English and Old Frisian

Stephen Laker

1. Introduction[1]

Opinions are divided on whether palatalization of **-k(k)-* and **-g(g)-* in Old English and Old Frisian resulted from a shared development or arose independently. Earlier scholarship asserted that there was a link. Theodor Siebs wrote that the beginnings of palatalization (but not assibilation) 'liegen in der englisch-friesischen, das heißt der kontinentalen Periode'. Karl Luick thought that palatalization initiated 'noch zur Zeit der anglofriesischen Gemeinschaft'. Alistair Campbell concluded that there was 'nothing to show that the sensitivity of *k* and *g* to the nature of following vowels does not date back to a period when English and Frisian were in sufficient contact to develop some common characteristics, but it certainly continued long after the period', and in his grammar he maintained that palatalization 'doubtless began in the continental period, for it is a major link of Old English and Old Frisian'.[2]

Some investigators, however, have argued that palatalization and assibilation were independent changes in Old English and Old Frisian. They argue – Richard Hogg, Patrick Stiles and Hans Frede Nielsen – that English and Frisian do not share the same relative chronology of sound changes prior to palatalization, concluding that Frisian and English must have gone their separate ways before palatalization even initiated.[3] These scholars do not

---

[1] I would like to thank Rolf Bremmer, Robert Mailhammer, Karling Rottschäfer, and, especially, Patrick Stiles for giving me valuable comments on this article; however, they are in no way to be associated with the suggestions made in it.

[2] T. Siebs, 'Geschichte der friesischen Sprache', *Grundriß der germanischen Philologie I*, ed. H. Paul, 2nd edn. (Strassburg, 1901), 1152–464, at 1288; K. Luick, *Historische Grammatik der englischen Sprache* (Stuttgart, 1914–1940; repr. Oxford, 1964), §637; A. Campbell, 'Some Old Frisian Sound-changes', *Transactions of the Philological Society* (1939), 78–107, at 106, and his *Old English Grammar* (Oxford, 1959), §486.

[3] See R. M. Hogg, 'Old English Palatalization', *Transactions of the Philological Society* (1979), 89–113, esp. 89–91; P. V. Stiles, 'Remarks on the "Anglo-Frisian" Thesis', *Friesische Studien* II, ed. V. F. Faltings, A. G. H. Walker and O. Wilts [= NOWELE Suppl. 12 (1995)], 177–220, at 194–96; H. F. Nielsen, 'Frisian and the Grouping of the Older Germanic Languages', *Handbuch / Handbook*, 512–23, at 519–21.

seem to question that there was a general Old English palatalization though; but, unlike Siebs, Luick and Campbell, they are unspecific about whether it initiated before or after the settlement of Britain.

In response to arguments against a shared Old English and Old Frisian development, Robert Fulk, in the forerunner to this volume, presented an alternative chronology and interpretation of Anglo-Frisian sound changes which aimed to bring English and Frisian back to a common dialect at the time when velars were palatalized. Subsequently, Frederik Kortlandt responded to Fulk's paper, criticizing many points of his chronology and offering several revisions while at the same time agreeing with the main thrust of it, namely that palatalizaton of velars initiated when Old English and Old Frisian formed a linguistic unity, Anglo-Frisian.[4]

In this paper I argue that older scholarship was right to place the beginnings of palatalization in the continental period. I then take up the debate about relative chronology, and show that three out of four of the main arguments against a shared process of palatalization carry no weight while a fourth is inconclusive. However, ultimately it is questionable whether recourse to relative chronology is the ideal approach for assessing whether palatalization was a shared development or not, especially since the origins of palatalization are unknown. In particular, the genealogical (or *Stammbaum*) method based on relative chronology cannot adequately deal with sound-change resulting from dialectal diffusion within language continua, and since Patrick Stiles[5] has presented good arguments to show that we are dealing with a language continuum, the genealogical approach is bound to have its limitations.

2. Palatalization in Old English and Old Frisian

First it may be useful to outline the three environments in which palatalization occurred, they were: 1. Initially: here **k* and **g* were palatalized by all front vowels (except front vowels deriving from *i*-umlaut, a condition which holds for velar palatalizations in all positions) and the palatal approximant *j*. 2. Medially: **-k(k)-*, **-gg-* were palatalized before **i*, **j*, while **-g-* was palatalized between all front vowels. 3. Finally: **-k* was palatalized by preceding front vowels in Old English only, while **-g* was palatalized by preceding front vowels in both languages. Some examples are given in Fig. 1. Unlike Old Frisian, palatalized velars are not usually indicated in Old English orthography. In order to indicate them, the convention of a super-

---

[4] R. D. Fulk, 'The Chronology of Anglo-Frisian Sound Changes', *Approaches*, 139–54; F. Kortlandt, 'The Origin of the Old English Dialects Revisited', *ABäG* 51 (1999), 45–51.

[5] Stiles, 'Remarks', 205–12.

script dot (*ċ*, *ċċ*, *ġ*, *ċ*) will be adopted when citing Old English forms – this approach leaves open the possibility of the velar plosives being either palatalized or assibilated which is very convenient, since assibilation cannot be dated with precision (FV = front vowel not derived from *i*-umlaut):

	K			
	k* + *FV	***-k-* + *i*, *j***	***-kk-* + *i*, *j***	***i* + *-k***
WGmc	**kin-* 'chin'	**bruki* 'breach'	**þrukkjan* 'press'	**dīk* 'ditch'
OE	*ċinn*	*bryċe*	*þryċċan*	*diċ*
OFris	***ts**in*	*bre**ts**e*	*thri**tz**a*	*di**k***
	G			
	g* + *FV	***-g-* + *i*, *j***	***-gg-*, *-ng* + *i*,*j***	***FV* + *-g***
WGmc	**geld-* 'tax'	**hugi-* 'mind'	**wiggja* 'horse'	**dag* 'day'
OE	*ġield*	*hyġe*	*wiċġ*	*dæġ*
OFris	***i**eld*	*he**i***	*wi**ds**e*	*de**i***

Fig. 1: Palatalization and assibilation of **k* and **g* in OE and OFris[6]

In brief, palatalized **k* ultimately yields assibilated reflexes but **g* shows two outcomes of palatalization: either it merges with the palatal approximant *j* or it assibilates, yielding OE /dʒ/, OFris *dz*. Many scholars explain this twofold development by assuming that **g* differed phonetically according to position at the time of palatalization. By this analysis, the reflex *j* can be derived from palatalization of a voiced velar fricative /ɣ/, and the assibilated variants *dʒ* and *dz* from the voiced velar plosive [g], which existed after **n* (i.e. in the combination **ng*), and in the geminate **gg*.[7] Finally, many scholars[8] – what

[6] I am aware that there is more dialectal variation in medial and final positions than presented here; however, some of the main issues will be discussed in section 4 of this paper. For more detailed overviews, see K. D. Bülbring, *Altenglisches Elementarbuch* (Heidelberg, 1902), §§491–500; Campbell, *Old English Grammar*, §§426–29; Siebs, 'Geschichte der friesischen Sprache', 1288–302.

[7] See W. G. Moulton, 'The Proto-Germanic Non-syllabics (Consonants)', *Toward a Grammar of Proto-Germanic*, ed. F. van Coetsem and H. L. Kufner (Tübingen, 1972), 141–73, at 173; M. Schulz, *Untersuchungen zum anlautenden velaren /g/ im Altenglischen*, PhD disseratation (Göttingen, 1978); D. Minkova, *Alliteration and Sound Change in Early English* (Cambridge, 2003), 113–20.

[8] E.g. Siebs, 'Geschichte der friesischen Sprache', 1288; J. Wright and E. M. Wright, *Old English Grammar* (Oxford, 1925), 162–63; R. M. Hogg, *A Grammar of Old English. I. Phonology* (Oxford, 1992), 257–58; Fulk, 'The Chronology', 146; Minkova,

ever their view is on the relationship between the Old English and Old Frisian palatalizations – distinguish between an earlier process of palatalization and a later process of assibilation, the latter occurring much later and showing variation in Old English and Old Frisian. In other words, the velar plosives **k* and **g* were naturally palatalized somewhat before front vowels (i.e. [c] and [ɟ]), yet these must surely have been followed by some form of secondary articulation too, probably a palatal off-glide, so as to induce dentalization and assibilation: **k* > **c*^{j} > **t*^{j} > OE /tʃ/, OFris *ts* and **g* > **ɟ*^{j} > OE /dʒ/, OFris *dz*.

3. The history of palatalization

If we want to establish whether palatalization of velars was a shared or independent development of pre-Old English and pre-Old Frisian we should first try to estimate when palatalization took place. If the balance of probability indicates that palatalization of velars had already initiated before the Anglo-Saxon settlement of Britain around the mid-fifth century then the prospect of it being a shared development increases in likelihood. In order to assess when palatalization initiated, it will be easier to first establish when it stopped and then to work back in time.

Most important for assessing when palatalization stopped has always been the question of when *i*-umlaut started, since velars were not palatalized before front vowels resulting from *i*-umlaut, e.g. OFris *kening* 'king' < PreOFris **kuning* and OE *kyn* 'kin' < **kunni*. Although there is still some uncertainty on the date of *i*-umlaut, Karl Luick's sixth-century dating provides one workable estimate for English, especially since it has found subsequent support from a detailed study of place-name evidence by Richard Coates.[9] Indeed, it is difficult to suggest a much later date because *i*-umlaut is already represented in the earliest attestations of Old English, e.g. in the Franks Casket runic inscription **wylfi** (< Pre-OE **wulβi* 'she-wolf') from about the late seventh century. For Old Frisian, an early dating for *i*-umlaut looks probable too, based on the personal-name **æniwulufu** (< **auni-*) found on the Folkstone Coin runic inscription, *c.* 600–650, which is usually thought to be Frisian.[10] Failing this, Gysseling provides early Old Frisian attestations of unrounded *i*-umlaut in the name **Hrēðgǣr* (< **Hrōþi-*), appearing in copies of documents which ultimately date to the late eighth century, as

Alliteration and Sound Change, 90–113.

[9] Luick, *Historische Grammatik*, §350. For a discussion of the place-name evidence see R. Coates, 'On an Early Date for OE *i*-Mutation', *Linguistic and Stylistic Studies in Medieval English*, ed. A. Crépin (Amiens, 1984), 25–37; at 31, Coates argues that *i*-umlaut cannot have been operative long after AD 500 in English.

[10] See J. Insley, 'The Personal Name **Āniwulf* / **Ǣniwulf*', *Old English Runes and their Continental Background*, ed. A. Bammesberger (Heidelberg, 1991), 172–74.

Hredgaerus (AD 793), *Hredgerus* (AD 796, 805).[11] Assuming, then, that *i*-umlaut took place by about the sixth century in Old English and between the sixth and eighth centuries in Old Frisian, the usual inference is that palatalization of velars stopped in these languages at the same time.

Some scholars, however, have claimed that palatalization of velars could continue after *i*-umlaut, arguing that rounded front vowels from *i*-umlaut did not have the same palatalizing effect as the older inherited non-rounded front vowels. If this is so, and it is most doubtful (see discussion below), palatalization of velars could conceivably have continued as a sound-change somewhat longer, perhaps into the seventh century. But a date much later than this seems improbable for Frisian, since the North Frisian settlements began in around the seventh or eighth century, and while these dialects are thought to have developed independently for many centuries, they show the same palatalizations as in Modern West and East Frisian. The situation in English is much more problematic, however. If Coates is right that *i*-umlaut cannot have been operative long after AD 500 – nobody, it seems, has yet challenged his arguments – then there is a complication, since it is quite certain that velars were still undergoing palatalization after this date, perhaps until the mid-seventh century, as place-name evidence indicates.

During the Anglo-Saxon migrations and settlement of Britain, which began in the early to mid fifth century, Romano-British place-names containing **k* and **g* were taken into Old English and show palatalization before front vowels, e.g. Cheviot (Northumberland), Chevening (Kent) < Brit. **keṽn-* 'ridge', Yeavering (Northumberland) < Brit. **gaβr-* 'goat', Cheetham (Lancashire) < **kɛ̄d-* 'forest'. The distribution of the last mentioned place-name element – **kɛ̄d* 'forest' – is presented in Map 1. In the fifth century **kɛ̄d* 'forest' had a mid-front vowel **ɛ̄* (or possibly a diphthong **ɛi*) which caused palatalization and subsequent assibilation of preceding **k* (> *c^j > *t^j > *tʃ*) in many dialects of English. Evidently, there are few exceptions to *k*-palatalization. Those exceptions which do exist, e.g. Coedmoor, Hengoed, Pencoyd, are found in the vicinity of the present-day Welsh border, which in former times was further east, hence there was no early British to Old English shift in this area. More exceptions are found in west Devonshire, e.g. Penquit, and in the North, e.g. Culgaith, Tulketh, Penketh, Alkincoats, Clesketts, Bathgate, Pencaitland.

---

[11] M. Gysseling, 'Het oudste Fries', *IB* 24 (1962), 1–26, at 18.

Map 1: Place-names containing Late British *kε̄d 'forest'[12]

[12] I have made this map using R. Coates, 'Gazetteer of Celtic Names in England (except Cornwall)', R. Coates and A. Breeze, *Celtic Voices, English Places: Studies of the Celtic Impact on Place-Names in England* (Stamford, 2000), 263–345. Some Scottish place-names have also been added to the map using W. J. Watson, *The Celtic Place-Names of Scotland* (Edinburgh, 1926), 381–82

It is tempting to explain away the northern forms with Scandinavian influence. However, the areas in question were settled late, and the forms could just as easily continue British pronunciations: Lothian fell to Bernicia in AD 638 (according to the Irish annals), and areas west of the Pennines and north of the Ribble were absorbed by Northumbria after the mid-seventh century.[13] Finally, there is a conspicuous example of non-palatalization in southern Lincolnshire, the district name Kesteven, and, perhaps, the more doubtful Ketton in Rutland. But aside from these few examples palatalized forms abound.

One way of explaining both early *i*-umlaut and continuing palatalization would be to use once more the argument that palatalization was still an ongoing phonetic process, though not before rounded front vowels. But although this explanation has been offered several times before, and although it seems logical on the face of it, scholars who favour this interpretation have a tendency never to cite living languages which attest such a typology. By contrast, many languages can be cited which have palatalization of velars before both rounded and unrounded front vowels, as Salmons (this volume) demonstrates.[14] An alternative solution, then, is to assume that a phonemic contrast between palatalized and non-palatalized velars already existed prior to *i*-umlaut and the creation of rounded front vowels, as has been argued for by some scholars.[15] In such a case it would be possible to assume that the velars of Romano-British place-names were palatalized on adoption into English in accordance with the phonotactic properties of Anglo-Saxon. In

[13] See K. H. Jackson, *Language and History in Early Britain* (Edinburgh, 1953), 208–09 and 218.

[14] Further languages showing palatalization before both rounded and non-rounded front vowels are listed in D. N. S. Bhat, 'A General Study of Palatalization', J. H. Greenberg, *Universals of Human Language*. II. *Phonology* (Stanford, 1978), 47–92. It has obviously been harder for Bhat to find languages which show palatalization before non-rounded front vowels only, but Bhat (p. 61) notes that in English 'velar palatalization did not take place before the vowel *i* derived through umlaut from *u*', which brings us full circle. However, the notion that there was palatalization after **i* (short, long or nasalized) but not after rounded front vowels has also been used by linguists studying the historical phonology of Slavic, see W. Vermeer, 'Leading Ideas in the Study of the Progressive Palatalization of Proto-Slavic', *International Journal of Slavic Linguistics and Poetics* 44–45 (2002– 03), 377–94, at 383–84, 387 and footnotes 15 and 21.

[15] See F. Cercignani, 'The Development of */k/ and */sk/ in Old English', *The Journal of English and Germanic Philology* 82 (1983), 313–23 and A. Liberman, 'Palatalized and Velarized Consonants in English against their Germanic Background, with Special Reference to *i*-umlaut', *Studies in the History of the English Language* III, ed. C. M. Cain and G. Russom (Berlin, 2007), 5–36.

other words, there was sound-substitution, but otherwise no new process of palatalization occurred before rounded front vowels.[16]

To be sure, early Brittonic place-names were assimilated to Anglo-Saxon phonology by a form of sound-substitution. For instance, the voiced velar plosive *g appeared in intervocalic position or between a vowel and a resonant in Late British. But in Old English only the voiced velar fricative *ɣ (when palatalized: [ʝ]) was found in these positions, with the plosive *g only occurring in gemination or after *n. As a consequence, the Brittonic *g was usually replaced by OE *k* (or occasionally *-gg-*) in these positions, e.g. *Eccles* (in Lancashire and many other place) from Late British *eglēs* (cp. Modern Welsh *eglwys* 'church'), ultimately from Vulgar Latin *eclesia*.[17] By a similar token, the Brittonic property of having unpalatalized velars adjacent to front vowels was not reflected in Anglo-Saxon phonotactics. The evidence suggests that there was an early process of sound-substitution, thus **k* was palatalized and later assibilated, i.e. $*c^j > *t^j > tʃ$.[18] This explanation of palatalization of Brittonic place-names upon assimilation seems the most likely scenario, especially given the narrow time-frame of Anglicization of large sweeps of present-day England during the fifth and sixth centuries.[19]

The evidence suggests that Siebs, Luick and Campbell were right to conclude that palatalization was a pre-Conquest phenomenon. Their judgement, however, was based primarily on the inference that the close similarities with Frisian bespoke a continental origin for English palatalization. Now the

---

16 Here I follow the premises of dating sound change outlined by Theo Vennemann, who has drawn attention to the often overlooked fact that following a specific sound change a language may continue to adapt loanwords to its newly defined phonetic/phonological system. Such adaptations, or sound-substitutions, may continue for centuries after the sound change has taken effect, indicating that loanwords can be extremely precarious for dating sound changes. See further T. Vennemann, 'Betrachtung zum Alter der Hochgermanischen Lautverschiebung', *Althochdeutsch*, ed. R. Bergmann, H. Kolb and K. Matzel, 2 vols. (Heidelberg, 1987) I, 29–53, at 32.

17 See further Jackson, *Language and History*, 556–57, and K. Cameron, '*Eccles* in English Place-names', *Christianity in Britain, 300–700*, ed. M. W. Barley and R. P. C. Hanson (Leicester, 1968), 87–92.

18 Support for later assibilation has also been argued for on the basis of English alliterations, for which see Minkova, *Alliteration and Sound Change*, Chapter 3.

19 I should also point out that there is a further possible factor to consider, namely the possibility of Vulgar British Latin influence especially in southern lowland Britain which could have had the effect of palatalizing Brittonic place-name elements, such as **kɛ̄d* 'forest', before the advent of the Saxons. This possibility should not be ruled out. However, I doubt whether it would account for all the toponymic evidence, and we should not forget that there is evidence elsewhere for sound-substitution of Brittonic place-names in Pre-Old English. For a discussion of British Latin influence on Brittonic and Old English see P. Schrijver, 'The Rise and Fall of British Latin: Evidence from English and Brittonic', *The Celtic Roots of English*, ed. M. Filppula, J. Klemola and H. Pitkänen (Joensuu, 2002), 87–110, esp. 108.

evidence from Romano-British place-names also provides another useful argument in favour of a continental origin of palatalization in pre-Conquest Anglo-Saxon dialects, which in turn provides a more likely scenario than the idea of palatalization only emerging in Old English dialects after the settlement of Britain – for instance, by a form of later cross-sea contact, as envisaged by Hans Kuhn.[20]

4. The debated chronology of palatalization

If we can agree that palatalization of velars was a property of pre-Conquest Anglo-Saxon dialects and that the homeland of the Anglo-Saxons was northern Germany and parts of Denmark, i.e. close or adjacent to areas where Frisian is or was spoken, we may also like to conclude that palatalization was a shared areal feature of parts of West Germanic. From this prehistoric areal configuration, dialects other than Old English and Old Frisian have later emerged. It is well-known that there is sporadic evidence of palatalized velars in Old Dutch and Middle Dutch which has been ascribed to a prehistoric substrate language usually designated as Ingvaeonic or Frisian.[21] Secondly, there is sporadic orthographic evidence for palatalization in Old Saxon, which, as a close ancestor to Anglo-Saxon, is perhaps hardly surprising.[22] Yet due to the subsequent Franconicization of Old Dutch and the High German influence, especially since the eighth century, on Old Saxon, these dialects are less useful for the present enquiry. This leaves only Old English and Old Frisian, and in this narrower sense the term Anglo-Frisian is often understood.

Assuming, then, that palatalization of velars was an areal feature shared by varieties of Germanic spoken along a large stretch of land in the proximity the North Sea Coast, it seems reasonable to ask how this shared feature originated, such as whether it developed in one or more areas before spreading to other dialects, whether it reflects an archaism lost in other dia-

---

20 See H. Kuhn, 'Zur Gliederung der germanischen Sprachen', *ZfdA* 86 (1955), 1–47, at 32, and 'Friesisch und Nordseegermanisch', *UW* 4 (1955), 37–46, at 42.

21 The designation of this substrate has been influenced by personal ideologies in the past, see E. Hoekstra, 'K. H. Heeroma: strider en tsjûger foar it ABN. Oer de gearhing tusken taalkunde, taalpolityk en nasjonale identiteit', *UW* 44 (1995), 51–68.

22 For a detailed survey of the evidence, see S. Krogh, *Die Stellung des Altsächsischen im Rahmen der germanischen Sprachen* (Göttingen, 1996), 203–13. Briefly, Krogh thinks that a connection between palatalization in Old Dutch and that in Old English and Old Frisian is possible. However, Krogh rejects a connection with Old Saxon because of evidence for palatalization of velars before front vowels resulting from *i*-umlaut. Krogh is right to notice this difference, but it does not eliminate the possibility that palatalization of velars initiated before Old Saxon *i*-umlaut. Due to the scanty data supplied by Old and Middle Dutch, as well as Modern Dutch dialects, the relative chronology of palatalization and *i*-umlaut cannot be established here.

lects, or whether it developed by some form of prehistoric language contact (e.g. with Vulgar Latin), to name but a few possibilities. Unfortunately nobody knows. But one way of assessing the validity of a shared prehistoric change has been to consider questions of relative chronology. If a single coherent Anglo-Frisian chronology cannot be developed, then it can be argued that Old English and Old Frisian were two separate dialects at the time of palatalization rather than a single language. In this sense, Hogg, Stiles and Nielsen have argued (see note 3) that palatalization was an independent development in Old English and Old Frisian.

However, Robert Fulk has shown that if we look at Anglo-Saxon through the same chronological spectacles as we do Anglo-Frisian, then we are forced to conclude that palatalization was an independent change in Old English too.[23] Suffice it to say that two dialects or varieties can share a linguistic development yet variation as well. Another aspect to consider when deducing a relative chronology is that palatalization can have a long life span. Already Campbell described how sensitivity of *k* and *g* 'continued through the periods of Anglo-Frisian fronting, breaking, and retraction before consonant groups and before back vowels'.[24] Although there is disagreement about which changes did take place while palatalization as a development was active, the fact that palatalization can straddle other sound changes in a relative chronology complicates any analysis and must be taken into consideration. This problem is particularly well known in Frisian studies because, despite the fact that palatalization of velars had been phonologized at the latest after *i*-umlaut, a second process of palatalization and assibilation of *k* (as well as *t* and *d*) re-occurred in West Frisian dialects in about the fifteenth century.[25] Therefore, it is with these considerations in mind that the following four chronological issues should be addressed.

4.1 Breaking and palatal diphthongization

Since there is general agreement that the sound-change known as breaking was independent in both Old English and Old Frisian,[26] all phonological processes which postdate breaking must be independent in both English and

---

23 Cp. Fulk, 'The Chronology', 141: 'The Old English dialects themselves show a similar divergence at an early date. When WGmc *ā* was fronted [...], it presumably developed first to *ǣ*, which remains in West Saxon, but then changed further to *ē* in other Old English dialects as well as in Old Frisian. The raising of *ǣ* to *ē* must have taken place quite early in Old English, since it precedes breaking, as demonstrated by forms like Kentish *nēor* "nearer" and Mercian *nēolǣcan* "approach" and *nēowest* "vicinity".'

24 Campbell, *Old English Grammar*, §426.

25 See Siebs, 'Geschichte der friesischen Sprache', 1294–95; J. J. Loopstra, *De Assibilatie in de Oudfriese Oorkonden* (Haarlem, 1935), 72–137.

26 See Stiles, 'Remarks', 194–95 and, implicitly, D. Boutkan, 'On Labial Mutation and Breaking in Old Frisian', *Approaches*, 77–88.

Frisian. In this vein, Patrick Stiles has argued that Old English breaking 'is demonstrably earlier than palatalization as a phonemic change', and draws into consideration 'WGmc. **kerl* (cf. G *Kerl*), which yields OE *ċeorl* 'churl' by breaking, NOT † *ċierl* by palatal diphthongization, a change clearly dependent on the prior existence of palatalization.'[27] Stiles' wording is noteworthy: 'palatalization as a phonemic change', his intentional use of 'phonemic' would seem to indicate that palatalization as an allophonic change may have preceded breaking. But in fact Stiles is quite adamant that even phonetic palatalization cannot be 'Anglo-Frisian' when he later writes: 'palatalization as merely a phonetic tendency cannot be pushed further back to an "Anglo-Frisian" stage'.[28] Stiles provides, implicitly, two chronologies of sound change (1a–b), whereby only one can produce the desired outcome, namely (1a). But although the chronology given in (1a) will produce the desired Old English output *ċeorl*, whereas (1b) will not, it is possible to propose an alternative chronology that places palatalization before breaking (1c).

(1)

a.		b.		c.	
Input	**kerl*	Input	**kerl*	Input	**kerl*
Breaking	**ceorl*	Palataliz.	**ċerl*	Palataliz.	**ċerl*
Palataliz.	**ċeorl*	Palatal Diph.	**ċierl*	Breaking	**ċeorl*
OE	*ċeorl*	OE	***ċierl*	OE	*ċeorl*

The problem with Stiles' analysis is the assumption that palatal diphthongization must immediately follow or occur contemporaneously with palatalization,[29] but there is no evidence to suggest this must have been the case. In fact there is more reason to believe that palatalization was not contemporaneous, since palatal diphthongization – in contrast to palatalization of velars – is not found in all Old English dialects.[30] So while Stiles' analysis shows convincingly that palatal diphthongization follows breaking, it does not prove that palatalization follows breaking either as a phonemic change or not.

---

[27] Stiles, 'Remarks', 194.

[28] *Ibid.* 196.

[29] Karl Luick estimated that palatalization of velars initiated at the end of the fourth or the beginning of the fifth century, and thought that palatal diphthongization probably immediately followed the change. But it is clear that he knows no proof that this must have been the case when he writes: 'Die (ältere) Palataldiphthongierung hat sich wohl unmittelbar an diesen Wandel angeschlossen.' See Luick, *Historische Grammatik*, §291.

[30] It should be noted that palatal diphthongization, whatever its debated status as a sound change, occurred only in West Saxon and 'North' Northumbrian. But in the latter short **e* was generally unaffected by it. Consequently, the example OE *ċeorl* can serve as a test case for West Saxon dialects only.

4.2 Breaking and palatalization of the voiceless fricative

Another argument in favour of the chronology breaking then palatalization is the evidence from breaking before **h* (phonetically a velar or uvular fricative, [x] or [χ], in post-vocalic positions).[31] The situation is summarized by Patrick Stiles as follows:[32]

> Phonetic palatalization of the velars in Old English led to a phonemic split in the case of the stops *k* and *g* and the voiced fricative ʒ [= IPA [ɣ], SL]. It also affected the voiceless fricative *h*, although here it did not lead to a phonemic split (cf. Hogg 1992:§2.60 and references). However, because breaking only took place before velar consonants, the voiceless fricative *h* must have been unaffected by any phonetic palatalization in English at the time of the earlier change of breaking.

Stiles then cites the following data in favour of this argument:

Pre-OE * *wīh* > Breaking **wīoh* > OE *wēoh* 'idol'
Pre-OE **nǣh* > Breaking **nǣah* > OE *nēah* 'near'
Pre-OE **hlæχχjan* > Breaking **hlæaχχjan* > OE *hliehhan* (with *i*-umlaut) 'to laugh'

It seems logical then to place the palatalization of **h* at the same time as *k* and *g* in the history of English. Consequently, breaking must surely have occurred before palatalization in order to yield the outcomes of breaking cited above. Fulk, however, has argued that 'it is an unreliable assumption that because *h* was not palatalized in this word [i.e. Pre-OE **hlæhhjan* 'laugh', SL] at this time, nor could other consonants have been palatalized.[33]

If we look to Old Frisian, we find palatalization of **k* and **g*, yet the evidence for palatalization of *h* is ambiguous.[34] One finds OFris *siuht(h)* 'he

---

31 For a detailed discussion see Hogg, 'Old English Palatalization', 89–113.

32 Stiles, 'Remarks', 196.

33 Fulk, 'The Chronology', 145. Note that Bülbring, *Altenglisches Elementarbuch*, §§491–501, differentiates 'Früh-urenglischen Palatalisierungen von ʒ, *g*, *k*, *gg*, *kk*' from a later 'urenglische' palatalization of *χ*.

34 Patrick Stiles (p.c.) points out to me that the voiceless fricative *h* seems to have been palatalized in Old Frisian when *i* stood in the next syllable, as indicated by the following words which failed to undergo breaking: OFris *plicht* 'duty'(< **plih-ti-*), OFris *wicht* 'weight'(< **wih-ti*), *secht* 'illness'(< **suh-ti*). However, Boutkan explains these forms otherwise in 'On Labial Mutation and Breaking', 82–83 and fn. 39. Boutkan (*ibid.*) maintains that *-*xt*- as well as **xs*- had a strong velar character, such that they 'inhibited the fronting of PGmc **a* to *e*, e.g. *nacht* "night", *achta* "eight", *fax* "hair".' Further, he thinks that there was only breaking of **e* (not **i*), and that unrounding of *i*-umlauted **u* to *e* postdated breaking in forms such as *secht* 'illness'. In fact, breaking is attested in this

sees' (< *sehiþ) vs. OFris *leith*, *līth* 'he lies' (< *legiþ*) and OFris *riucht*, *riocht* 'right' (< *reht-*) vs. OFris *rein* 'rain' (< *regna-*).[35] This situation has continued into Modern East Frisian and Standard West Frisian where *χ* did not develop a palatal allophone [ç] before or after front vowels, while it has done so in some North Frisian dialects. The allophonic distribution /χ ~ ç/ is quite common cross-linguistically. For example, it has developed in Standard German but not in Swiss German or Standard Dutch, it has evolved in the North Frisian dialects of Moring and Helgoland, but not in the East Frisian of Saterland or on Wangerooge (now extinct).[36] Indeed, there seems to be no conclusive evidence that in pre-Old English the palatalization of **χ* and the velars **k* and **g* were parallel developments, instead of independent innovations, occurring perhaps several centuries apart, as in several Frisian dialects. Ultimately, the observation that the voiced velar fricative does palatalize, while its unvoiced (probably uvular) counterpart does not, explains the apparent mystery[37] of why only the latter induces breaking in Old English, e.g. OE *feohtan* 'fight' (< **feht-*) vs. OE *segl* (**segl-*) 'sail'.

4.3 Palatalization in Old English before ⟨ea⟩ (< Gmc **au*)

A stronger argument that palatalization occurred independently, in the genealogical sense, in Old English and Old Frisian concerns the twofold development of **k* before Gmc **au*, which shows different reflexes in Old English and Old Frisian:[38]

---

form in OWFris *siuchte*, *siocht* also in ModWFris *sjocht(e)* and IsNFris *sjocht* (Amrum), cp. R. H. Bremmer Jr, An Introduction to Old Frisian (MS Leiden, 2006), §50.

35 Examples mainly involve the cluster **xt*, where **h* may have had a strong velar character (see last note). In intervocalic positions and finally, **h* was weakened and lost. Evidence for the palatalization of weakened **h* seems to be OFris *nēi*, *nēy* (< Gmc **nēhwō* 'nigh, near'). Cases of the intervocalic geminate *-hh-* followed by a front vowel are rare and almost confined to the Germanic etymon **hlahjan* 'to laugh'. However, Old Frisian has only **hlakkia*, which could reflect a unique *change* **-χχ-* > (**-χk-?*) > *-kk-* (for other such problematic cases in Old English, see K. Brunner, *Altenglische Grammatik* [Tübingen, 1965], §220, Anm.2). Alternatively, **hlakkia* could go back to an unexplained variant pre-form, i.e. cognate with ON *hlakka*. Nevertheless, several Modern Frisian dialects do show reflexes of the etymon with a velar fricative, and some dialects have a palatal reflex [ç] (e.g. Sylt *lachi*) while others do not (e.g. Saterland *laachje*), see Siebs, 'Geschichte der friesischen Sprache', 1305.

36 See E. Bauer, *Die Moringer Mundart* (Heidelberg, 1925), §85; W. Krogmann, *Helgoländer Wörterbuch* (Wiesbaden, 1957–1968), 5; P. Kramer, *Kute Seelter Sproakleere* (Rhauderfehn, 1982), 7; Siebs, 'Geschichte der friesischen Sprache', 1382.

37 See Hogg, 'Old English Palatalization', 96: '[W]e have not found any satisfactory solution to the problem of why [ʒ], unlike [x], did not cause breaking.'

38 Stiles, 'Remarks', 195.

> The difference between OE *ċeapian* 'to trade, buy' (with palatalization) and OFris. *kapia* 'to buy' (without) – both ultimately derived from Lat. *caupo* 'tavern-keeper; hawker' – demonstrates that palatalization took place in each language after changes which are unique to it.

This assumption is linked to the development of the Germanic diphthong **au* and its connection with fronting of Gmc **a* yielding OE *æ* and OFris *e*. It is more economical if the development of Gmc **au* to OE *æo*, and later *æa*, can be linked with a contemporaneous fronting of Gmc **a* > OE *æ* which also caused palatalization of preceding velars; otherwise two separate changes must be posited. By doing so, however, it seems that the fronting of Gmc **a* must also be seen as yet another coincidence common to Old English and Old Frisian, which is likewise uneconomical. At least four different ways around this issue have been proposed in the literature.

1) Karl Luick and, more recently, Kurt Goblirsch have argued that Gmc **a* was fronted contemporaneously in the diphthong **au* in Anglo-Frisian and thus the Germanic diphthong developed to **æa*, which was subsequently monophthongized to **ā* in Pre-Old Frisian.[39] According to Goblirsch, the change **æa* > *ā* resulted from *Akzentumsprung* (presumably, velar palatalizations in Frisian were then lost in the process). *Akzentumsprung* must then have been very early, however. Based on onomastic material, Maurits Gysseling has argued that Frisian monophthongization of **au* to *ā* can be dated to the eighth century on the basis of place-name evidence.[40] But runic evidence, notably the **skanomodu** inscription (< **skaun*- 'beautiful'), if it is Frisian, might suggest an even earlier date for monophthongization, around the sixth century.

2) Robert Fulk has offered a slightly different proposal to that of Luick and Goblirsch. He thinks that Gmc **a* was fronted contemporaneously in the diphthong **au* (as well as the diphthong **ai*) and that all three induced palatalizations in Anglo-Frisian. However, Fulk believes that the resulting diphthong **æu* changed back to **au* (not **ā*, which arose later still) in Pre-Old Frisian which caused depalatalization of preceding velars before assibilation took place, i.e. Anglo-Fris **kau*- > **cæu*- yielded: (1) OE *tʃæa*-, but (2)

[39] Luick, *Historische Grammatik*, §120; K. G. Goblirsch, 'Germanic *ai* and *au* in Anglo-Frisian', *ABäG* 33 (1991), 17–23.

[40] Gysseling, 'Het oudste Fries', 9–11. E.g. Middag (district of Groningen) from Gmc **augjō*- 'island in the sea' appears as *Midochi*, *Midach*, *Middach* in thirteenth- and fourteenth-century copies of a document from 786–87; Fivelgo (district of Groningen) from Gmc **gauja*- 'district' appears in an eleventh century copy of an early ninth-century document as *Fiuilga*; *Vronen* (North Holland) from Gmc **frauna*- 'lordly' appears as *Vranlo, Vronlo, Franlo* in eleventh- and twelfth-century copies of a document from the ninth century.

> PreOFris **kau-* > OFris *kā-*.[41] But Kortlandt has criticized Fulk's proposal, since it relies on pendulum-developments which, though not impossible, are uneconomical.[42] Thus, leaving aside the complex issue of the development of Gmc **ai*, which Fulk does not elaborate upon in detail, he must posit at least three stages of development for Old Frisian (**au* > **æu* > **au* > OFris *ā*), whereas Luick and Goblirsch's proposal has the merit of needing only two (**au* > **æa* > OFris *ā*).

3) Raymond Page has argued that Gmc **au* developed to **ā* not only in Old Frisian but also in earliest Old English before a development of raising and diphthongization before the earliest Old English texts (apparently the resulting **ā* must have been somehow distinct from **ā* < Gmc **ai*).[43] As such, the putative Old English diphthongization of **ā* could be compared to a similar process which affected West Frisian after the Middle Ages (OFris *ā* > ModWFris *ea*).

4) Finally, some scholars have argued that Gmc **au* was not subject to fronting in Old English until quite late.[44] By assuming that fronting of **au* was a later Anglo-Saxon development, which subsequently induced palatalization of preceding velars, the idea of an earlier Anglo-Frisian palatalization of velars need not be dismissed. For instance, Yakov Krupatkin has presumed that the development **au* > *ǣa* was part of a general Old English development of the Germanic diphthongs in *-u* which became incorporated into the long vowel system as front-back phonemes, i.e. the Old English high vowels *ī* and *ū* had a diphthongal counterpart *īu*, the mid vowels *ē* and *ō*, *ēo*, and the low vowels *ǣ* and *ā*, *ǣa*.[45] By this interpretation, the change **au* > *æa* was not dependent on fronting of short **a* at all.

---

41 Fulk, 'The Chronology', 151, 153.

42 See Kortlandt, 'The Origin of the Old English Dialects Revisited', 46.

43 R. I. Page, 'The Old English Rune *ear*', *Medium Ævum* 30 (1961), 65–79.

44 E.g. C. F. Koch, 'Angelsächsisch eâ (Grimms eá)', *ZfdP* 1 (1869), 339–44; Bülbring, *Altenglisches Elementarbuch*, §107, Anm. 2; J. Fourquet, 'Le système des éléments vocaliques longs en vieil-anglais', *Mélanges de linguistique et de philologie: Fernand Mossé in memoriam*, ed. A. C. Bouman (Paris, 1959), 148–60; Y. B. Krupatkin, 'From Germanic to English and Frisian', *UW* 19 (1970), 49–71; D. Hofmann, 'Zur Monophthongierung von germanisch *ai* und *au* im Altfriesischen und in seinen Nachbarsprachen', *Lingua Theodisca: Beiträge zur Sprach- und Literaturwissenschaft*, ed. J. Cajot and L. Kremer (Münster and Hamburg, 1995), 23–36, at 33; Kortlandt, 'The Origin of the Old English Dialects', 48.

45 Krupatkin, 'From Germanic to English and Frisian', 61. A similar proposal is offered by H. Pilch, *Altenglische Grammatik* (München, 1970), 83: 'Ggerm. [Gemeingermanisch] /iu/ gleitet von der hohen vorderen Komponente /i/ zur hohen hinteren Komponente /u/. Ggerm. /au/ gleicht sich dieser Bewegungsrichtung von vorn nach hinten an. Es verändert sich zu /æɑ/ mit tiefer vorderer Komponente [æ] und tiefer hinterer Komponente [ɑ]. Damit entsteht ein System zweier von vorne nach hinten gleitender Diphthonge, und zwar /iu/ mit hoher, /æɑ/ mit tiefer Zungenstellung'.

Thus, in addition to the traditional interpretation of the Germanic diphthong **au* in Old English and Old Frisian as favoured by Stiles, we find several quite different, competing proposals – the most likely of which seem to be (1) and (4), which are perhaps not mutually exclusive if (4) preceded (1). Undoubtedly, the development of the **au* is the core problem for the interpretation of the Anglo-Frisian subgrouping, and its interpretation remains very much a subjective one.

4.4 Different conditioning factors

Stiles has pointed out that the conditioning factors for palatalization in Old English and Old Frisian were different, noting contrasting reflexes of the voiceless velar: OFris *tser(e)ke* 'church', *dīk* 'ditch', *rīk(e)* 'rich' against OE *ċiriċe*, *dīċ*, *rīċe* with palatalization.[46] Both languages agree in evidencing palatalization before front vowels word initially, but differ medially and word finally.

The first difference is that only Old English palatalizes **k* after **i* (and less regularly other front vowels) in absolute final position. It seems likely, however, that, while **k* was palatalized after **i* in all Old English dialects, it never resulted in assibilation in this position in Northumbria and parts of Mercia.[47] Of the few examples where it can be proven that palatalization of **k* was due to preceding long or short **i*, e.g. *iċ* 'I', *dīċ* 'ditch',[48] *līċ* 'lich, corpse', *wīċ* '-wich', *piċ* 'pitch', *swilīċ* 'such', *hwalīċ* 'which', all are unassibilated at least in northern English dialects, but also in parts of the Midlands and East Anglia in Middle English and Modern English dialects. This lack of assibilation has been accounted for in different ways: 1. Due to frication of final **-k* under weak stress; 2. Analogical levelling in the paradigm, e.g. *dīċ* ~ *dīcas* 'ditch, dike' with a northern preference for the unpalatalized variant (in contrast to the South, which preferred the assibilated

46 Stiles, 'Remarks', 195–96. Note, however, that palatalization is attested in OFris *rīze* nt. 'riches, property', see *De Tweede Emsinger Codex*, ed. K. Fokkema, OTR 7 (The Hague, 1953), at 19, line 56. For this information, I am indebted to Anne Popkema. The *Oxford English Dictionary* (<www.oed.com>, accessed 16 June 2006) remarks that 'In ME. the use of the word may have been reinforced by F. *riche* (= Sp. *rico*, It. *ricco*), itself of Teut. origin. This would help to explain the early disappearance of the northern form *rike*.'

47 Palatalization did occur in Northumbrian, as is clear from runic evidence, but not assibilation. For the runic evidence see C. Ball, 'Inconsistencies in the Main Runic Inscriptions on the Ruthwell Cross', *Old English Runes*, ed. Bammesberger, 107–23, at 117—19.

48 The idea that English *dike* is an Old Norse loan and that English *ditch* is of native stock has been questioned in H. Ramisch, 'Re-examining the Influence of Scandinavian on English: the Case of *ditch/dike*', *Language History and Linguistic Modelling* [= Festschrift Fisiak], ed. R. Hickey and S. Puppel, 2 vols. (Berlin, 1997) I, 561–69.

variant); 3. Scandinavian influence.[49] What this all boils down to is the conjecture that the process of *k*-assibilation must have been the same across all Old English dialects. But it seems equally possible that, like in Frisian, **k* was only assibilated before front vowels in northern dialects of English.

Basing his arguments on place-name evidence, and apparently without knowledge of the Frisian parallels, John Watson also came to similar conclusions with regard to the lack of assibilation of **k* in Northumbrian English in absolute final position after front vowels:[50]

> In Northumbrian Old English, the phoneme *č* did not, in general, occur [in final position] at all. However, [...] the disappearance of final *-i* after a long syllable caused an originally medial *č* to stand in final position. Cf. the Lindisfarne form *bǣc* 'book' dat.sg. < **bōki* (John 20.30).

Watson's article is sometimes mentioned briefly in reference grammars, but is brushed aside with passing reference to Olga Gevenich's monograph on the palatalization of **k* in English place-names.[51] Gevenich argued, namely, that palatalization was a general Old English change, and that the lack palatalization in the North is due almost exclusively to Scandinavian influence.[52] What the grammars do no not seem to appreciate is that Watson never questioned the fact that velar palatalization occurred in all Old English dialects, but argued that the outcomes of it were not always the same.

The only paper which does attempt to reject Watsons thesis on the basis of actual data is that of Tae-Yong Pak.[53] In this paper, Pak is able to cite a few place-names which do in fact display palatalization of absolute final **k*: *Prestwich*, *Horwich*, *Reddish*.[54] But all of these toponyms are located in Southern Lancashire, and thus out of the Northumbrian region proper, which ought to be located approximately to the north of the River Lune (or, perhaps, the Ribble) in the west. The one other apparent example cited by Pak

---

49 See Hogg, *A Grammar of Old English*, 7.52, 7.41, 7.42, with references.

50 J. W. Watson Jr., 'Non-initial *k* in the North of England', *Language* 23 (1947), 34–49, at 49.

51 E.g. Brunner, *Altenglische Grammatik*, §206, Anm. 9; Hogg, *A Grammar of Old English*, 7.23, n.1.; O. Gevenich, *Die Palatalisierung von K > Č im Lichte der englischen Ortsnamen* (Halle/S., 1918).

52 Some aspects of this one-sided approach have been criticized in a review by E. Ekwall, *Anglia Beiblatt* 30 (1919), 221–28, and by George van Langenhove, 'The Assibilation of Palatal Stops in Old English', *A Grammatical Miscellany Offered to Otto Jespersen on his 70th Birthday*, ed. N. Børgholm, A. Brusendorff and C. A. Bodelsen (Copenhagen, 1930), 69–75.

53 T.-Y. Pak, 'Position and Affrication in Northumbrian Old English', *Linguistics* 82 (1972), 52–62.

54 *Ibid.* 56, 58.

is *Lintz* in County Durham, which is thought to derive from OE *hlinc* 'a rising ground, ridge'.[55] But this isolated example is quite dubious on account of its usual interpretation as a Normanized spelling pronunciation /ts/, which continues to this day. In other words, the one suspect Northumbrian example of suggested progressive palatalization of **k* unearthed by Pak only serves to bolster Watson's analysis.[56]

The second locus of variation between Old English and Old Frisian is in medial position. Medial position includes, however, a large number of Old English etyma which seemingly display palatalization in final position too, due to syncopation of a following **i* or **j* (i.e. different from *iċ* 'I', *dīċ* 'ditch', *piċ* 'pitch' etc., where **k* was never followed by **i* or **j*). Typical examples are from the *ja(n)*-stems (e.g. *lǣċe* 'physician', *mēċe* 'sword', *rīċe* 'kingdom', *gefylċe* 'troop', *fliċċe* 'flitch', *styċċe* 'piece', *mereċe* 'smallage', *wreċċa* 'wretch'; *weċġ* 'wedge', *hryċġ* 'ridge') and *jō(n)*-stems (e.g. *wiċċe* 'witch', *bierċe* 'birch', *sæċċ* 'strife', *spǣċ* 'speech', *cryċċ* 'crutch'; *bruċġ* 'bridge', *eċġ* 'edge', *heċġ* 'hedge', *myċġ* 'midge', *seċġ* 'sedge'). Such words – in particular those with geminate consonants resulting from West Germanic Gemination after a short root vowel – have reflexes with and without assibilation in the English dialects. The variation is often accounted for by Scandinavian influence.[57] But a problem with appealing solely to Scandinavian influence is that the non-palatalized forms occur in English dialects outside the main sphere of Scandinavian influence, such as in Rutland, Bedfordshire, Warwickshire, Worcestershire, Gloucestershire, Buckinghamshire, Herefordshire, Oxfordshire, Wiltshire, Somerset and Dorset.[58]

In light of the above facts, Karl Luick's proposal which focuses on the alternations of palatalized and non-palatatalized forms in the paradigms of nouns offers the best solution. Once **j* was lost, the palatalized consonant would have fallen in contact with either a following front or back vowel, depending on number and case. The general tendency is that front vowels are found in the singular and back vowels, the plural. It is possible, then, that either palatalized (later assibilated) consonants were generalized throughout the paradigm, or that non-palatalized velars were generalized. Luick points out that some nouns were especially prone to appear in the plural and are

---

55 *Ibid.* 58.

56 The evidence suggests that West Saxon and other southerly dialects of Old English show a different development from Northumbrian Old English and Old Frisian with respect to assibilation after *i*. The dialect configuration of Anglian and, especially, Northumbrian Old English and Old Frisian has been noticed by Fulk, 'The Chronology'. Another parallel is the lack of fronting of **a* before *-ld*, e.g. OE(Anglian) *cald*, OFris *cald* vs. OE(West Saxon) *ċeald* 'cold'.

57 E.g. R. Jordan, *Handbook of Middle English Grammar: Phonology*, trans. and rev. E. J. Crook (The Hague, 1974), §179.

58 See K. Luick, 'Zur Palatalisierung', *Anglia* 59 (1935), 274.

quite likely to have generalized the non-palatal variant and vice-versa. Such an explanation would account not only for the variation in English but also, sporadically, in Old Frisian too, e.g. *wigge* vs. *widze* 'horse' (< Gmc **wegja-*), *rīke* vs. *rīze* 'rich(es)' (< Gmc **rīkja-*), *wreke* vs. *wretse* 'revenge' (< Gmc **wrakja-*), *breke* vs. *bretse* 'breach, infringement' (< Gmc **brukja-*), *egge* vs. *edze* 'edge' (< Gmc **egjō-*).[59]

Thus, the conditioning factors for palatalization in Old Frisian and Old English are very similar, one difference being that in West Saxon dialects assibilation of **k* occurred not only before front vowels but also after them.

5. Conclusion

Palatalization of velars is probably the most striking phonological parallel of Old English and Old Frisian. Some scholars have argued that palatalization had shared Anglo-Frisian origins, others think it arose in both languages independently. In order to make headway in the debate, the absolute and relative chronology of palatalization must be worked out in more detail. Based on our present understanding of the chronology of the Anglo-Saxon settlement of England, and the evidence for palatalization in British Celtic place-name elements, palatalization of velars must have been active as a sound change at least until the early seventh century, i.e. later than the date of *i*-umlaut which, according to current estimations, took place no later than the sixth century. However, I have argued that palatalization started before *i*-umlaut and continued after it, too, namely by a form of sound-substitution. Significantly, my conclusions support those of earlier scholars who asserted that palatalization had initiated before the Anglo-Saxon settlement of Britain. In testing whether palatalization was a shared Anglo-Frisian development, further attention must be placed on the relative chronology of the change. If a shared coherent relative chronology cannot be developed for Old English

---

59 Stiles attaches special attention to the bird-name 'lark', which displays no palatalization in English but does in Frisian. However, most Old English scholars would assume that this *ōn*-stem noun did have palatalization in two out of its eight case forms in Old English, and that the palatalized forms were levelled out in early Middle English. Among the numerous spellings of this etymologically obscure word, three examples apparently showing palatalization are attested in early Middle English, namely *lauerche, Lauerchfeld, Liurochebere*, see *The Middle English Dictionary, ed.* H. Kurath, S. Kuhn and R. Lewis (Ann Arbor, MI, 1952–2001), s.v. *larke*. In Stiles' defence, however, it must be admitted that ⟨ch⟩-spellings for *k* are quite common in early medieval documents. Indeed ⟨ch⟩ is the rule before *e* and *i* in the Domesday Book (though the attestations given here do not stem from this source). For a discussion of the Frisian forms see N. R. Århammar, 'Die Lerche (Alauda) im Friesischen: ein Beitrag zum *Atlas Linguarum Europae*. Über Inlautassibilierung, unregelmäßige Lautentwicklung und "Lehnlautungen"', *Miscellanea Frisica: A New Collection of Frisian Studies* [= Festschrift Miedema], ed. N. R. Århammar *et al.* (Assen, 1984), 137–52.

and Old Frisian up to palatalization of velars, then, it is argued, palatalization must have arisen independently in both languages. Four arguments have been used to demonstrate that palatalization was, genealogically speaking, an independent development of Pre-Old English and Pre-Old Frisian. Upon a closer analysis of the facts, three out of four of these arguments do not stand up to scrutiny. Arguments based on palatal diphthongization (4.1) are weak, as it was a later development of certain Old English dialects and thus must be differentiated from an earlier process of velar palatalization which is found in all Old English dialects. The idea that the voiceless velar fricative ought to have undergone the same process of palatalization as *-*k(k)*- and *-*g(g)*- is contradicted by the Frisian evidence (4.2). Stiles' grounds for supposing that there were different conditioning factors for palatalization in Old English and Old Frisian are without foundation. Rather there are different later outcomes of palatalization in specific dialects (4.4). Further, Luick's idea that there were different outcomes of palatalization due to paradigmatic levelling is essentially proved by the Frisian data which, in turn, are confirmed by the English. However, one argument – the development of Gmc **au*, which allowed for palatalization in Old English but not in Old Frisian (4.3) – remains open to different interpretations, and thus leaves some room open for future debate. Above all, my discussion has shown that after so many decades the findings of Siebs, Luick and Campbell still can stand a critical test.

Die Sprache von Bernardus Rordahusim in der niederdeutschen Apokalypse der Baseler Handschrift F.VII.12, folio 211r–217r

Erika Langbroek

1. Einleitung

Seit etwa 1500 befindet sich in der Baseler Universitätsbibliothek die Papierhandschrift F.VII.12., die im 15. Jahrhundert geschrieben wurde.[1] Auf welchem Wege sie nach Basel gelangte, ist nicht bekannt. Die Handschrift besteht aus vier Teilen, die zu einem Konvolut zusammengebunden wurden. Den Inhalt der ersten drei Teile, f. 1–92, bilden lateinische Abhandlungen über die kirchliche Zeitrechnung. Der vierte und größte Teil, f. 93–219, enthält vieles: wissenschaftliche Traktate, Zitate aus patristischer Literatur, Exempla, Sprüche, Reime, Traureden, Arzt- und Farbrezepte und eine reimende Apokalypse; für die verschiedenen Texte des vierten Teils benutzte eine einzige Schreibhand die lateinische, niederländische, deutsche, friesische und niederdeutsche Sprache. Schon 1950 wurde von Buma auf diese Handschrift hingewiesen; 1957 und 1990 folgte dann die besondere Beachtung für drei friesische Traureden (f. 147r–148v) und ein lateinisches Ehetraktat (f. 148v).[2] Die Textausgabe der niederdeutschen Apokalypse (f. 211r–217r), mit deren Sprache ich mich hier befassen will, erschien 2006.[3]

[1] Vgl. M. P. van Buijtenen, 'Bernardus Rordahusim en zijn kring', *Archief voor de Geschiedenis van de Katholieke Kerk in Nederland* 1 (1959), 267–334, hier 296–97.

[2] Vgl. für die Traureden: W. J. Buma, 'Geestelijke literatuur in Oud-Friesland', *Trijeresom Ynliedingen hâlden yn de Fryske seksje fan it Ned. philologekongres* 1950 (Groningen und Djakarta, 1950), 5–50, hier 34–50; W. J. Buma, *Aldfryske houlikstaspraken, mei ynlieding, oantekeningen, nammelist, wurdboek en in Ingelske gearfetting* (Assen, 1957); Van Buijtenen, 'Bernardus Rordahusim'; W. J. Buma, 'Vertaling der Oudfriese huwelijkstoespraken', und K. Heeroma, 'Auteurschap en structuur der "Aldfryske houlikstaspraken"', *Archief voor de Geschiedenis van de Katholieke Kerk in Nederland* 1 (1959), 335–44 und 345–59; R. H. Bremmer Jr, 'Bad Frisian and Bad Low German: Interference in the Writings of a Medieval West Frisian', *Multilingua. Journal of Cross-Cultural and Interlanguage Communication* 16 (1997), 375–88; für das lateinische Ehetraktat, siehe Á. Orbán und M. F. van Gelderen, 'Ein lateinisches Ehetraktat in einer Baseler Handschrift aus dem 15. Jahrhundert und dessen Beziehung zu den drei altfriesischen Traureden in dem Manuskript', *Aspects*, 102–24. Die Baseler Houliktaspraken werden weiter mit BH angedeutet.

[3] E. Langbroek, 'Eine niederdeutsche Apokalypse in der Baseler Handschrift F. VII. 12, folio 211r–217r', *Niederdeutsches Jahrbuch* 129 (2006), 111–38.

2. Bernardus Rordahusim

Der Schreiber, der den vierten Teil schrieb, macht sich an zwei Stellen in der Handschrift bekannt: Auf f. 180r schreibt er: 'Finit*us et com*plet*us* p*er* me b*er*nardu*m* stude*n*te*m* te*mpor*is t*un*c hilde*n*sim Anno do*mi*ni M° cccc° xlv°', und auf f. 208r: 'Explicit co*mpu*t*us* sacerdotal*is* sc*ri*ptum per ma*nus* b*er*-nardi rordahusi*m* qui t*empor*is tu*n*c visitans hildensi*m* s*u*b a*nn*o domi*ni* 1445'. Er heißt also Bernardus Rordahusim, stammte daher aus westerlauwersschem Friesland, aus Reduzum (ca. 10 Kilometer südlich von Leeuwarden), und arbeitete 1445, als er Hildesheim besuchte, als Scriba.[4] Van Buijtenen nimmt an, dass er einige Zeit in der Stiftung der Devotio Moderna Lüchtenhof in Hildesheim verblieb, die um das Jahr 1440 von Westfalen aus gegründet wurde. Aus den Personenlisten der Stiftung Lüchtenhof erfährt man leider nichts über Bernardus, aber kennzeichnend ist seine Schrift: Es ist die für die Devotio Moderna berühmte Fraterschrift, die *textualis formata* und *bastarda*.[5] Aus dem Inhalt der abgeschriebenen Texte ist vielleicht zu schließen, dass er ein Geistlicher war oder werden wollte.[6]

Dass der Schreiber oder Abschreiber mit der friesischen Sprache bekannt war, zeigt sich am deutlichsten in den friesischen Traureden; obwohl sie eine friesisch-niederdeutsche Mischsprache aufweisen, überherrscht das Friesische. Die Vita von St. Hubertus (*Legenda de sancto Huegberto*), die den Traureden unmittelbar folgt,[7] zeigt aber eine mittelniederdeutsch-friesische Mischsprache, in der das Mittelniederdeutsche weit überherrscht.[8] Ob Bernardus auch in der längeren niederdeutschen Apokalypse am Ende des vierten Teils Spuren hinterlässt, die man als friesisch definieren könnte, wie in der Vita von St. Hubertus, wird noch zu untersuchen sein. Es ist sehr wahrscheinlich, dass Bernardus Rordahusim nach einer mittelniederdeutschen (oder mitteldeutschen) Vorlage gearbeitet hat. So weit mir bekannt ist, gibt es drei weitere Handschriften, die den Text dieser Apokalypse enthalten: Helmst. 389, f. 9vb–15ra, Helmst. 1211, f. 23r–50v (beide in Wolfenbüttel) und Ms. Theol. 2° 83, f. 194rb–199rb (in Lüneburg).[9] Dass eine der vier Handschriften den anderen als Vorlage gedient haben könnte,

---

4 Die Angaben sind nach Buma, *Aldfryske houlikstaspraken*, 14–15.

5 Van Buijtenen, 'Bernardus Rordahusim', 319–25.

6 *Ibid.* 318.

7 Buma, *Aldfryske houlikstaspraken*, 13. Die Vita von St. Hubertus wird weiter mit VH angedeutet.

8 Bremmer, 'Bad Frisian and Bad Low German', 378–84. Bei den von Bremmer genannten friesischen Beispielen könnten einige dem Niederdeutschen zugerechnet werden: *hillich* (379), *de(e)r-* 'da, dort' (380), *bringghen* (380) und eventuell *vier, wierde* (379).

9 Vgl. Hj. Psilander, *Die Niederdeutsche Apokalypse* (Upsala, 1901), VIII–IX.

zeigt sich nicht aus einer durchgeführten stemmatologischen Untersuchung.[10] Nach Transkribierung der Apokalypsetexte der Handschriften aus Wolfenbüttel und Lüneburg – Textausgaben liegen leider noch nicht vor – könnte man mit Sicherheit schließen, dass alle vier Apokalypsetexte zu einer Textfamilie gehören. Manche unklare Stelle im Baseler Text konnte mit Hilfe einer der drei norddeutschen Texte geklärt werden. Zum Beispiel: Bernardus Rordahusim füllt manchmal eine Zeile mit buchstabenartigen Zeichen aus; an diesen Stellen findet man in Helmst. 389 und 1211 ähnliche Zeichen. Nur in Lüneburg, Ms. Theol. 2° 83 wird deutlich, was mit diesen Zeichen gemeint sein könnte: Wenn bei der Wiedergabe des Bibeltextes ein neues Kapitel anfängt, wird in roter Tinte das Kapitel vermerkt, so zu Vers 60: *secundu*m ca*pitulum*, zu Vers 117: *terti*um ca*pitulu*m usw. Oft steht am Ende eines Kapitels das Wort *Glosa*, das auf exegetische Erklärungen hindeutet. Der Titel des Textes in Ms. Theol. 2° 83 heißt denn auch: *Apocalipsis tho dude myd der glosen*. Im Baseler Text werden die Kapitelandeutungen manchmal zu Kritzeln, meistens erscheint aber in der Zeile eine offene Stelle. Auch findet man an den Stellen, wo das Wort *Glosa* hätte stehen können, einen größeren Zwischenraum mit einem Paragraphzeichen.

Der Schreiber von Ms. Theol. 2° 83 nennt ebenfalls seinen Namen, nämlich in den Versen, die dem Text hinzugefügt wurden (925–30):

O Leue sote mylde here ihesu crist /
wente du gnedich vn*de* barmhertich bist /
So wes gnedich vnde hebbe leff /
de dit lest vnde scrifft /
joh*anne*s vrigdach /
dat sin name is Amen et cetera.

Auch in Helmst. 1211 macht der Schreiber sich bekannt, am Ende des der Apokalypse vorhergehenden Textes; außerdem nennt er die Jahreszahl (f. 22v):

Hyr endet tobias bock Ghescreuen in
den iaren vnses heren (durchgestrichen: MCCCCVII62etc)
MCCCCII vn*de* sestich Des anderen
sundaghes in der vasten Got si gelouet
va*n* ey*n*en arme*n* Broder herme*n* va*n* bedeli-
ke is et gescreuen Got si myt vns

[10] E. Langbroek und A. Roeleveld, unter Mitarbeit von E. Wattel, ‘Die “Umgebung” der niederdeutschen Apokalypse in Basel, F.VII.12: Ergebnisse einer stemmatologischen Untersuchung und einer Reimuntersuchung’, *ABäG* 63 (2007), 179–97.

Auffallend ist also, dass wir von drei Apokalypsetexten die Namen der Schreiber wissen.

3. Die Apokalypse

Bei den Apokalypsetexten geht es um sich paarweise reimende Gedichte; die Baseler Apokalypse hat 912 Verse; Helmst. 389 und Helmst. 1211 zählen 922 beziehungsweise 862 Verse, Ms. Theol. 2° 83 hat 920 Verse. In keiner der Handschriften setzten die Schreiber die Verse ab, und nirgends zeigt sich der reimende Charakter des Textes auf den ersten Blick. In Helmst. 389, 1211 und Ms. Theol. 2° 83 folgt nach den letzten Versen noch ein Explicit.[11]

In Wf (zweimal):

> Explic*it* Apocalipsis b*ea*ti ioha*n*nis /
> apostoli etc. etc. /
> EXPLICIT LIBER B*EA*TI IOHANNIS /
> APOSTOLI. (Wf923–26)

In Wo folgt:

> Dyt bock heuet hyr ey*n* ende /
> Got mote vns syne genade sende*n* /
> wan wy van hy*n*nen solle*n* scheyde*n* /
> so mote vns maria geleeden /
> AMEN (Wo863–67)

Maria wird auch in den abschließenden Versen von L genannt:

> Dat wy god alle moten schowen /
> Vnde ewichliken moten myd eme rowen /
> Des helpe vns allen tho same*n* /
> Maria vn*de* er leue kynd Amen (L921–24)

In Wo scheint der Text durcheinander geraten zu sein. Vergleichen wir Wo mit B, Wf und L, dann müsste man nach Wo 1–636 die Verse Wo 790–844, dann Wo 732–89 und schließlich Wo 637–731 und Wo 845–62 lesen. Außerdem fehlt in Wo ein größerer Textteil: nach Vers 260 fehlen 50 Verse.

[11] Die Hss. werden weiter verkürzt genannt: Basel F.VII.12 mit B, Helmst. 389 mit Wf, Helmst. 1211 mit Wo, Ms. Theol. 2° 83 mit L.

In allen Handschriften weicht die Reihenfolge der Bilder, die in den Apokalypsetexten gezeigt werden, einigermaßen von der in der Bibel ab.[12]

4. Die Sprache der Apokalypse

Der Frage soll nachgegangen werden, ob dem Scribenten Bernardus bei der Transkription der Apokalypse friesische Schreibgewohnheiten unterlaufen sind. Dazu soll sein Text sehr kritisch betrachtet werden. Auf den ersten Blick scheint der ganze Text der Apokalypse mittelniederdeutsch zu sein; aber viele für das Mittelniederdeutsche typische Schreibweisen könnte man im Friesischen auch antreffen. Als Beispiel werden die ersten 12 Verse des Textes zitiert; daneben wird von einigen Wörtern von mir die (fast) gleiche friesische Variante geschrieben:

(Text)	(friesische Schreibweise)
APPOKALIPSE IS DIT BOEK GHENAMT	is; dit, bok/boek, named
DAR I*N*NE IS VNS wunders vele beka*n*t	inne, wonders, folla, bekand/t
Dat besc*r*iuet vns jo*hannes* ewa*ngelis*ta	bi/besk/crivath/eth
To patmos in der insula	to/tho, in, der
des meres an eyn ende	des, meres, ende
Dar on domician*us* de keyser hen sende	de, keiser, hen, sende
Dorch had de bose tyra*n*ne	hat, de
To leyde dem heyligh*en* ma*n*ne	to/tho, leyde, heylig(h), manne
Dat he den hillighe rechten louen nicht	dene
en merde	en, merde (?)
Vn*de* dat wolke tho gode kerde	folk, to/tho, gode, kerde
Alse he tho asya hadde ghedan	alse, to/tho
Des gheliik wolde he ok tho rome began	des, lik(e), wolde, to/tho

Bei dieser Arbeitsweise, bei der von jeder Verszeile die jeweiligen friesischen Wörter aufgezählt werden, werden zwar die großen Sprachübereinstimmungen zwischen dem geschriebenen Mittelniederdeutschen und dem Friesischen aufgezeigt, sie besagen aber nicht, dass Bernardus sich weniger gut im Mittelniederdeutschen auskannte. Dass er seiner Vorlage im Allgemeinen treu war, zeigen folgende Verse (1–6), die den vier Textvarianten entnommen sind:

[12] Die Länge und die Reihenfolge der Apokalypse in B, Wo, Wf und L weichen ab von der von Psilander, *Die Niederdeutsche Apokalypse*, aus verschiedenen Fragmenten rekonstruierten niederdeutschen Apokalypse. Nach Psilander (S. VIII–IX) sind Wo, Wf und L stark gekürzt, die Handschrift B kannte er nicht; auf Apok. 1–13 folgt in B, Wo, Wf und L Apok. 17, 18, 20, 14, 21. Psilanders Rekonstruktion zählt insgesamt 2566 Verse; sie kennt bei den erzählten 'Bildern' aus der Bibel keine Umstellung.

B1 APPOKALIPSE IS DIT BOEK GHENAMT
Wo1 Apocolipsis is dyt ey*n* boch genant
Wf1 APocalipsis ys en boych genant
L1 Apocalipsis is dit bok ghenant

B2 DAR I*N*NE IS VNS wunders vele beka*n*t
Wo2 dar jnne vns vele wonders vert bekant
Wf2 dar y*n*ne vns wu*n*ders wert vele bekant
L2 Dar inne vele wunders wert bekant

B3 Dat bescr*i*uet vns jo*hannes* ewa*ngelis*ta
Wo3 Dat bescriuet vns johan*ne*s de hillige ewangelista
Wf3 Dat bescref ioha*n*nes Ewa*n*gelista
L3 Dat bescrift sunte ioh*ann*es ewangelista

B4 To patmos in der insula
Wo4 to pachmos jn dem insula
Wf4 tho patmos in der Insula
L4 To pathmos in deme insula

B5 des meres an eyn ende
Wo5 jn des meers ellende
Wf5 An des meres elle*n*de
L5 In des meres elende

B6 Dar on domician*us* De keyser hen sende
Wo6 dor dar en de konynck damycianus hen sende
Wf6 dar en de ko*nn*i*n*g damasian*us* hen sende
L6 Dar ene de keyser domicianus he*n*ne sende

Bei Wf, Wo und L ist wahrscheinlich von norddeutschen Schreibern auszugehen. Die Unterschiede zwischen den vier Varianten sind wohl hauptsächlich auf niederdeutsche Mundartunterschiede zurückzuführen. Eine Mundartuntersuchung der drei Parallelhandschriften zeigt folgendes: Wf ist sehr wahrscheinlich ein westfälischer Text, eventuell aus dem Grenzgebiet mit dem Nordniederdeutschen. Wo ist zweifellos ein westfälischer Text. Der Lüneburger Text zeigt vor allem nordniederdeutsche und westfälische Kennzeichen. Es könnte sein, dass er ebenfalls dem Grenzgebiet des Nordniederdeutschen und Westfälischen entstammt.[13]

[13] Vgl. für die Mundartuntersuchung Anhang 2, 3 und 4. Siehe hierzu R. Peters, 'Katalog sprachlicher Merkmale zur variablenlinguistischen Erforschung des Mittelniederdeutschen. I–III', *NW* 27 (1987), 61–93; 28 (1988), 75–106; 30 (1990), 1–18, im

Daher wird bei folgender Untersuchung von einer alphabetischen Wörterliste Gebrauch gemacht, die ich vom Wortmaterial der Baseler Apokalypse gemacht habe. Typisch friesische lexikologische Kriterien, wie Bremmer sie für die St. Hubertusvita zusammenstellte,[14] gelten hier nicht, da der Scribent nach mnd. oder md. Vorlage arbeitete. Er gebraucht also, um einige Beispiele zu nennen, mnd. *eder*, *edder* statt fries. *jefta*, mnd. *rauwen* statt fries. *resta* oder mnd. *allerleye* statt fries. *enigre hande*, mnd. *dunker* statt fries. *thiuster*. Bei der Suche nach friesischen Spuren gehe ich daher vom Mittelniederdeutschen und den (Un-)Möglichkeiten in mittelniederdeutscher Sprache aus. Es werden zum Vergleich die entsprechenden Wörter aus Wo, Wf und L zitiert. Bei der Besprechung kommen folgende Punkte vor:

a. Welche Formen sind im Mnd. unmöglich?
b. Welche Formen sind im Mnd. eigentlich unmöglich?
c. Was fällt auf, aber wäre im Mnd. und im Fries. möglich?
d. Was fällt so auf, dass es erklärt werden muss?
e. Schlussfolgerungen.

4a. Welche Formen sind im Mittelniederdeutschen unmöglich?

4a1. *Ingwäonismen*:
Viele der für das (Alt-)Friesische typischen Ingwäonismen fehlen im Baseler Text; so trifft man nirgends die friesischen Wörter *ōther*, *tōth* und *tēth*, *mūth*, *kūthe* ('kannte'); 'uns' trifft man im Mnd. zwar als *ūs* und *uns* an, es erscheint hier nur als *vns*, *wns*, *vnser-*. Für 'ander' findet man *ander(-)* in B184, 310, 399, 574, 638, 639, 667, 796, 812. Für 'Zähne' findet man *tenen* in B483, für 'Mund' *munt* in B394, 488, 606, 776, *mund(e)* sieht man sogar zehnmal. 'Kannte' kommt nicht vor; Nur *fīf* findet seine Entsprechung; 'fünf(te)' kommt vor als *wiiff* in B474 und *wiiffte* in B407; die Formen könnten aber auch mnd. sein.

4a2. B93 *Nu* schille gy *alle rechte vorstan*
[Wo92 solle gy Wf91 schulle gy L93 schole gy]
Sonstige Formen des Verbs 'sollen' sind in B: (du) *schalt*, (er) *scal*, *sal*, (wir, sie) *scolen*, *scollen*, *scullen*, *schullen*, *sullen*, (er) *scholde*, *scolde*, (sie)

Folgenden: Peters. Für eine vergleichbare Untersuchung, siehe E. Langbroek und A. Roeleveld, 'Ein stemmatologischer Versuch. "Dith is de kranshals" im Hartebok. Textvergleiche mit den überlieferten sonstigen Kranshalsgedichten', *ABäG* 60 (2005), vor allem 185–86, 194–98.

14 Vgl. Bremmer, 'Bad Frisian and Bad Low German', 382.

scholden, scolden, solden.[15] Befremdend ist nicht so sehr die wechselnde Orthographie von *s-*, *sc-*, *sch-*, sondern der Vokal *-i-* in *schille gy*. Die Normalformen des Infinitivs und der Präs. Pluralformen, mit Umlautfaktor, sind im Mnd. *schülen*, *schölen*, *schült*, *schölt*. Der Umlaut wurde durch analoge Übertragung aus dem Optativ verursacht, was doch bei 'sollen' nie zur *i*-Schreibung führte.[16]

Im Friesischen ist folgende Entwicklung zu sehen: *u* > *ü* > *e* > *i*, wo das Optativsuffix *-in* Umlaut bewirkt hat.[17] Für das westerlauwerssche Friesisch ist es so, dass die Singularformen *skil* (*skel*) verursachen, dass für früheres **skula* (Inf.), *skulath* (Plur. Präs. Ind.) **skilla* (**skella*), *skilleth* (*scellet*) eintritt.[18]

4a3. B768 *Eyn* dyar *gan vte des wilden mers g[ ]nde*
B810 *Dyt* dyar *dat aldus vte dem mere is ghegan*
B812 *Dat ander* dyar *dat dar quam van der eerden*
[Wo765 deyr Wf777 der L775 deir]
[Wo655 deyr Wf820 deyr L818 deir]
[Wo657 -- Wf822 der L820 deir]

Für das Wort 'Tier' oder 'Tiere' gebraucht Bernardus neben *dyar* fünfmal *dere* (Akk./Dat.Sg.), einmal *deyr*, einmal *dyer*, einmal *dere* (Pl.).[19] Für die Form *dyer* ließe sich im Mnd. eine Erklärung finden: Das mnd. *ē* < germ. *eu* (in germ. **deuza*; as. *dior*) konkurriert mit *i* (*y*, *ie* [d.i. Diphth.], vor allem im östlichen Gebiet (Lasch §113); archaisierende Schreibungen kommen unter hd. und ndfries. Einfluss vor (Lasch §114); einige Male kommt *dēr* 'Tier' mit *i* vor (Lasch §115).

---

15 Vgl. *schalt* [40, 119], *scal, sal* [164, 293, 358, 538, 621, 642], *scolen, scollen, scullen, schullen, sullen* [42, 120, 360, 600, 620, 665, 697, 764, 876], *scolde* [378, 580, 875], *scholden, scolden, solden* [28, 230, 234, 285, 291, 292, 472, 887, 890, 891].

16 Vgl. A. Lasch, *Mittelniederdeutsche Grammatik* (Halle/S., 1914), §53, 422 A.3 und 443; im Folgenden: Lasch. Im Wisbyer Stadtrecht, im Kieler Rentebuch (also in nördlichen und russischen Texten) findet man das *y* als Schreibweise für umgelautetes *u*; vgl. Lasch §45 u. §45 A.2.

17 W. L. van Helten, *Altostfriesische Grammatik* (Leeuwarden, 1890), §282; im Folgenden: van Helten.

18 G. Gosses, *De Friesche oorkonden uit het archief van het St. Anthony-Gasthuis te Leeuwarden. I. Een bijdrage tot de kennis der historische grammatika van het Westfriesch* (Amsterdam, 1939), §161, A.3. Vgl. auch BH II 24, III 125 *schil*, BH III 131, 133 *schillet*.

19 Vgl. *dere* [779, 783, 797, 800, 824], *deyr* [796], *dyer* [651], *dere* Pl. [410].

Germ. *eu* entwickelt sich im Friesischen aber zu *ia* bei *a*, *e*, *o* der Folgesilbe.[20] Folglich kann das dreimalige *dyar* nur als friesische Interferenz betrachtet werden.

4b. Welche Formen sind im Mnd. eigentlich unmöglich?

4b1a. B43 *Van* onbeginne *went an den ende*
[Wo42 anbegynne Wf42 anbegynne L43 ambeginne]

Sonstige Schreibungen für 'Anfang', *aenbeginne* und *ambeghin*, kommen jeweils einmal vor.[21] An diesen Stellen bevorzugen Wo, Wf und L *anbegyn(ne)*, *ambeghin*. Die Schreibung *a* > *o* findet man vor *ld*, *lt*; einige mnd. Dialekte behalten das *a* bei (Lasch §93). Nur im Merseburgischen scheint *a* > *o* vor Nasal vorzukommen. Die Fälle sind nach Lasch (§92 Anm.) den Frisismen des Gebietes beizuzählen. Ist dies der Fall, dann könnte die Vorsilbe *on-* unter friesischem Einfluss stehen.
Im Friesischen entwickelt sich germ. *a* vor Nasalen (ohne folgende Spiranten) zu *o*, wie in *onbijenn*, obwohl es viele Schwankungen gibt: z.B. *man* / *mon*, *nama* / *noma*, *land* / *lond;*[22] auch die Schreibung im Westfriesischen wechselt zwischen *oen* und *aen.*[23]

4b1b. B320 *Van der werelt* [a]n begange
[Wo266 aneghange Wf318 anevange L316 ane vange]

Bei *[a]n begange* ist natürlich unsicher, welcher Anfangsvokal gemeint ist. Die Zusammensetzung ist im Mnd. ungebräuchlich; normalerweise findet man *anbegin*, *anegin*, *angank*, *anegank*, *anegenk*. Das Wort scheint eine Mischform zu sein von *anbegin* und *anegank*. Bei dieser Mischform könnte das friesische *-gang* / *-gong* / *-gung* oder das Verb *bigunga* eine Rolle gespielt haben. Eine solche Vermischung trifft man nicht in den drei anderen Apokalypsetexten.

4b2a. B125 *Siin anlaet was* hem *groen vnde roed*
B785 *Siin mund ward* hem *wp ghedan*
[Wo124 eme Wf123 em L125 em]
[Wo783 eme Wf795 em L793 eme]

Das Pronomen personale 'ihm' oder 'ihn' kommt in diesem Text vor als:

om 5	*ome* 6	*one* 4	*hem* 2
oem 1	*on* 7	*enne* 1	

[20] W. Steller, *Abriss der altfriesischen Grammatik*, Sammlung kurzer Grammatiken germanischer Dialekte, C. Abriss Nr. 5 (Halle/S., 1928), §20. Vgl. für *dyar* auch BH II 37, VH 178, 181, 188, 190, 191, 196, 198, für *dier* VH 171,172, 177, 184, für *dyer* VH 169.
[21] Vgl. *aenbeginne* [B213], *ambeghin* [B83].
[22] Steller, *Abriss*, §4.
[23] Gosses, *De Friesche oorkonden*, §65.

Lasch (§353) bemerkt zu dem *h*, dass manche Schreiber das *h* fälschlicherweise weglassen oder hinzufügen, wie bei *hunsen* < *unsen* und *heres* < *eres*. Wäre von einer irrtümlichen Hinzufügung eines *h* auszugehen und wäre ursprünglich in beiden Fällen *em* anzunehmen, dann befremdet *em* trotzdem, weil der Scribent sonst die ostfälische Schreibweise *om(e)*, *oem*, *on(e)* bevorzugt. Nach Lasch (§404 A.3) begegnet *hem* in Texten aus dem niederdeutschen Ostfriesland.[24] Es fällt aber auf, dass man nur in zwei Fällen eine niederdeutsch-ostfriesische Form antrifft (vgl. auch Peters 4.5.1.9/10.).

Die fries. Formen *him* / *hem* / *hine* / *hene* könnten den Schreiber aber beeinflusst haben. Sowohl in BH als in VH findet man hem. Außerdem ist hier Einfluss des Niederländischen *heme*, *hem* nicht auszuschließen.[25]

4b2b. B833 *Die moeten myt* hore *in dat affgrunde sencken*
[Wo678 er Wf843 er L841 er]

Das Pronomen personale (mit) ‘ihr’ oder (von) ‘ihnen’ kennt in diesem Text mehrere Formen:

or 3 *ore* 3
oer 4 *hore* 1

Die Schreibung *or(e)* statt *er(e)* kommt vor allem im Ostfälischen vor. Nach Peters (4.5.1.13.) findet man *hore* im Ostniederländischen und im niederdeutschen Ostfriesland. Sonst ist das Anfangs-*h* sehr ungebräuchlich. Es mutet natürlich fremd an, wenn nur bei einer Form ein ostniederländisches oder niederdeutsch-ostfriesisches Element auftreten würde. Vielleicht gilt hier ebenfalls die Bemerkung von Lasch, dass das *h* nur falsch hinzugefügt wurde.

Nicht aber im Westfriesischen: da gibt es die Formen *hira* / *hire* / *hera* / *here.*[26]

Bei dem Pronomen possesivum Plur. und Fem. Sg. ‘ihr-’ sieht man im Baseler Text ebenfalls Formen mit und ohne Anfangs-*h*. Neunmal kommt *oer*, 35mal *or-* und insgesamt achtmal *hore-* vor. In all diesen Fällen haben Wo, Wf und L *er-*. Die weitaus gebräuchlichsten Formen *oer* und *or-* sind für das Ostfälische kennzeichnend, *hore* könnte nur im Ostniederländischen oder im niederdeutschen Ostfriesisch ihre Berechtigung haben. Wie schon bei dem Pronomen personale *hore* gesagt wurde, muten die Formen mit

---

[24] Mit dem niederdeutschen Ostfriesland ist das Gebiet östlich des Dollarts gemeint.

[25] Vgl. J. Franck, *Mittelniederländische grammatik, mit Lesestücken und Glossar* (Leipzig, 1910; Nachdr. Arnheim, 1971), §210.

[26] Gosses, *De Friesche oorkonden*, §106; vgl. auch Steller, *Abriss*, §83. Vgl. BH fries. *hyaren, hemmen*, mnd. *hoer, horen*.

Anfangs-*h* fremd an. Offen bleibt, ob auch hier das friesische *hira* etc. eine Rolle gespielt hat.[27]

4b3. B98 *Betekent sine godheyt* llutter *ende claer*
[Wo97 lutter Wf96 lutter L98 lutter]

Noch einmal kommt 'rein' vor: *lutteren* (B603). In der anlautenden altnd. Verbindung *hl* schwindet das *h*. Ob das *ll* für eine intensivere Aussprache als einfaches *l* steht, bleibt unklar.

Im Altfriesischen wechseln die anlautenden Verbindungen *hw*, *hr*, *hl*, *hn* unter Verlust des *h* mit *w*, *r*, *l*, *n*, z.B. in *hlid* und *lid.*[28] Im Codex Roorda (ca. 1480) trifft man noch die Form *hlutter*. Es wäre also möglich, dass *llutter* eine friesische Interferenz ausweist.

4b4. B474 Masten *wiiff manen pine van on liden*
[Wo423 mosten Wf476 mosten L474 Mosten]

Präteritumformen von *moten* 'müssen, mögen' sind fünfmal *moste*, zweimal *mosten* und einmal *masten*. Normalerweise findet man im Mnd. *mōste(n)*, *moste(n)*, *muste(n)*. Für die *a*-Schreibung gibt es keine Erklärung, es sei denn, der Schreiber hat irrtümlicherweise ein *a* geschrieben oder das *o* in seiner Vorlage in *a* geändert, wie es oft im Nnd. und Ofäl. passierte; die volle Durchführung der Schreibung *a* für *o* geschah im Laufe des 15. Jahrhunderts (jedoch nicht bei mosten) (vgl. *a* < *o*, Lasch §85ff.). Eine andere Möglichkeit wäre, dass Analogie das a bewirkt hat; vgl. dazu die fries. Form *machte* neben *muchte*, *mochte*[29] für mnd. mochte. In allen Fällen, wo in B *moste(n)* geschrieben wird, steht in L meistens *mochte(n)*. Vergleicht man nun die Fälle, wo B *mochte(n)* schreibt (B274, 561, 678, 745), dann findet man in Wo und L ebenfalls *mochten*, in Wf einmal *machten*. Ich weise noch kurz darauf hin, dass Wf (Helmst. 389) ein westfälischer Text mit nordniederdeutschen Kennzeichen ist.[30] Die *a*-Schreibung für *o* kommt ja gerade im Ndd. viel vor.

4c. Was fällt auf, wäre aber im Mittelniederdeutschen und im Friesischen möglich

4c1. B506 *Dat bedudet ores herten* erghe
[Wo457 arghe Wf510 erge L508 arge]

---

[27] Für das Mittelniederländische vgl. Franck, *Mittelniederländische Grammatik*, §45: 'dunkelfarbiges *-r* hinter Vokal zeigt sich in Nebenformen von *hare*: *hör(e), hore, hoor*'.

[28] Steller, *Abriss*, §45 A.2. Vgl. dazu H. Nijdam, 'Loss of Old Frisian *h* in Initial Consonant Clusters', *ABäG* 51 (1999), 81–104.

[29] Steller, *Abriss*, §104 V.8; vgl. Gosses, *De Friesche oorkonden*, §143.

[30] Vgl. Anhang 3.

Das Wort *erghe* sollte mit *halsberge* ein Reimpaar bilden, wie in Wo, Wf und L; in B505 wurde aber *hals bande* geschrieben. Wo und L haben mit *halsberg(h)e* : arg(h)e also einen unreinen Reim. In B802 findet man das Adj. *arghen (raed)* (vgl. Wo647, Wf812, L810 argen), in nicht-reimender Position. Im Altsächsischen wurde *a* vor einer *r*-Verbindung nicht umgelautet; im Mnd. sieht man aber ein umgelautetes *a* in *-werdich* (vgl. Lasch §58, 3).[31] Auch im Komparativ des Adj. findet man ebenfalls umgelautete und unumgelautete Formen neben einander: *arger*, *erger* (Lasch §393).
Im Friesischen wird *a* vor *rg* oft zu *e*: erg; im Westfriesischen kommt *arg* neben *erg* vor.[32]

4c2. B437 Dat die schep der van voersunken
B572 Grod wunder scholde der werden gheseyn
[Wo386 dar Wf439 dar L437 dar]
[Wo522 dar Wf577 dar L575 dar]

Der Schreiber verwendet für 'da, dort' sehr oft *dar* (mehr als zwanzigmal), einmal *daer* und zweimal *der*. Nach Lasch erscheint schon früh e für a durch Abschwächung in einer Reihe gewöhnlich nebentönig oder unbetont gebrauchter Partikeln: *dār* > *dar* > *der* 'dort' (Lasch §80 u. 83 A.1). Es fragt sich nur, warum in B zweimal der erscheint, wo die Normalform doch dar ist; die Parallelhss. weisen nur dar auf.
Das westfriesische Wort für 'dort' lautet *deer*, *der*, wo sich aus *a* ein Nebenton *e* entwickelte, außerdem findet man *dar*, *daer.*[33]

4c3. B281 *Disse enghel vor mit* grimme
[Wo -- Wf279 grimme L279 grymme]

Dieser Vers fehlt in Wo; in B, Wf und L reimt *grimme/grymme* auf *stempme/stempne*. Die Reimposition *stemme* : *gremme* kommt auch einmal vor in B139/40, während Wo, Wf und L *grimme/grymme* : *stemme/stempne* bevorzugen. Ob im Mnd. die Normalform gram ist, ist unklar. Im As. findet man *gram* (< germ. **grama*) und *grim* (< germ. **gremma).*[34] Ein umgelautetes *a* kann unter Umständen zu *i* werden: vor dentalen und gutturalen Nasalverbindungen und vor *l*-Verbindungen, die hier aber keine Rolle spielen. Vielleicht ist in diesem Beispiel das für das Ostfälische *i* statt *e* zu

31 Ein Textbeispiel aus B ist B537 *weruet.*

32 Gosses, *De Friesche oorkonden*, §56; Steller, *Abriss*, §3 A.2. Vgl. BH I 98 *erga* (Akk. Pl.).

33 J. S. H. Boersma, *De Friesche oorkonden uit het archief van het St. Anthony-Gasthuis te Leeuwarden. II. Een bijdrage tot de kennis der historische grammatika van het Westfriesch* (Amsterdam, 1939), §3 u. §11. Vgl. auch Steller, *Abriss*, §23 A.2. In BH trifft man neben *der* auch *daer*.

34 F. Kluge, *Etymologisches Wörterbuch der deutschen Sprache*, 23. Aufl., bearbeitet von E. Seebold (Berlin und New York, 1995), 333 und 338.

finden, wie bei *stidde, schipper* (statt *stede, schepper*) zu sehen ist (Lasch §140; Peters 1.1.1.).
Dass bei allen Apokalypsetexten mit Beeinflussung von fries. *grimm* gerechnet werden muss, ist unwahrscheinlich.

4c4. B557 *Dat war ludet vnde is* dach *gheloghen*
[Wo507 doch Wf562 doch L560 doch]
Sonstige Formen von 'doch' sind *doch* (viermal) und *doech* (dreimal). Im Mnd. entwickelt sich *a* < *o* einige Male vor stimmlosen Spiranten *f, ch.* In westfälischen Texten könnte dies Abschwächung sein (vgl. Lasch (§85); Lasch fragt sich, ob *dach* < *doch* in einem ostfälischen Fall eine nebentönige Entwicklung sein kann.
Das fries. *thach* entwickelte sich aus germ. *au* zu fries. *ā*.[35] Beeinflussung ist hier nicht ausgeschlossen.

4c5. B269 *Die den* vyer *winden dat werden*
B283 *De* vyer *enghelen alzo Tho*
B343 *De* vyer *vnde twentich oltheren*
B302 *De* wyer *enghele de in der werelt stan*
B405 *Die* wierde *enghel bleys dorch noet*
[Wo -- Wf276 ver L267 veer]
[Wo -- Wf281 ver L281 ver]
[Wo289 vere Wf341 ver L339 veer]
[Wo -- Wf300 ver L299 ver]
[Wo354 verde Wf407 (derde) L405 verde]
Für 'vier', 'vierte' und Zusammensetzungen mit 'vier' trifft man in B außer den oben erwähnten Fällen viele Schreibweisen:

ver (B149)	*veyer* (B271)
weer (B147, 268)	*weyer* (B305)
vere (B134, 175)	*ver(diehalliff)* (B631)
veyr (B347)	*veere(halff)* (B791)
weyr (B303, 515, 539, 540, 620)	*weyr*(kant) (B906)

Man könnte vor allem aus den Schreibweisen in direkter Nähe der oben erwähnten Fällen (bei B268, 271, 303, 305, 347) schließen, dass der Schreiber bei 'vier' oder 'vierte' keine feste Orthographie hatte. Wohl erscheint mnd. *ver*, aus germ. **fewar*, mitunter als *vir*, denn mit *ē* konkurriert auch *ī* (y, ie); außerdem wäre *vir* als Zahlwort leicht der Entlehnung ausgesetzt (Lasch §113, 115 u. 397 A.1).
Ein ähnlicher Fall, dass *ē* mit *ī* (y, ie) wechselt, könnte neben B461 *vor leysen*, B494 *worleset*, B206 *woerleyset* in B440 *woerliezen* [vgl. Wo389 *verlesen*; Wf442 *verlesen* L440 vor--] vorliegen.

---
[35] Steller, *Abriss*, §19

Es wäre möglich, dass bei der wechselnden Schreibweise von 'vier(te)' das friesische *fiar*, *fiuwer*, *fiower*, *fior* mitgespielt hat,[36] und bei 'verlieren' das fries. *-liasa*.

4c6. B637 *Dat teyende* dyel *vel nedder van der stad*
[Wo589 deyl Wf642 del L640 deyl]

Sonst kommt 'Teil' vor als:

deel 1
deil 5
deyl(e) 6[37]

In B404, mit *deyl*, wurde *dil* gestrichen. Die anderen Apokalypsetexte bevorzugen nur *del*, *deil*, *deyl*. Es könnte sich natürlich um einen Schreibfehler handeln: *ye* statt *ey*. Aber das *ē* < germ. *ai* in mnd. del entwickelt sich manchmal zu *i*, in *dīl*, *ordīl* (Lasch §145, 1). Vielleicht hat außerdem eine Rolle gespielt, dass *e* vor *l*-Verbindungen zu *i* wird (Lasch §137).
Im Altfriesischen ist die Normalform *del*, im Westfriesischen entwickelt sich *ē* > *ī*; man trifft da oft *diel* neben *deel*.[38]

4c7. B434 *Betekent den* duwel *myt sinem heer*
[Wo383 duuel Wf436 duvel L434 duuel]

Sonstige Beispiele in B für *duwel*, *duwels*, *duwele* sind B210, 549, 525, 556. Weiter trifft man *duuel* (B720, 735), *duuele* (B710, 716) und *duvels* (B189). Nach Lasch (§290, 291) tritt im 15. Jahrhundert *w* häufig für *v* ein.
Bremmer bringt die Änderung von *v* in *w* zwischen Vokalen, besonderes nach Vokalen in der Anfangssilbe, als Beispiel für Frisismen in der Vita von St. Hubertus.[39] Vgl. weiter unten für die allgemeine unsichere Schreibung des *f*, *v*, *u*, *w* (4c9.).

4c8. *Metathese des* r

Die Metathese des *r* neben kurzem Vokal ist eine im Nd. (und Ndl.) sehr verbreitete Erscheinung. Als feste Gruppen entwickeln sich *tr*, *vr* vor Vokal, *r* + Dental (*rd*, *rt*, *rst*, *rs(ch)*, *rn*), jedoch nicht *rnd*, also *bernen* und *brande*. Als Beispiele nennt Lasch (§231) u.a. *vrüchten*, *derde* < *dridde*, *bersten*, *born*. In B findet man *bernen* (B430), *bernende* (B400, 706), *branden* (B143), *brenden* (B328); für 'dritte' *derde* (B193), *dredde* (B403) und

---

36 Vgl. auch Bremmer, 'Bad Frisian and Bad Low German', 379. In VH findet man (Z. 20, 24, 185) *wier*, (Z. 70) *wyer*, (Z. 31) *wierde*.

37 B686 *deel*; B397, 402, 406, 427, 451 *deil*; B404, 412, 493, 520, 529, 657 *deyl(e)*.

38 Boersma, *De Friesche oorkonden*, §15 *deel*, §20 *diel*, §38 *diel, deel*, §118 *deel*, §128 *diel*.

39 Bremmer, 'Bad Frisian and Bad Low German', 378; VH (Z. 29) *duwel*.

dridde (elfmal).[40] Für *born* findet man *bornen* (B360). Vgl. weiter die folgenden Formen und ihre fries. Entsprechung: (fünfmal) *dorch* – fries. *thruch*; (zweimal) *gras* – fries. *gers*, *gres*; (zwölfmal) *ros*, *roes*, *rosse* – fries. *hars*, *hors*. B kennt also Formen mit und ohne Metathese.

4c9. *Unsicherheit bei der Schreibung* f/v/u *und* w

Wie schon bei 4c5. (*wierde*, *woerliezen*) und 4c7. (*duwel*) zu sehen ist, wird in B *w* statt *v/u* geschrieben. Das umgekehrte kommt auch häufig vor. Die Beispiele werden nach Anlaut und Inlaut getrennt:

u/v/f > *w*, im Anlaut (außer *weer* etc. 'vier'):

wntfaen B666, neben *vntfan* (*entfan*, *ontfaen*, *ontfaed*, *ontfengh*, *ent*--)
wn vorwunnen B277; 'un-' sonst immer *vn*
wp B34, *wppe* in sehr vielen (mehr als 50) Fällen, neben *vppe* (13x)
wt B16 und in zehn weiteren Fällen, neben *vt*, *ut*, *vte* (insgesamt 20x)
wal B859 'Fall', neben *vael* (B454), *val* (B858)
wel B637, *weel* B408 'fiel', neben *vel* (3x), *vellen* (6x)
wel B36, *wele* B323, *wil* B328, 517, 793 'viel(e)', neben *vele* (4x), *vel* (1x), *vil* (5x)
walsche(-) B444, 801 'falsch', *walscheyt* B445, neben *valsche*(-) (7x)
werne B407, neben *verne* (B256, 844)
wyent B222, *wienden* B237, *wyenden* B634, neben *vient* (B182), *viande* (B179)
wiiff B474, *wiiffte* 'fünf(te)' B407
winden B795, *want* B128 'finden, fand', neben *vint* (B802, 866), *vunden* (B334)
wlammen B101, neben *vlammen* (B70), *flammen* (B436)
wloech B416, 739, *wloeck* B512 'flog'
wolk B836, 875, *wolke* B10, 633 'Volk', neben *volk* (B444, 682, 817)
wor B318, (7x) *woer* 'vor', neben *vor* (8x)
wor- (6x), *woer-* (17x) 'ver-', neben *vor* (27x), *voer* (5x), *ver* (18x)
worde B280 'führte', neben *vorde* (B194)
wort B678 'fort', neben *vort* (B62, 593, 703)
woyte(-) B75, 671, 697, 775, neben *voet* (B111), *vote* (B80, 574)
wreysliik B141, 208, *wreysliick* B769, *wreysliken* B525, neben *vresliik* (B479), *vreysliken* (B523)
wro B36 'früh', neben *vro* (B198, 284, 342, 518)
wronbe B81, 95 'heilig', neben *vrouwe* (wrs. statt *vronwe*, B118)
wroyde B388 'Freude', neben *vroyde*(-) (B236, 351, 424, 630), *froyde* (B461)

[40] Vgl. für die Varianten Lasch §399: *dridde, drudden, derde (dirde, darde), dörde (dröde, dürde).*

wul na B210
wur B163, 370, *wuer* B379, 408, 454, 528, 555 'Feuer', neben *vur* (B425)
wurich B524, 545, 601, *wurighe* B433, neben *vurich* (B185), *vurighen* (B706), *vürne* (B571)
wns B220, 222, 884, neben *vns* (B2, 3, 166, 537, 733, 820)
u/v > *w*, im Inlaut (außer *duwel(-)*):
liewes B184 'Leib', neben *lyues* (B426), *liue* (B563, 662), *lyue* (B738)
ower B88, 169, 193, neben *over* (B237), *ouer* (neunmal), *auer* (4x)
voerderwen B563
w > *v*, nur im (Silben-)Anlaut (außer *vere* etc. 'vier'):
ghevant B65 [normal: *gewāt*, vgl. aber *gewandstricker*], neben *wande* (B137, 326, 349)
ghevolt B187, *ghevalt* B546 'Gewalt', neben *ghewalt* (B710, 814)
van B246 'wann, wenn', neben *wan* (B703), *wen* (B287, 702)
venede B155 'weinte', neben *wenen* (B901)
vere B253 'wäre', neben *were* (B774, 821), *weren* (15x)
viiff B502, *vyue* B858 'Weib', neben *wiiff* (8x), *wyue*(s) (B482, 503, 737)
vint B246 'Wind', neben *wint* (B867), *winden* (B269, 303)
vol B340 'wohl', neben *wol* (10x), *wal* (B797)
voldaet B346, neben waldat (B103)
volken B567 'Wolke', neben *wolken* (B595, 597, 881)
vrake B237 'Rache', neben *wrake* (B227)

Wie aus den obigen Fällen klar wird, wechselt die Orthographie, was *v/u* und *w* betrifft, stark. Nach Lasch erscheint westgerm. *f* in mnd. Texten anlautend als stimmloses *v* und später auch als *f* (§288), wie vielleicht bei *flammen* (B436) und *froyde* (B461) zu sehen ist. Bei Fremdwörtern wie *figūre* und *forme* ist *f* im Anlaut üblich. Vielleicht wurde *flammen* noch als Fremdwort betrachtet. Gegen die Tatsache, dass *flammen* und *froyde* noch als Fremwörter betrachtet werden könnten, sprechen übrigens die Formen *wlammen* (B101) / *vlammen* (B70) und *wroyde* (B 388) / *vroyde* (B 236, 351, 424, 630). Inlautend steht *v*, *u* für den stimmhaften Laut; während *u* im Anlaut nur beschränkt auftritt, ist *u* im Imlaut nicht selten. Später, besonders im späteren 15. Jahrhundert, tritt *w* häufig für *v* ein (Lasch §290). Lasch bemerkt außerdem (§291), dass *v* nicht selten für *w* im Anlaut eintritt, besonders in flüchtigen Schriftstücken oder bei ungeübten Schreibern. In der Inlautschreibung tritt *w* später auch für germ. *f* und stimmh. *b* an die Stelle des *v* und ist in vielen Dialekten mit inlautend *f*, *v* zusammengefallen (in einen labiodentalen Laut) (Lasch §291, 292). Der Vokal *u* kann ebenfalls mit *u*, *v*, *w* wiedergegeben werden; im Allgemeinen steht *v* im Anlaut, *u* im Inlaut (Lasch §179). Also sind alle Variationen, die Bernardus anwandte, durchaus möglich, aber es muss bemerkt werden, dass die Paralleltexte Wo,

Wf und L keine solche Variierung zeigen. Das Problem ist, dass hier von einem flüchtigen Schriftstück bestimmt nicht die Rede ist. Und einen ungeübten Schreiber kann man Bernardus nicht nennen, es sei denn, dass er ungeübt in der Niederschrift der mittelniederdeutschen Sprache(n) war.

Für das Friesische kann man bemerken, dass germ. *w* in altwestfriesischen Texten anlautend oft nur *v*, *u* geschrieben wird; intervokalisches *w* ist, außer in der Nachbarschaft von hellen Vokalen (germ. *i*, *ī*, *e*, $\bar{e}_2$, *ai*) erhalten;[41] vgl. hierzu *duwel(-)*, *ower*, *liewes* (< germ. **leiba*). Im Anlaut hört man im Friesischen das germ. *f* normalerweise als *f*, obwohl oft *v* oder *w* geschrieben wird.

4d. Was fällt so auf, dass es erklärt werden muss?

4d1. B471 *Auer* ane *was gheboden Vnde raden*
[Wo304 en Wf456 em L354 --]

Das Pronomen personale 'ihnen' kommt in diesem Text vor als:

oen 1 *one* 1
on 2 *ane* 1

Nach Lasch (§404 A.3) ist der Vokal im Dativ Plur. – Normalformen im Mnd. sind *em*, *en*, *öm*, *jüm* – durch Zerdehnung aus *i* entstanden. *Ome* findet man namentlich in ostfälischen Texten; eme herrscht auf dem übrigen Gebiet vor. Vereinzelt kommt auch *ame* vor, das ein offenes *ä* darstellen mag: *eäme*, *eäne*. Die Form ane könnte also mnd. sein.
Das fries. Pronomen personale *him* oder das fries. Demonstrativum *tha* können keine Rolle gespielt haben.

4d2. B384 *Die god noech* dan *wel an mannighen teken besunder*
[Wo333 don Wf386 don L384 doen]

Der Infinitiv *dan* 'tun' fällt auf, denn sonst trifft man *doen* (B429, 816). Das westfäl. *a* für gemeinnd. *ō* < germ. *au* gilt hier nicht, denn das *ō* in *don* stammt aus germ. *ō* (Lasch §87). Es könnte ein Fall der Analogiewirkung sein, da im Nnd. und Ofäl. allgemein *o* > *a* wurde (vgl. Lasch §85; 89).
Im Altfriesischen entwickelt sich germ. ō vor dunklem Vokal der Folgesilbe zu *u*; in der Lautverbindung *ūa* wird sodann das *u* unter Akzentverlegung zu *uā*; z.B. *duā*.[42] Die altwestfries. Form *dwān* des Infinitivs ist Analogiebildung nach *gān* und *stān*.[43] Friesischer Einfluss wäre also eine der Möglichkeiten. Aber ein Schreibfehler ist nicht auszuschließen.

4d3. B898 *Vnde* orde *enen stempne des die vppe den throne saed*
[Wo845 horde Wf908 horde L906 horde]

---

41 Vgl. Steller, *Abriss*, §27 u. A.1, 2.

42 Steller, *Abriss*, §16 A.3.

43 *Ibid.* §107 A.3; Boersma, *De Friesche oorkonden*, §81: *dwaen*.

Weitere Formen von 'hören' sind: *horet* (B521), *horde* (B249, 535), *ghehoert* (B61). Vielleicht ist dies einer der seltenen Fälle, dass der Ausfall des *h* (wie in einem enklitischen Wort) in der Schreibung ausgedrückt ist (wie in: "*vn e warp* für *vnde he* ..."; Lasch §352), weil *Vnde* dem Wort *orde* vorangeht.
Nach Steller[44] schwindet im Friesischen anlautendes *h* in einigen Fällen, *alf* neben *half*, *ēta* neben *hēta*.

4d4. B791 *Went oet* waer *dat wol veerdehallf hundert jar*
[Wo789 wart Wf801 waret L799 waret]

Obschon man in diesem Vers ohne Textvergleiche mit Wo, Wf und L in B791 eine 'moderne' Präteritumform des Verbs wesen zu lesen glaubt – *waer* statt *was* (wie in B319) –, muss wohl ein Schreibfehler vorliegen; wahrscheinlich ist eine Präsensform des Verbs *waren* 'währen' gemeint. Friesischer Einfluss ist auszuschließen.

4e. Schlussfolgerungen

4e1. *Die von Bernardus benutzte niederdeutsche Sprache*

Zuerst wird hier das Niederdeutsch von Bernardus Rordahusim besprochen. Und es muss gesagt werden, dass der Schreiber Bernardus sich einigermaßen in den mittelniederdeutschen Mundarten auskannte. Aber in Anhang 1, wo versucht wurde (mit Hilfe der von Peters hervorgehobenen linguistischen Variablen), die von Bernardus gebrauchte mittelniederdeutsche Mundart zu bestimmen, wird deutlich, dass er sich beim Abschreiben des Apokalypsetextes nicht nur einer einzigen Mundart bediente. Besonders auffallend ist eine große Unentschlossenheit, was die Orthographie betrifft. Obwohl man sagen muss, dass aus den gezeigten Beispielen in Anhang 1 klar wird, dass das Nordniederdeutsche manche Kennzeichen mit dem Westfälischen und manche Kennzeichen mit dem Ostfälischen teilt, sieht man doch Schreibweisen, die ausschließlich in einer Mundart anzutreffen sind. Als nur west- und nordniederdeutsch kann man eigentlich die Orthographie von *vrinden*, *twalff*, *hem*, *hore* und *wo* (also 5 Fälle) bezeichnen. Formen, die man nur westfälisch einstufen kann, sind *ghewalt*, *scullen*, *bode (gode*, *louen)*, *over*, *edele (hemel)*, *neder (weder)*, *weten*, *koning*, *oghe (ok)*, *satten*, *konde*, *doet*, *vorstornisse*, *mensche* (obwohl es statt *mynsche* nur einmal vorkommt), *derde*, *inghesegelen*, *heyligh*, *wal* (also in 18 Fällen). Typisch ostfälisch sind *leddich*, *konninghe*, *mek (juk)*, *vrochten*, *dredde*, *ek*, *ome (one)*, *o(e)t*, *or(e) (oer)*, *one (ane)*, *sek*, *dusse*, *wuer* (also 13 Fälle). Ein wichtiges Argument für das Ostfälische könnten die Pronomina (*ek*, *mek*, *ome*, *one*, *oet*, *juk*, *sek*) darstellen, denn sie findet man durch den ganzen

---

[44] *Abriss*, §45 A.1.

Text hindurch. Aber die als typisch westfälisch einzustufenden Formen überwiegen hier. Die Unsicherheit bei west- und ostfälischen Formen könnte mit dem Schreibort Hildesheim zusammenhängen, denn obwohl er einer der Hauptschreiborte des Ostfälischen ist, liegt diese Stadt unweit von der Leine, einem Nebenfluss der Weser. Die Weser bildete die Grenze zwischen dem West- und Ostfälischen. Und weiter könnte das West- und Norddeutsche Bernardus von seiner Heimat her am vertrautesten gewesen sein. Außerdem schrieb Bernardus im vierten Teil der Handschrift manchen niederländischen Text ab.[45]

4e2. *Friesische Spuren*

Weiter hat die Untersuchung nach den friesischen Interferenzen in seiner Orthographie ergeben, dass es nur wenige Formen gibt, die als ausschließlich friesisch zu interpretieren wären: *schille gy*, *dyar*, die Vorsilbe *on-* (von *onbeginne*), *vyer/wyer* und *woerliezen* und eventuell *[a]n begange*, *dan* für *don* 'tun'. Die Pronomina *hem* und *hore* könnten aus dem niederdeutsch-ostfriesischen Gebiet stammen. Nähme man jedoch für die *h*-Schreibung friesischen Einfluss an, dann wäre *ore* (*hore* ohne *h*) dem Ostfälischen zuzurechnen, aber zweimal *em* (*hem* ohne *h*) 'ihm/ihn' dem Nordniederdeutschen oder Westfälischen. Wahrscheinlich können *orde* für *horde* und die *ll*-Schreibung bei *llutter* durch das Friesische beeinflusst sein. Offen bleibt, ob friesischer Einfluss bei *der*, *dach*, *duwel* und mit Analogiewirkung bei *masten* mitgewirkt hat; *duwel* könnte überhaupt im Fries. und im Mnd. die gebräuchliche Form sein.

4e3. *Varianten und Schreibfehler*

Obwohl *grymme* und *erghe* friesisch anmuten, weist Textvergleich mit Wo, Wf und L (vor allem in Reimposition) auf geläufige Formen. Das Fehlen typisch friesischer Ingwäonismen zeigt, dass Bernardus seiner (wahrscheinlich norddeutschen) Vorlage getreu folgte. Die Wörter mit Metathese folgen den im Mnd. geltenden Regeln. Für die Schreibung *dyel* findet sich im Mnd. und eventuell im Fries. eine Erklärung. Bei *waer* ist nur von einem Schreibfehler auszugehen. Eventuell muss man bei *dan* von einem Schreibfehler ausgehen.

4e4. *Der Wechsel bei* u/v/f/ *und* w

Was bleibt, ist der besonders auffallende Wechsel bei *u/v/f* und *w*. Der könnte bestätigen, dass Bernardus keine feste Orthographie wählen konnte. Friesischer Einfluss wäre eine der Möglichkeiten für die auftretende Variierung.

[45] Vgl hierzu BH 9–15 (bl. 97v, 105r–105v, 123ar, 129r, 130r–145r, 146r, 149r–150r, 169r–174r, 174–177r, 208v, 209v, 210r–210v).

Insgesamt muss man feststellen, dass Bernardus im Apokalypsetext von weniger Frisismen Gebrauch machte als in der *Legenda de sancto Huegberto* (f. 149r–150r). Diese Vita folgte direkt den friesischen Traureden (f. 147v–148v).[46] Es könnte natürlich sein, dass das Friesische der Traureden die Schreibweise der Vita mehr als die der erst am Ende der Handschrift erscheinenden Apokalypse beeinflusst hat. Außerdem ist die Vita kein reimender Text. Obwohl die reimenden Verse bei Bernardus nicht abgesetzt sind (auch nicht in Wo, Wf und L), könnte die Vorlage abgesetzte Verse enthalten haben, wodurch der mnd. Reim und die mnd. Orthographie bei Bernardus meistens erhalten blieb. Die friesischen Formen sind ihm wahrscheinlich unbewusst aus der Feder geflossen.

[46] *Ibid.* 13.

Anhänge

Anhang 1

Anmerkung zu Anhang 1–4: Die unter dem Namen Peters genannten Nummern beziehen sich auf die von Peters numerierten unterscheidenden Merkmale. NB. ‘tl.’ = tonlange.

Basel, Hs. F. VII. 12				
Peters	Formen	(w)nnd	(s)wfäl	ofäl
1.1.1. Uml. a	stede, schepper	+	+	-
1.1.2. a > o vor ld, lt	ghewalt	+	+ (süd)	-
1.1.5.3. a > e vor rK	scharp, stark, vordarf	+	+	-
1.2.1. tl. ū	scullen	-	+	-
1.2.2. tl. ō	boden, gode, louen	-	+	-
tl. ǖ	over [meistens]	-	+	-
	auer [4x]	+	-	+
1.2.3. Kzg. vor -el	edele, hemel	-	+	-
	himmel	+	-	+
Kzg. vor -er	neder, weder	-	+	-
	nedder, wedder	+	-	+
Kzg. vor -en	weten	-	+	-
Kzg. vor -ich	leddich	-	-	+
Kzg. vor -ing	koning	-	+	-
	konninghe	-	-	+
1.3.7. ô1, ö1	don, broder	+	+	-
1.3.8. ô2, ö2	oghe, ok	-	+	-
1.4.3. ft > cht	deyl-, woenhafftich	+	-	+
2.1.5. ‘bringen’	bringhen	+	-	+
2.1.7. Rückumlaut	satten	-	+	-
2.1.9.2. ‘können’	konde	-	+	-
2.1.10.2. ‘tun’	doet [deyt nur Reim]	-	+	-
‘sehen’	stunt, stunden	+	-	+
2.4. Einheitskasus	my, dy, v	+	+	-
	mek, juk	-	-	+
2.5.2.2. -nisse/-nüsse	vorstornisse	-	+	-
4.2.2.1. ‘Mensch’	mynsche [14x]	+	-	+
	mensche [1x]	-	+	-
4.2.2.8. ‘Freund’	vrinden	+ (west)	-	-
	vrunt	+	-	+
4.2.6.3. ‘opfern’	offeren	+	+	-
4.2.7.3. ‘fürchten’	vrochten	-	-	+

Basel, Hs. F. VII. 12				
Peters	Formen	(w)nnd	(s)wfäl	ofäl
4.2.7.10. 'Siegel'	seghele inghesegelen	+ -	- +	+ -
4.3.4. 'heilig'	hilligh, hilgh heyligh	+ -	- +	+ -
4.4.5. 'zwölf'	twalff twolff	+(west) +	- -	- +
4.4.9. 'dritte'	dridde dredde derde	+ - -	- - +	+ + -
4.5.1.1. 'ich'	ik ek	+ -	+ -	- +
4.5.1.9/10. 'ihm, ihn'	om(e), on(e) hem	- +(ostfri)	- -	+ -
4.5.1.11. 'es'	id o(e)t	+ -	+ -	- +
4.5.1.13. 'ihr-'	hore or(e), oer	+(ostfri) -	- -	- +
4.5.1.14. 'ihnen'	on(e), ane	-	-	+
4.5.2. 'sich'	sik sek	+ -	+ -	- +
4.5.3.1. 'dies-'	desse disse dusse	+ + -	+ - -	- + +
4.5.4.4. 'derselbe'	sulue	+	-	+
4.6.1.1. 'wo'	wuer	-	-	+
4.6.1.3. 'wie'	wo	+	-	-
4.6.4.1. 'so'	aldus (al)sus	+ +	+ -	- +
4.6.4.4. 'wohl	wol wal	+ -	- +	+ -
im Ganzen		31+/31-	28+/34-	29+/33-

Die Orthographie ist unsicher, denn für und gegen das Nordniederdeutsche spricht fast gleich viel; bei den westfälischen und ostfälischen Kennzeichen überwiegen die negativen Argumente.

Anhang 2

Wolfenbüttel, Helmst. 1211				
Peters	Formen	(w)nnd	(s)wfäl	ofäl
1.1.1. Uml. a	stede, schepper	+	+	-
1.1.2. a > o vor ld, lt	halden	-	+(süd)	-
1.1.5.3. a > e vor rK	scharp, stark, vordarf	+	+	-
1.2.2. tl. ō tl. ǖ	boden, gode, loueden over	- -	+ +	- -
1.2.3. Kzg. vor -el Kzg. vor -er Kzg. vor -en Kzg. vor -ich Kzg. vor -ing	edele, hemel neder, weder weten ledich konynck	- - - - -	+ + + + +	- - - - -
1.3.7. ô1, ö1	don, broder	+	+	-
1.3.8. ô2, ö2	ogen, ok	-	+	-
1.4.3. ft > cht	deilaftich wonachtich	+ -	- +	+ -
2.1.5. ‘bringen’	brynghen	+	-	+
2.1.7. Rückumlaut	setten [Prät.]	+	-	+
2.1.9.2. ‘können’	konde	-	+	-
2.1.10.2. ‘tun’ ‘stehen’	doet [deyt nur Reim] stond	- -	+ +	- -
2.4. Einheitskasus	my, dy, ju	+	+	-
2.5.2.2. -nisse/-nüsse	vorstornisse	-	+	-
4.2.2.1. ‘Mensch’	mensche	-	+	-
4.2.2.8. ‘Freund’	vront	-	+	-
4.2.6.3. ‘opfern’	offeren	+	+	-
4.2.7.3. ‘fürchten’	vorchten	-	-	+
4.2.7.10. ‘Siegel’	segel jnghesegelen	+ -	- +	+ -
4.3.4. ‘heilig’	hilg	+	-	+
4.4.5. ‘zwölf’	twelff	-	+	-
4.4.9. ‘dritte’	derde	-	+	-
4.5.1.1. ‘ich’	ik ek	+ -	+ -	- +
4.5.1.9/10. ‘ihm/ihn’	em(e), en(e)	+	+	-
4.5.1.11. ‘es’	et	+	+	-
4.5.1.13. ‘ihr-‘	er(e)	+	+	-
4.5.1.14. ‘ihnen’	en(e)	-	+	+
4.5.2. ‘sich’	sic	+	+	-

Wolfenbüttel, Helmst. 1211				
Peters	Formen	(w)nnd	(s)wfäl	ofäl
4.5.3.1. 'dies-'	dusse	-	-	+
4.5.4.4. 'derselbe'	selue	-	+	-
4.6.1.1. 'wo'	war	-	+	-
4.6.1.3. 'wie'	wo	+	-	-
4.6.4.1. 'so'	aldus	+	+	-
4.6.4.4. 'wohl'	wal	-	+	-
im Ganzen		17+/26-	34+/9-	9+/34-

Deutlich ist, dass Helmst. 1211 ein westfälischer Text ist. Typisch für das Nordniederdeutsche ist nur: wo; für das Ostfälische nur vorchten, ek und dusse. Typisch westfälisch sind halden, boden (gode, louen), over, edele (hemel), neder (weder), weten, ledich, koninck, ogen (ok), wonachtich, konde, doet, stond, vorstornisse, mensche, vront, jnghesegelen, twelff, derde, selue, war und wal.

Anhang 3

Wolfenbüttel, Helmst. 389				
Peters	Formen	(w)nnd.	(s)wfäl.	ofäl.
1.1.1. Uml. a	stede, schepper	+	+	-
1.1.2. a > o vor ld, lt	ald, gewalt	-	+ (süd)	-
1.1.5.3. a > e vor rK	scharp, stark, vordarf	+	+	-
1.2.1. tl. ū	s(ch)ullen	-	+	-
1.2.2. tl. ō tl. ǖ 	boden, gode, loven baden over auer	- + - +	+ - + -	- + - +
1.2.3. Kzg. vor -el Kzg. vor -er Kzg. vor -en Kzg. vor -ich Kzg. vor -ing 	edele, hemel hemmel neder, weder weten ledich konink konnynck	- + - - - - -	+ - + + + + -	- + - - - - +
1.3.7. ô1, ö1	don, broder	+	+	-
1.3.8. ô2, ö2	ogen, ok	-	+	-
1.4.3. ft > cht 	delaftich wonnachtich	+ -	- +	+ -
2.1.5. 'bringen'	brenghen	-	+	-
2.1.7. Rückumlaut	setten [Prät.]	+	-	+
2.1.9.2. 'können'	konde	-	+	-

Wolfenbüttel, Helmst. 389				
Peters	Formen	(w)nnd.	(s)wfäl.	ofäl.
2.1.10.2. 'tun 'stehen'	dot [deyt nur Reim] stunt	- +	+ -	- +
2.4. Einheitskasus	my, dy, iv iuk	+ -	+ -	- +
2.5.2.2. -nisse/-nüsse	vorstornisse	-	+	-
4.2.2.1. 'Mensch'	mensche mynsche [1x]	- +	+ -	- +
4.2.2.8. 'Freund'	vrunt vrenden	+ -	- +	+ -
4.2.6.3. 'opfern'	offeren	+	+	-
4.2.7.3. 'fürchten'	vrochten	-	-	+
4.2.7.10. 'Siegel'	jngesegelen	-	+	-
4.3.4. 'heilig'	hilg	+	-	+
4.4.5. 'zwölf'	twelff	-	+	-
4.4.9. 'dritte	dridde derde	+ -	- +	+ -
4.5.1.1. 'ich'	ik ek	+ -	+ -	- +
4.5.1.9/10. 'ihm/ihn'	eme, ene	+	+	-
4.5.1.11. 'es'	et	+	+	-
4.5.1.13. 'ihr-'	er-	+	+	-
4.5.1.14. 'ihnen'	em en	+ -	- +	- (+)
4.5.2. 'sich'	sik sek	+ -	+ -	- +
4.5.3.1. 'dies-'	desse disse dusse	+ + -	+ - -	- - +
4.5.4.4. 'derselbe'	sulue selue	+ -	- +	+ -
4.6.1.1. 'wo'	war	-	+	-
4.6.1.3. 'wie'	wo	+	-	-
4.6.4.1. 'so'	(al)dus (al)sus	+ +	+ -	- +
4.6.4.4. 'wohl'	wol	+	-	+
im Ganzen		28+/29-	35+/22-	20+/37-

Helmst. 389 ist sehr wahrscheinlich ein westfälischer Text, eventuell aus dem Grenzgebiet mit dem Nordniederdeutschen. Nur nordniederdeutsch sind *em*, *disse*, *wo*; nur ostfälisch *konnynck*, *iuk*, *vrochten*, *ek*, *sek*, *dusse*; aber nur westfälisch sind *ald (gewalt)*, *s(ch)ullen*, *boden (gode, loven)*, *over*, *edele (hemel)*, *neder (weder)*, *weten*, *ledich*, *konink*, *ogen (ok)*, *wonnachtich*, *brenghen*, *konde*, *dot*, *vorstornisse*, *mensche*, *vrenden*, *jngesegelen*, *twelff*, *derde*, *selue*, *war*.

Anhang 4

Lüneburg, Ms. Theol. 2° 83				
Peters	Formen	(w)nnd	(s)wfäl	ofäl
1.1.1. Uml. a	stede, schepper	+	+	-
1.1.2. a > o vor ld, lt	halden, alt, (ghe)walt, -ualt	-	+(süd)	-
1.1.5.3. a> e vor rK	scharp, stark, vordarf	+	+	-
1.2.1. tl. ū	s(ch)ullen	-	+	-
1.2.2. tl. ō tl. ǖ	boden, gode, loven over	- -	+ +	- -
1.2.3. Kzg. vor -el Kzg. vor -er Kzg. vor ich Kzg. vor -ing	edder, hemmel nedder, wedder neder, weder leddich konynghe	+ + - + -	- - + - +	+ + - + -
1.3.7. ô1, ö1	doen, broder	+	+	-
1.3.8. ô2, ö2	ogen, ok	-	+	-
1.4.3. ft > cht	delaftich, wonaftich	+	-	+
2.1.1. Einheitsplur.	-en [8x]	+	-	+
2.1.5. 'bringen'	bryngen	+	-	+
2.1.7. Rückumlaut	satten	-	+	-
2.1.9.2. 'können'	konde	-	+	-
2.1.10.2. 'tun' 'stehen'	dot [deyt nur Reim] stund	- +	+ -	- +
2.4. Einheitskasus	my, dy, iu	+	+	-
2.5.2.2. -nisse/ -nüsse	vorstornisse	-	+	-
4.2.2.1. 'Mensch'	mynsche	+	-	+
4.2.2.8. 'Freund'	vrunt	+	-	+
4.2.6.3. 'opfern'	offeren	+	+	-
4.2.7.3. 'fürchten'	vruchten	+	+	-
4.2.7.10. 'Siegel'	jngesegele	-	+	-
4.3.4. 'heilig'	hilgh	+	-	+
4.4.5. 'zwölf'	twelff	-	+	-
4.4.9. 'dritte'	drudde	+	-	+
4.5.1.1. 'ich'	ik	+	+	-
4.5.1.9/10. 'ihm/ihn'	eme, ene	+	+	-

Lüneburg, Ms. Theol. 2° 83				
Peters	Formen	(w)nnd	(s)wfäl	ofäl
4.5.1.11. 'es'	id	+	+	-
4.5.1.13. 'ihr-'	er-	+	+	-
4.5.1.14. 'ihnen'	en	-	+	(+)
4.5.2. 'sich'	sik sek	+ -	+ -	- +
4.5.3.1. 'dies-'	desse	+	+	-
4.5.4.4. 'derselbe'	sulue	+	-	+
4.6.1.1. 'wo'	wor	+	-	-
4.6.1.3. 'wie'	wo	+	-	-
4.6.4.1. 'so'	aldus (al)sus	+ +	+ -	- +
4.6.4.4. 'wohl'	wol	+	-	+
im Ganzen		29+/15-	27+/17-	16+/28-

Ms. Theol. 2° 83 zeigt vor allem nordniederdeutsche und westfälische Kennzeichen. Es könnte sein, dass die Handschrift dem Grenzgebiet vom Nordniederdeutschen und Westfälischen entstammt. Nur westfälisch sind jedoch *halden (ald, (ghe)walt, -ualt)*, *s(ch)ullen*, *boden (gode, loven)*, *over*, *neder (weder)*, *konynghe*, *ogen (ok)*, *satten*, *konde*, *dot*, *vorstornisse*, *jngesegele*, *twelff*. Nur ostfälisch ist *sek*; nur nordniederdeutsch sind *wor*, *wo*. Das westfälische Element herrscht also vor.

Bedingungssätze in altfriesischen Rechtstexten

Rosemarie Lühr

1. Problemstellung

Während nahezu alle anderen frühen Rechtsquellen des westeuropäischen Festlandes nur als Übersetzungen ins Mittellateinische überliefert sind, sind mit Ausnahme der lateinisch geschriebenen *Lex Frisionum* die altfriesischen Rechtsquellen in der Muttersprache abgefasst. Sie sind daher von einzigartigem Wert sowohl für die westeuropäische Rechtsgeschichte als auch für die germanische Rechtssprache.[1] Nun hat jede Fachsprache Besonderheiten, die sie von der Normalsprache unterscheiden. Während bei einer Fachsprache im Allgemeinen die Lexik auffällt, ist es bei der Rechtssprache auch die Syntax. Das wichtigste Kennzeichen ist wohl die Häufigkeit von Bedingungssätzen: Die Protasis beschreibt den Tatbestand, d.h. den Inbegriff von Tatsachen, an deren Eintreten der Gesetzgeber eine bestimmte Folge knüpfen will, und die Apodosis umschreibt eben diese Folge. Schon in der ältesten Quelle der lateinischen Rechtssprache, in den Zwölftafelgesetzen, kommen solche Bedingungssätze vor:

(1) Tabula I. 1–3 (um 450 v. Chr.)
SI IN IUS VOCAT, ITO.
'wenn der Kläger jemanden vor Gericht ruft, soll dieser gehen'.
SI CALVITUR PEDEMVE STRUIT, MANUM ENDO IACTIO.
'wenn er Ausflüchte macht oder ein Bein bereitstellt (d.h. fliehen will), soll er Hand auf (ihn) legen (d.h. ihn festnehmen)'.[2]

Während aber die Römer die lapidare Kürze des Zwölftafel-Stils bald aufgegeben haben, haben sie die durchsichtigen konditionalen Strukturen stets beibehalten. Insbesondere haben sie gegenüber den Zwölftafelgesetzen, wo oftmals das Subjekt erschlossen werden muss, dieses später eindeutig bezeichnet. Z.B. kann das Subjekt in der Protasis ein Appellativ sein:

---

[1] N. E. Algra, 'Grundzüge des friesischen Rechts im Mittelalter', *Handbuch / Handbook*, 555–70, hier 556.

[2] R. Düll, *Das Zwölftafelgesetz. Texte, Übersetzungen und Erläuterungen* (München, 1971).

(2) Imperatores Diocletianus et Maximianus Augusti et Constantius et Maximianus nobilissimi Caesares Sosio (3. Jh. n. Chr.)
Si servus ignorante domino vel sciente et prohibere nequeunte res tuas vi rapuit, dominum eius apud praesidem provinciae, si necdum utilis annus excessit, quadrupli, quod si hoc effluxit tempus, simpli noxali iudicio convenire potes.
'Wenn ein Sklave dir deine Sache gewaltsam entrissen hat, ohne dass der Herr davon wusste, oder wenn er zwar davon wusste, es aber nicht verhindern konnte, dann kannst du den Herrn beim Provinzstatthalter mit der Halterhaftungsklage belangen: wenn die Jahresfriest seit Klagmöglichkeit noch nicht verstrichen ist, auf das Vierfache' (Exempla Iuris Romani 58)[3]

Auch kommen Indefinitpronomina vor, wenn unbestimmt ist, um welche Person genau es sich handelt:

(3) Paulus, Ad edictum praetoris XIX (2./3. Jh. n. Chr.)
Si quis servum meum vel filium ludibrio habeat licet consentientem, tamen ego iniuriam videor accipere, veluti si in popinam duxerit illum si alea luserit.
'Wenn jemand mit meinem Sklaven oder Sohn Possen treibt, dann widerfährt mir ersichtlich trotz dessen Zustimmung eine Injurie, z.B. wenn er ihn in eine Kneipe führt oder Würfel mit ihm spielt.' (Exempla Iuris Romani 60)

Eine andere Form der Bezeichnung eines indefiniten Subjekts findet sich in freien Relativsätzen. Wie die Protasis in konditionalen Strukturen, erscheinen solche Relativsätze an der Spitze des komplexen Satzes. Semantisch sind solche Satzgefüge eine Variante des konditionalen Gefüges.

(4) Bonifaz III (13. Jh.)
Qui ad agendum admittitur, est ad excipiendum multo magis admittendum.
'Wer zum Klagen zugelassen wird, ist um so mehr zum Einwenden zuzulassen.' (Lateinische Rechtsregeln und Rechtssprichwörter Q-23)[4]

Während aber in (1) bis (3) das Subjekt zwischen Neben- und Hauptsatz wechselt, herrscht in dem Gefügesatztyp (4) Subjektidentität.

---

3 M. Fuhrmann und D. Liebs, *Exempla Iuris Romani. Römische Rechtstexte* (München, 1988).

4 D. Liebs, *Lateinische Rechtsregeln und Rechtssprichwörter* (Darmstadt, 1983).

Das römische Recht hat im Mittelalter eine weite Verbreitung erfahren. Für den germanischen Bereich ist insbesondere das Wirken Karls des Großen von Bedeutung. So sieht man die Entstehung der lateinischen *Lex Frisionum* im Zusammenhang mit seiner Gesetzgebung (802/803), selbst wenn viele Fragen zur Genese dieses Textes unbeantwortet bleiben müssen. Er ist die älteste Aufzeichnung des friesischen Rechts und nur durch den 1557 in Basel erschienenen Druck des Basilius Johannes Herold (1514–1567) überliefert. Die handschriftliche Vorlage ist nicht bewahrt. Es soll aber Ende des 9. Jh.s in der Remigiusabtei zu Reims ein Kodex vorhanden gewesen sein, der u.a. die *Lex Frisionum* enthielt.[5]

Die Frage ist nun, ob die Sprache des römischen Rechts die mittellateinischen Versionen der Germanenrechte, hier der *Lex Frisionum*, beeinflusst hat. Von hier aus könnten dann auch lateinisch-volkssprachliche Interferenzen in den altfriesischen Fassungen zustande gekommen sein.

2. Bedingungssätze der *Lex Frisionum*

Sämtliche Typen von Bedingungssätzen der lateinischen Beispiele kommen auch in der *Lex Frisionum* vor. Zu *si* + Appellativ wie in (2) vgl.:

> (5) De homicidiis Tit. I 'Von Totschlägen'
> §1 Si nobilis nobilem occiderit, LXXX sol(idos) comp(onant).
> 'Wenn ein Edler einen Edlen tötet, büße er 80 Schillinge.'[6]

Zu *si* + Indefinitpronomen wie in (3) vgl.:

> (6) Thiubda. Tit. III 'Diebstahl'
> §8 Si quis in furto deprẹhensus fuerit et ab ipso qui eum deprehẹndit furti arguatur et negaverit, iuret uterque solus et ad examinationem ferventis aquẹ iudicio dei probandus accedat
> 'Wenn jemand beim Diebstahl ergriffen wird und von demjenigen, der ihn ergreift, des Diebstahls beschuldigt wird und leugnet, schwöre jeder von beiden allein und komme zur Prüfung des siedenden Wassers, um durch Gottesurteil erprobt zu werden'

Eine Variante ist die Verbindung mit einem dem Substantiv nachgestellten *quislibet*:

> (7) De homine in turbo occiso. Tit. XIIII 'Von Tötung eines Mannes bei einem Auflauf'
> Si homo quislibet in seditione ac turba populi fuerit interfectus ...

[5] *Lex Frisionum*, K. A. Eckhardt und A. Eckhardt, Hg. (Hannover, 1982), 11, 22.

[6] *Ibid.* 34–35. Alle weiteren Zitaten aus der *Lex Frisionum* basieren auf dieser Ausgabe.

'Wenn irgendein Mann bei einem Aufruhr und Volksauflauf umgebracht wird ...'

und

(8) De farlegani. Tit. IX 'Von Hurerei'
Si femina quaelibet homini cuilibet fornicando se miscuerit, componat ad partem regis weregildum suum
'Wenn irgendeine Frau sich mit irgendeinem Mann fleischlich vermischt, büße sie an den Teil des Königs ihr Wergeld'

Auch substantivisch kommt *quislibet* vor; vgl. mit der Konjunktion *quodsi*:

(9) De homicidiis Tit. I 'Von Totschlägen'
§12 Quodsi quaelibet ex praedictis personis hoc homicidium se perpetrasse negaverit, iuxta quod summa precii occisi mancipii fuerit ęstimata, maiori vel minori sacramento se excusare debebit.
'Wenn jedoch irgendeine von den vorgenannten Personen diesen Totschlag begangen zu haben leugnet, muss sie gemäß dem, was die Wertsumme des getöteten Unfreien geschätzt wird, mit größerem oder kleinerem Eide entschuldigen'

Und zum freien Relativsatz wie in (4), vgl.:

(10) De mordrito. Tit. XX 'Vom Mord'
Qui obsidem occiderit, novies eum componat.
'Wer einen Geisel tötet, büße sie neunfach.'

Bedingungssätze mit *si* + Appellativ oder Indefinitpronomen als Subjekt und freie Relativsätze beschreiben also in der *Lex Frisionum* wie im Klassischen Latein und Spätlatein ein Vergehen; die sich darauf ergebende strafrechtliche Folge wird dann im Hauptsatz ausgedrückt.

3. Bedingungssätze in den altfriesischen Rechtstexten

3.1. Vergleich mit der *Lex Frisionum*

Vielfältiger ist das Bild der Bedingungssätze in der volkssprachlichen friesischen Überlieferung – das Datenmaterial ist in der Regel dem Ersten Rüstringer Codex, dem sogenannten Asegabuch, entnommen, weil die Rüstringer Handschrift R_1 unter den altfriesischen Handschriften zu den ältesten gehört (um 1300).[7] Zwar übersetzen Wybren Jan Buma und Wilhelm Ebel in ihrer Textausgabe die Einleitung von Bedingungssätzen und verwandten Strukturen in der Regel mit dem Wort ‘wenn’.[8] Zu unterscheiden sind aber:

a) freie Relativsätze z.B. mit Einleitewort *hwa* ‘wer’ oder verallgemeinernde Relativsätze z.B. mit Einleitewort *hwasa*[9] ‘wer auch immer’[10]
b) Bedingungssätze mit Konjunktion, z.B. *jef* ‘wenn’ oder *sa* ‘wenn’, eigentlich ‘so’
c) Bedingungssätze mit Spitzenstellung des finiten Verbs

Von diesen haben nur die freien Relativsätze und die Bedingungssätze mit Konjunktion eine Entsprechung in den Nebensatzstrukturen der *Lex Frisionum*. Bedingungssätze mit Spitzenstellung des finiten Verbs gibt es dagegen generell im Lateinischen nicht. Doch verfügt das Lateinische über verallgemeinernde Relativsätze. In der *Lex Frisionum* kommen sie in folgenden Positionen vor: Das verallgemeinernde Relativpronomen erscheint in vorangestellten verallgemeinernden Relativsätzen adjektivisch, und zwar vor oder hinter seinem Bezugswort; vgl. zur Voranstellung:

(11) Wlemarus: Hoc totum in triplo componatur. Tit. III. ‘Dies alles werde dreifach gebüßt.’
§46 Quodcunque membrum percussum ita debilitatum fuerit, ut ibi inutile pendeat, medietate componatur, quam componi debuit, si penitus fuisset abscisum.
‘Welches geschlagene Glied auch immer so geschwächt wird, dass es alsdann unbrauchbar herabhängt, werde mit der Hälfte gebüßt, wie es gebüßt werden müsste, wenn es gänzlich abgeschlagen wäre.’

Und zur Nachstellung:

---

7 T. S. B. Johnston, ‘The Old Frisian Law Manuscripts and Law Texts’, *Handbuch / Handbook*, 571–94, hier 576.

8 *Das Rüstringer Recht*, W. J. Buma und W. Ebel, Hg., AR 1 (Göttingen, 1963), *passim*. Alle weiteren Zitaten aus dem Rüstringer Recht basieren auf dieser Ausgabe.

9 Zur Entstehung der verallgemeinernden Relativpronomina im Germanischen, vgl. R. Lühr, ‘Universale Konzessivsätze im Ahd.’, *Indogermanistik – Germanistik – Linguistik. Akten der Arbeitstagung der Indogermanischen Gesellschaft, Jena 18.–20.09.2002*, M. Kozianka, R. Lühr und S. Zeilfelder, Hg. (Hamburg, 2004), 345–59. Anders T. Leuschner, ‘Nebensatzkonnektoren des Typs “W-Wort + Partikel(n)” (Deutsch wer auch immer usw.) im Germanischen. Eine intragenetische Typologie aus areallinguistischer Sicht’, *Studia Germanica Gandensia* (2001: 2), 3–26.

10 Vgl. die Übersetzung ‘whoever’ von R. H. Bremmer Jr, ‘Insults Hurt: Verbal Injury in Late Medieval Frisia’, *Approaches*, 89–112, hier 92; G. van der Meer, ‘Relative Markers in the Old West Frisian Manuscript Jus Municipale Frisonum’, *UW* 36 (1987), 71–90, hier 83.

(12) Wlemarus: Hoc totum in triplo componatur. Tit. III. 'Dies alles werde dreifach gebüßt.'
§27 Os quodcunque ferro praecisum fuerit, ter IIII solid(is) componatur. 'Welcher Knochen auch immer durch das Eisen abgeschnitten wird, werde mit dreimal drei Schillingen und einer Tremisse gebüßt.'

Sonst erscheinen verallgemeinernde Relativsätze innerhalb von Satzgefügen:

(13) Forresni. Tit. II 'Anstiftung.'
§3 … sin vero homicida infra patriam est, expositor nihil iuret, sed tantum inimicitias propinquorum occisi hominis patiatur, donec cum eis quoquomodo potuerit in gratiam revertatur.
'… wenn aber der Totschläger in der Heimat ist, schwöre der Anstifter nichts, sondern erdulde nur die Fehde der Verwandten des getöteten Mannes, bis er mit ihnen, auf welche Weise auch immer er kann, ins Einvernehmen zurückkehrt.'

Anders verhält es sich in der volkssprachlichen Überlieferung. Sehr häufig erscheinen vorangestellte verallgemeinernde Relativsätze[11] mit einem verallgemeinernden Relativpronomen ohne Bezugswort. Das Relativpronomen vertritt dabei entweder einen Kasus, z.B. den Nominativ:[12]

---

[11] Zum Modusgebrauch vgl. E. Herrmann, 'Altertümliches und Eigentümliches im Friesischen', *Nachrichten aus der neueren Philologie und Literaturgeschichte* 2 (1938), 99–126; G. J. de Haan, 'Syntax of Old Frisian', *Handbuch / Handbook*, 626–36, hier 633.

[12] Andere Verbindungen sind weitaus seltener; vgl. etwa:
(i) Die alten Rüstringer Küren:
Alsa monich hus **sa** ma barnde, alsa monich hundred merka tha liodon to fretha. R_1 VIII 3
'So oft man ein Haus niederbrennt, so oft (hat man) dem Volke hundert Mark als Friedensgeld (zu zahlen)'; *Das Rüstringer Recht*. Buma und Ebel, Hg., 78–79.
(ii) Die Hunsingoer Bußtaxen II
Hu fir sa mon orne onfiucht, weder sa <a> achnem sa honden sa foten sa mith ene bernande skide, **hu fir sa**rne a onfiucht, nowet diura te betane tha en tuede lif … . H IX 2
'Wie heftig ein Mann auch einen anderen angreift, es sei an Augen oder Händen oder Füßen oder mit einem brennenden Holzscheit zur Brandlegung, wie hart er ihm auch zusetzt, (so ist das doch) nicht höher als (mit) zweidrittel Wergeld zu büßen ...', *Das Hunsingoer Recht*, W. J. Buma und W. Ebel, Hg., AR 4 (Göttingen, 1969), 62–63. Alle weiteren Zitaten aus dem Hunsingoer Recht basieren auf dieser Ausgabe.

(14) Die neuen Rüstringer Küren[13]
Thit is thi thredda kere: **Sa hwasa** fiucht, thi skil fiuchta opa sinne einene hals and opa sina eina haua. R_1 IX 3
'Dies ist die dritte Küre. Wer auch immer sich schlägt, der soll dies auf seinen eigenen Hals und sein eigenes Vermögen tun.'

oder ein Adverb. Dabei handelt es sich eigentlich um ein Lokaladverb der Bedeutung 'wo auch immer'. Wie aber deutsch *wo* in *zu dem Zeitpunkt, wo* temporale Bedeutung annehmen kann, ist *sa hwersa* neben seiner lokalen Bedeutung 'wo auch immer' auch temporal aufzufassen, und zwar als 'wann auch immer'.

(15) Die fünf Ausnahmen von der 17. Küre
Thet fifte: **Sa hwersa ma** enne menotere bifari mith falske tha mith fade an sina skrine ieftha an sina skate, an sina helde tha an sina bigerdele, sa ne mi hi therumbe nena witha biada. R_1 VII 6
'Fünftens: Wann auch immer man einen Münzer mit falschem oder zu geringhaltigem Gelde in seinem Schrein oder in seinem Schoß, in seinem Behältnis oder in seiner Gürteltasche ertappt, so darf er sich deswegen nicht um Unschuldseid auf die Reliquien erbieten.'

Die vorangestellten verallgemeinernden Relativsätze in den Rechtsquellen sind also ein echt altfriesischer Sprachgebrauch. Sie sind nicht durch Interferenz mit dem Latein zustande gekommen.

3.2. Semantik und Pragmatik der Bedingungssätze

3.2.1. *Semantik*

In der Literatur werden verallgemeinernde Relativsätze als universale Irrelevanzkonditionalia bezeichnet. Sie unterscheiden sich dadurch von einfachen Bedingungssätzen, dass sie einen konditionalen Zusammenhang zwischen einer ganzen Reihe von Antezedenzbedingungen in der Protasis zu einem Konsequens in der Apodosis herstellen. Konditionalia mit einem Allquantor implizieren also ebenso wie einfache Bedingungssätze ihr Konsequens. Unter den Bedingungen der universalen Irrelevanzkonditionalia ist aber mindestens eine, die 'in einem prinzipiellen Konflikt zu dem im Konsequens

[13] In den neuen Rüstringer Küren, einem jüngeren Stück im Asegabuch, kommen auch andere textabschnitteinleitende Bedingungssätze vor:
Die neuen Rüstringer Küren
Thit is thi fifta kere: **Alther** en rike mon ene otheron sin lif onawint ... R_1 IX 5
'Dies ist die fünfte Küre: Wo auch immer ein reicher Mann einen andern ums Leben bringt ...'.

genannten Sachverhalt steht'. Dadurch ergibt sich eine Beziehung zu den sogenannten skalaren Irrelevanzkonditionalia;[14] vgl.:

(16) **Wer auch immer** einen Mord begeht, **selbst wenn** es ein Regierungschef ist, wird bestraft.

Indem ein Sprecher ein derartiges Irrelevanzkonditionale verwendet, stimmt er zwar mit der Prämisse überein, den sich aus (16) ergebenden Schluss, dass ein Regierungschef eine Sonderstellung innehat und so nicht so hart zu bestrafen ist wie ein normaler Bürger, er akzeptiert ihn aber nicht.

Da bei universalen Irrelevanzkonditionalia auch Eigennamen exemplifizierend hinzugesetzt werden können:

(17) **Wer (immer)** solche Dinge sagt, z.B. der Hans vorhin, sollte zurechtgewiesen werden.

haben universale Irrelevanzkonditionalia eher zum referentiellen als zum indefiniten Gebrauch Beziehung.[15]

Auch freie Relativsätze sind generalisierend verwendbar:

(18) **Wer** einen Mord begeht, selbst wenn es ein Asega ist ...

Die Generalisierung ist jedoch nicht explizit bezeichnet.

Weiterhin können die mit Konjunktion eingeleiteten Bedingungssätze generische Bedeutung haben, wenn sie 'konditional-hypothetisch' verwendet sind. So kommen für die Rechtssprache Konditionalia in Betracht, 'die auf den allgemeinen Fall abheben und von der Konkretisierung einzelner Personen und Gegenstände absehen'.[16] Es sind 'event-conditionals', also zentrale Adverbialsätze, die das Matrix-Prädikat modifizieren.[17] Gleichfalls 'konditional-hypothetisch' und generisch können Bedingungssätze mit Spitzenstellung des Verbs gebraucht werden.

Von ihrer Semantik her unterscheiden sich die genannten Bedingungssätze also wenig. Dennoch muss es gravierende Unterschiede in ihrem

---

[14] E. König, 'Konzessive Konjunktionen', *Semantik. Ein internationales Handbuch der zeitgenössischen Forschung*, A. von Stechow und D. Wunderlich, Hg. (Berlin und New York, 1991), 631–39, hier 635–36.

[15] G. Zifonun, L. Hoffmann und B. Strecker, *Grammatik der deutschen Sprache*, 3 Bde. (Berlin und New York, 1997) III, 2274.

[16] *Ibid.* 2283.

[17] L. Haegeman, 'Conditional Clauses: External and Internal Syntax', *Mind & Language* 18 (2003), 317–39, hier 339.

Gebrauch geben, da diese Nebensätze in den altfriesischen Rechtstexten eine bestimmte textstrukturelle Distribution haben.

3.1.2. *Pragmatik*

Hier kommt die Informationsstruktur dieser Sätze, also die Topik-Kommentar- und Fokus-Hintergrund-Gliederung, ins Spiel:[18] der Fokus stellt die vom Sprecher in einem gegebenen sprachlichen Kontext als wichtig hervorgehobene Information dar, während durch den Hintergrund die weniger wichtige Information gekennzeichnet wird. Demgegenüber ist das Topik der Ausgangspunkt des Satzes, d.h. die Entität, über die eine Aussage getroffen wird.

Mit der Topik-Kommentar-Gliederung hängt die Rahmenbildung zusammen, wie Äquivalente in Sprachen, die über overte Topik-Marker verfügen, zeigen. So dienen die unmarkierten Konditionalia – das sind die Bedingungssätze, die mit einer Konjunktion eingeleitet sind –, oftmals der Rahmenbildung; vgl.:

(19) If the team win, they will receive a commendation from the president.

Joachim Jacobs definiert dabei Rahmenbildung auf folgende Weise:[19]

> Frame-setting
> In (X Y), X is the frame for Y if X specifies a domain of (possible) reality to which the proposition expressed by Y is restricted.

Für (19) bedeutet dies, dass die Proposition, der Inhalt des Hauptsatzes (*they will receive a commendation from the president*) auf bestimmte Situationen (those *in which the team wins*) eingeschränkt wird.[20]

Auch das verallgemeinernde Relativadverb *sa hwersa* 'wo auch immer', 'wann auch immer' in Irrelevanzkonditionalia ist ein rahmenbildendes Element. Das zeigt der Vergleich mit althochdeutschen Adverbien wie ahd. *thô* 'da, damals' und *thar*. In (20) wird *thar* dabei zur Einführung eines neuen Diskursreferenten verwendet:

---

[18] Vgl. auch G. van der Meer, 'On the Position of the Old Frisian Verbs and Pronouns', *Aspects*, 311–35, hier 317, 330, 332, zur 'functional sentence perspective' und zum 'Gesetz der wachsenden Glieder' im Altfriesischen.

[19] 'The Dimensions of Topic-comment', *Linguistics* 39 (2001), 641–81, hier 656.

[20] Zu *if* als Topik-Marker vgl. E. Sweetser, *From Etymology to Pragmatics. Metaphorical and Cultural Aspects of Semantic Structure* (Cambridge, 1990), 125ff.

(20) Tatian 81,36
erant autem ibi lapideę hydrię
thar uuarun steininu uuarfaz
'Dort waren steinerne Wasserfässer'[21]

Auch Verberststellung (= VI) erscheint im Althochdeutschen bei der Etablierung eines neuen Diskursreferenten:

(21) Tatian 35,29
Et pastores erant in regione eadem
uuarun thô hirta in thero lantskeffi
'Da waren Hirten in jener Gegend'[22]

Daneben kommt Verberststellung auch vor, wenn im vorangegangenen Diskurs der Referent bereits genannt ist, und zwar bei typischen Gruppen von Verben, wie Verba dicendi, Verben der Bewegung oder Verben, die Beginn und Wandel einer Situation beschreiben; z.B.:

(22) Tatian 126,5/6
Phariseus autem coepit intra se / reputans dicere
bigonda ther phariseus innan imo / ahtonti queden
'Als er darüber nachgedacht hatte, begann der Pharisäer zu sprechen ...'

Auch im Altisländischen[23] ist in solchen 'Inversionssätzen' das Subjekt stets Topik, also bereits eingeführt.[24] Gerd Enno Rieger[25] fügt hinzu, dass Verberstsätze eine 'Präzisierung' mit sich bringen können. Zwar ist die Inversion in Nebensätzen seltener, doch kommt sie gerade in konditionalen Strukturen vor:

---

[21] R. Hinterhölzl, S. Petrova und M. Solf, 'Diskurspragmatische Faktoren für Topikalität und Verbstellung in der ahd. Tatianübersetzung (9. Jh.)', *Approaches and Findings in Oral, Written and Gestural Language. Working Papers of the SFB 632, Interdisciplinary Studies on Information Structure* 3 (Berlin, 2005), 143–82, hier 152.

[22] *Ibid.* 152.

[23] Zum folgenden, vgl. K. Donhauser, M. Solf, M. und L. E. Zeige, 'Informationsstruktur und Diskursrelationen im Vergleich: Althochdeutsch – Altisländisch', *Grenzgänger. Festschrift zum 65. Geburtstag von Jurij Kusmenko*, A. Hornscheidt, Hg. (Berlin, 2006), 73–90.

[24] Halldór Ármann Sigurðsson, *Um frásagnarumröðun og grundvallarorðaröð í fornislensku* (Reykjavík, 1994), 138.

[25] 'Die Spitzenstellung des finiten Verbs als Stilmittel des isländischen Sagaerzählers', *Arkiv für Nordisk Filologi* 83 (1968), 81–139, hier 98.

(23) Ólafs saga ins helga
Þá hljóp at Áslákr Fitjaskalli ok hjó með øxi í hǫfuð Erlingi, svá at stóð í heila niðri; **var** (VI) þat þegar bana-sár; **lét** (VI) Erlingr þar líf sitt.
'Da lief Áslákr herbei und hieb mit der Axt Erlingi ins Haupt, so dass sie tief im Hirn stecken blieb; war das dann eine Todeswunde, ließ Erlingi da sein Leben.'[26]

Demgegenüber nimmt in Irrelevanzkonditionalia mit substantivischem *sa hwasa* bzw. *hwa* das verallgemeinernde oder einfache Relativpronomen eine vom Verb geforderte Kasusstelle im Satz ein; Sätze mit *sa hwasa* sind dann Subjektsätze, Sätze mit *sa hwamsa* usw. Objektsätze. Vgl. mit Präpositionalobjekt:

(24) Die Vierundzwanzig Landrechte
Thit is thet en and twintegoste londriucht: **To hwamsa** ma en lond and en erue askie and tospreke, sa ondwarde thi, ther mat him toaskie, and quethe: ... R_1 IV 21
'Dies ist das einundzwanzigste Landrecht: Von wem auch immer man ein Grundstück und Erbe fordert und ihn deswegen gerichtlich belangt, so antworte der, von dem man es fordert, und spreche: ...'

Der weitaus häufigste Typ sind hier aber die Subjektsätze. Informationsstrukturell bestehen sie im Falle von:

(25) **Wer immer** das tut, wird bestraft.

aus dem Topik *wer immer das tut* und dem Kommentar *wird bestraft* bzw. aus dem Hintergrund *wer immer das tut*, und dem Fokus *wird bestraft*. Auch solche Sätze haben die Aufgabe, neue Diskursreferenten einzuführen, der Ausdruck dafür ist jedoch kein Appellativ wie z.B. in (11) und (12), sondern ein verallgemeinernder Relativsatz. Es erfolgt als keine Referenzfestlegung auf eine bestimmte Person oder Personengruppe.

4. Distribution der altfriesischen Bedingungssätze

4.1. Indefinite Referenz

Das auffallendste syntaktische Merkmal der altfriesischen Rechtstexte sind zweifellos die Irrelevanzkonditionalia jeweils zu Beginn einer Küre, eines Landrechtes usw. – freie Relativsätze mit einem einfachen Relativpronomen

[26] *Heimskringla. Nóregs konunga sǫgur af Snorri Sturluson*, Finnur Jónsson, Hg., 4 Bde. (Kopenhagen, 1893–1900) II, K. 176 (S. 406/16–18).

kommen in dieser Position im Datenmaterial nicht vor.[27] M. Szadrowsky beschreibt die verallgemeinernden Relativsätze auf folgende Weise:[28]

> Ein wesenhaftes 'wer' steht an der Spitze, kein bedingendes 'wenn'. Ein Subjektsatz ist die 'gegebene' Umschreibung für ein Subjekt, wenn auch der Nachsatz eigentlich einen Bedingungssatz 'voraussetzt'. Auch ein relatives Akkusativ- oder Dativobjekt ist leibhaftiger als eine Bedingung.

Substantivische verallgemeinernde Relativpronomina werden jedoch, wie in 3.1.2. bemerkt, zur Einführung neuer, noch nicht bestimmter Referenten verwendet.[29] So wird z.B. zu Beginn einer Küre oftmals keine bestimmte Person oder Personengruppe genannt; vgl. (14); ferner ebenfalls mit Referenzidentität zwischen dem Subjekt des Irrelevanzkonditionale und dem Hauptsatz:

> (26) Die alten Rüstringer Küren
> Thit is thi thredda kere: **Sa hwasa** enne mon sle and thes nena iechta ne lede, thet hi thritich merk breke R_1 VIII 4
> 'Wer auch immer einen Mann erschlägt und deswegen kein Geständnis vor Gericht ablegt, der verwirkt dreißig Mark'

Auch das Genus bleibt offen. Der Rechtssatz gilt vielmehr für jedermann. Auf wen er zutrifft, wird erst im aktuellen Rechtsfall konkretisiert.

Eine Variante mit dem rahmensetzenden Element *sa hwersa* und dem Indefinitpronomen *ma* 'man'[30] liegt in (27) vor. Wie die Konditionalsätze mit Konjunktion oder Verbspitzenstellung dient hier aber auch der Konditionalsatz insgesamt der Rahmensetzung. Verallgemeinerndes *sa hwersa* 'wo auch immer', 'wann auch immer' weist dabei ebenfalls darauf hin, dass die Bedingung erst in einem bestimmten Fall konkretisiert wird.

---

[27] Eine jüngere Einleitungsformel ist offensichtlich die Verbindung *jef ther* in dem Fragesatz:
Die Rüstringer Priesterbußen (2. Teil)
Jef ther en papa lemid werth fon ena leya, hu monich pund hach hi to bote fori tha sigun wiena? R_1 VIII 1 ['Wenn da ein Geistlicher von einem Laien verstümmelt wird, wie viel Pfund kommen ihm zur Buße für die sieben Weihen zu?'].

[28] 'Stil und Syntax der altfriesischen Rechtssprache', *BGdSL* 83 (1961), 80–131, hier 113.

[29] Vgl. A. Bor, 'Relative Markers in Old East Frisian', *UW* 36 (1987), 21–48, hier 40.

[30] Vgl. dazu T. L. Markey, *Frisian* (The Hague, Paris and New York, 1981), 137–38; D. Boutkan and S. M. Siebinga, *Old Frisian Etymological Dictionary* (Leiden, 2005), 325.

(27) Die fünf Ausnahmen von der 17. Küre
Thet other: **Sa hwersa ma** wif nedgie and hiri wepinroft folgie folk and thi frana and hiu hered werthe, sa is thet al iechta; erost there wiue hiri withirield R_1 VII 3
'Die zweite: Wann auch immer man eine Frau notzüchtigt und das Volk und der Frana ihrem Notgeschrei folgen und sie gehört wird, so ist die Tat vollends unleugbar; zuerst (soll man) der Frau Schadenersatz (leisten)'

Wie *sa hwa sa* ist auch *sa hwersa ma* genusindifferent.

Eine weitere Variante besteht aus rahmensetzendem *sa hwersa* und *en mon* 'ein Mann':

(28) Die vierundzwanzig Landrechte
Thit is thet siuguntinde londriucht: **Sa hwersa en mon** tha otheron sin god to haldande deth, sa is thet riucht, thet hit him ondwarde thes selua dis, ther hit hebba wili R_1 IV 17
'Dies ist das siebzehnte Landrecht: Wann auch immer jemand einem andern sein Gut in Verwahrung gibt, so ist das Rechtens, dass dieser es ihm an demselben Tage, wo er es haben will, zurückgebe …'

4.2. Genusbezogene indefinite Referenz

Da neben *sa hwersa en mon* auch *wif* vorkommt, bietet das verallgemeinernde Relativadverb *sa hwersa* auch den Anschluss einer genusbezogenen Referenz. Auch in (29) geht es bei den Substantiven um neue indefinite Diskursreferenten:

(29) Die Vierundzwanzig Landrechte
Thit is thet sextinde londriucht: **Sa hwersa en mon ieftha en wif** steruat, and hiara erue and otheres hiara god leuath ... R_1 IV 16
'Dies ist das sechzehnte Landrecht: Wann auch immer ein Mann oder eine Frau stirbt, und sie ihr Land und ihr sonstiges Gut herlassen …'

Vgl. auch:

(30) Die vierundzwanzig Landrechte
Thit is thet achtatinde londriucht: **Sa hwersa en wif** ena monne bitegath, thet hi se nedgad hebbe, wili hi ia, sa betere hiri mith fullere bote R_1 IV 18

'Dies ist das achtzehnte Landrecht: Wann immer eine Frau einen Mann beschuldigt, dass er sie genotzüchtigt habe, so soll er, wenn er bekennen will, es ihr mit voller Buße engelten'

4.3. Gattungsbezogene Referenz

4.3.1. *neuer Diskursreferent*

Werden Appellativa, die nicht der Genusunterscheidung dienen, mit verallgemeinerndem *sa hwersa* verbunden, handelt es sich in der Regel ebenfalls um Personenbezeichnungen: Wie auch sonst bei der Einführung von Diskursreferenten kann der indefinite Artikel verwendet werden:

(31) Die neuen Rüstringer Küren
Thit is thi twilifta kere: **Sa hwersa en aldirmon** deth ene vnriuchte lhiene (= hliene) and thi redieua him nelle nawet folgia, sa skil hi tha liodon hundred merka sella. R_1 IX 12
'Dies ist die zwölfte Küre: Wann auch immer ein Ältermann ein falsches Zeugnis ablegt und der Redjeve ihm nicht beistimmen will, so soll er dem Volke hundert Mark entrichten.'

Auch mit qualifizierenden Adjektiven verbundene Appellativa erscheinen in Verbindung mit *sa hwersa* und indefinitem Artikel:

(32) Die neuen Rüstringer Küren
Thit is thi forma nia kere: **Sa hwersa** cumth en erm mon to tha warue clagande, thet ma tha erma er skil riuchta er ma tha rika. R_1 IX 1
'Dies ist die erste neue Küre: Wann auch immer ein armer Mann mit einer Klage vor Gericht erscheint, so soll man dem Armen eher Recht sprechen als dem Reichen.'

Neben dem indefiniten Artikel kommt auch der definite Artikel vor.

(33) Die alten Rüstringer Küren
Sa hwersa thi redieua misfari thruch bede tha thruch panninga, thet hi unriuchte thinge and thes londes kere wende, and hi thes birethad werthe mith werde ... R_1 VIII 14
'Wenn der Redjeve auf Bitten oder um Geld unrichtig handelt, so dass er ungerecht urteilt und von der Landesküre abweicht, und er dessen mit Zeugenbeweis überführt wird ...'.

Im altfriesischen Recht ist der Redjeve zwar als Kollegialrichter und Amtsträger bekannt.[31] Da diese Personengruppe in (33) aber nicht unmittelbar

---

[31] *Das Hunsingoer Recht*, Buma und Ebel, Hg., 150.

vorerwähnt ist, gilt sie ebenfalls als neu eingeführt. Neben dem Singular kommt auch der Plural vor. In beiden Fällen dient der definite Artikel der Generalisierung:

(34) Die alten Rüstringer Küren
Thit is thi fiarda kere: **Sa hwersa** tha redieua enne menene warf kethe, fretho to tha thinge and fretho fon tha thinge bi twam iechtiga ieldon and bi twam hundreda merkon alle heroge monnon. R_1 VIII 5
'Wann immer die Redjeven eine allgemeine Volksversammlung ansagen, so soll bei Strafe von zwei im Nichtleugnungsfall zu zahlenden Wergeldern und (einer Brüche von) zweihundert Mark für alle gehorsamen Männer auf dem Wege zum Gericht und vom Gericht Friede herrschen.'

Eine weitere Art der appellativischen Referenz begegnet in (35): Auf abschnitteinleitendes *sa hwersa tha redieua* folgen die verallgemeinernden Ausdrücke *sa hwelik bonnere ieftha hodere* und *sa hwelik aldirmon*.

(35) Die alten Rüstringer Küren
Sa hwelik bonnere ieftha hodere ouer thes redieua willa and sine hliene fari oua enne mon, thet hi thritich merk breke ... **Sa hwelik** aldirmon sa thera wedda awet ouirte, ther thi redieua hlige, thet hi se selua ielde. R_1 VIII 14
'Welcher Bonnere oder Hodere auch immer gegen des Redjeven Willen und dessen Ausspruch einen Zwangsvollstreckungszug gegen jemand führt, so verwirke er eine Brüche von dreißig Mark ... Welcher Ältermann auch immer auch nur die geringste Buße, die der Redjeve auferlegt, nicht beitreibt, so zahle er sie selbst.'

Bonnere, Hodere und Ältermann sind Vollstreckungsbeamte,[32] die den Weisungen des Redjeve zu folgen haben. In der Textstruktur kommt diese Hierarchie dadurch zum Ausdruck, dass für die Bezeichnung des Bonnere, Hodere und Ältermann ein anderer verallgemeinernder Ausdruck als bei der des Redjeve gewählt wird. Es ist ein adjektivisches verallgemeinerndes Relativpronomen und hat ebenfalls die Funktion, einen neuen Diskursreferenten einzuführen.[33]

---

32 *Das Rüstringer Recht*, Buma und Ebel, Hg., 161, 163, 168.

33 In den 'Neuen Rüstringer Küren' kommt auch *sa hwelik* zu Beginn einer Küre vor: Die neuen Rüstringer Küren
Sa hwelik redgeua sa thes is tha erma wernande, thi skil wesa alla skeldon egengen. R1 IX 3 ['Welcher Redjeve auch immer das dem Armen verweigert, so soll er mit vollem Recht seines Amtes entsetzt werden'].

4.3.2. *bridging*

Während in den bisherigen Fällen das mit *hwersa* verbundene Subjekt einen neuen Diskursreferenten bezeichnet, liegt in (36) eine andere Art der Referenz vor:

> (36) Die alten Rüstringer Küren
> Tha wi Frisa kersten wrdon, tha urief us thi kinig Kerl, sa hwersa alle liode enne kere kere, thet hi stede and stalle were bi londes legore and bi lioda libbande. R_1 VIII 1
> 'Als wir Friesen Christen wurden, da gewährte uns König Karl, dass, wann auch immer das ganze Volk eine Küre beschlösse, sie gültig und fest sein sollte, solange das Land stünde und Menschen lebten.'

wi Frisa wird in Verbindung mit *sa hwersa* durch *alle liode* wieder aufgenommen. Gegenüber *wi Frisa* betont aber das Adjektiv *alle* den Aspekt der Gesamtheit. Es herrscht also eine Art Teil-Ganzes-Beziehung, wie sie für sogenannte *bridging*-Relationen typisch ist: Der Referent ist mit einem vorerwähnten Diskursreferenten kompatibel und muss akkomodiert werden.[34] Es ist somit keine anaphorische Referenz wie bei Identitätsanaphern gegeben, weshalb sich die nominale Fügung *alle liode* in Verbindung mit *sa hwersa* zur Einleitung einer Rechtssatzung eignet.

4.4. Anaphorische Referenz

Anaphorische Referenz kommt dagegen vor allem durch pronominale Wiederaufnahme zu Stande. Für diese Referenz stehen nun Konditionalsätze mit Konjunktion oder Spitzenstellung des Verbs zur Verfügung.

> (37) Die vierundzwanzig Landrechte
> Thit send tha siuguntine liodkesta and tha fiuwer and twintich londriucht, ther alle Frisa mith hiara fia kapadon and mith riuchte bruka skilun, **ief** se moton R_1 IV 25
> 'Dies sind die siebzehn Volksküren und die vierundzwanzig Landrechte, die alle Friesen sich mit ihrem Gelde erkauft haben und die sie Rechtens in Anwendung bringen dürfen, wenn sie können'

und

> (38) Die alten Rüstringer Küren
> Thit is thi siugunda kere: **Sa hwasa** mith woniron an en godishus fore, thet hi hundred merk breke. **Deth** hi eniga monne enigene skatha binna tha godishuse ieftha buta, a twibete and twifrethe. R_1 VIII 8

[34] C. Umbach, '(De)accenting Definite Descriptions'. MS 2001.

'Dies ist die siebente Küre: Wer auch immer mit Kriegsknechten eine Kirche besetzen sollte, der verwirkt eine Brüche von hundert Mark. Tut er jemandem innerhalb oder außerhalb der Kirche irgendwelchen Schaden, so hat er dafür in jedem Falle doppelte Buße und doppeltes Friedensgeld zu zahlen.'

In (39) zeigt die Ellipse von *kind* in *thet leste* die enge Verknüpfung mit *thera kinda allerek* in dem vorausgehenden Satz. Denn ein substantivisches Bezugswort kann nur weggelassen werden, wenn in dem unmittelbar vorhergehenden Text dieses Wort vorkommt:

(39) Die alten Rüstringer Küren
Thit is thi sexta kere and thi warth mith ethon bisweren: **Sa hwersa** twa sinhigen se and kinda tein hebbath and hiara other forifalle, thet thera kinda allerek otheron leue; **sterue** thet leste, thet ma thet got inna twa dele. R1 VIII 6
'Das ist die sechste Küre und die wurde mit Eiden beschworen: Wo auch immer zwei Eheleute sind und sie Kinder gezeugt haben und deren eines stirbt, da soll jedes Kind sein Gut auf die andern vererben; stirbt das letzte (Kind), so teile man das Gut in zwei Teile.'

5. Textstrukturelle Funktion

Während die Irrelevanzkonditionalia mit verallgemeinerndem Relativpronomen oder Relativadverb in den angeführten Beispielen abschnitteinleitende Funktion haben, befinden sich die mit Konjunktion oder mit Verb eingeleiteten Relativsätze innerhalb eines Textabschnitts. Die Relationen, die diese Bedingungssätze zu ihrer textuellen Umgebung haben, lässt sich am besten mit der Centering Theory beschreiben, da diese Theorie referentielle Unterschiede der Entitäten im Diskurs berücksichtigt: So ist jede Entität ein potentieller Kandidat für das 'Center', eben die Entität, die die Textkohärenz gewährleistet. Zum einen gibt es 'forward-looking Centers', die nach folgender Hierarchie grammatikalischer Funktion als Referenzträger in Frage kommen:

Subjekt >> Objekt >> Adverbiale etc.

Die Anordnung besagt, dass im Falle von Koreferenz das Subjekt des folgenden Satzes das bevorzugte Center ist. Zum anderen ist die Verbindung des Centers zur vorigen Äußerung von Bedeutung. Es ist zu prüfen, ob irgendein referentieller Ausdruck der Vorgängeräußerung als Center der aktuellen Äußerung gewählt wird oder ob es derjenige referentielle Ausdruck ist, der gleichzeitig das Center der Äußerung davor war. Auch für dieses 'backward-looking Center' ergibt sich eine Hierarchie, nämlich:

Continue >> Retain >> Smooth Shift >> Rough Shift

Vgl. dazu die Beispiele:

Continue: (A) **Die Grabungsleiter** trinken einen starken Kaffee. (B) Etwas Aufmunterung können **sie** wohl gebrauchen.
Retain: (A) **Die Grabungsleiter** trinken einen starken Kaffee. (B) Neue Aufgaben warten auf **sie**.
Smooth Shift: (B) Neue Aufgaben warten auf **sie**. (C) **Diese** gelten als überaus schwierig.
Rough Shift: (B) Etwas Aufmunterung können **sie** wohl gebrauchen. (C) Zur **Aufmunterung** trug auch eine Begebenheit bei der gestrigen Grabung bei.[35]

Betrachtet man nun noch einmal (38), so wird hier das indefinite Subjekt des Irrelevanzkonditionale durch das Subjekt *hi* in einer Continue-Relation wieder aufgenommen:

(38) Die alten Rüstringer Küren
Thit is thi siugunda kere: **Sa hwasa** mith woniron an en godishus fore, thet hi hundred merk breke. **Deth** hi eniga monne enigene skatha binna tha godishuse ieftha buta, a twibete and twifrethe. R_1 VIII 8
'Dies ist die siebente Küre: Wer auch immer mit Kriegsknechten eine Kirche besetzen sollte, der verwirkt eine Brüche von hundert Mark. Tut er jemandem innerhalb oder außerhalb der Kirche irgendwelchen Schaden, so hat er dafür in jedem Falle doppelte Buße und doppeltes Friedensgeld zu zahlen.'

Auch die Retain-Relation tritt bei den Konditionalsätzen mit Spitzenstellung des Verbs auf; vgl. (40) mit der Wiederaufnahme des Subjekts des vorausgehenden Nebensatzes (*thet kind*) durch das Objekt *him*:

(40) Die Vierundzwanzig Landrechte
Sa hwersa thiu moder hiri kindis erue urkapath tha urwixlath mith hiri frionda rede, er thet kind ieroch se, **like** him the kap, alsa hit ieroch se, sa halde hit ne; **likere** him *nicht, so* ... R_1 IV 2
'Wann auch immer die Mutter den Grundbesitz ihres Kindes mit Zustimmung ihrer Verwandten verkauft oder vertauscht, bevor das Kind mündig

[35] A. Speyer, 'Die Bedeutung der Center-Theorie für die Vorfeldbesetzung des Deutschen' (Ms. Philadelphia 2007).

ist, so soll dieses, gefällt ihm der Verkauf, sobald es mündig ist, ihn gelten lassen; gefällt er ihm aber nicht, so ...'

Des weiteren belegen enklitische Pronomina am Verb die enge Textkohärenz von Konditionalsätzen mit Verberststellung: Denn enklitische Pronomina eignen sich wie 0-Pronomina in besonderem Maße für eine Continue-Relation.[36] In (41) herrscht diese Relation zwischen zwischen dem 0-Pronomen des thet-Satzes der Apodosis des Irrelevanzkonditionale und dem folgenden Konditionalsatz:

(41) Die alten Rüstringer Küren
Thit is thi siuguntinda kere, thet ma anda londe nen long sax ne droge. **Sa hwasa** thermithi enne mon sloge, thet hine mith twam ieldon gulde and ma him sine ferra hond opa tha thingstapule ofsloge. **Ac wndader**ne, thet mam thet sax thruch sine ferra hond sloge midda alle Riostringon. R_1 VIII 18
'Dies ist die siebzehnte Küre, dass man im Lande kein langes Messer tragen solle. Wer auch immer einen Mann damit tötete, der sollte ihn mit doppeltem Wergeld büßen und man sollte ihm die rechte Hand auf dem Dingstapel abhauen. Und verwundet er ihn, sollte man ihn inmitten aller Rüstringer das Messer durch die rechte Hand schlagen.'

Oftmals ist auch ein Konditionalsatz mit Verberststellung durch *ac* 'und' angeschlossen; vgl. dreimaliges formelhaftes *ac* + Verb in (36):

(42) Die gemeinfriesischen Siebzehn Küren
Thit is thiv sextinde liodkest and thes kiningis Kerles ieft, thet alle Frisa mugun hiara feitha mith tha fia capia ... **Ac wrth**ere vrwnnen and urdeld anda liodthinge mith riuchtere tele and mith asega dome and bi lioda londriuchte, bi skeltata bonne and bi keyseres orloui ieftha sines weldiga boda, fon falske tha fon fade, so hach ma [Ms. hina] sine ferra hond opa tha thingstapule of to slande umbe tha twa deda. **Ac hebbe** hi haueddeda eden, nachtbrond ieftha othera morthdeda, sa skil hi ielda mith sines selues halse alle liodon to like thonke bi asega dome and bi lioda londriuchte, thet is, thet ma hini skil opa en reth setta. **Ac hebbe** hi thivuethe den bi Frisona kere, **ief** hit an tha fia nebbe, sa hach ma hini to hwande. R_1 III 16
'Dies ist die sechzehnte Volksküre und König Karls Privileg, dass alle Friesen ihre Blutschulden durch Geld und Gut sühnen dürfen. ... Und wird einer im Volksgericht auf eine gültige Klage hin und durch Urteil

[36] M. A. Walker, A. K. Joshi and E. F. Prince, 'Centering in Naturally Occurring Discourse: an Overview', *Centering Theory in Discourse*, M. A. Walker, A. K. Joshi und E. F. Prince, Hg. (Oxford, 1998), 1–28, hier 5.

des Asega und nach dem Landrecht des Volkes, auf Befehl des Skeltata und mit der Erlaubnis des Kaisers oder von dessen Bevollmächtigtem schuldig gesprochen und verurteilt wegen Münzfälschung oder Münzverringerung, so soll man ihm wegen dieser beiden Taten die rechte Hand auf dem Dingstapel abhauen. Und hat er Halsverbrechen begangen, Nachtbrand oder sonstige Mordtaten, so soll er durch Urteil des Asega und nach dem Landrecht des Volkes mit seinem eigenen Leben büßen, um alle Leute in gleichem Maße zu befriedigen, das heißt, man soll ihn aufs Rad flechten. Und hat er einen Diebstahl im Sinne der friesischen Küren verübt, so soll man ihn, wenn er es nicht in Geld und Gut hat, hängen.'

Da textverknüpfende Elemente möglichst eng an den Vorgängersatz anschließen, knüpfen die Konditionalsätze mit Spitzenstellung des Verbs unmittelbar an den vorangehenden Satz an. Im Bedingungsgefüge stehen sie also vor der Apodosis. Dagegen können die mit *ief* eingeleiteten Konditionalsätze auch zwischengestellt werden; vgl. (42); ferner:

(43) Die alten Rüstringer Küren
Thit is thi fiftinda kere: **Sa hwersa** en prester ieftha en skeltata ieftha otheres hwelikera honda mon sa thet were, ther en lengad god fon houi hede, **ief** hi forifelle and kindar lefde, ther thet lengade god upnema machte, sa hwet sa thi were, ther tha riuchta erua thet god underwnne, thet hi hundred merk breke. R1 VIII 16
'Dies ist die fünfzehnhte Küre: Wann auch immer ein Priester oder ein Skeltata, oder was für ein Mann es sonst auch sein mochte, ein Lehngut vom Hofe hätte, soll, wenn dieser stürbe und Kinder hinterließe, die das Lehngut in Besitz nehmen könnten, derjenige, wer er auch wäre, der dem gesetzlichen Erben das Gut entzöge, eine Brüche von hundert Mark entrichten.'

Auch außerhalb des Rüstringer Rechts finden sich mit Konjunktion eingeleitete Bedingungssätze in solchen Positionen; vgl. zur Stellung im Nachfeld des Hauptsatzes:

(44) Die Hunsingoer Bußtaxen II
Uversa ma ene prestere en raf deth, sin bote a mith fiardatuede skillenge achta warue te betane, **alsa fir** sat nen licraf nis. H IX 4
'Wann auch immer man einen Raub an einem Priester verübt, (so hat man) die ihm gebührende Buße je zu dreizweidrittel Schillingen achtmal zu entgelten, sofern es sich nicht um Ausplündern bis auf die Haut handelt.'

Der Unterschied in der Stellung der mit Konjunktion oder Verb eingeleiteten Nebensätze zeigt sich dabei an Textstellen, die beide Typen von Konditionalsätzen aufweisen; vgl. die Stellung der formelhaften Fügung *ief hit selua nawet nebbe* in (42) mit der in (45):

(45) Die gemeinfriesischen Siebzehn Küren
Sa hwersa en mon sa erga deda dede, thet hi nedgade widua ieftha megitha ieftha enis otheres monnis wif, **werth** hi mith werde tha mith compe vrwnnen, sa hach thet wif to bote twilif merk ... Thet is riucht, thet him sina friond therto helpe, **ief** hit selua nawet nebbe, thruch thet hia ne mugun him nawet undkuma, hiara berena blode. R_1 III 15
'Wann auch immer ein Mann solche schlimmen Taten beginge, dass er Witwen oder Jungfrauen oder die Frau eines anderen Mannes notzüchtigte, wird er dessen mit Zeugenbeweis oder durch gerichtlichen Zweikampf überführt würde, so kommen der Frau als Buße zwölf Mark zu ... Das ist Recht, dass ihm seine Verwandten dabei helfen, wenn er es selbst nicht hat, deswegen, weil sie ihn, ihren Blutsfreund, nicht im Stich lassen dürfen.'

Was nun weitere Unterschiede zwischen den mit Konjunktion oder Verb eingeleiteten Bedingungssätzen an solchen Textstellen angeht, so zeigen die Bedingungssätze mit Spitzenstellung des Verbs eine referentiell engere textuelle Verbindung als die mit Konjunktion: So erscheint in (46) das Subjekt des Vorgängersatzes in dem mit *ac willath* eingeleiteten Konditionalsatz in einer Continue-Relation wiederum als Subjekt. Dagegen ist in dem durch *sa* eingeleiteten Konditionalsatz das Objekt *en bern* durch *sin kind* bzw. *sinis kindis kind* wieder aufgenommen. Also liegt Smooth Shift vor. Gleiches gilt für den Wechsel von *mith fiuwer modermegon and mith achta federmegon* zu dem Subjekt *sina friond* in dem mit *ief* eingeleiteten Satz:

(46) Die Vierundzwanzig Landrechte
Thit is thet sexte londriucht: **Sa hwersa** twene brother send and thi other thenne en wif halath and bi there wiue thenne en bern tivcht, sa weldegath him sin feder efter sine degon enne riuchtene swesdel. **Sa** sin kind ieftha sinis kindis kind hini urleuath, sa thes kindis alder nawet ne leuath, sa wili thet kind dela and thi fidiria nele and queth thet, thet hi ena kni niar se: sa hach thet kind thenne an tha were to tiande mith fiuwer modermegon and mith achta federmegon, **ief** him sina friond helpa willath. Ac **willath** hini sina friond eta withon urtia, sa hach thet kind thenne framde man mith sina fia te kapande, ther mith him gunge to tha withon stonda, and halde iuen godene del ediles lauon, thach thet kind se wel ena halua kni biefta. R_1 IV 6

'Dies ist das sechste Landrecht: Wo auch immer es zwei Brüder gibt und der eine dann eine Frau heimführt und darauf mit der Frau ein Kind zeugt, so wendet sein Vater ihm einen gesetzlichen Erbteil nach seinem Tode zu. Wenn sein Kind oder sein Kindeskind ihn überlebt, während des Kindes Vater nicht (mehr) lebt, so will das Kind die Erbschaft [*seines Großvaters*] teilen und der Vatersbruder will es nicht und sagt, dass er um einen Grad näher verwandt sei; dann soll das Kind mit vier mütterlichen und mit acht väterlichen Verwandten den Besitz an sich ziehen, wenn seine Angehörigen ihm helfen wollen. Und wollen seine Verwandten es bei der Eidesleistung auf die Reliquien im Stich lassen, so soll das Kind darauf mit seinem Gelde fremde Männer kaufen, die mit ihm zum Eide vor die Reliquien treten, und es soll einen gleich großen Anteil an der Hinterlassenschaft des Großvaters bekommen, obgleich das Kind wohl um einen halben Grad zurücksteht.'

Zwar kommt auch Wiederaufnahme mit Pronomen oder 0-Pronomen in den mit Konjunktion eingeleiteten Bedingungssätzen vor, wie die Beispiele (42), (43) und (45) deutlich machen. Doch werden auch Appellativa als Diskursreferenten eingeführt. In (47) weist das Possessivpronomen *hiri* in *hiri brother* in einer Retain-Relation auf *hiri – hiv – dochter* zurück:

(47) Die Vierundzwanzig Landrechte
Thit is thet fiarde londriucht: **Sa hwersa** feder and moder hiara dochter eine fletieue ieuath and hia utbeldath mith afta gode and mith hiara fria erue, and thenne lede mith kape tha mith wixle of tha liodgarda ana enne otherne, and tha hionon hiara god misgunge and hiara meni aken werthe and hia an thet god unriuchte spreka willat, sa hach hiv to wetande hiri god mith twam dedethon. Ac **ief** hiri brother tha fletieua brida wili and tiona, sa mot hiu se tiona and halda mith twam hondon anda withon buta stride. R1 IV 4
'Dies ist das vierte Landrecht: Wann auch immer Vater und Mutter ihrer Tochter eine Aussteuer geben und sie mit ihrem rechtmäßigen Gut und mit ihrem freien erblichen Grundbesitz abfinden, und sie diesen dann durch Verkauf oder durch Tausch aus dem Familiengut in ein anderes bringt, und das Gut der Eheleute zurückgeht, und ihre Angehörigenzahl wächst, und sie das Gut [*der Tochter*] zu Unrecht anfordern wollen, so soll sie mit zwei Tateiden vor Gericht beschwören, dass ihr das Gut gehöre. Und wenn ihr Bruder die Aussteuer an sich bringen und beanspruchen will, so darf sie diese ohne (gerichtlichen) Zweikampf mit zwei (Eides-)Händen auf die Reliquien beanspruchen und behalten.'

Auch eine weitere Art von Perspektivenwechsel findet sich in den mit Konjunktion eingeleiteten Bedingungssätzen: Während in (48) in dem Irrelevanzkonditionale der Ankläger der Agens ist, ist in den *jef*-Sätzen der Angeklagte Patiens bzw. Agens. Zwischen *to ena monne* und *him* vollzieht sich also ein Smooth Shift, während *hi* in *jef hi bisoke* unmittelbar als Subjekt fortgesetzt ist.

(48) Die gemeinfriesischen Siebzehn Küren
Thit is thiu achtande liodkest, thet nen husmon with sinne hera to felo ne stride. **Sa hwetsa** (Ms. hwersa) ma ther von thes kininges haluon sochte (Ms. fochte) to ena monne, **jef** hit him urkome, thet hi sinere hauedlesne skeldich were, **jef** hi bisoke, thet hine sikurade mith twilif monnon an tha withon, mith fiuwer frilingon and mith fiuwer ethelingon and mith fiuwer lethslachton R_1 III 8
'Dies ist die achte Volksküre, dass kein Hausmann mit seinem Herrn zu sehr streite. Was immer man da einem Mann von Seiten des Königs zur Last legt – wenn das ihm nachgewiesen würde, dass er seine Hauptlösung schuldig wäre, so soll er, wenn er leugnet, sich mit zwölf Männern auf die Reliquien freischwören (nämlich) mit vier Frilingen und mit vier Ethelingen und mit vier Letslachten.'

Und in (49) wechselt die Rolle des Beklagten vom Patiens im Irrelevanzkonditionale zum Agens im *jef*-Satz. Dazwischen steht aber ein Verberst-Konditionalsatz mit einem Subjekt in einer Retain-Relation (*sin god ieftha sin erue*), während der mit *jef* eingeleitete Bedingungssatz mit dem Subjekt des Irrelevanzkonditionale neu einsetzt.

(49) Die gemeinfriesischen Siebzehn Küren
Thit is thiv fiuwertinde liodkest: **sa hwersa** en ungeroch kind ut of londe lat werth thruch sellonge tha thruch hirigongar, **werth** sin god ieftha sin erue urset tha urseld, **jef** thet kind to londe kumth and to sina liodon, mi hit thenne bikanna brother and swester and to nomande wet sine nesta friond and sinne feder and sine moder, mi hit sines eina erues enigene ekker bikanna, sa hach thet kind .... R_1 III 14
'Dies ist die vierzehnte Volksküre: Wann auch immer ein unmündiges Kind aus dem Lande weggeführt wird durch Verkauf oder durch Heergang, wird sein Gut oder sein Grundbesitz (darauf) verpfändet oder verkauft, so soll, wenn das Kind (später wieder) ins Land zu seinen Leuten kommt und es dann Bruder und Schwester wiedererkennen kann und seine nächsten Verwandten und seinen Vater und seine Mutter zu nennen weiß und es irgendeinen Acker seiner Grundstücke erkennen kann, das Kind ... .'

6. Fazit

Mit Konjunktion eingeleitete Bedingungssätze haben also in den mit Irrelevanzkonditionalia beginnenden Textabschnitten eine besondere textstrukturelle Funktion: Sie lenken auf das Topik zurück oder führen ein neues Diskurstopik ein, wozu dann in der Apodosis neue Information hinzukommt. Geht ein Konditionalsatz mit Verbspitzenstellung einem solchen mit Konjunktion eingeleiteten Bedingungssatz voraus, so ist dieser enger an den vorausgehenden Text angeschlossen.[37] Somit ergibt sich folgendes Schema:

I zur Einleitung in einen allgemeinen Rechtsfall:
a) universales Irrelevanzkonditionale zur Einführung eines indefiniten Diskursreferenten
b) rahmensetzendes universales Irrelevanzkonditionale mit einem indefiniten oder appellativischen neuen Diskursreferenten
II zur Präzisierung des allgemeinen Falls:
mit Verb eingeleiteter Konditionalsatz mit anaphorischer Referenz
III zur Rücklenkung oder Neuetablierung des Topiks:
mit Konjunktion eingeleiteter Konditionalsatz mit anaphorischer Referenz oder einem neuen Diskursreferenten[38]

Vergleicht man noch einmal die Apodosis-Strukturen der lateinischen Konditionalsätze in der *Lex Frisionum*, so unterscheiden sich diese wesentlich von der volkssprachlichen Textstruktur: Wie bemerkt, sind die verallgemeinernden Relativsätze zwischengestellt. Zuweilen sind sie aber mit der Aufzählung der Entitäten verbunden, die unter den verallgemeinerten Begriff fallen können:

(51) De homicidiis. Tit. I 'Von Totschlägen'
§13 Si servus nobilem seu liberum aut litum nesciente domino occiderit, dominus eius, cuiuscunque condicionis fuerit homo qui occisus est, iuret hoc se non iussisse et multam eius pro servo bis simplum componat.
'Wenn ein Knecht einen Edlen oder Freien oder Halbfreien ohne Wissen des Herrn tötet, schwöre sein Herr, er habe dies nicht befohlen, welchen Standes auch immer der Mann war, der getötet ist, und büße dessen Sühne zweimal einfach für den Knecht.'[39]

---

[37] Nach Szadrowsky, 'Stil und Syntax', 117, ist jedoch die dritte Bedingung der zweiten deutlich untergeordnet.

[38] Szadrowsky, 'Stil und Syntax', 119 drückt dies folgendermaßen aus: 'Man muss ganze Satzungen lesen, um zu prüfen, was die ungebrochene Wucht des Hauptsatzes bedeutet. Atem schöpft der Gesetzsprecher zu markigem Einsatz der Hauptsache'.

[39] Siehe Fußn. 6.

Auch Konditionalsätze mit Konjunktion *si* werden auf diese Weise verwendet:

(52) Haec Wlemarus addidet 'Dies fügte Wlemar hinzu':
Si quis servum aut ancillam, caballum, bovem, ovem vel cuiuscunque generis animal vel quodcunque homo ad usum necessarium in potestate habuerit, arma, vestem, utensilia quęlibet et pecuniam, alii ad auferendum exposuerit, si ille qui abstulit patria profugerit, expositor tertiam portionem compositionis exsolvat
'Wenn jemand einen andern anstiftet, Knecht oder Magd, Pferd, Rind, Schaf oder ein Tier irgendwelcher Art, oder was immer ein Mann zu notwendigem Gebrauch in Gewalt hat, Waffen, Kleidung, irgendwelche Gebrauchsgegenstände und Geld wegzunehmen, bezahle der Anstifter, wenn jeder, der wegnahm, der Heimat entflieht, den dritten Bruchteil der Buße'

(53) De homicidiis Tit. I 'Von Totschlägen'
§11 Si quis homo, sive nobilis sive liber sive litus sive etiam servus, alterius servum occiderit, componat eum iuxta quod fuerit adpretiatus ...
'Wenn irgendein Mann, er sei Edler oder Freier oder Halbfreier oder auch Knecht, eines andern Knecht tötet, büße er ihm gemäß dem, wie er bewertet wird ...'

(54) Wlemarus
§68 Si caballus aut bos aut quodlibet animal homini vulnus intulerit ...
'Wenn ein Pferd oder Rind oder irgendein Tier einem Menschen eine Wunde beibringt ...'

Im Altfriesischen sind derartige Spezifizierungen dagegen selten; vgl.:

(55) Die Vierundzwanzig Landrechte
sa hwetsa therunder bisken is, dolch sa dath, sa mi thi thredkniling efter thes otheres dathe spreka R_1 VI 8
'Was auch immer dabei geschehen ist, es sei Verwundung oder Totschlag, so darf der Verwandte im dritten Grade nach des anderen Tode Klage erheben'

Diese Unterschiede machen noch einmal deutlich, dass die Textstruktur der Bedingungssätze in den altfriesischen Rechtstexten wirklich ein einheimischer Sprachgebrauch ist. Durch die unterschiedlichen Referenzmöglichkeiten volkssprachlicher Konditionalsätze war ein stufenweises Fortschreiten vom allgemeinen Rechtsfall (Irrelevanzkonditionalia) zum spezielleren

(Bedingungssätze mit Spitzenstellung des Verbs) möglich. Dann erfolgte gegebenenfalls ein Rückgriff auf das Diskurstopik oder die Einführung eines neuen solchen Topiks (Konditionalsätze mit Konjunktion), wenn eine weitere Ausformulierung der allgemeinen Rechtsbedingung notwendig war.

Dat nye lantrecht. Altfriesisches Recht im fünfzehnten und sechzehnten Jahrhundert – Nachleben oder Neuanfang?

Henk D. Meijering

EINFÜHRUNG

Gerbenzons Untersuchungen zu einigen friesischen Rechtsbüchern des 15. Jahrhunderts, vorgelegt in einer Dissertation aus dem Jahre 1956,[1] sind zwar sehr reichhaltig, sie bieten aber nicht alle Ergebnisse seiner Forschungsarbeit. Es war noch ein zweiter Band vorgesehen, eine Studie, in der er namentlich die *Jurisprudentia Frisica* hätte analysieren wollen, eine mehr oder weniger systematisch eingerichtete Sammlung von Paragrafen, in der die damals noch brauchbaren Elemente aus dem altfriesischen Recht mit kanonistischen Bestimmungen verbunden wurden. Dieses Buch ist niemals herausgekommen, aber 1989 erschien in zwei Heften der *Tijdschrift voor Rechtsgeschiedenis*[2] dasjenige, was Gerbenzon dreißig Jahre davor vielleicht noch nicht für publikationsreif hielt, was aber im Grunde genauso reichhaltig war wie die Dissertation aus dem Jahre 1956.

Nun geht es mir nicht um die von Gerbenzon durchgeführte Analyse. Es ist unwahrscheinlich, dass ein Nichtkanonist wie ich seinen Beobachtungen auch nur einiges hätte hinzufügen können. Wesentlich ist aber in diesem Zusammenhang der Rahmen, in den Gerbenzon die Handschrift, die die *Jurisprudentia Frisica* als Hauptbestandteil enthält,[3] stellt. Mit Recht sieht er die *Jurisprudentia-Frisica* – und die ganze *Excerpta-legum*-Tradition, in der sie steht – als einen Versuch, das altfriesische Recht den Anforderungen der modernen (das heißt der spätmittelalterlichen) Zeit anzupassen. Das bedeutet nicht, dass es die Absicht des Autors oder Auftraggebers der

---

[1] P. Gerbenzon, *Excerpta legum. Onderzoekingen betreffende enkele Friese rechtsboeken uit de vijftiende eeuw* (Groningen und Jakarta, 1956).

[2] P. Gerbenzon, 'Aantekeningen over de *Jurisprudentia Frisica*. Een laat-vijftiendeeeuwse Westerlauwers-Friese bewerking van de *Excerpta legum*', *TRG* 57 (1989), 21–67 und 339–74.

[3] Kodex Roorda (weiterhin Ro).

Sammlung war, das traditionelle, ideologische[4] Recht ganz abzuschaffen. Das Manuskript fängt ja mit Texten an, die auch den Beginn von Textträgern wie der *Inkunabel des Freeska Landriucht* (D) oder der Handschrift *Jus Municipale Frisonum* (J) bilden: *Haet is riucht* ['Was ist Recht?'] und das *Ältere Sceltariucht* ['Älteres Schulzenrecht'; ÄS]. Was am Ende des fünfzehnten Jahrhunderts deren Bedeutung für die Rechtspraxis war, ist unklar, aber ohne den ideologischen Gefühlswert dieser oder ähnlicher Texte konnte man anscheinend nicht zurechtkommen. Diese ideologische Textsammlung bricht aber in Ro mitten in einem Artikel des ÄS ab, und das unterstreicht eher das Gewicht dieser traditionellen Texte, als dass man daraus schließen könnte, dass sie ihre Bedeutung verloren hätten. Gerbenzon hat nämlich Grund zu der Annahme, dass gerade als der Kopist diese ideologischen Texte abschrieb, die Inkunabel auf den Markt kam (ca. 1485). Es ist nicht bekannt, wie hoch deren Auflage war (uns liegen jetzt noch neun Exemplare vor), aber eben dadurch, dass sie erschien, hatte es keinen Sinn mehr, noch weitere altfriesische ideologische *Handschriften* zu kopieren. Das gilt für den Anfang der Handschrift Ro noch umso stärker, als ihre Darstellung der altfriesischen Texte mit der von D verwandt ist, mit lateinischen Allegaten, die mit denen von D übereinstimmen, ja sogar noch ausführlicher sind.

Gerbenzon schließt eins seiner Kapitel resignierend ab: Der Autor oder die Autoren der *Excerpta legum* in deren verschiedenartigen Textgestalten hätten ein modernisiertes, 'gelehrtes' friesisches Recht angestrebt, das in das frühe sechzehnte Jahrhundert passte. Sie erkannten, dass das *Freeska Landriucht* seine Zeit gehabt habe, aber auch sie könnten den Lauf der Geschichte weder voraussagen noch regulieren oder eindämmen. Nach dem Jahre 1498, als Friesland dem Herzog Albrecht von Sachsen übergeben wurde, sei die JF 'weggeschwemmt'.[5]

In diesem Beitrag geht es um die modernisierende Tendenz im spätmittelalterlichen altfriesischen Recht. Tatsächlich ist diese Tendenz im Westerlauwersschen Friesland[6] abrupt abgebrochen worden. Das heißt aber nicht, dass das modernisierte friesische Recht nicht an anderen Orten weiterlebte, und dass die Entwicklung westlich der Lauwers nicht schon früher und in größerem Umfang eingesetzt habe. Gerbenzon hat immer einen Blick für diese neuen Entwicklungen gehabt, aber weil man sich im Hauptstrom

---

[4] Das Wort 'ideologisch' bezieht sich auf die friesische Freiheitsideologie, was immer man davon auch halten mag.

[5] Gerbenzon, 'Aantekeningen', 61.

[6] Um das schwerfällige Adjektiv 'westerlauwerssch' möglichst wenig zu verwenden, bezeichne ich Friesland, westlich der Lauwers, weiterhin als Westfriesland und dessen Sprache als Westfriesisch. Im Rahmen dieses Beitrags wird das nicht zu Missverständnissen führen.

der altfriesischen Philologie namentlich auf die friesischsprachige Überlieferung richtete, und dann auch noch auf die der 'klassischen', ideologischen Texte, blieb längere Zeit unbeachtet, dass die mittelalterliche friesische Gesellschaft, auch was ihre Gesetzgebung und Rechtssetzung anbelangt, dabei war, sich auf die moderne Zeit einzustellen. Dass das nicht zu Lasten der Überlieferung der 'klassischen' Rechtsliteratur geschah, sahen wir schon angesichts der ursprünglichen Absicht des Autors oder Auftraggebers von Ro, dem Text, der jetzt den Löwenanteil der Handschrift bildet, der *Jurisprudentia Frisica*, eine Sammlung von Rechtstexten, ähnlich der in D, vorauszuschicken. Auch die Handschrift J (um 1530) bezeugt dieses Interesse. Was Westfriesland anbelangt, kommt diese Modernisierung zum Ausdruck

1. in der Anpassung an auch außerhalb Friesland geltendes Recht: kanonistische Sammlungen, und ansonsten lateinische Allegate zu 'klassischen' altfriesischen Rechtstexten;
2. in infolge gesellschaftlicher Entwicklungen andersartigen Rechtstextsorten: Stadtrechte;
3. im Gebrauch einer anderen Sprache als das Friesische: Niederländisch;
4. in einem anderen Medium: dem Buchdruck; die *Inkunabel des Freeska Landriucht* sollte für mehr als ein Jahrhundert das einzige gedruckte friesischsprachige Buch bleiben.

Die modernisierenden Elemente in oben stehender Aufzählung sind in der früheren Forschung durchaus bemerkt und erwähnt worden. Dass aber auch der *Inhalt* der klassischen, ursprünglich ideologischen Texte beteiligt war, ist noch zu wenig beachtet worden. Ich konzentriere mich auf die westfriesische Überlieferung und deren Rezeption in den Groninger Ommelanden. Diese Rezeption – die die durch den Ablauf der politischen, und damit auch der legislativen Geschichte abgebrochene westfriesische Entwicklung widerspiegelt – war möglich, weil das altfriesische Recht in den Ommelanden bis zum Jahre 1601 in Kraft blieb. Ostfriesland behielt das altfriesische traditionelle Recht noch länger (bis 1809), aber da handelt es sich im Grunde um eine inhaltliche Pervertierung desselben Rechts unter Beibehaltung des ursprünglichen Wortlauts. Es diente nur den Ansprüchen des gräflichen Hauses.[7]

Altfriesisches Recht in den Groninger Ommelanden

Für die Erforschung erneuernder Tendenzen im westerlauwersschen altfriesischen Recht ist also die Überlieferungslage in den Groninger Ommelanden von Bedeutung. Genauso wie in Westfriesland sind auch hier nur

[7] W. Ebel, *Das Ende des friesischen Rechts in Ostfriesland* (Aurich, 1961).

wenige vollständig überlieferte ideologische friesischsprachige Handschriften bewahrt geblieben: die beiden Hunsingoer Kodizes und das Manuskript, das wir als die Fivelgoer Handschrift (F) kennen. Sicherlich hat es mehr davon gegeben, wir kennen noch Fragmente, *membra disiecta*, aber schon der Sprachwechsel und infolge dessen das Entstehen niedersächsischer Übersetzungen wird einer ungestörter Überlieferung friesischsprachiger Texte nicht förderlich gewesen sein. Die Anwesenheit dieser niedersächsischen Ommelander Handschriften hat also dieselbe Wirkung auf das Weiterleben friesischer handgeschriebener Rechtsquellen gehabt, wie die Inkunabel das in Westfriesland hatte.

Die altfriesische Handschrift F ist in ihrem ersten Teil – der von westfriesischen Quellen beeinflusst worden ist – am stärksten ideologisch gefärbt, also gesamtfriesisch ausgerichtet. Die Texte des zweiten Teiles haben eine beschränktere geografische Reichweite. Das ist auch der Sachverhalt in den übersetzten Ommelander Handschriften: Auch da ist ein ideologischer Kern, zu dem fast immer die *Siebzehn Küren* und die *Vierundzwanzig Landrechte* gehören, und andere Texte, die sich nur auf die Ommelanden beziehen.[8] Manche von diesen 'Groninger' Rechtsquellen gehen auf eine altfriesische Vorlage zurück, die aber nicht unbedingt aus Westfriesland stammen muss. Wir kennen nämlich 'einheimische' Groninger Texte, von denen es plausibel oder sogar beweisbar ist, dass es sich um Übersetzungen aus dem Altfriesischen handelt. Ihre in den Ommelanden entstandene Vorlage besitzen wir aber nicht mehr. Tom Johnston hat die Übertragung und Überlieferung von einigen von diesen, hauptsächlich aus dem Groninger Westerkwartier stammenden Rechtsquellen genau dargelegt.[9]

Es sind aber nicht diese 'einheimischen' Ommelander Texte, um die es mir geht. Ich widme mich den Texten, deren altfriesisches Gegenstück nur in der westfriesischen Überlieferung erhalten ist, oder die mit dem 'westfriesischen' Teil von F verwandt sind. Anhand dieser Texte erhalten wir – wenn auch indirekt, denn es handelt sich um Übersetzungen – Einsicht in die Entwicklung in Westfriesland, dem Gebiet, in dem die friesische Sprache bewahrt blieb, während – nicht ohne Ironie – das altfriesische Recht dort früher als in Groningen oder in Ostfriesland aufgegeben wurde. Aber schon in der westfriesischen Rechtsüberlieferung des fünfzehnten Jahrhunderts sind modernisierende Tendenzen nachweisbar. Ich hoffe zeigen zu können, dass man damals schon versuchte, das altfriesische Recht inhaltlich anzupassen, und auch – aber dann geht es um eine andere Modernisierung –, dass

[8] T. S. B. Johnston, *Codex Hummercensis (Groningen, UB, PEIP 12). An Old Frisian Legal Manuscript in Low Saxon Guise* (Leeuwarden, 1998), 46–89. Vgl. auch T. S. B. Johnston, 'The Middle Low German Translations of Old Frisian Legal Texts', *Handbuch / Handbook*, 587–94.

[9] Johnston, *Codex Hummercensis*, passim.

man schon in Westfriesland bereit war, sich der konkurrierenden Volkssprache, des Niederländischen, zu bedienen. Es handelt sich dabei zwar nicht um die klassischen Rechtsquellen als Ganzes, sondern um Teile daraus, die in kanonistische Sammlungen aufgenommen wurden. Ich werde mich dabei auf die *Rechten ende Wilkoeren* (RW) konzentrieren, eine Sammlung, von der namentlich Gerbenzon nachgewiesen hat, wie eingehend sie aus den klassischen altfriesischen Quellen geschöpft hat.

Die Einordnung der altfriesischen Textfragmente in die *Rechten ende Wilkoeren*

Wir sind nur durch die Ommelander Überlieferung mit den RW vertraut; allgemein wird aber angenommen, dass ihre erste Fassung friesischsprachig war. Gerbenzon gibt eine ausführliche Darstellung der Struktur.[10] Johnston weicht zwar in Einzelheiten von Gerbenzon ab, aber im Großen und Ganzen ist er derselben Ansicht.[11] Der wichtigste Teil der RW (oder vielleicht sogar die eigentlichen RW) bilden die Paragraphen 1–144.[12] Dieser Teil (RW-I) enthält wohl westfriesisches Material, aber auch andere Quellen sind verarbeitet worden (am augenfälligsten wohl der *Text des Rechtes* [RW 55–87, mit einigen eingefügten Bestimmungen anderer Herkunft] und *Godes Recht* [im Großen und Ganzen RW 89–144]). Eine gewisse Systematik in der Ordnung der Artikel fehlt nicht, wenn diese auch eher den verarbeiteten Quellen zu verdanken ist als der Arbeit des Autors selber. Gerbenzons tief schürfende Analyse basiert im Grunde auf RW-I. Die übrigen Artikel (RW-II), also die Paragraphen 149–202, betrachtet er als einen Zusatz,[13] der aus westfriesischem, noch zu verarbeitendem Material besteht. Übrigens sind einige von diesen im Ursprung ideologischen altfriesischen Bestimmungen sowohl in RW-I als auch in RW-II vertreten, was ebenfalls darauf hinweist, dass RW-II noch nicht integriert worden war. Zwei Handschriften bieten nach der Meinung Gerbenzons innerhalb von RW-I eine leicht abweichende Fassung, was für ihn Anlass zu der Schlussfolgerung war, es handele sich um eine gesonderte Gruppe (RW-var.).[14] Diese Textform sei aber erst nach der Übersetzung aus dem Altfriesischen entstanden, eine Meinung, der sich Johnston anschließt.[15]

Bei der vorbereitenden Arbeit für eine Ausgabe des Archetypus aller aus dem Westfriesischen ins Niedersächsische übersetzten Rechtsquellen (an der

[10] Gerbenzon, *Excerpta legum*, 156–79 und 428–45.

[11] Johnston, *Codex Hummercensis*, 49–59.

[12] Aus praktischen Gründen behalte ich Gerbenzons Nummerierung bei.

[13] Die Paragrafen 145–48, die nur in einigen Handschriften vorkommen, und zudem nicht in derselben Textgestalt, lasse ich außer Betracht.

[14] Gerbenzon, *Excerpta legum*, 444 und 445.

[15] Johnston, *Codex Hummercensis*, 53–57.

die RW stark beteiligt sind) stieß ich auf eine Gruppe von Handschriften, die eine andere Fassung der RW bieten als RW (und RW-var.?). Es handelt sich da hauptsächlich um RW-II, wohl aber um einige dort fehlende, ebenfalls aus dem Altfriesischen übersetzte Bestimmungen erweitert, und auch mit Einfügung einiger Artikel, die sich ansonsten in RW-I finden. Diese erweiterte Fassung von RW-II bezeichne ich vorläufig als RWX. Nicht nur in diesen Ergänzungen, sondern auch in der Formulierung einzelner Paragrafen weist RWX oft eine größere Verwandtschaft mit ihrem altfriesischen Gegenstück auf als RW(-II). Im Folgenden werde ich also regelmäßig auf die RWX-Fassung verweisen.

Bis jetzt habe ich RWX nur anhand von drei Manuskripten kollationieren können.[16] Nun hat sich mittlerweile herausgestellt, dass RWX sich auch in den zwei Handschriften, die Gerbenzon als RW-var. zusammenfasst, findet. Es wäre also möglich, dass RWX mit RW-var. identisch ist, zwar mit der Einschränkung, dass in ersterer Gruppe von Handschriften RW-I fehlt, jedenfalls in der von Gerbenzon dargestellten vollständigen Form. Vermutlich ist auch Johnston zu diesem Schluss gekommen.[17] Auch Gerbenzon war sich dessen wahrscheinlich bewusst,[18] aber da er ausschließlich auf Grund von Kriterien aus RW-I zu der RW-var.-Gruppe kommt, konnten die Manuskripte, die nur RWX enthalten, nicht mit berücksichtigt werden. RWX und RW-var. seien also vermutlich identisch, aber vorläufig lege ich sie noch nicht zusammen. Sowohl Gerbenzon als auch Johnston nehmen eine gemeinsame Vorlage von RW und RW-var. an, die schon niedersächsisch ist. Sie schätzen die Bedeutung von RW-var. hoch ein. Johnston ist da noch am explizitesten: Der Autor von RW-var. 'copied material from a "normal" version of that compendium, supplementing it with new material translated directly from an Old Frisian manuscript from west of the Lauwers'.[19] Das kann sich kaum auf RW-var. beziehen in der Gestalt wie Gerbenzon die Fassung charakterisiert hat. Gemeint ist also wohl RWX, und damit ist ihr Verhältnis sowohl zu der 'Normalform' von RW wie zu der friesischsprachigen Überlieferung geklärt.

Ich werde mich in dieser Abhandlung namentlich mit dem Weiterleben westfriesischen Rechts in den *Rechten ende Wilkoeren* befassen. Für den Autor der RW sind die westfriesischen Rechtsquellen eine Art von Steinbruch: Abhängig von der von ihm intendierten Struktur übernimmt er einzelne Paragrafen, wobei der ursprüngliche Aufbau der Vorlage nicht unbedingt berücksichtigt ist. In den Ommelander Handschriften finden sich aber auch vollständig übersetzte Texte. Einigen von ihnen hat der Autor

16 Groninger Archieven, GAG q3B, RAG OA 61 und RAG OA 310.

17 Johnston, *Codex Hummercensis*, 55 und 56.

18 Gerbenzon, *Excerpta legum*, 444.

19 Johnston, *Codex Hummercensis*, 56.

einen Platz in RW gegeben, andere Texte kommen separat in den Handschriften vor. Es wird sich herausstellen, dass die inhaltliche Anpassung nicht in allen Kategorien in derselben Weise verlaufen ist. Das Korpus der Ommelander Handschriften als solches und jede Handschrift an sich bilden nämlich nicht ein homogenes Ganzes. Die unterschiedlichen Bestandteile, sowohl die ursprünglich altfriesischen als auch die Groninger regional ausgerichteten und die auf die Stadt Groningen bezogenen Texte sind in ungleicher Weise integriert worden.

WESTFRIESISCHES RECHT IN DEN *RECHTEN ENDE WILKOEREN*

Es handelt sich hier nur um die Verarbeitung von westfriesischen klassischen Rechtsquellen in den RW. Gerbenzon hat die Struktur des ganzen Textes und die Intention des Autors in extenso wiedergegeben. Es geht durchaus nicht um eine wörtliche Übersetzung der friesischen Vorlage: Die Texte sind weitgehend angepasst worden, vermutlich schon im Rahmen der friesischsprachigen *Rechten ende Wilkoeren*, jedenfalls aber in den niedersächsischen Handschriften. Die niedersächsischen, aus dem Westfriesischen übersetzten Texte können wir nur mit ihrem jeweiligen Gegenstück in den klassischen Rechtshandschriften vergleichen – die friesischsprachige RW-Zwischenstufe besitzen wir ja nicht mehr. Für die westfriesischen Paralleltexte verweise ich immer auf die Handschrift J, auch auf die von den Herausgebern verwendete Nummerierung.[20] Es handelt sich hier um eine zuverlässige moderne Ausgabe dieser Handschrift, und fast alle in Betracht kommenden altfriesischen Texte finden sich in ihr.

Der Autor der RW hat bei der Eingliederung des altfriesischen Materials eine Auswahl getroffen: Viele Paragrafen nahm er wohl auf, andere ließ er außer Betracht. Sehr intensiv machte er Gebrauch von dem *Sceltariucht* ['Schulzenrecht'], sowohl das sogenannte *Ältere* (ÄS) wie das *Jüngere* (JS). Der Ordnung wegen weise ich darauf hin, dass diese beiden Rechtsquellen wohl den Löwenanteil von RW-II und RWX bilden, dass diese beiden Sammlungen aber auch andere Texte enthalten (zum Beispiel die *Swarta swengen* ['Verbrechen, für die nur der Papst Absolution erteilen kann'], *Skakraf* ['gewaltsamer Raub'], *Wenden* ['Ausnahmen'] *von der 17. Küre*). Das Verfahren des Autors kann aber hinreichend anhand von ÄS und JS dargelegt werden. Dabei geht es um nachfolgende Fragen:

Welche Paragrafen werden wohl aufgenommen, und damit auch: welche nicht? Welche Auswahlkriterien gelten dabei für den Autor? In welchen Angelegenheiten weicht der niedersächsische Text von der überlieferten altfriesischen Parallelfassung ab? Handelt es sich dabei um terminologische

---

20 *Westerlauwerssches Recht. I. Jus Municipale Frisonum*, W. J. Buma und W. Ebel, Hg., unter Mitwirkung von M. Tragter-Schubert, AR 6/1–2 (Göttingen, 1977).

Änderungen (zum Beispiel weil der Übersetzer nicht mehr ganz mit der friesischen Sprache vertraut war), oder hat ein anderes Rechtssystem diese Anpassungen herbeigeführt? Nicht alle Paragrafen aus ÄS und JS sind aber in angepasster Form aufgenommen. Die Gründe dafür verdeutlichen die Auswahlkriterien des Autors. Im Falle von ÄS und JS hat der Autor die altfriesischen Rechtsquellen 'ausgeschlachtet'. Einige Texte nimmt er aber vollständig auf. Auch dafür soll eine Erklärung gefunden werden.

Den Schulzenrechten entnommene Paragrafen

In RW (im Wesentlichen also RW-II) finden sich folgende Paragrafen aus ÄS (oft bearbeitet, und manchmal stark gekürzt): 1–3, 7–11, 13, 30, 31, 33, 35, 36, 38, 43–47, 49, 53, 56, 58, 60, 64–69, 73, 74 und 79. Die Reihenfolge der Paragrafen ist in RW oft eine andere als in ÄS selber.[21] In RWX fehlen 9, 73 und 74, dafür enthält diese Fassung die zusätzlichen Artikel 12, 22–25, 41, 50, 70 und 71. RW und RWX überlappen sich oftmals. Letztere Fassung geht ja auf RW zurück unter nochmaliger Heranziehung einer altfriesischen Vorlage. Allerdings gibt es auch in RW Stellen, die besser als in RWX die altfriesische Lesart wiedergeben.

Aus JS hat der Autor nachfolgende Paragrafen entlehnt: 1–7, 22–26, 28, 29, 32, 33, 35, 36 und 41 (bis auf zwei Bestimmungen alle RW-II). RWX hat noch zusätzlich: 12–14, 27, 30, 31, 39 und 40.

Detailanalyse einiger Paragrafen aus den Schulzenrechten

Eine Analyse der Übersetzungs- und Bearbeitungsstrategie in einigen Paragrafen der Schulzenrechte soll einer globalen Charakterisierung der sich auf diese beiden Quellen beziehenden Artikel in RW vorangestellt werden. Diesen Artikeln liegt letztendlich eine altfriesische Quelle zugrunde, und ich glaube nachweisen zu können, welche Beweggründe das Verhalten des Autors bestimmt haben. Dann richtet sich die Aufmerksamkeit auf zwei Gruppen von altfriesischen Bestimmungen, die in der niedersächsischen Bearbeitung kein Gegenstück haben.

Zuerst ÄS 1, in dem beschrieben wird, wie der Einzug des Grafen in Westfriesland vor sich gehen soll. Ich zitiere nach der Ausgabe von Buma *et al.*, und übernehme auch die dort abgedruckte Übersetzung. Die niedersächsische Fassung ist in den Beispielen die von RW-II oder RWX. Ich übersetze nur die Stellen, die von dem altfriesischen Text abweichen. In beiden Fassungen sind übrigens diese Abweichungen, insoweit sie in diesem

---

21 Vgl. für die Abweichungen in der Reihenfolge Gerbenzon, *Excerpta legum*, 436–441, wo auf die synoptischen Editionen beider Rechtsquellen verwiesen wird: W. Steller, *Das altwestfriesische Schulzenrecht* (Breslau, 1926), und B. W. van Klaarbergen, *Das altwestfriesische jüngere Schulzenrecht* (Drachten, 1947).

Zusammenhang relevant sind, durch Kursivdruck hervorgehoben.

ÄS 1: Djt is landriocht der Fresena. Dy greuwa, deer oen Freesland griouwa wessa schel, dy schel wessa *fulre berte bern* ende zijn riocht onferlerren. Hij schel toe Sudamoeta jnkomma (ende komma)[22] ti Fraenkere *jn dat del* mey *werdere* were, mey des konynges iefte, mey brieff ende mey jnsighele. Deer aeghen hem dae Fresen toe ontfaene ende riochtes toe *stedegiane*. Deer aech hem dy aesgha enen ferde toe delane *ende hi self toe bannane*, dat hem emma wald ief onriocht dwe. Deer aeghen dae lioede den ferde toe sterkiane. Deer aegh dy griouwa aller mannalikum sijn *len* toe iewane, *als hijt oen sijnre were hede, one fia-ieftem*. Soe des griouwa kompst keth is, soe is zijn frede binna der *komste dy* daedslagha fyouwer ende sextich punda.
['Dies ist Landrecht der Friesen. Der Graf, der in Friesland Graf sein soll, soll von vollehelicher Geburt sein und sein Recht nicht verwirkt haben. Er soll zu Tacozijl ins Land kommen, und in den Bezirk Franeker gehen mit gültigem Anspruch, (d.h.) mit königlichem Privileg, mit Brief und Siegel. Dort sollen die Friesen ihn empfangen und sein Recht bestätigen. Dort soll der Asega ihm den Frieden erteilen und soll er selbst gebieten, dass keiner ihm Gewalt oder Unrecht antun soll. Darauf soll das Volk diesen Frieden bekräftigen. Dann soll der Graf jedem sein Lehen bestätigen, wie er es in seinem Besitz hatte, ohne Geldleistung. Wenn die Ankunft des Grafen bekanntgemacht ist, so beträgt sein Friedensgeld für jeden Totschlag während seines Aufenthaltes vierundsechzig Pfund'.]
RW-II 149: Dyt ys recht Vressen lantrecht. De graue de in Vresslant greue vessen sal, he sal wesen *van groeten gheslachten geboren* ende syn recht onverloren. He sal tho Suydermude (RWX: Sude)[23] inkomen, tho Franeker myt *weerender* weere ende myt des koninghes gyften, myt breue ende myt segel. Dar egen em de Vressen tho ontfangen ende rechte tho *geuen*. Darna hort den rechter enen vrede tho maken dat se nemant geuelt noch onrecht en don; ende de luyden soellen em de vrede helpen sterken. Darna horet den greue alder mallyck syn *recht* tho geuen. Wanner des greuen thokumpst gekundyget ys, soe yst vrede bynnen synre *kumste. Dee* doetslach ys veer ende xx punt (RWX: *De* doet tho lxiiij punt *to broke*).

Für die Entstehungszeit der RW, und sicher für die der Übersetzung, ist die Beschreibung des gräflichen Einzugs ein Anachronismus. Dieser Paragraf

---

[22] Nicht in J; von Buma *et al.* ergänzt aus den Parallelhandschriften D, Ro und Unia (= U). Die Stelle fehlt aber auch in RW(X) und in der mittelniederländischen Bearbeitung von Kodex Dousa (vgl. *Landrecht der Vriesne: tekstuitgave en commentaar*, Ph. H. Breuker, Hg. [Leeuwarden, 1996], 18).

[23] Vgl. J, wo Buma *et al.* zwar *Sudamoeta* lesen, wo aber in der Handschrift steht: *suda moeta jn komma*.

und auch der nachfolgende, der die Heerfahrtsverpflichtung der Friesen beschreibt, bilden den ideologischen Auftakt zu der Rechtsquelle. Von praktischer Bedeutung waren sie wohl nicht mehr, jedenfalls nicht was den Einzug des Grafen betrifft. Kleinere Anpassungen an die rechtliche und politische Lage der späteren Zeit findet man trotzdem, sowohl im Wortlaut wie auch in den Auslassungen. So könnte zum Beispiel die Übersetzung von *mey werdere were* auf militärische Begleitung des Grafen hinweisen, nicht aber auf seinen Rechtsanspruch. Auch die Wiedergabe von *len* durch *recht* – und die Auslassung der Stelle, die im Altfriesischen folgt, beschreibt ein anderes Verhältnis zwischen dem Grafen und den friesischen Rechtspflichtigen. Der letzte Satz des friesischen Textes wird in RW(X) durch zwei Sätze wiedergegeben,[24] eine Folge davon, dass afr. *frede* 'Friedensgeld' als 'Rechtsschutz', oder sogar 'Frieden' im modernen Sinne aufgefasst wird.

Und obwohl der Autor sich bemüht hat, seine Vorlage noch einigermaßen zu bearbeiten und somit den Text auch den Umständen seiner Zeit anzupassen, ist doch der Hauptgrund, dass der erste Paragraf des ÄS übernommen wurde, die ideologische Färbung – und damit Legitimation –, die die RW dadurch erhielten.

Weitgehende Anpassungen, aber unter Beibehaltung des Inhalts, finden wir im folgenden Artikel.

ÄS 36: Dit is riocht, aldeer *di fria Fresa* op en eerwe *thijnghia* wol, dat hi oen dat *banne thing* coma scol *mey sijn thijngmanne, mit afte greetwerde greta schol* ende bitighie him dis, dat hi een eerue oen zijn wer habbe onriochte, der hi him mey riochte toerema schel. Soe aegh hem di oera toe andriane ende fregia hem, hweer dat eerwa lidzie. Soe aegh hem dy *aesga* toe delane, dat hi hem dat eerua wise *mit stewe ende mit thinghe*; dat thyng scol wessa *wr sauwen nachten dis sella deis oppe dae eerua.*
['Dies ist Recht, dass der freie Friese, wenn er ein Grundstück beanspruchen will, mit seinem Vorsprecher in das gebotene Gericht kommen, mit vorschriftsmäßiger Klage (seinen Gegner) ansprechen und ihn dessen bezichtigen soll, dass er unrechtmäßig ein Grundstück im Besitz habe, das er ihm nach Recht abtreten solle. Dann soll der andere ihm antworten und ihn fragen, wo das Grundstück liege. Dann soll der Asega ihm auferlegen, dass er ihm das Grundstück eidlich und gerichtlich bezeichne; das Gericht soll nach sieben Nächten an demselben Tage auf dem Grundstück stattfinden'.]
RW-II 161: Dyt ys recht: Waer *een* op een arue *spreket ende secht dattet em tho hoert*, soe sal he gaen totten *rechte* (RWX: *rechter*) ende *spreken* ende betyeden (RWX: betyen) den anderen man de dat arue heft, dat he

[24] Die Interpunktion in RW(X) stammt zwar von mir, ist aber syntaktisch bedingt.

an synre were onrecht arue hebbe, dat he myt recht rumen sal. Soe sal de ander hem antworden ende vragen waer dat dat arue legge. Soe sal em de *rechter* dat beden dat he dat arue wysse *myt synen eede*, ende dat sal he doen *bynnen vij dagen.*

Inhaltlich weichen beide Fassungen nicht von einander ab: Es geht um das Verfahren in einem Rechtsstreit um ein Grundstück. Die juristischen Formulierungen sind aber weitgehend vereinfacht. Im fünfzehnten Jahrhundert gab es auch in Westfriesland keinen Asega mehr. Dafür steht das Wort *rechter.* Das Verfahren ist modernisiert worden: Veraltete Formeln sind durch allgemeine Bezeichnungen ersetzt worden: *mit afte greetwerde greta* und *mit stewe ende mit thinghe.* Im letzten Satz des Paragrafen ist zwar die Periode von sieben Tagen beibehalten worden, aber ist das Verfahren ein anderes.

Im Falle der Bearbeitung von ÄS 1 sahen wir, wie der Autor oder der Übersetzer das altfriesische Wort *frede* 'Friedensgeld' uminterpretierte zu 'Rechtsschutz' oder vielleicht zu 'Frieden im modernen Sinne'. Ähnliches finden wir im nachfolgenden Beispiel, wo *strid* 'Gerichtsstreit' als Kampf im militärischen Sinne aufgefasst wird. Zwar zeigt die Fortsetzung des Artikels, dass es sich auch um einen Gerichtsstreit handelt, aber die Hinzufügung *in heeruaert* ist unmissverständlich – und weist dadurch darauf hin, dass Autor und/oder Übersetzer den Text nicht verstanden haben!

ÄS 30, 31: Dit is riocht: als die sonne sigande js *ende dio ku dae clewen dene decht*, soe ne toer di fria Fresa efterdam *an da strijde withstaen* des deis, *omdat hij eer gret ne was.*
Dit is riocht, dat dy fria Fresa des greuwa ban tiulda ne thoer ner des schelta efter sonna sedle.
['Dies ist Recht: Wenn die Sonne sinkt und die Kuh die Klauen (unter sich) nieder tut – d.h. sich niederlegt –, so braucht sich der freie Friese danach an dem Tage nicht vor Gericht zu verantworten, weil er nicht eher darauf angesprochen war.
Dies ist Recht, dass der freie Friese weder des Grafen noch des Skelta Banngewalt nach Sonnenuntergang zu folgen braucht'.]
RW 164: Dit is recht: Na der sonnen vnderganck so sal de vrye Vrese niet *to stryde staen in heeruaert ende nyet to rechte staen* ende geen ban lyden, *dat ys scade van wanantwort* ['Nichterscheinen vor Gericht'] off des gelyck van greuen off van schulten[25] *off van deken off anders recht in Vreslant.*

Manchmal konnte der altfriesische Text ohne allzu große Änderungen übersetzt werden. In den mir jetzt bekannten Fassungen des folgenden Paragrafen liegen zwar Missverständnisse vor, die aber vermutlich nicht aus dem

25 *van greuen off van schulten* fehlt in RWX.

niedersächsischen Archetypus stammten. Ich gebe hier sowohl die RW- wie die RWX-Fassung wieder, weil sie in ihren Unterschieden zu einander ihr verschiedenartiges Verhältnis zu der altfriesischen Vorlage zeigen.

> ÄS 7: Dit is riocht, dat di fadir ne aegh sine dochter nennen man to jaen wr hir willa, omdat se nautes an wald ne aegh in were[26] here ledena. Ende ief hi se iout wr hir willa ende wr hir wald ende hir dan oen dae onwilla misschijd, soe aegh hi dat toe betan *mey ferda ende mey festa* alsoe, ief hi se mey sine handen wrslain habba.
> ['Dies ist Recht, dass ein Vater seiner Tochter keinen Mann gegen ihren Willen geben darf, weil sie lediglich Gewalt über ihr Glieder hat. Und wenn er sie gegen ihren Willen und gegen ihren Wunsch (in die Ehe) gibt und ihr dann durch ihre Widerwilligkeit Böses widerfährt, so hat er das mit Friedensgeld und Fasten abzubüßen, wie wenn er sie mit eigenen Händen erschlagen hätte'.]
> RW 47: Dyt ys recht dat dee vader neet en ys schuldych de dochter eenen man tho geuen tegens oren wyllen, om se nychtes en eeget tho wolden dor oer sulues leeden. Off see or ouer wyllen ende oer jn onwyllen mysselycke myschede, soe ys dat dee vader schuldych tho boeten off he dat suluen gedan hadde.
> RWX 47: Dit is recht: De vader eget nenen manne syne dochter to geuen ouer hoer wille, daromme dat se ghenen willen hebben sal an oer lichaem. Ende gefft he se ouer willen ende oer iet misquaeme oft qwades to komet, so sal de vader myt vrede ende myt feste boten likerwijs oft he se myt synes selues hant doet geslagen hadde.

Der Autor übernahm also nur die Paragrafen, die für die juristische Praxis seiner Zeit noch Relevanz besaßen, aber auch er konnte nicht völlig auf die Aufnahme von Texten mit nur freiheitsideologischer Tendenz verzichten. Wenn nötig passte er seine Texte durch Vereinfachungen oder Auslassungen den Umständen seiner Zeit an. Wenn dies nicht mehr möglich war, zum Beispiel weil ein Rechtsverfahren beschrieben wurde, das selbst durch weitgehende Anpassungen nicht mehr aktualisiert werden konnte, ließ er die diesbezüglichen Paragrafen außer Betracht.

Es erübrigt sich, hier das Vorgehen des Autors in derselben Weise mit Zitaten darzulegen, wie dies oben geschah, schon deshalb, weil keine niedersächsischen Texte vorliegen. Als Beispiel einer völlig veralteten Rechtsbestimmung führe ich ÄS 57 an, den Artikel, der das Verfahren in der Klage beim Grafengericht beschreibt. Nicht nur weil es im fünfzehnten Jahrhundert kein Grafengericht mehr gab, nicht nur weil man in der Rechts-

---

[26] Hs. *in toere*, was von Buma *et al.* wohl nicht zu Unrecht emendiert wird. Vgl. aber in RW das genauso unverständliche *dor*, das – hier wie an anderen Stellen – auf eine gemeinsame Vorlage von J und RW in deren altfriesischer Gestalt hinweisen könnte.

sprechung weder Asega noch Königszeugen mehr kannte, sondern auch, weil im Falle von *wrheerghenisse* ['Ungehorsam (gegen das Gericht)'] ein so kompliziertes Verfahren angewandt wird, dass sich der Paragraf nicht mehr zu einer praktikablen Bestimmung zusammenstreichen lassen würde.

Es finden sich in den beiden Schulzenrechten aber auch sehr praktisch anwendbare Paragrafen, die nicht von dem Autor bearbeitet und später übersetzt wurden. Als Beispiel gebe ich die Artikel JS 9–11 und ÄS 14–21, die u.a. die Verpflichtungen der freien Friesen hinsichtlich Bau und Instandhaltung von Wegen, Deichen und Sielen beschreiben. Warum gerade diese Bestimmungen nicht berücksichtigt wurden, ist nicht klar. Es könnte sein, dass sie sich nach der Meinung des Autors nicht für Aufnahme in die RW eigneten, da es sich in dieser Sammlung hauptsächlich um prozessrechtliche Bestimmungen handelt (aber JS 12–14 sind wohl aufgenommen worden – sei es auch nur in RWX!). Es könnte aber auch sein, dass gerade ihr praktischer Charakter die Aufnahme verhinderte: Aus Westfriesland und den Ommelanden besitzen wir zahlreiche Deich- und Sielrechte, bei deren Anwendung die entsprechenden alten Bestimmungen interferierend wirken könnten. Aber nicht nur durch die wohl in RW aufgenommenen Paragrafen, sondern auch durch die nicht berücksichtigten werden die Auswahlkriterien des Autors erkennbar.

Zusammenfassende Charakterisierung der *Rechten ende Wilkoeren*

Auch hier beschränke ich mich auf die Paragrafen, die aus dem Älteren oder dem Jüngeren Schulzenrecht entlehnt worden sind. Bei der Einarbeitung von Bestimmungen aus anderen altwestfriesischen Rechtsquellen verfährt der Autor übrigens nach denselben Grundsätzen wie im Falle von ÄS und JS. Wir sahen schon, dass die ersten zwei Paragrafen wegen ihres ideologischen Gehalts aufgenommen wirden. Das gilt auch für ÄS 3 (RW 112; RW[X] 151): das Recht des freien Friesen, seine Taten auf die Reliquien zu beschwören. Dann folgen, in der Reihenfolge der altfriesischen Quelle, aber jeweils mit der Nummerierung von RW:

ÄS 7 (RW[X] 47): Verheiratung der Tochter (s. oben).
ÄS 8 (RW[X] 152): Vormundschaft über eine Witwe. (Auch der kurze Paragraf RW 113 geht auf ÄS 8 und 9 zurück).
ÄS 10 (RW[X] 153): Nichtzahlung des Muntschatzes.
ÄS 11 (RW[X] 154): Verpflichtung des Sohnes, der Mutter zwölf Jahre lang für jedes Jahr ihrer Obhut einen bestimmten Betrag zu bezahlen.

ÄS 12 (RWX 154-a):[27]: Der Sohn darf sich im Falle von Vernachlässigung von dieser Verpflichtung freischwören.
ÄS 13 (RW[X] 155: Jüngerer Bruder heiratet als erster.
ÄS 22–25 (RWX 156–158): Bewaffnung bei der Landesverteidigung.
ÄS 30, 31 (RW[X]) 164): Anwesenheitsverpflichtung bei Rechtsstreit usw. (s. oben).
ÄS 33 (RW[X] 159): Verfahren bei Vergewaltigung oder Entführung einer Frau.
ÄS 35b-II, c (RW[X] 160): Teilung der gemeinen Mark.
ÄS 36 (RW[X] 161): Rechtsstreit um Grundstück (s. oben).
ÄS 38 (RW[X] 56): Verkauf von Land ohne Zustimmung des Erben.
ÄS 41 (RWX 162): Gottesurteil (in ÄS) – oder vielleicht richterliches Urteil (in RWX).
ÄS 43–47 (RW[X] 43–47 [±]): Zusammenfassung und Berichtigung der das Gottesurteil behandelnden Bestimmungen (Auch in ÄS 44a-I, 43 [RW 57] handelt es sich um das Gottesurteil).
ÄS 49 (RW[X] 58): Streit zwischen Pächter und Grundherrn.
ÄS 50 (RWX 165): Rechtsanspruch einer schwangeren Frau.
ÄS 53 (RW[X] 166): Tod eines Fremdlings.
ÄS 56 (RW[X] 167): Pflügen usw. auf dem Land eines anderen Mannes.
ÄS 58, 60 (RW[X] 168): Ladung des Friesen vor das Grafengericht (ÄS) oder vor ein Gericht schlechthin (RW[X]).
ÄS 64-I (RW 115, RW[X] 169): Zeugnis eines Toten.
ÄS 65 (RW[X] 163): Streit um einen offenen Graben und den dazugehörigen Grund (ÄS) oder bloß um ein Grundstück (RW[X]).
ÄS 66, 67 (RW[X] 170): Verfahren bei der Hausdurchsuchung nach gestohlenem Gut (Auch 66c-II, d [RW 116]).
ÄS 69, 68 (RW[X] 171): Nachlassprozess.
ÄS 70, 71a (RWX 172): Erbschaftsfragen.
ÄS 79 (RW[X] 196, 197): Sündhafter oder sonst wie inkorrekt handelnder Richter (*Asega* in ÄS).

In oben stehender Übersicht ist darauf verzichtet worden, die jeweiligen Unterschiede zwischen den altfriesischen und den niedersächsischen Fassungen zu beschreiben. Das gilt auch für die nachfolgende Übersicht der aus JS aufgenommenen Paragrafen. Übrigens fällt auf, dass der Autor im Falle von JS seine Vorlage oft kürzt, sie inhaltlich aber weniger ändert als in den Paragrafen aus ÄS. Das *Jüngere Sceltariucht* trägt seinen Namen also mit Recht.

[27] Da ich Gerbenzons Nummerierung beibehalten habe, werden die zusätzlichen Artikel (immer in RWX) in dieser Weise bezeichnet.

JS 1a–1d (RW[X] 184): Zusammenfassung einiger Formulare, die beschreiben, wie man eine Klage vorbringen soll.
JS 1e (RW[X] 186): Eid auf die Reliquien bei Haargriff usw. (in D Teil der *Willküren der Fünf Dele*, in U daran anschließend).
JS 2 (RW 138): Aufbrechen eines Hauses.
JS 2–4 (RW[X] 187): Aufbrechen eines Hauses; Haussteuer.
JS 5 (RW[X] 188): Verfahren bei Nichtzahlung der Haussteuer.
JS 6 (RW[X] 189): Viehraub.
JS 7 (RW[X] 190): Schlägerei in einem Hause.
JS 12 (RWX 190-a): Weg um den Hauptort einer Dorfmark herum (JS) oder zu einem Dorf, wo Recht gesprochen wird (RWX).
JS 13a (RWX 190-b): Instandhaltung eines Siels.
JS 14 (RWX 190-c): Weg an der Innenseite eines Deichs.
JS 22, 23 (RW[X] 199): Graben im Land eines anderen Mannes.
JS 24 (RW[X] 200): Bestohlener söhnt sich mit dem Dieb aus mit Übergehung des *scelta*, *schulte*.
JS 25 (RW[X] 201): Bestrafung eines gefangenen Diebes.
JS 26 (RW[X] 202: Fundgut.
JS 27 (RWX 202-a): Tod eines Fremdlings.
JS 28 (RW[X] 191): Pfändung eines Schiffs.
JS 29a (RW[X] 192): Grundstücksklage.
JS 30a (RWX 192-a): Besitz einer Frau.
JS 31 (RWX 190-d): Verantwortlichkeit des Herrn für seinen Knecht.
JS 32 (RW 137): Knecht bestiehlt Herrn.
JS 32, 33 (RW[X] 193): Knecht bestiehlt Herrn.
JS 35a (RW[X] 194): Klage wegen Lähmung oder Verwundung.
JS 36 (RW[X] 135): Unerlaubtes Reiten eines Pferdes.
JS 39 (RWX 194-a): Dorfmarkgraben (JS) oder Graben zwischen Gerichtsbezirken (RWX).
JS 40 (RWX 194-b): Schau eines Deiches.
JS 41 (RW[X] 195): Pfändung.

Dass es sich in den altfriesischen klassischen Rechtsquellen und in den *Rechten ende Wilkoeren* zwar um vergleichbare, aber nicht mehr um dieselben Rechtssysteme handelt, wird einigermaßen verwischt durch die etymologische Gleichheit der Terminologie: Die Funktion des altfriesischen *scelta* ist eine andere als die des niedersächsischen *schulte*, und *ordel* bezeichnet im altfriesischen Kontext das Gottesurteil, im niedersächsischen ein richterliches Urteil. Doch findet eine terminologische Vereinfachung statt: Die Bezeichnungen *asega* und *frana* fehlen in RW(X). Ihre Entsprechung ist dann *rechter*, das einige Male auch die Übersetzung von *scelta* ist, wenn auch in RW(X) *schulte* die allgemeine Entsprechung von *scelta* ist.[28]

Unterschiede in der Terminologie müssen aber nicht immer auf Änderungen im Rechtssystem basieren. Auch abnehmende Kenntnisse der altfriesischen Sprache beim Autor oder beim Übersetzer sollten wir in Betracht ziehen. Beides ist möglich im Falle von dem *wilda witzenes floed* ['die Flut des wilden Wikingers']: Die Normannen bildeten im 14./15. Jahrhundert nicht mehr eine Gefahr, aber die verunstaltete Form *witzenes* weist doch auf Unverständnis hin. In ÄS 64-I (RW[X]) 169) ist *bodeldeel* ['Erbteil'] viel spezifischer als *tijl guet off ... tilbar guet, dat synnen mobilia*, und in demselben Paragrafen, sowie er in RW-I 115 vorliegt (er ist doppelt überliefert worden), ist *bede* unverständlich. Die niedersächsische Entsprechung von ÄS 13 (RW[X] 155) ist inhaltlich korrekt. Der Übersetzer könnte hier also auf *taekeres iefte* ['Gabe an den Schwager'] verzichten, er ließ aber wohl den Ausdruck unübersetzt, weil er ihn nicht mehr verstand. Völlig unverständlich ist die Übersetzung von *dera tolwa sawen* ['mit sieben von den zwölf (Gemeindezeugen)'] in JS, 5, 6 und 29a: in RW 188, 189 bzw. 192 *myt souen tollen* ['mit sieben Zöllen'], in RWX 188 und 189 *myt synen tollen* ['mit seinen Zöllen'] und in RWX 192 *myt synen tallen* ['mit seinen Zahlen (oder Bezahlungen?)'.] Wir sollten übrigens dem Übersetzer solche Fehlinterpretationen nicht zu schwer anrechnen: Auch in den altfriesischen Handschriften finden sich manchmal entstellte, jedenfalls nicht ohne Weiteres verständliche Lesarten.

Vollständig in die Ommelander Handschriften aufgenommene altfriesische Rechtstexte

Oben habe ich angedeutet, dass der Autor von RW die beiden Schulzenrechte – und auch einige andere Rechtsquellen – als eine Art von Steinbruch betrachtete: Er wählte sich die Paragrafen aus, die in die von ihm angestrebte Struktur passten, übrigens mit der Einschränkung, dass er die in RW-II zusammengestellten Bestimmungen noch nicht verarbeitet hatte. Es finden sich in den Ommelander Rechtshandschriften aber auch vollständig rezipierte Texte, sowohl im Rahmen von RW als auch als selbständige Texte.

Zur ersteren Kategorie gehört das *Rudolfsbuch* (RW 2–18) in der nach Gerbenzon so bezeichneten RW-Fassung.[29] Es ist nicht gerade modernes Recht, wenn sich auch die historisch-ideologischen reimenden Teile nicht in der Übersetzung finden. Das *Rudolfsbuch* kommt in einer abweichenden

[28] Vgl. für eine ausführlichere Darstellung dieser Bezeichnungen, nicht nur in RW(X), sondern auch in den Ommelander Handschriften überhaupt: J. C. Krolis-Sytsema, '*Frana* und *Schulte* in den Ommelander Rechtshandschriften', *Aspects*, 242–54.

[29] *Rudolfsboekmateriael*, P. Gerbenzon, Hg., Estrikken 32 (Groningen, 1961), 85–123.

Fassung (Gerbenzons wxy-Fassung)[30] in einigen anderen Handschriften auch außerhalb der *Rechten ende Wilkoeren* vor. In diesen Handschriften fehlt RW übrigens nicht, aber dann wohl in der Gestalt von RWX.

Die *Willküren von Upstalsboom* (RW 88) sind ohne große Änderungen in zahlreichen Handschriften vertreten. Es handelt sich um die Kurzfassung, die sich gut mit der von D und U vergleichen lässt.[31] Das Statut wird manchmal in anderen Rechtsquellen zitiert, sowohl in altfriesischen als auch in niedersächsischen Handschriften.[32] Wenn die einzelnen Paragrafen auch manchmal einen ziemlich unbestimmten Charakter hatten, war anscheinend der Text zu seiner Zeit doch noch praktisch anwendbar.

Letzteres kann nicht gesagt werden von den separat rezipierten Rechtsquellen. Bis auf vereinzelte Ausnahmen tragen die einen ideologischen Charakter. Das gilt vor allem für die *Siebzehn Küren* und die *Vierundzwanzig Landrechte*, die in sechsundsiebzig Handschriften auf uns gekommen sind. Damit kommen sie in höherer Frequenz im Ommelander Handschriftenkorpus vor als jeder andere Text auch immer. Keine anderen Texte sind in ihrem gegenseitigen Verhältnis auch so eingehend erforscht worden wie diese beiden.[33] Dass sie hauptsächlich eine ideologische Funktion hatten (wie in den ersten Paragrafen in ÄS), geht auch daraus hervor, dass die Rechtsterminologie viel weniger den Umständen der Überlieferungszeit angepasst worden ist als in den Paragrafen, die der Autor von RW den sonstigen klassischen Texten entnommen hatte. So wird der *frana*, dessen terminologische Entsprechung in RW *rechter* ist, noch erwähnt, manchmal übrigens mit einer erläuternden Ergänzung: *frana, dat is de schulte*.[34] Auch Etyma, die der Übersetzer von RW sicher nicht unübersetzt aufgenommen hätte, wie *clepschilde* ['Abgabe in klingender Münze'], finden sich.[35] Die Texte kennen wir in zwei Fassungen, einer längeren, die dem in F überlieferten altfriesischen Text sehr verwandt ist, und einer kürzeren, – die aber auch auf eine altfriesische Vorlage zurückgeht. Es fragt sich, ob diese Texte den niedersächsischen Zeitgenossen noch verständlich waren. Für uns jedenfalls ist eine sinnvolle Interpretation oft nur durch Vergleich mit einem altfriesischen Paralleltext möglich.[36] Das gilt nicht nur für die späten Abschriften: Auch für die Interpretation der ältesten überlieferten

---

30 *Ibid.* 124–40.

31 H. D. Meijering, *De Willekeuren van de Opstalsboom (1323). Een historisch-filologische monografie* (Groningen, 1974), 24–66.

32 *Ibid.* 284 und 285.

33 J. C. Sijtsema (weiterhin: Sytsema), *De 17 Keuren en de 24 Landrechten in de Ommelander rechtshandschriften* (Amsterdam, 1998).

34 *Ibid.* 212.

35 *Ibid.* 210.

36 *Ibid. passim.*

Fassung in dem Kodex Sickinghe ist die nahe Verwandtschaft beider Texte mit denen in F sehr hilfreich.

Die Kurzfassung weist in ihren Anpassungen und Auslassungen einen moderneren Charakter auf, wenn sie auch manchmal eine alte, nicht in den friesischen Handschriften vorkommende Überlieferung repräsentiert.[37] Amüsant ist, dass die Normannen im zwanzigsten Landrecht in 'Holländer' transformiert worden sind![38]

In den von mir bis jetzt kollationierten Handschriften, die die abweichende Fassung der *Rechten ende Wilkoeren* enthalten (also RWX), steht immer die Kurzfassung der Küren und Landrechte. Das Umgekehrte gilt nicht: Es kommen auch Handschriften vor, die sowohl diese Kurzfassung wie auch RW in der 'normalen' Gestalt enthalten.[39] Wir sahen auch, dass sich Gerbenzons wxy-Fassung des *Rudolfsbuchs* nur in RWX-Handschriften findet. Diese Handschriften sind auch wesentlich für die Überlieferung einiger westfriesischen Bußregister in niedersächsischer Übersetzung.[40] Sie sind alle verhältnismäßig junge Handschriften mit einem 'gelehrten' Charakter,[41] die aber oft eine alte friesische Vorlage widerspiegeln.

Die Sage von *König Karl und König Redbad* besteht aus zwei Teilen: das Kreuzordal, das entscheidet, wer von den beiden Königen Herr über Friesland sein wird, und die Sage von der Findung des Rechts. Wahrscheinlich besteht ein Zusammenhang zwischen diesem Text und dem *Älteren Sceltariucht*, genauso wie die gleichfalls pseudohistorisch-ideologisch gefärbten *Magnusküren* mit den *Siebzehn Küren* verbunden sind.[42] Auch das *Westfriesische Marktrecht* steht separat, jedenfalls außerhalb der *Rechten ende Wilkoeren*, in den Ommelander Rechtshandschriften. Dieser Text war wahrscheinlich noch im fünfzehnten und sechzehnten Jahrhundert praktisch anwendbar. Auffällig ist, dass in den drei von mir kollationierten RWX-Handschriften das *Marktrecht* der Sage von *König Karl und König Redbad* unmittelbar vorangeht. Könnte das bedeuten, dass die ebenfalls amüsante Fehlübersetzung zu Anfang der Sage (in allen Handschriften!) durch die Positionierung beider Texte 'getriggert' wurde: *Doe de koninck Karel ende*

---

37 Vgl. J. C. Krolis-Sytsema, 'De weirekke tsiende Kêst. Oer in ûnbekende ferzy fan de 17 Kêsten', *IB* 55 (1993), 83–95.

38 Sytsema, *17 Keuren*, 280.

39 *Ibid.* 125.

40 H. D. Meijering, *Ommelander handschriften als spiegel van de Oudfriese rechtsliteratuur. Proeve van een editie* (Opende, 2005).

41 Vgl. zum Beispiel Hs. Groninger Archieven RAG OA 61, die den übersetzten Text mit den aus D übernommenen – oder jedenfalls mit denen von D verwandten – lateinischen Allegaten ergänzt.

42 P. N. Noomen, '*Hachens en Wachens*: Feit en fiksje yn midsieusk Fryslân', *Speculum Frisicum. Stúdzjes oanbean oan Philippus H. Breuker*, R. H. Bremmer Jr, L. G. Jansma en P. Visser, Hg. (Leeuwarden und Leiden, 2001), 3–22, hier 3–6.

de konynck Radbad van den markede in dat lant quamen ['Als König Karl und König Radbod von dem Markt in das Land kamen'] aus *Dae di koning Kaerle ende di koning Redbad fan Danemerckum* ['Dänemark'] *jn dat land komen*?

Die Ommelander Handschriften enthalten relativ zahlreiche lokale und regionale Sendrechte: Achtkarspelen, Hunsingo und Fivelgo, Fivelgo, Farmsum, Loppersum, Usquert, Humsterland, Langewold, Vredewold. Keiner von diesen Texten hat eine westfriesische Vorlage, wahrscheinlich überhaupt keine friesische. Doch ist auch das *Allgemeine Westfriesische Sendrecht* sehr häufig vertreten. Bis auf drei Ausnahmen handelt es sich dann um die 'Fivelgoer' Fassung, und zwar mit der dort fehlenden Lage.[43] Trotz des verhältnismäßig hohen Alters dieser Rechtsquelle und – damit zusammenhängend – ihrer ideologischen Ausrichtung wird ihre praktische Verwendbarkeit auch eine Rolle gespielt haben. Es bestehen auch zwei oder drei Kurzfassungen, auf die im nächsten Paragrafen näher eingegangen wird.

Modernisierungen, nicht in Westfriesland sondern in den Ommelanden

Bis jetzt handelte es sich um modernisierende Anpassungen im altwestfriesischen Recht, die aber wohl hauptsächlich in den niedersächsischen Übersetzungen erkennbar wurden.

In Westfriesland gab es nach 1504 für diese modernen Texte keine Verwendungsmöglichkeit mehr, im Gegensatz zu den Ommelanden, wo sie bis zum Jahre 1601 im Gebrauch blieben. Auch hier waren aber selbständige neue Entwicklungen möglich. In zwei Handschriften (Groninger Archieven GAG q9B und RAG q127 [2x]) finden wir drei mit einander verwandte Kurzfassungen des *Allgemeinen Westfriesischen Sendrechts*, die eindeutig nicht auf die überlieferte niedersächsische, 'Fivelgoer' Fassung zurückgehen. Sie fangen nämlich mit dem Paragrafen an, in dem Papst Leo III. den Friesen das Sendrecht gab (J IX, 24), einem Artikel, der nicht nur in F, sondern auch in der niedersächsischen entsprechenden Fassung fehlt. Der Text in Hs. GAG q9B ist leidlich vollständig, wohl aber ohne ideologische und ansonsten veraltete Elemente. Hs. RAG q27, 125v–128v, bringt denselben Text, aber weniger vollständig. Der Text in derselben Handschrift, 124r–125v, fängt auch mit dem Papst Leo an, es folgt dann noch die Entsprechung von J IX, 25, aber der Text beschränkt sich weiterhin auf Verfahrensfragen: die Einberufung des Sendgerichts (etwa J IX, 25) und ein in allen Einzelheiten beschriebenes Berufungsverfahren. Inhaltliche Fragen werden nicht behandelt. Dafür enthält dieselbe Handschrift aber andere,

---

[43] Vgl. P. Gerbenzon, 'Teksthistoaryske oantekening by de Fivelinger tekst fan it Syndrjocht', *UW* 12 (1963), 75–80.

regionale Sendrechte: die Sendrechte von Loppersum und von Hunsingo und Fivelgo. Letzterer Text verweist auch auf die *olden zeendtbreuen*. Die Kurzfassung des *Allgemeinen Sendrechts* bietet also den Rahmen für ansonsten praktisch verwendbare Texte. In der Symbiose mit regionalen kirchenrechtlichen Texten erhielt das alte Sendrecht noch im sechzehnten Jahrhundert eine neue Funktion.

Die altfriesische Überlieferung wird durch zahlreiche Bußregister gekennzeichnet. Einige von den westfriesischen Registern sind in den Ommelanden rezipiert worden.[44] Trotzdem sind da diese Bußtaxen nicht zahlreich vertreten, was erstaunlich ist, da es sich doch um praktisch verwendbare Texte handelt. Am häufigsten kommt noch das sogenannte *'Westerlauwerssche' Bußregister* vor, insgesamt in neun Handschriften. Schon Johnston bemerkte, dass das *'Westerlauwerssche' Bußregister* 'an otherwise rare one within the corpus of Low Saxon Ommeland manuscripts' war.[45] Ein in diesen Handschriften aber sehr häufig vertretenes Bußregister findet sich im *Ommelander Landrecht, 1448*, und zwar das erste Buch *van wondinge*.[46] Letzteres Register wird die Übersetzung der altfriesischen Bußtaxen verdrängt haben, was auf Reflexion über die Funktion beider Texte, also auch des ursprünglich westfriesischen, hinweist. Zwar lässt sich das nicht durch eine komplementäre Verteilung beider Register über die Handschriften nachweisen, denn in sechs von den neun Manuskripten, die das *'Westerlauwerssche' Bußregister* enthalten, kommt auch das *Ommelander Landrecht* vor. Aber in einem von diesen sechs Handschriften wird das Verhältnis beider Register explizite beschrieben: In Groninger Archieven, RAG q146, wird das Bußregister eingeleitet mit diesem Satz: 'Hyer ... begynt dat boeck van wondinge ende ander quade wercken, als van dat olde lantrecht ende niet van dat nye lantrecht' (83r), während die Überschrift des Landrechts lautet: 'Hier na beschreuen beghint dat nye landt recht van wondinge ende van allen anderen quaden daden off warcken' (11v).

Mit dem Ausdruck *dat Nye lantrecht* ist dann eine neue Form von modernisiertem altfriesischem Recht vorgestellt worden. Es lohnt sich, dessen Inhalt näher zu umschreiben. Auf den ersten Blick scheinen sich die Bezeichnungen 'Altes Landrecht' und 'Neues Landrecht' in den oben angeführten Zitaten nur auf die beiden Bußregister zu beziehen. Ich habe aber Gründe, diesen Begriffen einen weitreichenderen Inhalt zu geben. Zunächst

---

44 Meijering, *Ommelander handschriften*, 23–49.

45 Johnston, *Codex Hummercensis*, 81.

46 Der Text ist – nach verschiedenen Handschriften – dreimal herausgegeben worden: K. von Richthofen, *Friesische Rechtsquellen* (Berlin, 1840), 315–20; D. Simonides, *Die Hunsigoer Küren vom Jahre 1252 und das Ommelander Landrecht vom Jahre 1448* (Assen, 1938), 83–90; *De Tweede Emsinger Codex*, ed. K. Fokkema, OTR 7 (Den Haag, 1953), 46–55.

einmal werden die westfriesischen Bußregister, wenn sie separat vorkommen, niemals als 'Landrecht' bezeichnet. Im Gegenteil sogar: In den Handschriften werden manchmal die Begriffe 'Landrecht' und 'Bußen' unterschieden.[47] Auch die Art, wie die niedersächsische Übersetzung des *'Westerlauwersschen' Bußregisters* in der Handschrift RAG q146 bezeichnet wird, bestätigt diese Feststellung. Dass das sogenannte *Ommelander Landrecht, 1448* als 'Landrecht' bezeichnet wird, ist – abgesehen von einer vereinzelten Erwähnung wie im obenstehenden Zitat – nachmittelalterlich,[48] und besagt also nichts über die Weise, wie man im fünfzehnten oder sechzehnten Jahrhundert den Text betrachtete. Das stärkste Argument, das sogenannte *Ommelander Landrecht, 1448* als einen Teil einer weit größeren Sammlung von Texten aufzufassen, die dann durchaus den Titel 'Landrecht' beanspruchen könnte und somit das 'Neue Landrecht' darstellt, entnehmen wir dem direkten Kontext dieses Landrechts in zahlreichen Ommelander Handschriften. In vielen von diesen Manuskripten folgt dem zweiten Buche des *Ommelander Landrechts* regulär ein drittes Buch, das aus zwei Erbrechten besteht, und zwar jene von Hunsingo und Fivelgo, bzw. von Fivelgo. Dann folgt ein viertes Buch, mit als Inhalt das *Bündnis der Stadt Groningen und der Ommelanden des Jahres 1482* und Teile des *Ordelboks*.[49] Es handelt sich aber nicht immer um Groninger, auf Altfriesisch oder auf Niedersächsisch abgefasste Texte. Auch westfriesische Rechtsquellen, wie die *Siebzehn Küren* und die *Vierundzwanzig Landrechte*, finden sich später in diesen Handschriften, dann aber in der abweichenden Reihenfolge 24 Lr – 17 K.[50] Hinzu kommt, dass es sich dabei um Manuskripte handelt, die die Kurzfassung der *Excerpta legum* enthalten.[51] Eine sehr explizite Strukturierung finden wir in der Handschrift Groningen UB, PEIP 24, die zu Anfang ein Register enthält mit nachfolgender Aufzählung: Buch I und II: *Ommelander Landrecht, 1448;* III: Erbrechte; IV: *Ordelbok*; V: Kirchliche Rechte,

---

[47] Zum Beispiel in der Überschrift des Textes, der unter dem Namen *Van walddethum* ('Von den Gewalttaten') bekannt ist (J, XXVI,1): *vrgadereth jn tha landriuchte and jn manighere botem*. Auch die Formulierung im '*Westerlauwersschen' Bußregister* IV,22 (*Codex Aysma*, W. J. Buma, P. Gerbenzon und M. Tragter-Schubert, Hg. [Assen und Maastricht, 1993], 496) weist auf denselben Sachverhalt hin.

[48] T. D. Wiarda, *Asega-Buch, ein Alt-friesisches Gesetzbuch der Rüstringer* (Berlin und Stettin, 1805, XXXIX) bezeichnet es als *Gröninger Landrecht*, und Richthofen, *Altfriesische Rechtsquellen* (315) als *Landrecht für Fivelgo, Hunsingo und die Stadt Groningen von 1448*.

[49] So ist z.B. die Konstellation in der Handschrift Groningen Universiteitsbibliotheek, PEIP 32; vgl. P. Gerbenzon und H. D. Meijering, 'Inhoudsopgaven van Ommelander rechtshandschriften, 1', *Meidielingen Stúdzjerjochting Frysk* 1 (Amsterdam, 1972), 82.

[50] Es handelt sich dann namentlich um die Gruppe h' im Stemma der langen Fassung (Sytsema, *17 Keuren*, 124).

[51] Die Handschriften D1–D11, und auch E, bei Gerbenzon, *Excerpta legum*, 23–39.

1531; VI: Kirchliche Rechte, 1530; VII: *Vierundzwanzig Landrechte*; VIII: *Siebzehn Küren*, Tabelle, *Excerpta legum*. Zwar trägt diese Kompilation nicht die Überschrift 'Neues Landrecht', aber bei näherer Erforschung des ganzen Handschriftenkorpus wird sich vermutlich herausstellen, dass dieses durchaus die angemessene Bezeichnung gewesen wäre.

Dieses neue Landrecht steht also neben dem modernisierten westfriesischen Landrecht, dessen Kern die *Rechten ende Wilkoeren* bilden. Es hat den Anschein, dass wir es mit zwei konkurrierenden Sammlungen zu tun haben, die aber beide das klassische altfriesische Recht zu modernisieren beabsichtigen, und somit beide die Bezeichnung 'Neues Landrecht' beanspruchen können. Die zweite Sammlung, das oben beschriebene *Nye Lantrecht*, basiert zum Teil auf Groninger Ommelander Quellen, aber auch in dieser Sammlung fehlen westfriesische Quellen nicht: die *Vierundzwanzig Landrechte* und die *Siebzehn Küren*, und als auffälliger Konkurrent der *RW* die *Excerpta legum*. Die Überlieferung in den Ommelander Rechtshandschriften tendiert zu einer komplementären Verteilung zwischen den letztgenannten Quellen.[52] In beiden Fällen ist von einem Weiterleben des westfriesischen Rechtes in den Ommelanden die Rede, wenn auch die die *RW* enthaltende Sammlung interessanter ist, einmal weil der Autor die klassischen altfriesischen Quellen in weit größerem Umfang aufnimmt, und zum anderen weil diese von ihm intensiv bearbeitet werden. Die zweite Sammlung, die als 'Neues Landrecht' bezeichnet wird, enthält wohl klassische Quellen, die *Küren* und die *Landrechte*, aber diese werden unverändert aufgenommen. In diesem Beitrag konzentriere ich ich mich denn auch auf das Weiterleben altfriesischen Rechts in ersterer Sammlung, in der Hauptsache also in den *Rechten ende Wilkoeren.*

Abschliessende Bemerkungen: Wo wurden die *Rechten ende Wilkoeren* übersetzt?

In den Ommelanden wurde westfriesisches Recht mit all seinen Erneuerungen rezipiert. Wir sahen, dass sich diese Modernisierung auch nach der Rezeption fortsetzte. Es ging uns aber an erster Stelle um die Rechtsentwicklung in Westfriesland, wobei wir uns namentlich auf die *Rechten ende Wilkoeren* richteten. Es steht fest, dass diese Sammlung ursprünglich auf Friesisch abgefasst wurde, wenn wir auch keine friesischsprachige Fassung mehr besitzen: Der Autor von RW bearbeitete Paragrafen aus den klassischen altfriesischen Rechtshandschriften, und sein Text wirkte wieder auf andere Rechtssammlungen, die wir durchaus in altfriesischer Gestalt

52 Vgl. die Inhaltsbeschreibungen der die *Excerpta legum* enthaltenden Handschriften bei Gerbenzon, *Excerpta legum*, 24–49.

kennen.[53] Die *Rechten ende Wilkoeren* seien dann erst bei der Rezeption in den Ommelanden übersetzt worden. Es fragt sich, ob dies der Fall ist.

An fünf Stellen in RW verwendet der Übersetzer nämlich das Adverb *alhyr* ['hier']. Dieses Wort fehlt im entsprechenden friesischen Paragrafen: Es ist der Übersetzer, der hiermit seinen Standort andeutet, und der ist, jedenfalls an diesen Stellen, nicht das östlich der Lauwers liegende Rechts- und Sprachgebiet, sondern Westfriesland. Es handelt sich um nachfolgende Stellen:

a. RWX 35 (Acht Domen, 2): 'syner moder voersprake; dath heth al hir een *voermunder*' ['Verteidiger seiner Mutter; das heißt hier Vormund'.]
b. RWX 175 (Acht Domen, 4): 'Alle anstoruen guet, dat al hyr *lawe* heth' ['Alle durch Vererbung erworbene Besitzungen, die hier Hinterlassenschaft heißen'.]
c. RW(X) 185 (Ausnahmen von der 17. Küre, 1): 'twe vaen optheen; dat heetet allhyr een *schuw* (RWX *schewe*)' ['zwei Fahnen aufrichten; das heißt hier ein Notzeichen, ein Signal'; neufr. *sjeau, sjou.*]
d. RW(X) 163 (ÄS 65): 'dat ys dat em de rechter dat lant tho vonden hebbe; dat heet alhyr een *vredeban'* ['dass der Richter ihm das Grundstück zuerkannt hat; das heißt hier eine gerichtliche Kaufbestätigung'.]
e. RWX 177 (Swarta swengen, 2): 'Dyt is ene grote sunde; dat heet alhyr *swaert sweng*' ['Dies ist eine schwere Sünde; das heißt hier eine niederträchtige Missetat'.]

Das erste Beispiel (a) besagt noch wenig: Sowohl das Wort *voersprake* als auch *voermunder* kommt an beiden Seiten der Lauwers vor. Auch Beispiel (b) ist noch nicht beweiskräftig: Das Wort *lawa* ist sowohl altwestfriesisch wie altostfriesisch, wenn man sich auch fragen könnte, warum da das Wort 'hier' steht, und nicht etwa 'früher'. Im dritten Beispiel (c) finden wir ein Wort, das in abgewandelter Form auch jetzt noch zur westfriesischen Sprache gehört. Es kommt aber auch im Mittelniederdeutschen vor,[54] also könnte es auch zur Groninger Mundart gehören. Die beiden letzten Beispiele sind aber aussagefähiger: Die Etyma *vredeban* (afries. *ferdban, fretheban)* und *swarta sweng* in der hier angewendeten Bedeutung sind eindeutig westfriesisch. Das heißt in Verbindung mit dem Adverb *alhyr*, dass die Übersetzung aus dem Altfriesischen in Westfriesland zustande gekommen ist. Damit ist nicht bewiesen, dass die ganzen *Rechten ende Wilkoeren* schon in Westfriesland übersetzt worden sind; es könnte sich auch um vereinzelte

---

53 Das *Autentica Riocht* und die *Aysma*-Sammlung; vgl. das Schema in Gerbenzon, *Excerpta legum*, 155.

54 A. Lasch und C. Borchling, *Mittelniederdeutsches Handwörterbuch* (Neumünster, 1956–..), s.v. *schûwe.*

Paragrafen handeln, aber dies besagt durchaus, dass man sich bei Texten, die auf dem klassischen altfriesischen Recht basieren, auch in Westfriesland einer anderen Sprache bedienen konnte, und zwar einer, die der neuen Zeit angehörte.[55]

Aber genauso wie in Westfriesland im Falle der *Jurisprudentia Frisica* am Ende des fünfzehnten Jahrhunderts wurden auch ein Jahrhundert später in den Groninger Ommelanden die *Rechten ende Wilkoeren* 'weggeschwemmt'. Zu gleicher Zeit kam ein anderes modernes, also auch 'neues' Landrecht außer Gebrauch, das zum Teil auch auf westfriesischem Recht basierte. Wir erhalten somit auch durch dasjenige, was im sechzehnten Jahrhundert in den Ommelanden hervorgebracht wurde, durchaus ein Bild davon, wie sich in Westfriesland ein modernes friesisches Recht hätte entwickeln können!

[55] Ich lasse hier das niederländischsprachige *Sceltariucht* in der Hs. Dousa außer Betracht (siehe Breuker, *Landrecht der Vriesne*). Die Herausgeber äußern sich nicht über Herkunft oder Zielgruppe des Textes. Die Sprache ist aber sicherlich nicht niedersächsisch.

Gallows in Late Medieval Frisia

Johannes A. Mol

Introduction[1]

Gallows were a familiar sight in the landscape of fifteenth-century Frisia. I am not thinking here primarily of temporary installations erected for executions in the town square to be dismantled afterwards, but rather of permanent constructions of wood or iron upon which the corpses of miscreants were exhibited after the execution, until they decomposed. For this purpose, wagon-wheels were attached onto poles nearby the gallows to serve as platforms upon which the beheaded and broken bodies of criminals were laid. Frisia between the Vlie and the Lauwers, the area on which my research is focussed in particular, counted at least forty such gallows-and-wheel constructions prior to 1515. Set high upon natural elevations, beside busy thoroughfares and waterways or beyond the dyke, these structures stood out conspicuously in the landscape and were intended to be seen from afar.

Despite their emphatic position in public spaces and the significance which they thus acquired for the general public, little attention has been paid to the history of the gallows, neither in the Low Countries nor elsewhere in Western Europe. General histories of crime and criminal law devote only marginal attention to this phenomenon; studies of state building entirely pass it by.[2] This neglect has nothing to do with the morbid nature of the subject.

---

[1] This is a translated and somewhat adapted version of my 'Galgen in laatmiddeleeuws Friesland', *De Vrije Fries* 86 (2006), 95–140.

[2] The most detailed information is given by D. A. Berents, 'Galg en rad: "wrede straffen" in laat-middeleeuws Utrecht', *Misdaad, zoen en straf. Aspekten van de middeleeuwse strafrechtsgeschiedenis in de Nederlanden*, ed. H. A. Diederiks and H. W. Roodenburg (Hilversum, 1991), 85–101; idem, *Het werk van de vos. Samenleving en criminaliteit in de late middeleeuwen* (Zutphen, 1985); and his *Misdaad in de Middeleeuwen*, 2nd ed. (Utrecht, 1984). Also see K. J. Frederiks, *Het Oud-Nederlandsche Strafrecht*, vol. 1 (Haarlem, 1918); R. His, *Das Strafrecht des deutschen Mittelalters*, 2 vols. (Weimar, 1935), 80; L. T. Maes, *Vijf eeuwen stedelijk strafrecht. Bijdrage tot de rechts- en cultuurgeschiedenis der Nederlanden* (Antwerpen, 1947), and R. C. van Caenegem, *Geschiedenis van het strafrecht in Vlaanderen van de XIe tot de XIVe eeuw* (Brussels, 1954); cf. C. Gauvard, *'De grace especial'. Crime, état et societé en France à la fin du Moyen Age* (Paris, 1991).

After all, there is plenty of literature on the hangman and his job.[3] The most likely reason for this dearth of studies would seem to be a lack of source material regarding the construction, distribution and function of the gallows in the Middle Ages. Localisable illustrations on maps, prints and paintings begin to appear only in the sixteenth century; few reports and administrative documents are extant which predate 1500, and the gallows themselves have perished. Hardly any foundations survive of even the sturdiest structures from early modern times. At most, archaeologists may now and then come across a skull and some bones of the hanged, self-buried as it were at the place of execution.[4]

There is, however, one trajectory which the historian of the gallows may follow with profit: onomastics. Gallows are often memorialised in the names of fields, water courses and other landscape features, such as in *Galge(n)-berg* (Gallows Hill), *Galgeduin* (Gallows Dune), *Galgefenne* (Gallows Fen), *Galgekamp* (Gallows Pitch), *Galgerak* (Gallows Reach), *Galgeveld* (Gallows Field), *Galgewater* (Gallows Water), *Galgewier* (Gallows Rise), *Galgeweel* (Gallows Pool). Such names, whether in Dutch or in Frisian, have retained their gallows component after the eponymous construction had fallen into disuse and had subsequently decayed or been demolished. These names can be inventoried and localised, after which it can be concluded whether they indeed refer to the former presence of a gallows. Such names represent the primary material for this essay. I have assembled them with the help of the huge collection of names of fields and water bodies put together at the Frisian Academy in the 1940s and 1950s.[5] Important in this connection is the institute's historical Geographic Information System (GIS), because it allows us not only to locate the physical position of gallows but

---

[3] See the detailed bibliography in G. Wilbertz, *Scharfrichter und Abdecker im Hochstift Osnabrück: Untersuchungen zur Sozialgeschichte zweier 'unehrlicher' Berufe im nordwestdeutschen Raum vom 16. bis zum 19. Jahrhundert* (Osnabrück, 1979); P. Spierenburg, *The Spectacle of Suffering. Executions and the Evolution of Repression: from a Pre-industrial Metropolis to the European Experience* (Cambridge, 1984); and H. Klemetillä, *Epitomes of Evil. Representations of Executioners in Northern France and the Low Countries in the Late Middle Ages* (Leiden, 2005). For the Netherlands, cf. F. de Wit Huberts, *De beul en z'n werk* (Amsterdam, 1937).

[4] Kind information from Wijnand van den Sanden who is preparing a publication on the archeological finds at the former gallows of Assen.

[5] The collection contains both archival and 'living' toponyms. The former category refers to field names from various administrative sources and also, for example, from newspaper advertisements for the sale of land. Such names may be mapped by linking them with those appearing in the earliest land registers. The names in the latter category were orally collected from farmers, farm hands and others, cf. J. J. Spahr van der Hoek, 'Stân fan saken oangeande de toponymesamlingen', *Fryske Nammen* 1 (1976), 111–13 (with map).

also their owners, thereby giving some indication of who may have been involved in the setting up and maintenance of the gallows.[6]

The number, distribution and function of gallows in Frisia are particularly worthy of study in relation to the extraordinary social and political developments of this region in the Middle Ages. It is known that gallows were built not only to instil fear and trembling and to act as a deterrent; they also served as a reminder of a ruler's power and authority.[7] In this way the holder of high jurisdiction, i.e. he who held the right to condemn to death, made it clear to his own subjects and to visitors alike that they found themselves in an independent jurisdiction. The message conveyed that disturbances of the peace would not be left to the victim's relatives to be corrected but would be severely dealt with by the authorities on behalf of the community. The gallows thus symbolised the monopoly on violence held by a governing authority. Simultaneously, the gallows would seem to have been intended to disseminate a concept of the necessity for painful capital punishment, a concept which in its turn was intimately connected with the development of the modern territorial state.

The object, then, of my essay is to establish how the application of the death penalty, the erection of such penal sites and the exhibition of punished miscreants relates to the decentralised communal government as found everywhere in Frisia between the Vlie and the Lauwers during the late Middle Ages. This region had been free of feudal authority since the middle of the thirteenth century which implied that per land (*terra*) the local elite itself practised government and exercised legal rights under the leadership of judges elected by the people.[8] The free Frisian lands themselves were the holders of high domain. They recognised that this right derived in the first place from the sovereignty of the Holy Roman Empire, to which they considered themselves to belong at least nominally. These communally governed lands were in fact fairly loosely organised confederations, without much political machinery and with only a minimum of administrative infrastructure. Until far into the fifteenth century they had no chancery at their disposal or buildings or any other centralised facilities. Most lands and their sub-districts had, so to speak, nothing more than their seal.

Given these circumstances, the question arises as to why the (possible) application of the death penalty by using gallows-and-wheel constructions ever found favour amongst these independent mini-territories, and what

6 To be found at <www.hisgis.nl> with detailed information.

7 A. Erler, 'Galgen', *Handwörterbuch zur deutschen Rechtsgeschichte*, ed. A. Erler, *et al.* (Berlin, 1971) I, cols. 1375–78, at 1376.

8 General: O. Vries, *Het Heilige Roomse Rijk en de Friese vrijheid* (Leeuwarden, 1986), 14–27; *idem*, 'Geschichte der Friesen im Mittelalter: West- und Ostfriesland', *Handbuch / Handbook*, 538–50, at 542–48.

purpose they served. The question is the more pressing in regard to the Frisian lands precisely because the Frisians are known to have clung so tenaciously to the Germanic system of compensation. Many crimes, including manslaughter, which elsewhere had long become liable to the death penalty, were dealt with in Frisia by paying compensation. This custom does not imply that Old Frisian law texts fail to mention hanging or beheading. They certainly do. But these texts emphatically radiate the sense that the legal order, once violated, may be restored through pecuniary reparation.

I have chosen the year 1515 for the end date of my investigation. This is the year in which Duke George of Saxony passed his authority over the Frisian lands to the west of the Lauwers to Charles V of Habsburg. The date of the end of Frisian autonomy, 1498, might seem a more obvious choice. In that year George's father Albert captured the region and centralised its government, amongst other things by establishing an overarching Court of Law in Leeuwarden with far-reaching legal jurisdiction. Various scholars assume that this Court from the start exercised capital punishment on behalf of all of the Frisia lands west of the Lauwers, and that as a result all executions after 1498 took place in Leeuwarden.[9] On closer examination, however, this appears not to have been the case.[10] Even though Duke George's intention may have been to centralise the 'painful penal code' and to try in Leeuwarden all capital crimes perpetrated in Frisia west of the Lauwers, it took until 1515 before the towns and *grietenien* (rural judicial districts) officially abandoned their right to execute and exhibit sentenced miscreants.

1. Compensation versus the death penalty in Old Frisian law

Eloquent and programmatic for the strongly compensation-based character of the medieval Frisian judicial system is the sixteenth of the *Seventeen Statutes*, which contains a collection of legal regulations possibly dating back to the twelfth century and in force for all of Frisia, from the Vlie in the west to the Weser in the east. The sixteenth statute states in so many words 'that all Frisians may compensate their (violation of the) peace with their money and goods'.[11] On account of this statute, allegedly granted by Charle

---

[9] J. S. Theissen, *Centraal gezag en Friesche vrijheid. Friesland onder Karel V* (Groningen, 1907), 40; A. H. Huusen, Jr., *Veroordeeld in Friesland. Criminaliteitsbestrijding in de eeuw der Verlichting* (Leeuwarden, 1994), 11.

[10] As pointed out to me by my colleague Paul Baks, e.g. on account of a sentence of a wrongdoer in Wommels in 1514: Dresden, Sächsisches Hauptstaatsarchiv, Loc. 10374/9, fols. 55–59.

[11] *Jus Municipale Frisonum*, ed. W. J. Buma and W. Ebel, AR 6/1–2 (Göttingen 1977) I, 144–45: 'Djo sextundiste kest is, dat alle Fresen hiare ferde bete mey hiara fia. Truch dat schelleth Fresen wessa oen Saxena merkum wtor stok ende wtor stupa ende wtor schera ende wtor fillane ende wtor pina binna settena merkum'. Cf. N. E. Algra, *17*

magne, the Frisians remained exempt from imprisonment, rod, fetters and other painful punishments not only in their own lands but also throughout the Saxon duchy. This right immediately makes clear that the Frisian system had resisted the application of corporal punishment long after its neighbouring regions had accepted it. In a plea for more attention for this very particular Frisian development, the Göttingen medievalist Ernst Schubert speaks of a 'dezidierte, aber keineswegs konsequente Ablehnung der Blutgerichtsbarkeit, der Lebens- und Körperstrafen'.[12] We know that the Frisian system of compensation dates back at least as far as the late eighth century: in the pages of the *Lex Frisionum* every transgression and injury is regulated by a certain amount of money. These payments, and hence the practice of compensation, were of a remarkably structured and continuous character, for a great number of tariffs recur again and again in hardly altering sums in late-medieval compensation registers that have survived for the various Frisian judicial districts.[13] Essential here is that even manslaughter can be settled by paying a full *wergeld.*

This is not to say that Old Frisian Law is lacking in clauses that allow for the death penalty for serious misdeeds. Searching the rich collection of surviving law texts for capital crimes reveals stipulations on capital offences which were liable for the death penalty, such as violent robbery, church robbery, arson, forgery and high treason. 'Murder must be compensated with murder' is a recurring proverbial wisdom found in the various provisions.[14] Schubert is aware of this but judges the fact to constitute a paradox in Frisian law.[15] In his view, the contradiction is only apparent, because he simultaneously feels able to establish that in many Frisian regions the death sentence for serious crimes could ultimately be avoided by compensation until well into the sixteenth century. For a long time, according to Schubert, the Frisians considered settlement in money or goods a fully valid alternative

Keuren en 24 Landrechten (Doorn, 1991), 313–14, who explains how this provision refers to buying off blood feuds: instead of *ferde* 'peace', older versions have *feitha*, *inimicitia* 'enmity'.

12 E. Schubert, 'Vom Wergeld zur Strafe: die übersehene Bedeutung der friesischen Rechtsquellen zur Interpretation eines epochalen mittelalterlichen Wandels', *Tota Frisia in Teilansichten. Hajo van Lengen zum 65. Geburtstag*, ed. H. Schmidt, W. Schwartz and M. Tielke (Aurich, 2005), 97–120, at 97–99.

13 D. J. Henstra, *The Evolution of the Money Standard in Medieval Frisia: a Treatise on the History of the Systems of Money of Account in the Former Frisia (c.600–c.1500)* (Groningen, 2000), 14–16.

14 E.g. in the conclusion of the sixteenth Statute and in the twenty-fourth Landlaw; see *Das Rüstringer Recht*, ed. W. J. Buma and W. Ebel, AR 1 (Göttingen, 1963), 40–41, and 58–59: 'Morth mot ma mith morthe kela, til thiu thet ma tha ergon stiore' [Murder must be paid for with murder in order to avert the evil ones]; cf. N. E. Algra, *Oudfries recht 800–1256* (Leeuwarden, 2000), 193 and 295.

15 Schubert, 'Vom Wergeld zur Strafe', 109.

to painful execution. It was even a necessary alternative, given the absence of any practical infrastructure to support the execution of the death penalty in Frisia. There were, after all, neither castles nor strongholds and hence no secure prisons for the detention of criminals awaiting trial, sentence and execution. Nor were there professional executioners available to deal with the dirty work associated with this form of justice. The first hangmen arrived in larger Frisia only around 1500, and then more in particular in towns such as Groningen and Emden – it was the town that gave birth to the hangman. In short, Old Frisian law applied the death penalty only in exceptional cases '... für die zwar Lösungen gesucht, aber keine praktische Vorkehrungen getroffen wurden'.[16] Elsewhere,[17] Schubert says that despite its presence in the law codes capital punishment played no part in general patterns of judicial punishment in Frisia until the sixteenth century.

In his essay, Schubert neglects to test this hypothesis against other than normative sources. The reluctance for Frisian authorities to implement capital punishment until about 1500 is a hard fact for Schubert. He uses it to comment on theories that have been postulated by legal historians regarding the whys and wherefores in German penal law of the transition from a system of compensations to that with capital punishment. It will become clear that my enquiry into the administration of justice, and more particularly the implementation of gallows, follows quite another line. New data concerning the death penalty and gallows-and-wheel constructions collected from place-names and narrative sources gives occasion to question the validity of Schubert's hypothesis. Upon closer inspection, there is also reason to challenge his analysis of neck-and-head clauses in the law texts.

To begin with, I shall examine in some detail the consequences of the afore-mentioned sixteenth Statute. Here, *hauddeda*, (' "head-deeds", capital crimes') are explicitly referred to, that is crimes for which a perpetrator must pay with his head in order to satisfy the community. The most serious crimes were nightly arson and other surreptitious deeds. For these felonies the punishment was breaking on the wheel, while thieves were led to the gallows – that is, those thieves who were unable to compensate.[18] The *Wenden* ('Exceptions') to the sixteenth of the *Seventeen Statutes* as found in the Fivelgo and Hunsingo manuscripts list just three *mordseka* ('evil cases') for which a free Frisian may lose his neck: church robbery, high

---

[16] *Ibid.* 111.

[17] *Ibid.* 101.

[18] *Das Rüstringer Recht,* ed. Buma and Ebel, 40–41: 'Ac hebbe hi haueddeda eden, nachtbrond ieftha othera morthdeda, sa skil hi ielda mith sines selues halse alle lioden to like thonke ..., thet is, thet ma hini skil ope en reth setta. Ac hebbe hi thivuethe den bi Frisona kere, ief hit an tha fia nebbe, sa hach ma hini to hwande'.

treason and church arson.[19] In other texts, however, mention is made of the death penalty for the thief who is caught red-handed while burgling and stealing at night.[20] Such a punishment speaks for itself considering that a thief does not generally possess the means by which to recompense his crime. Thus he was made to pay a still heavier price for his furtive behaviour. The way in which he was executed implied a complete loss of honour: he was blindfolded with a black cloth and hanged by the neck on the *northalda bam* or *northalda tre*: the (wretched) north-facing, leafless tree: the gallows.[21] For severe misdeeds, such as robbery with murder and church robbery, the sentence was breaking of the bones with subsequent exhibition upon the nine or ten-spoked wheel: *thet tian spetzie fial*.[22] How the punishment was to be carried out is described at length in a legal provision entitled *Fan en Schaekraef* ('Of violent robbery'), probably originating from the thirteenth century. Article eight describes three cases of violent robbery: one in a house, one on board a ship and one involving a travelling tradesman.[23] Importantly, the article stipulates the exhibition of the convict's corpse so that people might 'learn to avoid dreadful deeds'.

In short, murder for robbery, theft and nightly arson were capital offences under Old Frisian law at least since the twelfth century; a perpetrator could no longer compensate these crimes with money and goods. Later texts reiterate the provisions in such cases, explaining them in a relatively consistent manner. For example, the late thirteenth-century *Brocmonna Bref*, originating from Brokmerland in East Frisia, makes clear in several places that both

---

19 *Das Hunsingoer Recht*, ed. W. J. Buma and W. Ebel, AR 4 (Göttingen, 1969), 46–47; *Das Fivelgoer Recht*, ed. W. J. Buma and W. Ebel, AR 5 (Göttingen, 1972), 170–71. The Emsigo version counts five exceptions, including violent robbery in a forest, see *Das Emsiger Recht*, ed. W. J. Buma and W. Ebel, AR 3 (Göttingen, 1967), 92–93. Otherwise, we find a number of such cases in the *Lex Frisionum*, ed. K. A. Eckhardt and A. Eckhardt (Hanover, 1982), Tit. V: 'Of people who may be killed without compensation'. They include thieves caught in the act, arsonists and desecrators of sanctuaries.

20 For example, in extrapolation of the twenty-fifth Land law: Das *Emsiger Recht*, ed. Buma and Ebel,VII, §§ 35–36, pp. 94–95. See also the provisions *De Duplici Malo*, §§ 1–2; *ibid.* 134–37.

21 *Das Hunsingoer Recht*, ed. Buma and Ebel, 90–91: 'And sa ach hi bi riuchta thene swarta lappa and thene smerta knotta and the nordalde tre'. Cf. His, *Das Strafrecht der Friesen im Mittelalter* (Leipzig, 1901), 195–96.

22 Mentioned in the *Wenden op de Zestiende Keur* (Exceptions to the Sixteenth Statute): *De eerste en de tweede Hunsinger Codex*, ed. J. Hoekstra, OTR 6 (The Hague, 1950), 58 (VI, 6).

23 *Jus Municipale Frisonum*, ed. Buma and Ebel, I, 250–51; cf. the variant in *Jurisprudentia Frisica of Friesche regtkennis. Een handschrift uit de vijftiende eeuw*, ed. M. de Haan Hettema, 2 vols. (Leeuwarden, 1835) II, 180–83.

murder for robbery and theft were liable to capital punishment.[24] The value of the stolen goods was relevant, but no amount was specified. It seems that it was left to the judges to decide what value would tip the balance. The *Ommeland Land Law of 1448*, agreed between the Frisian lands (*terrae*) of Fivelgo and Hunsingo and the city of Groningen on the basis of older Frisian law, concludes its article on fatal arson with the instruction that if a man has been found guilty, the damage will be doubly recovered from his goods '... ende den schuldinghen te rechten an syn lyf' ['... and the convict to be executed to death'].[25] As for thieving: the perpetrator must hang if the value of the stolen goods exceeded that of an old shield (gold coin). The *Joure Market Law* of 1466 offers the same sentence: 'is it een schild ald ieldis ofte daer toe bowa, soe schilma hem zyn riucht dwaan'.[26] The same measure is to be found abundantly in a treaty concluded in 1491 between Groningen on the one side, and the town of Dokkum, a number of monasteries, various village communities and diverse prominent figures from Oostergo on the other.[27] If we compare these provisions with the norm that prevailed in similar circumstances elsewhere in the northern Netherlands and in northern Germany we scarcely find any differences. At most, the sums and amounts outlined were somewhat lower beyond the boundaries of Frisia west of the Lauwers.[28]

In its judgement of manslaughter, Frisia demonstrated its singularity in relation to surrounding areas, because this deed could be compensated by the payment of a *wergeld*.[29] We must realise, however, that compensation was possible only if the felon was capable of procuring the vast sum which was demanded in recompense for manslaughter and grievous bodily harm. Only members of the nobility and freeholders had at their disposal substantial assets in terms of property, kinsmen or personnel. Upon this point Frisian law is to the point: he who cannot compensate in money or goods must do so with his blood. The sixth statute of the *New Riustring Statutes*

---

24 *Das Brokmer Recht*, ed. W.J. Buma and W. Ebel, AR 2 (Göttingen 1965), 82–83: *Brokmer Brief*, §§130, 132.

25 D. Simonides, *Die Hunsigoer Küren vom Jahre 1252 und das Ommelander Landrecht vom Jahre 1448* (Assen, 1938), 94–95.

26 *Oudfriesche Oorkonden*, ed. P. Sipma, 3 vols. (The Hague, 1927–1941) II, no. 66, p. 86: 'If it is a shield in old currency or more, then he must be executed'.

27 *Pax Groningana: 204 oarkonden út it Grinzer gemeente-archyf oer de forhâlding Grins-Fryslân yn de fyftjinde ieu*, ed. M. G. Oosterhout *et al.* (Groningen, 1975), no. 47, p. 69: 'Jtem wellick menssche de steelt bouen eenen olden fransschen schilt den deeff salmen hangen [...]. Jtem alle stratenschenders ende nachtrouers de misdoen in onsen verbonde de rechtmen an oir lyff'.

28 The amounts elsewhere vary between five and sixteen shillings, see Berents, *Misdaad in de Middeleeuwen*, 82–83; Berents, *Werk van de vos*, 69 and 71–72.

29 His, *Strafrecht des deutschen Mittelalters*, II, 80.

states that the *blata* ('poor man') who was apprehended immediately after committing manslaughter in a violent quarrel, must pay with his neck; there was to be no 'peace' (= money) for his head.[30] A search for *blata* in Old Frisian law texts results time and again in finding variations on the theme. It underlines once more the intricate relationship between honour, property and law in medieval Frisian society.[31]

In view of the absence of a practical organisation for carrying out executions, may we conclude from the many legal provisions concerning death penalties that they were merely there for the purpose of deterrence? And would judges have circumnavigated this predicament by handing down sentences of exile or compensations? I do no think so. In the first place, the lack of information concerning trial procedures in Old Frisian laws should not lead us to assume that any serious organisation was lacking too. Information is also sadly deficient regarding the precise way in which court sessions were conducted. Nevertheless, between the lines of the provisions on death penalties some indications are certainly to be found of concrete arrangements for capturing, sentencing and executing felons who had forfeited their lives.

The law *Fan en Schaekraef*, dealing with cases of violent robbery, is a good example in point. It contains an almost lyrical plea to the members of the legal community to stop immediately whatever they are doing the moment a clarion of bells alerts them to pursue robbers or thieves. Freely translated, the text reads as follows: 'everyone, young or old, hungry or thirsty, warm or cold, hearing the signal shall immediately heed it and pursue God's enemies'.[32] One need not have to have seen many Westerns to imagine what sort of posse might have been set in motion by the *grietman* (judge of a rural district) when cattle or goods had been stolen and the thief was rumoured not to be far off.

Concerning the actual execution: the *Younger Magistrates' Law* which related to Frisia west of the Lauwers, assumed that the *banner* ('officer of

30 *Das Rüstringer Recht*, ed. Buma and Ebel, 85: 'Alder thi blata falt enne mon, werth hi tohond bigengen, sa mot hi riuchta mith tha halse and thet lif ac fretholas biliua'. Compare the treaty of 1491 between Groningen with Oostergo, mentioned above: 'gebreket hem Jn den guede, hie betale mit den bloede'.

31 So in the eleventh provision of the *Old Riustring Statutes*: *Das Rüstringer Recht*, ed. Buma and Ebel, 81–82; *Brokmer Brief*, §128: *Das Brokmer Recht*, ed. Buma and Ebel, 82–83; *Emsigo Penningschuldboek* ('Book of Debts'), §§29–30: *Das Emsiger Recht*, ed. Buma and Ebel, 216–17; and *Hunsingo Satutes of 1252*, §§29–30: *Das Hunsingoer Recht*, ed. Buma and Ebel, 120–21.

32 *Jus Municipale Frisonum*, ed. Buma and Ebel, I, 250–51: 'Is hi ald, js hi iong, deer dae kedene heerth, is hi torstich, js hi hongerich, js him hete, is him kalde, soe ne ach deer nen man soe lange toe bidiane, dat hi zijn weed bewandelia moeghe, mer hia schelleth dae Goedis fianda fulghia'.

the court') was the one who tied the convicted thief and conduced him to the gallows. At this point, the thief's victim was given the choice whether to execute the criminal himself or to pay someone else to do it.[33] In the thirteenth century, it was still customary in the Frisian lands, as it was elsewhere, for the victim himself or one of his kinsmen to carry out the execution as a form of judicially approved revenge. According to a treaty between Rüstringen and Bremen signed in 1220, the victim himself carried out punishment on the robber.[34] In the early fourteenth century this would seem to have been the normal procedure in Brokmerland too. Whoever caught the thief – supposedly the latter's victim – had his goods returned and in addition a silver mark, after which he himself was entitled to execute the sentence: 'and sa vrdue hine selwa'.[35] The Bolsward bylaws of 1451 prescribe that the victim who had his goods stolen, should execute the thief himself or pay someone else to do it for him. If he was not prepared to pay, he forfeited the right to have his stolen goods returned to him and the alderman was to take care of (or arrange for) the execution of the sentence.[36] In short, law sources afford us a clear glimpse of the posse, the gallows, and the man who pulled the chord.

2. Execution and exhibition: town and country

My examination of the texts has demonstrated that the application of capital punishment involved more than just the execution. The execution did not end with the hanging, beheading or breaking on the wheel. The corpse had to be exhibited, partly as an additional punishment or revenge on behalf of the community and partly as a deterrent. The afore-mentioned law text *Fan en Schaekraef* stipulates that the violent robber, after mutilation, had to be given a place beyond the dyke high upon a wheel that had never before been used on a wain. There '…no wind is to blow upon him, no man to look upon him, no dew to bedew him and no sun to shine upon him, so that everyone might learn from this that misdeeds are to be avoided'.[37] The internal contra-

---

[33] *Jus Municipale Frisonum*, ed. Buma and Ebel, I, 224–25: 'So aeg di bannere him to bindane ende ti dere rode ti ledane … . Soe aegh di man dyne kerre, her hi dyn tiaef hwe soe hyt mit sijn goed winne'.

[34] His, *Strafrecht der Friesen*, 198 n. 4: 'spoliator capitalem sententiam per manus spoliati subibit'.

[35] *Das Brokmer Recht*, ed. Buma and Ebel, §132, p. 82.

[36] V. Robijn, *Het recht van een vrije Friese Stad. De stadboeken van Bolsward van 1455 en 1479* (Hilversum and Leeuwarden, 2005), c. XCI, p. 128.

[37] 'Soe aegh ma him wtor dike toe ferane ende deer en boem toe ferane, en tial toe brengane, deer eer oen wayne ne kome, him der op ti settane, hi zijn eynde deerop ti nymane. Him aegh nen wynd ti biwaine, nen man ti bisiane, nen dau ti bidauwen, nen senne ti bischinen, mer datter alle lioede oen merke, dat ma eergha deda wrmide.'

diction of this poetic but macabre passage might be read to mean that the punished man must be banished wholly from the cosmos as a person but that his ashes had to serve as an ever-visible lesson to the community. The 'placing beyond the dyke' lends extra symbolic weight to this ambivalent message. The convict after all ends up on the border between land and sea, in the margin of society, facing the malevolent world beyond. This element is reminiscent of the death penalty clause for the desecrator of pagan sanctuaries given in the *Lex Frisionum*: whoever violates a sanctuary (*fana*) must be carried to the sea shore, suffer castration there and is offered as a sacrifice to the god whose temple he has violated.[38] Important too, however, is that the executed violent robber whose corpse is exhibited on the waterline should be visible from afar. The same applies to the thief who gets the rope. He must hang 'bi tha wie', that is, adjacent to the public highway.[39]

These are rather general provisions which, charged as they are with symbolism, appear in numerous judicial sources throughout Europe.[40] All emphasise that the execution of the death sentence was a public affair. As many of the public as possible would be gathered together for the execution which was surrounded by many rituals. But also afterwards, by its display to the community for many months, the corpse of the miscreant had to illustrate how dearly he had paid with a grisly fate for his violation of social order. The exemplification and striking fear into the hearts of the people were thereby more important than any avenging and banishing from society of the criminal. Execution and exhibition belonged together from the beginning and served one and the same goal.[41]

Before we can compile an inventory for Frisia of the tools and further practical constructions instrumental in achieving this goal, we must consider whether execution and exhibition could simultaneously serve both functions and, if so, under what circumstances. In other words, were the gallows-and-wheel used in Frisia for both execution and exhibition or were they constructions that served first the one and then the other purpose? From the judicial-historical literature it appears that almost all the large towns of the Middle Ages and Early Modern era in fact had a separate exhibition gallows which were situated on a clearly visible spot beyond the city wall, embankment or moat. Such exhibition structures are often referred to in Dutch sources as the *gerecht* ('justice', compare German *Hochgericht*). Thither the criminals' corpses were brought after execution, usually in a ritual and

[38] *Lex Frisionum*, Note XI, I: *De honore templorum*.

[39] J. Grimm, *Deutsche Rechtsalterthümer*, 4th ed., 2 vols. (Leipzig, 1899) II, 259.

[40] *Ibid.* 257; see also the literature mentioned in footnote 3 above.

[41] In practice it would seem that exhibition often did not take place, sometimes owing to a mitigation of the sentence, but also at the request of the relatives of the sentenced man if they considered it their duty to give him a decent burial.

humiliating manner, to be hung up or otherwise exposed, prey to rats and ravens until they had decomposed.

Frisian, like Dutch and German, has just one technical term for both structures: *galge* (gallows). In French and English the two may be discriminated through the use of two separate terms.[42] The execution gallows, which may be single in the form of a knee, or double in the shape of a 'T' (whence the plural form *gallows* in English), is in French called *potence* (after the noose made of willow twigs) or *patibule* (from Latin *patibulum*, also used for the traverse of the cross used for the execution of Christ). The exhibition gallows is mostly referred to in French as *gibet* or *fourche de gibet*; *fourche* (from Latin *furca*) points to the fork-construction atop the supporting posts, in and upon which the crossbeam rests for the hanging. The French word *gibet* is perpetuated in the English word *gibbet.*

Some of the seventeenth-century city gibbets in the Netherlands are well known. That of Utrecht, for instance, was situated on the Vaartse Rijn, a good distance south of the city moat.[43] Still better known, thanks to drawings made by Rembrandt, Reinier Vinkeles and others, is the Amsterdam *gerecht*, located in the Volewijk on the north bank of the river IJ.[44] As for the north of the Netherlands, the Groningen exhibition gallows, situated on the south-side of the town during the sixteenth century, certainly deserves to be mentioned. The historiographer Sicke Benninge records its demolition by German troops on the occasion of the siege of Groningen by Albert, duke of Saxony, in 1500. It was reputed to have been an expensive construction of heavy iron beams on pillars of costly Bentheim stone.[45]

The custom of erecting separate scaffolds for execution and exhibition within and without the town is relatively old. The gallows place in Brussels, on the Flotsenberg west of the city, already existed in 1233.[46] In Gent,

---

42 Maes, *Vijf eeuwen stedelijk strafrecht*, 296–98.

43 The execution of those who had committed serious crimes took place at the Neude, where a scaffold and separate knee-shaped gallows stood for this purpose: Berents, *Misdaad in de Middeleeuwen*, 39–42; *idem*, *Werk van de vos*, 70.

44 H. G. Jelgersma, *Galgebergen en galgevelden* (Zutphen, 1978), 37–41.

45 *Chronickel der Vriescher landen en der stadt Groningen, door Sicke Benninghe*, ed. M. Brouerius van Nidek, *Analecta Medii Aevi* (Amsterdam and Middelburg, 1725), 1–432, at 59–60. The execution itself took place in Groningen, usually on the Great Market; see F. J. Bakker and A. H. Huussen, Jr., 'Het oudste Groningse Register van criminele en andere zaken en De bekentenis van Johan Stenbar (1475–1547)', *Verslagen en Mededelingen van de Stichting tot Uitgaaf Bronnen Oud-Vaderlandse Recht,* n.s. 7 (1992), 43–92, at 47.

46 In the beginning of the fifteenth century this gibbet was rebuilt into a sturdy, triangular walled construction fourteen rods long, with openings and cantilevers, the gallows and wheel situated within. All … 'mit ene dobbele slote om de dode lichamen als sy vanden gherechte vallen daer inne te verwarene vor de beesten diese sliten ende eten mochten als honden ende andere beesten' ['… with a double ditch in order to protect the

wrongdoers were exhibited at the place of execution for a long time after their death during the eleventh century. This conclusion may be drawn when the chronicler Walter of Terwaan remarks that the corpses of some miscreants were removed from the noose only after their decomposition began badly to affect the air in the marketplace.[47] The need for prompt separation of the two locations soon became evident to the town administration in densely populated trading towns. It proved difficult for town administrators and lords to combine the obvious need for permanent deterrence with their other equally important role in promoting concentration of economic activities. The solution which they found for this dilemma was the establishment of a place of exhibition at a short distance from the town, where the bodies of wrongdoers could be well seen but where their rotting away would not hinder those living nearby too much. One thing is certain, after all: living and working in the vicinity of a gallows field was no pleasure. ‘The ghastly sight and smell of the dead, half-rotten miscreants put there to hang and display’[48] motivated people living on the Vaartse Rijn in Utrecht to seek relocation of the gallows field in 1674.

Public annoyance with gallows-and-wheel constructions cannot have posed such a problem in the countryside. In the first place there were fewer such constructions there, and less often bodies to put on show. The towns were of course more densely populated and lodged more wealth, which resulted in more criminal activity. The chance of criminals getting caught was also commensurately higher in towns than in the countryside. In the second place, in the countryside it was easier for administrators to choose and set up a location for the gallows field while bearing in mind the prevalent wind direction, so that the people living in its vicinity would be less troubled. By implication, and in contrast to urban gallows, these rural constructions also served as a place of execution. Separation of function was not only unnecessary but also too costly for the often much less prosperous country districts. In the Groningen Ommelanden, where *redgers* (‘rural judges’) continued to exercise their right of sentencing people to death until 1795, the condemned were both executed and exhibited at the same place outside the village in the seventeenth and eighteenth centuries.[49] There is no reason to assume that procedures were different in earlier centuries. Consequently, when drawing up an inventory of gallows in medieval Frisia, we

corpses after having fallen from the gibbet from the beasts, such as dogs and other animals, which might tear and eat them’], F. Vanhemelryck, *Misdadigers tussen rechter en beul 1400–1800* (Amsterdam, 1984), 193.

47 Van Caenegem, *Strafrecht in Vlaanderen*, 171.

48 Berents, *Werk van de vos*, 7.

49 J. Frima, *Het strafproces in de Ommelanden tusschen Eems en Lauwers van 1602–1749* (Amersfoort, 1920), 390.

can take it for granted that, some town gallows excluded, by far the majority was intended for execution and exhibition alike.

3. Gallows in or near towns and *grietenien*

Care must be taken when tracking down gallows through toponyms. Not every name with *galg(e)* need point to a former place of execution or exhibition. It may occasionally concern a nick-name or some memorial event, as is the case with *Galgenhuis* (Gallows House) in the village of Stiens, where around1870 someone was said to have hanged himself.[50] More often, however, the *galg-* element in a place-name appears to derive not from the penal apparatus but rather from Dutch *gagel* 'gale, bog-myrtle' (*Myrica gale*), an aromatic plant in great demand in the Middle Ages for making gruit (or grut), a herb mixture used for bittering and flavouring beer. Gale may grow to a metre in height and is found on slightly acidic, moist soil that is poor in calcium, such as peat bogs and alongside old riverbeds. Because this plant is known in Frisian as *galje* or *gaalje*, it regularly features in field names such as *Galjefjild* and *Galjemeden*. When identifying sites, it is important therefore constantly to check whether the toponym under review might refer to a site that might have been a habitat of this plant. In view of the damp habitat of the plant, such a confusion is less likely in toponyms compounded with *wier* 'clay mound', *berg* 'hill', and words indicating 'high'.[51]

From *galje*, which can erode to *galge* by way of such intermediate phases as *galleg* and *gallege*, it is a small step to *galle*[52] and *gale*. In the latter case extra care must be taken, because *gale* may also derive from the Frisian personal name *Gale*, often appearing in toponyms. To avoid the risk of confusion, forms with single 'l', such as *Galekampen* and *Galefennen*, have been excluded from my inventory.

---

50 For this information I should like to thank Mr. D. Th. Reitsma, Stiens.

51 There are doubts concerning interpretation of the adjacent *Galiefinne* and *Galiekamp*, southwards on the through road from Twizel to Drogeham (cadastral plots Kooten C9 and Drogeham F189–190), lying on either side of the border between the villages of Kooten and Drogeham, see S. de Haan, 'Fjildnammen yn Droegeham en Harkema-Opeinde neffens de floreenkohieren', *Nieuwsblad van Noord-Oost Friesland,* 30 Nov. 1988, 8. The road lies so high and dry here that it would not present an obvious habitat for gale. Though lack of hard evidence actually forbids this conclusion, it is tempting to consider this the location of the gallows of Achtkarspelen. The gallows of this *grietenie* is nowhere else to be found.

52 See, for example, the *Galgekamp* 'gallows field', Sexbierum, which also turns up in the sources as *Gallekamp*.

Frisia west of the Lauwers and its political division in the fifteenth century: the *terrae*, the *grietenien* and the cities.

Westergo	Oostergo	Zevenwouden	
1.Menaldumadeel	9. Leeuwarderadeel	17.Utingeradeel	24.Kollumerland
2.Franekeradeel	10.Ferwerderadeel	18.Engwirden	25.Achtkarspelen
3.Barradeel	11.Westdongeradeel	19.Doniawerstal	26.Smallingerland
4.Baarderadeel	12.Oostdongeradeel	20.Haskerland	27.Opsterland
5.Hennaarderadeel	13.Dantumadeel	21.Schoterland	28.Ooststellingwerf
6.Wonseradeel	14.Tietjerksteradeel	22.Oosterzeeïngerland	29.Weststellingwerf
7.Wymbritseradeel	15.Idaarderadeel	23.Mirderland	
8.Gaasterland	16.Rauwerderhem		

Taking into account these and other uncertainties, I have been able to compile a file of about thirty 'gallows' place-names for the present-day Dutch province of Fryslân.[53] The list may be split into various categories, of which the two that are devoted to towns and to *grietenien*, respectively, are the most significant. In addition to these two is a category covering the

53 The internal inventory is available on <www.hisgis.nl> in a separate layer 'galgen'.

remainder of the 'other high seignories' that includes not only the islands of Terschelling and Ameland,[54] but also the parish of Burum near the river Lauwers that enjoyed judicial exemption since all the landed property withinits borders belonged to the Cistercian Jerusalem Abbey, also known as Gerkesklooster.

In terms of gallows sites belonging to the eleven Frisian towns, no fewer than nine can be identified and localised. Of Harlingen no record whatsoever has survived, whilst for Dokkum all that is currently known is that in 1491 there was a wheel in or nearby the town, upon which after his execution Groningen troops placed a nobleman whom they considered a traitor. Because gallows and wheels always went together as exhibition apparatus it may be taken that a gallows was also built at this place. For the remaining nine towns, the position of the gallows is more or less precisely locatable. That of Staveren reputedly was situated on land beyond the dyke, between the harbour and the Rode Klif near Scharl. The Workum gallows was situated somewhere south of the sluice, whilst that of Sloten was built near the canal connecting the town with the Sloten Lake. For the remaining towns the place of the gibbet can even be located on the cadastre.

Regarding the *grietenien*, no fewer than sixteen gallows can be traced. It is still uncertain how many *grietenien* we should take into account before 1500. The traditional number since the sixteenth century has been thirty, less one: the Bildt. This future district came into being after it had been reclaimed from the sea and enclosed by dykes only in 1505. Other districts, such as Hemelumer Oldeferd, for a long time formed a whole with a neighbouring district, in this case Gaasterland. Other *grietenien* again were split up into parts that were later reunited. In whatever way they are counted, the sixteen districts for which I have recovered the gallows in any case cover more than half of the districts. They are, in alphabetical order: Baarderadeel, Barradeel, Dantumadeel, Ferwerderadeel, Franekeradeel, Hemelumer Oldeferd (and Gaasterland), Kollumerland, Menaldumadeel, Oostdongeradeel, Ooststellingwerf, Smallingerland, Tietjerksteradeel, Westdongeradeel, Weststellingwerf, Wonseradeel and Wymbritseradeel. Hennaarderadeel may also be added to this number, because we know that in Wommels, the biggest village of the district, another miscreant was beheaded in 1514.[55] The decapitation must have taken place at the place of execution for this district, although it is not possible for me to localise it with any precision. Finally, it would seem that the later central gallows of Leeuwarden, on the towpath to Harlingen, originally belonged to Leeuwarderadeel. There was also a

[54] In the sixteenth century, Terschelling and Ameland were already separate high seignories that retained this status even after 1580, when the States of Friesland attained sovereign status.

[55] Dresden, Sächsisches Hauptstaatsarchiv, Loc. 10374/9, fols. 55–59.

gibbet on the Vliet, some miles east of the town, which in 1580 was referred to as the *olde gerecht*. Because of that name the construction will have been out of function by then for some time.[56] This would seem to have been the town scaffold rather than the one lying to the south-west of Leeuwarden. The former was closer by and easily reached from the Brol, which was still the site of the Leeuwarden execution place in the early sixteenth century.[57] Following this identification, only ten out of about thirty *grietenien* remain for which I have found no data. These districts were situated, probably not coincidentally, in the middle, east and south of the present-day province of Fryslân – areas which are poorly documented for the Middle Ages: Achtkarspelen,[58] Doniawerstal, Engwirden, Haskerland,[59] Idaarderadeel, Lemsterland, Rauwerderhem, Opsterland, Schoterland and Utingeradeel.

Before 1515, then, every (sub-)*grietenie* very probably possessed its own gallows. Or should we say that, apart from the towns, every rural district in any case had the right to set up its own gallows, and to use and maintain it? A specification of 1540 mentions *Baerderadeels galge* in so many words.[60] And in his account of the Groningen interference in northern Oostergo, written around 1585, the chronicler Johan Rengers van Ten Post refers emphatically to the presence of rural-district gallows, to wit those of Kollumerland, Oostdongeradeel and Westdongeradeel. The gallows of Kollumerland was said to have been beside the fortified house of the (Groningen) castellan inhabited in 1583 by the nobleman Sippe Meckama, a site then still called *Galgevenne*. It had long disappeared by Johan Rengers' time, of course, but a certain Wittie Douwes of Anjum, in the presence of the village parson, stated to Rengers '… that he had himself seen heads hanging there'.[61]

Only the administration of rural judicial districts in the person of the *grietman* was eligible to take the initiative of setting up a gallows. This prerogative appears from a witness statement, made in 1558, referring to the

---

56 See the *Liber Beneficiorum* from 1580, Leeuwarden, Stadsarchief, inv. Singels, no. 269, fol. 10: 'het Olt Gerecht op het Vliet, … nae die zijde nae Huijsum toe'; cf. W. Dolk, *Leeuwarder straatnamen* (Leeuwarden, 1997), 48 (*Olde Galgefenne*).

57 Here the rebellious burgomaster Wybe Saeckles, who sided with the Duke of Guelders, was beheaded in 1516, see 'Landboek van Keimpe Martena', *Groot Placaat en Charterboek van Vriesland*, ed. G.F. thoe Schwartzenberg en Hohenlansberg, 3 vols. (Leeuwarden, 1768–1778) II, 97.

58 However, compare note 50.

59 See the *Joure Market Law of 1466* which provides for the pronouncement and implementation of death sentences; *Oudfriesche oorkonden*, ed. Sipma, II, no. 66.

60 *Leuwerderadeels aenbrengh gemaect int jaer 1540*, ed. J. A. Mol (Leeuwarden 1989), 95: 'In Westerlant daer Baerderadeels galge stond'.

61 *Werken van den Ommelander edelman Johan Rengers van Ten Post*, ed. H. O. Feith, 2 vols. (Groningen, 1852–1853) I, 108.

establishment of the borderline between the districts of Vredewold (Groningen) and Opsterland (Frisia). Pretty well all of the very elderly witnesses declared before *grietman* Ipo Haeyma, who was investigating the matter, that the border lay by the Friesche Palen ('Frisian boundary') and that the late Bonne Vukema, when he was the land administrator for Vredewold, 'had set up a gallows on the northern side of the aforementioned [Friesche] Palen […], and had there ordered to be hanged a certain Menko Nekens'. The execution had taken place about sixty years previously, shortly before 1500. The witnesses further gave evidence that Sywert Fossema, *grietman* for Vredewold at the time, had thirty years later re-erected the scaffold which his predecessor Bonne Vukema had put up for the execution of another miscreant.[62] Because Vredewold bordered immediately on the Frisian districts of Achtkarspelen and Opsterland west of the Lauwers, it is likely that its legal practice differed little much around 1500 from places to the west and south of the Friesche Palen. One way or another, the gallows at the Friesche Palen would seem not to have been the first in Vredewold, for as early as 1385 there is mention of a *Zudgalgha* (southern gallows) somewhere beside one of the water outlets of the five parishes of Vredewold.[63] The name would lead us to assume that at the same time in the adjacent district of Langewold there must have been a northern gallows as a counterpart.

That rural judicial districts and towns alike had the right to erect a gallows will not be self-evident to every reader. After all, the original holder of the *hagista riocht* ('highest right') in free Frisia after the demise of feudal rule was the land (*terra*) which may be seen as a communally governed continuation of the districts previously ruled by a count. In Frisia west of the river Lauwers there were three such 'counties' during the High Middle Ages: Westergo, Oostergo and Zuidergo, of which the last one had merged with Westergo in the thirteenth century. Still later, in reclaimed regions to the east and south of Westergo and Oostergo a number of small additional lands, such as Opsterland, emerged which succeeded in claiming autonomy for themselves. Through the absence of a count, these *terrae* granted permission for the founding of towns and gave them the right to exercise capital punishment. For example, in 1392, when the *grietmannen* and their co-judges of the Leppa – the southern half of Oostergo comprising Leeuwarderadeel, Tietjerksteradeel, Smallingerland and Idaarderadeel – conferred Leeuwarden the right to hang and behead.[64] At the time, Oostergo and Westergo had for a long time known judicial sub-districts designated with

---

62 *Groot Placaat en Charterboek van Vriesland*, ed. Schwartzenberg, III, 441–42.

63 *Oorkondenboek van Groningen en Drenthe*, ed. P. J. Blok *et al.*, 2 vols. (Groningen, 1896–1899) II, no. 746.

64 *Oudfriesche Oorkonden*, ed. Sipma, II, no. 3.

deel ('part'), a name which intrinsically indicates subordination. Their *grietmannen* were entitled to deal with non-capital offences. They were also involved in the exercise of high justice, but only at a central level, as members of the governing body of the *terra*.

Problematic is the time when the *grietman* and his co-judges took control of capital punishments and why they thought it necessary to exercise this right in actuality and demonstrate it in public by exhibiting the bodies of executed criminals. In order to arrive at an answer, it is useful first to review the location of the various gallows places.

4. Visible locations

Exhibiting the dead beyond the dyke, as stipulated in the law on *Schaekraef*, would appear to be more than a symbol-laden fiction. An actual location beyond the dyke can be demonstrated for at least six of these gallows sites.[65] The most clearly localizable site is probably that of Oostdongeradeel. According to Johan Rengers van Ten Post, the gallows was just north of Ezumazijl on land beyond the dyke beside the Lauwers Sea, close to a water outlet. At Workum, on the south-west coast of Westergo, the gallows was likewise located in the vicinity of a key junction of waterways. Such a location was not coincidental. The exhibition of a corpse in the border zone between land and water was especially effective; at such spots the process of decay could be witnessed by many. In this regard, the position of the Ameland gallows on the open mud flats between Hollum and Ballum was equally well chosen. The main thoroughfare passed by it and the scaffold was supremely visible to small ships passing through a gully just to the south of the island. Good visibility was also enjoyed by the gallows of Staveren, beyond the dyke behind Scharl and just to the south-east of the town. This gallows will also have served as a landmark, not far from the southern entrance to the harbour, and have sent out signals different, perhaps, from a lighthouse but just as clear and constituting just as good a reference point for sailors voyaging to and from Kampen or Amsterdam. When it appears in the sources for the first and last time in 1516, the gallows of Menaldumadeel, in a corner of the former Bildtland in Dijkshorne near Beetgumermolen, was no longer visible from the sea, since The Bildt had been definitively closed in by dykes in 1505. It was used in that year to hang a

[65] It may be supposed that these gallows beyond the dyke were among the oldest in Frisia, given the sacral character of the sentence being carried out in the border zone between land and sea. If so, the aspect of visibility would play a less important role. This seems unlikely to me, however, as in all instances we are dealing with constructions from towns and *grietenien* which with respect to their jurisdiction emancipated only later from the *terrae* of Westergo and Oostergo.

thief who had stolen twenty cows in The Bildt,[66] so that the inhabitants of the new land could take good note of the justice that was meted out to those who gravely trespass the law.

Not every Frisian gibbet lay at the edge of the sea, of course. Yet, the motivation of good visibility from the water could also be applied in districts situated on one of the great lakes. Wymbritseradeel, for example, was bordered on in the east by the Sneek lake. Its gallows was placed beside the Kruiswater, where the shipping lane from Sneek to Joure crossed the waterway from the south-west to the north-west in the direction of Leeuwarden, before meeting the huge water body of the Sneek lake. The gallows of Tietjerksteradeel would appear to have been on an elevation jutting into Bergum Lake, while that of Sloten marked the entrance to the Sloten canal from the Sloten lake.

What the sea and the lakes were to the districts in the north-west and middle, the heath was to those in the south-east: endless vistas with low horizons against which a gallows might stand out sharply. The gallows of Smallingerland and Ooststellingwerf each took up a position high on the moors at the farthest extremity of the district – right on the northern border with the adjacent country and close by a through road from which it might be clearly viewed. It seems that the gallows of Oostellingwerf even had its own hill raised for the purpose. On his *Nieuwe Kaart van Friesland* ('New Map of Friesland'), Eekhoff drew a piece of raised land within the parcel that accommodated the gallows, designating it *Galgeberg*.[67] And to cross the border between Opsterland and Groningen once more: when the *grietman* of Vredewold wanted to erect a new gallows for the execution of a wrongdoer in the 1490s, he found a suitable spot on the heath, beside the road that crossed the western border near Frieschepalen.[68]

From these seven cases it appears that the scaffold-builders selected a combination of good visibility within a spacious expanse and a spot on the outermost edge of the district, in addition to exhibition on a relatively busy route for through traffic, or even a crossroads. This was obviously done to demonstrate justice.[69] All the other gallows places that I have been able to localise score equally well for visibility along major thoroughfares. However, they do not appear in the margin but precisely in the middle of the district. The best examples are the gallows of Barradeel, Ferwerderadeel,

---

[66] H. Sannes, *Geschiedenis van Het Bildt*, 4 vols. (Franeker, 1951–1957) I, 63.

[67] W. Eekhoff, *Nieuwe atlas van de provincie Friesland, bevattende kaarten van de dertig grietenijen of gemeenten, met de daarin gelegene elf steden en haar grondgebied, alsmede van de eilanden Ameland en Schiermonnikoog* ... (Leeuwarden, 1849–1859; repr. The Hague, 1970).

[68] See note 61.

[69] E. von Künssberg, *Rechtliche Volkskunde* (Halle/S., 1936), 162–63.

Wonseradeel and Weststellingwerf. In Barradeel, the *Galgekamp* was situated halfway along the part of Barradeel that bordered on the Slachte, an important defensive inner dyke that divided the district in two. In Ferwerderadeel, the *Galgemorgen* lay on the road that went from Ferwerd past the Bethania Monastery near Foswerd to Waaxens. In Weststellingwerf, the traveller using the interregional route from Steenwijk by way of Oudeschoot and Haskerdijken to Leeuwarden, or back, would pass the gallows about a mile to the south-east of the church in Wolvega. In Wonseradeel, the gallows had been raised on the *terp* of the Wonser Weeren, beside the through road that connected the centrally situated Wons with Makkum and the southernmost villages of this *grietenie*. The gallows of Dantumadeel, too, enjoyed a central position, erected at the intersection of two important waterways: the Geestmer canal and the Galgediep, which ran from Rinsumageest to Veenwouden.

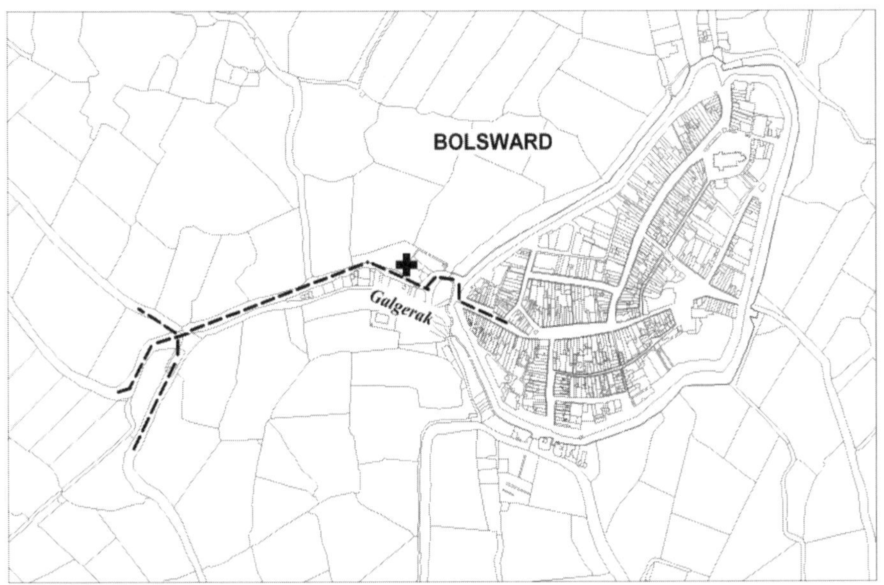

Visibility: the gallows of Bolsward within a stone's throw of the city moat

For anyone who approached or left the towns it was simply impossible to miss the gallows. It is remarkable that not only in Workum but also in Bolswerd, IJlst and Hindelopen the gallows were less than a hundred metres from the town centre, again beside the main road, whether by land or water. Apparently, the intention was that the citizens in particular should be confronted daily with the stringency of the law. Like that of Sloten, the gallows of Sneek was somewhat remoter, half a kilometre beyond the

Noorderpoort (North Gate), on the Hemdijk to IJlst. As for the gallows of Franeker, which lay even farther outside the town, we have seen that it was probably also used by the *grietenie* of Franekeradeel. These gallows possibly originally also served as the scaffold for the older and larger district of Franeker Ouddeel and the Leppa. Their central position on an important regional land and waterway corresponds with that of the gallows in Barradeel and Weststellingwerf.

5. The owners of gallows and gallows lands

Who were the owners and hence also the probable builders of the gallows? It would seem obvious to point to the administrators of towns and *gritenien*. Confirmation of their involvement may be found in connection with the huge plot of gallows land at Wolvega, which in 1832 still belonged to the *grietenie* of Weststellingwerf; but whether this was the case as early as 1500 is difficult to say.[70] We may be more certain, at least in relation to the gallows itself, about the district of Vredewold where a little before 1500 the *grietman* had erected a gallows near Friesche Palen for the hanging of Menko Nekens.[71] From this episode we may deduce that the *grietman* was responsible for the construction of the gallows, while the *grietenie* defrayed the costs.

In the Ommelanden, where the rural courts held on to the right to exercise capital punishment until 1795, the land upon which the scaffold stood was also bought by the districts. In Kantens, where no permanent gallows was available, the judge signed a provisional contract in 1727 by which he purchased half an acre of land for sixty carolus guilders, '… hetwelcke geemployeert sal worden tot een rigtplaatse' ['to be used as a place of execution'].[72] He needed it for the hanging of Rintje Jacobs, a farmer convicted of incest and infanticide. The transaction eventually failed to take place, because the convicted man had escaped and fled across the territorial border.

It is hard to establish whether both the gallows and the land upon which it stood were in the possession of the Frisian *grietenien* prior to 1515. As for the gallows situated beyond the dyke, it is known that the open land of the mud flats beyond the dyke belonged of old to the one whose farm bordered on the inside of the dyke. His was the right, so to speak, of reclamation and expansion into the newly accreted land. However, this right did not go entirely undisputed. It was overturned when The Bildt was enclosed by

70 The plot of land is not registered in the fiscal land registers (*floreenkohieren*) of 1700, probably because it was not taxed then. This could indicate a public function; other explanations are also possible.

71 See note 61.

72 Frima, *Strafproces in de Ommelanden*, 390–91.

dykes around 1500, and the new landlord, Duke Albert of Saxony, claimed this land. But the majority of newly cultivated polders along the Frisian sea coast would seem to have ended up belonging to the owners of land immediately behind the dyke. In other words, potential gallows land originally lay in private hands. One may imagine, however, that so long as the salt marshes remained unsuitable for arable land and fit only for grazing sheep, the councils of lands or *grietenien* would have had no objection to a piece of it being used for the general public weal.

On land within the dykes we find two types of owner. Around 1500, the majority of gallows plots of which the owners can be traced were in the possession of either church funds, or of descendants of chieftains (*haedlingen*) or rich freeholding peasants who at some time had possibly participated in administrating the district. To begin with the last category: the land upon which was the gallows of Franeker, Franekeradeel, and possibly also Franeker Oud Deel,[73] belonged to Eedwer Sjaerda in 1510. She was heiress to the Franeker nobleman Sicke Douwes Sjaerda who, although an Aylva on his father's side, had taken over the imperium of the early fifteenth-century Sjaerda family.[74] Both his father's father-in-law, Sicka, after whom he had been named, and his own father had ruled over Franekeradeel during the last quarter of the fourteenth and the first decades of the fifteenth century. The surviving register of the judicial procedure for Franekeradeel for the years 1406 to 1438 shows that this dynasty of chieftains owned so many enfranchised homesteads in this district that for about half of the period they were able to appoint the *grietman*. It is therefore probable that the Sjaerdas, on account of their judicial functions, had ordered the gallows to be erected on their own land. Another possibility is that they had taken it over from a previous chieftain.

A similar connection may be found between the office of *grietman* and the ownership of gallows land in IJlst and Sloten. The *Slootmanna galgha* recorded in 1496 stood on the Sloten Lake, near the entrance of the canal leading up to this small town. Retrospective research into land ownership indicates that the land on which it was situated belonged to the Harinxma family in 1700. Their forefathers had founded the small town of Sloten in the early fifteenth century and had ruled it for long after as urban chieftains. The *Galgeland* in IJlst was in 1542 the demonstrable property of Sytse Harinxma of the eponymous chieftain family, related to the Harinxmas of

73 The district of Franeker before autonomy was granted to its five sub-divisions.

74 *Friese testamenten tot 1550*, ed. G. Verhoeven and J. A. Mol (Leeuwarden, 1994), no. 77, p. 149.

Sloten. For the whole of the fifteenth century they had ruled IJlst as urban lords.[75]

Striking once more is the case of Rinsumageest, where the gallows plot bordered on ground backing onto Tjaarda Estate. This estate, including its keep, represented the centre of power from which for much of the sixteenth century the Tjaardas and their judicial predecessors exercised hegemony in Dantumadeel and a large area of northern Oostergo.

Eloquent in this respect is the gallows place belonging to the south-western *fiarndel* (quarter) of Tietjerksteradeel. Like so many other ones in the fifteenth century, this large *grietenie* had to cope with centrifugal forces urging the judges of the quarters of which it was comprised to decentralise the administration of justice and government.[76]

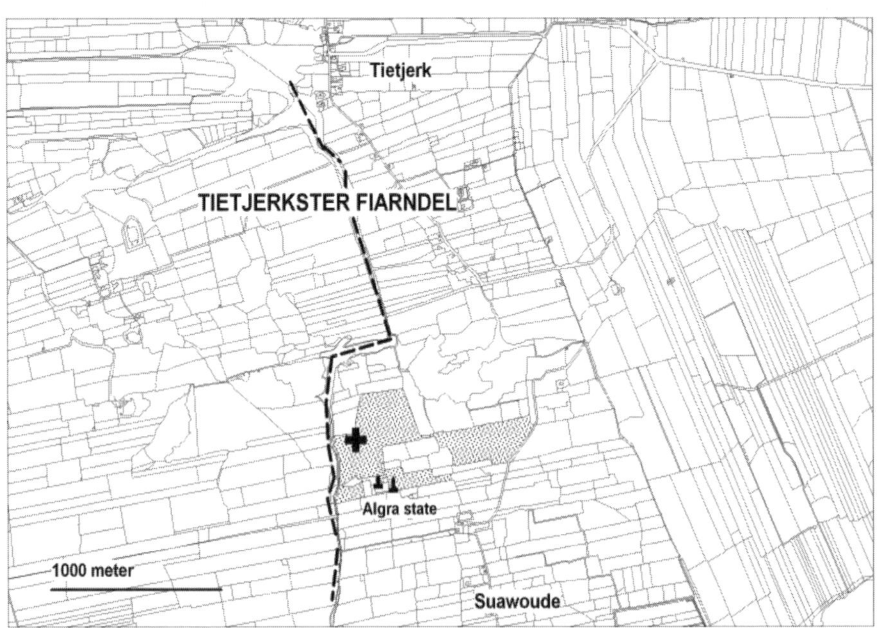

Builders and chronology: gallows on the land of Ghield Aelgera, freeholder and *grietman* of the Tietjerk *fiarndel*, built around 1490

For example, in 1481 the Tietjerk *fiarndel* formed an independent alliance with the town of Leeuwarden in order to gain protection and end

[75] 'Item ick selfs in der Ilst ben bruycken ses pondematen, hiettende dat Galgelant', see Leeuwarden, Tresoar, Archief Tjaardastate, inv. no. 421 (T313).

[76] Compare the situation in Baarderadeel, where around 1440 the various quarters greatly dissented one another's share in the criminal proceedings and the places at which this should be carried out: *Oudfriesche Oorkonden*, ed. Sipma, II, no. 26.

violence and legal insecurity.[77] One of the stipulations of the treaty was that the town and the *grietnie* would together choose the *grietman*. The document ends with the conclusion that the *fiarndel* would be 'al heel afwessa fan Tyetzerkeradeel ende hiara riuchten' ['entirely separate from Tietjerksteradeel and its legal rules']. As a result, it now formed an independent sub-*grietenie*. The alliance with Leeuwarden would seem not to have lasted long because this town, after the 'beer uprising' of 1487, fell once more under the custody of the mighty chieftains of the Schiering faction.[78] The Tietjerk quarter, however, retained its autonomy. In 1491 its three villages of Rijperkerk, Tietjerk and Suawoude together joined the great alliance between the town of Groningen and a number of chieftains and monasteries in Oostergo.[79] Tietjerk was represented by the rich freeholder Ghield Aelgera, the owner of a local estate and a great deal of land. It can be no coincidence that a *Galgewier* may be traced precisely to the property of the Aelgera Estate, at a well visible spot on the waterway that connects the three named villages.[80] The names of the *grietmannen* may not have come down to us, but we are surely not jumping to conclusions when we assume that Ghield Aelgera exercised the office of *grietman* himself and erected a gallows on his own land in the interests of justice in the three villages under his wing. Freeholders and chieftains in their office of *grietman* had to provide the means of execution and demonstration in order to support their authority. What would have been simpler for them but to build these constructions on their own property?

From circa 1500 onwards, as I have briefly remarked, gallows land may also be found in the possession of church funds. This was the case, for example, in Leeuwarden, where more than half of the *Galgefenne* in 1501 belonged to Dom Tzalling, a chantry priest. In that year he willed it to a new memorial fund, founded by himself to be associated with St Vitus's church in Leeuwarden.[81] In Sneek, the *Galgeland* outside the North Gate on the Hemdijk belonged to St Barbara's fund, founded in the late fifteenth-century. And in Ferwerderadeel in 1700, St Martin's church in Ferwerd is registered as the owner of the *Galegemorgen*. How these church funds became owners of gallows lands may only be guessed. It is not unthinkable

---

[77] *Ibid.* no. 91; compare no. 102 of the same (April 1482) in which also the Trynwâlden, the north-western quarter of Tietjerksteradeel, is registered as a separate *grietenie*, among others by Leeuwarden, to ensure that *herich riucht* ('proper law') was also carried out here.

[78] M. Schroor, 'Leeuwarden tussen Middeleeuwen en Nieuwe tijd', *Leeuwarden 750–2000. Hoofdstad van Friesland*, ed. R. Kunst *et al.* (Franeker, 1999), 78–109, at 87.

[79] *Pax Groningana*, ed. Oosterhout *et al.*, no. 61, p. 83.

[80] On Algra Estate, see P. N. Noomen, *De stinzen in middeleeuws Friesland en hun bewoners* (Hilversum, [forthcoming]).

[81] *Friese testamenten*, ed. Verhoeven and Mol, no. 63, p. 122.

that such funds owed these gallows lands to administrators of a *grietenie* or town who approached fund administrators to allow them to build gallows on their land. But it is also possible that the lands came into their possession through gifting on the part of the builders or owners of gallows or their descendants. Vicarages and church fabrics, after all, were often the chosen recipients of supplementary memorial gifts by families of substance. We must therefore leave unresolved the question of whether the taboo on gallows represented an extra motive for these families to donate such lands.

6. When and why

In the period when counts still reigned over Frisia, exercise of the death penalty lay in the hands of the count who, as a servant of the king, practised this right with the help of prominent judicial officials recruited from within his region. In the course of the thirteenth century the count's rule was set aside in Frisia and responsibility was assumed collectively by the administrations of county districts, now independent. These districts called themselves *universitates terrae* ('land communities'), of which Westergo and Oostergo were the most important. In other words, these communally administrated lands as such were not novel entities. They had also earlier had sub-divisions within which the law was enacted at a lower level by the count's bailiffs. Their task was now taken over by *grietmannen* and their co-judges, who were elected from the ranks of freeholders. From their independency onwards, the *terrae* were governed by boards of judges comprised of representatives of the *grietmannen* and co-judges of the separate districts. The members of such a board are represented one by one on the thirteenth-century seal of Oostergo: a total of eighteen persons in two groups of nine, nine for the northern part and nine for the southern part of the land. These boards of judges regularly convened to conduct administrative business concerning the whole region, such as interregional alliances, but also for higher judicial matters. The council dealt with all cases that exceeded a fixed amount of compensation, and in addition functioned corporately as a court of appeal. The sources describe their competence as the *hagista riocht* ('highest domain').[82] In Franeker Oud Deel, this right was known as the *keysers riocht* because it was considered to stem from the emperor. High domain included as a matter of course the right to judge capital offence. Supposedly, the thirteenth-century process of communalisation initially will have brought little change in the judicial practise, trial procedure and the

82 G. Overdiep and J. C. Tjessinga, *De rechtsomgang van Franekeradeel 1406–1438* (Franeker, 1950), 146–52.

jurisdiction itself. Westergo and Oostergo, together with their sub-districts,[83] will each have had their own gallows even before the period of Frisian Freedom began. This supposition implies that around 1250 there may have been no more than five gallows lands in all of Frisia west of the Lauwers.

In view of the relatively small number of five gallows, we may ask when the proliferation of these penal instruments occurred. In what period did towns and *grietenien* each acquire their own gallows-and-wheel? Or put another way: taking as a point of departure that the right to execute and exhibit criminals flowed from the right to exercise capital punishment, when did the administrative boards of the *terrae* begin to allow towns and sub-districts within their lands to pronounce sentences on 'neck and head'? At first sight these questions would seem easy to answer for the Frisian towns by taking as a starting point the year when they obtained their municipal rights. But this is tricky, because for many a Frisian town it is unclear when they acquired their independent status. With the exception of Staveren,[84] municipal rights in Frisia were not conferred by a count or any other lord, so that we have little documentation on this matter. Furthermore, consideration must be given to the fact that not every settlement with urban dimensions immediately exercised capital punishment or was allowed to exercise it. Trade centres and places with central functions were first and foremost interested in obtaining market privileges with their accompanying judicial rights. Gaining the right of high criminal justice belonged to a later phase in the process of becoming independent. This becomes especially apparent in the case of Franeker: in 1401 and 1417,[85] the town community was granted market rights and many other privileges by the administration board of Franeker Oud Deel but not the permission to exercise high justice. Only in 1474 did the town of Franeker receive this right, from the confederated towns and *grietenien* of Westergo.[86]

In as far as we know, Leeuwarden was the first town to which a *terra* granted the right to exercise high justice, an authority conveyed by the *grietmannen* of the Leppa in 1392. However, the year may not be taken as a

[83] For Westergo: Franeker Oud Deel, Wonseradeel and Wymbritseradeel; for Oostergo: the Northern Nyogen and the Leppa.

[84] As early as the eleventh century, Staveren possessed market and other privileges which were confirmed and enhanced by the Count of Holland in the thirteenth century. Consequently, until 1411 Staveren may be considered as having been a town that belonged to Holland.

[85] *Oudfriesche Oorkonden*, ed. Sipma, II, nos. 7 and 10.

[86] *Ibid.* no. 77.

datum antequem because the phrasing of the privilege expressly refers to the right as exercised 'of old'[87] by the alderman and magistrates.

It is more difficult to give a date with respect to the other nine towns. The earliest municipality rights for Bolsward and Workum date from 1399.[88] But because they were granted by Albert, duke of Bavaria and count of Holland, who ruled over Frisia for only a short while, it is questionable how firmly founded they were or whether Westergo and Wonseradeel consented after Albert's departure. The practising of capital punishment was the implicit reserve of the bailiff who bore this authority on behalf of the count in the towns named, which does not exclude the possibility of Bolsward and Workum themselves being allowed to erect a gallows. The Bolsward bylaws of 1455, adopted by Sneek in 1456, mentions the hanging of miscreants. This means that in these years both towns must have had a gallows at their disposal. That Sneek also before this time had such a penal instrument may be deduced from a document of 1424 which survives only in copy. In it, the administrators of Wymbritseradeel grant rights to the council of IJlst to judge all misdeeds, including capital crimes, such as deadly arson, in the same way as in Sneek.[89] However, this document has recently been conclusively proven to be spurious,[90] so that the *datum antequem* for IJlst is 1450. In this year, a committee of priests from Wymbritseradeel confirmed that the *eheer* (co-judge to the *grietman*) Epa Harinxma had rightfully dealt with all judicial cases *cleyn ende groot* ('small and large') presenting in IJlst.[91]

We have no data for Dokkum, Hindeloopen and Sloten.[92] Dokkum is present in the sources as an urban settlement as early as 1298; Hindeloopen (1368) and Sloten (1422) make their appearance somewhat later. In view of Franeker, all these little towns do not necessarily have had the right of high jurisdiction as from these years. This was neither the case for Sneek and

---

87 *Ibid.* no. 3 (19 July 1392): '… thet dy aulderman a Lyouwerth ende sine schepenan moghen ende moeten vp halden ende wr riochta alle misdeghe lyoede ther misdwaet a Lyouwerd deys jefta nachtes with enghen bur jefta engghen wte bur … als hya al eer tijt fan aldis habbeth biriucht wr hals ende wr haud.'

88 *De oorlogen van hertog Albrecht van Beieren met de Friezen in de laatste jaren der XIVe eeuw*, ed. E. Verwijs (Utrecht, 1869), 509–16, esp. 511: '… quaeden feyten die aen tlijf gaen.'

89 *Oudfriesche Oorkonden*, ed. Sipma, II, no.11 (20 June 1424).

90 O. Vries, '*Al ting sonder falikant*. Die Arglistformel in den altfriesischen Urkunden', *UW* 46 (1997), 150–68, at 163: the *narratio* seems to be derived from a real charter, but the closing ratification and dating with the formula *Al ting sonder falicant* ('everything without deceit') implies that it cannot be much later than about 1470.

91 *Groot Placaat en Charterboek van Vriesland*, ed. Schwartzenberg, I, 538.

92 See the facts cited by J. C. M. Cox, *Repertorium van de stadsrechten in Nederland. 'Quod vulgariter statreghte nuncupatur'* (The Hague, 2005), 88, 138 and 216.

IJlst, two towns which had presented themselves as communities of burghers since 1317. One weighty argument in this connection is the fact that up until the beginning of the fifteenth century the Frisian *terrae* west of the Lauwers had granted the towns no role in the political decision making.[93] Only in 1426 did the towns belonging to the *mena reed der steddena* ('the general council of the towns') win representation in the diet, the highest board of the *terrae* that up until then had been run by prelates, *grietmannen* and co-judges. If the councils of the lands were thus attempting to keep the towns politically impotent for as long as possible, then the same strategy probably also applied to the room they gave to the towns in matters judicial. Moreover, it should also be borne in mind that Westergo and Oostergo with their sub-districts attached so much importance to high jurisdiction that they sabotaged negotiations with William IV in May 1345. They were quite ready to follow the count of Holland on military expeditions and were even prepared to grant him permission to build castles, but 'dat hoghe gerecht en woudens sij hem nyet verlyen' ['... they did not want to confer to him the right of high domain'].[94] For all these reasons I am inclined – leaving Leeuwarden and Staveren aside – to date the building of gallows in or near the Frisian towns to not earlier than the second decade of the fifteenth century.[95]

If it seems a challenge chronologically to place the granting of high jurisdiction to the towns, facts relating to the countryside are equally difficult to interpret, perhaps even more so. Dates are known for only three *grietenien*: Kollumerland, the Tietjerk quarter of Tietjerksteradeel, and Vredewold immediately east of the Lauwers. The erection of gallows in Kollumerland can be associated with the encroachment of power from the town of Groningen into Oostergo in the second half of the fifteenth century. In 1467, Groningen concluded a thirty-year treaty with Kollumerland to avert all violence and robbery. The most significant stipulation of the treaty was the building of a small block-house at Kollum. A group of military was to be housed there under leadership of a castellan to warrant the preservation of the jurisdiction.[96] This *casteel* was indeed built, fortified by bulwarks and moats. It lay to the north village centre, west of the Ried. After the Groningen gar-

---

[93] O. Vries,'De stêden oan it roer. It tiidrek fan stedske supremasy yn Fryslân (1482–1486)', *IB* 62 (2000), 73–99, at 75.

[94] J. A. Mol, 'Graaf Willem IV, de Hollands-Friese oorlog van 1344/1345 en de Friese kloosters', *Negen eeuwen Friesland-Holland. Geschiedenis van een haat-liefde-verhouding*, ed. Ph.H. Breuker and A. Janse (Zutphen and Leeuwarden, 1997), 94–108, at 102.

[95] No gallows is known for Harlingen. The same applies to fifteenth-century market places, such as Joure, which did not succeed in attaining autonomy.

[96] *Pax Groningana*, ed. Oosterhout *et al.*, no. 19.

rison had been expelled by the Duke of Saxony, it was acquired in about 1500 by Feye Riemersma, also known as Meckema, whose father-in-law had, ironically enough, opposed its building. Johan Rengers van Ten Post, writing in 1583, noted that the gallows of Kollumerland was placed beside the former castellan's house. Because the treaty of 1467 provided for the application of the death penalty for thieves, murderers, rapists and nightly robbers, it seems reasonable to assume that the Groningen forces had erected this gallows in the same year.[97]

It may also be assumed that the gallows of the aforementioned Tietjerk *fiarndel* was built with the co-operation of the Groningen forces, shortly after 1491. There was already a gallows in Tietjerksteradeel, on the banks of Bergum Lake, but it is clear that at this time the *grietman* and his co-judges were no longer capable of maintaining justice in all parts of their jurisdiction. Why else would this Tietjerk quarter have sought an alliance with Leeuwarden in 1481? As it is, this treaty still proceeded from the idea that capital cases (*deer an't lyf gaet*) would be sentenced by the town. This means that the judicial authorities in the *fiarndel* appropriated capital rights only after the rupture with Leeuwarden in 1487, most probably even after their alignment with the Dokkum treaty of 1491. In Vredewold, east of the Lauwers, we have already seen that the *grietman* took the initiative of setting up a gallows just before 1500.

In these three cases it would seem that the building of a gallows resulted from a desire to offer inhabitants judicial security. The ruling judges had to show, by whatever means, that justice would be done. The Frisian lands adduce several reasons in the written treaties by which they placed themselves under the protection of the city of Groningen. Conspicuous amongst these reasons is the great dissatisfaction over the lack of punishment meted out in cases of violence often stemming from an increasing assumption of power by chieftains and the inability of the overarching lands to moderate this.[98] The strong arm needed to seize wrongdoers and bring them to justice effectively was willingly lent by the expansive city of Groningen.

This was in accord with practice already well established in the Ommelanden, where the radiation of judicial security was promoted energetically by the highest levels of power. In 1427, the Focke Ukena Statutes, voluntarily accepted by the lands between Ems and Lauwers, stipulated that each *ampt* ('sub-district') of these lands had to have erected a gallows before

97 See the entry for Meckema in Noomen, *De stinzen in middeleeuws Friesland* [forthcoming].

98 *Pax Groningana*, ed. Oosterhout *et al.*, no. 16 (Achtkarspelen 1458), no. 17 (Opsterlân 1461), no. 19 (Kollumerlân 1467).

Whitsuntide,[99] so that 'alman ziin goed dat hem God verleent, desto vredeliker moghe broken' ['... every man may even more peacefully enjoy his good which God has lent him']. This new organisation of jurisdiction[100] had no place any longer for the existing diets and the chamber of Groningen chieftains as courts of appeal – the East Frisian 'chieftain' Focke Ukena who tried to establish a territorial lordship in the region was trying to repel as far as possible the powerful reach of the city of Groningen. Yet, his intention was to give top-down form to the monopoly on violence, which included fighting criminality. In this respect, Focke Ukena was adopting the recent territorial political programme of the Tom Brok dynasty realised east of the river Ems.[101] The Ommeland chieftains who supported Ukena will have seen the model opportunistically, namely as a possibility to strengthen their position of power locally. However, Focke Ukena's judicial reform was probably never introduced. The city of Groningen launched a successful counteroffensive, recovered and even extended its influence in the Ommelanden, also by concluding treaties with the Westerkwartier (the lands west of the city), Hunsingo and Fivelgo. It is not known whether these treaties provided for the erection of regional gallows. Given the later politics of Groningen in relation to Frisian lands, it seems extremely likely that in this matter it would have adopted the politics of Focke Ukena.

For *grietenien* in Frisia west of the Lauwers that were less enamoured by the Groningen ambitions the motivation to radiate a sense of judicial security in turbulent times must nonetheless have weighed heavily. Increasingly widespread partisanship and military escalation of feuding through the taking on of foreign mercenaries was unbalancing the political system, leading to growing criminality; and this in turn gave rise to the need for symbols of strict and severe justice at local level.

The question is, however, whether the proliferation of gallows in the countryside can be ascribed only to these event-related factors. After all, the three datable examples concern only the final phase in the period of the gallows, when sub-*grietenien* and split-off parts desired judicial autonomy. It cannot be other than that self-sufficiency on the part of the 'ordinary' *grietenien* preceded this, probably shortly after the majority of towns had won the right to exercise capital punishment from the lands, so in the course

99 *Ostfriesisches Urkundenbuch*, ed. E. Friedländer, 2 vols. (Emden, 1878–1881; repr. Wiesbaden, 1968), nos. 367, 1769: provision is also made herein for the hanging on this gallows of all thieves convicted of stealing 'over' four guilders.

100 W. J. Formsma, 'De middeleeuwse vrijheid', *Historie van Groningen, Stad en Land*, ed. W. J. Formsma *et al.*, 2nd ed. (Groningen, 1981), 77–106, at 97–99.

101 H. van Lengen, 'Bauernfreiheit und Häuptlingsherrlichkeit im Mittelalter', *Ostfriesland. Geschichte und Gestalt einer Kulturlandschaft*, ed. K.-E. Behre and H. van Lengen (Aurich, 1996), 113–34, at 128–31.

of the fifteenth century, roughly between 1425 and 1475. The process of transferring high judicial power and other rights from the overarching level of lands to towns and districts points to nothing more than a fragmentation and erosion of the power of the lands and their councils. This process indisputably led to a weakening in the structure of communal administration, which in turn resulted in instability. But it was, as such, a process with its own dynamics. This is clear from the Groningen Ommelanden, where the judicial system within the lands became more and more decentralised until there were judicial districts comprising no more than a single hamlet. In contrast to the case of Frisia west of the Lauwers, the system in the Ommelanden was able to carry on functioning without cover from the land councils simply because the city of Groningen filled the power vacuum.

The gallows, then, are also indicators of a self-timing political and judicial fragmentation process whereby both *grietenie* and town, whether or not under the leadership of dominant chieftains, demanded their self-evident autonomy. This development is traceable to some degree in relation to Franeker Oud Deel which in the first half of the fifteenth century had to relinquish power and custodial responsibilities to the newly existent subdistricts of Barradeel, Menaldumadeel, Franekeradeel, Baarderadeel and Hennaarderadeel.[102] Initially, the *grietmannen* of these districts came to Franeker, each to deal with the judicial business of their individual districts, but by 1440 the *grietman* of Baarderadeel was already administering the law in Baard.[103] Whether he and his colleagues in the other sub-districts by then also addressed cases demanding the death penalty is not known. I think that this is improbable because the rulers of the Franeker Oud Deel hesitated until 1474 to award the town of Franeker the right of high criminal justice. However this may be, within the given constellation the gallows was meant to demonstrate hard-won independence rather than to radiate judicial power.[104]

There is, finally, another indication that signalling of autonomy was as much, or even more so, the purpose of these instruments than deterrence, containment and prevention of crime. This indication lies in the relatively high number of gallows in proportion to the number of wrongdoers actually sentenced to death and the size of the population. It is useful in this con-

---

[102] See the thorough survey by Overdiep and Tjessinga, *De rechtsomgang van Franekeradeel*, 145.

[103] *Oudfriesche Oorkonden*, ed. Sipma, II, no. 26.

[104] It is also as a symbol of autonomy that gallows were targeted during sieges and other enemy actions: its destruction undermined, as it were, the authority of the party under siege; see Spierenburg, *Spectacle of Suffering*, 57–58. There are no known examples relating to Frisian lands, but revealing in this context is the toppling of the Groningen gallows by Saxon soldiers that besieged the town in September 1500; see note 44.

nection to know that after 1515 only one gallows was available for the whole of Frisia (the one to the south-west of Leeuwarden). During the sixteenth century no more than four or five people per year were executed for the entire province,[105] and not even every one of these was exhibited after the execution. There is no reason to assume that in the fourteenth and fifteenth centuries more people were hanged, beheaded or broken on the wheel than during the sixteenth century. On the contrary, research into the frequency of death sentencing in Europe in this period teaches us that strict punishment came into its own only after 1500.[106] There are, it is true, few statistics available, but what figures we have confirm the trend sketched above.[107] In Mechelen in the Southern Netherlands, the population of which vacillated at around 25,000 in the fifteenth and sixteenth centuries, 203 and 255 wrongdoers, respectively, were sentenced: an average of two to 2.5 per year. In Brussels, with its population of about 35,000 in the second half of the fifteenth century, the hangman was called upon to fulfil his duty 535 times in the fifteenth century, and 488 in the sixteenth century,[108] which is about five times per year. This figure complies with that of the North-German port town of Lübeck, of similar size. There 471 sentences were carried out over a period of ninety years (1371–1460). This relatively high number may be associated with the extensive judicial region, which extended well beyond the walls of the town. In Frankfurt am Main, judges gave out only 318 death sentences in the 160 years between 1401 and 1560, an average of no more than two per year. Nearer to Frisia, in the town of Utrecht, with a population of about 10,000 inhabitants at the turn of the sixteenth century, the fifteenth century certainly saw no more than two men executed per year.[109] These statistics are, all in all, not so shocking. We may indeed conclude from them that there was always someone dangling on the end of a rope in the large cities of Europe. However, even taking an average of five per year for Frisia west of the Lauwers, with an estimated population around 1511 of about 70,000 people, this figure – twice as many as in the sixteenth century – still implies that very few people were exhibited upon its dozens of gallows-and-wheels. The data for Vredewold indicate that after

[105] R. S. Roarda, *It Algera-Algra skaei, 1425–1955*, vol. 1 (Leeuwarden, 1956), 28, gives a figure of 529 executed persons for the period 1519–1600 (against only 129 in the seventeenth century); but these 529 included more than 100 'heretics' and a great number of rebels. In normal circumstances no more than four to five criminals were sentenced to death.

[106] Berents, 'Galg en Rad', 91–92, 94, 99.

[107] Many of the relevant facts are provided by Maes, *Vijf eeuwen stedelijk strafrecht*, 387–89.

[108] F. Vanhemelryck, 'De beul van Brussel en zijn werk (XIV–XIX eeuw)', *Bijdragen voor de Geschiedenis der Nederlanden* 19 (1964–1965), 181–216, at 185–87.

[109] Berents, *Misdaad in de Middeleeuwen*, 38.

the execution of Menko Nekens thirty years passed before another criminal was sentenced to hang there.[110] In the meanwhile the gallows stood rotting. Things will not have been much different in many other *grietenien* and towns.

Conclusion

What is the result of my inquiry into the function, number and distribution of exhibition scaffolds in Frisia west of the Lauwers? First of all, I have made clear that the death sentence was indeed carried out in this part of late-medieval Frisia despite the fundamental principle of traditional Frisian Law that the Free Frisian had the right to compensate with money even the gravest misdeeds, including manslaughter. It is impossible to say how often death sentences were executed. There must have been practical procedures and supporting actions for which the lands were the responsible authority charged with the execution. Secondly, my investigation has shown that by the end of the fifteenth century pretty well every town and *grietenie* had its own gallows-and-wheel. The gallows stood without fail in a prominent, eye-catching position; for the towns this would be near the outer town wall or moat, beside a thoroughfare; for the *grietenien* in the middle or precisely on the edge of the judicial area, but always visible from afar. It is difficult to date the erection of gallows in the individual towns and *grietenien* detached from the interrelation between the lands and their earliest sub-districts. Because the erection of gallows was the result of the transference of an extraordinarily essential right from overarching to regional and even to local level, it seems that we are dealing with a process of communal decentralisation. The available data suggests to me that the majority of Frisian towns were unable to exercise capital punishment and consequently build a gallows much before the second quarter of the fifteenth century. It may be taken that the *grietenien* were not lagging far behind in acquiring this right. The implication of this late date is that the gallows identified in my paper were in actual use for only a relatively short period of time. As far as their general function is concerned, in Frisia as in other towns and rural districts throughout the Europe of those days the gallows served both as a deterrent for the prevention of crime and as a demonstration to subjects and strangers alike that the town or the *grietenie* was completely independent in judicial matters. In this respect, Frisia west of the Lauwers is exceptional for its large number of gallows. If we may assume that no more criminals were sentenced to death on average in Frisia than elsewhere during the fifteenth century, then given the size of population we have reason enough to infer that corpses hung relatively infrequently upon the Frisian gallows-and-wheels.

---

[110] See note 61.

Therefore, in as far as both functions may be separated, their symbolic function in spreading an aura of judicial and political independence was more important than their warning function. The sparse number of datable facts, however, forces us to be circumspect. Further research into the distribution and chronology of gallows in the Frisian lands east of the Lauwers, especially in the Ommelanden and Ostfriesland, may offer some clarification here.[111]

[111] My thanks are due to Onno Hellinga, Otto Knottnerus, Han Nijdam and Oebele Vries for their many directions, facts and comments.

Die voraltfriesischen Personennamen der Runeninschriften auf dem Webschwert von Westeremden, dem Schwertchen von Arum und anderen Denkmälern

Robert Nedoma

I

Das Corpus der auf uns gekommenen friesischen Runeninschriften ist nicht allzu umfangreich; nach derzeitigem Kenntnisstand handelt es sich um ca. zwanzig Texte meist kürzeren oder kürzesten Umfangs.[1] Nicht alle Inschriften sind hinreichend lesbar, und nicht alle hinreichend lesbaren Inschriften sind auch hinreichend deutbar; nicht zuletzt ist auch die Morphologie der in den Runeninschriften bezeugten voraltfriesischen sprachlichen Formen bisweilen schwer zu beurteilen. Daß eine vergleichsweise große Vielfalt verschiedener Inschriftenträger entgegentritt (Gruppen bilden immerhin Kämme und Kammzubehör sowie Münzen),[2] erschwert die Interpretationsarbeit zusätzlich, da nicht immer mit bestimmten 'Wirkungsabsichten' der runenpigraphischen Texte und von bekannten Formularen bzw. Textsorten ausgegangen werden kann. Dennoch steht außer Frage, daß ein näherer Blick auf die karge runenepigraphische Überlieferung, die das

---

[1] Eine heutigen Ansprüchen genügende handbuchartige Gesamtedition der friesischen Runeninschriften fehlt. Die klassische Abhandlung ist K. Düwel und W.-D. Tempel, 'Knochenkämme mit Runeninschriften aus Friesland. Mit einer Zusammenstellung aller bekannten Runenkämme und einem Beitrag zu den friesischen Runeninschriften', *Palaeohistoria* 14 (1968 [1970]), 353–91; jüngere Materialzusammenstellungen bieten A. Quak, 'Runica Frisica', *Aspects*, 357–70: 360 ff.; K. Düwel, 'Friesen: Runen-Inschr[iften]', *Reallexikon*, X,1–2 (1998), 28–29; T. Looijenga, 'Checklist Frisian Runic Inscriptions', *Frisian Runes and Neighbouring Traditions*, T. Looijenga und A. Quak, Hg. (= ABäG 45 [Amsterdam und Atlanta, 1996]), 91–108: 91 ff.; Dies., *Texts & Contexts of the Oldest Runic Inscriptions*. The Northern World 4 (Leiden, 2003), 299 ff.; C. Giliberto, *Le iscrizioni runiche sullo sfondo della cultura frisone altomedievale*. Göppinger Arbeiten zur Germanistik 679 (Göppingen, 2000), 49 ff.

[2] Kämme (4): AMAY, HOOGEBEINTUM, OOSTUM, TOORNWERD; Kammzubehör (2): FERWERD, KANTENS; Münzen (4): FOLKESTONE, HARLINGEN, SCHWEINDORF, UNBEKANNTER FUNDORT (in London aufbewahrter Goldsolidus).

alte Friesland zu bieten hat, die Mühe lohnt: schließlich ergeben sich von hier aus wichtige Erkenntnisse über einen Sprachstand, der uns sonst aufgrund der Quellenlage – die literarische Überlieferung setzt ja erst mehrere Jahrhunderte nach der friesischen 'Runenzeit' ein – weitgehend verborgen bleibt.

II

Eine der am besten deutbaren friesischen Runeninschriften, vielleicht sogar 'the simplest of the inscriptions'[3] überhaupt, ist auf dem vorderen Teil eines 21 cm langen Webschwerts aus Eibenholz angebracht, das aus einer bei Westeremden (Gemeinde Loppersum, Prov. Groningen, Niederlande) gelegenen Terp stammt; Objekt und Text ('WESTEREMDEN I') gehören wohl spätestens in das (späte) 8. Jahrhundert bzw. (frühe) 9. Jahrhundert.[4] Die nicht übermäßig sorgfältig eingeritzte rechtsläufige Runeninschrift ist mit hinreichender Wahrscheinlichkeit **a$_2$dug$_2$islu ⁝ m͡eþ̣g$_2$isuhḷdu** (**a**$_2$ = ᚨ, **g**$_2$ = ᛄ) zu lesen.[5]

---

3 R. I. Page, *An Introduction to English Runes*, 2nd ed. (Woodbridge, 1999), 100.

4 Die stratigraphische Datierung von A. E. van Giffen, 'Mededeeling omtrent het systematisch onderzoek, verricht in de jaren 1928, 1929 en 1930', *Jaarverslag van de Vereniging voor Terpenonderzoek* 13–15 ([1928–]1931), 16–46: 24 ist *opinio communis*, eine genauere zeitliche Bestimmung mit naturwissenschaftlichen Methoden scheint (bislang) noch nicht vorgenommen worden zu sein. – In der dargebotenen Form nicht nachvollziehbar Looijenga, 'Checklist', 96 f.; Dies., *Texts & Contexts*, 311 ('No date').

5 J. M. N. Kapteyn, 'Zwei Runeninschriften aus der Terp von Westeremden', *BGdSL* 57 (1933), 160–226: 160 ff. (Abb.: Taf. 1); H. Arntz und H. Zeiß, *Gesamtausgabe der älteren Runendenkmäler*. I: *Die einheimischen Runendenkmäler des Festlandes* (Leipzig 1939; im folgenden zitiert als: *ERF*), Nr. 37 (Abb.: Taf. XXXIV und XLIV). Vgl. ferner Quak, 'Runica Frisica', 364; Düwel, 'Friesen: Runeninschriften', 28; Giliberto, *Iscrizioni runiche*, 89 ff.; Looijenga, 'Checklist', 91 und 96 f.; Dies., *Texts & Contexts*, 311 f. Die ältere Literatur verbucht U. Schnall, *Bibliographie der Runeninschriften nach Fundorten*. II: *Die Runeninschriften des europäischen Kontinents*. Abh. Akademie der Wissenschaften in Göttingen, Philolog.-Histor. Kl., 3. F., 80 (Göttingen, 1973), 85.

Abweichend von der herrschenden Praxis (sog. Dickins-Page-System) verwende ich für die (anglo-)friesischen Runeninschriften hier und im folgenden ein nicht-interpretatives Transliterationssystem, für das gilt: **a**$_1$ = ᚫ ('**æ**'), **a**$_2$ = ᚪ und (exklusiv fries.) ᚨ ('**a**'), **a**$_3$ = ᚩ ('**o**'), **o** = ᛟ, **g**$_2$ = ᛄ ('**j**'). Der wesentliche Vorteil dieser (nur) auf den ersten Blick weniger übersichtlichen Methode besteht in der Eineindeutigkeit: die graphemische Ebene wird nicht verlassen, und es wird keine Vorentscheidung über tatsächliche oder vermeintliche Graphem-Phon(em)-Korrelationen getroffen. – Was die Transliteration von ᛄ als **g**$_2$ betrifft, so bleibt unklar, ob die 'Sternrune' ᛄ in Friesland als Abkömmling der alten *j*-Rune ᛃ, ᛃ, ᛅ (wie in Skandinavien) entstanden ist: rein formal handelt es sich eher um eine alte *g*-Rune ᚷ **g**$_1$ mit einem Diakritikon ᛁ (das dann wohl [+ palatal] indiziert; das 'Basiszeichen' ᚷ ist in den friesischen Runeninschriften nicht belegt); vgl. auch D. Parsons, 'Anglo-Saxon Runes in Continental Manuscripts', *Runische Schriftkultur in kontinental-skandinavischer und -angelsächsischer Wechselbeziehung*, K. Düwel et al.,

Abb. 1: Webschwert von Westeremden (nach Arntz, *ERF*, Taf. XLIV: Abb. 37).

Eine Besonderheit stellt die Tripelbinderune Nr. 9-11 **meþ̣** dar,[6] deren letzter Bestandteil (i.e. Winkel des **þ**) schwer zu erkennen ist. Auffällig ist ferner der überlange untere Zweig von Rune Nr. 16 ᚺ **h**, der sogar den Stab der nachfolgenden Rune kreuzt; in der Frage, ob es sich bei dieser Rune (i.e. Nr. 17) um ein **l** oder ein **i** handelt, entscheiden sich sowohl Kapteyn als auch Arntz letztlich für **l**.[7] Daß in oder zwischen den Runen Nr. 16 und 17 noch eine i-Rune ᛁ 'versteckt' wäre,[8] ist eine alte, methodologisch jedoch kaum rechtzufertigende Annahme, die heutzutage auch keine Fürspreche-(rinnen) mehr findet.[9]

Ohne Zweifel handelt es sich um einen Dreiworttext, in dem zwei zweigliedrige Anthroponyme, **$a_2$du-$g_2$islu** m. und **$g_2$isu-hḷdu** f., durch die Präposition *meþ* '(gemeinsam) mit' (+ Dat.; afries. *mith*, *mit*, ae. *mið*, *mid*, as. *mið*, *mid(i)*, *med*[10], mnd. *mit*, mnl. *met*, *mit*, ahd. *mit(i)*, aisl. *með*, got. *miþ* etc.) verbunden sind. Der Männername steht mit einiger Bestimmtheit im

---

Hg., Reallexikon, Ergänzungsbd. 10 (Berlin und New York, 1994), 195–220: 202 ff. Zur ᛡ-Rune allgemein U. Schwab, *Die Sternrune im Wessobrunner Gebet*, Amsterdamer Publikationen zur Sprache und Literatur 1 (Amsterdam, 1973), 76 ff. pass.

6 Dazu zuletzt M. MacLeod, *Bind-Runes. An Investigation of Ligatures in Runic Epigraphy*, Runrön 15 (Uppsala, 2002), 71 pass.

7 Kapteyn, 'Zwei Runeninschriften', 164; Arntz, *ERF*, 384 f. Unentschieden Looijenga, *Texts & Contexts*, 311. Um eine Eibenrune ᛇ kann es sich entgegen einer Annahme von E. Seebold ('Die Überlieferung des älteren Fuþark', *Old English Runes and their Continental Background*, A. Bammesberger, Hg., Anglistische Forschungen 217 [Heidelberg, 1991], 439–569: 510) nicht handeln.

8 Kapteyn, 'Zwei Runeninschriften', 164 f. (der überlange untere Zweig des ᚺ vertrete 'zugleich das Zeichen ᛁ = i'); Arntz, *ERF*, 385 f. ('entweder im rechten Hauptstab des ᚺ oder in dem des ᛚ enthalten').

9 Dazu jüngst M. MacLeod, 'Hidden Bind-Runes', *ABäG* 53 (2000), 21–31: 31.

10 Zwei Belege im *Freckenhorster Heberegister*, Hg. E. Wadstein, *Kleinere altsächsische Sprachdenkmäler*, Niederdeutsche Denkmäler 6 (Norden und Leipzig, 1899), 28, Z. 22 und 35, Z. 38.

Nom. Sg. auf **-u**, der als vor-afries. -ə̣ < urgerm. *-*az* zu interpretieren ist[11]

[11] So vor allem W. Krause, *Handbuch des Gotischen* (München, ³1968), §34 Anm. ('Murmelvokal'); Ders., *Die Sprache der urnordischen Runeninschriften* (Heidelberg, 1971), §6 Anm. 2; Düwel, 'Knochenkämme', 365 *pass.*; H. F. Nielsen, 'Unaccented Vowels in the Frisian Runic Inscriptions', *Miscellanea Frisica: in nije bondel Fryske stúdzjes*, N. R. Århammar et al., Hg., Fryske Akademy 634 (Assen, 1984), 11–19: 13; Ders., 'Unaccented Vowels in Runic Frisian and Ingvaeonic', *Old English Runes*, Bammesberger, Hg., 299–303: 300 f.; 'Developments in Frisian Runology: a Discussion of Düwel & Tempel's Runic Corpus from 1970', *Frisian Runes*, Looijenga und Quak, Hg., 123–30: 125 ff.; Ders., *The Early Runic Language of Scandinavia. Studies in Germanic Dialect Geography* (Heidelberg, 2000), 93; Quak, 'Altfriesische und altenglische Runen', *Old English Runes*, Bammesberger, Hg., 287–98: 288; B. Odenstedt, 'On the Transliteration of the ᚨ-Rune in Early English and Frisian Inscriptions', *Festskrift Ottar Grønvik*, J. O. Askedal et al., Hg. (Oslo, 1991), 53–69: 55; J. Hines, 'Coins and Runes in England and Frisia in the Seventh Century', *Frisian Runes*, Looijenga und Quak, Hg., 47–62: 47. – An sicheren oder immerhin wahrscheinlichen Belegen für **-u** im Nom. Sg. maskuliner *a*-Stämme sind neben **a$_2$dug$_2$islu** anzuführen: 1. **ska$_2$nomodu** UFO (in London aufbewahrter Goldsolidus), 576–600/610 (Männername *-*mōdaz*); 2. ⌜**w**⌝**ela$_2$du** (⌜**w**⌝ = ᚹ) SCHWEINDORF, spätes 6. oder frühes 7. Jh. (wohl Männername **Wē$_2$-landaz*, belegt auch als fränk. VELANDU Gen., 7. Jh. [Ebersheim], *Corpus inscriptionum Latinarum* XIII, Nr. 7260; oder Appellativ?); 3. **a$_1$niwulufu** FOLKSTONE, vor/um 650 (Männername *-*wulfaz*); 4. **ka$_3$bu** TOORNWERD, wohl 8. Jh. (**kambaz* m. 'Kamm'); 5. **ha$_2$buku** OOSTUM, spätes 8. oder frühes 9. Jh. (Männername **Habukaz*). Demgegenüber ist **ka$_2$bu** OOSTUM als Akk. Sg. (**kamba^n*) zu fassen. – Nicht in diesen Zusammenhang gehören die beiden auf dem Franks Casket (Runenkästchen von Auzon; um 700) bezeugten exquisiten Formen **fla$_3$du** = ae. *flōdu* 'Flut' (*u*-Stamm, wohl Nom. Sg.) und **g$_1$iuþea$_2$su** = ae. *Juþeas* 'die Juden' (Nom. Pl., mit unberechtigtem *u*) oder *Juþeas (s)u[m]* 'einer der Juden (Gen. Pl.)'.

Anders wird das für die friesischen Runeninschriften charakteristische **-u** beurteilt z.B. von J. Insley, 'The Personal Name **Āniwulf*/**Ǣniwulf*' [Appendix 2 ad M. Blackburn, 'A Survey of Anglo-Saxon and Frisian Coins with Runic Inscriptions'], *Old English Runes*, Bammesberger, Hg., 172–74: 173 f. (**-u** als Instrumentale), P. V. Stiles, 'Remarks on the "Anglo-Frisian" Thesis', *Friesische Studien II*, V. F. Faltings et al., Hg., NOWELE Suppl. 12 (Odense, 1995), 177–220: 190 (**-u** zum Teil alte Instrumental-Ausgänge, zum Teil Ausgänge des Nom. Sg. femininer *ō*-Stämme); A. Bammesberger, 'Runic Frisian *Weladu* and Further West Germanic Nominal Forms in *-u*', *NOWELE* 33 (1998), 121–32 (rechnet v.a. mit [Einzel-?]Übernahme von *-u* aus dem Paradigma der *u*-Stämme). Rundum zufriedenstellend ist keine dieser Annahmen: einerseits träte, wie H. F. Nielsen ('Ante-Old Frisian: A Review', *NOWELE* 24 [1994], 91–136: 120) zu Recht einwendet, in den friesischen Inschriften eine unerklärlich große Anzahl an Dativen bzw. Instrumentalen entgegen, anderseits ist auch die Annahme eines interparadigmatischen Ausgleichs aus systemischen Gründen (eindeutiges -*Ø* würde ja durch mehrdeutiges **-u** ersetzt) nicht wirklich attraktiv, und **ska$_2$nomodu** UFO (Goldsolidus, 576–600/610) schließlich ist entgegen Stiles (u.a.) angesichts des problematischen 'Sitzes im Leben' wohl kaum als Frauenname zu fassen.

(kaum Akk. Sg. *-*a*^{n}, was jedoch rein formal gleichermaßen möglich ist).[12] Daß hier -**u** für altes *-*az* (bzw. *-*a*^{n}) steht, deutet auf durchgeführte Reduktionsprozesse, wobei als *output*-Lautung am ehesten an einen geschlossen realisierten Zentralvokal zu denken ist, phonetisch also etwa [ə̣] (demnach 'obermittelhoch'; der mittlere Zentralvokal [ə] wäre wohl durch -**e**- bezeichnet worden). Der Frauenname steht hingegen im Dat. Sg. auf -**u** = vorafries. -*u* (< *-*ju* < *-*iju* < urgerm. *-*ijō*, ursprünglicher Instrumental)[13]. Was die Textsorte betrifft, so handelt es bei 'A. mit G., A. samt G.' entweder um die Schenker des Webschwerts (und des Webstuhls?) oder, etwas weniger wahrscheinlich, um dessen Besitzer.

Keine besonderen Deutungsprobleme verursacht im letzten Segment der Inschrift der Frauenname **g$_2$isuhḷdu** = vor-afries. *Gīsə̣ h(i)ldu* (wohl [ʝi:°]), der fast zeitgleich, und zwar in dem kurz vor 829 entstandenen *Polyptychon*

---

[12] Nicht zu überzeugen vermag eine Interpretation von **a$_2$dug$_2$isl-u** als Dat. Sg. (urgerm. *-*aī* > *-*ē* > afries. ae. -*e*; zu erwarten wäre demnach -**e**) oder als Instr. Sg. (urgerm. *-*ei* Lokativ > *-*ī* > ae. -*i*, -*e*, afries. -*e*; zu erwarten wäre demnach wohl -**i**); ohne Reflexe im literarisch bezeugten Altfriesischen (oder Altenglischen) einen (ursprünglichen) Instrumental auf -*u* (< *-*ū* < urgerm. *-*ō*) wie im Althochdeutschen und Altsächsischen anzusetzen, wie u.a. Arntz, *ERF*, 386 f. und M. Gysseling, *Corpus van middelnederlandse teksten (tot en met het jaar 1300)*. II: *Literaire handschriften*, Teil 1: *Fragmenten* ('s-Gravenhage, 1980), 14 (sub L) wollen, verfängt jedenfalls nicht. – Zum Instr. Sg. der maskulinen *a*-Stämme auf -*i*, -*e* im 'Anglo-Friesischen', s. W. L. van Helten, *Altostfriesische Grammatik* (Leeuwarden, 1890), 125 f. (§152 Anm.); Th. Siebs, 'Geschichte der friesischen Sprache', *Grundriß der germanischen Philologie*, I, H. Paul, Hg., 2. Aufl. (Straßburg, 1901), 1152–464: 1139 (§152,4); I. Dahl, *Substantival Inflexion in Early Old English Vocalic Stems*. Lund Studies in English 7 (Lund etc., 1938), 46 ff. und 61; K. Brunner, *Altenglische Grammatik* (Tübingen, 1965), 195 f. (§237 Anm. 2).

[13] Nielsen, 'Unaccented vowels', 13 f.; Th. Klein, 'Die Straubinger Heliand-Fragmente: altfriesisch oder altsächsisch?', *Aspects,* 197–225: 217; Stiles, 'Remarks', 189 f. Etwas anders dagegen St. Krogh, *Die Stellung des Altsächsischen im Rahmen der germanischen Sprachen*. Studien zum Althochdeutschen 29 (Göttingen, 1996), 346 f. (echter Instrumental). Im literarisch bezeugten Altfriesischen geht der Dat. Sg. der *(j)ō*-Stämme dann auf -*e* (-*i*), -*a* oder auch -*Ø* aus; vgl. z.B. van Helten, *Altostfriesische Grammatik*, 137 (§166) und 138 (§168β–γ); Siebs, 'Geschichte', 1341 f. (§153,4); W. Steller, *Abriß der altfriesischen Grammatik mit Berücksichtigung der westgermanischen Dialecte des Altenglischen, Altsächsischen und Althochdeutschen* (Halle/S., 1928), 38 (§52 mit Anm. 1); D. Boutkan, *A Concise Grammar of the Old Frisian Dialect of the First Riustring Manuscript*. NOWELE Suppl. 16 (Odense, 1996), 71 f. – Nielsen, 'Unaccented vowels', 14, erwägt alternativ auch analogische Übernahme des -*u* < *-*un* < *-*ūn* aus dem Paradigma der femininen *(j)ōn*- Stämme, was jedoch lautlich schwierig ist: nach *u* ist auslautendes *n* noch im Altfriesischen in Fällen wie *hulpun* Prät.Pl.Ind. 'halfen' bewahrt (van Helten, *Altostfriesische Grammatik*, 84 f. [§107γ]), sodaß für die voraltfriesische Runeninschrift -**un** zu erwarten wäre; vgl. Krogh, *Stellung des Altsächsischen*, 345 f.

Irminonis, auch als westfränk. *Gisohildis* bezeugt ist.[14] Der schon im altgermanischen Onomastikon gut zu belegende Namenstamm *Gīsa-* gehört zu mnd. *gīse* (wohl m.) 'Geisel' und 'mhd.' (niederrhein.-ripuar.) *gîse* dass.[15] In der Kompositionsfuge zeigt sich ein 'Bindevokal' nach schwerer Silbe; daß hier (**g**$_2$**is**)-**u**- für altes *(Gīs)-a-* steht, läßt wie im Falle des Nom. Sg. der maskulinen *a*-Stämme (s. vorhin) an einen geschlossen realisierten Zentralvokal [ə̣] denken. Die Wiedergabe des Hinterglieds vor-afries. *-h(i)ldu* Dat. durch **-hl̥du** schließlich folgt einem von Ottar Grønvik entdeckten Prinzip,[16] demzufolge die Sequenz *CVRC* in den älteren Runeninschriften durch (*CR̥C* ersetzt und durch) ‹CRC› repräsentiert werden kann. Dabei kann im 'Vorkontext' Konsonanz fehlen, der eliminierte Vokal ist durchwegs Hochzungenvokal, und im 'Nachkontext' steht durchwegs ein Obstruent, sodaß die Grønviksche Substitutionsregel in modifizierter Form wie folgt lautet: $C_0URT \rightarrow C_0R̥T$ ‹C_0RT›.[17] Das in allen Epochen germanischer Namengebung überaus häufig entgegentretende Hinterglied **-heldijō-* f.,[18] runenepigraphisch z.B. auch in **þuruþhild** = vor-ahd. (fränk.) *Þ^{u}ruþ-hild* FRIEDBERG, 567–600,[19] stellt sich zu ae. *hild* 'Kampf, Krieg', as. *hildi* Dat.Sg.

---

[14] XV,54; ferner auch *Gisoildis* VI,31 und XVII,5: *Das Polyptychon von Saint-Germain-des-Prés*, D. Hägermann et al., Hg. (Köln etc., 1993), 134, 42 und 147. Vgl. E. Förstemann, *Altdeutsches Namenbuch*. I: *Personennamen*, 2. Aufl. (Bonn, 1900 = München und Hildesheim, 1966), 645; M.-Th. Morlet, *Les noms de personne sur le territoire de l'ancienne Gaule du VIe au XIIe siècle*. I: *Les noms issus du germanique continental et les créations gallo-germaniques* (Paris, 1968 = 1971), 110.

[15] Zum Namenstamm *Gīsa-* zuletzt R. Nedoma, *Personennamen in südgermanischen Runeninschriften*. Studien zur altgermanischen Namenkunde I,1,1 (Heidelberg, 2004), 200 ff. (LNr. 15, C.3.; mit Lit.). – Die altgermanischen Belege sind zu eruieren über H. Reichert, *Lexikon der altgermanischen Personennamen*. II: *Register*, erstellt von R. Nedoma und H. Reichert (Wien, 1990; im folgenden zitiert als: *LaN* II), 522.

[16] O. Grønvik, 'Über den Lautwert der Ing-Runen und die Auslassung von Vokal in den älteren Runeninschriften', *IF* 90 (1985), 168–95: 186 und 191 f.

[17] Dazu ausführlich R. Nedoma, 'Noch einmal zur Runeninschrift auf der Gürtelschnalle von Pforzen', *Alemannien und der Norden*, H.-P. Naumann et al., Hg., Reallexikon, Ergänzungsbd. 43 (Berlin und New York, 2004), 340–70: 348 ff. – Weitere Beispiele für Grønviks Regel in modifizierter Form sind 1. **wlþuþewaz** THORSBERG, um 200 (*RäF*, Nr. 20) = urn. *W(u)lþuþewaz* m.; 2. **birgŋgu** OPEDAL, (3./)4. Jh. (*RäF*, Nr. 76) = urn. *birg(i)ngu* f. *ō*-St. 'Begräbnis, Bestattung'; 3. **ltahu** PFORZEN I, 567–600 (Neufund) = vor-ahd. *(I)ltahu* f. *ō*-St., Instr. Sg. (in lokativischer Funktion) 'an der "Ilzach"'; 4. **-brg** OETTINGEN, 551–600 (Neufund) = vor-ahd. *-birg* Frauenname; 5. **uþfnþai** CHARNAY, 551–600 (*RäF*, Nr. 6) = ogerm. (wohl burgund.) *u(n)þf(i)nþai* 3. Pers. Sg. Konj. I 'möge herausfinden'. – Die Standardedition ist W. Krause und H. Jankuhn, *Die Runeninschriften im älteren Futhark*. I: *Text*. II: *Tafeln*. Abh. Akademie der Wissenschaften in Göttingen, Philolog.-Histor. Kl., 3. F., 65 (Göttingen, 1966; hier und im folgenden zitiert als: *RäF*).

[18] Liste altgermanischer Belege: *LaN* II, 542 ff.

[19] *ERF*, Nr. 16; *RäF*, Nr. 141.

'Kampf, Kampfesmut', ahd. *hiltiu* Dat.Sg. 'Kampf', aisl. *hildr* 'Kampf, Krieg'.[20]

Das Hinterglied des im ersten Segment der Inschrift genannten Männernamens **$a_2$du-$g_2$islu** = vor-afries. *-gīslə̣* (wohl [-ɟi:°]) < **-gīslaz* ist ebenfalls schon aus altgermanischer Zeit zu belegen, runenepigraphisch z.B. in **asugisalas** = urn. *A(n)su-gīs*^{a}*las* Gen., KRAGEHUL, Anfang 6. Jh.,[21] ferner auch in fries. *Aldgislus* 7. Jh. (*rex*).[22] Appellativische Relata sind ae. *gīsel*, ahd. *gīsal*, aisl. *gísl* m. 'Geisel, Bürge', langob. *gīsel* 'Bürge, Zeuge' etc. (< **gīsla-*, wohl aus urgerm. **geis(s)la-*).[23] Im Vorderglied schließlich haben bereits Kapteyn und, wenn ich das recht beurteile, auch die gesamte nachfolgende Forschung die Monophthongierung /au/ > /ā/ durchgeführt gesehen, indem man **$a_2$du-** als vor-afries. *Ādu-* < **Auda-* gefaßt hat[24] (zu ae. *ēad* n.

---

[20] Zu den Namenelementen **Heldija-* bzw. **-helda-* m., **-heldijō-* f. zuletzt E. Felder, *Die Personennamen auf den merowingischen Münzen der Bibliothèque nationale de France*. Abh. Bayer. Akademie der Wissenschaften, Philosoph.-Histor. Kl., N.F. 122 (München, 2003), 205 f.; Nedoma, *Personennamen*, 311 f. (LNr. 42, C.3.; mit Lit.).

[21] *RäF*, Nr. 27. Liste weiterer altgermanischer Belege: *LaN* II, 542 ff.

[22] Zwei Belege in der *Vita Wilfridi* des Eddius Stephanus (c. 26 und 27), ein Beleg in Bedas Kirchengeschichte (V,19): W. Levison, Hg., 'Vita Wilfridi I. episcopi Eboracensis auctore Stephano', *Passiones vitaeque sanctorum aevi Merovingici [IV]*, B. Krusch und W. Levison, Hg., MGH, Scriptores rerum Merovingicarum 6 (Hannover und Leipzig 1913), 163–263: 220, Z. 7 (*Aldgislo*, Var. *-giso*) und Z. 21 (*Aldgislum*, Var. *-gelsum*); *Venerabilis Baedae opera historica*, C. Plummer, Hg. (Oxford, 1896) I, 326 (*Aldgilso*, Var. *-gislo*) bzw. *König Alfreds Übersetzung von Bedas Kirchengeschichte*, J. Schipper, Hg., Bibliothek der angelsächsischen Prosa 4 (Leipzig, 1899), 664 (*Eadgylse*, Var. *-gylsse*, *-gilse*, *Aldgilse*).

[23] Zum Namenstamm *Gīsla-* zuletzt Nedoma, *Personennamen*, 304 ff. (LNr. 40, C.1.; mit Lit.). – Das ganz ähnlich lautende Namenelement *Gīsila-*, das zu langob. *gīsil* 'Pfeil, Pfeilschaft' und aisl. *gísli* m. 'Schistock' zu stellen ist, bleibt an sich fern, wenngleich natürlich auch sekundäre Vermischung stattgefunden haben kann und wird; vgl. R. Nedoma, 'Geisel: Sprachliches, Namenkundliches', *Reallexikon*, X,5–6 (^{2}1998), 572–73. Unbegründete Ablehnung bei Felder, *Personennamen*, 181.

[24] Kapteyn, 'Zwei Runeninschriften', 162 f. ('beweist unzweideutig die fries. form des namens'); so ferner u.v.a. auch Arntz, *ERF*, 386; Krause, *Handbuch des Gotischen*, §34 Anm.; P. Sipma, 'Eat oer Fryske runen', *Fryske Stúdzjes. Festschrift J. H. Brouwer*, K. Dykstra et al., Hg., Studia Germanica 2 (Assen, 1960), 67–76: 73; Gysseling, *Corpus* II,1, 14 (sub L); H. T. J. Miedema und A. R. Reith, 'De verhouding tussen de oudgermaanse namen Adugisl, Eadgils en Athils', *Naamkunde* 21 (1989), 65–71: 65 ff.; Insley, '*Āniwulf/*Ǣniwulf*', 173; Nielsen, 'Unaccented Vowels', 12; Ders., 'Unaccented Vowels' (1991), 300; Ders., 'The Beginnings of a "Frisian" Runic Corpus', *Philologia Frisica anno 1993* (1994), 210–22: 216 und 217; Ders., 'Developments', 126 Anm. 5 und 128; Ders., *Early Runic Language*, 93; Stiles, 'Remarks', 189; Krogh, *Stellung des Altsächsischen*, 276; Looijenga, 'Checklist', 96; Dies., *Texts & Contexts*, 312; Giliberto, *Iscrizioni runiche*, 90 f. und 121 pass.; U. Timmermann, 'Altfriesische Personennamen', *Handbuch / Handbook*, 657–70: 662. Ein wenig reservierter äußert sich nur Quak, 'Runica Frisica', 364 ('dürfte ... sein'); Ders., 'Friese persoonsnamen in de oudste

'Reichtum, Wohlstand, Glück', as. *ōd* n./m.? 'Besitz, Wohlstand, Glück', aisl. *auðr* m. 'Reichtum, Schatz, Fülle' etc.).[25] In diesem Fall würde in wfränk. *Audegiselus* bei Venantius Fortunatus (spätes 6. Jh.; ein *maior domus regiae*) eine Entsprechung aus altgermanischer Zeit vorliegen,[26] weitere Gegenstücke aus späterer ('nachaltgermanischer') Zeit wären sodann ae. *Ēadgīls* 7. Jh.,[27] hispanogot. *Odisclus* 10. Jh.[28] und awn. *Auðgísl* 10. Jh.[29]

Obzwar Kapteyns Deutung zweifellos das Richtige treffen kann, ist festzuhalten, daß es sich nur um eine von insgesamt drei gleichwertigen Möglichkeiten handelt: die Runenfolge **a**$_2$**du-** kann nämlich auch ein Namenelement **Ada-* oder ein Namenelement **Anda-* bergen[30]– mit 'Nicht-Repräsentation' des Nasals vor homorganem Obstruenten.[31] In diesen

bronnen', *Friezen. In bondel stúdzjes oer persoansnammen*, R. A. Ebeling et al., Hg., Fryske Nammen 10 (Ljouwert, 1996), 155–69: 166 ('vermoedelijk').

[25] Zum Namenstamm *Auda-* zuletzt Felder, *Personennamen*, 69; Nedoma, *Personennamen*, 191 f. (LNr. 12, C.1.; mit Lit.). – Liste altgermanischer Belege: *LaN* II, 469 f.

[26] *Vita S. Germani* XLIV/122: *Venanti Honori Clementiani Fortunati presbyteri Italici opera pedestria*, B. Krusch, Hg., MGH, Auctores antiquissimi 4,2 (Hannover, 1885 = 1995), 20, Z. 39 (Var. *Audi-*). Weitere westfränkische Belege verzeichnen Förstemann, *Personennamen*, 194 (sub *Audegisel*; ab dem 7. Jh.) und Morlet, *Noms de personne* I, 44 (sub *Odgisilus*).

[27] Der früheste Beleg findet sich in Bedas Kirchengeschichte (IV,25 [23]): *Venerabilis Baedae opera historica*, Plummer, Hg., I, 266 (*Aedgils*, Var. *Edgisl*) bzw. *König Alfreds Übersetzung*, Schipper, Hg., 503 (*Eadgyls*, Var. *Ed-*, *Eed-*). Ferner ist der Name in der Urkundenüberlieferung und in der Heldendichtung (*Bēowulf*, V. 2392 [Sohn des Schwedenkönigs Oht(h)ere] ~ aisl. *Aðils*; *Wīdsīþ*, V. 93) bezeugt; die Belege verbucht W. G. Searle, *Onomasticon Anglo-Saxonicum* (Cambridge, 1897), 181.

[28] Beleg bei J. M. Piel und D. Kremer, *Hispano-gotisches Namenbuch. Der Niederschlag des Westgotischen in den alten und heutigen Personen- und Ortsnamen der Iberischen Halbinsel* (Heidelberg, 1976), 92 (§31,7). – Das Hinterglied *-(g)iscl-* ist durch Substitution von germanischem [sl] durch romanisches [skl] (mit epenthetischem *k*) zu erklären; Lit. bei Nedoma, *Personennamen*, 304 (LNr. 40, C.1.).

[29] Belege bei E. H. Lind, *Norsk-isländska dopnamn ock fingerade namn från medeltiden* (Uppsala und Leipzig, 1905–1915), 97 f.

[30] Nedoma, *Personennamen*, 146 f. – Ambig ist auch die Runenfolge **ado** auf der Büchse von Gammertingen, ca. 551–575 (*ERF*, Nr. 17; *RäF*, Nr. 161), die als Männername vor-ahd. (obd.) *Ado* oder *A(n)do* zu fassen ist; s. ebd., 141 ff. (LNr. 2).

[31] $C_0VNT \rightarrow C_0\tilde{V}T$ ‹C_0VT›; dazu etwa Ė. A. Makaev, *The Language of the Oldest Runic Inscriptions. A Linguistic and Historical-Philological Analysis*. Kungl. Vitterhets Historie och Antikvitets Akademiens Handlingar, Filolog.-filosof. ser. 21 (Stockholm, 1996 [zuerst 1965]), 52 f.; H. Williams, 'The Non-Representation of Nasals before Obstruents: Spelling Convention or Phonetic Analysis?', *Proceedings of the Third International Symposium on Runes and Runic Inscriptions, Grindaheim 1990*, J. E. Knirk, Hg., Runrön 9 (Uppsala, 1994), 217–22: 217 ff.; Nedoma, 'Noch einmal zur Runeninschrift', 352. – Sichere friesischen Belege sind: 1. ⌜**w**⌝**ela**$_2$**du** = vor-afries. *°lo(n)də* m., SCHWEINDORF, spätes 6. oder frühes 7. Jh.; 2. **ka**$_3$**bu** = vor-afries. *kɔ(m)bə* 'Kamm'

beiden, bisher offenbar noch nicht in Betracht gezogenen Fällen würde Rune Nr. 1 **a**$_2$ für ein aus dem Urgermanischen ererbtes /ă/ (≠ /æ/ ~ **a**$_1$) stehen wie zum einen (scil. in der Folge C_0_+C vor V [– palatal])[32] in **ha**$_2$**da**$_2$ = vor-afries. *Had(d)a* m., HARLINGEN, spätes 6. oder frühes 7. Jh. (= ae. *H(e)ada*, *H(e)adda* 7. Jh.[33]) und **ha**$_2$**buku** = vor-afries. *Hab-ukə̣* m., OOSTUM, spätes 8. oder frühes 9. Jh. (afries. *hauk*, ae. *h(e)afoc* 'Habicht'), zum anderen (scil. in der Folge C_0_NC ‹C_0_C›) in **ka**$_2$**bu** = vor-afries. *kɔ(m)bə̣* m. Akk., OOSTUM (= ae. *camb* 'Kamm') und, nebentonig, ferner in ⌜**w**⌝**ela**$_2$**du** = vor-afries. *°lɔ(n)də̣* m., SCHWEINDORF, spätes 6. oder frühes 7. Jh. (= fränk. VELANDU Gen.).[34] Was die Kompositionsfuge betrifft, so ist **u** nach Ausweis des zweiten Anthroponyms der Westeremdener Runeninschrift, **g**$_2$**is-u-hl̩du** f., die zu erwartende Wiedergabe von Fugenelement **a* > *ə̣* nach schwerer Silbe (i.e. nach Vorderglied **Auda-* gemäß traditioneller Ansicht oder eben auch nach Vorderglied **Anda-*).[35] Für die Vertretung von 'Bindevokal' **a* nach leichter Silbe (i.e. nach Vorderglied **Ada-*) indessen mangelt

---

TOORNWERD, wohl 8. Jh.; 3. **ka**$_2$**bu** = vor-afries. *kɔ(m)bə̣* Akk., 'Kamm' OOSTUM, spätes 8. oder frühes 9. Jh.

[32] Die Kontextbedingungen für die Bewahrung bzw. Revelarisierung von haupttonigem urgerm. /ă/ im Altfriesischen sind nicht in allen Punkten klar, vor allem aufgrund intra- und auch interparadigmatischer Analogiewirkungen. Grundsätzlich wird *a* jedenfalls vor einem schwachtonigen velaren (besser: nicht-palatalen) Vokal in ursprünglich offener Silbe nicht aufgehellt; s. etwa van Helten, *Altostfriesische Grammatik*, 4 f. (§4α); Siebs, 'Geschichte', 1179 f. (§11,5); C. B. van Haeringen, 'Zur friesischen Lautgeschichte', *BGdSL* 44 (1920), 27–53: 40 und 47; vgl. ferner zuletzt Krogh, *Stellung des Altsächsischen*, 144. Formen wie afries. *gled* Adj. 'glatt' (ae. *glæd* 'glänzend') sind durch Schwund (des Reflexes) von stammbildendem *a* vor Eintritt der Aufhellung zu erklären (wgerm. **glad* < urgerm. **gladaz*), in der friesischen 'Runenzeit' ist jedoch der Reflex von schwachtonigem *-a-* in der Kompositionsfuge zweigliedriger Anthroponyme als *-u-* = *-ə̣-* (auch nach schwerer Silbe) noch bewahrt, sodaß in einem Vorderglied urgerm. wgerm. **Ada-* > vor-afries. *Adə̣-* die Aufhellung vor schwachtonigem Fugenvokal *ə̣* [– palatal] unterblieben sein wird, da auch keine Beeinflussung durch ein appellativisches Relatum mit aufgehelltem haupttonigen *æ* stattgefunden hat. (Eine friesische Entsprechung des Adjektivs ahd. *ata-haft* Adj. [s. sofort im Haupttext] ist jedenfalls nicht bezeugt.)

[33] Belege bei Searle, *Onomasticon*, 275 (*Hada*, *Hadda*) und 281 f. (*Heada*, *Headda*).

[34] Vgl. oben, Anm. 11.

[35] Nicht schlüssig zu erklären ist hingegen die Kompositionsfuge des zweigliedrigen Männernamens **ska**$_2$**n-o-modu** UFO (in London aufbewahrter Goldsolidus), 576–600/610. Ist hier mit Ersatz von urgerm. **skaunija-* (oder **skauni-*) Adj. 'schön' (got. *skaun(ei)s** *i-* oder *ija*-Stamm, ahd. as. *skōni*, ae. *scīene*, afries. *skēne* an sich *ija*-Stämme) durch **skauna-* zu rechnen (so z.B. A. Bammesberger, '**skanomodu**: Linguistic Issues', *Britain 400–600: Language and History*, Ders. und A. Wollmann, Hg., Anglistische Forschungen 205 [Heidelberg, 1990], 457–66: 463), wobei sodann vor dem labialen Nasal *m* ein 'Bindevokal' *ɔ* (wiedergegeben durch **o**) entgegentritt?

es den friesischen Runeninschriften an überzeugenden Beispielen;[36] die Annahme, daß **u** auch in diesem Fall für einen 'reduzierten' Vokal in der Kompositionsfuge steht, ist jedoch nicht weiter problematisch.

Der Namenstamm *Ada-* ist aus altgermanischer Zeit nicht übermäßig frequent, jedoch hinreichend belegt,[37] z.B. in skir.(?) *Adaric(h)* 5. Jh. (Chron. min.), ogot. *Aderit* 6. Jh. (Papyrusurkunde), wfränk. *Adovarius* 6. Jh. (Gregor Tur.),[38] aus späterer ('nachaltgermanischer') Zeit ferner in wfränk. *Adegis* 9. Jh. (Paris),[39] ahd. *Atolf* 9. Jh. (St. Gallen; mit lautverschobenem *t*)[40] etc.; in anderen Einzelsprachen ist *Ada-* dagegen schwer nachzuweisen: afries. ae. as. *Ă̄d-*, awn. *Ă̄ð-* etc. sind mehrdeutig (**A/Ai/Auda-*, **Aþ/da-*). Das Namenelement *Ada-* gehört wohl zu ahd. *ata-haft* Adj. 'ununterbrochen, fortwährend' (Grundbedeutung etwa 'mit *continuitas* behaftet').[41] Etwas häufiger im altgermanischen Onomastikon bezeugt ist hingegen der Namenstamm *Anda-*,[42] etwa in ogot. *Andagis* Gen., 5. Jh. (Jordanes), burgund. *Anda(ha)ri* Gen., 5./6. Jh. (Lex Burgund.) und wfränk. *Andulfus* 6. Jh. (Venantius Fortunatus),[43] dazu später z.B. in afries. *Andulf* 10. Jh. (Werden), as. *Andger* 9. Jh. (Corvey), wfränk. *Andegis* 9. Jh. (Paris), ahd. *Antolf* 9. Jh. (Fulda, St. Gallen).[44] Appellativische Relata sind aisl. *andi* m. 'Atem, Hauch, Geist' und (mit Bedeutungswandel '[heftiger] Atem' → 'Erregung' wie in lat. *animus*) ae. *anda*, ahd. *anto* m. 'Zorn, Eifer, Neid', as. *ando* m. 'Zorn, Ärger' etc. (urgerm. **an-dan-* : **an-man-* > afries. *omma*, *amma* m. 'Atem, Hauch'); in einzelnen Fällen – wie etwa bei ogot. *Andvit*

---

36 Zu **eda$_1$:ba$_3$da$_2$** ARUM s. unten, III.

37 Die in Frage kommenden Bildungen finden sich in *LaN* II, 468 f. s.v. *aþ-* eingeordnet.

38 Einzelbelege bei H. Reichert, *Lexikon der altgermanischen Personennamen*. I: *Text* (Wien, 1986; im folgenden zitiert als: *LaN* I), 10 f.

39 *Polyptychon*, Hägermann, Hg., 141 (*Polyptychon Irminonis* XVI,27). Vgl. Förstemann, *Personennamen*, 155; Morlet, *Noms de personne* I, 14.

40 Belege bei Förstemann, *Personennamen*, 158 (dort s.v. *Atha-* verbucht).

41 N. Wagner, 'Adaric und ahd. atahaft', *Beiträge zur Namenforschung* N.F. 24 (1989), 310–17: 314 ff.; zustimmend Nedoma, *Personennamen*, 144 f. (LNr. 2, C.1.2.; mit weiterer Lit.); abwägend Felder, *Personennamen*, 44.

42 Liste altgermanischer Belege: *LaN* II, 461 f.

43 Einzelbelege in *LaN* I, 49 ff.

44 *Rheinische Urbare*. II: *Die Urbare der Abtei Werden a. d. Ruhr*. A: *Die Urbare vom 9.–13. Jahrhundert*, R. Kötzschke, Hg., Publikationen der Gesellschaft für Rheinische Geschichtskunde 20,2 (Bonn, 1906), 47, Z. 27 (afries. *Andulf*); *Die alten Mönchslisten und die Traditionen von Corvey*, K. Honselmann, Hg., Veröffentlichungen der Histor. Kommission für Westfalen, X: Abhandlungen zur Corveyer Geschichtsschreibung 6,1 (Paderborn, 1982), 91 (Nr. 53; as. *Andger*); *Polyptychon*, Hägermann, Hg., 77 (wfränk. *Andegis* IX,186); Förstemann, *Personennamen*, 105 (ahd. *Antolf*).

6. Jh. (Cassiodor)[45] – mag es sich auch um morphologisch-semantisch motivierte Bildungen (sog. Primärkombinationen) mit Präfix **anda-* 'entgegen' (betont got. *anda-*, ae. afries. *and-*, *ond-*, ahd. *ant-*, aisl. *and-* etc.) handeln.

Die Bildungen (Transponate) **Adagīslaz* und **Andagīslaz* sind in der germanischen Namengebung nicht zweifelsfrei nachzuweisen: hispano-got. *Adiscle* 9. Jh. (Katalonien)[46] ist ambig (**Aþa-* oder **Ada-*?) und hispano-got. **Andisclus*[47] unsicher; immerhin lassen sich jedoch mit wfränk. *Adegis* 9. Jh. und mit ogot. *Andagis* Gen., 5. Jh., wfränk. *Andegis* 9. Jh. (s. vorhin) für beide Anthroponyme immerhin 'anklingende' Parallelbildungen beibringen.[48] Die unsichere bzw. fehlende Bezeugung stellt indessen keine große Hypothek dar: so etwa hat – um hier nur *ein* Beispiel anzuführen – auch der in der Runeninschrift auf der Gürtelschnalle von Pforzen (567–600; Neufund)[49] entgegentretende Frauenname **a͡ïlrun** = vor-ahd. *Ailrūn*[50] keinerlei Entsprechungen im altgermanischen Onomastikon oder in der späteren Namenüberlieferung; insbesondere in früherer Zeit fließen die Quellen nicht eben reichlich. In jedem Fall aber war die germanische Personennamengebung seit alters her insofern 'offen', als sowohl morphologisch-semantisch 'sinnvolle' Primärkombinationen als auch pragmatisch determinierte, mit-

---

45 Beleg in *LaN* I, 51 (s.v. *Andvit* 2). Ogot. (und vandal.) **Andwīts* etwa 'Schlagfertiger', 'Vergelter': F. Wrede, *Über die Sprache der Ostgoten in Italien*, QF 68 (Straßburg, 1891), 126. Ein nordisches Gegenstück scheint in runenschwed. **antuitr** vorzuliegen; Belege bei L. Peterson, *Nordiskt runnamnslexikon*, 5. Aufl. (Uppsala, 2007), 23 (s.v. *Andvēttr*).

46 Beleg bei D. Kremer, *Die germanischen Personennamen in Katalonien. Namensammlung und Etymologisches* (Barcelona, 1969–1972), 68 (§18,II,5) bzw. Piel und Kremer, *Hispano-gotisches Namenbuch*, 62 (§ 3,7). – Zu *-(g)iscl-* mit epenthetischem romanischen *k* vgl. oben, Anm. 28.

47 Zwei mögliche Belege ebd., 74 (§14,3): verbaut in dem Patronymikon *Andiscliquiz* und/oder dem Toponym *Andixo*?

48 Bei einigen Männernamen ist ein Wechsel *-gis(c)l* ~ *-gis* im Hinterglied auch bezeugt, z.B. langob. *Elmi-gisilus* = *Hilme-gis* 6. Jh., langob. 'Ιλδι-γσάλ = 'Ιλδί-γης 6. Jh.; dazu M. Schönfeld, *Wörterbuch der altgermanischen Personen- und Völkernamen* (Heidelberg, 1911, ²1965), 30 (s.v. *Arnigisclus*); N. Wagner, 'Zu einigen Personennamen aus Quellen zur gotischen Geschichte', *Würzburger Prosastudien* II. *Untersuchungen zur Literatur und Sprache des Mittelalters. Festschrift Kurt Ruh*, P. Kesting, Hg., Medium Aevum 31 (München, 1975), 19–33: 28 mit Anm. 57; Nedoma, 'Geisel', 573.

49 Die Inschrift auf der Gürtelschnalle von Pforzen ist ausführlich dokumentiert und interpretiert in dem Sammelband *Pforzen und Bergakker. Neue Untersuchungen zu Runeninschriften*, A. Bammesberger und G. Waxenberger, Hg., Historische Sprachforschung, Ergänzungsheft 41 (Göttingen, 1999), 15–118 (Beiträge von V. Babucke, P. Pieper, K. Düwel, U. Schwab, T. Looijenga, E. Seebold, N. Wagner, R. Nedoma, H. Eichner und A. Bammesberger).

50 Zu vor-ahd. *Ailrūn* N. Wagner, 'Zu den Runeninschriften von Pforzen und Nordendorf', *Historische Sprachforschung* 108 (1995), 104–12: 106; ferner Nedoma, *Personennamen*, 168 ff. (LNr. 6, C.; mit weiterer Lit.).

unter nur wenig 'sinnhafte' oder überhaupt 'sinnlose' Sekundärkombinationen grundsätzlich jederzeit (neu)gebildet werden konnten. Sowohl **Audagīslaz* > vor-afries. *Ādəgīslə̣* m. als auch die beiden Bildungen **Adagīslaz* > vor-afries. *Adəgīslə̣* m. und **Andagīslaz* > vor-afries. *Āndəgīslə̣* m. können ohne weiteres (ursprünglich) durch Namenvariation entstanden sein,[51] i.e. durch mechanische Kombination geläufiger Namenelemente, von denen eines (oder selten beide) aus den Elternnamen bzw. aus Namen anderer Verwandter übernommen wird (Typ afries. *Antulf – Burgolf* 9. Jh., Vater und Sohn).[52]

Nach alldem ergibt sich, daß **a$_2$du**- keineswegs zwingend die Durchführung des Lautwandels urgerm. /au/ > vor-afries. afries. /ā/ und kraft dessen die friesische Herkunft des runenepigraphischen Texts indiziert.[53] (Als einziger zuverlässiger früher Beleg für monophthongiertes /ā/ < /au/ in den friesischen Runeninschriften verbleibt sonach **ska$_2$nomodu** = vor-afries. *Skānomōdə̣* m. auf dem in London aufbewahrten Goldsolidus unbekannter Herkunft, zu datieren 576–600/610.)[54] Für die Frage der Provenienz der Inschrift auf dem Webschwert von Westeremden verbleiben freilich noch drei weitere Indizien, und zwar geographischer, epigraphischer und lingui-

---

51 An Primärkombinationen braucht wohl für keinen der drei Fälle gedacht werden; weder für 'Reichtum, Glück' + 'Bürge, Geisel' noch für 'beständig' + 'Bürge, Geisel' oder für '(Geist,) Zorn' + 'Bürge, Geisel' drängen sich wirklich schlagende morphologisch-semantische Modellierungen auf. – Zum Problem der Konstruktionsbedeutung bzw. des 'Sinngehalts' altgermanischer Anthroponyme demnächst R. Nedoma, 'Schrift und Sprache in den südgermanischen Runeninschriften', *The* fuþark *and Its Development*, A. Bammesberger und G. Waxenberger, Hg., Reallexikon, Ergänzungsbd. 51 (Berlin und New York, 2006), 109–56: 121 ff.

52 *Traditiones et antiquitates Fuldenses*, E. F. J. Dronke, Hg. (Fulda, 1844), 44 (Nr. 25). – Mitunter sind die 'freien' Namenelemente auch zusätzlich durch Alliteration verbunden, z.B. afries. *Eisbern – Altbern* 9. Jh. (Brüder; ebd., 47 [Nr. 65]) oder ahd. *Heribrant – Hiltibrant – Hadubrant* (Großvater, Vater und Sohn im *Hildebrandlied*).

53 Hinzuzufügen ist, daß auch im Altsächsischen teilweise ‹a›-Schreibungen (scil. für /ɔː/ < /au/) auftreten; vgl. zusammenfassend Krogh, *Stellung des Altsächsischen*, 283 f. (mit Lit.).

54 Anders D. Hofmann, 'Zur Monophthongierung von germanisch *ai* und *au* im Altfriesischen und in seinen Nachbarsprachen', *Lingua theodisca. Beiträge zur Sprach- und Literaturwissenschaft. Festschrift Jan Goossens*, J. Cajot et al., Hg., Niederlande-Studien 16, 2 Bde. (Münster, 1995) I, 23–35: 32 (**a$_2$** als 'unvollkommene Schreibung' für /au/; dies ist nicht mehr als eine *ad hoc*-Annahme). – Wie das Vorderglied des Männernamens **a$_1$niwulufu** auf dem vor bzw. um 650 zu datierenden Tremissis von Folkestone zu beurteilen ist (Insley, '**Āniwulf*/**Ǣniwulf*', 173: vor-afries. *Ǣni*- < **Auni*-, zu datieren in die Zeit vor 600), lasse ich hier offen. Ein später Beleg ist sodann **ka$_2$ta$_1$** = *kā°* < urgerm. **kautō$^{(n)}$* f. 'Knöchel' auf dem Knochen von Southampton (*Hamwic*; dazu unten, IV).

stischer Art:[55] zum einen deutet der Fundort (in seit alters her friesischem Gebiet), zum anderen die typisch friesische Variante ᚨ der Rune $\mathbf{a}_2$ und schließlich der exklusiv im Korpus friesischer Runeninschriften auftretende Ausgang -**u** (= ə̣) im Nom. Sg. der maskulinen *a*-Stämme mit großer Wahrscheinlichkeit darauf, daß es sich ‘dennoch’ um einen voraltfriesischen runenepigraphischen Text handelt.

III

Abb. 2: Schwertchen von Arum (nach Arntz, *ERF*, Taf. VI: Abb. 6)

---

55 Freilich ist keines der drei ins Treffen geführten Indizien für sich genommen beweiskräftig: 1. Objekte wie der Brakteat von Hitsum-A (Inschrift **fozo g**$^{\mathbf{u}}$**/**$_{\mathbf{r}}$**oba**; K. Hauck et al., *Die Goldbrakteaten der Völkerwanderungszeit.* 3 Bde, Münstersche Mittelalter-Schriften 24 [München, 1985–1989], Nr. 76) sind wahrscheinlich Importware (anders E. Seebold, ‘Wie friesisch ist der Brakteat von Wurt Hitsum?’, *Frisian Runes*, Hg. Looijenga und Quak, 181–98). – 2. $\mathbf{a}_2$ ᚨ (mit dem Diakritikon in der Mitte des oberen Zweigs) tritt in Friesland selbst noch zwei weitere Male (scil. ARUM, OOSTUM) entgegen, ist aber auch einmal in England bezeugt, und zwar auf dem Knochen von Southampton (*Hamwic*), der freilich allem Anschein nach friesischer Provenienz ist; s. D. Hofmann, ‘Eine friesische Runeninschrift in England’, *UW* 25 (1976), 73–76 = *Gesammelte Schriften.* II (Hamburg, 1989), 376–79. – 3. Schließlich kann, worauf H. F. Nielsen (‘Runic Frisian *skanomodu* and *aniwulufu* and the Relative Chronology of Monophthongization and *i*-Mutation’, *Festschrift Hans Bekker-Nielsen.* NOWELE 21/22 [Odense, 1993], 81–88: 83; ‘Developments’, 128 f.) zu Recht aufmerksam macht, finales **u** an sich auch *-u* < *-*ū* < *-*ō* im Nom. Sg. der femininen *ō*-Stämme wiedergeben, was allerdings nicht für gegenständliches *Ādə̣-/Adə̣-/Andə̣-gīslə* gilt: wegen des Hinterglieds handelt sich eindeutig um einen Männernamen. – Abwägend und zusammenfassend zur ‘Frisizität’ von Runeninschriften zuletzt vor allem Nielsen, ‘Ante-Old Frisian’, 112 ff.; Ders., ‘Developments’, 123 ff.; Ders., ‘Friesen: The Linguistic Provenance of the Frisian Runic Corpus’, *Reallexikon*, X,1–2 (1996), 29–34: 30 ff.; Quak, ‘Runica Frisica’, 357 ff.; Düwel, ‘Friesen: Runeninschriften’, 29; Giliberto, ‘Criteria for the Formation’, 156 ff.

Ebenfalls aus Eibenholz gefertigt ist ein kleines, 23 cm langes Schwert, das aus einer Terp bei Arum (Gemeinde Wûnseradiel [Wonseradeel], Prov. Friesland, Niederlande) geborgen wurde und am ehesten in das 6./7. Jahrhundert, vielleicht aber auch erst in das 8. Jahrhundert zu datieren ist.[56] Auf einer Seite der 'Klinge' ist in Richtung auf den Griff eine rechtsläufige Runenfolge **eda$_1$:ba$_3$da$_2$** (**a$_2$** = ᚨ; als Trenner 2–4 Kerben) angebracht.[57]

Auffällig ist die an sich für südgermanische Runeninschriften charakteristische Form der *b*-Rune mit weiter auseinandergezogenen Winkeln, die in den friesischen Runeninschriften aber auch auf der Kammschale A von Oostum (**ka$_2$bu**; spätes 8. oder frühes 9. Jh.) entgegentritt.[58] Vor der Runeninschrift (also links davon) sind drei aneinandergrenzende Rauten ungleicher Größe angebracht; bei diesen 'paraschriftliche' Zeichen handelt es sich am ehesten um Zeilenfüllsel oder Markierungen des Textbeginns.[59]

---

56 P. C. J. A. Boeles Jr, 'Het zwaardje van Arum', *71. Verslag der Handelingen van het Friesch Genootschap van Geschied-, Oudheid- en Taalkunde te Leeuwarden* (1898–1899), 41–50: 46 (7.–10. Jh.); Ders., 'Nogmaals het zwaardje van Arum en de Hadamunt', *De Vrije Fries* 20 (1906), 190–203: 193 (6.–9. Jh.); Ders., *Friesland tot de elfde eeuw. Zijn oudste beschaving en geschiedenis* ('s-Gravenhage, 1927), 195 (Mitte oder Ende der zweiten Terpenperiode, die ca. 400 bis Mitte 8. Jh. datiert wird); Arntz, *ERF*, 112 f. (550–650); Boeles, *Friesland tot de elfde eeuw. Zijn vóór- en vroege geschiedenis* ('s-Gravenhage, 1951), 348 und 590 (550–650). Da das Objekt (scil. im Jahre 1895) 'unfachmännisch' geborgen wurde und sich daher die Fundschicht nicht sicher rekonstruieren läßt, gibt es weniger echte Anhaltspunkte für die Datierung als im Falle des Webschwerts von Westeremden: auch im Falle des Schwertchens von Arum sind offenbar (noch) keine naturwissenschaftlichen Methoden zur Altersbestimmung eingesetzt worden. Zu Fundkontext und Fundgeschichte vor allem Boeles, 'Nogmaals het zwaardje', 192 ff.; Arntz, *ERF*, 106 und 113. Die Runeninschrift wurde erst im Jahre 1899 entdeckt, und zwar von Pieter C. J. A. Boeles. – Looijenga ('Checklist', 91 und 96; Dies., *Texts & Contexts*, 309) und Giliberto (*Iscrizioni runiche*, 51) setzen das Schwertchen in das späte 8. Jh., begründen diese Datierung aber nicht.

57 Boeles, 'Het zwaardje', 42 ff. (Abb.: Fig. I); Ders., 'Nogmaals het zwaardje', 190 ff. (Abb.: Pl. II); Ders., *Friesland* ([1]1927), 194 f. und 258 (Abb.: Pl. XXVII,18 und XLII,4); Ders., *Friesland* ([2]1951), 347 f. (Abb.: Pl. XXX,18 und XLVII,4); *ERF*, Nr. 6 (Abb.: Taf. VI). Vgl. ferner Quak, 'Runica Frisica', 360; Düwel, 'Friesen: Runeninschriften', 28; Giliberto, *Iscrizioni runiche*, 51 ff.; Looijenga, 'Checklist', 91 und 96; Dies., *Texts & Contexts*, 309. Die ältere Literatur verzeichnet Schnall, *Bibliographie*, 12 f.

58 Inwieweit auch Rune II,2 auf dem Stab von Britsum (Datierung unklar) hier anzuführen ist, bleibt unklar: der etwas größere Abstand zwischen den (gerundeten) Buckeln mag durch die ornamentale Ausführung des Zeichens bedingt sein (Stab sechsfach, Buckel dreifach geritzt); die Buckel der zweiten *b*-Rune der Inschrift (I,5; Stab fünffach, Buckel dreifach geritzt) sind jedenfalls nicht bzw. nur minimal auseinandergezogen.

59 Arntz (*ERF*, 115 f.) erblickt darin zwei gegenständig eingeritzte 'liegende' *o*-Runen ᛟ, H. Harder ('Die Runeninschrift des Holzschwertes von Arum', *Archiv für das Studium der neueren Sprachen und Literaturen* 170 [1936], 218–19: 218) hingegen drei *ŋ*-Runen ◇; beide Autoren vertreten begriffsrunische Deutungen (Arntz: 'Besitz, Besitz'; Harder: 'Ing, Ing, Ing'). Derartige Verfahrensweisen bzw. Interpretationen finden heutzutage

Schon in der älteren Forschung hat man dem Schwertchen, dessen Spitze verkohlt ist,[60] symbolische Funktion zuerkannt; man hat darin ein Zeichen zum Aufgebot des Heeres (also ein Mobilmachungssignal) gesehen[61] oder auch den Ausweis bzw. die Legitimation eines Boten.[62] Wirklich erhärten lassen sich jedoch diese Annahmen nicht; es kann sich genausogut um simples K(leink)inderspielzeug handeln.[63] Auf spielerischen Gebrauch würde jedenfalls der Umstand hindeuten, daß der Griff ziemlich stark abgenutzt ist:[64] derartig deutliche Gebrauchsspuren würde man bei einem symbolisch-repräsentativen Gegenstand nicht unbedingt erwarten.

Was die Runeninschrift betrifft, so konkurrieren heutzutage im wesentlichen zwei Deutungen: zumeist erblickt man in der Sequenz **eda**$_1$**:ba**$_3$**da**$_2$

---

wohl kaum mehr Zustimmung. – An der Spitze des Schwertchens haben Arntz (*ERF*, 114 ff.) und andere darüber hinaus ein 'sehr schwach angedeutetes' bäumchenartiges Zeichen erkannt; sollte es sich tatsächlich um eine intendierte Ritzung handeln, bleiben Funktion und Bedeutung unklar.

60 Ob die Verkohlung ursprünglich ist, wie der Finder, ein Schiffer namens Wieger Sijtsma, dann im Zuge einer näheren Befragung etwa ein Jahrzehnt nach der Auffindung (!) angegeben hat (Boeles, 'Nogmaals het zwaardje' [1906], 193 f: 'juist dezer dagen'), bleibt unsicher: es kann sich auch um eine Schutzbehauptung Sijtsmas handeln.

61 So zuerst G. Neckel, 'Kleine Beiträge zur germanischen Altertumskunde', *BGdSL* 33 (1908), 459–82: 462 ('Seine form lässt vermuten, dass [...] das kriegsaufgebot seine ursprüngliche funktion war'). Als Parallele denkt Neckel an den (aisl.) *herǫr* im alten Skandinavien, der als Alarmsignal bzw. Ruf zu den Waffen diente; literarisch ist der Einsatz eines 'Kriegspfeils' vielfach belegt, z.B. Saxo Grammaticus, *Gesta Danorum* V,5,5; *Egils saga Skalla-Grímssonar*, c. 3; Snorri Sturluson, *Heimskringla*, *Óláfs saga helga*, c. 39; *Stadtrecht des Magnus Hákonarson* III,3. Vgl. ferner etwa J. Grimm, *Deutsche Rechtsalterthümer*, I, 4. Aufl. (Leipzig, 1899) = J. und W. Grimm, *Werke*, Abt. I, 17 (Hildesheim etc., 1992), 222 f.; P. Herrmann, *Erläuterungen zu den ersten neun Büchern der Dänischen Geschichte des Saxo Grammaticus*. II: *Kommentar: Die Heldensagen des Saxo Grammaticus* (Leipzig, 1922), 346.

62 Arntz, *ERF*, 112 ('eine Legitimation für den Boten, der mit dem Symbol umherzog'). Die ebd. erwogene (und dann zurückgestellte) Alternative, das Schwertchen sei 'ein Symbol dafür, daß der Meineidige durch Schwert und Feuer umkommen soll', hat deutlich weniger für sich.

63 Dem Einwand von Arntz, das Objekt könne 'wegen seiner Kleinheit kein eigentliches Kinderspielzeug gewesen sein' (*ERF*, 119), kann ich nicht folgen: so etwa ist das kleinere von zwei in Staraja Ladoga gefundenen hölzernen Spielzeugschwertern aus dem 8. oder 9. Jh. (*Wikinger, Waräger, Normannen. Die Skandinavier und Europa 800–1200*. Katalog der Ausstellung Paris 1992, Berlin 1992, Kopenhagen 1992/1993 [Mainz, 1992], 301 [Nr. 279]), dessen erhaltener Teil 13,9 cm mißt und für das man wohl ungefähr die doppelte Gesamtlänge veranschlagen wird, nicht viel größer als das Schwertchen von Arum. – Für 'technische' Beratung in diesem Zusammenhang danke ich Jakob Schnell (Wien) sehr herzlich. Zum Thema Spielzeugschwerter im Mittelalter jüngst (kurz und knapp) I. Gabriel, 'Spiel und Spielzeug', *Reallexikon*, XXIX (2005), 354–63: 357.

64 Vgl. Arntz, *ERF*, 118.

ein Kompositum *edœboda* 'renuntius',[65] bisweilen wird der runenepigraphische Text jedoch auch als Zueignung 'für E., den Boten' gefaßt.[66] Andere Interpretationen werden demgegenüber nur vereinzelt vertreten und kommen – aus unterschiedlichen Gründen – auch nicht in nähere Betracht.[67]

---

[65] Th. von Grienberger, 'Zwei Runeninschriften aus Norwegen und Friesland', *ZfdP* 42 (1910), 385–97: 395 ff. (Präfix **eda-* > ae. as. anfränk. *ed-* 'wiederum' ~ **eþa-* > afries. *eth-*, *et-*, als Grundelement **budan-* > afries. *boda*; das Schwertchen sei 'am ehesten ein legitimierendes abzeichen, glaublich für einen boten'). Die Interpretation als 'renuntius' findet sich ferner etwa bei Arntz, *ERF*, 120 und 456; W. Krause, *Was man in Runen ritzte*, 2. Aufl. (Halle/S., 1943), 33 f. ('möglicherweise'); Nielsen, 'Unaccented vowels' (1984), 17; Ders., 'Unaccented Vowels' (1991), 300; R. W. V. *Elliott, Runes: an Introduction*, 2. Aufl. (Manchester und New York, 1989), 42; Odenstedt, 'Transliteration', 55; Giliberto, *Iscrizioni runiche*, 55 f.

[66] W. J. Buma, *Frieslands Runeninscripties* (Groningen und Djakarta, 1957), 24 ff. ('voor Ede, [de] bode': **eda**$_1$ = *-æ* als Dat. Sg. eines maskulinen *n*-Stamms, was jedoch lautlich nicht angeht). So z.B. auch H. T. J. Miedema, 'Dialect en runen van Britsum en de oudste anglofriese runeninscripties', *Taal en Tongval* 26 (1974), 101–28: 114; Düwel, 'Friesen: Runeninschriften', 28 ('"für Eda, den Boten" [als Rechtszeichen]'); Ders., *Runenkunde*, 3. Aufl., Sammlung Metzler 72 (Stuttgart und Weimar, 2001), 86 f.; Ders., 'Kämme mit Runeninschriften', *Die deutsche Sprache in der Gegenwart. Festschrift Dieter Cherubim*, St. J. Schierholz et al., Hg. (Frankfurt/M., 2001), 11–22: 12; abwägend Quak, 'Runica Frisica', 360. – Auch Gysseling, *Corpus* II,1, 11 (sub G) faßt **eda**$_1$ = *-æ* als Dat. Sg. eines *a*-Stammes (*boda* aber als Nom. Sg. eines Anthroponyms *Boda*).

[67] 1. Die ganze Runenfolge als zweigliedrigen Männernamen zu fassen (so S. Bugge, 'Das Runendenkmal von Britsum in Friesland', *ZfdP* 40 [1908], 174–84: 181; L. Musset, *Introduction à la runologie*. Bibliothèque de philologie germanique 20 [Paris, 1965], 210), vermag aus morphologischen Gründen nicht zu überzeugen: *n*-Stämme als Hinterglieder sind in der altgermanischen Anthroponymie extrem selten; vgl. Nedoma, *Personennamen*, 317 (LNr. 43, C.3.1.). – 2. Die alte Interpretation als 'Eidbote', jüngst wieder von Looijenga ('Checklist', 96; Dies., *Texts & Contexts*, 309) vertreten, trifft – wie bereits W. L. van Helten kurz nach der Entdeckung der Inschrift (brieflich bei von Grienberger, 'Zwei Runeninschriften', 395 mit Anm. 2) festgestellt hat – ebenfalls schwerlich das Richtige: daß /þ/ in urgerm. **aiþa-* m. 'Eid' (> afries. as. *ēth*, ae. *āð* etc.) durch eine *d*-Rune wiedergegeben wäre, ist nicht mehr als eine *ad hoc*-Annahme; unerwartet käme auch das Fugenelement **(ed)-a**$_1$-, denn nach schwerer Silbe zeigt sich in den friesischen Runeninschriften sonst **-u-** = vor-afries. -ə̣- (s. oben, II). – 3. Aus epigraphischen Gründen nicht zu halten ist die Lesung/Deutung von W. Krogmann, *Zur Frage der friesischen Runeninschriften*, Estrikken 2 (Grins, 1953), 19 ff. (*ēdlboda* 'Krankheitsbote'), die in rezent(er)en Publikationen wieder Urständ feiert, z.B. bei Th. L. Markey, *Frisian*, Trends in Linguistics, State-of-the-Art Reports 13 (The Hague etc., 1981), 52; K. S. Bussmann, *Diphthongs in Frisian. A Comparative Analysis of Phonemic Inventories Past and Present* (Heidelberg, 2004), 1 Anm. 1 (ohne Referenz). – 4. Problematisch ist schließlich auch die Lesung/Deutung von A. Bammesberger, 'Ingvaeonic Sound Changes and the Anglo-Frisian Runes', *Old English Runes*, Bammesberger, Hg., 389–408: 404 Anm. 41; Ders., 'Frisian and Anglo-Saxon Runes: from the Linguistic Angle', *Frisian Runes*, Looijenga und Quak, Hg., 15–23: 20 (**edæbanda**, sodaß sich ein Nomen agentis *banda* 'Binder' ergebe): die angenommene orthographische Oszillation ᚠ ~ ᚨᚾ ist nicht zu erhärten. – Gegen alle vier referierten Interpretationen ist zudem einzuwenden, daß

Formal einwandfrei, ist die Deutung von **eda$_1$:ba$_3$da$_2$** als vor-afries. *edæboda* 'renuntius' aus epigraphischen Gründen problematisch, denn aus den älteren Runeninschriften (im älteren Fuþark oder im anglo-friesischen Fuþork) ist kein einziges auch nur einigermaßen überzeugendes Beispiel dafür beizubringen, daß man Trenner innerhalb eines Wortes, sozusagen Intrapunktionen, gesetzt hätte.[68] Ferner will auch der 'Sitz im Leben' nicht wirklich einleuchten, denn es bliebe unklar, warum der sich mit seinem Schwertchen legitimierende Gesandte in der Runeninschrift als '*re*nuntius' bezeichnet wäre: für den/die Adressaten/-in einer Botschaft bliebe eine Legitimation '*zurück*kehrender Bote' referentiell leer, und bei dem/der Adressanten/-in der Botschaft braucht sich der Gesandte nicht legitimieren.

Epigraphisch einwandfrei, ist sodann die Deutung von **eda$_1$:ba$_3$da$_2$** als Zueignung bzw. Widmung *Edæ boda* 'für E., den Boten' aus formalen Gründen schwerlich zu halten, denn es zeigt sich kein Reflex eines Suffixes, mit dem (ursprüngliche) Kurzformen zu zweigliedrigen Männernamen gebildet werden. In der germanischen Anthroponymie sind vor allem **-an-* oder auch **-(i)ja-* in dieser Funktion produktiv, sodaß für den Dativ der voraltfriesischen Entsprechung von afries. *Edo* m., 10. Jh. (Utrecht;[69] mit latei-

die Kerben nach Rune Nr. 3 **a$_1$** schwerlich als 'Intrapunktion' zu nehmen sind (s. oben und sofort, Anm. 68). – Einen Überblick über die tastenden Deutungsversuche der ältesten Forschung bietet Arntz, *ERF*, 118 ff.

68 Vgl. bereits S. Gutenbrunner, *Die germanischen Götternamen der antiken Inschriften*. Rheinische Beiträge und Hülfsbücher zur germanischen Philologie und Volkskunde (Halle/S., 1936), 40 Anm. 1; Arntz, *ERF*, 120; Buma, *Frieslands Runeninscripties*, 23 f. Daß **a$_1$** und **b** trotz der zwischen diesen beiden Runen gesetzten Trenner auch nicht weiter voneinander entfernt sind als andere Runen der Inschrift, ist für die Funktion als Interpunktion (für die Funktion, eine Wortgrenze zu signalisieren) nicht relevant. – Aus der älteren runenepigraphischen Überlieferung hat man in der rezenten Forschung, soweit ich sehe, lediglich die Folge **ulu:hari** auf einem der drei sog. Weser-Runenknochen (5. Jh.) als 'intrapunktiertes' Kompositum zu deuten versucht. Schon aus lautlichen Gründen kann es sich hier jedoch entgegen P. Pieper, *Die Weser-Runenknochen. Neue Untersuchungen zur Problematik: Original oder Fälschung*, Archäologische Mitteilungen aus Nordwestdeutschland, Beiheft 2 (Oldenburg, 1989), 182 f. (**Wulþu-h°*) und E. H. Antonsen, 'The Weser Runes: Magic or Message?', *Festschrift Hans Bekker-Nielsen*, 1–20: 14 = Ders., *Runes and Germanic Linguistics*, Trends in Linguistics, Studies and Monographs 140 (Berlin und New York, 2002), 326 (**Uw(w)a/ila-h°*) um kein zweigliedriges Anthroponym handeln; s. Nedoma, *Personennamen*, 328 ff. (LNr. 45, C.0.2.).

69 *Diplomata Belgica ante annum millesimum centesium scripta*, M. Gysseling und A. C. F. Koch, Hg., Bouwstoffen en studiën voor de geschiedenis en de lexicografie van het Nederlands 1 (Brussel, 1950), I: *Teksten*, 339 (Nr. 195). Zu afries. *Edo* m. vgl. ferner Quak, 'Friese persoonsnamen', 167; da der Haupttonvokal offenbar lang ist (*Ēd-* < **Aid-*; s. sofort), bleibt ae. *Eda* m. aus lautlichen Gründen fern (≠ *Ād-* < **Aid-*).

nischem Ausgang *-o* statt originär-afries. *-a*) runenepigraphisches (**ed**)-$\mathbf{a}_2$[70] bzw. -$\mathbf{a}_2$**n** (afries. *bod-a* Dat. Sg. m. *n*-St. 'Bote'; ae. *bod-an* < urgerm. *$^{(*)}$*-ani*) oder auch **-e** (afries. ae. *end-e* Dat. Sg. m. *ija*-St. 'Ende' < **-je* < **-ije* < **-ijē* < urgerm. **-ijai̯*) zu erwarten wäre; demgegenüber ist eine stark flektierte Form (**ed**)-$\mathbf{a}_1$ = *-æ* (afries. *ēth-e* Dat. Sg. m. *a*-St. 'Eid', ae. *āð-e*, früh-ae. *-æ* < **-ǣ* < **-ē* < urgerm. **-ai̯*) mit den in der altgermanischen (Kurz-)Namenbildung herrschenden Regularitäten[71] nicht zu vereinbaren.

Für **eda**$_1$ bietet sich indessen eine andere, einwandfreie Deutung an, und zwar als Nom. Sg. einer mit *n*-Suffix gebildeten (ursprünglichen) Kurzform zu einem zweigliedrigen Frauennamen. Der Ausgang -$\mathbf{a}_1$ = *-æ* ist der für das Voraltfriesische lautgesetzlich zu erwartende Reflex von urgerm. **-ō*^{n} (afries. ae. *tung-e*, früh-ae. *-æ* Nom. Sg. f. *ōn*-St. < **-a* < **-ɔ* < **-ō* < **-ō*^{n}).[72] Das zugrundeliegende Namenelement ist wohl als *Ēda-* < **Aida-* zu be-

[70] Genau diese Runenfolge ist überliefert auf dem Kamm von 'Amay' (Fundort unsicher; 6. oder 7. Jh.), allerdings nach einer Bruchstelle: sonach läßt sich nicht entscheiden, ob die Inschrift vollständig ist (in diesem Fall wäre **ẹda**$_2$ ein *n*-stämmiger männlicher Kurzname *Ēda* im Nom. Sg.) oder ob es sich etwa um den Schlußteil einer Herstellerinschrift *[N.N.* (auf der anderen Seite?) *d]ēda* 'N.N. tat, machte' handelt; vgl. Düwel, 'Knochenkämme', 370 f.; Ders., 'Friesen: Runeninschriften', 28.

[71] Dazu grundlegend G. Müller, 'Starke und schwache Flexion bei den eingliedrigen germanischen Männernamen', *Gedenkschrift William Foerste*, D. Hofmann und W. Sanders, Hg., Niederdeutsche Studien 18 (Köln und Wien, 1970), 215–31; ferner etwa A. Bach, *Deutsche Namenkunde*. I,1–2: *Die deutschen Personennamen*, 2. Aufl. (Heidelberg, 1952–1953 = 3. Aufl. 1978), §41,2 und §96 ff.; Wagner, 'Personennamen', 23 ff.; D. Geuenich, *Die Personennamen der Klostergemeinschaft von Fulda im früheren Mittelalter*. Münstersche Mittelalter-Schriften 5 (München, 1976), 90 ff.; zuletzt Th. Andersson, 'Personennamen', *Reallexikon*, XXII (2003), 589–614: 597 ff. (mit Lit.). – Auf einen (ganz groben) Nenner gebracht, steht in der germanischen Namengebung der größeren Gruppe der (ursprünglich) mittels Reduktion plus Derivation gebildeten Kurzformen aus zweigliedrigen Anthroponymen (Typen afries. *Thiad-a* m. < **-ō*, *Thiad(d)-i* m. < **-ijaz* zu 'Vollnamen' wie afries. *Thiadbrand* m.) eine kleinere Gruppe von 'konvertierten', mit Nullableitung modellierten Simplizia auf Basis von Ethnonymen bzw. Personengruppen (z.B. ahd. *Swāb*, woneben *n*-stämmiges ahd. *Frieso* etc.) appellativischen Substantiva (insbesondere Bezeichnungen aus dem Komplex Beruf, Beschäftigung, Stand, Familie, sodann Waffen, Tiere und Abstrakta, z.B. as. *Karl* 'Mann', ae. *Bil* 'Schwert', vor-afries. *Habukə* OOSTUM, ae. *Wīg* 'Kampf') und Adjektiva (z.B. urn. *Wakraz* 'wach, aufmerksam', woneben *n*-stämmiges afries. *Snello* etc.) gegenüber. Ohne hier den Sachverhalt in seiner ganzen Breite aufzurollen, ist bei **eda**$_1$ auf dem Schwertchen von Arum (: **Aida-*, zu ae. *ād* 'Feuer, Scheiterhaufen' etc.) jedenfalls kein direkter ('motivierter') Bezug auf ein nominales Appellativum gegeben, der eine Flexion als *a*-Stamm 'rechtfertigen' würde.

[72] S. etwa Siebs, 'Geschichte', 1241 (§69); K. Luick, *Historische Grammatik der englischen Sprache*. I,1 (Leipzig, 1921 = Oxford und Stuttgart, 1964), 267 ff. (§299,3, §301,3 und §324); H. Krahe, *Germanische Sprachwissenschaft*. I: *Einleitung und Lautlehre* (Berlin, 1942 u.ö. [^{7}1969]), 124 f. (§126,2); vgl. Nielsen, 'Unaccented vowels' (1984), 17; Ders., 'Unaccented Vowels' (1991), 301; Odenstedt, 'Transliteration', 64.

stimmen,[73] das in Anthroponymen wie ogot. Αἰδοΐγγου Gen., 5. Jh. (Malchos) oder skir. *Aedico* 5. Jh. (Chron. min.) entgegentritt,[74] ferner aus der späteren Namenüberlieferung etwa in langob. *Aidualdus* 8. Jh. (Farfa), früh-ahd. *Aitpald* 8. Jh. (Salzburg) und ae. *Ādhysi* 9. Jh. (Durham).[75] Der Namenstamm **Aida*- gehört zu ae. *ād* 'Feuer, Scheiterhaufen', ahd. *eit* dass., as. *ēd* 'Scheiterhaufen',[76] afries. *ēd* 'Brennstoff, Torf'[77] (urgerm. **aida*- m.).[78] Die Runenfolge **eda**$_1$ = *Ēdæ* f. (oder phonetisch genauer: *Ę̄dæ*) gibt demzufolge die vorafr. Entsprechung von fränk.(-as.) *Aeda* f., 8./9. Jh. (Hrotsuith)[79] und

---

[73] Urgerm. /ai/ wird im Altfriesischen in der Position vor Dentalen bevorzugt (aber nicht exklusiv) als /ē/ fortgesetzt (wie etwa in *brēd* Adj. 'breit' < urgerm. **braida*-); dazu vor allem H. F. Nielsen, 'Germanic *ai* in Old Frisian, Old English and Old Norse', *IF* 88 (1983 [1984]), 156–64; Hofmann, 'Zur Monophthongierung', 26 ff.; Krogh, *Stellung des Altsächsischen*, 274 ff. (mit Lit.). – Nicht gänzlich auszuschließen, aber dennoch wenig wahrscheinlich ist die Anknüpfung an einen nur undeutlich greifbaren kurzvokalischen Sekundärstamm *Ĕd(a)*-, der sich je nach Umfeld aus verschiedenen Quellen zu speisen scheint. Für das 'intern' (scil. in einheimisch-germanischer Runenschrift in einheimisch-germanischem kulturellen Milieu) überlieferte friesische Anthroponym **eda**$_1$ kommen jedenfalls durch romanischsprachige Tradierende verursachte Lautsubstitutionen oder Ablautentgleisungen (nach fremden Mustern) schwerlich in Frage, sodaß die lautlich und semantisch gut fundierte Verbindung mit ae. *ād* 'Feuer, Scheiterhaufen' etc. bzw. der Ansatz eines langvokalischen *Ēdæ* ohne Zweifel weitaus mehr für sich hat. – Daß der Namenstamm **Haidu*- (zu got. *haidus** 'Art und Weise', ahd. *heit*, ae. *hād* 'Person, Stand, Art', afries. -*hēd(e)* etc.) zugrundeliegt, wie Looijenga ('Checklist', 92; *Texts & Contexts*, 303 ad **ẹda**$_2$ 'AMAY' alternativ) erwägt, ist nicht anzunehmen: im Voraltfriesischen (und im Altfriesischen) hat kein Schwund von anlautendem /h/ stattgefunden, und mit romanischen Interferenzen braucht nicht gerechnet zu werden (vgl. vorhin).

[74] Einzelbelege in *LaN* I, 16 und 244 (s.v. *Edico*); Liste weiterer Belege: *LaN* II, 454. – Keltischer Herkunft ist wohl 'wfränk.' *Aidus* 7. Jh. (Ep. Merov.; LaN I, 16). Ein bekannter Namenträger ist air. *Áed*, latinisiert *Aidus*, Bischof von Sléibte (gest. 700), dem Muirchú seine *Vita Patricii* widmete; weitere Belege verbucht A. Holder, *Alt-Celtischer Sprachschatz*. 3 Bde. (Leipzig, 1896–1907 = Graz, 1962) I, 64 f.

[75] Einzelbelege bei W. Bruckner, *Die Sprache der Langobarden*, QF 75 (Straßburg, 1895 = 1969), 219 (langob. *Aidualdus*); Förstemann, *Personennamen*, 46 (früh-ahd. *Aitpald*); Searle, *Onomasticon*, 3 (ae. *Ādhysi*).

[76] Hapax legomenon: Wadstein, *Kleinere altsächsische Sprachdenkmäler*, 96, Z. 14.

[77] K. Fokkema, *Nei wider kimen. Kar út syn fersprate skriften* (Groningen, 1969), 98.

[78] Vgl. z.B. Kaufmann, *Ergänzungsband zu Förstemann, Personennamen* (München und Hildesheim, 1968), 25 (s.v. *Aid*-); N. Wagner, 'Ostgermanisch-alanisch-hunnische Beziehungen bei Personennamen', *Studien zur deutschen Literatur des Mittelalters*, R. Schützeichel, Hg. (Bonn, 1979), 11–33: 29 (mit Lit.); Felder, *Personennamen*, 50.

[79] *[Annales, chronica et historiae aevi Carolini et Saxonici]*, G. H. Pertz, Hg., MGH, Scriptores [in folio] 4 (Hannover, 1841 = Stuttgart, 1982), 306 (*bis*) und 316. Vgl. Förstemann, *Personennamen*, 448; Schlaug, *Personennamen*, 53.

as. *Aeda* f. (Totenbuch Merseburg zum 28.IX.)[80] wieder, vgl. ferner das Hypokoristikon wfränk. *Aidelina* f., 9. Jh. (Paris)[81].

Das zweite Segment der Inschrift, **ba$_3$da$_2$**, birgt entweder das Appellativum afries. ae. *boda*, as. *bodo*, ahd. *boto*, aisl. *boði* m. 'Bote, Herold' (urgerm. **budan-*) oder eine (ursprüngliche) *n*-stämmige Kurzform zu einem zweigliedrigen Anthroponym mit Namenstamm **Buda-* > **Boda-* (schwundstufig zu urgerm. **beuda-* 'bieten')[82] im Vorder- oder Hinterglied. Aus altgermanischer Zeit ist das Namenelement **Buda-* > **Boda-* in Bildungen wie wfränk. *Bodegisilus* 6. Jh. (Venantius Fortunatus etc.)[83] zu belegen oder, im Hinterglied, auch runenepigraphisch in **arsiboda** = langob. *Arsibodā̆* f. Gen., BEZENYE B, 550–568.[84] Dazu kommen aus späterer Zeit auch direkte Entsprechungen von **ba$_3$da$_2$**, z.B. afries. *Bodonis* Gen., 14. Jh. (Willküre von Wildinghe [Wûnseradiel];[85] mit lateinischem Ausgang *-o* statt originär-afries. *-a*), spät-ae. *Boda* 11. Jh. (Domesday Book), ahd. *Boto*, *Poto* 8. Jh. (St. Gallen etc.), langob. *Bodo*, *Poto* 8. Jh. (Pavia etc.).[86] Ob Appellativ oder Anthroponym, es kann sich bei **ba$_3$da$_2$** um einen Nominativ Sg. **-a$_2$** = *-a* (afries. ae. *-a* m. *n*-St. < *-*ɔ* < *-*o* < *-*ō̃* < urgerm. *-*ō̃*) handeln wie bei **ha$_2$da$_2$** = vor-afries. *Had(d)a* m., HARLINGEN, spätes 6. oder frühes 7. Jh. (= ae. *H(e)ada*, *H(e)adda* 7. Jh.[87]) oder bei **tuda$_2$** BERNSTERBUREN (*bis*), vor oder um 800, das wohl als vor-afries. *Tūd(d)a* m. mit Entsprechungen in ae.

---

80 *Die Totenbücher von Merseburg, Magdeburg und Lüneburg*, G. Althoff und J. Wollasch, Hg., MGH, Libri memoriales et necrologia N.S. 2 (Hannover, 1983), 12 (sub *e 6*; nicht unbedingt dieselbe Person wie die vorhin genannte fränk.-[as.] *Aeda*, die Frau Billungs). Vgl. Schlaug, *Personennamen*, 53. – Die Schreibung *Ae-* deutet auf einen noch offen realisierten (monophthongischen) Reflex von altem /ai/; dazu J. H. Gallée (und H. Tiefenbach), *Altsächsische Grammatik*, 3. Aufl. (Tübingen, 1993), 70 (§89) und 73 (§93,2).

81 *Polyptychon*, Hägermann, Hg., 141 (*Polyptychon Irminonis* XVI,30). Vgl. Förstemann, *Personennamen*, 46; Morlet, *Noms de personne* I, 27.

82 Zum Namenstamm **Buda-* > **Boda-* zuletzt Felder, *Personennamen*, 105 ff. (ad wfränk. *Bŏd-*); Nedoma, *Personennamen*, 207 ff. (LNr. 16, C.3.; mit Lit.).

83 Belege: *LaN* I, 145. – Bei Venantius Fortunatus erscheint altes /au/ noch durchwegs als ‹au› (z.B. in *Audegiselus*, *Launebodis* Gen., *Lauto* etc.), sodaß im Vorderglied gewiß *Bŏde-* und nicht *Bōde-* < **Baudi-* vorliegt.

84 *ERF* Nr. 27–28; *RäF* Nr. 166. Zu Inschrift und Namen ausführlich Nedoma, *Personennamen*, 202 ff. (LNr. 16).

85 *Oudfriesche oorkonden* II, P. Sipma, Hg., OTR 2 ('s-Gravenhage, 1933), 3 (Nr. 2, a. 1379).

86 Diese und weitere Belege bei Searle, *Onomasticon*, 109 (spät-ae. *Boda*); Förstemann, *Personennamen*, 320 (ahd. *Boto*, *Poto*); Bruckner, *Sprache der Langobarden*, 237 (langob. *Bodo*, *Poto*). – Wfränk. *Bodo* (Belege bei Morlet, *Noms de personne* I, 59 f.) ist ambig: es kann (**Buda-* >) **Boda-* oder (**Baudi-* >) **Bōdi-* vorausliegen.

87 Belege bei Searle, *Onomasticon*, 275 (*Hada*, *Hadda*) und 281 f. (*Heada*, *Headda*).

Tud(d)a 7. Jh.,[88] as. *Tudo* 9. Jh.[89] sowie ahd. *Zuto* 9. Jh., *Zutto* 8. Jh. (St. Gallen)[90] zu fassen ist, vgl. ferner das um ein *l*-Suffix erweiterte Deminutivum hispano-got. *Tudila* 9. Jh.[91]. Durchaus möglich, jedoch etwas weniger wahrscheinlich ist sodann eine Interpretation als Dativ Sg. auf -$\mathbf{a}_2$ = *-a* (afries. *-a*, ae. *-an* m. *n*-St. < urgerm. *^(*)^*-ani*): in diesem Fall müßte die für das Altfriesische charakteristische Generalisierung von *-a* im Singular-Paradigma der maskulinen *n*-Stämme[92] bereits in der 'Runenzeit' durchgeführt worden sein (wogegen *-an* im Altenglischen erhalten ist).

Für die Zweiwortinschrift auf dem Schwertchen von Arum bieten sich demnach folgende drei Deutungsmöglichkeiten:

---

[88] Belege ebd., 460 und 579; auf das Nebeneinander von **tuda**$_2$ und ae. *Tud(d)a* hat bereits Quak ('Zur Runeninschrift von Bernsterburen', *ABäG* 34 [1991], 19–21: 19; Ders., 'Friese persoonsnamen', 168) hingewiesen. – Ae. *Tuda, Tudda* m. ist häufig bezeugt (z.B. in Bedas Kirchengeschichte, in der Angelsächsischen Chronik oder im *Liber vitae Dunelmensis*); ob es sich um einen ursprünglich keltischen Namen handelt, wie meist angenommen wird (z.B. von M. Redin, *Studies on Uncompounded Personal Names in Old English* [Uppsala, 1919], 71; H. Ström, *Old English Personal Names in Bede's History. An Etymological-phonological Investigation*. Lund Studies in English 8 [Lund, 1939], 77), ist fraglich: in Betracht kommt vor allem eine wohl 'kindersprachlich' bzw. expressiv vereinfachte Variante einer (ursprünglichen) Kurzform zu einem zweigliedrigen germanischen Anthroponym mit Namenstamm **Þeuda-* im Vorderglied (zu ae. *þēod*, as. *thiod(a)*, afries. *thiād*, ahd. *diot* etc. 'Volk, Menge, [Pl.] Leute' < urgerm. **þeudō-* f.); vgl. Kaufmann, *Ergänzungsband*, 354 f. (ad *T(h)ūd-*). Ein aus altem /eu/ entwickeltes /ū/ zeigen z.B. auch *Thudelindi* f. Gen., 7. Jh. (Ebersheim; *Corpus inscriptionum Latinarum* XIII, Nr. 7260) oder auch runenepigraphisches **luda**$_2$ = ae. *Lūd(d)a* HARFORD FARM, eingeritzt ca. 630/640–660/670 (: **Leudi-*); dazu Nedoma, *Personennamen*, 427 (LNr. 78, C.1.). Wenn die Interpretation als 'überformtes' **Þeudan-* das Richtige trifft, muß es sich bei **tuda**$_2$ = vor-afries. *Tūd(d)a*, ae. *Tūd(d)a* samt as. *Tūdo*, früh-ahd. *Zūt(t)o* und hispano-got. *Tūdila* (Belege sofort, Anm. 88–90) um früh verselbständigte und 'fossilierte' Kurznamen handeln, denn Neubildung aus den regulären Formen afries. *Thiada* m., 10. Jh. (Werden; *Urbare*, Kötzschke, Hg., 53 [§23]), ae. **Þēoda* bzw. as. *Thiado*, früh-ahd. *Thiodo* etc. kommt wegen des abweichenden konsonantischen Anlauts (*Þ-* ≠ *T-*, ahd. *Z-*) und des abweichenden Diphthongzweitteils (*a/ɔ/o* ≠ *u*) nicht in Frage. – Daß ae. *Tuda, Tudda* aus dem Germanischen zu erklären ist, schließt natürlich keineswegs aus, daß die Bildung auch eine keltische 'Nebenquelle' hat.

[89] *Traditionen*, Honselmann, Hg., 91 (Nr. 51). Vgl. Schlaug, *Personennamen*, 157. Zwei weitere altsächsische Belege verzeichnet Förstemann, *Personennamen*, 1412.

[90] *Subsidia Sangallensia*. I: *Materialien und Untersuchungen zu den Verbrüderungsbüchern und zu den älteren Urkunden des Stiftsarchivs St. Gallen*, M. Borgolte et al., Hg., St. Galler Kultur und Geschichte 16 (St. Gallen, 1986), 631 (s.v. *t 18*; *Zuto* a. 811, *Zutto* a. 768). Vgl. Förstemann, *Personennamen*, 1676 (s.v. *Zot* verbucht).

[91] Beleg bei Kremer, *Personennamen*, 209 (§177,1,II) bzw. Piel und Kremer, *Hispanogotisches Namenbuch*, 266 (§271,41).

[92] Van Helten, *Altostfriesische Grammatik*, 55 (§66ε; 'in folge von jüngerer apocope') und 84 (§107α); Siebs, 'Geschichte', 1265 f. (§108); Steller, *Abriß*, 42 (§60 Anm. 2).

(1) ‘E. [und] B.’ (asyndetische Namen zweier Schenkender, einer Frau und eines Mannes, jeweils im Nominativ)[93] oder, etwas weniger wahrscheinlich,

(2a) ‘E. dem B.’ (Name der Schenkerin im Nominativ, Name des Beschenkten im Dativ) bzw.

(2b) ‘E. dem Boten’ (Name der Schenkerin im Nominativ, appellativische Bezeichnung des Beschenkten im Dativ).

Aufgrund der letztlich nicht zu erhellenden Funktion des Inschriftenträgers – K(leink)inderspielzeug?; Botenstab??, Mobilmachungssignal???, auch andere Gebrauchszwecke sind ohne weiteres denkbar – läßt sich zwischen den drei angeführten Alternativen keine endgültige Entscheidung treffen.

IV

Was die Sukzession urgerm. *-ō*^{n} > *-ō > *-ɔ > *-a > vor-afries. *-æ* > afries. *-e* (bzw. früh-ae. *-æ* > ae. *-e*) betrifft, stellt sich abschließend die Frage, ob bzw. inwieweit auch andere Sequenzen mit finalem -$\mathbf{a}_1$ in den friesischen Runeninschriften als schwach flektierte Nom. Sg. auf *-æ* zu fassen sind.

Stimmig ist eine derartige ‘innere Deutung für die Runenfolge **mura**$_1$ auf dem Kammfutteral von Ferwerd (6./7. Jh.):[94] daß hier eine Besitzerinschrift vor-afries. *Mur(r)æ* f. (Nom. Sg. *ōn*-St.) vorliegt, hat alle Wahrscheinlichkeit für sich.[95] Da in der germanischen Anthroponymie zweigliedrige Bildungen mit Namenelement *Mū̆r(r)-* nur unsicher zu belegen sind,[96] wird es sich bei

[93] Die formal mögliche Interpretation ‘E. [und] der Bote’ kommt aus ‘äußeren’ Gründen kaum in Betracht.

[94] Das erste Zeichen lese ich mit Boeles (‘De runeninscripties van het Friesch Museum’, *De Vrije Fries* 35 [1939], 83–95: 89 ff.; *Friesland* [²1951], 354); Düwel (‘Knochenkämme’, 370 f.; ‘Friesen: Runeninschriften’, 28), Quak (‘Runica Frisica’, 362) und anderen als *m*-Rune ᛗ. Deutlich weniger plausible Lesungsvorschläge bieten Arntz (*ERF*, 208: Binderune **l͡t** = *t[i]l* ‘für’), Looijenga (‘Checklist’, 92 f.; *Texts & Contexts*, 303: **m͡e** = *me* ‘mir’) sowie Giliberto (*Iscrizioni runiche*, 68: **m͡e͡t** für *meþ* ‘mit’). – Daß sich der Lautwert von Rune Nr. 4 $\mathbf{a}_1$ nicht bestimmen lasse (so Odenstedt, ‘Transliteration’, 64; Looijenga, ‘Checklist’, 92; *Texts & Contexts*, 303: ‘may be transcribed either **a** or **æ**’), will nicht recht einleuchten.

[95] Ein (formal möglicher) Akk. Sg. eines femininen *ō*-Stamms *-æ* < urgerm. *-ō*^{n} kommt von der ‘äußeren’ Deutung her nicht in Betracht. – Eine Interpretation als Dat. Sg. eines maskulinen *a*-Stamms (so Gysseling, *Corpus* II,1, 13 [sub J]) vermag nach dem oben (III) Gesagten nicht zu überzeugen. Buma erblickt in **mura**$_1$, wenn ich ihn recht verstehe, einen Nom. Sg. eines maskulinen *n*-Stamms, dessen *-æ* er durch ‘reductie van de slotvocaal’ *-a* erklärt (*Frieslands Runeninscripties*, 19 und 26): dies ist eine *ad hoc*-Annahme, die nicht erhärtet werden kann.

[96] Zwei dunkle Bildungen wfränk. *Murailpus* m., 8. Jh., *Murieldis* f., 12. Jh. verbuchen Förstemann, *Personennamen*, 1138 und Morlet, *Noms de personne* I, 170 (s.v. *Mur-*). – Hispano-got. *Murila* 6. Jh. ist Variante von *Maurila* (Piel und Kremer, *Hispano-*

mura$_1$ um einen (ursprünglichen) Übernamen handeln.[97] Als Ableitungsgrundlage bietet sich das Onomapoetikon mnd. *murren* 'brummen, murren', mnl. *morren* 'brummen, knurren', früh-nhd. *murren*, aisl. *murra* 'murren, knurren', aschwed. *morra* 'brummen, murren' etc. (**murrōn-* sw. Vb.) an, sodaß vor-afries. *Murræ* demnach als 'die Murrende, Mürrische' o.ä. zu fassen ist.[98] Derivat und Derivationsbasis stehen demnach im gleichen Verhältnis wie aisl. *Snorri* m. 'der Murrende, Mürrische' o.ä.[99] und mnd. *snurren, snorren* 'schnarren, brummen, surren, murren', nl. *snorren* 'brummen, surren', mhd. *snurren* 'rauschen, sausen, brummen', schwed. (16. Jh.) *snurra* 'schnarren, brummen' (**snurrōn-* sw. Vb.).

Auch die Gegenstandsbezeichnung **ka**$_2$**ta**$_1$ auf dem Knochen von Southampton (*Hamwic*; 7.–9. Jh.) ist wahrscheinlich als Nom. Sg. eines *n*-stämmigen Femininums auf vor-afries. *-æ* zu bestimmen.[100] Zwar flektiert

gotisches Namenbuch, 202 [§ 182,3]), und 'langob.' *Murus* 11. Jh. ist Variante von *Maurus* (Maria Giovanna Arcamone et al., 'Personenregister', *Codex diplomaticus Amiatinus. Urkundenbuch der Abtei S. Salvatore am Montamiata*. III,2: *Register*, [Tübingen, 1998], 110). Wie monetarisch bezeugtes ae. *Morre* m. (Redin, *Studies*, 128) zu beurteilen ist, lasse ich dahingestellt.

97 Vgl. J. Winkler, *Friesche Naamlijst (Onomasticon Frisicum)* (W. Dijkstra, *Friesch Woordenboek (Lexicon Frisicum)* [IV]; Leeuwarden, 1898), 264 (*Morre*) und 266 (*Murra*); Quellenangaben fehlen jedoch in Winklers Werk stets, sodaß die Belege nur von beschränktem Wert sind.

98 Gysseling (*Corpus* II,1, 13 [sub J]) hat – offenbar im Anschluß an Sipma, 'Fryske runen', 70 – die Konjektur *M[a]uræ* vorgeschlagen: dies ist methodologisch bedenklich, vor allem aber lautlich (*au* sollte zu *ā* geworden sein) wie sachlich (zum Mauren-Namen?) nicht angängig. – Fern bleibt jedenfalls auch das lateinepigraphisch mehrfach bezeugte Anthroponym *Murra* m. f. (z.B. *Corpus inscriptionum Latinarum* X, Nr. 45 [m.] und V, Nr. 2530 [f.]; zu gr. μύρρα 'Myrrhe); dazu I. Kajanto, *The Latin Cognomina*. Societas Scientiarum Fennica, Commentationes Humanarum Litterarum 36,2 (Helsinki, 1965), 335.

99 Erhellend ist eine Passage der *Eyrbyggja saga* (c. 12): *hann [Þorgrímr] var heldr ósvífr í æskunni, ok var hann af því Snerrir kallaðr ok eptir þat Snorri* 'er war ziemlich eigensinnig in seiner Jugend, und er wurde deswegen *Snerrir* genannt und danach *Snorri*' (*Eyrbyggja saga*, H. Gering, Hg., Altnordische Saga-Bibliothek 6 [Halle/S., 1897], 29). *Snerrir* muß eine *ija*-Bildung zu *o*-stufigem **snarrōn-* (ä. dän. *snarre* 'knurren, mürrisch reden', mnd. *snarren* 'schnarren, murren, brummen, schwatzen', mnl. *snarren* 'schnurren, brummen, [jd.en] anfahren', mhd. *snarren* 'schnarren, schmettern, schwatzen' etc.) sein, die wegen der Synonymie bzw. Homoionymie mit *Snorri* von der Sippe aisl. *snarr* Adj. 'schnell, scharf' (**snarha-*), *snerra* f. 'Kampf' etc. fernzuhalten ist.

100 Vgl. Looijenga (*Texts & Contexts*, 324), die – ohne nähere Erläuterung allerdings – einen *ōn*-Stamm ansetzt. – Aus lautlichen Gründen abzulehnen ist die Deutung als Nom. Sg. eines femininen *ō*-Stamms (Hofmann, 'Friesische Runeninschrift', 74 f.: **-a**$_1$ = *-æ* < *-u* < urgerm. **-ō*; zu erwarten wäre indessen eine Form auf *-u* wie in **g**$_2$**isuhḷdu** Dat. Sg., WESTEREMDEN I, s. oben, I). Daß es sich um einen Akk. Sg. eines femininen *ō*-Stamms handelt (Nielsen, 'Unaccented vowels' [1984], 17: 'to designate the object in question'), ist ebenfalls nicht anzunehmen, und zwar aus (morpho)syntaktischen

afries. *kāte* f. 'menschlicher (Finger-)Knochen, Fingerglied' (in der Regel) stark,[101] doch ist im Altfriesischen (wie in anderen altgermanischen Sprachen) bei den femininen Substantiva ein Schwanken zwischen *ō*- und *ōn*-Flexion nicht ungewöhnlich:[102] in den Flexionsparadigmata sind nur drei (von acht) Positionen distinkt, und zwar Gen., Dat. und Akk. Sg. *-e* (*ō*-Stämme) gegenüber *-a* (*ōn*-Stämme). Tatsächlich sind auch im Falle von *kāte* schwache Kasusformen belegt (*katha* Dat. Sg., J XXIII,114)[103], sodaß auf dem Runenknochen von Southampton der nominativische *slot* im Basisformular der Textsorte Gegenstandsbezeichnung ('[dies ist] _')[104] offenbar mit einem (ursprünglichen und/oder neben einem *ō*-Stamm existierenden) *ōn*-Stamm **ka$_2$ta$_1$** = vor-afries. *kātæ* f. < urgerm. **kautō^n* auszufüllen ist.

Was schließlich das Knochenplättchen von Hantum (keine begründete Datierung; Funktion unklar) betrifft, so hat von den bisher vorgeschlagenen Interpretationen die Annahme einer Ritzer- oder Besitzerinschrift **ị:a$_1$ha$_1$:k** = vor-afries. *ik Æhæ* 'ich, Ä.' (mit 'rahmendem' *ik* 'ich')[105] noch am meisten für sich. Tentativ kann ein schwach flektierter Frauenname vor-afries. *Æhæ* Nom. Sg. angesetzt werden, für den in langob. *A(c)ha* f., 9. Jh. (Mailand)[106] eine Entsprechung vorläge;[107] maskuline Gegenstücke würden sodann ae.

Gründen: im Formular ist die Leerstelle 'Gegenstand' mit einer Nominativ-Ergänzung zu besetzen, vgl. **binisþitabinisþtạ** = adän. *bēn es þet(t)a, bēn es þ[e]t(t)a* 'Knochen ist dies, Knochen ist dies' LUND, Knochen III (L. Jacobsen und E. Moltke, *Danmarks Runeindskrifter*. 4 Bde. [Kopenhagen, 1941–1942], Nr. 302). Vgl. dazu vor allem Düwel, 'Knochenkämme', 369 f.; Ders., 'Kämme mit Runeninschriften', 17; Ders., 'Zu einem merkwürdigen Inschriftentyp: Funktions-, Gegenstands- oder Materialbezeichnung?', *Forschungen zur Archäologie und Geschichte in Norddeutschland. Festschrift Wolf-Dieter Tempel*, U. Masemann, Hg. (Rotenburg [Wümme], 2002), 279–89: 282 ff.

101 Das ablautende Zubehör – mnl. *cōte* f. 'Gelenk, Würfel' (nnl. *koot*), mnd. *kōte*, *kute* f. 'Knöchel, Astragalus, Fußfessel [bei Pferden], Huf, Klaue'; wohl aus dem Niederdeutschen entlehnt ist nhd. *Köte*, *Kote* f. 'Knöchel [bes. am Pferdefuß]' – gibt für die Frage der ursprünglichen Flexion von afries. *kāte* < urgerm. **kautō(n)*- keinen Aufschluß.

102 Vgl. van Helten, *Grammatik*, 137 (§ 165 Anm. 1).

103 *Westerlauwerssches Recht*. I: *Jus municipale Frisonum*, W. J. Buma und W. Ebel, Hg., AR 6/1–2 (Göttingen, 1977), 450 (*bi this thuma katha*).

104 Vgl. vorhin, Anm. 99.

105 Düwel, 'Friesen: Runeninschriften', 28; Ders., *Runenkunde*, 87 (jeweils mit Vorbehalt). – Auf der anderen Seite des Knochenplättchens ist eine rechtsläufige lateinepigraphische Folge ABA angebracht.

106 *Codex diplomaticus Langobardiae*, G. Porro Lambertenghi, Hg., Historiae patriae monumenta 13 (Torino, 1873), 352 (Nr. 214, a. 861; *Aha*, *Ahani* Dat.) und 372 (Nr. 222, a. 862; *Acha*). Vgl. Bruckner, *Sprache der Langobarden*, 219.

107 Eine andere Deutung findet sich bei Quak ('Friese persoonsnamen', 167), der **a$_1$ha$_1$** mit Formen wie *Agi*, *Ago* verbindet; unerklärt bleibt aber, warum *g* durch **h** wiedergegeben sein sollte.

Aehcha m., 7./8. Jh. (Kent)[108] und ahd. *Aho* m., 9. Jh. (Reichenau)[109] darstellen. Zu analysieren wären diese Bildungen als (ursprüngliche) Kurzformen zu zweigliedrigen Anthroponymen mit Vorderglied *Aha-* (wohl zu got. *aha* m. 'Sinn, Verstand')[110], z.B. in ahd. *Ahlindis* f., 8. Jh. (Weißenburg), wfränk. *Achildis* f., 9. Jh. (Paris), langob. *Ahaldus* m., 8. Jh.[111] Auffällig ist allerdings, daß von den in Frage kommenden zweigliedrigen Namen, soweit ich sehe, nur eine einzige Bildung – ahd. *Ahaberti* m. Gen., 8. Jh. (Murbach)[112] – das zu erwartende Fugenelement *a* nach leichter Silbe zeigt; berücksichtigt man dazu die vergleichsweise schwache Bezeugung (in althochdeutschen, westfränkischen und langobardischen Namen), so ist der Ansatz eines Primärstamms *Aha-* nicht über jeden Verdacht erhaben. Da auch die Lautgestalt eines *n*-stämmigen Femininums vor-afries. *Æhæ* nicht sicher zu erhellen ist,[113] muß es, was $\mathbf{a_1ha_1}$ HANTUM betrifft, letztlich bei einem *non liquet* bleiben.[114]

---

108 *Cartularium Saxonicum: a Collection of Charters Relating to Anglo-Saxon History*, W. de Gray Birch, Hg., 3 Bde. (London 1887–1893), Nr. 97 (a. 697 oder 712) und Nr. 98 (a. 700 oder 715). Vgl. Searle, *Onomasticon*, 6. In ae. (kent.) *Aehcha* gibt ‹ae› wohl das Produkt der Brechung (und Ebnung?) *a* > *ea* (> angl. *æ*?) wieder; vgl. *The Oldest English Texts*, H. Sweet, Hg., Early English Text Society OS 83 (London, 1885 = 1966), 494 (**Eahha*). – Zu dem 'Namennest' *Achae** f., 6./7. Jh., *Acha* m., 9. Jh. und *Echha* m., 9. Jh. s. Redin, *Studies*, 81 (*Acha* m. als Variante von *Acca*), 94 f. (*Aehcha* m. bleibt unerklärt, *Echha* m. wird als Variante von *Ecca* oder *Ecga* gefaßt) und 116 (*Achae** f. womöglich **Eahhe*); M. Boehler, *Die altenglischen Frauennamen*, Germanistische Studien 98 (Berlin, 1930), 206 (*Achae** f. als **Alh°*; verweist auf *Ahhere* 9. Jh., der auch als *Alhhere* erscheint); Ström, *Personal Names*, 58 f. (*Achae** f. als **Alh°*).

109 *Das Verbrüderungsbuch der Abtei Reichenau*, J. Autenrieth et al., Hg., MGH, Libri memoriales et necrologia N.S. 1 (Hannover, 1979), 34 (sub a 129). Vgl. Förstemann, *Personennamen*, 15.

110 Bruckner, *Sprache der Langobarden*, 219; Kaufmann, *Ergänzungsband*, 24.

111 Belege bei Förstemann, *Personennamen*, 23 (ahd. *Ahlind*, sub *Ackilinda* verbucht) und 22 (wfränk. *Achildis* [*Polypt. Irm.* II,111 und IV,33], sub *Agohildis* verbucht); Morlet, *Noms de personne* I, 21 (wfränk. *Achildis*, sub *Aghildis* verbucht); Bruckner, *Sprache der Langobarden*, 291 (langob. *Ahaldus*).

112 *Alsatia aevi Merovingici, Carolingici, Saxonici, Salici, Suevici diplomatica*, J. D. Schöpflin, Hg., 2 Bde. (Mannheim, 1772–1775), I, 58 (Nr. 69, a. 794; eine neuere Edition ist mir nicht bekannt). Vgl. Förstemann, *Personennamen*, 43.

113 Unklar bleibt nämlich, ob man im Friesischen mit einem aufgehellten Reflex von altem *a* in der Position vor *h* zu rechnen hat. – Siebs ('Geschichte', 1179 [§ 11,3]) bezweifelt dies, indem er auf afries. *sach* (saterländ. *saȝ*) Prät. Sg. 'sah' mit erhaltenem bzw. revelarisiertem *a* (~ *sēgon, sēgen* Prät. Pl. 'sahen') verweist; wenn diese Bedenken zu Recht bestehen, wäre die Lautgestalt von vor-afries. *Æhæ* f. (: **Ahō*^{n}) schwer zu erklären.

114 Die Inschrift auf dem Schwertgriff von Raskwerd (9. Jh.) lasse ich hier angesichts der unsicheren Lesung ($\mathbf{ekuma_1\d{d}kla_3ka_2}$?, °$\mathbf{\d{d}ita_3ka_2}$?) und der schwierigen Segmentierung beiseite.

Treffen aber die Ausführungen zu **eda**$_1$ ARUM, **mura**$_1$ FERWERD und **ka**$_2$**ta**$_1$ SOUTHAMPTON das Richtige, so ist nunmehr mit dem Ausgang -**a**$_1$ = -*æ* des Nom. Sg. der femininen *ōn*-Stämme (neben -**a**$_2$ = -*a* im Nom. Sg. der maskulinen *n*-Stämme, -**u** = -ə̣ im Nom. Sg. der maskulinen *a*-Stämme und -**u** = -*u* im Dat. Sg. der femininen *ō*-Stämme) ein weiteres Flexiv der voraltfriesischen Substantiva 'dingfest' gemacht worden – weitere Aufschlüsse sind von zukünftigen Funden zu erwarten: *uerba docent, exempla trahunt.*

Die altfriesischen Eidesbezeichnungen

Anne Tjerk Popkema

0. Einführung[1]

Ein prominentes Teilgebiet der altgermanischen, deshalb auch der altfriesischen Rechtsterminologie bildet das Eidesverfahren: der Eid war ja eines der wichtigsten Beweismittel des altgermanischen Rechts. Daher war die altgermanische Eidesterminologie schon häufig und auf tiefgehende Weise Forschungsobjekt.[2] Jedoch spielte die altfriesische Eidesterminologie, trotz der großzügigen Beachtung, die dem altgermanischen Eidesverfahren schon zuteil wurde, bei den komparativen Untersuchungen der altgermanischen Eidesterminologie oft die zweite Geige. Nicht nur der erst relativ späte Anfang der altfriesischen Überlieferung, der für manche vergleichende Forschungen Schwierigkeiten bildet, sondern auch die qualitativ minderwertige Lage, in der die altfriesische Lexikographie sich bedauerlicherweise noch heute befindet, ist wohl mit Grund für jene untergeordnete Rolle. Dazu muss aber bemerkt werden, dass auch die Beachtung seitens der Altfrisistik und der friesischen Historiker selbst eher gering bemessen war. Obwohl die Aussage, 'die Eidesterminologie zeigt in den germanischen Sprachen bemerkenswerte Konstanz'[3] für die meisten altgermanischen Sprachen wohl zutreffen wird, sichert die obenerläuterte 'friesische' Lage jedoch ebenso die Behauptung, dass die altfriesischen Quellen bei den vergleichenden Untersuchungen nur teilweise einbezogen wurden. Eventuelle Abweichungen zur altgermanischen Eidesterminologie ließen sich für das Altfriesische also bisher nicht völlig feststellen. Dieser Aufsatz beabsichtigt, ein beschrei-

---

[1] Ich danke Prof. Dr. Jarich Hoekstra (Christian-Albrechts-Universität Kiel) für seine wertvollen Bemerkungen.

[2] Eine gute Einführung in das Eidesverfahren und die Eidesterminologie bieten beispielsweise H. Brunner, *Deutsche Rechtsgeschichte* I–II, 2. Aufl., bearb. von C. von Schwerin (Leipzig und München, 1906–1928) II, 512–28 und 568–76; HRG, s.v. *Eid*; K. von Amira, *Germanisches Recht* I. *Rechtsdenkmäler*. II. *Rechtsaltertümer*, 4. Aufl., bearb. von K. A. Eckhardt (Berlin, 1960–1967) II, 166–70. Für das altfriesische Eidesverfahren bietet die folgende Literatur einiges, vor allem aber Rechtshistorisches: M. S. van Oosten, 'Inleidende beschouwingen over het oudere Friese bewijsrecht', *TRG* 18 (1950), 440–76; R. P. Cleveringa, *Het oud-Friese 'kestigia'*. Verhandelingen KNAW, Nieuwe Reeks 66.4, Afd. Letterkunde (Amsterdam, 1959).

[3] *Reallexikon*, s.v. *Eid*, §1.

bendes Inventar eines Teils der altfriesischen Eidesterminologie, und zwar der Eidesbezeichnungen, darzubieten und somit zur altfriesischen lexikologischen Forschung beizutragen. Hoffentlich wird eine derartige Wortfelduntersuchung Wissenschaftler beim Erforschen der germanischen Eidesterminologie zum stärkeren Einbeziehen des Altfriesischen anstoßen und befähigen.

Wie gesagt wird die vorliegende Arbeit sich auf Eidesbezeichnungen, also auf Substantive, die den Begriff 'Eid' ausdrücken, beschränken: es würde hier ja einfach zu weit führen, den ganzen Bereich der altfriesischen Eidesterminologie zu untersuchen. Im Fall des Altfriesischen beziehen die bisherigen lexikologischen Forschungen im Bereich der Eidesbezeichnungen sich hauptsächlich auf mit afr. *ēth* 'Eid' gebildete Komposita.[4] Zwar sind mitunter Bedeutungs- und Verwendungsunterschiede einiger dieser Zusammensetzungen erläutert worden, es gibt jedoch noch eine Menge anderer Substantive, deren semantische Entwicklung zu einer Bedeutung 'Eid' geführt hat. Aus den altfriesischen Quellen konnten, außer (Zusammensetzungen mit) *ēth*, die nachfolgenden Hauptwörter, aus denen sich also das altfriesische Wortfeld 'Eid' zusammensetzt, gesammelt werden: *dēd, handtrowe, kest, lāda, riucht, stef* und *wīthe*. Zunächst werden diese Substantive und die Bedeutungsentwicklungen, die zu einer eidesbezüglichen Verwendung führten, erläutert. Ihnen wird jedoch ein ziemlich großzügiger Abschnitt, in dem *ēth* und sämtliche Zusammensetzungen mit *ēth* berücksichtigt werden, vorausgehen.

Vorangehend müssen aber noch einige Bemerkungen zur Forschungsweise gemacht werden. Erstens sind einige Begriffe, die an sich eidliche Verfahren darstellen (wie zum Beispiel *lēd* und *oflēdene*, beide 'Übernahme der Haftung', *onbrins* 'eidliche Erhärtung einer Klage' oder auch *undgung* 'eidliche Reinigung') nicht aufgenommen. Diese Rechtsverfahren fanden zwar unter Eidesleistung statt, aber die Begriffe selber sind meiner Meinung nach nicht als reine Eidesbezeichnungen zu verstehen. Es sei aber gerne zugegeben, dass man sich darüber wohl streiten könne. Andere Beispiele von außer Betracht gelassenen Substantiven sind *sikeringe* 'Freischwörung', *stowinge* 'Eidesstabung' und *sweringe* 'Schwörung', die nicht so sehr als Eidesbezeichnung, sondern als Deutung der Tätigkeit des Schwörens bzw. der Vereidigung zu verstehen sind.

Zweitens muss hier bemerkt werden, dass nur kurze Angaben bezüglich der sprachgeographischen, innerfriesischen Verteilung der Eidesbezeichnungen und ihrer germanischen Entsprechungen geboten werden.[5] Wegen

[4] Vgl. vor allem N. E. Algra, 'Eedsfoarmen yn it âldfryske rjocht', *UW* 12 (1963), 80–89.

[5] Im Fall von Vergleichen mit den Nachbarsprachen ist meistens die hervorragende Online-Version des *Deutschen Rechtswörterbuchs* (*DRW*) in Betracht genommen.

des beabsichtigten lexikologischen Charakters wird in diesem Aufsatz vor allem die semantische Entwicklung der Wörter berücksichtigt.

Drittens werden, obwohl alle altfriesischen Quellen in der Forschung einbezogen worden sind, nur beispielsweise Belegstellen aufgeführt. Wegen derer allgemeinen Zugänglichkeit wird, wenn Auswahl möglich ist, aus den kritischen Ausgaben der von Buma und Ebel begründeten Reihe *Altfriesische Rechtsquellen* zitiert.

Ein zum Beschreiben der Eidesbezeichnungen besonders geeignetes Hilfsmittel ist die Einstufung der Eide als entweder 'promissorisch' oder 'assertorisch'. Hinsichtlich des Eides heißt es im HRG:

> der Eid tritt im Rechtsleben auf als assertorischer E. (Wahrheitseid) oder als promissorischer E. (Gelöbniseid). Der assertorische E. ist vor allem der Eid des Klägers, des Angeklagten, des Zeugen; er betrifft in der Regel die Richtigkeit behaupteter und bereits eingetretener Tatsachen. [...] Der promissorische Eid betrifft das eigene Verhalten des Schwörenden in der Zukunft: etwa Herrschereide, [...], Bürgereide, Amtseide'.[6]

Für weitere Einstufung ist für die assertorischen Eide der Unterschied 'Eineid'-'Eid mit Eideshelfern' wichtig. Der Eineid wurde logischerweise nur von einer Person geschworen, im Fall von einem assertorischen Eid mit Eideshelfern wurde aber der Schwörende von Mitschwörenden gestützt; dabei war die Zahl der Mitschwörenden unterschiedlich.[7]

1. Bezüglich *Ēth*[8]

1.1. Das Simplex *ēth* 'Eid'[9]

Wie für die anderen germanischen Sprachen, wird für das Altfriesische das Hyperonym und somit die wichtigste Eidesbezeichnung des zu untersuchenden Wortfeldes, vom Maskulinum *ēth* gebildet. Afr. *ēth*, das im westerlauwersschen Altfriesischen oft als *ēd* erscheint,[10] begegnet in den

---

[6] *HRG*, s.v. *Eid*, §1.

[7] Vgl. *HRG*, s.v. *Eideshelfer*. Bezüglich der Zahl der Eideshelfer im altfriesischen Recht, siehe S. Kalifa, 'Note sur la nature de la conjuration dans la Frise du Moyen Age. A propos d'ouvrages récents', *L'année sociologique*, 3e série (1957–1958), 417–26.

[8] Bei jedem Abschnitt sind beispielsweise relevante Literaturangaben zum zu behandelnden Wort aufgeführt, die grundsätzlich als Hilfe zu weiterer Forschung gemeint sind. Falls einer davon bestimmte Aussagen entnommen wurden, wird die Titel in einer Fußnote aufs neue explizit aufgeführt.

[9] Vgl. Fußnote 2.

[10] Im Kodex Unia (U) begegnet dreimal die Schreibung *ath*, z.B. W. Steller, *Das altwestfriesische Schulzenrecht* (Breslau, 1926), 156. Ob es sich dabei um Schreibfehler oder um Variante von *ēth* handelt, ist eine komplizierte Frage, auf die hier nicht eingegangen werden kann.

frühesten osterlauwersschen Quellen bis in die Spätzeit der altfriesischen Überlieferung. Überdies ist es in einer Unmenge von festen Verbindungen, Zusammensetzungen und Ableitungen nachzuweisen.

Die Bedeutungsentwicklung von afr. *ēth* lässt sich, trotz der großen Anzahl der Belegstellen und der Vielgestaltigkeit der zahlreichen Ausdrücke, relativ einfach beschreiben. Als Hyperonym des Begriffes 'Eid' ist es mit genau dieser allgemeinen Bedeutung vom Germanischen ins Friesische übergegangen, wobei es als 'Gewährleistung für die Zuverlässigkeit des eigenen Wortes durch Einsatz eines Gutes für dessen Wahrheit' dient.[11] Als solches funktioniert *ēth* im ganzen altfriesischen Zeitraum.

Sonst gibt es im Grunde nur eine deutliche Bedeutungserweiterung. Sie muss schon in frühaltfriesischer Zeit stattgefunden haben, weil derer Ergebnis sich schon in den frühesten Quellen und beiderseits der Lauwers nachweisen lässt. Wo der Eid als Amtseid, also zum promissorischen Einschwören eines gerichtlichen oder verwaltungsmäßigen Funktionärs, abgenommen wurde, konnte *ēth* nämlich auch zur Bezeichnung von dessen Amt, Amtsbereich oder Amtszeit verwendet werden. Vergleiche aus dem Zweiten Rüstringer Kodex (R_2):

> mi hi thenne bewera mit thesse keron and mit friseske riuchte (an) hodere ondwarde and godera lioda, sa sitte hi and sine ethe wel mith eron ...
> 'kann er (...) sich dann mit (Berufung auf) diese Küren und nach friesischem Rechte in Gegenwart der Hodere und glaubwürdiger Leute verteidigen, so walte er weiterhin in allen Ehren seines Amtes...'[12]

Im Ausgang des fünfzehnten Jahrhunderts scheint diese Verwendung aber nicht mehr gebräuchlich zu sein. In den Nachbarsprachen begegnet jene Verwendung erst in nachmittelalterlicher Zeit.[13]

1.2 Weitere Eidesbezeichnungen mit *ēth*

bōdelēth 'Vermögenseid'[14]
Mit diesem Terminus wird der Eid, den der Verwalter eines Vermögens über dessen vollständige Bewahrung zu schwören hat, bezeichnet. Dieser asser-

---

[11] Von Amira und Eckhardt, *Germanisches Recht*, II, 167.

[12] *Das Rüstringer Recht*, W. J. Buma und W. Ebel, Hg., AR 1 (Göttingen, 1963), 156–57 (B VIII 8).

[13] Vgl. *DRW*, s.v. 2 *Eid*: Bezirk. Die einzige nichtfriesische Belegstelle (*ein man der im eid gesessen ist*) bezieht sich auf nachmittelalterliche Zeit.

[14] J. Grimm, *Deutsche Rechtsaltertümer,* I–II, 4. Aufl. bearb. von A. Heusler und R. Hübner (Göttingen, 1899) II, 562; S. Kalifa, *Pré-droit et procédures dans la Frise du moyen âge*, Estrikken 9 (Groningen, 1955), 63 (mit französischer Übersetzung); Algra, 'Eedsfoarmen', 83–84; N. E. Algra, *Oudfries recht 800–1256* (Leeuwarden, 2000), 332–33.

torische Eineid begegnet nur einige Male in den westerlauwersschen Quellen. Im *Älteren Schulzenrecht* werden äußerliche Bedingungen sowie die, teilweise paraphrasierte, Eidesformel dieses Eides aufgeführt.[15] Im Mittelniederländischen (*boedeleet*) und Mittelniederdeutschen (*budeleed*) begegnen Entsprechungen.[16]

borgersēd 'Bürgereid, Eid des Neubürgers'[17]
In der Überschrift eines wahrscheinlich 1517 in das (sonst meist niederländischsprachigen)[18] Sneeker Bürgerbuch eingetragenen altfriesischen Eidesformulars heißt es *borgers eedt.*[19] Es gibt keine weiteren altfriesischen Belegstellen dieses Wortes. Entsprechungen in den Nachbarsprachen sind recht spärlich: die wenigen Belegstellen begegnen erst ab dem Ende des fünfzehnten Jahrhunderts im Mittelhochdeutschen und erst ab dem sechzehnten Jahrhundert im Mittelniederdeutschen.[20] Im Mittelniederländischen ist der 'Bürgereid' nicht belegt. Gemäß dem Wortlaut der Formel zielte der Bürgereid auf Treue und Gehorsam gegenüber Stadt und (bereits eingeschworenen) Bürgern sowie gegenüber dem heutigen oder auch künftigen Stadtrat.[21] Afr. *borgersēd* bezeichnete also einen promissorischen Eid.

Es ist bemerkenswert, dass der Rechtsterminus 'Bürgereid' zwei unterschiedliche Rechtsbegriffe deckt. Gemäß Ebel bezeichnete er ursprünglich den 'bei jeder Ratsumsetzung von der versammelten Bürgerschaft geleisteten Gesamtschwur, die coniuratio reiterata'.[22] In den deutschen Städten ging das Verfahren so vor, dass an dem Tag, an dem der Ratswechsel stattfand ('Schwörtag'), 'dem neuen Rat Treue und Gehorsam geschworen, der Bürgerschwur durch den Eid des Rats beantwortet, und mit dem Eide die Pax und die Verbindlichkeit des gesamten, aus diesem Anlaß verlesenen Stadtrechts erneuert (wurde)'.[23] Neben dieser Verwendung von 'Bürgereid'

---

15 Vgl. Steller, *Das altwestfriesische Schulzenrecht*, 36.

16 Vgl. DRW, s.v. *Bodeleid.*

17 A. S. Miedema, *Sneek en het Sneeker Stadrecht* (Sneek, 1895), 103–07; P. Sipma, 'De âlde Snitser eedformules', *Frysk Jierboek* (1937), 129–35, hier 135; ausführlich zum deutschen Bürgereid: W. Ebel, *Der Bürgereid als Geltungsgrund und Gestaltungsprinzip des deutschen mitteralterlichen Stadtrechts* (Weimar, 1958).

18 O. Vries, 'Aldfryske ynskriuwingen yn it boargerboek fan Snits', *UW* 36 (1987), 55–56, hier 55.

19 Vgl. Sipma, 'Snitser eedformules', 135.

20 Vgl. DRW, s.v. *Bürgereid.*

21 Siehe Sipma, 'Snitser eedformules', 135.

22 Ebel, *Der Bürgereid*, 15–16. Bis der Publikation Ebels wurde der Bürgereid schlechthin als der Einzeleid des Neubürgers interpretiert. Der Begriff 'Bürgereid' im ursprünglichen Sinn scheint nicht mit einem volkstümlichen Terminus in den westgermanischen Sprachen vertreten zu sein, fehlt ja auch im DRW, wo nur die Sekundärbedeutung aufgelistet ist.

23 *Ibid.* 22–23.

im ursprünglichen Sinn, hat der Begriff die Bedeutung 'Einzelbürgereid des Neubürgers' bekommen, die als 'geschichtlich und begrifflich sekundäres Gebilde' zu betrachten ist.[24] Dem Wortlaut der Formel ist nicht ohne weiteres zu entnehmen, um welche der zwei Bedeutungen es sich bei dem friesischen Eid handelt.[25] Es liegt aber nahe, in ihm den Eid des Neubürgers zu erkennen. Erstens, weil es in mehreren Stadtbüchern schon einige Belegstellen gibt, die das Bestehen des Neubürgereides bestätigen.[26] Zweitens, weil, meines Wissens, in den mittelalterlichen friesischen Quellen deutliche Beweise mangeln, dass es den periodischen Gesamtschwur, also den Bürgereid im ursprünglichen Sinn, in den friesischen Städten überhaupt gegeben haben muss.[27]

dēdēth 'Tateid'[28]

Der Tateid ist ein assertorischer, mit Eideshelfern zu leistender 'Bestätigungseid', der im Zusammenhang mit Eigentums- und Besitzrechtsstreitigkeiten zur Erhärtung der Rechtmäßigkeit einer vom Beklagten als 'Tatsache' angeführten Rechtslage dient. Durch seine Ableistung wird ein bestehendes, aber vom Kläger angefochtenes Rechtsverhältnis gerichtlich anerkannt, da durch den Tateid der Nachweis erbracht wird, dass die Tatsachenbehauptungen des Beklagten (Eigentümers, Besitzers) wahr sind und deshalb der augenblickliche Zustand rechtmäßig ist'.[29] Gemäß derselben Quelle kann der Tateid 'n u r mit Eideshelfern geleistet werden'. Afr. *dēdēth* begegnet in den beiden Hauptmundarten und ist vom Ausgang des dreizehnten Jahrhunderts

---

24 Ebel, *Der Bürgereid*, 16.

25 Vgl. *ibid.* Fn. 14: es 'sei vermerkt, daß es nicht immer ausgemacht ist, welchen Eid die älteren Stadtrechtsquellen meinen, wenn sie den Wortlaut des "burger eydts" verzeichnen. Es geht nicht an, diese Formeln schlechtweg als solche des Neubürgereides zu betrachten. Der Wortlaut des Gesamteides und des Einzeleides ist häufig, ja meist derselbe.'

26 In den Stadtbüchern der westerlauwersschen Städte Bolsward, Sneek und Leeuwarden wird auf den Eid des Neubürgers verwiesen, siehe *De Friesche stadrechten*, A. Telting, Hg. ('s-Gravenhage, 1883), 20 (Bolsward [1455], §XXXV), 153 (Bolsward [1479], §38), 107 (Sneek, §142), 220–21 (Leeuwarden, §14 – mit der niederländischen Eidesformel, von einer Überschrift *Vanden eede der borgeren* versehen). Der *Franeker Bürgerbrief* aus 1417 (O II 10) enthält keinen Verweis auf den Bürgereid.

27 Hier ist auf die Behauptung Ebels, *Der Bürgereid*, 37, 'dass sich die Schwureinung, zunehmend von Süden nach Norden hin, abschwächt und auflöst' hinzudeuten.

28 S. J. Fockema Andreae, 'Dedeth, dedjuramentum', *Album Kern* (Leiden, 1903), 161–63; Grimm, *Rechtsaltertümer,* II, 562; Algra, 'Eedsfoarmen', 85; *Die 'Fivelgoer' Handschrift. I–II*, B. Sjölin, Hg., OTR 12–13 ('s-Gravenhage, 1970–1975) I, 183–84; Algra, *Oudfries recht*, 123 Fn. 61 und 347.

29 *Die 'Fivelgoer' Handschrift*, Sjölin, Hg., I, 183–84, wo es diesbezüglich 'frdl. Mitteilung des DRWb durch Herrn Dr. W. Bührer' heißt. Herr Dr. Heino Speer des DRW hat mir freundlicherweise mitgeteilt, dass die Mitteilung Herrn Bührers nur auf altfriesischen Belegstellen basierte.

bis ins sechzehnte Jahrhundert nachzuweisen. In den Nachbarsprachen gibt es für afr. *dēdēth* keine wörtlichen Entsprechungen.

dīkattaēd 'Eid des Deichgeschworenen'[30]
Dieser promissorische Eid bildet den Amtseid des Deichgeschworenen. Das Wort ist nur einmal belegt und zwar in der westerlauwersschen Handschrift Jus Municipale Frisonum (J), in der Überschrift der diesbezüglichen Eidesformel.[31] Die Eidesformel ist, mit nur kleinen Unterschieden und mit der Überschrift *Thir atthena stawinga*, 'Die Eidstabung der Atten', auch in Kodex U überliefert.[32] Obwohl es auch in den mittelalterlichen Nachbarsprachen den Begriff 'Deichgeschworene' gab und es somit einen diesem Amt zugehörenden und dem *dīkattaēd* wohl entsprechenden Eid gegeben haben muss, scheint der Terminus an sich nicht nachzuweisen zu sein.

ēhēraēd 'Eid des Dorfrichters'[33]
Auch auch dieses Kompositum ist nur einmal im Altfriesischen und zwar in der Überschrift der diesbezüglichen Eidesformel im westerlauwersschen J, überliefert worden.[34] Und geradeso ist die Eidesformel dieses promissorischen Amtseides des Dorfrichters auch in U überliefert, dort aber mit der abweichenden Überschrift *Homa thin gaes gretman, therma asinga hat, in that riocht stawia scil* 'Wie man den Gretmann des Bezirkes, den man 'asinga' nennt, in das Richteramt einschwören soll'.[35] Weil der *ēhēra* ein typisch friesisches Begriff darstellt,[36] sind wörtliche Entsprechungen dieses Eides logischerweise in den Nachbarsprachen nicht belegt.

ēth der wird 'Gefährdeeid; Zeugeneid'[37]
Nur in den späteren Quellen begegnet die Eidesbezeichnung *ēth der wird*, wörtlich 'Eid der Wahrheit'. Aus dem sich ausdrücklich auf diesen Eid beziehenden, mit einer Überschrift *de juramento calumnie* versehenen Abschnitt im kanonischen Rechtstext *Processus Judicii*, ist abzuleiten, dass der Eid beim Anfang des Prozesses von Kläger und Beklagtem geschworen

---

30 J. P. Winsemius, *De historische ontwikkeling van het waterstaatsrecht in Friesland* (Franeker, 1947), 47–48; P. Heck, *Die altfriesische Gerichtsverfassung. Mit sprachwissenschaftlichen Beiträgen von Theodor Siebs* (Weimar, 1894), 365.

31 Vgl. *Westerlauwerssches Recht I. Jus Municipale Frisonum*, I–II, W. J. Buma und W. Ebel, Hg., AR 6/1–2 (Göttingen, 1977), 634–37 (§XXXVIII, Überschrift).

32 *Unia Apographa* (Oxford, Bodleian Library, MS Junius 49), fol. 42r.

33 Heck, *Altfriesische Gerichtsverfassung*, 333.

34 *Westerlauwerssches Recht*, Buma und Ebel, Hg., 634 (§XXXVII, Überschrift).

35 *Unia Apographa*, fol. 41v. Meine Übersetzung.

36 Vgl. DRW, s.v. *ehera*.

37 Algra, 'Eedsfoarmen', 88. Bezüglich des Zeugen und des Zeugeneides: Brunner und von Schwerin, *Deutsche Rechtsgeschichte*, II, 528–37; von Amira und Eckhardt, *Germanisches Recht*, II, 170–71.

wurde.[38] Die Parteien gaben einander die eidliche Versicherung, dass sie nur die Wahrheit sprechen, keine betrügerische Beweisführung vorbringen und den Prozessvorgang nicht absichtlich frustrieren würden. Sonst ist auch auf einen (mittelniederländischen) Abschnitt der Sneeker Rezessbücher (SnR) hinzuweisen:

> Dit js *juramentum de calumpniae*. Inden eersten seit N, dattet geestelic ende waerlic recht si, dat die parten die in recht staen moeten een eedt der waerheit doen, alsmen myt recht dat begheert, ende is gheheten in des paus rechten *juramentum de calumpnia*.
> 'Dies ist *juramentum de calumpniae*. Erstens sagt N, dass es geistliches und weltliches Recht sei, dass die Parteien, die vor dem Gericht stehen, einen Gefährdeeid leisten sollen, falls man dies rechtens verlangt, und (der) heißt, gemäß dem kanonischen Recht, *juramentum de calumpniae*'.[39]

Somit ist dieser Eid als promissorischer Eid zu betrachten. In der deutschen rechtshistorischen Literatur wird das *juramentum calumpniae* als 'Gefährdeeid' bezeichnet.[40]

Der Begriff *ēth der wird* hat aber noch eine zweite Verwendung bekommen, die ausschließlich in SnR begegnet, vergleiche:

> Op den vors. dei is Jancka toe zeens hier mey riocht citeerd om een eed der wird toe dwaen ende toe sidzen, hat hem kondich is om dae scortinge, deer dirck moller ende herman toe zeens meymankorum habbet
> 'Am vorhergenannten Tag ist Jancka zu Sens rechtens vorgeladen worden zum Schwören eines Wahrheitseides und zum Bezeugen, was ihm in Bezug auf den Streit, den Dirck Moller und Herman zu Sens miteinander haben, bekannt ist'.[41]

Weil der Zeuge nicht eine der zwei Parteien ist, kann also nicht von einem 'Gefährdeeid' die Rede sein. Es wäre besser, *ēth der wird* hier als 'Zeugeneid' zu übersetzen. In dieser Verwendung dient der *ēth der wird* zur Bestätigung der Wahrheit einer Beschreibung von einem Ereignis in der Vergangenheit und ist somit als assertorisch zu betrachten.

---

[38] Vgl. die Überschrift *de juramento calumnie* 'vom Wahrheitseid' des sich ausdrücklich auf diesen Eid beziehenden Abschnitts; siehe für die Emsinger Fassung: *Das Emsiger Recht*, W. J. Buma und W. Ebel, Hg., AR 3 (Göttingen, 1967), 246–47 (§21), dort *eeth der werde* genannt.

[39] SnR, Nr. 3118. Meine Übersetzung. Dieser Abschnitt wird von Algra, 'Eedsfoarmen', 88 Fn. 6, ungenau als das Eidesformular des *ēth der wird* bezeichnet.

[40] Vgl. DRW, s.v. *Gefährdeeid*: *calumnien- oder gefärdeid*. Weitere Informationen bez. des Gefährdeeides: Brunner und von Schwerin, *Deutsche Rechtsgeschichte*, II, 456–58.

[41] SnR, Nr. 4649. Meine Übersetzung.

fēknianēth 'Reklamationseid'[42]

Dieser assertorische Eineid begegnet nur zweimal: einmal als *feknian eth* und einmal als *feknie eth.*[43] Beide Belegstellen sind in der osterlauwersschen Fivelgoer Handschrift (F) überliefert. Der erste Teil des Kompositums bildet wohl ein Präsenspartizip zum altfriesischen Verb *fēknia* 'reklamieren'.[44] Es besteht keine Übereinstimmung darüber, ob er vom Kläger oder vom Beklagten zu schwören sei, ob er also als Unschulds- oder Klageeid betrachtet werden müsste. Gemäß Buma und Munske ist er als Klageeid anzusetzen,[45] weil mit dem *fēknianēth* 'gekauftes Gut innerhalb bestimmter Frist als fehlerhaft reklamiert werden' konnte. Der Eid beinhaltete also '(ursprünglich) den Vorwurf des Verkaufsbetrugs. Ob dieser Sinn dem friesischen Terminus noch beigelegt wurde, steht dahin, da *fēknia* bereits etymologisch isoliert ist und vielleicht nicht mehr wörtlich verstanden wurde'.[46] Dagegen wollte Sjölin ihn wohl eher, gemäß seiner Deutung 'Eid (des Verkäufers) im Falle der Reklamation' als Unschuldseid ansetzen,[47] eine Erklärung, der ich mich hier anschließe. Eine wörtliche Entsprechung von afr. *fēknianēth* in den Nachbarsprachen ist nur in einer mittelniederdeutschen Übersetzung der erwähnten Fivelgoer Belegstellen nachzuweisen (mnd. *feken eet*).[48]

fiāēth 'Fahrniseid'[49]

Dieser sich auf bewegliche Habe beziehende Eid ist vor allem wegen des ausführlichen Eidesformulars, das nur im Zweiten Emsinger Kodex (E_2)

42 W. J. Buma, 'Thi feknian eth', *IB* 25 (1963), 255–64; *Die 'Fivelgoer' Handschrift*, Sjölin, Hg., I, 187–88; H. H. Munske, *Der germanische Rechtswortschatz im Bereich der Missetaten. Philologische und sprachgeographische Untersuchungen. I. Die Terminologie der älteren westgermanischen Rechtsquellen* (Berlin und New York, 1973), 174.

43 Vgl. *Die 'Fivelgoer' Handschrift*, Sjölin, Hg., I, 187–88.

44 Vgl. Buma, 'Thi feknian eth', 262.

45 Bzw. *ibid.* und Munske, *Germanische Rechtswortschatz*, 174.

46 *Ibid.*

47 *Die 'Fivelgoer' Handschrift*, Sjölin, Hg., I, 187. Dr. O. Vries wies mich auf einen im *Frysk Ynstitút* der *Rijksuniversiteit Groningen* aufbewahrten, nicht veröffentlichten Aufsatz (mit dem Titel 'Jitris: thi feknian-eth') des 1970 verstorbenen Rechtshistorikers Meinte Oosterhout hin. In diesem Aufsatz wird aufgrund Rechtslogik erörtert, dass der *fēknianēth* wahrscheinlich vom Verkäufer geschworen wurde.

48 Vgl. Buma, 'Thi feknian eth', 259.

49 K. von Richthofen, *Altfriesisches Wörterbuch* (Göttingen, 1840), s.v. *fiaeth*; F. Buitenrust Hettema, 'Fres(is)ka', *TNTL* 9 (1890), 307–24; W. L. van Helten, *Zur Lexicologie des Altostfriesischen*, KAW, NR 9, Afd. Letterkunde (Amsterdam, 1907), 122–25; Grimm, *Rechtsaltertümer*, II, 562; O. Postma, 'Swierrichheden by it oersetten fen de *fiaeth* út it Emsiger rjucht', *Frysk Jierboek* (1938), 168–73 (mit westfriesischer Übersetzung); K. Nauta, *Die altfriesischen allgemeinen Bußtaxen. Texte und Untersuchungen* (Assen, 1941), 135; Kalifa, *Pré-droit*, 63–66 (mit französischer Übersetzung); Algra, 'Eedsfoarmen', 83–84; K. Fokkema, 'De Fia-eed', *IB* 12 (1950), 69–82; T. D. Hill, 'Two Notes on the Old Frisian *Fia-eth*', *Approaches*, 169–78; Algra, *Oudfries recht*, 332.

vollständig überliefert ist,[50] schon oft und von ganz unterschiedlichen Perspektiven aus untersucht worden. Afr. *fiā* (wörtlich 'Vieh') bezieht sich hier auf Besitz, mit dem wohl Geld gemeint wurde. Der *fiāēth* wurde als assertorischer Unschuldseid geschworen und ist als Eineid zu betrachten.

Obwohl der *fiāēth* einmal im Vierzehnten Landrecht gemäß U, J und der Inkunabel Druck (D), (dort im Fünfzehnten Landrecht),[51] begegnet und dazu noch einmal im Bussregister *Bireknada Bota* gemäß J (es fehlt an der Parallelstelle in D), war es im westerlauwersschen Friesland vielleicht ein ziemlich unbekannter Begriff: aus den nur vier westerlauwersschen Belegstellen sind zwei entstellt.[52] In den osterlauwersschen Quellen begegnet *fiāēth* aber ziemlich häufig. Als wörtliche Entsprechung von afr. *fiāēth* begegnet nur mnd. *vēhēd*,[53] jedoch ausschließlich in Übersetzungen von altfriesischen Texten.

fogedēd 'Vogteid, Eid des Kirchenvogts'
Wie bei *ēhēraēd* und *dīkattaēd* ist auch diese Bezeichnung des promissorischen Amtseides des Kirchenvogts nur einmal und nur in der Überschrift des diesbezüglichen Eidesformulars im westerlauwersschen J überliefert.[54] Der Paralleltext in U zeigt die Überschrift *Ho dat ma da foeghden den eed stowiet* 'wie man den Kirchenvögten den Eid stabt'.[55] Obwohl der Begriff '(Kirchen) Vogt' in mehreren germanischen Sprachen vertreten ist, weisen sie keine wörtlichen Entsprechungen des afr. *fogedēd* auf.

forma ēth 'Ersteid'[56]

---

[50] Vgl. *Emsiger Recht*, Buma und Ebel, Hg., 102–06 (§I). Bruchstücke dieses Eidesformulars sind auch in E_1 (vgl. *ibid.* 16 (§I)) und in der sogenannten Hs. Mone überliefert, vgl. *De Tweede Emsinger Codex*, K. Fokkema, Hg., OTR 7 ('s-Gravenhage, 1953), 66–67.

[51] Siehe K. von Richthofen, *Friesische Rechtsquellen* (Göttingen, 1840), 65.

[52] Im Vierzehnten Landrecht in U heißt es *mith ene fria ethe* (*Unia Collationes* [Oxford, Bodleian Library, Ms. Junius 109], 74) und in den *Bireknada Bota* gemäß J heißt es *flaethe*, vgl. *Westerlauwerssches Recht*, Buma und Ebel, Hg., 494 Fn. 647.

[53] Vgl. von Richthofen, *Friesische Rechtsquellen*, 65 Fn. 12 und 88 Fn. 7.

[54] *Westerlauwerssches Recht*, Buma und Ebel, Hg., 636–39 (§XXXIX Überschrift).

[55] *Unia Apographa*, fol. 42v. Meine Übersetzung.

[56] Van Helten, *Zur Lexicologie des Altostfriesischen*, 137; R. P. Cleveringa, 'De vóóreed in het Ommelander recht', *Akademiedagen* 6 (1953), 34–35; Algra, 'Eedsfoarmen', 85–88; *Die 'Fivelgoer' Handschrift*, Sjölin, Hg., I, 188–89. Dass *forma ēth* nicht als Kompositum (wie Sjölin, *Die 'Fivelgoer' Handschrift*, II, s.v. *formaeth* offenbar tut), sondern als attributive Verbindung analysiert werden sollte, zeigt sich wohl aus den *Hunsinger Küren* gemäß F: *jefta hi vngunge thes mith xij ethum thera sibbista liwa, jefta thi clachere layne thene forma sunder witherstride* 'oder er schwöre mit zwölf Eiden seiner nächsten Verwandten davon frei, außer wenn der Kläger den ersten (Eid des Beklagten) ohne (dessen) Widerrede ablehnt', so *Das Fivelgoer Recht*, W. J. Buma und W. Ebel, Hg., AR 5 (Göttingen, 1972), 198–99.

Obwohl die unfrequente Verbindung *forma ēth* schlichtweg 'erster Eid' bedeuten konnte, womit also einfach der erste einer Reihe von Unschuldseiden bezeichnet wurde, wie es in dem Ersten Rüstringer Kodex (R_1) auftaucht,[57] wurde in den anderen Fällen, bei denen *forma ēth* übrigens immer als Objekt zum Verb *laina* begegnet, ein spezifischer Eid gemeint. Es ist vor allem die Deutung dieses Ausdrucks *thine forma ēth laina* gewesen, die zur Diskussion in der Literatur geführt hat. Wie Sjölin,[58] möchte ich mich Algra anschließen, der darlegt, dass dieser Ausdruck sich auf die Eidesscheltung bezieht.[59] Eine der Arten der Eidesschelte bestand darin, dass der Scheltende 'dem Schwörenden die Hand von den Reliquien oder überhaupt von dem Gegenstande wegzog, der beim Eide berührt werden sollte. Die Verlegung des Eides musste erfolgen, ehe die Eidhelfer geschworen hatten'.[60] Demgemäß sei der Ausdruck *thine forma ēth laina* wohl so aufzufassen, dass der vom Kläger oder Beklagten selbst zu schwörende Ersteid, 'gelogen geheißen', also gescholten wird. Zum Verb *laina* gestellt, bezieht *forma ēth* sich also ausdrücklich auf den, zuerst zu leistenden, assertorischen Eid des Hauptschwörenden, eine Verwendung, die nur im osterlauwersschen Altfriesischen begegnet. Es gibt keine Entsprechungen in den Nachbarsprachen.

fremethe ēth 'Fremdeid, Eid eines Nichtverwandten'[61]

Die Eidesbezeichnung *fremethe ēth* begegnet zweimal, aber nur im sogenannten *Pfennigschuldbuch* gemäß dem osterlauwersschen Dritten Emsiger Kodex (E_3).[62] Er ist als assertorischer Eineid zu betrachten. Dass *fremethe* hier als 'nicht verwandt' zu deuten sei, geht aus dem üblichen Gebrauch dieses Adjektivs im Altfriesischen hervor. Der *fremethe ēth* ist also als ein Eid, bei dem die Eideshelfer nicht verwandt sein dürfen, zu verstehen.[63] In den Nachbarsprachen gibt es keine wörtlichen Entsprechungen dieser Eidesbezeichnung.

fretheēth 'Sühneid, Urfehde'[64]

---

57 *Das Rüstringer Recht*, Buma und Ebel, Hg., 88 (§X 5).

58 *Die 'Fivelgoer' Handschrift*, Sjölin, Hg., I, 188.

59 Algra, 'Eedsfoarmen', 86.

60 Brunner und von Schwerin, *Deutsche Rechtsgeschichte*, II, 576.

61 Algra, 'Eedsfoarmen', 85.

62 *Das Emsiger Recht*, Buma und Ebel, Hg., 210 (§V 2).

63 Die Deutung Algras, 'Eedsfoarmen', 85 ('in eed, dy't "troch in oar dien wurde moat"' ['einen Eid, der "von einem anderen geleistet werden soll"']) ist also wohl zu tilgen.

64 R. His, *Das Strafrecht der Friesen im Mittelalter* (Leipzig, 1901), 216; Kalifa, *Prédroit*, 66 (mit französischer Übersetzung); Algra, 'Eedsfoarmen', 88; K. de Vries, '"Ick wijbe etis ...". In Snitser "Hafturfehde" út 1515', *Studia Frisica in memoriam Prof. Dr. K. Fokkema 1898–1967 scripta*, H. D. Meijering, H. T. J. Miedema und Y. Poortinga, Hg. (Groningen, 1969), 112–16; O. Vries, 'De "Hafturfehde", in bysûndere foarm fan

Wegen seiner großen Bedeutung im friesischen Fehdewesen als Akt beim Sühnen einer Fehde war dieser promissorische Eid schon oft Forschungsobjekt. Im Altfriesischen ist *fretheēth* (wörtlich 'Friedeneid'), das in verschiedenen Formen auftaucht (wie *frethēth, frēdeēd, ferdēd*), nur in westerlauwersschen Quellen auf uns gekommen (in J ist sogar die ganze Eidesformel überliefert worden).[65] Dessen ungeachtet zeigt das in einer wohl aus Groningen stammenden Urkunde aus dem Jahre 1340 überlieferte mnd. *vrethe ethe*, dass dieser Terminus in Teilen des osterlauwersschen Frieslands mindestens bekannt gewesen sein muss, obwohl in Ostfriesland die Bezeichnung mnd. *orveyde* üblich war.[66] Weitere wörtliche Entsprechungen gibt es übrigens in den Nachbarsprachen nicht: dort wurde der gleiche Begriff üblicherweise mit Entsprechungen von 'Urfehde' oder 'Sühneid' bezeichnet.[67]

fulēth 'Volleid, Zwölfereid'[68]

Nur im osterlauwersschen F wird, einmal, der *fulēth* erwähnt: *lithscilda ende meinesna is en ful eth binna xxv panningum* '(Für Leugnung von) Trinkschulden und Gesindelohn unter fünfundzwanzig Pfennigen ist ein Volleid (erforderlich)'.[69] Von Sjölin, dem ich mich hier anschließe, wird *fulēth* als 'Zwölfereid' erklärt.[70] Er wird sich wohl von der Verwendung des Begriffes 'Volleid' bei anderen germanischen Stämmen inspirieren lassen haben,[71] weil den altfriesischen Belegstellen diese Zahl von zwölf Eideshelfern nicht zu entnehmen ist. Der *fulēth* war also ein assertorischer Unschuldseid, der (wahrscheinlich) mit zwölf Eideshelfern geleistet werden sollte.

hondēth 'Handeid'[72]

Nur in F ist afr. *hondēth* überliefert, von einer wohl gekürzten oder 'zusammengefassten' Eidesformel gefolgt: *en nates hondeth: sa help iv tha trowa, ther thi nat tha nat schildich is, sa j thes rawis vnschildich se* 'der

---

de "freedeed"', *UW* 29 (1980), 95–102; O. Vries, '*Ick ontsidse jemme ende jemme onderseten*. Bemerkungen zum friesischen Fehdewesen sowie zur Fehdeterminologie', *Tota Frisia in Teilansichten. Hajo van Lengen zum 65. Geburtstag*, H. Schmidt, W. Schwarz und M. Tielke, Hg. (Aurich, 2005), 122–41, hier 131.

[65] *Westerlauwerssches Recht*, Buma und Ebel, Hg., 638–41 (§XLI, die Eidesbezeichnung in der Überschrift).

[66] Vgl. Vries, '*Ick ontsidse jemme*', 131.

[67] Vgl. Grimm, *Rechtsaltertümer*, II, 561–62.

[68] *Ibid.* 562; Cleveringa, '*Kestigia*', 8.

[69] *Das Fivelgoer Recht*, Buma und Ebel, Hg., 148–49 (§XII 12).

[70] *Die 'Fivelgoer' Handschrift*, Sjölin, Hg., I, 341–42 (§XIII 12).

[71] Vgl. Brunner und von Schwerin, *Deutsche Rechtsgeschichte*, II, 520–22 und von Amira und Eckhardt, *Germanisches Recht*, II, 169.

[72] Van Helten, *Zur Lexicologie des Altostfriesischen*, 182; Brunner und von Schwerin, *Deutsche Rechtsgeschichte*, II, 527 und 572; Algra, 'Eedsfoarmen', 83–84.

Handeid eines Sippegenossen (lautet): Möge Euch so die Treue helfen, die der eine Sippegenosse dem anderen schuldet, wie Ihr am Raube unschuldig seid'.[73] Gemäß Brunner betrachte man den Handeid als 'einen minderwertigen Eid, der mit Berührung der Hand eines Sippegenossen in der Weise abgelegt wird, dass dessen Heil den Einsatz des Eides bildet. (...) Der Eid, der (...) als ein dem Waffeneid gleichwertiger Eid geschworen wird, (scheint) die Bedeutung gehabt zu haben, dass die berührte Hand dem Meineidigen Verderben bringen solle'.[74] Der Sippegenosse 'bleibt passiv, etwa wie die Waffe, auf die man Eide leistet'.[75] Somit ist der Handeid für einen assertorischen Eineid zu halten. Wörtliche Entsprechungen sind in den Nachbarsprachen nicht belegt: Brunner erwähnt nur die lateinischen Äquivalente, Eide *in manu proximi* 'zur Hand des Nächstverwandten' und *in manu liti* 'zur Hand des Liten'.[76]

Obwohl, wie gesagt, *hondēth* nur in F begegnet, muss hier auf eine Belegstelle in D hingewiesen werden, in der wohl die gleiche Art Eidesleistung stattfindet, die Eidesbezeichnung an sich jedoch von *handtrowe* vertreten wird (siehe dort).

lēdēth 'Leiteid, Eid des Fehdeführers'[77]

Mit diesem promissorischen Eid beschwört der Leiter einer Fehdepartei, dass er die Haftung (afr. *lēde* 'Leite') des Fehdeunternehmens übernimmt. Afr. *lēdēth* ist nur in den Überschriften der diesbezüglichen Eidesformel in J und U überliefert.[78] Der Behauptung gemäß, dass die zur Übernahme der Haftung übliche Terminologie als 'eigenständig friesisch'[79] zu betrachten sei, sind in den Nachbarsprachen keine wörtlichen Entsprechungen von afr. *lēdēth* nachzuweisen.

mēnēth 'Meineid'[80]

Gemeingermanisch und auch in den zwei altfriesischen Hauptmundarten häufig nachzuweisen, ist der Begriff 'Meineid'. Darunter ist 'die strafbare Handlung eines Falscheids vor Gericht (vereinzelt auch einer anderen Institution) sowie der Bruch eines Gelöbnisses, mit dem ein besonderes Ver-

---

73 *Das Fivelgoer Recht,* Buma und Ebel, Hg., 148–49 (§XII 7).

74 Brunner und von Schwerin, *Deutsche Rechtsgeschichte*, II, 572.

75 *Ibid.* 527.

76 *Ibid.*

77 His, *Strafrecht der Friesen,* 65–68 und 364–65 (Text des *lēdēth* gemäß U); Algra, 'Eedsfoarmen', 88; Algra, *Oudfries recht*, 175; Vries, '*Ick ontsidse jemme*', 134.

78 Bzw. *Westerlauwerssches Recht*, Buma und Ebel, Hg., 638–39 (§XL, Überschrift) und His, *Strafrecht der Friesen*, 364–65 (gemäß U).

79 Vries, '*Ick ontsidse jemme*', 134.

80 Grimm, *Rechtsaltertümer*, II, 558–60 (bez. der germanischen Entsprechungen); Brunner und von Schwerin, *Deutsche Rechtsgeschichte*, II, 876–78; HRG, s.v. *Meineid*; Munske, *Germanische Rechtswortschatz*, 180 und 272–73.

halten versprochen wird (promissorischer Eid), insb. von zu besonderer Treue verpflichteten und dazu vereidigten Personen'[81] zu verstehen. Der assertorische wie der promissorische Eid konnte also zu Meineid führen. Neben dem altfriesischen Kompositum begegnet auch der Cluster *thi mēna ēth* (oder eine ähnliche Form) 'der falsche Eid'.[82]

mensingēd 'Verteilungseid'[83]

Dieses in den Nachbarsprachen nicht mit Entsprechungen vertretene Kompositum begegnet nur im westerlauwersschen *Älteren Schulzenrecht* (gemäß D und J; U zeigt nur *ēth*). Der erste Teil der Zusammensetzung ist, gemäß Ahlsson, wahrscheinlich als Verbalabstraktum von afr. *mendza* 'mengen, mischen' zu betrachten.[84] Von den vielen Deutungen trifft jene von Buma ('Eid, mit dem beschworen wurde, dass das Weideland der Dorfmark von neuem in Parzellen aufgeteilt werden musste') meiner Meinung nach am meisten zu.[85] Mit dem *mensingēd* wurde, gemäß dem der Belegstelle vor angehenden Abschnitt, auf die Reliquien beschworen, *dat dio ieertele ommen se ende hij mey mara riochte dela schelle dan hit lengra aldus staen schel* 'daß die Jahrzahl abgelaufen ist und er es mit größerem Recht abteilen darf als daß es länger so ungeteilt liegen bleiben soll'.[86] Der Verteilungseid ist also assertorisch und, wegen des Kontextes und der Verwendung des Singulars an allen Stellen, als Eineid zu betrachten.[87]

---

81 DRW, s.v. *Meineid.*

82 Munske, *Germanische Rechtswortschatz*, 180, setzt ein wohl unberechtigtes Kompositum *mēnaēth* mit Kompositionsvokal an.

83 Von Richthofen, *Altfriesisches Wörterbuch,* s.v. *mensinged*; W. L. van Helten, *Zur Lexicologie des Altwestfriesischen*, Verhandelingen KAW, vol. 1, nr. 5, afd. Letterkunde (Amsterdam, 1896), 36; F. Swart, *Zur friesischen Agrargeschichte* (Leipzig, 1910), 144–49 (mit Edition der friesischen Parallelstellen und deutscher Übersetzung); L.-E. Ahlsson, *Die altfriesischen Abstraktbildungen* (Uppsala, 1960), 72; Algra, 'Eedsfoarmen', 88; N. E. Algra, *Ein. Enkele rechtshistorische aspecten van de grondeigendom in Westerlauwers Friesland* (Groningen, 1966), 69.

84 Ahlsson, *Altfriesische Abstraktbildungen,* 72

85 W. J. Buma, *Vollständiges Wörterbuch zum westerlauwersschen* Jus Municipale Frisonum (Leeuwarden, 1996), s.v. *mensengēd.* Jedoch trifft die dazugestellte Übersetzung 'Sonderungseid' nicht zu.

86 *Westerlauwerssches Recht*, Buma und Ebel, Hg., 88–89 (§III 34a).

87 In Algra, *Ein,* 69 ('Vandaar dat er één hemriks-vertegenwoordiger werd aangewezen door het zweren van een "mensingeed"' ['deswegen, dass ein Vertreter des Dorfgebiets durch das Schwören eines Verteilungseides bestimmt wurde']) wird 'door het zweren' ['durch das Schwören'] wohl als wegen eines Schreibfehlers entstelltes 'voor het zweren' ['zum Schwören'] zu betrachten sein: sonst würde die Behauptung Algras eine offenbare Fehlinterpretation des Begriffes darstellen.

nēdēd 'Noteid, erzwungener Eid'[88]

An einigen westerlauwersschen Belegstellen begegnet *nēdēd*. Die Erklärung 'erzwungener Eid' geht deutlich aus den Belegstellen, die einander alle gleichen, hervor, wie zum Beispiel aus dem Kodex Furmerius (Fu):

> alle need panden, need eeden, need loffenisse, need burgen, -sikeringe, need brieuen ende need onthietinghe ende alla finsene fry ende quyt toe wessen
>
> 'alle erzwungenen Pfandsetzungen, erzwungenen Eide, erzwungenen Gelöbnisse, erzwungenen Bürgschaften, (erzwungenen) Reinigungen, erzwungenen Urkunden und erzwungenen Versprechen und alle Gefangenen (sollen) frei und erledigt sein'.[89]

Obwohl es in den Nachbarsprachen wörtliche Entsprechungen von afr. *nēdēd* gibt, beziehen sie sich alle ausschließlich auf das Prozessverfahren und sind somit semantisch völlig abweichend.[90]

nīelandsēd 'Neulandseid'[91]

Mit dem Begriff 'Neuland' wird das vom Wasser abgewonnene und eingedeichte Land bezeichnet. Das Kompositum *nīelandsēd* begegnet nur einmal, und zwar in einer westerlauwersschen Urkunde des Jahres 1427,[92] die die Instandhaltung der Neulandsdeiche in der Gegend von der Stadt Sneek behandelt. Es wird festgestellt, dass Einwohner des Dorfes Bozum einen *nīelandsēd* leisten sollten,[93] weil die Jurisdiktion über sämtliches Neuland in jener Gegend turnusgemäß den umliegenden Dörfern Bozum, Sânleane

---

[88] Algra, 'Eedsfoarmen', 88.

[89] *Fryske Stikken út Codex Furmerius*, I–II, P. Gerbenzon, W. J. Buma u.a., Hg., Estrikken 33–34 (Groningen, [1963]) I, 134 (§12). Meine Übersetzung. Es verdient zu bemerken, dass das in diesem Zitat begegnende Kompositum *nedbrief* vom DRW, s.v. *Notbrief*, fälschlich als 'Drohbrief' statt als 'erzwungene (d.h. unter Zwang aufgestellte) Urkunde' interpretiert worden ist. Sonst ist der Eintrag *Notbürgensicherung* im DRW (dort als 'Kompositum?' gedeutet), der ausschließlich auf dem oben zitierten Abschnitt basiert, zu tilgen. Es handelt sich hier wahrscheinlich um ein Kompositum **needsikeringe* 'erzwungene Reinigung', wobei das Erstelement *need-* wohl entweder wegen Konjunktionreduktion oder wegen eines Schreibfehlers weggelassen wurde.

[90] Vgl. DRW, s.v. *Noteid*, I und II. Das DRW zeigt hier, neben der friesischen, zwei weitere Verwendungen des Begriffes 'Noteid' auf: 'vom Richter einer der vor Gericht erschienenen Parteien auferlegter Eid zur Klärung, ob das Klagebegehren begründet ist' und 'ein Eid, der bezeugt, daß der in dieser Prozeßsituation erforderliche Eid mit Eideshelfern nicht geleistet werden kann'.

[91] Algra, 'De Nijlânseed', *UW* 13 (1963), 1–4. Obwohl dieser Aufsatz mit dem Titel 'De Nijlânseed' veröffentlicht ist, handelt es sich überhaupt nicht um diesen Eid, sondern nur um einige rechtshistorische Aspekte des Neulandes. Weil aber die hier zu behandelnde Belegstelle im Aufsatz kurz aufgeführt wird, wird er hier trotzdem erwähnt.

[92] O II 14.

[93] Es heißt wörtlich *nīelandsēd ferra* 'Neulandseid führen'.

und Lutkewierum zustand.[94] Bis zu ihrem Turnus sollten die Bozumer mit diesem promissorischen Eid wohl die (also befristete) Jurisdiktion des Nachbardorfes über das ihnen zugehörende Neuland anerkennen. Obwohl der Terminus 'Neuland' für neu eingedeichtes Land auch außerhalb des Friesischen üblich war,[95] sind in den Nachbarsprachen keine wörtlichen Entsprechungen von afr. *nīelandsēd* nachzuweisen.

rēdsliōdenaēd 'Eid der Ratsleute'[96]

Ein zweites Sneeker Eidesformular (siehe *borgersēd*) ist das des Eides der Ratsleute, des *rēdsliōdenaēd*, wie es in der Überschrift heißt. Dieser promissorische Amtseid wurde von denjenigen Ratsleuten, die dem sogenannten *Riocht ende Reed* 'Recht und Rat' beitraten,[97] an dem Schwörtag (siehe *borgersēd*) geleistet. Die Wahl der Mitglieder des neuen Sneeker *Riocht ende Reed* fand am 31. Dezember und der faktische Ratswechsel am 1. Januar statt. Die Amtseide der beitretenden Schöffen und Ratsleute wurden jedoch erst am 2. Januar abgenommen.[98] Gemäß Miedema suggeriere die Verwendung des Pronomens *jemma* 'ihr' in der Eidesformel, dass die Leistung als Gesamtschwur abgenommen wurde.[99] Obwohl es keine wörtlichen Entsprechungen in den Nachbarsprachen gibt, wird mhd. *ratseid* dem altfriesischen Terminus semantisch wohl genau entsprechen.[100]

---

[94] Algra, 'De Nijlânseed', 4, bezüglich dieses Abschnitts der Urkunde: 'Yn 'e Boazumer kontreijen wie nijlân njonken mear doarpen ûnder ien gerjocht brocht en dêr gong it rjocht "om" oer de doarpen' ['im Gebiet bei Bozum wurde Neuland in der Nähe von mehreren Dörfern unter einem Gericht angeordnet und dort wurde die Gerichtsbarkeit den Dörfern turnusgemäß zuteil'].

[95] Vgl. DRW, s.v. *Neuland* I.

[96] A. Telting, *Het Oud-Friesche Stadrecht. Een schets* (Leiden, 1882), 139–44; Miedema, *Sneek en het Sneeker Stadrecht*, 99–101; Sipma, 'Snitser eedformules'.

[97] Der *Riocht ende Reed* von Sneek setzte sich aus zwölf Leuten zusammen, unter denen es vier Ratsleute (*rēdsliōde*) und acht Schöffen (*skeppenen*) gab. Grundsätzlich beschäftigten die Ratsleute sich mit der städtischen Geschäftsführung und die Schöffen mit der Gerichtsbarkeit, obwohl diese Trennung nicht absolut war (Miedema, *Sneek en het Sneeker Stadrecht*, 64–71). Zwar ist auch die Eidesformel des promissorischen Schöffeneides überliefert, die dazugehörige altfriesische Eidesbezeichnung jedoch nicht. Obwohl die Ausgabe der Formel des Schöffeneides bei Miedema, *ibid.* 94–95, suggeriert, dass sie mit dem Terminus *Schepenen eed* überschrieben wurde, Herr Hessel Jaasma, Gemeente-archief von Sneek, konnte mir jedoch sagen, dass diese Überschrift in der Handschrift (Sneek, Oud Archief Sneek, nr. 56, fol. 60), wie die Ausgabe bei *Friesche Stadrechten*, Telting, Hg., 137, schon vermuten lässt, nicht begegnet.

[98] Telting, *Oud-Friesche Stadrecht*, 139.

[99] Miedema, *Sneek en het Sneeker Stadrecht,* 101.

[100] Vgl. DRW, s.v. *Ratseid.*

sliuchte ēth 'schlichter Eid'[101]

Nur im westerlauwersschen Altfriesischen, und zwar dreimal, ist *sliuchte ēth* überliefert.[102] Es begegnet immer in der Phrase *nāt hāgera bikomria then up ēn sliuchten ēth*, was, gemäß Cleveringa, als 'nicht mehr beschlagnahmen als das, was der Beklagte mit einem schlichten Unschuldseid zurückerhalten kann' zu deuten sei.[103] Die Phrase bezieht sich auf die Praxis der außergerichtlichen Pfandnahme, 'ein(en) Akt erlaubter und rechtlich geregelter Selbsthilfe'.[104] Kurzgesagt bestand der Akt darin, dass ein Gläubiger die Zurückzahlung einer gewetteten Schuld durch Pfandnahme abzwingen dürfte. Statt *sliuchte ēth* begegnet an ähnlichen Belegstellen einfach *ēth* oder *sīn selvis ēth* oder auch *kest.*[105] Mit dem altfriesischen *sliuchte ēth* ist also wohl ein assertorischer Eineid gemeint, der in diesem Fall vom Beklagten zum Freischwören von einer Anklage wegen nicht rechtzeitig zurückbezahlter Schuld geleistet wurde.

Damit ist aber noch nicht das Adjektiv *sliucht* gedeutet worden. Es verdient diesbezüglich erstens zu bemerken, dass es im Lateinischen das so genannte *iuramentum planum* gab, das von Brunner als 'in schlichten Worten geschworener und ungestabter Eid (Eid ohne *vare*)' interpretiert wurde.[106] Sonst ist auf die Tatsache, dass sich *sliucht* auch mit Substantiven wie *werd* 'Wort', *spreke* 'Aussage' und *lofnisse* 'Versprechen' kombinieren lässt, aufmerksam zu machen. Vergleiche aus dem Kodex Aysma (A): *dat hy da forwerth ende swerringha ende lowingha al scildich is to halden, al hede hijt nat mer dan mit ene sliuchta werde spritzen* 'dass jemand durchaus verpflichtet ist, sich an den Vertrag und den Eid und das Versprechen zu halten, (...) auch wenn er solches nicht weiter als mit einem schlichten Wort erklärt hätte'.[107] Unter *sliucht* wird hier wohl 'weniger feierlich, einfach, schlicht' verstanden. Der *sliuchte ēth* ist also wohl als ein weniger feierlich abgenommener Eid zu interpretieren. Eventuell könnte die Vereidigung

---

101 Cleveringa, '*Kestigia*', 30 und 41–42; Algra, 'Eedsfoarmen', 88.

102 O II 129, O II 154 und SnR, Nr. 42 (Ausgabe und niederländische Übersetzung der letzteren bei Cleveringa, '*Kestigia*', 75–77).

103 *Ibid.* 76. Meine deutsche Paraphrase.

104 Brunner und von Schwerin, *Deutsche Rechtsgeschichte*, II, 585.

105 Vgl. Cleveringa, '*Kestigia*', 29 und 41–42.

106 H. Brunner, *Forschungen zur Geschichte des deutschen und französischen Rechtes* (Stuttgart, 1894), 327 Fn. 4.

107 *Codex Aysma. Die altfriesischen Texte*, W. J. Buma, P. Gerbenzon und M. Tragter-Schubert, Hg. (Assen und Maastricht, 1993), 128–29 (§I 179). Auf ähnliche Weise wird das Wort auch im Mittelhoch- und Mittelniederdeutschen verwendet, siehe DRW, s.v. *Mundlobde* und *Antwort*, I 16.

ohne Eideshelfer[108] oder ohne Sachberührung oder auch ohne Nachsagen der vollständigen Eidesformel stattgefunden haben.

strīdēth 'Kampfeid'[109]
Hinsichtlich des Zweikampfes im *Älteren Schulzenrecht* heißt es im *Register* zu J: *strijdeed fan ayder ig* 'Kampfeid jeder Partei'.[110] Dies schließt sich der Erklärung des DRW von Kampfeid als 'von den Parteien vor dem gerichtlichen Zweikampfes geleisteter Eid'[111] genau an. Dieser 'Kampfeid' sollte also von beiden gerichtlichen Parteien vor dem Anfang des gerichtlichen Zweikampfes geleistet werden und ist somit als eine Art Hyperonym zu diesen zwei assertorischen Eiden zu betrachten. Dabei bildete der Eid des Beklagten einen Leugnungseid, der vom Kläger zu leistende Eid einen Gegeneid zur Scheltung des Beklagteneides.[112]

Mit dem *strīdēd* wurde im Altfriesischen aber auch spezifisch der Leugnungseid des Beklagten bezeichnet, vergleiche aus dem *Älteren Schulzenrecht* (gemäß J): *soe is dat riocht, dat hi etta fyfta thinghe den strijdeed swerra scol ende den wedereed hera* 'Da ist es Recht, daß er am fünften Gerichtstermin den Streiteid schwören und den Gegeneid anhören soll'.[113] Hier ist *strīdēd* also wohl besser als 'Kampfeid (des Beklagten)' zu deuten. Wörtliche Entsprechungen gibt es in den Nachbarsprachen nicht.

tolewaēth 'Eid des Mitglieds des Zwölferkollegs'[114]
Im westerlauwersschen Altfriesischen kann mit der substantivierten Kardinalzahl *tolewa* das Kollegium der sogenannten 'Zwölfer', das aus zwölf

[108] Dafür spricht vielleicht die folgende Brunnersche Behauptung: 'Der Voreid [...] wird entweder als Eineid oder mit Helfern geschworen. Jenen können wir den schlichten, diesen den verstärkten Voreid nennen', Brunner und von Schwerin, *Deutsche Rechtsgeschichte*, II, 456–57.

[109] Von Amira und Eckhardt, *Germanisches Recht*, II, 173–74. In U begegnet als Parallele zu *strīdēth* einmal das Hapaxlegomenon *ēthstrīd* (*Unia Apographa*, fol. 27r). Ob es sich hier um einen Schreibfehler oder ein eigenständiges Substantiv handelt, ist eine schwierige Frage, auf die hier nicht eingegangen wird. Afr. *ēthstrīd* wurde von Hofmann in den Berichtigungen zu Holthausens Angaben übrigens zu Unrecht als nicht auffindbar qualifiziert, F. Holthausen und D. Hofmann, *Altfriesisches Wörterbuch*, 2., verbesserte Aufl. (Heidelberg, 1985), 137.

[110] *Westerlauwerssches Recht*, Buma und Ebel, Hg., 30–31 (§I 16).

[111] DRW, s.v. *Kampfeid.*

[112] Vgl. von Amira und Eckhardt, *Germanisches Recht*, II, 173: 'Zwei Eide stehen einander gegenüber: Leugnungseid des Beklagten und Gegen-(Scheltungs-)Eid des Klägers (...)'.

[113] *Westerlauwerssches Recht*, Buma und Ebel, Hg., 96–97 (§III 44a). Die Tatsache, dass *strīdēd* hier mit 'Streiteid' statt 'Kampfeid' übersetzt worden ist, hat sich wohl nicht aus inhaltlichen Gründen ergeben und ist also eher auf Inkonsistenz zurückzuführen.

[114] Heck, *Altfriesische Gerichtsverfassung*, 345–49; H. Jaekel, *Forschungen zur altfriesischen Gerichts- und Ständeverfassung* (Weimar, 1907), 184–85; Winsemius, *Historische ontwikkeling*, 51–53.

Gemeindegeschworenen zusammengesetzt war, bezeichnet werden. Die einzelnen Mitglieder konnten ebenfalls mit der Kardinalzahl *tolewa* oder auch mit der Ordinalzahl *tolfta* bezeichnet werden. Die Zusammensetzung *tolewaēth*, die den vom Zwölfermitglied zu leistenden promissorischen Amtseid bezeichnet, begegnet nur zweimal, und zwar in der diesbezüglichen Eidesformel gemäß U und J (in U mit der Ordinalzahl zusammengesetzt, also als *tolftaēth* erscheinend).[115] In den Nachbarsprachen gibt es keine Entsprechungen.

ūtstāfsēd 'vollständig vorgetragener Eid'[116]
Der *ūtstāfsēd*, der im Altfriesischen nur zweimal und nur in den westerlauwersschen SnR begegnet,[117] bezeichnete wohl einen Eid, dessen Formel bis zu Ende vorgesagt wurde. Dies lässt sich freilich aus der Bedeutung von mnl. *utestaven*[118] schließen. In dem aus dem späten fünfzehnten Jahrhundert stammenden westerlauwersschen Kodex Roorda (Ro) begegnet sonst *ūtstowed ēd*, vergleiche: *dyo pyne is allyck fan een gueden lowinge dan fan een wtstowed eed* 'die Strafe ist im Fall eines glaubwürdigen Versprechens gleich wie im Fall eines völlig vorgesagten Eids'.[119] Sonst ist hier noch auf das *Bolswarder Sendrecht* gemäß J hinzuweisen, wo *hi en swerra enen stouwenden eeth* 'es sei denn, er schwöre einen feierlich vorzusprechenden Eid'[120] begegnet. Mit diesen Begriffen konnte eventuell jeder Eid, dessen Formel völlig vor- und nachgesprochen wurde, bezeichnet werden.

wederēd/withēth 'Gegeneid, Eid der Gegenpartei'[121]
Wie oben (siehe *strīdēth*) erläutert wurde, war der 'Gegeneid, Eid der Gegenpartei' Teil des Kampfeidesverfahrens, bei dem der Beklagte einen Leugnungseid (*strīdēth*) leistete, der vom *wederēd* des Klägers gescholten

---

[115] *Westerlauwerssches Recht*, Buma und Ebel, Hg., 640 (§XLII 3) und *Unia Apographa*, fol. 42r.

[116] Algra, 'Eedsfoarmen', 88.

[117] SnR, Nr. 104 und 496.

[118] MNW, s.v. *utestaven*: 'ten volle "staven", geheel voorzeggen, een eed'. Im Mittelniederländischen begegnet das Verb übrigens nur als adjektivisches Präteritalpartizip zu *eed* (*wtgestaefdes eed*).

[119] *Jurisprudentia Frisica of Friesche regtskennis. Een handschrift uit de vijftiende eeuw*, I–III, M. de Haan Hettema, Hg. (Leeuwarden, 1834–1835) I, 178 (§23:10). Meine Übersetzung.

[120] *Westerlauwerssches Recht*, Buma und Ebel, Hg., 594–95 (§XXXIII 2).

[121] Grimm, *Rechtsaltertümer*, II, 561; Algra, 'Eedsfoarmen', 85; von Amira und Eckhardt, *Germanisches Recht*, II, 173–74. Obwohl die Etymologie von *with* und *withir* – aus dem sich, wohl unter mittelniederländischem Einfluß, *weder* ergeben hat – unterschiedlich ist, entsprechen die beiden Formen einander semantisch völlig. Gemäß D. Boutkan und S. M. Siebinga, *Old Frisian Etymological Dictionary* (Leiden und Boston, 2005), s.v. *with* 1, 2 (sic) ist *with* als eine analogische Rückbildung aus *withir* zu betrachten.

werden konnte. Der Terminus *wederēd* kann in jenem Kontext also als 'Kampfeid des Klägers' interpretiert werden und begegnet als solcher dreimal im westerlauwersschen Altfriesischen (in U als *withēth*).[122] Der *wederēd* war ein assertorischer Eineid. Zwar gab es wörtliche Entsprechungen in anderen germanischen Sprachen (zum Beispiel den *wedredus* der Franken),[123] mit denen wurden jedoch andere Eidesbegriffe bezeichnet.

wīthēth 'Eid auf die Reliquien'[124]
Ein im ganzen altfriesischen Gebiet häufig begegnender Eid ist der *wīthēth*, der als assertorischer Eid mit Eideshelfern zu betrachten ist. Der Erstteil dieses Kompositums, *wīthe*, bedeutet 'Reliquie' (siehe *wīthe*). Eine Entsprechung von *wīthēth* gibt es gemäß Grimm im mhd. *wīheth*.[125] Die seit der Christianisierung übliche Praxis, beim Schwören Reliquien(behälter) zu berühren,[126] hat dazu geführt, dass schon in den frühesten altfriesischen Quellen der Terminus *wīthēth* erwähnt wird. In gleicher Bedeutung begegnet auch afr. *wīthe* (siehe dort).

Exkurs: *wroegh eden*[127]
Ein Problemfall, der meiner Meinung nach zu interessant ist um in einer Fußnote versteckt zu sitzen und deswegen hier aufgeführt wird, ergibt sich im *Westerlauwersschen Sendrecht* (gemäß J). In einer Überschrift heißt es dort: *om wroegh eden*, gefolgt von: *Als ma wroeght eden, deer swerren sint om landkaep*

---

122 Vgl. Steller, *Das altwestfriesische Schulzenrecht*, 90.

123 Vgl. Brunner und von Schwerin, *Deutsche Rechtsgeschichte*, II, 456. Der fränkische *wedredus* 'Widereid' wurde beim Anfang des Klageverfahrens geleistet und diente zum Beschwören, dass die Klage nur aus genügenden Verdachtsgründen erheben wurde.

124 Grimm, *Rechtsaltertümer*, II, 562; Algra, 'Eedsfoarmen', 84. Kalifa, 'Note sur la nature de la cojuration', 422 (oben, Fn. 7), zeigt bezüglich *wīthēth* eine offenbare Fehlinterpretierung, indem er behauptet: 'la cojuration appelée "withēth", c'est à dire "contre-serment"'. Diese Erklärung basiert auf Nauta, *Bußtaxen*, 157, der afr. *withēth* fehlerhaft als 'Gegeneid' übersetzt. Vielleicht hat Nauta sich unglücklicherweise von Steller, *Das altwestfriesische Schulzenrecht*, 205, inspirieren lassen, bei dem die, meines Wissens, einzige Belegstelle im Altfriesischen, wobei *withēth* tatsächlich 'Gegeneid' bedeutet, begegnet. Sonst ist hier auf Buma, *Vollständiges Wörterbuch*, s.v. *wedēth* hinzuweisen: dieses im *Register* zu J überlieferte Kompositum – *secka, deer nen wedeeden habbeth*, Buma und Ebel, *Westerlauwerssches Recht*, 44 (§I 64) – ist als fehlerhaft für *wīthēth* zu betrachten, weil die entsprechende Belegstelle in der Handschrift *fan secken sonder witheden* (*ibid.* 200 [§XI, Überschrift], mit dem offenbar 'Eide auf die Reliquien' gemeint werden, aufweist. Das von Buma, *Vollständiges Wörterbuch* aufgenommene Lemma *wedēth* 'Unschuldseid mit Einsatz eines Pfandes (*wed*)' ist also zu tilgen.

125 Grimm, *Rechtsaltertümer*, II, 562.

126 Vgl. Brunner und von Schwerin, *Deutsche Rechtsgeschichte*, II, 573, und von Amira und Eckhardt, *Germanisches Recht*, II, 168.

127 Algra, *Oudfries recht*, 37.

ende om goldkaep (...)'Wenn man Eide rügt, die wegen Landkaufs und Goldkaufs (...) geschworen sind'.[128] Obwohl in der Originalhandschrift die Trennung der Wörter *wroegh* und *eden* deutlich sichtbar ist,[129] transkribierten die Herausgeber die Überschrift als *om wroegheden*, also ungetrennt, und übersetzten sie als 'von Rügeeiden'. An den Parallelstellen dieses Zitats in D und U ist diese Phrase nicht belegt. Aus dem dieser Überschrift folgenden Abschnitt ergibt sich, dass es sich hier um das Rügen von anderer Leute Eidesbruch handelt. Die Übersetzung der Herausgeber 'von Rügeeiden' trifft also nicht zu.[130] Besser als die Transkription und Übersetzung von Buma/ Ebel hinzunehmen, wäre es, meiner Meinung nach, hier zu emendieren. Es dienen sich zwei einigermaßen attraktive Möglichkeiten an: entweder kann zu *om wroeghed eden* 'von gerügten Eiden' (also mit als Adjektiv verwendetem Partizip des Verbs *wrōgia* 'rügen') emendiert werden, oder zu *om wroegh fan eden* 'von Rüge von Eiden' (wobei also von einer Ellipse der Präposition *fan* ausgegangen wird). In beiden Fällen ist 'Eid' dabei wohl als 'Meineid' zu verstehen.[131] Nicht nur ergeben beide Emendierungen keine unüberwindlichen paleografischen Schwierigkeiten, sondern sie würden beide auch viel besser mit dem Inhalt des Artikels übereinstimmen: das Rügen eines eventuellen Eidesbruches.

Eine wörtliche Entsprechung des deutschen Begriffes 'Rügeeid', zu verstehen als 'Eid des Rügegeschworenen', oder ein anderer Terminus, der diesem Begriff inhaltlich genau entspricht, ist im Altfriesischen nicht belegt. Dessen ungeachtet lässt sich im altfriesischen Sprachmaterial ein Abschnitt nachweisen, der wohl belegt, dass es im mittelalterlichen Friesland diesen Begriff 'Rügeeid' gegeben hat:

> alle tha helganeman, ther triewest send, agen tofara tha sinethe te suerane alsa, thet hia alle thet ruogie, ther to ruogia stonde, and thet se nena vnriuchte ruoga ne ruogia. And alle tha, ther hia bi hira ethe ruogiat, thet se vrwnnen se; alle tha, ther hia vnskeldigiat, thet se siker se
> 'alle Kirchenvögte, die ja am glaubwürdigsten sind, haben vor dem Sendgericht zu schwören, dass sie alles rügen, was gerügt werden soll, und dass sie keine falsche Rüge erheben. Und alle diejenigen, die sie bei ihrem Eide rügen, sollen als überführt gelten; alle die, welche sie für unschuldig erklären, sollen schuldlos sein'.[132]

---

[128] *Westerlauwerssches Recht*, Buma und Ebel, Hg., 188–89 (§IX 38, Überschrift).

[129] Siehe Ljouwert, Tresoar, Hs. R5, fol. 57v.

[130] Dies lässt sich durch die Übersetzung Algras stützen, da er 'aangaande het wroegen van eden' ['bezüglich des Rügens von Eiden'] interpretiert; Algra, *Oudfries recht*, 37.

[131] In der Fortsetzung des zitierten Artikels heißt es ja: *Brect him dera ladena, soe is hi des mena eed al sciuldich* 'Fehlen ihm die Unschuldseide, so ist er des Meineides völlig schuldig', *Westerlauwerssches Recht*, Buma und Ebel, Hg., 188–89 (§IX 38).

[132] *Das Emsiger Recht*, Buma und Ebel, Hg., 148–49 (§VIII 15). Obwohl Brunner diese Quelle nicht nennt, sei seine Erörterung des Rügeverfahrens wohl auch auf diese altfriesische Formel zu beziehen: 'Das Rügeverfahren beginnt damit, daß der Richter die glaubwürdigsten und angesehensten Männer des Untersuchungsbezirkes vorladet und

Obwohl der diesbezügliche *terminus technicus* 'Rügeeid' hier nicht erwähnt wird, bezieht die Phrase *bi hira ethe* sich wohl auf ihn. Es handelt sich bei diesem, also nicht mit einem friesischen Terminus vertretenen, aber schon im friesischen Beweisverfahren vorhandenen Eid um einen promissorischen Eid.

2. Sonstige Eidesbezeichnungen

dēd 'Tateid'[133]

Die Grundbedeutung des Femininums *dēd*, einer Kurzform von *dēde*, ist 'Tat, Handlung'. Jedoch gibt es im osterlauwersschen F einige Belegstellen, wo *dēd* als eine Bezeichnung für 'Eid' verwendet zu sein scheint. Vergleiche aus der Fünften Küre in F: *achma to haldana and ded sunder strid mith xij monnum on tha withum* '(diese) darf man mit Tateiden ohne gerichtlichen Zweikampf behalten, (und zwar) mit zwölf Männern auf die Reliquien'.[134] An Parallelstellen dieser Küre begegnet konsequent das Kompositum *dēdēth.*[135] Die Zuverlässigkeit der Belegstellen von *dēd* geht aus der Tatsache hervor, dass sie in einem ähnlichen Kontext an anderen Stellen auftaucht, wobei Parallelstellen schon wieder *dēdēth* aufweisen.[136] In jeder der drei Belegstellen begegnet es in einer festen Verbindung: *an(d) ded uter/sunder strid* 'mit Tateiden, ohne gerichtlichen Zweikampf'.[137]

Die Bedeutungsentwicklung lässt sich folgendermaßen skizzieren: aus der Grundbedeutung 'Tat' ergab sich die Bedeutung 'Tatsache'. Stützend auf die Zusammensetzung *dēdēth* (siehe dort), in der das Element *dēd-* schon diese Bedeutung 'Tatsache' hat, konnte *dēd* sich zu einer spezifischen Bedeutung 'Eid zur Erhärtung der Rechtmäßigkeit einer Tatsache' weiterentwickeln. Daraus lässt sich schließen, dass *dēd* und *dēdēth* als synonym zu betrachten sind und dass *dēd* also, wie *dēdēth*, als 'Tateid' zu übersetzen

---

ihnen einen Eid abnimmt, daß sie bestimmte von vornherein genannte Verbrechen rügen werden, oder daß sie schlechtweg die Wahrheit aussagen werden über das, was der Richter sie fragen werde', Brunner und von Schwerin, *Deutsche Rechtsgeschichte*, II, 640.

133 *Die 'Fivelgoer' Handschrift*, Sjölin, Hg., I, 183–84.

134 *Das Fivelgoer Recht*, Buma und Ebel, Hg., 30–31 (§III 5).

135 Vgl. J. Hoekstra, *Die gemeinfriesischen siebzehn Küren* (Assen, 1940), 90–92 und 126.

136 Vgl. *Die 'Fivelgoer' Handschrift*, Sjölin, Hg., I, 252 (§IV 7) und 338 (§XIII 2). Merkwürdigerweise listet Sjölin, *Die 'Fivelgoer' Handschrift*, II, s.v. *ded*, die genannten Belegstellen in seiner Wortliste bei der Bedeutung 'Tatsache' auf: die Bedeutung 'Tateid' fehlt.

137 Übrigens lässt auch *dēdēth* sich einmal in einer ähnlichen Phrase aufweisen, im Einundzwanzigsten Landrecht gemäß J: *aldeermey moet ick mijn eerwa bihalda wtor stryd mey twam dededum* 'damit darf ich mein Erbe ohne gerichtlichen Zweikampf mit zwei Tateiden behalten', *Westerlauwerssches Recht*, Buma und Ebel, Hg., 164–65 (§VIII 28).

und somit für einen assertorischen Eid mit Eideshelfern zu halten ist. Obwohl es in den Nachbarsprachen Entsprechungen von *dēd* gibt, ist eine Bedeutung im Bereich der Eidesleistung nur für das Altfriesische nachzuweisen.

handtrowe 'Handeid'

Das Femininum *handtrowe* war von alters her eine Bezeichnung des Begriffes 'Versprechen durch Handschlag'. Diese Originalbedeutung ist im Altfriesischen, im folgenden Abschnitt der sogenannten *Willküren des Upstalsboom* nachzuweisen, vergleiche (gemäß Ro):

> so habba wy meenlick seth, dat jewelick riuchter (...) alle lyued deer to drywa mit riuchte and mit eed swerringha jefta mit handtrouwen deer in syne deel se (...), datse dyne helliga ferd ewelick halde
> 'so haben wir zusammen bestimmt, dass jeder Richter (...) alle Leute, die in seinem Bezirk sind, mit Recht und mit dem Schwören eines Eides oder mit Versprechen durch Handschlag verpflichten solle, dass sie den heiligen Friedensbann ewig einhalten'.[138]

Diese Deutung trifft aber bei einigen anderen altfriesischen Belegstellen nicht zu, wie in den sogenannten *Willküren der fünf Delen* (gemäß D): *so schil di man an sine nates hand faen ende suara dat him god alsoe helpe ende riuchte hand trowa, so hi dera deda onschieldich se* 'so soll der mann an seines genossen hand fassen, und schwören dass ihm gott also helfe und handtreue richte, wie er, je nachdem er, an den vorher genannten verbrechen unschuldig sei'.[139] Die ziemlich allgemeine Richthofensche Übersetzung 'Handtreue' ist wohl, wegen des Anfassens der Hand des Sippegenossen, wie das ja auch bei der Leistung des *hondēth* stattfand (siehe dort), spezifischer als 'Freischwörung durch Handeid' zu deuten. Dass der Terminus *ēth* durch *trowe* ersetzt werden konnte, hat eventuell mit der von Brunner behaupteten Minderwertigkeit dieser Eidesform zu tun.[140] Die Erklärung von *handtrowe* als eine Art Eidesleistung lässt sich mit auf Grund vom Anfang des Textes, dem dieser Abschnitt gehört, rechtfertigen: der Text fängt nämlich mit der Überschrift *Hiir sint lada scrioun* 'hier sind Reinigungseide aufgelistet' an.[141] Überdies wird die Deutung vom DRW unterstützt: hierin sind, neben dieser altfriesischen Belegstelle, auch einige Belegstellen aus dem Mittelhochdeutschen aufzufinden, bei denen der Begriff 'Handtreue' auf ähnliche Weise verwendet wird, wie beispielsweise im Stadtrecht von

---

[138] H. D. Meijering, *De Willekeuren van de Opstalsboom (1323). Een filologisch-historische monografie* (Groningen, 1974), 67. Meine Übersetzung.

[139] Von Richthofen, *Altfriesisches Wörterbuch*, s.v. *hondtriuwe.*

[140] Wie oben, Fußnote 74.

[141] Siehe von Richthofen, *Friesische Rechtsquellen*, 476.

Adelsheim von 1572: *da er sich dessen mit der handtreu, dass er solches nicht gehört, entschuldigen kan.*[142] Im Mittelniederländischen und im Mittelniederdeutschen scheint keine ähnliche Verwendung von Entsprechungen von *handtrowe* überliefert zu sein.

kest 'fakultativer Eid'[143]

Die Grundbedeutung des Femininums *kest* ist 'Wahl', aus der sich im frühesten Altfriesischen schon die Bedeutung 'gewählte Satzung, Küre' ergeben hat. In jener Verwendung begegnet *kest* in beiden friesischen Hauptmundarten. Im westerlauwersschen Altfriesischen haben aber Bedeutungserweiterungen stattgefunden, von denen eine zu der Bedeutung 'fakultativer Eid' geführt hat. Als solche ist sie für *kest* mehrfach überliefert, vergleiche zum Beispiel: *nentra orum to bikomrien hagera dan en kest* 'von keinem anderen mehr zu beschlagnahmen als das, was mit einem fakultativen Eid zurückerhalten werden kann'.[144] An ähnlichen Stellen begegnet *ēth* oder *sliuchte ēth* (siehe dort).

Eine Urkunde des Jahres 1425 zeigt, was mit *kest* als Eidesbegriff wohl gemeint ist:

> Renyk foers. des lettera waer deys den keller kestghed mith twam, thet ber Dowa ne wrald neen ayndom in dis foers. land hawen had (...) ende thi keller foers. tha kest on nomad ende ful een al last habbet 'vorhergenannter Renyk forderte den Kellermeister am zweiten Gerichtstag zur fakultativen Eidesleistung auf, mit zwei (Eideshelfern zu schwören?), dass Bruder Dowa dieses vorhergenannte Landstück nie in Eigentum gehabt hat (...) und der vorhergenannte Kellermeister hat den fakultativen Eid akzeptiert und vollständig geleistet'.[145]

Der Beklagte bekam also die Wahl, entweder selber den Eid zu leisten oder nicht, so dass sich der *kest* wohl als 'fakultativer Eid' interpretieren lässt. Das Ablehnen der Eidesleistung konnte dazu führen, dass der Beklagte mit einem Eid des Klägers überführt wurde, vergleiche aus SnR: *dijthia brwnssin hat marten tyernazin op een kest set (...) ist seck dat marten den kest myt syn wyff naet dwaen willet (...) soe scel dythia ende syn wyff den kest dwaen* 'Dijthia Brwnssin hat Marten Tyernazin zu fakultativer Eidesleistung aufgefordert (...). Falls Marten und seine Ehefrau den fakultativen Eid nicht

---

142 DRW, s.v. 1 *Handtreue*, III.

143 S. J. Fockema Andreae, 'Tekstverklaring van oud-nederlandsche rechtsbronnen', *Rechtsgeleerd Magazijn* 7 (1888), 503–25, hier 503–17; W. L. van Helten, 'Oudfriesch *kestigia, kesta, kest* enz., Nederlandsch *custen, custinge* enz.', *TNTL* 14 (1895), 297–99; Cleveringa, '*Kestigia*', 29–30.

144 O II 187. Meine Übersetzung.

145 O I 42. Meine Übersetzung.

leisten wollen (...), dann sollen Dythia und seine Ehefrau den fakultativen Eid leisten'.[146] Die Zahl der zu leistenden Eide wird von Fall zu Fall wohl unterschiedlich gewesen sein. Aus einer Urkunde lässt sich der assertorische Charakter der Eidesleistung sichern: *een keste to laestane, dat is on da helgem to onswarane* 'einen fakultativen Eid zu leisten, dass heißt, sich auf die Reliquien freizuschwören'.[147] Genaue Entsprechungen sind in den Nachbarsprachen nicht belegt.[148]

lāda 'Reinigungseide'[149]

Schon His, dem Sjölin sich anschließt, hat mit Hilfe der zwei Homonyme von ae. *lād* ('Reinigung' und 'Führung, Weg') gezeigt, dass die Verbalableitungen *lāda* und *lēde* semantisch getrennt werden müssen: das Pluraletantum *lāda* bedeutet 'Reinigungseide', *lēde* bedeutet 'Übernahme der Haftung'.[150] Dessen ungeachtet werden diese beiden altfriesischen Wörter in neuerer lexikographischer Literatur immer noch als phonologische Varianten betrachtet.[151] Darum ist hier eine Erörterung der Etymologie der beiden Wörter zu versuchen.

Diesbezüglich sei erstens die vorgenommene Interpretation von *lāda* als Pluraletantum zu erläutern. In der Literatur wird das häufig begegnende *lāda* immer ohne weiteres als Plural zu **lāde* betrachtet, eine Form, die meines Wissens überhaupt nicht überliefert ist.[152] Wenn in einer Quelle *lāda* erwähnt werden, jedoch nur ein Unschuldseid geschworen werden sollte, wird eine andere Eidesbezeichnung verwendet. Dies zeigt zum Beispiel eine

---

[146] SnR, Nr. 3834. Meine Übersetzung.

[147] O II 31. O. Vries, *Correcties op P. Sipma, Oudfriesche Oorkonden I–III, aangevuld met een overzicht van de schrijvershanden*, Estrikken 64 (Groningen, 1984), 52, ließt *keste* statt Sipmas Transkription *teste*. Vries ergänzt, dass er sich seiner Lesung nicht völlig sicher ist.

[148] Im Mittelniederländischen ist jedoch einmal der Terminus *custeet* belegt, vom DRW, s.v. *Kusteid* als 'Eid des Klägers und seiner Eideshelfer zur Bekräftigung der Anklage' definiert. Das MNW, in dem diese einzige Belegstelle ebenfalls verarbeitet wurde, definiert (in meiner Übersetzung) 'Eid der Hauptperson und seiner Eideshelfer, zum Beweis, dass eine Anklage unbegründet ist; Unschuldseid'. Hier soll auch auf den DRW-Eintrag *Kustboteid* 'der Gegenpartei abgeforderter Eid' hingewiesen werden.

[149] Grimm, *Rechtsaltertümer*, II, 490 und 563; Brunner und von Schwerin, *Deutsche Rechtsgeschichte*, II, 574; Sjölin, 'Afr. *lâde* 'Reinigung'. Zu einer Stelle der Hunsingoër Küren', *Fryske stúdzjes oanbean oan Prof. Dr. J. H. Brouwer op syn sechstichste jierdei*, K. Dykstra u.a., Hg. (Assen, 1960), 85–87 ; W. J. Buma, 'Oer Aldfrysk *lare* en *lawe*', *UW* 17 (1968), 1–4; *Die 'Fivelgoer' Handschrift*, Sjölin, Hg., I, 204–05.

[150] His, *Strafrecht der Friesen,* 65–66; Sjölin, 'Afr. *lâde*', 85.

[151] Vgl. Holthausen und Hofmann, *Altfriesisches Wörterbuch*, s.v. *lâde* 2 und Buma, *Vollständiges Wörterbuch*, s.v. *lâde*.

[152] Zwar setzt Sjölin, *Die 'Fivelgoer' Handschrift*, II, s.v. *dedlade* einen femininen Akkusativ an, die in dem einschlägigen Abschnitt begegnende Form *dedlatha* wäre jedoch mit gleicher Berechtigung als Plural anzusetzen.

Belegstelle in J, wo es in der Überschrift eines Abschnitts heißt: *thit sint tha latha.*[153] Wo von keinem oder nur einem Eid gesprochen wird, begegnet niemals der Singularterminus **lāde*, sondern immer *(nēne) ēth*. Somit wäre *lāda* wohl besser als Pluraletantum zu betrachten. Es muss hier aber bemerkt werden, dass die angelsächsische Entsprechung *lād* auch als Singular erscheint, so dass die eventuelle Entwicklung zur Beschaffenheit eines Pluraletantums nur für das Altfriesische zutrifft.

Mit der Interpretation von *lāda* als Pluraletantum ist aber die Behauptung, dass *lēde* und *lāda* etymologisch zu trennen sind, noch nicht bewiesen: der Singular von *lāda* könnte ursprünglich **lāde* gewesen sein. Hier ist aber auf den unterschiedlichen Vokalismus hinzuweisen, der zeigt, dass afr. *lāda* und *lēde* sich nicht zum gleichen Zeitpunkt aus dem zugrundeliegenden Verb entwickelt haben können. *Lēde* ist wohl als ein mit *e*-Suffix gebildetes Verbalabstraktum anzusetzen. Eine derartige Verbableitung wird von der Tatsache, dass es neben *lēde* auch *lēdene* in der gleichen Bedeutung gibt, unterstützt: gemäß Ahlsson 'liegen Formen mit *-e* und *-ene* nebeneinander vor'.[154] Die Ableitung kann entweder schon als urgermanische oder als altfriesische Entwicklung angesetzt werden. Im ersten Fall entstand *lēde* aus dem Verbalwurzel germ. **laid-* 'leiten', weil das Suffix '*-i* (<*īni*) (...) in der Regel Umlaut der Wurzelsilbe (bewirkte)',[155] und also zu *lēde* führen musste. Im zweiten Fall entstand es erst später, aus dem schon umgelauteten Verb afr. *lēda*. Obwohl *lāda*, wie *lēde*, wohl ursprünglich ein Verbalabstraktum ist, wäre eine derartige Etymologie für *lāda*, die auf einer Verbalableitung mit Suffix *-e* beruht, abzulehnen, weil sie den abweichenden Vokalismus nicht erklären kann: *lāda* hätte sonst ja auch Umlaut aufzeigen müssen. Überdies ist für *lāda* nicht eine semantisch vergleichbare Nebenform mit einem Suffix *-ene* nachzuweisen, im Gegensatz zu *lēde*. Ein ursprünglicher Singular **lāde* zum Pluraletantum *lāda*, wie es meistens in der Literatur erscheint, ist meiner Meinung nach also abzulehnen, so dass für *lāda* eine alternative Etymologie anzusetzen ist. Die Frage, wie sie genau aussehen muss, bleibt hier unbeantwortet; dass sie aber irgendwie an germ. **laid-* 'leiten' anzuknüpfen ist, scheint wohl plausibel zu sein.[156]

Aus den Belegstellen zeigt sich *lāda* als Bezeichnung für mehrere, assertorische Reinigungseide. Da *lāda* (im Kompositum *dēdlāda*, siehe unten) im

---

[153] *Westerlauwerssches Recht*, Buma und Ebel, Hg., 422 (§XXI 109, Überschrift).

[154] Ahlsson, *Altfriesische Abstraktbildungen*, 1. Leider behandelt Ahlsson weder *lēde* noch *lāda*.

[155] *Ibid.*

[156] Vielleicht liegt Konversion des Grundmorphems des Verbs vor (wie etwa *fal* aus *falla* oder auch *strīd* aus *strīda*). Eine solche suffixlose Bildung wurde die Abwesenheit von Umlaut erklären können. Für eine solche deverbale Bildung spricht eventuell auch die Abwesenheit eines Suffixes in aeng. *lād*.

westerlauwersschen Altfriesischen ganz häufig, im osterlauwersschen Altfriesischen dagegen nur im *Westerlauwersschen Sendrecht* in F begegnet,[157] so lässt sich wohl vermuten, dass es als typisch westerlauwerssch zu betrachten sei. Falls dies zutrifft, wird es, aufgrund der angelsächsischen Entsprechung, schon lange vor dem Anfang der altfriesischen Überlieferung (etwa 1200) aus dem osterlauwersschen Altfriesischen verschwunden sein.[158] Mit *lāda* ist weiterhin das Kompositum *dēdlāda* gebildet worden.[159] Vergleiche aus dem *Westerlauwersschen Sendrecht* (gemäß F):

> jef hi him bitigat thes thredda deis, thet hi vrherich wesin hebbe, sa is thi deken niar mith fior leyem (hine) to bithiugane than hi tha dedlatha to biadane
> 'wenn er ihn am dritten Tage beschuldigt, dass er ungehorsam gewesen sei, so ist der Dekan näher berechtigt, ihn mit vier Laien zu überführen, als er, die Reinigungseide anzubieten'.[160]

In Bezug auf die Deutung sei auf ein Zitat Sjölins hinzuweisen. Demnach bezeichnet dieser Eidesbegriff einen 'Reinigungseid, der zur Klageabweisung dient. Durch seine Ableistung kann sich der Beklagte vor Gericht freischwören oder eine von seinem Gegner (Kläger) bezweifelte Tatsache

---

[157] Sjölin (*Die 'Fivelgoer' Handschrift*, I, 204–05) möchte die überlieferte Form *lawa* 'Absolution' zu *latha* emendieren, siehe *ibid.* 384–85 (§XXII 20). Ich möchte jedoch vorschlagen, an die Feminina ae. *lēaf* und mhd. *loube* 'Erlaubnis' (früh-nhd. *Laube*) anzuknüpfen und ein Femininum afr. **lāwe* zu rekonstruieren.

[158] Überdies scheint *lāda* nur in typisch westerlauwersschen Texten zu begegnen, obwohl ich dazu auch westerlauwerssche Bußregister rechne, die wahrscheinlich von jeher auf eine allgemein-friesische Vorlage zurückzuführen sind. In allgemein-friesischen Rechtstexten wie den *Siebzehn Küren* oder den *Vierundzwanzig Landrechten* ist *lāda* nicht nachzuweisen.

[159] Im *Westerlauwersschen Sendrecht* gemäß J begegnet einmal *dedleda* (vgl. *Westerlauwerssches Recht*, Buma und Ebel, Hg.,172 [§IX 12]), das meiner Meinung nach als fehlerhaft für *dedlada* zu betrachten ist (obwohl grundsätzlich die Möglichkeit, dass hier spätaltwestfriesische Vokalerhöhung vorliegt, nicht auszuschließen ist). Sonst begegnet im *Autentica Riocht* die Kombination *scalkis lada*: *Thet Autentica Riocht. Met inleiding, glossen, commentaar en woordenlijst*, J. H. Brouwer, Hg. (Assen, 1941), 56. Hierbei betrachtet Brouwer *scalkis* als Genitiv singular von *skalk* 'booswicht', *ibid.* 231. Somit nimmt er stillschweigend ein Kompositum *scalkislada* an, wie auch Buma u.a., *Codex Aysma,* 227 (§I 281), die den Begriff in der Parallelstelle in A als 'Unschuldseide für ehrenrührige Delikte' übersetzen. Ich möchte hier jedoch die Möglichkeit vorbringen, *scalkis* als Adverb, etwa mit einer Bedeutung 'auf unzuverlässige Weise' zu betrachten (vgl. nnl. *schalks* 'schelmisch, schalkhaft'). Obwohl es keine weiteren Belegstellen eines dergleichen Adverbs gibt, scheint mir diese Interpretation wegen des Kontextes besser geeignet zu sein. Das Adverb würde sich dann also auf die Weise der Eidesleistung beziehen.

[160] *Das Fivelgoer Recht*, 66–67, Buma und Ebel, Hg. (§VIII 17).

erhärten'.[161] Obwohl Sjölin *dedlatha* hier, meiner Meinung nach, also zu Unrecht als Singular ansetzt (siehe Fußnote 152), sind gegen die semantische Deutung Sjölins grundsätzlich keine Einwände vorzubringen. Das gilt aber nicht für die Fortsetzung des Zitats: 'Dabei bleibt es (...) unerheblich, ob ein sog. Eineid geschworen wird oder Eideshelfer zugegen sind. Hierin liegt wohl der entscheidende Unterschied zum Tateid, der nur mit Eideshelfern geleistet werden kann. Es steht deshalb zu vermuten, dass Tateid und Tatleite zwei nur in ihrem (ihnen vom Gericht beigemessenen) Wert unterschiedliche Beweismittel für die gleiche Sache darstellen'.[162] Falls die oben erläuterte Interpretation von *lāda* als Pluraletantum zutrifft, müsste daraus folgen, dass auch mit *dēdlāda* mehrere Eide gemeint wurden. Deswegen lässt die zitierte Vermutung bezüglich des Unterschieds zwischen 'Tateid' und 'Tatleite' sich nicht mit Hilfe von *dēdlāda* begründen. Der Begriff *dēdlāda* bezieht sich also wohl auf mehrere assertorische Unschuldseide, die mit Eideshelfern geleistet werden sollten. Das Element *dēd* deutet, wie in *dēdēth* (siehe dort), auf die Tatsache, weswegen Klage erhoben wurde, hin.

riucht 'Reinigungseid'
In F wird hinsichtlich des Angriffs auf ein ungeborenes Kind folgendes erwähnt: *hwasa hit bifiucht iefta birawat, thribete to betane jefta mith thrim riuchtum to riuchtane* '(wenn) jemand es angreift oder beraubt, (so hat er das) dreifach zu büßen oder sich mit der dreifachen Eideszahl zu reinigen'.[163] Entsprechungen begegnen in allen Nachbarsprachen,[164] so dass sich diese eidesbezügliche Bedeutung entweder schon im Urgermanischen entwickelt hat oder erst nach dem Anfang des Friesischen aus einer Nachbarsprache entlehnt worden ist. Aus den altfriesischen Belegstellen stellt sich heraus, dass es sich um einen assertorischen Reinigungseid handeln muss.

stef 'gestabter Eid'[165]
Wie in den Nachbarsprachen wurde afr. *stef* in der altfriesischen Eidesterminologie als *terminus technicus* verwendet: im Altfriesischen begegnet zum Beispiel der bildliche Ausdruck *et steve stonda* 'einen Eid ablegen' (wörtlich 'zum [Eid]stab stehen').[166] Es scheint jedoch eine Bedeutungserweiterung von 'Stab' stattgefunden zu haben, die zur Bedeutung 'gestabter Eid' geführt hat. Ein Beweis für diese semantische Entwicklung ist übrigens lediglich im Rüstringer Altfriesischen zu finden. Vergleiche aus R_1: *sa hach*

---

161 Wie Fußnote 29.
162 Wie Fußnote 161.
163 *Das Fivelgoer Recht*, Buma und Ebel, Hg. 134–35 (§XI 1).
164 Vgl. DRW, s.v. *Recht* X.
165 Algra, 'Eedsfoarmen', 89.
166 Vgl. z.B. *Das Rüstringer Recht*, Buma und Ebel, Hg., 48 (§IV 8).

thet kind thenne altheroua to gungande uter stef and uter strid 'so soll das Kind ohne gestabten Eid und ohne (gerichtlichen) Zweikampf (...) darauf wieder Besitz davon ergreifen'.[167] An den meisten Parallelstellen dieser Küre begegnet nur *uter stride* oder ähnliches, die Parallelstelle im Ersten Emsiger Kodex (E_1) zeigt dagegen *sa ach hi te farane uther ethar and vter strijd oppa sijn ein erue* 'so soll er (...) ohne Eide und ohne (gerichtlichen) Zweikampf sein eigenes Erbe in Besitz nehmen'.[168] Auf Grund dessen lässt sich, in Fällen wie in der zitierten Rüstringer Fassung, auf eine Übersetzung von *stef* als 'gestabter Eid' schließen.

wīthe 'Eid auf die Reliquien'

Afr. *wīthe*, das gemäß Boutkan und Siebinga vom Verb *wīa* 'weihen' abgeleitet wurde,[169] bedeutet 'Reliquie' (siehe auch *wīthēth*). Im vorchristlichen Beweisverfahren wurde oft auf bestimmte Sachen, wie auf Waffen, Schiff oder Ross, oder auch auf eigene Körperteile geschworen. Nach der Christianisierung wurde der Eid 'unter Handauflage auf den Altar oder dessen Abbreviaturen: Reliquienbehälter ("auf die Heiligen"), Evangelienbuch, Kreuz, unter Niederknien'[170] geleistet. Daher konnte sich für *wīthe* aus der Bedeutung 'Reliquie' eine Bedeutungserweiterung zu 'Eid auf die Reliquien' ergeben. Diese Neubedeutung ist schon in den ältesten Quellen häufig nachzuweisen, vergleiche aus der Siebzehnten Küre (gemäß R_1): *bihalua fif thingon, thes ne mi thi fria frisa nena witha biada* 'mit Ausnahme von fünf Sachen, deretwegen der freie Friese sich nicht zum Unschuldseid auf die Reliquien erbieten darf'.[171] Afr. *wīthe* könnte wohl als typisch osterlauwerssches Altfriesisch betrachtet werden: wo es für osterlauwerssche Belegstellen westerlauwerssche Parallelstellen gibt, zeigen die westerlauwersschen Quellen konsequent *wīthēth* statt *wīthe* auf.[172] In den Nachbarsprachen

---

[167] *Ibid.* 40–41. Rechtshistorisches zum Ausdruck *uter stef and uter strid* bei Cleveringa, '*Kestigia*', 50.

[168] *Das Emsiger Recht*, Buma und Ebel, Hg., 26–27 (§III 14).

[169] Boutkan und Siebinga, *Old Frisian Etymological Dictionary*, s.v. *withe*, unter Bezug auf Ahlsson, *Altfriesische Abstraktbildungen*, 135, der dort aber auch die nicht von Boutkan und Siebinga erwähnte Möglichkeit, dass *wīthe* eventuell von einem Adjektiv **wīh* 'heilig' abgeleitet sei, aufführt.

[170] Von Amira und Eckhardt, *Germanisches Recht*, II, 168.

[171] *Das Rüstringer Recht*, Buma und Ebel, Hg., 42–43 (§III 17).

[172] Vgl. beispielsweise die Siebzehnte Küre in Hoekstra, *Siebzehn Küren*, 117–22 und 130, wo die Handschriften H, F, R_1 und E_1 *wīthe* zeigen, J, D und U aber Varianten zu *wīthēth* aufweisen. Es ist hier jedoch auf die einzige westerlauwerssche Belegstelle, in den *Bireknada Bota* gemäß J, hinzuweisen: *jef hit an tha withem warria welle* 'falls er es auf die Reliquien erhärten will', siehe *Westerlauwerssches Recht*, Buma und Ebel, Hg., 528–29 (§XXVIII 278); die Parallelstelle in D zeigt *wytedum*, siehe von Richthofen, *Friesische Rechtsquellen*, 473.

gibt es zwar wörtliche Entsprechungen,[173] keine hat sich jedoch zu einer eidesbezüglichen Bedeutung entwickelt.

3. Schlussbemerkungen

Im Vorhergehenden ist ein beschreibendes Inventar der altfriesischen Eidesbezeichnungen dargeboten, in dem für jede einzelne die semantische Entwicklung erläutert und eine Übersetzung gegeben wurde. Somit ist das Hauptanliegen der Untersuchung, zur altfriesischen lexikologischen Forschung beizutragen, vollzogen worden.

Das Ganze überschauend, fallen einige Sachen auf: zum Beispiel, dass die promissorischen Eide nur mit der Eidesbezeichnung *ēth* bezeichnet werden, dass also alle Eidesbezeichnungen, die sich erst später (oder auch, wie *lāda* und *riucht*, schon im Vorfriesischen) ergeben haben, nur assertorische Eide bezeichnen. Sonst fällt auf, dass altfriesische Amtseidesbezeichnungen aus dem osterlauwersschen Friesland überhaupt nicht auf uns gekommen sind und dass westerlauwerssche Amtseidesbezeichnungen erst seit der zweiten Hälfte des fünfzehnten Jahrhunderts nachzuweisen sind. Auf der Ebene der Sprachgeographie fällt sich auch erkennen, dass manche Eidesbezeichnungen an beiden Seiten der Lauwers nicht gleichermaßen üblich waren. Das im osterlauwersschen Altfriesischen ziemlich häufig erscheinende *wīthe* scheint im westerlauwersschen Altfriesischen konsequent von *wīthēth* vertreten zu sein. Umgekehrt findet sich östlich der Lauwers kaum das im westerlauwersschen Friesland frequente *lāda.*

In Bezug auf die komparative Lexikologie hat es sich herausgestellt, dass sich bei manchen Wörtern, deren wörtliche Entsprechungen zwar auch über die friesischen Grenzen hinaus verwendet wurden, semantische Entwicklungen durchsetzen konnten, die zu bezüglichen Bedeutungen führten und als eigenständig friesisch zu betrachten sind (zum Beispiel *kest, wīthe* und *stef*). Sonst ist auf Eidesarten, die es anscheinend nur im friesischen Gebiet gegeben hat, hinzuweisen, wie den *fēknianēth*, den *fremethe ēth* oder auch den *mensingēd.*

Es hat sich gezeigt, dass die in der Einführung aufgeführte Behauptung, die Terminologie der germanischen Sprachen zeige 'bemerkenswerte Konstanz', sich bezüglich der Eidesbezeichnungen zwar unleugbar, aber nur teilweise vom Altfriesischen bestätigen lässt. Es hat sich nämlich ebenfalls herausgestellt, dass die altfriesische Eidesterminologie sich oft einen eigenen Weg sucht, der zu Eidesbezeichnungen geführt hat, die es nicht oder nicht

---

173 Nur in den älteren Sprachstufen, vgl. got. *weihiða* 'Weihe', ahd. *wīhida* 'consecratio, propitiatorium, reliquiae', as. *wīhitha* 'Reliquie', siehe Ahlsson, *Altfriesische Abstraktbildungen*, 135.

in der gleichen Verwendung in den Nachbarsprachen gab. Genau wann und wie sich diese einmaligen Verwendungen ergeben haben, ist eine Frage, die wegen mangelhafter Überlieferung oder eines nur schwer zu interpretierenden Kontextes oft nicht oder nur teilweise beantwortet werden konnte.

Es lässt sich vermuten, dass sich Ähnliches auch für andere Teilgebiete der altfriesischen Eidesterminologie konstatieren lässt. Deswegen konnte zum Beispiel eine lexikologische Untersuchung der sich auf das Eidesverfahren beziehenden Verben genauso nützlich sein. Solche Forschungen könnten nicht nur der altfriesischen und der komparativen altgermanischen Lexikologie, sondern auch für Rechtshistoriker von Nutzen sein. Was lässt sich durch Vergleichen des Eidesverfahrens, wie es in den altfriesischen Quellen, jedoch auch schon in der *Lex Frisionum*, zutage tritt, über dessen Kontinuität und Änderungen sagen? Wie sah die 'alltägliche' Schwurpraxis im mittelalterlichen Friesland aus? Überdies könnten Beurteilungen von sprachgeographischen Aspekten der altfriesischen Eidesterminologie zu interessanten rechtshistorischen Forschungen anregen: hat sich das Eidesverfahren im osterlauwersschen und westerlauwersschen Friesland unterschiedlich entwickelt? Falls ja: wie, wann und wieso haben sich diese Entwicklungen ergeben? Diese und ähnliche Fragen dürfen Aufgabe künftiger Forschungen sein. Hoffentlich können die obenstehenden Ausführungen dazu anregen.

Abkürzungen

DRW *Deutsches Rechtswörterbuch. Wörterbuch der älteren deutschen Rechtssprache* (Weimar, 1914–..). <http://drw-www.adw.uni-heidelberg.de/drw/>

HRG *Handwörterbuch zur deutschen Rechtsgeschichte*, A. Erler und E. Kauffmann, Hg. (Berlin, 1964–1998).

MNW *Middelnederlandsch Woordenboek*, E. Verwijs, J. Verdam, Hg. ('s-Gravenhage, 1885–1971).

O *Oudfriesche oorkonden* I–III, P. Sipma, Hg., OTR 1–3 ('s-Gravenhage, 1927–1941) und *Oudfriese Oorkonden* IV, O. Vries, Hg., OTR 14 ('s-Gravenhage, 1977).

SnR *Snitser Recesboeken 1490–1517*, M. Oosterhout, Hg. (Assen, 1960).

Gender Semiotics, Anglo-Frisian *wīf*, and Old Frisian Noun Gender

Irmengard Rauch

0. Introduction

Charles Sanders Peirce understood his ingenious category *abduction* to be so fundamental that he compared it to the instincts of feeding and breeding. He wrote: '… all human knowledge up to the highest flights of science, is but the development of our inborn animal instincts'.[1] And Thomas Sebeok displaced the Sapirean dictum that 'language is the sign system par excellence',[2] with his conviction that 'Genetic copying is the semiotic process par excellence'.[3] Genetic copying, reproduction and thus sex/gender is *the* fundamental signifying experience. If, in fact, we should grant this to be the case (although one could argue for genetic copying as a hyponym of *language*, depending on one's definition of language), if Sebeok's genetic copying is primary and Sapir's language is relegated to secondary position, we obviously expect to find a great deal of genetic copying, reproduction, and sex/gender in language itself. For Western translationists the equivalence in the Heinrich Heine poem *Ein Fichtenbaum steht einsam* between the German masculine noun '*der Fichtenbaum*: English "the spruce tree"' and the German feminine noun '*die Palme*: English "the palm tree"' ever remains a notorious and challenging case in point. The German wording overtly displays *sexual tension* between the anthropomorphized protagonist (spruce tree) and the object of its dream (the palm tree), an equivalence which is quasi-unattainable in the English translation.

1. Linguistic gender and semiotic effect

Linguistic research on language gender is enormous; it reaches from the innermost core of language, viz. sound, to the outermost layer of language

---

1 C. S. Peirce, *Collected Papers of Charles Sanders Peirce. I–II: Principles of Philosophy and Elements of Logic*, ed. C. Hartshorne and P. Weiss (Cambridge, MA, 1932) II, 754.

2 Echoed by T. Todorov, 'Literature and Semiotics', *The Tell-Tale Sign: A Survey of Semiotics*, ed. T. A. Sebeok (Lisse, 1975), 97–102, at 97.

3 T. A. Sebeok, *The Sign and Its Masters* (Austin, 1979), 120.

material, i.e., discourse. So, e.g., in phonology/metrics we speak of *masculine* rhymes as those in which the final syllable of a line is stressed, while the final syllable is unstressed in a *feminine* rhyme. At the other end of the grammatical spectrum, i.e., at the discourse level, language has experienced several waves of feminist grammar in the last half of the twentieth century which subsequently intersected with the PC language wave of the nineties, underscoring matriarchical or woman-speak alongside patriarchical (*PUD* = patriarchical universe of discourse) or man-speak.[4]

Surely, observations on the discourse level are overtly sex-related, while the phonological example of feminine and masculine rhyme requires sex-metaphorical understanding of the analogues, thus German 'männlich stumpf' = 'blunt, lifeless, impassive' and German 'weiblich klingend' = 'ringing, melodic'. Still less sex-related is the concept of grammatical gender as a formal category, i.e., as a noun class. So, e.g., Bantu linguists consider ten and twenty so-called *genders* based on morphology, i.e., prefixes suggestive of semantic features such as those which distinguish augmentation, e.g., *j-oka* 'giant snake', from dimunition, *ki-j-oka* 'tiny snake', from the residue, remaining animates, e.g., *mw-alimu* 'teacher', *jogoo* 'rooster'.[5] This is not so remote when one considers the diminutive suffixes in Frisian or in German which render nouns neuter regardless of their meaning, thus, e.g., Frisian *mantsje* 'little man' or German *Männlein*. In fact, more of the world's languages display formal gender rather than natural or semantic gender. Many are mixed. English belongs to a minority of languages, e.g., Dijari, an Australian aboriginal language, and some Dravidian languages such as those in India, Sri Lanka, Pakistan, which, with English are strict semantic gender languages, i.e., affixless English *man* and *little man* are both co-referential with *he*. No formal characteristic of the noun *man* identifies English gender; it is purely semantic, i.e., semiotically iconic, a Peircean *First,* and its coreferent *he* is nicely deictic, viz. a semiotic *Second* or index pointing to the noun *man*.[6] In comparison, while Frisian *mantsje* or German

[4] Cf. J. Penelope, *Speaking Freely: Unlearning the Lies of the Fathers' Tongues* (New York, 1990).

[5] Cited in G. G. Corbett, *Gender* (Cambridge, 1991), 47.

[6] Peircean categories exhibit the following correlations, as schematized in I. Rauch, *Semiotic Insights: The Data Do the Talking* (Toronto, 1999), 7:

Firstness	Secondness	Thirdness
freedom/life/freshness	otherness/cause-effect/ brute force	generality/continuity/habit
possibility	existence	law
might be	happens to be	would be
past	present	future
factual similarity	factual contiguity	imputed contiguity
sign	object	interpretant

Männlein produced through the diminutive suffix, a formal gender marker, are compulsively neuter, and therefore semiotic *Seconds*, they are conventionalized in the lexicon and are accordingly *Thirds*, i.e., symbols. Yet the underlying Frisian *man* and German *Mann* are as iconic as is English *man*.

2. ANGLO-FRISIAN *wīf*

To be sure, Frisian *wiif* and German *Weib* are as semantically iconic as *man/Mann* (above) in mirroring the object which they represent. The crucial difference resides in the fact that in both languages the noun representing the feminine person is of a grammatically neuter (Frisian 'non-common') gender. Indeed, in its past history throughout North-West Germanic, Old Norse *víf*, Old Frisian/Old Saxon *wīf*, Old High German *wīb* are all formal neuter, which has engendered a rich body of research, both synchronic and diachronic. Diachronically, etymologists consider an array of roots, e.g., the derivation from IE **sweip-* 'to move, swing, turn/swivel' interpreted as the one doing the house chores such as sweeping. Interestingly, but not far-fetched, it is reconstructed in Middle English to mean 'to copulate'.[7] The venerable Pokorny etymology for Anglo-Frisian *wīf* is IE **weip-*,[8] also glossed 'to turn, swing' and found in such words as Gothic *biwaibjan* 'to wind around, encircle, twist around', Old English *wǣfan* 'to clothe, wrap up, envelop', which intersects semantically with the IE root **webh-* 'to move back and forth, to weave'.[9] Where do we go from here? We perceive etymology as a bottomless pit. The reason for pursuing it here, is that recent world events lead toward the etymon meaning 'to clothe, wrap up, envelop' – the semantic concept of *burka.* Does this explain why *wīf* is neuter, i.e., does it display the ultimate semiotic rationale, or as Eco says, 'the fundamental characteristic of the sign is that I can use it to lie'?[10] Is a *cover-up* (cf. Old English *wǣfan* 'to clothe, wrap up, envelop', above) not a lie?

Yet the Anglo-Frisian language group (as is also the case with Old Norse *víf*) knew that the neuter *wīf* is a 'she', since the pronouns anaphoric or co-referential with *wīf* prevail as morphological feminines. Thus semantic

icon	index	symbol
syntax	semantics	pragmatics
abduction	induction	deduction

[7] Cited in A. Curzan, *Gender Shifts in the History of English* (Cambridge, 2003), 161, following D. Baron (*Grammar and Gender*, 1986) who cites Skinner's *Etymologicon linguae Anglicanae* (1671).

[8] J. Pokorny, *Indogermanisches etymologisches Wörterbuch* (Bern, 1959), 1115–16.

[9] Curzan, *Gender Shifts*, 162, points out the popularity of the Old English *wefan* 'to weave' etymology.

[10] U. Eco, 'Looking for a Logic of Culture', *The Tell-Tale Sign*, ed. Sebeok, 9–17, at 12.

congruence takes precedence over grammatical gender (but see section 3. below):

Būta mith thīnere āfta wīve skaltu godlike libba
'except with your lawful wife shall you live (a) godly (life)'
Old Frisian *Ten Commandments*, Sixth (First Riustring Ms.)
Godes engil ... them wībe gibōd, … tho siu erist that barn antfeng
'the angel of God commanded the woman, who first the child received'
Old Saxon *Heliand,* 445
Wæs sum wīf, sēo hæfde umtrumnesse gāst
'there was a certain woman, who had an unclean spirit'
Old English *Luke*, 13, 11

In stark contrast to the Anglo-Frisian habit, the neuter German *Weib* displays another semiotic gender configuration. Granted that German has a mixed semantic/grammatical gender system, anaphora to a neuter noun such as *Weib* or *Mädchen* yields a neuter pronoun, as seen, e.g., in the Old High German *Christ and the Samaritan Woman, 6: 'bat er sih ketrencan daz wīp thaz ther thara quam'* ('he bade the woman who came there to quench [his thirst]'). However, with the interesting intervention of proxemics, we can witness semantic gender taking precedence over grammatical gender in a citation such as that in Modern German from Thomas Mann's *Zauberberg*: '*Ein ... Mädchen stich dicht an Hans Castorp vorbei, indem es ihn fast mit dem Arme berührte, Und dabei pfiff sie ...*'. Proximally, grammatical gender prevails (*es*); distally semantic gender slips in/prevails (*sie*) in the anaphoric pronoun, whereby Peircean *Thirdness* (conventional 'it') yields to *Firstness* (iconic 'she'), both being *Seconds*, pointing to their referent ('girl').

In the switch from German *es* to *sie* we witness how a gender system might be on the move, i.e., we have a tiny example of how language might change. Not surprisingly, its teleology resides in iconicity, *Firstness*, abduction, Peirce's category for growth, creation (cf. section 0. above). Thus, while grammatical sex, i.e., semantic or natural gender, e.g., English *girl*, displays *Firstness* (iconic relative to its object), grammatical proxemics, pronominal gender congruence in the switch from German *es* to *sie* displays *Secondness* (indexical as to its object) and grammatical "lies", e.g., the neuter Anglo-Frisian *wīf* displays *Thirdness* (conventionalized as to its object).

3. Old Frisian Noun Gender

Clearly then, the Old Frisian sixth commandment citation in section 2 above bears witness to feminine coreference *thīnere* to a putative grammatically neuter noun *wīve,* but it differs from its Anglo-Frisian sibling dialects in its adjectival function where Old Saxon *them* and Old English *sum* are both neuter in grammatical agreement with *wībe* and *wīf*, respectively. Although marked neuter in the Old Frisian lexicon, the cited *wīve* is morphologically ambiguous as to gender since dative singular suffixal *-e* is gender neutral. Old Frisian *wīf* is not listed as heteroclitic, i.e., considered as attested with variable gender in the lexicon,[11] as opposed to, among other nouns, Old Frisian *here, hiri* masculine/neuter 'army', *bōk* feminine/neuter 'book', *kere* masculine/feminine 'privilege'.

Three genders for the Old Frisian noun system are affirmed throughout the literature, and Old Frisian grammars routinely display three gender paradigms often given with traditional genetic stem class provenance,[12] i.e., Gmc. *a, ō, i, u, n, r, nd*, root stems. Weak and strong stem type paradigms such as those of the First Riustring Manuscript offered by Boutkan,[13] in Figure 1A below, suggest the erosion of the historical stem class suffixes in part through neutralization of weakly stressed vowels to schwa and zero as seen, e.g., in the uniform dative singular depicting a strong stem type in *-e* or *-Ø* regardless of gender:

Figure 1A (Boutkan 2001)

		Strong	
	Masculine	Neuter	Feminine
Ns	*-Ø, -e*	*-Ø, -e*	*-e, -Ø. (-o)*
Gs	*-es, (-s), -Ø*	*-es*	*-e, (-Ø, -es)*
Ds	*-e, -Ø*	*-e, -Ø*	*-e, -Ø*
As	*-Ø, -e*	*-Ø, -e*	*-e, -Ø*
Np	*-a(r), -Ø, (–e)*	*-Ø, -a, -i, -o*	*-a, -Ø*
Gp	*-a (na)*	*-a (na)*	*-a, (-e, -Ø)*
Dp	*-on, (-Ø)*	*-on*	*-on*
Ap	*-a(r), -Ø, (–e)*	*-Ø, -a, -o (-ar),(-era)*	*-a, -Ø, -e*
		Weak	
Ns	*-a, -o*	*(-e)*	*-e*
Gs	*-a*	*(-a)*	*-a(n-)*
Ds	*-a*	*-a*	*-a*
As	*-a, -o*	*(-o)*	*-a*

[11] Cf. F. Holthausen, *Altfriesisches Wörterbuch*, rev. D. Hofmann (Heidelberg, 1985), 129.

[12] E.g., J. F. Hoekstra, 'Comparative Aspects of Frisian Morphology and Syntax', *Handbuch / Handbook*, 775–86, at 777, writes: 'The East Frisian and Mainland North Frisian dialects have retained the Old Frisian three gender system (cf. Bök. *di hün* (m.) 'the dog', *jü scheew* (f.) 'the table', *dåt uurd* (n.) 'the word')'. See also, e.g., W. Steller, *Abriss der altfriesischen Grammatik* (Halle/S., 1928), or B. Sjölin, *Einführung in das Friesische* (Stuttgart, 1969).

[13] D. F. H. Boutkan, 'Morphology of Old Frisian', *Handbuch / Handbook*, 620–26, at 622.

Np	*-a*	*(-on, -en)*	*-a*
Gp	*-ana, -ona*		*-(a)na*
Dp	*-on*	*(-non)*	*-on*
Ap	*-a*	*(-on)*	*-a*

Similarly the startling, almost a century earlier, minimal Old Frisian noun paradigms of Heuser,[14] in Figure 2A below, subvert the genetic stem classes and display what Heuser perceives as the unmarked desinence for each case. The neutralization of weak and strong stem types (as well as of all stem classes and all genders) is nicely visible in the uniform dative plural *-on, -um, -em:*

Figure 2A (Heuser 1903)

A. Starke Deklination.
Normalform.

		Masc.	Neutr.	Fem.
	N.A.	—	—	*-e*
Sing.	G.	*-es*	*-es*	*-e*
	D.	*-e*	*-s* [sic]	*-e*
	N.A.	*-ar, -a, -an*	*-o (-u), -e, -a*	*-a*
Plur.	G.	*-a*	*-a*	*-a*
	D.	*-on, -um, -em*		

B. Schwache Deklination

		Masc.	Neutr.	Fem.
	N.	*-a*	*-e*	*-e*
Sing.	G.	*-a*	*-a*	*-a*
	D.	*-a*	*-a*	*-a*
	A.	*-a*	*-e*	*-a*

N. *-a, -an* (Ntr. *-a, -on*)
G. *-ona, -ana, -ena*
D. *-on, -um, -em*
A. *-a, -an* (Ntr. *-a, -on*)

Depending on how it is read, most remarkable is the paradigm of Cummins,[15] in Figure 3A below, well over a century old, which indicates neither stem class, nor stem type (weak/strong) nor gender:

---

[14] W. Heuser, *Altfriesisches Lesebuch mit Grammatik und Glossar* (Heidelberg, 1903), 24–25. N.B.: p. 24, dative singular neuter *-s* is a typographical error.
[15] A. H. Cummins, *A Grammar of the Old Friesic Language* (London, 1887), 48.

Figure 3A (Cummins 1887)

1, SUMMARY OF THE DECLENSIONS.

Singular.

Nom.	
Gen.	*-es -is -e -a,* or same as nominative.
Dat.	*-a -e -i,* „ „
Acc.	*-a -e,* „ „

Plural.

Nom.	*-ar -a -e -u -an -en,* stem vowel changed, or same as nominative singular.
Gen.	*-a -ena -ane.*
Dat.	*-um -on -im -em.*
Acc.	same as nominative.

Cummins' schema may have been intended as no more than a summary of traditional noun paradigms since his fuller discussion (pp. 43–47) displays these paradigms arranged according to stem classes, stem types, and genders.

Returning to Figure 1A, Boutkan provides his inventory of the First Riustring Manuscript with the caveat that '(… endings containing *e* may also show *i,* those displaying *o* may also show *u* merely as phonological variants ["vowel balance"])'.[16] Even if granting Boutkan's vowel harmony/balance in the Riustring Manuscript for the moment, a gender neutral, stem class neutral, but not stem type neutral paradigm emerges in the strong noun desinences in Figure 1B below, where the residue is most numerous in the genitive singular but especially in the nominative plural and the accusative plural. But for the genitive singular *-a* and the dative singular *-a*, and perhaps the genitive plural *-ana*, the weak noun inflections show no gender neutralization:

Figure 1B

	Strong		
Ns	-e, -Ø	Np	*-a, -Ø*
Gs	*-es*	Gp	*-a*
Ds	*-e, -Ø*	Dp	*-on*
As	*-e, -Ø*	Ap	*-a, -Ø*

16 Boutkan, 'Morphology', 621.

Let us reconsider the already minimal Heuser paradigm of Figure 2 above, which displayed a dative plural neutral as to gender, as well as to weak or strong noun stem. A case can be made for further neutralization of the noun stem in the nominative plural but not without considerable residue. Figure 2B shows further gender neutrality in the dative singular and the genitive plural:

Figure 2B

		Masc.	Neutr.	Fem.
	N.A.	strong —	strong —	strong *-e*
		weak *-a*	weak *-e*	weak *-e* / A. *-a*
Sing.	G.	strong *-es*	strong *-es*	strong *-e*
		weak *-a*	weak *-a*	weak *-a*
	D.	strong *-e*	strong *-e*	strong *-e*
		weak *-a*	weak *-a*	weak *-a*
	N.A.	*-a*		
Plur.	G.	strong *-a*		
		weak *-ona, -ana, -ena*		
	D.	*-on, -um, -en*		

If we view Cummins' paradigm (cf. Figure 3A above) not labelled for noun class, noun type, or gender, details of noun inflection in traditional Old Frisian grammars such as Steller's[17] allow the checklist for gender given in Figure 3B:

Figure 3B

	Singular			
Nom.				
Gen.	*-es*	*-is*	*-e*	*-a*
	M	M	M	M
	F	F	F	F
	N	N	N	N
Dat.	*-a*	*-e*	*-i*	
	M	M	M	
	F	F	F	
	N	N	N	
Acc.	*-a*	*-e*		
	M	M		
	F	F		
		N		

17 Steller, *Abriss*, §§49–66.

					Plural	
Nom./	*-ar*	*-a*	*-e*	*-u*	*-an*	*-en*
Acc.	M	M	M		M	M
		F	F		F	F
		N	N	N	N	N
Gen.	*-a*	*-ena*	*-ana*			
	M	M	M			
	F	F	F			
	N	N	N			
Dat.	*-um*	*-on*	*-im*	*-em*		
	M	M	M	M		
	F	F	F	F		
	N	N	N	N		

Cummins' genitive plural *-ane* is written *-ana* in Steller, Heuser, and Boutkan and accepted as such. The accusative singular *-a* has alongside it a trigender *-e/-Ø* in the First Riustring Manuscript in figure 1A above, yielding overall a gender neutral accusative singular. The neutralization of the vocalic end syllable to schwa and zero in the case of final vowel is considerable,[18] affecting all derivational vowels, so that the lack of *-a* in the accusative singular for the neuter as well as the occurrence of *-u*[19] in the nominative plural for the neuter are not absolute certain gender markers. Even the seeming unambiguous *-ar* masculine of the nominative plural is compromised by cross-over neuter plurals in *-ar*, e.g., *hornar* 'horns'.[20] To be sure, the focus of this paper is on the viability of noun gender. Yet Figure 3B offers a ready springboard for consideration of possible number and case syncretism.

How well, then, do the desinential suffixes of Figure 3B adhere as gender signs, i.e., semiotically? We have utilized Peirce's universal categories of *Firstness, Secondness,* and *Thirdness* to extract the relationships of icon, index, and symbol, respectively (cf. section 2 above). Appealing to further attributes of Peirce's categories of *Firstness, Secondness,* and *Thirdness,* let

[18] Observations of end syllable neutralization pervade, e.g., Steller's presentation of the Old Frisian morphological paradigms, which are encapsulated in his statement in *Abriss*, §21: 'Die vollen endsilbenvocale des germ. (westgerm.) sind im afrs. im allgemeinen geschwunden oder zu *e* geschwächt'. Similarly, cf. Heuser, *Altfriesisches Lesebuch*, 36, n.1: 'Die volleren Endungsvokale *i* und *u* (*o*) herrschen [in the Riustring Ms.] … gegenüber abgeschliffenem *e* der anderen Texte'.

[19] Thus, congruent with note 18 above, Steller, *Abriss,* §50.1, writes that beside *-u*, *-o*, and *-a* 'schwächung der endung zu *-e*' occurs as well.

[20] *Ibid.* That final *-r* can be reduced to Ø, cf. Steller, *Abriss*, §29.3, as can *-m* > *-n* (§31.1), and *-n* > Ø (§32.4).

us apply to the Old Frisian data the relationships of possibility, necessity, and convention, respectively, to help reveal strategies at work in the machinery of linguistic change. The accusative singular masculine/feminine *-a* as well as the neuter plural *-u* are mere possibilities (Firsts) to indicate gender, while the *-ar* is conventionalized (a Third) as a masculine plural. The Old Frisian noun *wīf* as observed in *thīnere wīve* (section 2 above) is thus quasi genderless; it borrows its gender from adjectives and pronouns, which in Indo-European fashion act in servitude to the noun. Indeed, consideration ought to be given to listing *wīf* in the lexicon at the least with heteroclitic gender (feminine and neuter; cf. above). The volatility of the Old Frisian noun suffix morphology represents allographic swarming indicative of phonological neutralization of the sort *-V* > -ə > -*Ø* and *-m* > (*-n*) > -*Ø* which does not require tortured genetic justification. Phonological change engenders new growth encapsulated in the Peircean semiotic aphorism 'symbols grow'.[21]

---

21 Peirce, *Collected Papers*, II, 302.

What Old Frisian Can Tell Us about the History of *i*-Umlaut across West Germanic

Joseph C. Salmons

Introduction

In Germanic historical linguistics, and perhaps in historical linguistics generally, there is a clear and longstanding bias toward the oldest data, and perhaps even toward data from ancestors of the languages with the most widely spoken modern descendants.[1] As a result, relevant data from languages like Old Frisian have at times been ignored by scholars making far-reaching claims about Germanic. While Old Frisian is robustly attested only much later than Old High German, Old Saxon and Old English, it can nonetheless fill in critical pieces of broader West Germanic linguistic history, as Smith shows in her comparison of Old Frisian 'vowel balance' to patterns of syncope and apocope in Old Saxon, Old English and Old High German.[2] When it comes to *i*-umlaut, Germanic historical linguists might expect to find virtually nothing, given the salient and early general fronting of /a/ in Frisian, as well as the early unrounding of the reflexes of mid and high umlaut outputs.[3]

In this paper, I argue that Old Frisian data can provide decisive support for one of two competing views about the unfolding of West Germanic *i*-umlaut. One view sees umlaut as having arisen extremely early, well before

---

[1] This paper grows out of years of work and discussion with Greg Iverson, as well as Rob Howell, Dave Holsinger and Laura Catharine Smith, among others. Additional comments and discussions directly on this paper came from Greg Iverson, Monica Macaulay, and I happily acknowledge that help. The comments of an anonymous reviewer were greatly helpful as well.

[2] L. C. Smith, *Cross-Level Interactions in West Germanic Phonology and Morphology*. Ph.D. dissertation, University of Wisconsin-Madison, 2004.

[3] C. V. J. Russ, 'Umlaut in Frisian and the Germanic Languages: Some Thoughts on its Genesis and Development', *NOWELE* 28–29 [= Festschrift Nils Århammar] (1996), 501–12, provides an excellent general overview of how Frisian umlaut fits into the broader picture of Germanic, but that paper was written before the post-Twaddellian view (as defined below) was widely known, and thus he does not focus on the core issues treated here.

the dawn of directly recorded Germanic linguistic history, even Proto-Germanic, while the other view dates umlaut back to the dialectal period, ca. 7–8th century C.E., just before the emergence of our earlier extensive written documents in Germanic. I aim to show that Old Frisian evidence underpins the latter view, namely that umlaut was an emphatically dialectal phenomenon, in line with its traditional dating in Old Frisian and across West Germanic. Umlaut cannot date back to earliest Germanic, as argued by many in the classic American Structuralist tradition (Antonsen, Penzl, others). This paper thus brings the chronology of Old Frisian sound changes to bear on Germanic umlaut, following conservative and virtually theory independent assumptions about Frisian linguistic history. More importantly, it adds a distinct new type of argument to the debates over Germanic *i*-umlaut, namely from relative chronology, and does so in a theory-neutral way.

After a brief sketch of the two just-noted and fundamentally opposed views of umlaut (§1), I recapitulate some generally accepted points of Frisian phonological history (§2), showing that Frisian palatalization of velar stops had to pre-date the rise of even allophonic umlaut. In §3, I briefly outline arguments that changes in low vowels must have preceded umlaut, and that monophthongization of West Germanic **ai* and **au* almost surely did as well. §4 concludes.

While what follows may be largely a case of stating the obvious to Frisianists, the evidence reviewed here and its implications for a widespread view of umlaut across Germanic seem remarkably unknown among the broader community of Germanic linguists, at least on the topic of umlaut, and this, I hope, shows how Old Frisian data can be directly important for Germanic comparative linguistics.

1. Two competing views of umlaut

For present purposes, let us distinguish three approaches to how umlaut unfolded, with Twaddell's structuralist view chronologically in the center, flanked by earlier traditional or pre-Twaddellian views on one side and post-Twaddellian views on the other. I will focus on the Twaddellian or American Structuralist view of umlaut, and how it compares to a newer post-Twaddellian or 'Wisconsin School' view. The turning point at b, Twaddell's note of 1938,[4] anchors an analysis of Old High German umlaut firmly in classic phonemic theory, rigorously distinguishing the behaviour of conditioned or allophonic variants from the behaviour of independent phonemes. Whereas many earlier views had assumed that umlaut had unfolded gradually, one very direct implication of Twaddell's groundbreaking article

[4] W. Freeman Twaddell, 'A Note on Old High German Umlaut', *Monatshefte für deutschsprachige Literatur und Kultur* 30 (1938), 177–81.

is that all of *i*-umlaut happened at once, making it what Buccini calls a 'one-fell-swoop' approach.[5] That is, phonetically, *a* becomes *e* at the same time as all other back vowels are fronted, including *a* in 'blocking environments' (basically *h, l, r* plus obstruent) fronting (but not raising) to [æ].

Critically, of course, this means that umlaut took place PHONETICALLY at once, and was PHONOLOGIZED at some later point, which did not happen at once, but varied dialectally as umlaut 'triggers' – that is, *i, ī, j* – were lost, or at least weakened to schwa to the point that they were irrecoverable to speakers of that era. Phonetic, or more specifically allophonic, umlaut would naturally not be spelled, and only after phonologization would we expect to find it spelled.[6] While virtually all sources agree that umlauted vowels arose at some point before they were written,[7] Twaddell's analysis suggests that umlaut could readily have happened phonetically centuries before it was phonologized. While this does not follow by necessity from Twaddell's arguments, those arguments certainly open the door to proposing umlaut as an early Germanic phenomenon, and certainly not without some reason: Occam's Razor is often invoked in such historical scenarios and it is obviously parsimonious to posit umlaut as taking place only once in Germanic rather than individually in North Germanic and various West Germanic languages.[8]

This position is taken most explicitly and forcefully by Penzl and Antonsen, who project the development of umlaut allophones back remarkably far in Germanic (pre-)history. Penzl asserts that 'Umlautsallophone in der Grundsprache müssen wir wegen der Folgeentwicklung zu Umlautsphonemen in allen nordgermanischen und westgermanischen Sprachen annehmen', where the 'Grundsprache' in question is his 'Northwest

[5] A. F. Buccini, *The Development of Umlaut and the Dialectal Position of Dutch in Germanic*. Ph.D. dissertation Cornell University 1992, 69.

[6] For detailed discussion of this issue, see D. Fertig, 'Phonology, Orthography and the Umlaut Puzzle', *Diachronic and Syntactic Studies in Germanic Linguistics*, ed. R. Lippi-Green and J. C. Salmons (Amsterdam, 1996), 169–84.

[7] Not all scholars see things this way. E. H. Antonsen, '"Weil die Schrift immer strebt ...". On Phonological Reconstruction', *NOWELE* 43 (2003), 2–20, at 7, goes to considerable lengths to argue that generativists 'are reduced to taking LETTERS literally' (emphasis in original, JCS) and he sees generativists as holding the view that 'sound changes are taken not to have occurred until they are actually recorded in the manuscripts'. I do not understand how this follows from generative views of phonology, which – whether or not one accepts generative theories – have shown themselves fully capable of distinguishing allophones from phonemes both synchronically and in sound change.

[8] Scholars like Buccini stress the structuralist rejection of Sapirian 'drift' as a major motivation here, but this perhaps ultimately comes down to a theoretically-driven formulation of a view very close to Occam's Razor, as noted above.

Germanic'.[9] As Antonsen puts it more recently:[10] 'Suffice it to say that by *late* Proto-Germanic, all of the vowel phonemes in root syllables had developed positional variants that were dependent on the following vowel or semivowel' [again, emphasis in original, JCS], which he illustrates with an inventory including (in his transcription) [y] and [ȳ] as the allophones of /u/ and /u:/ in *i*-umlaut environments. On this view, all exceptions to *i*-umlaut – that is, forms which originally contained a tonic back vowel followed by an *i/j* in the following syllable but which do not show umlaut in modern Germanic – can ONLY be explained as analogical, a point made most explicitly perhaps by Antonsen in 1969 (and as will be exemplified momentarily).[11]

Until Buccini's dissertation,[12] directly relevant Netherlandic evidence was simply ignored in this entire line of research. Buccini called attention to the fact that western Netherlandic shows the reflexes of primary umlaut (umlaut of short *a* before *i, j*) but reflexes of only that limited process, not of broader *i*-umlaut. These facts, baffling on a Twaddellian analysis, fall out in a straightforward fashion from a view that has umlaut gradually unfolding in the dialectal period. On these points, the post-Twaddellian position returns to some aspects of the traditional, pre-Twaddellian view of umlaut's history.

More recent work has expanded along many parameters on Buccini's post-Twaddellian perspective, detailing an array of other problems created by the structuralist view, all of which dissolve under the assumption of a stepwise unfolding during the dialectal period, including where umlaut was blocked in early West Germanic,[13] how it spread over West Germanic,[14] how and when it came to be morphologized,[15] and how it unfolded somewhat

---

[9] H. Penzl, 'Zum *i*-Umlaut in den althochdeutschen Dialekten', *Folia Linguistica Historica* 16 (1995), 115–21, at 116.

[10] E. H. Antonsen, *Runes and Germanic Linguistics* (Berlin, 2002), 23.

[11] E. H. Antonsen, 'Zur Umlautfeindlichkeit des Oberdeutschen', *Zeitschrift für Dialektologie und Linguistik* 36 (1969), 201–07.

[12] See note 5.

[13] G. K. Iverson, G. W. Davis and J. C. Salmons, 'Blocking Environments in Old High German Umlaut', *Folia Linguistica Historica* 15 (1994), 131–48.

[14] R. B. Howell and J. C. Salmons, 'Umlaut Residues in Germanic', *American Journal of Germanic Linguistics and Literatures* 9 (1997), 83–111.

[15] D. J. Holsinger and J. C. Salmons, 'Toward "a complete analysis of the residues": On Regular vs. Morpholexical Approaches to Old High German Umlaut', *The Emergence of the Modern Language Sciences: Studies on the Transition from Historical-comparative to Structural Linguistics in Honour of E .F. Konrad Koerner*, ed. S. Embleton, J. E. Joseph and H.-J. Niederehe, 2 vols. (Amsterdam, 1999) II, 239–53.

differently in North Germanic than it did in West Germanic.[16] As Iverson and Salmons show,[17] *i*-umlaut cannot even be formulated coherently as a single phonological generalization of the sort so thoroughly familiar from the generative literature.[18]

At its core, these works all reflect an effort to find rigorous accounts of the complex data at hand – the attested products of *i*-umlaut were shaped, we argue, by vowel-to-vowel coarticulation and perception in its earliest stages, then by phonological principles, and only later reshaped by analogy. In particular, we have sought to account for sets of exceptional data as principled parts of umlaut's unfolding, as we have done with the Old High German blocking environments (OHG *mahti, starki*, etc.) and the Upper German umlautless residues (cf. German *suchen, um* < **sōkian*, **umbi*), and so on. We take such accounts to be inherently preferable on basic scientific grounds to undifferentiated appeals to analogy as the source of all wrinkles in umlaut.

No Twaddellian to date has responded in any significant way to any of the above post-Twaddellian positions in print, though Antonsen claims that all such views rest on nothing more than the confusion of letters and sounds,[19] repeating the mistakes of Grimm's early treatment of umlaut. Still, the classic phonemic perspective is proving surprisingly resilient, continued most vigorously by Americans like Penzl and Antonsen,[20] but also by some in Europe. West writes flatly that:[21]

> It is about time we stopped teaching primary and secondary umlaut as if it were holy writ: as Keller … convincingly shows, the fact that OHG scribes did not write the umlaut of [u] and so on has an orthographical, rather than a phonological explanation.

---

[16] G. K. Iverson and J. C. Salmons, 'The Conundrum of Old Norse Umlaut: Regular Sound Change versus Crisis Analogy', *Journal of Germanic Linguistics* 16 (2004), 77–110.

[17] G. K. Iverson and J. C. Salmons, 'The Primacy of Primary Umlaut', *BGdSL* 118 (1996), 69–86.

[18] Cf. P. Kiparsky, 'Linguistic Universals and Language Change', *Universals in Linguistic Theory*, ed. E. Bach and R. Harms (New York, 1968), 191–212; R. D. King, *Historical Linguistics and Generative Grammar* (Englewood Cliffs, NJ, 1969), 92–101.

[19] Antonsen, '"Weil die Schrift immer strebt ..."'.

[20] Penzl, 'Zum *i*-Umlaut in den althochdeutschen Dialekten'; *idem*, 'Zum Beweismaterial für den *i*-Umlaut im Nordisch-Westgermanischen', *American Journal of Germanic Linguistics and Literatures* 8 (1996), 93–104; Antonsen, *Runes and Germanic Linguistics*; 237–54; *idem*, '"Weil die Schrift immer strebt ..."'.

[21] J. West, review of H. Gross, *Einführung in die germanistische Linguistik* in *Webjournal of Modern Language Linguistics* 4–5 (1999–2000). Available on-line at http://wjmll.ncl.ac.uk/.

It is, then, perhaps worth evincing additional arguments for the post-Twaddellian view of umlaut's historical development. Old Frisian language history provides fodder for such arguments.

Underlying some part of the success of the Twaddellian view, I have long suspected, is that it makes an extremely early dating of umlaut virtually unfalsifiable: Since we cannot appeal to orthography for help in dating the change, showing when an allophonic pattern arose in prehistory can be maddeningly difficult. The basic approach I take below on this point is simple: If we can show, with reasonable certainty, that one or more Frisian-specific changes preceded allophonic *i*-umlaut, then umlaut simply cannot possibly date to Germanic or even West Germanic. This vitiates, I will argue, issues of spelling and allophonic status.[22]

2. The chronology of palatalization and umlaut in Frisian

A salient and characteristic change that distinguishes Frisian from other West Germanic languages (except English, which presents parallel evidence) is palatalization or assibilation of original velar stops to affricates before front vowels, while inherited **k* and **g* are continued before back vowels. These patterns are illustrated in (1).[23]

(1) Velar stop palatalization[24]

**k* + front V	+ back Vowel	+ umlaut of *o, u*	
tserl 'Kerl'	*komp* 'Kampf'	*kētha* 'künden'	< **kūðian* < **kunðian*
tserke 'Kirche'	*kāp* 'Kauf'	*kessa* 'küssen'	< **kussian*
tsin 'Kinn'	*kole* 'Kohle'	*kening* 'König'	< **koning*
	kuma 'kommen'	*kēla* 'kühlen'	

**g* + front V	+ back vowel	+ umlaut of *o, u*	
jeva 'geben'	*guma* 'Mann'	*gēde* 'Güte'	
jeld 'Geld'	*gold* 'Gold'	*gēla* 'verfolgen'	< **gōljan*
jēsel 'Geisel'	*gaderia* 'sammeln'	*gerda* 'gürten'	

---

[22] Throughout, I leave aside a variety of wrinkles in sound changes not directly relevant to the points at hand, for instance, in the conditioning of so-called brightening, or /a/ fronting. I see no possibility that these could change the basic thrust of the analysis.

[23] Throughout, data are drawn from W. Heuser, *Altfriesisches Lesebuch, mit Grammatik und Glossar* (Heidelberg, 1903), F. Holthausen, *Altfriesisches Wörterbuch*, rev. D. Hofmann (Heidelberg, 1985), K. von Richthofen, *Altfriesisches Wörterbuch* (Göttingen, 1840; repr. 1961), and other sources. Nothing here, to my knowledge, rests on the particulars of any singular piece of data.

[24] Old Frisian orthography is notoriously variable on this and other points. I simply use *ts* and *j* here for the palatals derived, respectively, from **k* and **g*. I also leave aside what are almost certainly lexical exceptions or variants.

Based on the fact that umlauted vowels pattern here with back vowels rather than front ones, i.e., do not trigger palatalization, Bremmer follows the thoroughly traditional view that palatalization must have preceded *i*-umlaut. That is, velar stop palatalization was not fed by *i*-umlaut. Were the chronology reversed, with umlaut earlier than palatalization, the 'king' word would be **tsening* rather than the attested OFris *kening*. As Bremmer notes, 'no such forms as ⁺*tsening* 'king' exist'.[25]

This assumes that palatalization was triggered purely by frontness, without reference to rounding. Fulk and Stiles at least note the possibility that rounding could have inhibited palatalization, that is, that palatalization might only pre-date the unrounding of front rounded vowels, not umlaut itself.[26] But we certainly expect palatalization to reflect frontness, other things being equal. Milroy gives the chronic patterns of palatalization before front vowels in Germanic linguistic history as a prototypical example of sound change driven by coarticulation.[27] The coarticulation in question is that a front vowel prompts fronting of an underlyingly velar consonant, and roundness is not obviously relevant here. For instance, in German, the salient post-vocalic alternations in dorsal fricatives evince the same pattern where German *Buch* 'book' has [x] but *Bücher* 'books' has [ç], like in the proper name *Bichel*. (I assume that it is universally agreed that such allophonic alternations must have preceded the phonemic split historically in Frisian.)

Cross-linguistically, palatalization is often restricted in various ways, for example triggered only or in its earliest historical stages only by high vowels (as in familiar changes from Romance and Slavic) and perhaps first taking place before long *i*.[28] It can also happen only with particular stops, as in the Frisian limitation to velars, whereas in many languages (see again Slavic), a broader range of stops split between velars and palatals. In a careful review of the phonetic literature, Guion shows that some acoustic effects of vowel coarticulation on preceding velar stops are greater with unrounded than with rounded front vowels.[29] This would seem to leave open the possibility of palatalization restricted only to front unrounded vowels. Such a pattern appears, however, unattested in Germanic, a topic to which we now turn.

---

25 R. H. Bremmer Jr, *An Introduction to Old Frisian*, §54 [forthcoming].

26 R. D. Fulk, 'The Chronology of Old Frisian Sound Changes', *Approaches*, 139–54; P. V. Stiles, 'Remarks on the Anglo-Frisian Hypothesis', *Friesische Studien II*, ed. V. F. Faltings, A. G. H. Walker and O. Wilts, *NOWELE* Suppl. 12 (Odense, 1995) 177–220.

27 J. Milroy, *Language Variation and Change* (Oxford, 1992), 21–22.

28 L. R. Palmer, *The Latin Language* (London, 1966), 158.

29 S. Guion, *Velar Palatalization: Coarticulation, Perception and Sound Change*. Ph.D. dissertation University of Texas at Austin 1996, at ch. 2.

Almost ninety years ago, van Haeringen adduced a convincing Swedish parallel, where Swedish palatalization 'ebensogut vor gerundeten wie vor ungerundeten vordervocalen durchgeführt wird: neu-schwed. *kyss, gynna; köra, göra* neben *kinkig, get, gärna*'.[30] That is, in all of these words, underlying velar stops (still spelled as such in the modern language) are realized as (palatal) fricatives, while *kaffe* and *gata* retain stop pronunciations before back vowels. In fact, while later changes have obscured patterns to some extent, Scandinavian generally palatalized velars before all front vowels early on, including in historical forms like *køyra* > *kjøyra*/ *kjøra* 'to drive'.[31]

In his classic treatment of Old English palatalization, Penzl notes the traditional view, adopted here for Old Frisian, that '"the process of palatalization had ceased" by the time of the *i*-umlaut, so that the velar allophone [k] was no longer affected by the new palatal vowels.'[32] Motivated directly by Twaddell's early date for the rise of umlaut allophones, he goes on to assert without evidence or argument that 'Proto-Old-English velar [k] was not affected by this *i*-umlaut.' Without explicit arguments or some supporting evidence, the traditional view is surely more straightforward.

In fact, like in the Swedish example above, palatalization processes throughout the history of Germanic appear sensitive only to frontness of the following vowel, never its rounding. Icelandic and Faroese, for example, underwent palatalization of velar stops after umlaut had taken place, the reverse of the relative chronology between the two changes in Frisian and English. We therefore find palatal rather than velar stops when a historical front vowel, rounded or not, followed an original velar. Árnason puts it simply:[33] The palatalization seems to have been an exceptionless change, triggered by the frontness of a following vowel. Later, this rule seems to have become inactive, since – when reorganization took place in the vowel system – the velar vs. palatal alternants kept their old distribution. Thus we have *kú* [k^{h}u:] 'cow' versus *kýr* [c^{h}i:r] from earlier [c^{h}y:r] 'cows', where an earlier umlauted vowel (since unrounded) triggered palatalization. Some historical back vowels were fronted only later in the history of Icelandic. In those cases, such as *köttur* 'cat' < *kǫttr*, the stops have remained velar, rather than becoming palatal.

---

30 C. B. van Haeringen, 'Zur friesischen lautgeschichte. I. Palatalisierung des *a*; *i*-umlaut; assibilierung von *k* und *g*', *BGdSL* 44 (1920), 27–53, at 33.

31 For brief handbook overviews, see E. Haugen, *The Scandinavian Languages* (London, 1976), 208, and *idem*, *Scandinavian Language Structures: A Comparative Historical Survey* (Minneapolis, 1982), 64–65.

32 H. Penzl, 'The Phonemic Split of Germanic *k* in Old English', *Language* 23 (1947), 34–42, at 41–42.

33 Kristján Árnason, 'Palatalization in Modern Icelandic: A Case for Historicism in Synchronic Linguistics', *Lingua* 46 (1978), 185–203, at 187.

In short, it is virtually impossible that *i*-umlaut could have happened prior to velar stop palatalization. Crucially, even allophonic umlaut can be excluded because the palatal pronunciation of stops was surely sensitive to actual articulation, not to phonemic or underlying representation.

3. The chronology of low vowel changes and umlaut

Low vowels do trigger palatalization, as in OFris *tsīse* 'cheese' and *tsetel* 'kettle', both Latin loans from *cāseum* and *catīnus* respectively. This, though, surely reflects the early fronting of low vowels and their backing/raising before coda nasals. This typically takes place in closed syllables and the fronting fails in environments much like the classic Old High German blocking conditions, especially coda *l*. Traditionally called 'Anglo-Frisian brightening', Versloot argues that this process is the oldest identifiable feature of Frisian.[34] His arguments rest in part on runic evidence, in particular the existence of *æ* and *o* runes, but while Frisian runic evidence may be suggestive, Page underscores the caution which is needed in interpreting it.[35] Still, specialists have long taken this point of relative chronology to be settled. Long ago, Campbell wrote of van Haeringen's arguments (see below) that they provide 'a final demolition of the view that fronting is later than *i/j* mutation'.[36]

(2) **a > e*, Old Frisian

**bak-*	*bek*	'back'
**gras-*	*gres/gers*	'grass'
**akr-*	*ekker*	'field, acre'

**a > o* before nasals, Old Frisian

**lam-*	*lom*	'lame'
**man-*	*mon*	'man'
**land-*	*lond*	'land'
**þank-*	*thonk*	'thanks'

The core point for our purposes is that the fronting process feeds palatalization while the backing process does not. That is, the original **a* triggers assibilation where it was fronted to *e* and not where it was back (or backed) and raised to *o*. This is illustrated in (3) with the lenis velar *g*.

---

[34] A. P. Versloot, 'Vergleichende Aspekte friesischer Lautgeschichte', *Handbuch / Handbook*, 767–74, at 767–68.

[35] R. I. Page, 'Frisian Runic Inscriptions', *Ibid.* 523–30.

[36] A. Campbell, 'Some Old Frisian Sound-Changes', *Transactions of the Philological Society* 1939, 78–107, at 93.

(3) Old Frisian fronting of original **a*, with palatalization of **g*

**gast*	*jest*	'guest'
**gat-*	*jet*	'hole, opening'
**gab-*	*jef*	'gave (pret.sg.)'

Old Frisian backing/raising of original **a* before nasal, with no palatalization of **g*

**gang*	*gong*	'gait, cf. Gang'
**gam-*	*gom-*	'pleasure, etc., cf. game'

Therefore, these changes must predate palatalization, and therewith *i*-umlaut.

The list of dialectal changes which took place before *i*-umlaut could be expanded, and it has been by a variety of scholars, though never, to my knowledge, with an eye to the topic at hand here. For instance, another piece of relative chronology involves the monophthongization of West Germanic **ai* and **au* with respect to umlaut. Nielsen has argued – persuasively to my mind – that monophthongization must precede umlaut.[37] Still, as Nielsen is careful to note, arguments have been mounted against this position by Dietrich Hofmann, and this example, unlike those sketched above, might be regarded as not yet completely resolved.

4. Conclusion

Any realistic reading of Frisian linguistic prehistory shows that a number of dialectal, Frisian-specific changes preceded *i*-umlaut, even in its allophonic form. I can find no source in the literature where the reverse has been proposed, and any such proposal would find a steep, rocky climb to acceptance. This then compels us to date umlaut, even umlaut *qua* allophonic process, far into the dialectal period, along the lines of traditional dates, perhaps as late as the eighth century C.E. The structuralist concern about 'confusion' of spelling and sound change is securely avoided here, because front allophones of underlying back vowels would have triggered palatalization. Moreover, while defenses of the Twaddellian position in recent years have tended to decry other views as 'hocus-pocus linguistics', no particular theoretical assumptions are employed above – as far as I can tell, the arguments given are thoroughly consistent with the notions of phonemicization put forward by Twaddell two-thirds of a century ago.

---

[37] H. F. Nielsen, 'Frisian and The Grouping of the Older Germanic languages', *Handbuch / Handbook*, 512–23, at 514–17; *idem*, *The Early Runic Language of Scandinavia: Studies in Germanic Dialect Geography* (Heidelberg, 2000), 117–18.

The particular chronology presented here fits broadly with a broader pattern of research into early Frisian.[38] And very similar arguments could naturally be built using English data, if one wanted to venture beyond the continent. In fact, consider some of the most recent detailed arguments about early Frisian chronology, namely the debate between Stiles and Fulk over the old 'Anglo-Frisian hypothesis'.[39] Both these authors, while they disagree about much, place *i*-mutation very late, after a whole set of changes that clearly post-date any notion of Germanic or even Northwest Germanic linguistic unity. All this work is consistent only with the dialectal unfolding of umlaut and thus adds new confirmation to the growing body of literature on Germanic umlaut since Buccini's dissertation. And while debate over the Anglo-Frisian hypothesis may go on, all interpretations of Frisian phonological history rest on justifiable relative chronologies that are fatal to the 'one-fell-swoop' view of umlaut.

---

[38] See Campbell, 'Some Old Frisian Sound-Changes', 104; M. Gysseling, 'Het oudste Fries (eerste deel)', *IB* 24 (1962), 1–26 (*passim*); Nielsen, *The Early Runic Language*', 247; *idem*, 'Frisian and the Grouping of the Older Germanic Languages', among many others.

[39] Summarized cleanly in Fulk, 'The Chronology of the Anglo-Frisian Sound Changes'.

Old Frisian Vowel Balance and its Relationship to West Germanic Apocope and Syncope

Laura Catharine Smith

1. Introduction[1]

A little more than one hundred years have passed since Wilhelm Heuser published his *Altfriesisches Lesebuch,* in which he first observed an alternation between the vowels *i~e* and *u~o* in the earliest Old Frisian texts, namely the Riustring manuscripts.[2] Called *Vocalbalance* or Vowel Balance one year later by Axel Kock, the scholar who was first to outline the conditions of the alternation, this pattern refers to the occurrence of *i* and *u* following short stem vowels as in *godi* 'God' (dat.sg.) and *skipu* 'ships' (nom.pl.), but *e* and *o* after long or polysyllabic stems as shown in *hūse* 'house' (dat.sg.) and *gerso* 'grass' (acc.pl.).[3] Early accounts of this alternation, including those by Kock and van Helten, tried to describe the environments where this alternation occurred, making reference to the shape of the word stem while attributing the alternation to differing levels of stress on the vowels in question.[4] Kock, for instance, noted that *i* and *u* were retained in syllables with a relatively strong accent but weakened to *e* and *o* respectively in weakly stressed syllables. More modern treatments, such as those recently found in Boutkan's grammar of the First Riustring manuscript or Versloot's overview of Frisian sound change, have simply revisited

[1] This paper stems from my dissertation, Laura Catharine Smith, *Cross-level Interactions in West Germanic Phonology and Morphology*, Unpublished Dissertation (Madison, WI, 2004), and from discussions with Joseph Salmons and Robert Howell. I am grateful for feedback on early versions of this paper from Joseph Salmons, Wendy Baker, Cary Johnson, and Dirk Elzinga. However, the usual disclaimers apply, most notably that any errors are my own.

[2] W. Heuser, *Altfriesisches Lesebuch mit Grammatik und Glossar* (Heidelberg, 1903).

[3] A. Kock, 'Vocalbalance im Altfriesischen', *BGdSL* 29 (1904), 175–193. Although Kock acknowledges Heuser's initial observation in his *Grammatik*, he was nevertheless the first scholar to describe the conditions for Vowel Balance in detail, including demonstrating how Vowel Harmony at times obscured the pattern. Kock called this phenomenon *Vocalbalance*. In this paper I shall use the equivalent English term 'Vowel Balance'.

[4] W. L. van Helten, 'Nachträge zur Vocalbalance und -harmonie im Altfriesischen', *BGdSL* 32 (1907), 517–32.

the data making reference to the role of stress placement similar to Kock's initial suggestion.[5] Unfortunately, these expositions have not situated the phenomenon within modern phonological theory – especially prosodic phonology – and thus have not taken advantage of the insights that such theories can provide to an analysis of Vowel Balance. Likewise, despite allusions that scholars have made to a similarity between Vowel Balance and the syncope and apocope of *i* and *u* elsewhere in West Germanic (Kock, Van Helten, etc.), these references have amounted to little more than a paragraph or footnote.

This paper reexamines Old Frisian Vowel Balance, providing a foot-based analysis of the phenomenon that not only accounts for the data, but that also subsequently provides the means for substantiating a connection between Vowel Balance and West Germanic apocope and syncope. Section Two presents data for Vowel Balance from the First and Second Riustring manuscripts in relation to Vowel Harmony. Vowel Harmony has at times obscured the effects of Vowel Balance causing *i* and *u* to surface as *e* and *o* after stems containing the midvowels. I note some other forces at work here, such as the differential behaviour of compounds and affixes as well as the influence of adjacent consonants, that account for the apparent exceptions to Vowel Balance. Next in Section Three, I present a foot-based analysis of the Vowel Balance data showing that *i* and *u* weakened to *e* and *o* respectively when they were in syllables that could not be footed with the initial foot of the stem. In Section Four, I show that the prosodic approach to Vowel Balance can also be adduced to account for apocope in Old Saxon *i*-stem nouns as well as syncope in Old High German *jan*-verbs. I then conclude in Section Five.

2. Vowel Balance in the Riustring manuscripts

Despite its name, Old Frisian Vowel Balance was not a widespread phenomenon across the Old Frisian dialects but was unique to the two Riustring

[5] D. Boutkan, *A Concise Grammar of the Old Frisian Dialect of the First Riustring Manuscript* (Odense, 1996); A. P. Versloot, 'Vergleichende Aspekte friesischer Lautgeschichte', *Handbuch / Handbook*, 767–75. In his book *The Germanic 'Auslautgesetze'* (Amsterdam, 1995), Dirk Boutkan does make reference to foot structure in his discussion of *u*-apocope in West Germanic. However, he fails to discuss this possibility with regard to Vowel Balance in Old Frisian, noting instead the role of stress placement attributed to the alternation of *i*~*e* and *u*~*o* by early scholars such as Kock and van Helten. This appeal to stress without reference to foot structure can likewise be seen in Versloot's brief overview of the process.

manuscripts, the oldest monuments of the Old Frisian language.[6] Although the First and Second Riustring manuscripts have been dated back to the late thirteenth century and the early fourteenth century respectively, when the other West Germanic languages were already in their middle periods, scholars have argued that these compilations of legal texts are actually based on earlier texts.[7] Nevertheless, as arguably the oldest Old Frisian texts, many scholars have assumed that the language found in the Riustring manuscripts represents the oldest form of Frisian.[8] Heuser, for instance, notes: 'Der nur in diesen beiden Denkmälern erhaltene weserfriesische Dialekt der alten Riostringer zeigt das Fries. in seiner altertümlichsten, edelsten Form, die aber mannigfach von der Sprache der übrigen Texte abweicht'.[9] Consequently, many assume the Riustring manuscripts to represent Old Frisian at a stage most reflective of its West Germanic roots. Thus, the discussion that follows on Old Frisian and Vowel Balance are perhaps better understood in terms of the Riustring dialect and early stages of Old Frisian rather than being indicative of Old Frisian in general, unless otherwise stated. With these things in mind, I now turn to a presentation of the data.

2.1 Vowel Balance: Data

Old Frisian shows a tendency towards a more general merger of all unstressed vowels to schwa.[10] The Riustring codices, however, differ from other Old Frisian texts by maintaining qualitative oppositions between stressed and unstressed vowels in the pairs *i~e* and *u~o*, oppositions that have been enshrined in the dialect as Vowel Balance. Boutkan has interpreted these alternations in terms of full versus reduced vowels, suggesting that *e* and *o* are simply reduced variants of *i* and *u* respectively.[11] The choice of variant is then determined by the shape of the word stem.

---

6 A similar pattern has also been noted for the Frisian dialect Wangeroogish in Kock, 'Vocalbalance', Heuser, *Altfriesisches Lesebuch*, and A. P. Versloot, 'Das Wangeroogische', *Handbuch / Handbook*, 423–29, at 426. However, this dialect is attested in texts much later around the turn of the nineteenth century and is thus not another example of Vowel Balance in the Old Frisian period.

7 Cf. *De Eerste Riustringer Codex*, ed. W. J. Buma, OTR 11 (The Hague, 1961) for a more detailed overview of the dating of the different manuscripts; see also Kock, 'Vocalbalance im Altfriesischen'. It has been argued that some parts of the manuscripts may stem from texts dating from almost one hundred years earlier.

8 However, see Rolf Bremmer's contribution to this volume, who argues against such an assumption.

9 Heuser, *Altfriesisches Lesebuch*, 36.

10 D. Boutkan, 'Phonology and Orthographic System of Old Frisian', *Handbuch / Handbook*, 613–20.

11 Boutkan, *A Concise Grammar*, 27.

As Kock first described, *i* and *u* are found in syllables following a short stem vowel, i.e. a light stem, as illustrated in (1a), while *e* and *o* appear after long, i.e. heavy, or polysyllabic stems as in (1b).[12]

(1) Vowel Balance Data from the First and Second Riustring Manuscripts

a. *i* and *u* appear after light stems, i.e. short stem vowels

i	*u*
i. In open final syllables:	
mith***i*** 'with'	mug***u*** 'can, may' (1pl.pres.ind.)
god***i*** 'God' (dat.sg.)	sun***u*** 'son' (nom./acc.sg.)
stid***i*** 'place' (acc./dat.sg.)	skip***u*** 'ship' (nom.pl.)
cum***i*** 'come' (3sg.pres.opt.)	skil***u*** 'should, must' (1sg.pres. ind.)
ii. In closed final syllables:	
god***is*** 'God' (gen.sg.)	skil***u***n 'should, must' (3pl.pres.ind.)
skip***is*** 'ship' (gen.sg.)	sik***u***r 'not guilty, predicative'
wet***i***r 'water' (nom./ acc.sg.nom.pl.)	mug***u***n 'may, can' (3pres.ind.)
ekim***i***n 'come' (past participle)	sin***u***th 'synodal court' (nom.sg.)
iii. In medial syllables:	him***u***le 'heaven' (dat.sg.)
god***i***lik 'godly, just'	sum***u***res 'summer' (gen.sg.)
to sem***i***ne 'together'	

b. *e* and *o* appear after heavy, i.e. long, and polysyllabic stems

e	*o*
i. After heavy stems ending in V̄C[13]	
stēn***e*** 'stone' (dat.sg.)	āg***o***n 'eye' (nom./acc.pl.)
hūs***e*** 'house' (dat.sg.)	bōk***o***n 'book' (dat.pl.)
fōr***e*** 'travel' (3sg.pret.opt.)	fīr***o***r 'further' (adv.)
liōd***e*** 'people' (nom.pl.)	clāth***o***n 'clothing' (dat.pl.)

[12] The terms 'light' and 'heavy' stems are often used as modern equivalents for the traditional labels 'short' and 'long' respectively when referring to stem shapes in Germanic. In this paper, the terms will be used interchangeably. However, it should be noted that the traditional description of the data refers to long versus short stems, see for instance Boutkan, *A Concise Grammar*, 27; Boutkan, *The Germanic 'Auslautgesetze'*; *Het Tweede Rüstringer Handschrift*, ed. W. J. Buma, OTR 8 (The Hague, 1954); and van Helten, 'Nachträge zur Vocalbalance und -harmonie im Altfriesischen'.

[13] Since vowel length is not indicated in the manuscripts, the convention of a macron will be used to indicate that the vowels are long underlying. However, this is only a linguisitic convention and should not be taken as a reflection of Old Frisian orthography.

ii. After heavy stems ending in VCC:

all*e* 'all' (adj.)
drocht*e*n 'Lord' (nom.sg.)
wrald*e* 'world' (dat./gen.sg.)
gers*o* 'grass' (nom.pl.)[14]
angl*o*n 'angel' (dat.pl.)

iii. After polysyllabic stems:

stapul*e* 'block' (dat.sg.)
himul*e* 'heaven' (dat.sg.)
tholad*e* 'endure' (3sg.pret.ind.)
wetir*o*n 'water' (dat.pl.)
hēlig*o*n 'holy' (dat.pl.)

The examples above are but a small selection of data illustrating Vowel Balance.[15] This process, as the data demonstrate, affected all lexical categories in Old Frisian: nouns, verbs, prepositions, adjectives and adverbs. As the forms in (1a) show, *i* and *u* were found following a light root initial syllable, namely one containing a short vowel followed by a single consonant (VC).[16] These full vowels were found in this environment regardless of whether *i* and *u* occurred finally in open syllables without a following consonant as in *godi* in (1.a.i), in final closed syllables as shown by *skilun* in (1.a.ii), or word medially as in *himule* from (1.a.iii). In the case of *ekimin* and *tosemine*, the prefixes *e-* and *to-* were not part of the root itself and thus do not contradict the requirement that *i* and *u* occur after the initial syllable of a light stem.

As for the reduced variants, *e* and *o* were evidenced after heavy stems, namely those with a long vowel plus consonant (V̄C), for instance *huse* and *clathon* in (1.b.i), or consisting of a vowel plus two consonants (VCC) as *wralde* and *gerso* illustrated in (1.b.ii). Examples such as *stapule* and *wetiron* from (1.b.iii) exemplify the third environment for the occurrence of the reduced vowels, namely following polysyllabic stems.

---

14 Although *gerso* is the result of metathesis from **grasu* this word is treated as a long stem based on the metathesised form in the literature on Vowel Balance. In the Riustring manuscripts this word only appears with metathesis, including in compound words such as *gersfal* 'the lopping off of a body part' (nom.sg.) indicating that despite its origin, *gers-* not *gras-* was the common form in this dialect.

15 Data are drawn from *De Eerste Riustringer Codex*; ed. Buma; *Het Tweede Rüstringer Handschrift*; ed. Buma; Kock, 'Vocalbalance'; Heuser, *Altfriesisches Lesebuch*; van Helten, 'Nachträge'; and Boutkan, *A Concise Grammar*. Since space does not permit an exhaustive listing of Vowel Balance forms, the interested reader is directed to these sources.

16 Most examples of Vowel Balance with the full vowels *i* and *u* qualify as light stems in that the stems are monosyllabic and end in -VC. However, examples like *himul-* or *sumur-* speak against this category applied to all words in this group since the vowel is found within the stem itself which is polysyllabic.

The alternation between the full and reduced vowels becomes even more apparent when pairs of words such as those in (2) are examined:

(2) Word pairs showing the effects of Vowel Balance:

a. godis 'God' (gen.sg.)	vs.	gōdes 'good' (gen.sg.)
b. fari 'travel' (3sg.pres.opt.)	vs.	fōre 'travel' (3sg.pret.opt.)[17]
c. fori 'before'	vs.	fōre 'travel' (3sg.pret.opt.)
d. skilu 'should, must' (1pl.pres.ind.)	vs.	skille 'should, must' (1sg.pres.opt.)

In these examples, the words in the left-hand column all have stems containing a short vowel and single consonant characteristic of the short stem vowel classification. The result is the appearance of the full vowels *i* and *u*. Conversely, the stems in the column on the right differ from their counterparts in the left-hand column primarily by the long vowel or double consonant. The heavier stem is in turn followed in the next syllable by the reduced vowel *e*. Although not depicted in the manuscripts, vowel length can be reconstructed by comparing these words with cognates in other Germanic languages. For instance, OHG *gott* 'God' also displays a short vowel as the *i* in OFris *godis* would suggest. On the other hand, the long *o* in OFris *godes* 'good' finds its counterpart in OHG *guot*, which derived its diphthong from an original long ō. That the occurrence of Vowel Balance can be used to determine the original length of the vowel was first suggested by Kock, where the appearance of *i* or *u* would point to a short stem vowel. The converse, however, is not necessarily the case: an *e* and *o* in an unstressed syllable are not always indicative of a long vowel in the stem due to the obscuring effects of Vowel Harmony.

2.2 The conflict between Vowel Balance and Vowel Harmony

One of the difficulties in assessing the Vowel Balance data has been that the reduced vowels *e* and *o* were not only found following heavy or polysyllabic stems. In some cases, these vowels occurred after stems with *e* and *o* in the root syllable due to a process of Vowel Harmony. As the examples in (3) illustrate, vowels often matched the height of the preceding midvowel as in (3):

---

[17] Although the contrast between *fari* and *fore* in (2b) is based in part on vowel quality, the distinction between the present and singular preterite stems of Class VI strong verbs also includes a contrast in vowel length. Indeed, vowel length was the original indicator of this contrast. This contrast in turn results in a differential behaviour of the inflectional endings across different tenses and forms of the same verb as (2b) illustrates.

(3) Old Frisian Vowel Harmony:

e	*o*
ker***e*** 'law' (nom.sg.)	freth***o*** 'peace' (acc.sg.)
slet***e***lon 'keys' (dat.pl.)	sker***o***n 'ploughshare' (dat.pl.)
ebrek***e***n 'break' (past participle)	fel***o*** 'much, many'
steu***e*** 'staff, stick' (dat.sg.)	hom***o***linge 'mutilation'

In all of the examples in (3), the stem vowel was short, precisely the environment for the retention of the full vowels according to the definition of Vowel Balance. However, rather than *i* or *u* appearing in the following syllable as we would expect, we find *e* and *o*. As Kock already observed in 1904, these reduced variants arose due to a process of Vowel Harmony with the midvowels of the stem. In each of these cases, the presence of *e* or *o* in the stem vowel triggered a lowering or reduction of the high vowels *i* and *u* in the following syllable(s).

As a result, Vowel Harmony is similar to Vowel Balance in that it leads to the reduction of *i* and *u* with one crucial exception, namely that the reduction takes place in precisely the environment where the full vowels are retained for Vowel Balance, in other words following a short stem vowel. Consequently, the output of Vowel Harmony is at times at odds with Vowel Balance, not only obscuring the Vowel Balance pattern but also making it difficult to identify in some instances. This is due in part to the fact that Vowel Harmony does not apply consistently throughout the data. For instance, *godis* 'God, gen.sg.' and *godi* 'God, dat.sg.' never occur as *godes* or *gode* respectively in the Riustring manuscripts despite the short *o* found in the stem syllable. Though it may be argued that this serves to retain the contrast with *gōde* 'good', the distinction in vowel length between the stem *god-* 'God' and *gōd-* 'good', would already contribute to the distinction between these words. A number of other examples of words with a short *e* or *o* in the root also failed to undergo Vowel Harmony such as *wetir* 'water' (nom./acc.sg., nom.pl.), *tosemine* 'together' and *fori* 'before' shown above in (1).[18] In all of these cases, the full vowels are expected by Vowel Balance to appear following the initial light syllable of the stem rather than the reduced variants prescribed by Vowel Harmony.

It is not always clear why in one instance, for example *kere* 'law', Vowel Harmony wins out, while in other cases, the pattern of Vowel Balance

[18] The failure of *fori* to reduce to *fore* is particularly interesting in light of a general propensity of function words to undergo reduction, e.g., *hini* 'he, acc.sg.' appears to reduce at times to *-ne* which then functions as a clitic in cases like *wndade (e)r (hi)ne* > *wndaderne* 'he shall wound him', from *De Eerste Riustringer Codex*, ed. Buma.

remains intact as in *godi* 'God' (dat.sg.). What does, however, become apparent is that at the time the Riustring codices were being written, Vowel Harmony did at times blur the Vowel Balance pattern. Boutkan and Kock have argued that Vowel Harmony was a later process than Vowel Balance[19] and as such would have upset the pattern that Vowel Balance would have established. Consequently, the contradictory Vowel Harmony data must be teased apart and set aside for a clear analysis of Vowel Balance to be proposed.

2.3 Additional Exceptions

Vowel Harmony, however, was not the only factor to produce apparent exceptions to Vowel Balance. Space does not permit an exhaustive account of every exception, real or apparent, yet a few trends can be highlighted to elucidate the interaction of Vowel Balance with other processes, such as suffixation, the influence of neighbouring sounds and the behaviour of compounds.[20]

2.3.1 *Derivational Suffixes and the Influence of Neighbouring Sounds*

A number of derivational suffixes failed to fully participate in Vowel Balance. For instance, the full vowels in *-ing* and *-ung* typically remained full even after heavy stems as illustrated in (4):

(4) The behaviour of suffix vowels in *-ing* and *-ung*:

After light stems (full vowels expected)	After heavy/polysyllabic stems (reduced vowels expected)
a. *-ing*	
kining/kyning 'king' (nom./acc.sg.)	Wepilinge 'River Wapel' (dat.sg.)
irth biuinge 'earthquake' (nom.sg.)	skilling 'shilling' (nom.sg.)
frilinga 'free man' (nom.pl.)	homolinge 'mutilation' (nom.sg.)
	ethelinga 'nobility' (nom.pl.)

[19] Boutkan, *A Concise Grammar*, 27; Kock, 'Vocalbalance'; In his chapter, 'Vergleichende Aspekte friesischer Lautgeschichte', 426, Versloot appears to suggest that Vowel Balance may have been a later process which in turn set aside the effects of Vowel Harmony in favour of the high vowels /i/ and /u/. This suggestion is at least proposed for Old Wangeroogish but may be applied to the Riustring dialect of Old Frisian.

[20] For a more detailed examination of the exceptions to Vowel Balance, the reader is directed to Boutkan, *A Concise Grammar*; *De Eerste Riustringer Codex*, ed. Buma; Kock, 'Vocalbalance'; and van Helten, 'Nachträge zur Vocalbalance und -harmonie im Altfriesischen'.

b. *-ung*

buwunga 'building' (acc.sg.)	fiardunge 'fourth of a mark' (acc.sg.)
ned skinunge 'legal justification' (gen.pl.)	BUT:
	sellonge 'sale, selling' (acc.sg.)
	horonge 'illegitimate birth' (nom.pl.)
	weder wondlonge 'weather change' (nom.pl.)

In the case of *-ing* in (4a), the suffix never appears as ***-eng* following heavy and polysyllabic stems as Vowel Balance would predict, e.g. *skilling* and *Wepilinge*, nor does the vowel weaken to *e* in a Vowel Harmony environment after stems containing *e* or *o* as *homolinge* and *ethelinga* illustrate.

The situation for *-ung*, however, is somewhat different. Unlike the invariable *-ing*, we do find examples of the reduced variant *-ong* in both manuscripts: *sellonge, horonge*, and *weder wondlonge*. However, in every case the reduced vowel could also potentially be attributed to Vowel Harmony. Compare for instance the environments where *-ung* occurs. None of the words have a stem with a midvowel *e* or *o* that could trigger Vowel Harmony. Conversely, every stem in the *-ong* examples contains either *e* or *o* that could trigger Vowel Harmony. A comparison with another suffix helps provide more insight.

A similar situation can be seen for *-ich/-ig* as shown in (5):

(5) The behaviour of the suffix *-ich/-ig*

After light stems	After heavy stems	Exceptions:
monich 'many'	plichtig 'obligated'	weldega
	ēnich 'few'	hēlegana
	weldich 'powerful'	unskeldech
	hēligana 'saints' (gen.pl.)	
	unskeldich 'not guilty'	

Again the data indicates that *-ich/-ig* frequently appeared after heavy stems, rather than the reduced *-ech/-eg*. However, as the exceptions in (5) illustrate, these reduced variants did nevertheless appear in the dialect. One possible interpretation of these alternate forms of the suffix would be that they have arisen as a consequence of Vowel Harmony as was suggested above for the alternation between *-ung* and *-ong*. Certainly in each case there is a preceding *e* in the stem which, it could be argued, triggered this reduction to the less frequently attested *helegana* and *unskeldech*. However, following van Helten, Boutkan suggests that the influence of the velar in this and other suffixes led to a neutralisation of *i~e* (and *u~o*).[21] According to this view, the presence of a following velar frequently led to the retention of the full vowel *i* as in *heligana* next to *helegana* or *skeldich* next to *skeldech*, even though Vowel Balance would normally predict a reduction of *i* to *e* in these circumstances. Boutkan also uses this approach to account, for instance, for the alternation between *-tich*/*-tig* versus *-tech*/*-teg* following heavy stems, as in *twintiga~twintega* 'twenty' (dat.fem.). Likewise, he argues for a velarised lateral in *blodilsa* 'bloody wound' (nom.sg.). This velar quality, he states, would account for the full vowel in this word in contrast to its reduced variant *blodelsa* 'bloody wound' (acc.pl.) which contains the more common *-elsa* form, as in *dreppelsa* 'threshold'.[22] In all of these examples, reduction would certainly be expected due first and foremost to Vowel Balance, for example, *twintiga* > *twintega*, or by means of Vowel Harmony (often in addition to Vowel Balance) such as in *heligona* > *helegona*, making the retention of the full vowel more striking. The result is a conflict between the reduction that arises from Vowel Balance and the retention of the full vowel in reduction environments according to Vowel Balance under the influence of the velar. At times Vowel Balance wins out, while at other times it is the influence of the neighbouring velar that prevails.

Velar consonants, however, are not the only sounds to have an apparent influence on the contrast between *i~e* and *u~o*. One prime example is the impact of a neighbouring *s*. Perhaps most visible in the masculine and neuter genitive ending, the expected contrast between *-is* after light stems but *-es* after heavy stems is frequently lost in favour of the *-is* ending regardless of stem type. Although we see doublets such as *berdis~berdes* 'beard, gen.sg.', which appear rarely in the data, we also see forms such as *goldis* 'gold, gen.sg.' which are found frequently throughout both manuscripts with no alternation in the genitive form. The influence of *-s* becomes more apparent when we note that *golde* 'gold, dat.sg.' with its reduced ending does exist, thereby providing evidence that this word was indeed affected by Vowel Balance in its other forms. From the perspective of Vowel Balance, the appearance of *-is* is certainly exceptional, however, when other dialects or manuscripts of Old Frisian are examined, we see that *-is* occurs quite regularly even when the reduced *-es* ending is expected. For instance, *-is* appears after masculine nouns in the Fivelgo Manuscript 47x as opposed to 51x for

21 Boutkan, *A Concise Grammar*, 28–32; van Helten, 'Nachträge'.

22 *Ibid.* 30. Unfortunately, Boutkan provides no explanation for the behaviour of velars.

the more expected *-es* ending.[23] An examination of other Germanic languages further reveals that this propensity towards a neutralisation in favour of *i* over *e* is not without parallels. Quak has argued that the regular genitive ending for masculine and neuter nouns in Old Dutch was *-is* (<**-es*).[24] Kock also notes that during the Reformation period, Danish had a similar pattern where *e* was the final vowel in all instances except before *s* where it surfaced as *i*.[25] He also observes that in the Old Swedish dialect of Södermannalag, *i* appeared before *s* instead of *e*. Later in Old Swedish when *i* > *e* in closed syllables, the *i* was retained before *s*.[26] The similar preference for *i* rather than the expected *e* before *s* in the Riustring manuscripts leads Boutkan to interpret the state of affairs 'as an indication for phonemic neutralisation, probably in favour of a high neutralisation product before *-s*'.[27] Whether this alternation between *-es* and *-is* is due to a phonemic neutralisation or in some cases to some other phonological conditioning needs to be further explored.[28]

When coupled with the influence of the velar consonants, this latter notion of neutralisation before *s* can be used to account for the variation between *frīsisk~frīsesk* 'Frisian'. Due to the long stem vowel, the commonly attested *e* of *-esk* would be expected. However, the *i* in *frisisk* could be accounted for as the result of the influence of both the *s* and the velar *k*.

Similar neutralisations before *r* and nasals, particularly *n,* have also been suggested by Boutkan.[29] The neutralisation before *r* would account for doublets such as *withir~wither* 'against' as well as the *i* in place of expected *e* after the long initial vowel in *mōdiran sunu* 'son of mother's sister' (acc.sg.). Likewise, assuming a neutralisation of *u* and *o* before nasals could account for the propensity of *u* to appear in *siugund-* 'second', *achtund-* 'eighth', *niugund-* 'ninth', etc., rather than the expected *o*. Certainly a neutralisation between *o~a* has also been noted, as in *heligana~heligona*

---

23 I am grateful to Rolf Bremmer for bringing this to my attention.

24 R. H. Bremmer Jr. and A. Quak, *Zur Phonologie und Morphologie des Altniederländischen* (Odense, 1992), 83.

25 Kock, 'Vocalbalance', 182.

26 *Ibid.*

27 Boutkan, *A Concise Grammar*, 28.

28 In some cases, it may be that the alternation between *-is* and *-es* is phonologically- (or morphologically-)conditioned. For instance, according to Bo Sjölin's edition of the Fivelgo manuscript, *Die 'Fivelgoer' Handschrift*, OTR 12 (The Hague, 1970), 114, the ending *-is* is found 30x after monosyllabic nouns ending in consonants versus 19x for *-es* in the same position. However, after nouns ending in *-ing*, *-is* only occurs 9x versus 25x for *-es*. Setting aside the fact that in twenty-four of those occasions, *-es* follows the same word, namely *keninges*, it could be argued that the occurrence of *-is* versus *-es* is conditioned by the phonemic and/or morphological shape of the preceding stem. I am grateful to Rolf Bremmer for bringing this to my attention.

29 Boutkan, *A Concise Grammar,* 31.

'holy one' (gen.pl.), keeping in line with the nasal influence found in Ingvaeonic.

To this point we have discussed the behaviour of the vowel pairs within word stems and endings. However, a similar alternation is also found in unstressed prefixes. For instance, both *i* and *e* can be found in prefixes in unstressed initial syllables, as in *bi slat* ~ *be slat* 'close (up)' (3sg.pret.ind.) or *bi seke~be seke* 'deny' (3sg.pres.opt.). When the behaviour of the suffixes outlined above and the influence of neighbouring consonants on the vowels *i, e, u,* and *o* are taken into consideration, it becomes clear that the effects of Vowel Balance, or more generally the alternations between *i~e* and *u~o* are at times obscured as Vowel Balance interacts with other influences at work in the language. That said, the effects of Vowel Balance (as well as Vowel Harmony) are most clearly attested in absolute final position, with the exceptions arising word medially or in closed syllables where the surrounding sounds can have an influence on the vowels.

2.3.2 *Behaviour of Compounds*

Before turning to an analysis of the Vowel Balance pattern, a group of examples can be addressed to account for some of the remaining data which seem at times to contradict the process at hand. This last set of exceptional forms is found in compound words. Typically, with regard to both Vowel Balance and Vowel Harmony, the individual words which combined to form compounds were treated separately as the examples in (6) illustrate:

(6) Treatment of compound words

a.	thing-stap**u**l**e** 'courtblock' (dat.sg.)	Vowel Balance: *u* and *e* in *stapule*
b.	dik-stath**u**l 'foot of dike' (acc.sg.)	Vowel Balance: *u* in *stathul*
c.	him**u**l-rik**e** 'kingdom of heaven' (dat.sg.)	Vowel Balance: *u* in *himul* and *e* in *rike*
d.	fidiran-sun**u** 'son of father's brother' (acc.sg.)	Vowel Balance: *u* in *sunu*
e.	mete-wund**e** 'measurable wound' (nom.sg.)	Vowel Harmony: *e* in *mete*; Vowel Balance: *e* in *wunde*

Both Vowel Balance and Vowel Harmony applied to the individual words before these words were put together to form their respective compounds. For instance in (6c), the *u* in *himul* was retained following the short vowel of the initial syllable, while *e* in *rike* resulted from Vowel Balance reduction after the long vowel *i* in the stem. These two words were then juxtaposed to form the compound.

In some compounds, however, this formulation was not as straightforward. Take for instance the doublets *nedwere~nedwiri* 'self-defence' (dat.

sg.) and *hirthstede~hirthstidi* 'fireplace' (dat.sg.). It could be argued that the first word in each pair, namely *nedwere* and *hirthstede*, arose when the two words forming the compound were treated separately. In this case, the first word of the compound would have been treated as a heavy stem, triggering the reduction of the stem vowel in *stidi* and *wiri* to *e*. Concomitant Vowel Harmony could then be adduced to account for the reduced final vowel *-e*. Van Helten and Boutkan have both noted that *stede* also exists as an alternate form for *stidi* in its simplex form, thus raising the possibility that this was considered a possible variant for the word 'place'. In the case of *nedwiri* and *hirthstidi*, two possible accounts can be proposed. First, *-were* and *-stede* were simply replaced in the compound word based on the preexisting simplex forms *wiri* and *stidi*. In the second possible account, Vowel Balance failed to apply to the second part of the compound because speakers treated the two words separately. In either case, it appears that there was a period of confusion for some of these words during which it was unclear as to whether to apply Vowel Balance to compounds as a whole, for example *hirthstede*, or to the individual words of the compound separately, for instance *hirth* + *stidi*.

This overview has sketched the types of opposing processes at work which at times disrupted the otherwise straightforward pattern of Vowel Balance. Although an exhaustive listing of every exception or even type of exception is beyond the scope of this paper, a large portion of those exceptions can be accounted for by means of the conflict between Vowel Harmony and Vowel Balance, the influence of neighbouring sounds such as *s* or *k*, and the treatment of affixes and compound words. At the least, these general examples can provide insight into which forms an analysis of Vowel Balance must be capable of accounting for and which do not fall under the purview of Vowel Balance. With these (apparent) exceptions set aside, I now turn to a prosodic account of Old Frisian Vowel Balance.

3. A Foot-based Account of Vowel Balance

As already noted, accounts of Vowel Balance have generally attributed the reduction of *i* and *u* to accent or stress placement. This is not surprising considering the widespread tendency for unstressed syllables to undergo reduction due to the *Auslautgesetze* or Laws of Finals that have been linked to stress placement in the history of Germanic. However, linguists have generally overlooked one other aspect of prosody as they have examined the Vowel Balance data: foot structure. By doing so, they have failed to capture the common thread that ties the variation of Vowel Balance together, namely that foot structure can provide a cogent and straightforward account for the occurrence of the full vowels in certain environments and reduced vowels in others.

Discussions of Vowel Balance have defined the process as follows: 1) full vowels are found after short stem vowels; and 2) reduced vowels appear after long or polysyllabic stems. These same environments can be roughly equated with what are referred to as light versus heavy (or polysyllabic) stems in discussions of apocope in Old Saxon *i*-stem nouns, syncope in Old High German *jan*-verbs,[30] Sievers' Law in Gothic,[31] and recently in the conundrum of umlaut in Old Norse,[32] to name but a few. Foot-based analyses have shed light on these problems in Germanic, underscoring the critical role of the moraic trochee in shaping the phonology and morphology of the Germanic languages historically.[33] To this end, it is fitting to examine Vowel Balance from the perspective of foot structure to determine if the moraic trochee can also provide an account of reduction there.

3.1 The Moraic Trochee in Germanic

As already noted, the primary foot-type in the early Germanic languages was the moraic trochee. To form this foot-type, individual sounds are grouped together to form syllables which are in turn grouped together to form feet. This is illustrated by the diagram of the Prosodic Hierarchy in (7):

---

[30] Smith, *Cross-level Interactions in West Germanic Phonology and Morphology* provides an account of both syncope in Old High German *jan*-verbs and apocope in Old Saxon *i*-stem nouns.

[31] Cf. Y. Kim, *Prosody and Prosodically-Motivated Processes from Germanic to Middle English*, Unpublished PhD Dissertation (Madison, WI, 2000), and E. Dresher and A. Lahiri, 'The Germanic Foot: Metrical Coherence in Old English', *Linguistic Inquiry* 22 (1991), 251–85.

[32] G. Iverson and J. Salmons, 'The Conundrum of Old Norse Umlaut: Sound Change versus Crisis Analogy', *Journal of Germanic Linguistics* 16 (2004), 77–110.

[33] The trochee has also been demonstrated to have a continued effect on some of the modern Germanic languages. In these cases, the moraic trochee has given way to the syllabic trochee that is helping shape morphological classes such as the plural system of German and Dutch as well as the Dutch diminutive system. The interested reader is directed to Smith, *Cross-level Interactions in West Germanic Phonology and Morphology*; L. C. Smith, 'The Resilience of Prosodic Templates in the History of West Germanic', *Historical Linguistics 2005: Selected papers from the 17th International Conference on Historical Linguistics, Madison, 31 July–5 August 2005*, ed. J. Salmons and S. Dubenion-Smith, eds. (Amsterdam, Forthcoming); R. Wiese, 'How Prosody Shapes German Words and Morphemes', *Interdisciplinary Journal for Germanic Linguistics and Semiotic Analysis* 6/2, (2001), 155-184; G. Booij, 'Phonological Output Constraints in Morphology', *Phonology and Morphology of the Germanic Languages*, ed. W. Kehrein and R. Wiese (Tübingen, 1998), 143–63; and H. van der Hulst and J. G. Kooij. 'Prosodic Choices and the Dutch Nominal Plural', *Phonology and Morphology of the Germanic Languages*, ed. W. Kehrein and R. Wiese (Tübingen, 1998), 187–98.

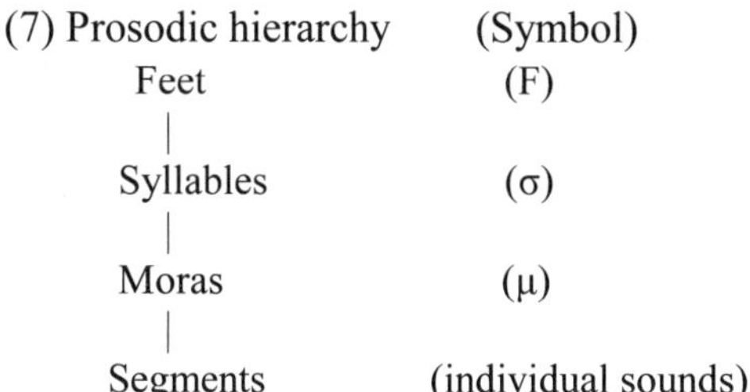

In the case of the moraic trochee, feet are constructed based on syllable weight, or in other words, the amount of segmental material found in the syllable rhyme. This segmental material is defined in terms of moras which contribute to the weight of a syllable.[34] According to this weight-sensitive foot, a syllable such as *wral* as in *wralde* in (8a) has two moras: one assigned to the vowel *a* and one to the coda *l*. As a heavy syllable, in other words, one that has two moras, it forms a foot on its own as indicated by the square brackets. However, since the next syllable, *de*, has only one mora assigned to the vowel *e* due to the lack of a coda, it is considered to be light and can therefore not form a foot on its own.

(8) a. Foot structure of OFris *wralde* 'world' (dat./gen.sg.)

F	Foot level (F=foot)
[H] L	Syllabic level (H=heavy syllable (2+ moras); L=light syllable (1 mora))
μμ μ	Moraic level (μ=mora)
[wral] de	Segmental level

b. Foot structure of OFris *stidi* 'place' (acc./dat.sg.)

F	Foot level
[L L]	Syllabic level
μ μ	Moraic level
[sti. di]	Segmental level ([...]=foot; .=syllable break)

c. Moraic trochee = [H] or [LL]

The moraic trochee is also formed by the sequence of two light syllables (or a light-heavy sequence). Together these two syllables form a foot that is equivalent to that formed by a single heavy syllable. This is illustrated in (8b)

---

34 Cf. E. Broselow, 'Skeletal Positions and Moras', *The Handbook of Phonological Theory*, ed. J. A. Goldsmith (Cambridge, MA, 1996), 175–205. Moras serve to indicate syllable weight in weight sensitive languages. Typically, one mora is assigned to each short vowel and single consonant found in coda position while long vowels are assigned two moras. Conversely, syllable onsets are argued to not contribute to syllable weight. This is certainly the case in Germanic. A syllable such as *cat* would thus have two moras, one from *a* and the second from *t*.

for *stidi* 'place' where the period denotes the syllable boundary. This equivalence between a heavy syllable and two light syllables with regards to foot construction stems from the notion of resolution that is observed in Germanic verse.[35]

3.2 Applying the Moraic Trochee to Old Frisian Vowel Balance

Using the moraic trochee as just described above, foot structure can now be assigned to the Vowel Balance data. Starting with the full vowels following the short vowels in stem initial position, we find the foot structures in (9). In all examples, the first foot is set apart from other feet, if any, by the double set of brackets.

(9) Full vowels following short stem vowels

a. Finally in open syllables	b. Finally in closed syllables
[[L L]] [[μ μ]] C_0V. Ci/u sti d*i* full go d*i* full ski p***u*** full	[[L H]] [[μ μμ]] C_0V. Ci/uC go d*i*s full we t*i*r full mu g***u***n full
c. Medially	**d. With prefixes**
[[L L]] [H] [[μ μ]] [μμ] C_0V. Ci/u CVC su m***u*** res full	[[L L]] L μ [[μ μ]] μ CV C_0V. Ci CV to se m*i* ne full

As the examples *stidi* and *godis* in (9a) and (9b) respectively demonstrate, the syllable containing the full vowel is footed with the first syllable via resolution. Likewise, the *u* in *sumures* in (9c) is footed with the initial syllable and also remains full in this position. The behaviour of words with prefixes is demonstrated in the final example *tosemine* in (9d). Since *to-* is not part of the root it fails to be footed. Instead, parsing of the syllables into feet begins with the syllable *se*, which is the first syllable of the root. As a consequence, the syllable *mi* is footed with the root initial syllable by means of resolution and the *i* remains full.

[35] Cf., e.g., Dresher and Lahiri, 'The Germanic Foot: Metrical Coherence in Old English', and A. Lahiri, T. Riad, and H. Jacobs, 'Diachronic Prosody', *Word Prosodic Systems in the Languages of Europe*, ed. H. van der Hulst (Berlin and New York, 1999), 335–422.

We can now compare the foot position of the reduced vowels with that of the full vowels given in (9) above. These are illustrated below in (10):

(10) Reduced Vowels after Heavy, i.e. Long, and Polysyllabic Stems

a. In open syllables after v̄C heavy stems	b. In closed syllables after v̄C heavy stems
[[H]] L [[μμ]] μ C_0v̄. Ci stē n*e̲* reduced hū s*e̲* reduced	[[H]] [H] [[μμ]] [μμ] C_0v̄. CuC bō k*o̲*n reduced clā th*o̲*n reduced
c. In open syllables after heavy VCC stems	d. In closed syllables after heavy VCC stems
[[H]] L [[μμ]] μ C_0VC. Ci/u wral d*e̲* reduced ger s*o̲* reduced	[[H]] [H] [[μμ]] [μμ] C_0VC. Ci/uC droch t*e̲*n reduced[36] ang l*o̲*n reduced[37]
e. In open syllables after polysyllabic stems	f. In closed syllables after polysyllabic stems
[[L L]] L [[μ μ]] μ C_0V. CV Ci sta pu l*e̲* reduced tho la d*e̲* reduced	[[L L]] [H] [[μ μ]] [μμ] C_0V. CV Ci/uC we ti r*o̲*n reduced he li g*o̲*n reduced

With the originally full vowels indicated on the CV-level, these examples demonstrate that reduction is based on the footing of *i* and *u*. In the examples *stene, wralde,* and *stapule* in (10a), (10c) and (10e), this is straightforward. In these cases, *i* and *u* are found in unfooted syllables word finally. In this position they are subject to reduction. However, footing alone is an insufficient condition for retaining the full vowel as *clathon*, *drochten* and *heligon* attest to in (10b), (10d) and (10f). In each of these cases, the reduced vowel appears in a footed syllable. What sets these examples apart from the

36 The letters ⟨ch⟩ represent the single phone [x] and thus only constitute a single consonant on the segmental level of the prosodic structure given in (10d).

37 Even if *anglon* were syllabified as *an.glon*, the result would be the same since the initial syllable would still be considered heavy making the stem also long and heavy.

cases we saw in (9), however, is that these syllables are not parsed with the initial foot. These latter examples underscore the observation that it is not enough for a syllable to be footed for *i* and *u* to remain full. Instead, what is critical is whether the vowel occurs in a syllable that is parsed within the initial foot. This vowel in question, either full or reduced, can be part of the root itself, for instance *sumures* or *wetir*, or it can be part of the suffix – especially the inflectional ending – as *skip**u*** and *gers**o*** indicate.

At this point a side-by-side comparison of the word pairs showing the effects of Vowel Balance from (2) above can be presented:

(11) A Direct Comparison of Light versus Heavy Stems

After a short stem vowel (light stem)	After a heavy stem
[[L L]]	[[H]] L
[[μ μ]]	[[μμ]] μ
C_0V. Ci	C0v̄. Ci
go d*i* 'God' (dat.sg.) full	gō d*e* 'good(s)' (dat.sg.) reduced
fo r*i* 'before' full	fō r*e* 'travel' (3sg.pret.opt.) red.

In these examples, it becomes immediately clear that foot structure does indeed play a critical role in whether the high vowels remain full or reduce. Whereas the full vowel *i* in *godi* and *fori* is found within the first foot of the word, the *i* in *+gō di > gode* and *+fō ri > fore* is not. Since *i* is not parsed within the first foot, it is subject to reduction, leading to a further distinction between these word pairs that goes beyond the length of the stem vowel.

Having shown that the distinction between *i* and *u* on one hand and *e* and *o* on the other is the product of foot structure, we can now show how this applies to compound words. Assuming that Vowel Balance affects individual words before they are brought together to form the compound, compounds can be analysed as illustrated below in (12). These examples include not only words that have been affected by Vowel Balance, but also how words that have undergone Vowel Harmony can interact with Vowel Balance words:

(12) Application of Vowel Balance (VB) and Vowel Harmony (VH) to Compounds

a. With Vowel Balance Only	b. With Vowel Harmony and Vowel Balance
[[L H]] + [[H]] L [[μ μμ]] [[μμ]] μ C_0V. CuC CV: Ci hi m*u*l + ri: k*e* Vowel Balance + Vowel Balance → himulrike	[[L L]] + [[H]] L [[μ μ]] [[μμ]] μ C_0V . Ci CVC Ci me t*e* + wun d*e* Vowel Harmony + Vowel Balance → metewunde

As (12a) shows, Vowel Balance applies first to the individual words before they are brought together to form the compound. For instance, *u* is retained in *himul* because it is footed with the initial syllable of the root by resolution. Next, in the case of **riki* > *rike*, the original full vowel *i* is not footed within the initial foot of the word and thus reduces to *e*. The resulting words are then brought together to form the compound *himulrike*.

Further evidence that the individual words are treated separately is found in *metewunde* in (12b). In the first word, the final *e* in *mete* arises as a result of Vowel Harmony. This is evident by the combination of two factors: 1) the failure of *i* to surface despite its being located within the initial foot and 2) the presence of the Vowel Harmony trigger vowel *e* in the stem *met-*. In the second word, Vowel Balance results in the final *e* surfacing in *wunde* since the original *i* is not footed with the initial heavy syllable. These two words which result from Vowel Harmony and Vowel Balance are then compounded, forming *metewunde*. Had Vowel Harmony and Vowel Balance applied post-compounding, then midvowels in *mete* could have potentially triggered Vowel Harmony in *wunde*, thereby producing *wonde*. However, this is not the case and the claim that both Vowel Balance and Vowel Harmony applied prior to compounding in these words is underscored.

It is possible, however, that there was some confusion as to whether these processes should be applied before or after compounding. This confusion may have been the source of the differential behaviour of some compounds. Consider for a moment the contrast between *hirthstede* and *hirthstidi* 'fireplace' illustrated in (13) below.

(13) Differential Behaviour of Compounds[38]

a. Compound Treated as Single Unit	b. Compound Treated as Two Separate Words
[[H]] [L L] [[μμμ]] [μ μ] C_0VCC CV Ci * hirth sti di Reduction Vowel Balance Vowel Harmony → hirthstede	[[H]] + [L L] [[μμμ]] [μ μ] C_0VCC CV Ci hirth + sti di Full → hirthstidi

The structure proposed for *hirthstede* in (13a) treats the two components of the compound as a single unit rather than as two separate words as the morphological boundary represented by the plus sign indicates in (13b). As a result, the first syllable *sti-* of *stidi* undergoes reduction to *ste-* because it is not footed with the initial syllable *hirth* to form the first foot of the word. Next, Vowel Harmony triggers the reduction of the final vowel in *-di* resulting in *-de*. Putting all of these components together, we arrive at the first variant of this noun, *hirthstede*.

The alternate form of this noun *hirthstidi* on the other hand is shown to result from the separate treatment of the two components of the compound. In the case of *hirth*, neither Vowel Balance nor Vowel Harmony apply. However, Vowel Balance does affect *stidi*. Since the final *i* is within the initial (and only) foot of the word, it remains full. These two words are then brought together to form *hirthstidi*.

This approach can also be described in terms of the prosodic word.[39] In (13a), the compound is treated as a single prosodic word and thus the two words that make up the compound are treated as a single unit. However, in (13b), each component is treated as a separate prosodic word and thus Vowel Balance applies to each prosodic word separately.

Before concluding, one further example of the interaction of Vowel Balance and derivation can be provided. Recall from §2.3.2 that some suffixes did not appear to interact with Vowel Balance. In these cases, exemplified by the suffix *-ing*, which lacks a reduced variant following heavy or poly-

---

[38] For a discussion of superheavy syllables in Germanic, the reader is directed to Smith, *Cross-Level Interactions in West Germanic Phonology and Morphology*; B. Hayes, 'Compensatory Lengthening in Moraic Phonology', *Linguistic Inquiry* 20 (1989), 253–306; and G. Booij, 'Phonological Output Constraints in Morphology', *Phonology and Morphology of the Germanic Languages*, ed. W. Kehrein and R. Wiese (Tübingen, 1998), 143–63.

[39] I am grateful to Dirk Elzinga for pointing this out to me.

syllabic stems, it could be argued that Vowel Balance applied first before the suffix was attached with subsequent resyllabification of the stem and suffix. An example is provided in (14):

(14) Suffixation of *-ing* after Vowel Balance

i. Apply Vowel Balance to stem	[[L H]] [[μ μμ]] C_0V. Ci We pi̲l Stem remains full
ii. Affix *-ing* to end of stem	[[L H]] + [H] [[μ μμ]] [μμ] C_0V. Ci VC We pi̲l + ing Stem remains full
iii. Resyllabify after Vowel Balance	We pi ling

In this example, the stem alone is subject to Vowel Balance as in (14i). Because the syllable containing the *i* is footed with the first syllable, the *i* remains full. In the second stage I propose, the suffix *-ing* is attached to the right edge of the stem as shown in (14ii). Finally, the word undergoes re-syllabification moving the *l* from the end of the stem final syllable into the onset of the syllable containing the suffix, resulting in the syllabification *We.pi.ling* seen in (14iii). As this example shows, the suffix is thus attached following the operation of Vowel Balance.

In the case of *-ong* where Vowel Harmony affects some forms, one additional step can be added to those given in (14) above.

(15) Suffixation of *-ung* after Vowel Balance

i. Apply Vowel Balance to stem	[[H]] [[μμμ]] C_0VCC sell Does not apply
ii. Affix *-ung* to end of stem	[[H]] + [H] [[μμμ]] [μμ] C_0VCC VC sell + ung Stem remains full

iii. Apply Vowel Harmony to whole word	sell + ong
iv. Resyllabify	sel.long

As (15i) shows, Vowel Balance applies first. Since the stem is monosyllabic, lacking either *i* or *u* in a second or third syllable, then Vowel Balance does not apply. Next the suffix *-ung* is affixed to the right edge of the stem as in (15ii) and Vowel Harmony then applies as in (15iii), causing the weakened variant of the suffix, *-ong*, to appear. Finally, this word undergoes resyllabification such that the final consonant of the stem becomes the onset of the final syllable as in (15iv). The ordering of Vowel Harmony and resyllabification can be reversed without changing the result of the derivation.[40] However, what is critical as both (14) and (15) illustrate is that Vowel Balance typically affects the stem first before the suffix is added. This actually highlights a fundamental difference between Vowel Balance and Vowel Harmony. While it appears that Vowel Balance does not cross over some morphological boundaries, or in other words some affixes are attached after the stems to which they attach have undergone Vowel Balance, Vowel Harmony appears to be more general in its application, able to affect the entire word even after suffixation has occurred.

As all of these examples have shown, a foot-based analysis of Vowel Balance provides a straightforward account of the process. In particular, where the high vowels *i* and *u* were not parsed within the first foot of a word, they were subject to reduction to *e* and *o* respectively. Conversely, where they did occur within the first foot, they remained full vowels except in cases where Vowel Harmony led to the change of *i* and *u* to *e* and *o*.

This approach has the advantage that it demonstrates the common ground between the two contrasting environments for Vowel Balance, namely the word-initial foot. Linguists have until now generally described the environment where the high vowels remained full in terms of the length of the stem vowel: *i* and *u* remain full after an initial short vowel. Conversely, the reduction of *i* > *e* and *u* > *o* has been defined in terms of stem shape: the high vowels reduce after heavy, i.e. long, or polysyllabic stems. The foot-based approach reveals the common thread that ties these two distinct environments together by showing the importance of the initial foot in maintaining full vowels in Old Frisian. In terms of prosodic templates, the initial foot permits the full range of vowel contrasts to occur. In other words, full vowels are licenced within the initial foot, but not necessarily so outside of the first foot

[40] There is also nothing to exclude the possibility that Vowel Harmony and resyllabification occurred at the same time.

of the word which leads to their reduction to *e* and *o*.[41] These prosodic templates constrain the shape that words or paradigms must have to be considered wellformed and are defined in terms of prosodic units such as syllables and feet.

A foot-based approach fits with the previous accent–based analyses such as that first proposed by Kock in that the domain of stress has been shown to be the foot in Germanic.[42] In Germanic, the first syllable of the root generally received the main stress of the word and was thus parsed within the initial foot of the word. We can thus consider the accent-based approach in terms of the foot. Consider for a moment Kock's original formulation of Vowel Balance for Old Norse which he subsequently applies to his analysis of Old Frisian: 'die älteren endungsvocale *i, u*,werden beibehalten in silben mit starkem levis (oder stärkerem accent), gehen aber in *e, o* über in silben mit schwächerem accent als starkem levis'.[43] According to Kock, the *starker levis* accent was the second syllable of 'kurzsilbiger wörter' such as the *u* in *gatu*. Translated into foot-structure terms, this would be the second syllable of a LL foot. Since the initial syllable carries main stress and is always within the initial foot, whether of the shape H or LL, this means that reduction takes place in syllables other than those found within the first foot of the word. In other words, it is the first foot of the word that protects *i* and *u* from undergoing reduction. The advantage of the foot-based approach over an accent-based approach is that it does not require assigning syllables to one of up to six different stress types as Kock's analysis required. As already stated, it captures instead the locus of retention versus reduction in terms of one structure: the initial foot.

A prosodic analysis also helps account for the at times exceptional behaviour of Vowel Balance with regards to Vowel Harmony and morphological processes such as suffixation and compounding. As Page states in his Prosodic Change Hypothesis, 'prosodic change proceeds by lexical dif-

---

41 For a further discussion of prosodic templates as applied to the Germanic languages, see Smith, *Cross-level Interactions in West Germanic Phonology and Morphology*; Smith, 'The Resilience of Prosodic Templates in the History of West Germanic'; D. Holsinger, *Lenition in Germanic: Prosodic Templates in Sound Change*, Unpublished Dissertation (Madison, WI, 2000); and L. C. Smith, J. Salmons and D. Holsinger, 'The Mediation of Perceptual Cues: Evidence from Cluster Reduction and Vowel Loss' [In Preparation].

42 Cf. Kim, *Prosody and Prosodically-Motivated Processes from Germanic to Middle English*. Kim provides an account of stress placement in the history of Germanic into Middle English and gives an overview of some of the different approaches that have been proposed for stress placement in Germanic.

43 Kock, 'Vocalbalance im Altfriesischen', 177.

fusion' and may be irregular.[44] According to this approach, 'the basic unit of change is the word' or even the word stem, not the sound.[45] In this way, we would expect to see some failure of words to undergo Vowel Balance or for there to be a certain level of confusion as to which suffixes participated or did not participate in Vowel Balance or even whether compounds should be treated as single units or the combination of the individual words. Thus, a prosodic approach to Vowel Balance not only elucidates where Vowel Balance occurred, but also suggests why at times it failed to occur in light of the Prosodic Change Hypothesis.

This type of foot-based account, however, is not unique to Old Frisian Vowel Balance. Similar prosodic analyses have been shown to account for apocope in Old Saxon *i*-stem nouns and for syncope in the Old High German *jan*-verbs, providing further evidence for the prosodic relationship between Vowel Balance in Old Frisian and other processes at work elsewhere in Germanic. Before concluding, I thus provide a brief overview of the impact of the moraic trochee in the Old Saxon and Old High German data to highlight this common prosodic thread that ties these processes together.

4.0 The foot in West Germanic apocope and syncope

The moraic trochee has been shown to play a key role in shaping the phonology and morphology of the early Germanic languages, including the West Germanic languages, the branch of Germanic to which Old Frisian belongs. In this section, I present further evidence for the moraic trochee's role in determining the fate of the high vowels in West Germanic as evidenced by apocope in Old Saxon *i*-stem nouns and syncope in Old High German *jan*-verbs. These changes in Old Saxon and Old High German differ, however, from the reduction of high vowels characteristic of Vowel Balance not only because they reflect vowel loss rather than reduction, but also because the loss in those languages is restricted to specific lexical classes in each case, for instance *i*-stem nouns and *jan*-verbs respectively, rather than a more general reduction of all high vowels regardless of word class as was the case in Old Frisian. Nevertheless, these phenomena all share a common thread: they are all prosodically-driven. With this in mind, I now turn to a discussion of the Old Saxon data.

4.1 Apocope in Old Saxon *i*-stem nouns

By the time the West Germanic languages were attested, the *i*-stem nouns had for the most part been absorbed into other noun classes in Old English

---

[44] R. Page, 'The Germanic Verschärfung and Prosodic Change', *Diachronica* 16 (1999), 297–334, at 299.

[45] *Ibid.*

and Old High German. However, in Old Saxon the alternation between the presence and absence of the linking vowel was still robust. As the Old Saxon data in (16) show, the loss or maintenance of the thematic vowel *i* depended on the shape of the preceding stem. In this noun class, *i* was lost following heavy or long stem nouns, namely those of the shape VCC and V:C, e.g., *fard* 'journey' and *thrād* 'thread'. Conversely, when the thematic vowel followed a light noun stem, i.e., one ending in a VC, e.g., *stedi* 'city', it was retained.

(16) Old Saxon Heavy versus Light Stems[46]

Heavy Stems		Light Stems
VCC	V̄C	VC
fard (f.) 'journey' gast (m.) 'guest' burg (f.) 'town, city' uurm (m.) 'worm'	quān (f.) 'woman' thrād (m.)'thread' wāg (m.) 'wave' brūd (f.) 'woman'	uuini (m.) 'friend' stedi (f.) 'city' seli (m.) 'room' friundskepi (m.) 'friendship'

Sample paradigms are provided in (17) for both the light and heavy masculine and feminine stems:

(17) Sample Declensions of Light / Heavy Masculine and Feminine *i*-Stems

		Masculine		**Feminine**	
		Light (VC)	**Heavy (VCC/V:C)**	**Light (VC)**	**Heavy (VCC/V:C)**
Sg.	**N**	uuin***i̲*** 'friend'	gast 'guest'	sted***i̲*** 'city'	fard 'journey'
	A	uuin***i̲***	gast	sted***i̲***	fard
	D	uuin*i̲*, *-ie, -ia, -ea, -e*	gast*e, -a*	sted***i̲***	ferd*i̲*, fard
	G	uuin***i̲***es, -**i**as, -es	gast*es*, *-as*	sted***i̲***	ferd*i̲*, *-e*[c]
	I	uuin***i̲***u, *-i*	gastu	----------[b]	----------
Pl.	**N**	uuin***i̲*, -*i*os**[a]	gest*i̲*, *-e*	sted***i̲***	ferd***i̲*,** *-e*
	A	uuin*i̲*, -***i***os[a]	gest***i̲*, -*e***	sted***i̲***	ferd***i̲***
	D	uuin***i̲***un, -***i***on	gest***i̲***un, *-m, -ion*	----------[c]	ferd***i̲***un, *-m*
	G	uuin***i̲***o	gest*i̲*o, *-eo*	----------	ferd***i̲***o

[46] The examples are all nom./acc.sg. forms. These data are from E. H. Sehrt, *Vollständiges Wörterbuch zum* Heliand *und zur altsächsischen* Genesis (Göttingen, 1925).

a. *-ios* reflects the extension of the *ja*-stem endings via analogy.
b. No instrumental forms exist for the feminine forms.
c. No forms have been attested in dative and genitive plural for this noun.

As the table shows,[47] the contrast between the *i*-full forms in the light stems and the *i*-less forms in the heavy stems is found primarily in the nominative and accusative forms. The presence or absence of umlaut serves to also further mark this contrast between the heavy and light stems. Simply put, where *i* was retained, i.e. in forms other than the nom./acc. singular, it triggered umlaut, e.g. *ferdi* (nom./acc.pl.)(*i,* umlaut), but in cases where it had been lost, namely in the nominative and accusative singular, we find a concomitant lack of umlaut as the form *fard* (no *i*, no umlaut) illustrates.

Similar to the trend we observed for the description of Old Frisian Vowel Balance, linguists have typically related the retention versus loss of *i* to the shape of the syllable immediately preceding the *i*, regardless of whether the word is monosyllabic, e.g., ⁺*wurmi* > *wurm* 'worm', or polysyllabic, e.g., *friundskepi* 'friendship'. As the table in (18) reveals, the description of the syllabic environment was in turn coupled with accent placement to account for the behaviour of *i*.[48]

(18) The development of PGmc. **i* in West Germanic

	Old Saxon	Old English	Old Hgh German
*i after unstressed syllable[49]	Ø nimis 'take' (2sg.ind.)	Ø nim(e)s(t)	Ø nimis(t)
*i after stressed long syllable	Ø wurm 'worm'	Ø wyrm	Ø gast 'guest'
*i after stressed short syllable	i wini 'friend'	e wine	i wini

[47] The table in (17) is a composite of forms drawn from R. L. Kyes, *Introduction to Old Saxon*, unpublished manuscript, and F. Holthausen, *Altsächsisches Elementarbuch*, 2nd edn (Heidelberg, 1921).

[48] Boutkan, *The Germanic 'Auslautgesetze'*, 39.

[49] *Ibid.* 438–39, Boutkan notes that *i* was lost in West Germanic following unstressed syllables in the dative singular of *n*-stem nouns and in the primary endings **-mi* (1sg.), **-si* (2sg.), **ti* (3sg.), and **-nti* (3pl.) which he reconstructs for the strong verbs. These reconstructions are supported by A. Bammesberger, *Der Aufbau des germanischen Verbalsystems* (Heidelberg, 1986), 105. Consequently, the final *i* was lost when the suffix followed an unstressed vowel, e.g., **nímisi* ('take' 2sg.pres.ind.) > *nímis*.

A description of this loss versus maintenance is simplified when foot structure is taken into consideration. Consider for a moment the examples in (19). With the syllables from the underlying forms parsed into feet, a clear pattern emerges.

(19) Foot Structure Before *i*-loss

Heavy		Light
[H] L [μμ] μ C_0VC. Ci far di > fard	[H] L [μμ] μ C_0V:. Ci tī di > tīd	[L L] [μ μ] C_0V. Ci se li > seli

As these examples demonstrate, the syllable containing *i* is unfooted following heavy stems. It is precisely in this position that the *i* is lost, as in *[far]di > fard* or *[tī]di > tīd*. Conversely, *i* is retained when the syllable containing the thematic vowel *i* is resolved with the preceding light syllable of a short stem as in *seli*. As result, the *i*-stem nouns come to end in a moraic trochee as depicted in (20):

(20)
[H]L → [H]
[L L] → [L L]

In terms of prosodic templates, it could be argued that the loss of *i* was driven by the need to fit these words to a template that required these words to end in a moraic trochee.[50]

This same approach can account for the failure of *i* to undergo syncope after trisyllabic light stems where the *i* is footed as *friundskepi* shows in (21):

(21) Trisyllabic short stem:
[H] [L L]
[μμμ] [μ μ]
friund. ske. pi 'friendship'

In sum, when the *i* can be footed and is thus mapped onto the template, it is retained.

At this point, we can compare the development in Old Saxon with that found in Old Frisian. This is diagrammed in (22):

50 Cf. Smith, *Cross-level Interactions in West Germanic Phonology and Morphology*, and Smith, 'The Resilience of Prosodic Templates in the History of West Germanic'.

(22) Old Saxon versus Old Frisian developments

Heavy		Light
[H] L [μμ] μ C_0VC. Ci OS far di > fard OFr wral de reduced ger so reduced	[H] L [μμ] μ $C_0\bar{v}$. Ci OS tī di > tīd OFr ske ro reduced	[L L] [μ μ] C_0V. Ci OS se li > seli OFr sti di full ski pu

As the examples in (22) demonstrate, the Old Frisian heavy and light stem forms correspond in shape to the forms from which the Old Saxon nouns were derived. In each case, the reduced vowels following the heavy stems in Old Frisian appear in unfooted syllables as *wralde* and *skero* illustrate. This matches the position in which the *i* is lost in Old Saxon, producing the forms *fard* and *tīd*. By contrast, when *i* and *u* are found in footed syllables, they remain full vowels in both Old Frisian, e.g. *stidi* and *skipu*, and Old Saxon, e.g. *seli*. Thus, although the vowels undergo reduction in Old Frisian rather than deletion as they do in Old Saxon, the foot plays a similar role in each case in determining whether the vowels would delete or reduce. As the Old Saxon example *friundskipi* demonstrates, however, it is not whether the high vowel is found within the first foot of the word that determines loss in Old Saxon as was the case in Old Frisian, but rather whether it is footed at all.

4.2. Syncope in Old High German *jan*-verbs

The syncope of *i* after West Germanic *jan*-verbs provides yet another instantiation of the role of the moraic trochee in determining vowel loss or reduction. In early Germanic, the preterite of the Class 1 weak verbs or *jan*-verbs was formed by adding a dental suffix, e.g., *-ta* or *-da*, to a stem + the connecting vowel *i* as in (23).

(23) Behaviour of *i* based on weight of stem

a. Light *ner-i-da > OHG nerita, OS nerida, OE nerede 'saved'
b. Heavy *hōr-i-da > OHG hōrta, OS hōrda, OE hīerde 'heard'
*drank-i-da > OHG drankta, OE drencte 'watered, soaked'
c. Polysyll. * mahal-i-ta > OHG mahalta 'vowed, pledged'

As the examples in (23) illustrate, the loss or maintenance of the linking vowel *i* was based on the weight of the preceding stem. For instance, when the stem was light, ending in a VC as in (23a), *i* was retained. However, the linking vowel underwent syncope after heavy stems, namely ones that ended in a VCC or VVC as in (23b), and after polysyllabic stems as in (23c). Additional examples from Old High German, where this pattern is most transparent, are provided in (24):

(24) OHG *jan*-verbs[51]

LIGHT	knussen	knusita	'to crush, pound'
	frummen	frumita	'to promote'
HEAVY	teilen	teilta	'to divide'
	wānen	wānta	'to mean'
	hengen	hangta, hancta	'to hang'
POLYSYLL.	nidaren	nidarta	'to lower'
	heilazen	heilazta	'to greet, hail'
	anazen	anazta	'to urge, drive on'

The description of syncope in Old High German *jan*-verbs is generally given in terms of morpheme boundaries: *i* underwent syncope after a heavy or polysyllabic stem immediately preceding the dental preterite suffix. This would lead us to examine the stem separately with regards to foot structure prior to affixing the preterite ending. Parsing the syllables into feet from left to right, the stem and connecting vowel are footed as in (25):

(25) Template mapping

a. Light (LL) and Polysyllabic (LLL>LH)	*b. Heavy (HL>H)*
F [L L] + ta μ μ CV CV + ta **i. Light** [*ne ri*] + ta <nerita> **ii. Poly.**[*ni da*] *ri* + ta <nidarta>	F [H] L + ta μμ μ C_0VC i + ta C_0VV Ci + ta **Heavy** [*tran*] *ki* + ta <trancta> [*hō*] *ri* + ta <hōrta>
	c. Polysyllabic (HHL>HH)
	[H] [H] L μμ μμ μ C_0VC CVC CV [*am*] [*bah*] *ti* + ta <ambahta>

[51] This table is based on W. Braune, *Althochdeutsche Grammatik*, ed. H. Eggers, 14th edn. (Tübingen, 1987).

As the examples in (25) show, the loss or retention of *i* was contingent upon whether or not it was footed. For instance, when the *i* could be footed as *nerita* demonstrates for light stems (25a.i), then it was retained thereby forming a resolved foot of the shape [LL] to which the dental preterite ending could be affixed. After other stems shown in (25), such as **trankita* > *trancta* in (25b), the *i* could not be footed with the stem and was subsequently lost. However, the polysyllabic examples of the shape HLL from the Otfrid and Notker texts serve as exceptions to the rule that *i* was retained when footed but lost when left unfooted.[52] Consider the example in (26). Here we see that a foot-based analysis cannot account for the loss of *i* for this stem type.

(26) ***Polysyllabic (HLL > HH)***
[H] [L L] + ta μμ μ μ C_0VC CV CV + ta C_0VV CV CV + ta [uuā] [fe ni] + ta > <*uuāfenda*>

Since *i* can be parsed into a resolved foot with the preceding light syllable, it would not be expected to be lost if foot structure alone were responsible for *i*-syncope. Consider the table in (27):

(27) Prosodic maxima and minima for *jan*-verb stems

Stem type	***Stem σ types***	***Example***	***# of morae***	***# of feet***	***# of syllables***
Light	L + L (< LL)	[ne.ri] + ta	2	1	2
Heavy	H (< HL)	[hōr] + ta	2+	1	1
Polysyll.	L + H (< LLL)	[ni. dar] + ta	2+	1	2
	H + H (<HHL)	[am] [baht] +ta	2+	2	2
	H + H (< HLL)	[hei] [laz] + ta	2+	2	2

As the table indicates, each word has at least one foot, with some polysyllabic stems having two. However, as the right-most column reveals, the

[52] Smith, *Cross-level Interactions in West Germanic Phonology and Morphology*. Other manuscripts such as Tatian and Isidor show a different behaviour of *i*-syncope following polysyllabic stems.

maximal number of syllables for any stem-type is two. Combining these two observations we can state that these stems have the following shapes: they all have at least one foot, but no more than two syllables, and by extension they have no more than two feet: Ft ≥ 1, σ ≤ 2; this is schematised in (28).

(28) a. Relation between stem and suffix in a templatic approach
X+preterite ending, where X≥ one foot and X≤ two syllables

b. OHG *jan*-verbs	
Foot:	[Ft] ([Ft])+[53]
Syllable:	σ (σ)
Moraic:	μ μ (μ) (μ)
Segmental:	Except with phonotactic violations[54]

Together these constraints form the prosodic template for the stem to which the dental preterite attaches. This template outlines the required shape that the stem must have to be considered well-formed. Consequently, the *i* in the HLL > HH polysyllabic stems is lost even though it can be footed as shown in (26), because the stem exceeds the two syllable maximum. The loss of *i* serves to remedy this violation of the disyllabic upper limit thereby bringing the stem in line with the constraints on stem shape and size, namely minimally one foot, but maximally two syllables.

Old High German and Old Frisian share in common the notion that it is not enough for the high vowels to appear in footed syllables. While in Old Frisian the *i* and *u* must be specifically parsed within the initial foot of the word, the situation in Old High German stipulates that *i* is lost when it is (a) not footed and (b) not within the first two syllables of the stem. Nevertheless, it is only through examining foot structure that we can adequately account for these phenomena.

5. Conclusions

At the beginning of this article I laid out two goals, first to provide an analysis of Old Frisian Vowel Balance and second to substantiate its relationship

---

53 The plus sign "+" indicates the edge to which the dental preterite ending is affixed.

54 Two possible interventions appear to have been used when syncope of *i* would have resulted in phonotactic violations: either syncope was blocked altogether as in (a) below or it was carried out with concomitant anaptyxis to break up the cluster as in (b). These interventions are illustrated with +*bauhnjan*:

a. Epenthesis	b. *i*-loss blocked
pauhh<u>a</u>nta	*bauhnida*
pouch<u>e</u>nta	*gabauhnita*

As a result, the stem violates the template but preserves the phonotactics.

with loss of *i* in the *i*-stem nouns and *jan*-verbs. To address the first goal, I have examined Vowel Balance in terms of the moraic trochee. Setting aside external influences that obscured the pattern such as Vowel Harmony, the influence of neighbouring consonants, compounding, and suffixation, I have argued that Vowel Balance is the product of foot structure. In particular, when the high vowel is footed within the initial trochee of the word, it remains full; however, when it fails to be parsed within this initial foot, even if it is found within a subsequent foot, it is subject to reduction.

Having shown the role of the moraic trochee in determining the fate of the high vowels *i* and *u* in Old Frisian, in other words their retention or reduction, we now have the means of addressing the second purpose of the paper, namely demonstrating the relationship between Vowel Balance and loss of *i* in the Old Saxon *i*-stem nouns and Old High German *jan*-verbs. For each of these latter phenomena, the moraic trochee was shown to account for the loss and maintenance of the *i*, either as the sole determining factor as was the case for Old Saxon, or in conjunction with another prosodic requirement like syllable count as the Old High German data illustrated.

Consequently, the Old Frisian data provide yet another piece of evidence for the critical role of prosody, especially involving the moraic trochee, in shaping the phonology and morphology of Germanic. Thus, although Kock's initial analysis of Old Frisian Vowel Balance was intended to emphasise its similarity to Vowel Balance in the old Nordic languages, especially Old Swedish, his intuition was right when he noted: 'so unterliegt es für mich keinem zweifel, dass ein und derselbe factor im afries. wie im aschw. (in den an. sprachen) beim zustandekommen der vocalbalance wirksam gewesen ist'.[55] This same conclusion can now be extended beyond Old Swedish to other processes such as syncope and apocope in West Germanic, which although superficially different from Vowel Balance have at their core one thing in common: they are all driven by foot-structure.

[55] Kock, 'Vocalbalance im Altfriesischen', 186.

The *Vita Siardi*: Inwardness, Community and Heavenly Bliss in Thirteenth-century Frisia

Ineke van 't Spijker

Historians of medieval Frisia have always had to struggle with the paucity of their written sources. Especially when it comes to narrative sources, little has remained – whether because of the effect of wars, nature, or, ironically, due to intensive use.[1] It is not surprising therefore that scholars have closely scrutinised one of the few written narrative sources available, the *Vitae abbatum Orti Sancte Marie* 'The Lives of the Abbots of Mariëngaarde' – and not infrequently they have deplored the lack of historical accuracy in part of this heterogeneous collection of hagio-biographies, especially in the Life of Siard. In this article I shall present the *Vita Siardi* from precisely the hagiographical perspective which has sometimes discredited it.

Mariëngaarde (Mary's Garden) was a Premonstratensian community founded just north of Leeuwarden in 1163. The complex of *Vitae* and *Gesta* about the earliest abbots of this monastery has been transmitted in a late fifteenth-century manuscript that is now in Brussels, but which must have been copied in Mariëngaarde.[2] As well as the *Vita Siardi*, the codex contains a *Vita* of the founder of the Premonstratensian order, Norbert, followed by the *Vita Fretherici*, about the founder of Mariëngaarde. The last chapters of the *Vita Siardi*, on the saint's death, were lacking even when a fifteenth-century scribe copied the work.[3] Both Lives are followed by accounts of *miracula*, which happened mostly at the holy man's grave. These reports were probably produced with a canonisation in mind.[4] The manuscript is completed by the *Libellus de vita et obitu atque miraculis fratris Herimanni Joseph in Steenvelt reconditi*, about the thirteenth-century saint from the Premonstratensian monastery at Steinfeld in Germany, who had spent some years in Mariëngaarde. The codex concludes with a collective Life of three

[1] See R. H. Bremmer Jr, *Hir es eskriven. Lezen en schrijven in de Friese landen rond 1300* (Hilversum and Leeuwarden, 2004), 11–17, on the dearth of written sources.

[2] For the following, see the Introduction to the new edition of the *Vitae*: *Vitae Abbatum Orti Sancti Marie. Vijf abtenlevens van het klooster Mariëngaarde in Friesland*, ed. H. T. M. Lambooij and J. A. Mol (Hilversum and Leeuwarden, 2001), 3–7. Henceforth *Vitae Abbatum*.

[3] See the *Vita Siardi*, in *Vitae Abbatum*, 318.

[4] N. Backmund, *Die mittelalterlichen Geschichtsschreiber des Prämonstratenserordens*, Bibliotheca Analectorum Praemonstratensium 10 (Averbode, 1972), 76, n. 116.

thirteenth-century abbots, the *Vita Sibrandi, Iarici et Ethelgeri.*[5] Finally, some blank folios at the end of the *Vita Siardi* were used in the sixteenth century to write a *Brevis Historia* of Mariëngaarde.

The *Vita Fretherici*, a vivid portrait of the founder of Mariëngaarde, was written by Sibrand, probably before he became abbot himself, that is before 1230. The collective Life of the three abbots was written by a contemporary, who, judging by the engaged tone of his narrative, was evidently involved in the events he related. The *Vita Siardi* was probably written not long after the saint's death in 1230; the *Miracula* that follow the truncated Life cover the period up to 1242.[6]

No consensus has emerged about the *Vita Siardi* among modern historians. The Dutch historian Jan Romein thought it of little interest, hardly deserving of a place in his history of Dutch historiography. Compared with the lively biographies in the *Vita Fretherici* and in the *Vita Sibrandi, Iarici et Ethelgeri*, the Life of Siard was an 'empty' work in Romein's opinion.[7] Wybrands, who first published these Lives, thought that the *Vita Siardi* was the dullest part of the whole.[8]

Reinier Post, however, was more positive. He drew attention to the many sermon-like passages that are attached to the hagiographical episodes in the *Vita Siardi.*[9] U. G. Leinsle read the *Vita* as an ascetic treatise, illustrating the virtues that made Siard a true follower of the *vita apostolica*. Thus, the *Vita* discusses meals and fasting (Chapters 2–5), dress (Chapters 6–7), work (Chapters 8–9), reading and discipline (Chapters 10–12), sleep and common prayer (Chapters 13–14), and finally the saint's relation to the outside world (Chapters 15ff.). Leinsle also argued that the author had some knowledge of philosophical issues, a point to which we shall return.[10] In his Introduction to the new edition of the *Vitae*, H. Th. M Lambooij sees in the *Vita* its theological justification of monastic life and an appeal, at a time when the first *élan* of the foundation was declining, to return to monastic discipline as

---

5 For the *Vita Norberti* (version B), see W. M. Grauwen, 'Inleiding tot de Vita Norberti B', *Analecta Praemonstratensia* 66 (1990), 123–202. The *Vita Hermanni Josephi* has been published in *Acta Sanctorum Bollandiana*, 7 April I (Antwerp, 1675), 686–714. On this vita, see Backmund, *Die mittelalterlichen Geschichtsschreiber*, 76–88.

6 See *Vitae abbatum*, 48; *Vita Siardi*, in *Vitae abbatum*, 348

7 J. Romein, *Geschiedenis van de Noord-Nederlandse geschiedschrijving in de middeleeuwen. Bijdrage tot de beschavingsgeschiedenis* (Haarlem, 1932), 67 and 71.

8 *Gesta Abbatum orti sancte Marie. Gedenkschriften van de abdij Mariëngaarde in Friesland*, ed. A. W. Wybrands (Leeuwarden, 1879), VIII–IX.

9 R. R. Post, *Kerkgeschiedenis van Nederland in de Middeleeuwen*, 2 vols. (Utrecht, 1952–1957) I, 242–43.

10 U. G. Leinsle, 'Aristoteles und die "Moderni" in der *Vita Siardi*', *Analecta Praemonstratensia* 58 (1982), 210–24.

embodied by Siard.[11] He also suggests that the 'real' Siard may be less apparent in his *vita* than in some remarks in the later Lives, where Siard is depicted in some of his administrative duties. Lambooij therefore wonders whether a slightly later chronicler, Menko, might have presented a more realistic picture of Siard, when he summarised the saint's career after observing a miracle that happened at Siard's grave in 1272:[12]

> This father had gloriously governed the church of Mariëngaarde for thirty-three years, and extended it in spiritual as well as temporal matters, while nevertheless afflicting himself not a little in fasting, waking and working. Hence through his holy way of life he not only excited many of his own community but many others in neighbouring places to the service of God. As a consequence, not only this miracle, but also several other ones took place at his grave.

The Lives of Fretheric and Siard clearly belong to hagiography. However, the hagiographical genre is well known for its range of biographical detail. These two Lives neatly illustrate this range. It is apposite to remark in this context that the boundaries between hagiography and historiography have recently been questioned.[13] These boundaries are extremely fluid, as is shown by the combination in one codex of the *Vitae* of both Fretheric and Siard and the joint *Vita* of Sibrand, Iarich and Ethelger. The latter one could be said to be more like a historical *Gesta abbatum* than a hagiographical *Vita*. The quotation from Menko's *Chronicle* also shows the fluidity between genres. In the following, I do not want to defend either the biographical veracity of the *Vita Siardi* nor its hagiographical distortion. It may be useful, however, to keep in mind the extent to which ideals, as presented in saints' lives, may have influenced the 'real life' of a person, and then in their turn reappear in the biography or hagiography of such a person. André

[11] *Vitae Abbatum*, 43–47.

[12] Menko, *Cronica Floridi Horti* 56, *Kroniek van het klooster Bloemhof te Wittewierum*, ed. H. P. H. Jansen and A. Janse (Hilversum, 1991), 442: 'Hic siquidem pater xxx et tribus annis ecclesiam Orti sancte Marie gloriose rexit et eam in spiritualibus ac temporalibus mirabiliter ampliavit, se nichilominus in ieiuniis, vigiliis et laboribus non modicum affligendo. Unde sancta conversatione sua non solum suam familiam, sed et multos in vicinis locis ad Dei servicium provocavit. Unde non solum hoc miraculum, sed et alia diversa ad eius sepulchrum contigerunt.'

[13] See, e.g., F. Lifschitz, 'Beyond Positivism and Genre: "Hagiographical" Texts as Historical Narrative', *Viator* 25 (1994), 95–113, who argues against isolating a hagiographical genre, offering an overview of historians' attitudes towards what, she demonstrates, they first had defined as hagiography.

Vauchez has shown how in the later Middle Ages this is increasingly the case.[14]

Elsewhere I have tried to analyse some such ideals in the *Vita Siardi* which the author managed to intertwine into his portrait of the saint.[15] I shall summarise these earlier findings here before presenting some aspects that may not have previously been noted with sufficient emphasis: Siard's inwardness and his relation to the community.

A TRADITIONAL SAINT

If, as Leinsle has demonstrated, the author of the *Vita Siardi* shows himself to be a conservative in the field of philosophy, he could also be called a conservative in hagiographical matters. For example, he often alludes to the *Canticum canticorum*. But whereas in the twelfth century, a tropological reading of the Song of Songs had gained pride of place, the author of the *Vita Siardi* interweaves the personal within an older ecclesiological perspective. Thus, when the author defends Siard's simple dress he refers to the dress of John the Baptist. He adds that, if there was no merit in such behaviour, the Holy Church would not have said: 'See, I am black and beautiful' (Cant. 1, 5).[16]

Siard's physical ascesis was connected with his care for the poor: the author explains how Siard gave his butter and porridge to a workman of the monastery, while taking bread and milk himself. The author then admonishes his brothers to take this as an example and leave food to the poor.[17] Physical ascesis such as fasting is also informed by Siard's desire to follow Christ and by a pervasive notion of the *vita angelica*: the saint, while still in the body, lives as if beyond the body. His moderation in food, connected to his *cura pauperum*, results in what is often called the *gratia lacrymarum*, the gift of tears.[18] Also, as he opened and prepared the 'room of his heart' for

---

[14] A. Vauchez, *La sainteté en Occident aux derniers siècles du Moyen Age d'après les procès de canonisation et les documents hagiographiques* (Rome, 1981), 621.

[15] See my 'Een matte biografie, een heiligenleven met allure. De dertiende-eeuwse "Vita Siardi"', *Het Noorden in het midden. Opstellen over de geschiedenis van de Noord-Nederlandse gewesten in Middeleeuwen en Nieuwe Tijd*, ed. D. E. H. de Boer, R. I. A. Nip and R. W. M. van Schaïk (Assen 1998), 187–99.

[16] *Vita Siardi*, ch. 6, in *Vitae abbatum*, 276. Henceforth *Vita Siardi*, followed by chapter number and page number.

[17] *Ibid.* 3, 254–56.

[18] *Ibid.* 4, 264: 'Sic ergo fuerunt sibi panes die prosperitatis et nocte adversitatis, lacrime ab intimis cordis affectibus erumpentes, ut movente dulci spiritu Ihesu Christi, intus cum Maria Magdalena humiliter et dulcissime debriatus, animam non siccam et aridam quasi terram, cum psalmo misrere mei Deus, ad Deum sublevaret; sed madentibus genis repletus aqua vivi fontis, quam mulier Samaritana ad puteum posita, adhuc carnalis ignorabat, dulciter absque ypocrisi ad excitationem fratrum, foras in faciem derivaret.'

the Holy Spirit, 'the Lord Jesus, entering his heart spiritually, celebrated symbolically the Eastermeal with the soul of the holy father', as a foretaste of the heavenly meal.[19] This complex of notions is then also connected with the texts of the Canticle as well as with the apocalyptic marriage supper of the Lamb (Rev. 19, 9).[20] Here, however, triumphal notions common in previous ages in this context are mitigated by a more intimate tone. On the other hand, for all the author's worry about the growing cold of love at the end of times (cf. Matt. 24, 12),[21] this concern sounds like the eternal complaint of any cultural pessimist. More 'modern' apocalyptic anxieties are absent.

Siard's care for the poor was more than a concomitant of his physical ascesis. He actively took food with him to give to the poor when some business took him outside the monastery.[22] He also took care of the physical needs of his chaplains.[23] This attitude was also part of his active life. The relation between action and contemplation and their proper order was a recurring issue in religious life as well in hagiography, often presented in terms of the story of Martha and Mary, or Leah and Rachel: in the Gospel story (Luke 10, 38–42) where Jesus visits the two sisters, he tells Martha, when she complains of doing the work while Mary is just listening to Jesus, that Mary (sometimes identified with Mary Magdalene) has chosen, in the Vulgate translation, the best part. Similarly, Jacob's marriage to Leah first, and then to Rachel (Gen. 29), came to symbolise the succession of the active and the contemplative life. Another metaphor that we see employed by the writer is derived from the Exodus texts on the tabernacle, where the outer curtains of goat's hair symbolise the active life by which the inside curtains of fine linen are protected.[24] All these figurae are used in the *Vita Siardi*.

The saint presents both positions as necessary, and emphasises their actual combination. He insists on sharing in the work, for example of carrying soil for the reparation of a dyke. His brothers were impressed with

---

[19] *Ibid.* 4, 264: 'Dicit enim Dominus in Apokalipsi: Si quis aperuerit mihi ianuam, introibo ad illum et cenabo cum illo, et ipse mecum (Rev. 3, 20). Quia ergo iste bonus pater Spiritui Sancto aperuit pulsanti, et cenaculum sui cordis Domino Ihesu stravit, ideo Dominus Ihesus cor eius spiritualiter ingrediens, typicum pascha (cf. Mat. 26, 17–18) cum eiusdem patris anima celebravit: ita videlicet ut iste pius pater transitum iam faceret a terrenis ad celestia, et adhuc in carne positus odorem celestis alimonie pregustaret in terris, quo sine interruptione super experientiam humanam, fruiturus cum sanctis et electis Dei erat in celis.'

[20] E.g., *ibid.* 4, 268: '[…] curramus in odore ungentorum tuorum (Cant. 1, 3) donec tollamur ab hac valle lacrimarum (Ps. 83, 7) et perveniamus ad vocatam cenam agni (Rev. 19, 9) Domini Ihesu Christi […].'

[21] *Ibid.* 5, 272.

[22] *Ibid.* 18, 308–10.

[23] *Ibid.* 19, 310.

[24] See G. Constable, 'The Interpretation of Mary and Martha', *Three Studies in Medieval Religious and Social Thought* (Cambridge, 1995).

this sign of humility – there was, from that day onwards, never a breach in the dyke. The author refers his readers to the example of Bernard of Clairvaux, who in a similar fashion wanted to share in the work on the field but at first did not know how to, and was turned away by the brothers. After praying to God, he became as competent as the others.[25] Siard shares in the working on the land, but also writes books and prepares the parchment himself.[26] During these writing activities, however, he had somebody read vigils to him. Similarly, while working on the land he, and following him the brothers, would pray and sing together. In this way, he was at the same time in the company of Martha and Mary.[27] The author emphasises the unity between the two sides: the fact that Mary and Martha are sisters is not devoid of a hidden meaning; it symbolises the unity of labour and contemplation in the religious person.[28] Later, during a journey outside the monastery, Siard is shown to receive the grace of contemplation because he first 'was united with Leah, he then also merited to succeed to the embrace of Rachel'. The author admonishes his readers to follow Siard's example and not to shrink from the 'labour of discipline', to wish to be 'inside the tabernacle as fine curtains rather than be troubled by labour outside and be shaken as the rough goat hair curtains'.[29]

---

[25] *Vita Siardi* 9, 284–86. See the *Vita Bernardi* 1, 4, 24, PL 185, cols. 225–368, at cols. 240D–41A. Earlier, in his criticism of luxury clothing, contrasted with Siard's simplicity (*Vita Siardi* 6, 274–78), the author quotes Bernard's *Apologia ad Guillelmum Abbatem*, X, 24–26, *Sancti Bernardi Opera*, ed. J. Leclercq and H. M. Rochais (Rome, 1963) III, 101–02.

[26] *Vita Siardi* 12, 292: 'Dedit igitur operam scribendi libros ad communes fratrum usus quatinus per dulcedinem scripturarum pervenirent ad Rachelis contubernium. Personaliter quoque quaternas de pargameno in suo secretario ad libros scribendos preparavit habens sibi in adiutorium legendi vigilias puerum sui monasterii […].'

[27] *Ibid.* 8, 280–82: 'Audivimus iam fratres, quomodo iste bonus pater, superflua devitans novit quasi unus ex fratribus humiliter vivere, et seipsum subditis suis bonorum operum exemplum, singulariter prebere, et contemplative vite dulcedinem cum Maria Magdalena degustare. Audiamus ergo qualiter novit esse et Martha, tamen absque sollicitudine et turbatione ergo plurima, et ex occupatione operis, illud unum necessarium non omittere, videlicet ut esset Maria audiendo, meditando, diligendo solum Dominum Ihesum, unicum verbum Patris, a quo anima necesse habet vivere et quiescere. Fuit vero cum Maria, simul et Martha: Maria, in interiori homine, Martha, in manuum labore.'

[28] *Ibid.* 8, 282: 'Nec vacat a misterio, quod iste fuerunt sorores. Nam propinquitas carnis, figurat in quolibet religioso et spirituali, unionem laboris et contemplationis.'

[29] *Ibid.* 19, 312: 'Quia ergo iste bonus pater se a sanctis laboribus discipline non absentavit, prius copulans sibi Lyam, ideoque meruit ad Rachelis succedere amplexus. Sed nos miseri fugientes labores sanctorum patrum, statim presumimus de Rachelis amplexibus, et dum nobis aliquod opus iniungitur, nobis excusationes confingimus, videlicet melius nos esse intus in tabernaculo ut cortina, quam exterius turbari laboribus et concuti ut saga cilicina (cf. Ex. 26, 1–7).' On the episode preceding this passage, see below, n. 57.

Shown to be following models of an earlier saint such as Bernard of Clairvaux, or of biblical models like Eliah, Siard is, above all, imitating the *forma Ihesu Christi*, for example in his fasting, or in his sleeping on a hard bed.[30] However, there is no trace here of the intimate familiarity with Jesus and with his mother Mary which became popular in the writings of, for example, the same Bernard of Clairvaux, and which was illustrated in the thirteenth-century *Vita Hermanni*.[31]

The author has succeeded in interweaving many hagiographical motifs into his *Vita*, thus making the life of the Frisian monks almost palpable – for example, in their work on the land and their maintenance of the dykes – as it was framed under a wider horizon of Christian saintliness. Uniting all these strands is the idea of the saint functioning as a model and example for the community, a model of abstinence, humility, simplicity – and of inwardness.

A PHILOSOPHY OF INWARDNESS

As the combination of working and singing has shown, the external life of labour is no obstacle to the 'life of the mind'. Following the passage about the working and singing monks, the author explains how maybe nobody will understand how sweet Siard's soul lived in God if God had not made this known to them. Yet, he recommends Siard's effort to know God through reason, even if God is ultimately incomprehensible, immediately connecting this effort to the work on the land:[32]

> Nothing pleases the holy soul so much as investigating God through reflective contemplation and to know him somehow by the force of reason, and not stay outside him. Even if she cannot comprehend him, yet through persistent investigation she is always growing, and is sweetly delighted [...]. Let us thus, brothers, love the farmer's life, created by the

---

30 *Ibid.* 13, 298.

31 See e.g. Bernard's *Sermones super Cantica, Sancti Bernardi Opera*, ed. J. Leclercq, C. H. Talbot, H. M. Rochais (Rome, 1957) I –II; *Vita Hermanni Josephi*, I, 3–4, p. 685; III, 18, p. 690. For the 'affective devotion' exemplified by these writings see now R. Fulton, *From Judgment to Passion: Devotion to Christ and the Virgin Mary, 800–1200* (New York, 2002).

32 *Vita Siardi*. 8, 282–84: 'Nichil enim melius libet sancte anime, quam consideratione investigare Deum et virtute rationis aliquantulum cognoscere, nec extra ipsum moram facere. Quem licet comprehendere non possit, tamen sedula investigatione mirabiliter semper crescit, et dulciter delectatur.[...] Ideoque fratres diligamus rusticationem, ab Altissimo creatam, et vestigia patris Sicardi sequamur, ut laboremus manibus nostris [...] laborando vigiliis et orationibus studeamus eorum beneficiis respondere, et quantum possumus exerceamus labores, ut eorum estibus facilius possimus condescendere.'

> Highest, and follow the steps of father Siard, and work with our hands [...]. Let us be ready to respond to their [i.e. the farmers'] service by our work of waking and praying, and let us do our work as much as we can, so that we may better meet their needs.

Later in the *Vita* the author denounces the teaching of Aristotle, and the custom of the Moderni to pay more attention to divisions and subdivisions in their preaching than to the issue of sins and virtues. Such attention results in envy rather than peace of mind.[33] However, the author does not seem to know more than the *logica vetus* and indeed seems only to have a muddled idea of it. Thus, when he argues that it is better to have in one's heart the virtues about which one can read in books, he explains this by saying that after all in a book there are no virtues, only the shapes of letters drawn with ink through which you can read and thus form words which are the signs and notes in the soul. What seems to be resonating here is Aristotle's distinction, possibly known in a monastery such as Mariëngaarde through Boethius' commentary on, and translation of, the *De interpretatione*.[34]

Earlier the author had told how Siard refused a dish that was specially prepared for him.[35] This anecdote provokes the author into emphasising the importance of communal unity. Here again, an excursus on words is incorporated. Someone may well claim to adhere to the apostolic injunction to communal possession, implied in the words 'nobody called anything their own' (Acts 4, 32). However, even if that person says 'our' instead of 'mine', this can hardly be called 'saying', but rather bringing forth some sound. The author further refers to Paul's 'no one can say, "Jesus is Lord" except by the Holy Spirit' (I Cor. 12, 3). He continues by pointing to the magpie, well able to produce sounds that imitate human words.[36] Nobody in their right mind, however, would hold that a magpie 'has what is signified by the words in its affect', even when you hear the bird form words by outer rattle. This again seems to resonate with the standard Aristotelian/Boethian notions mentioned before. The author concludes by appealing to his readers not to be as the magpie: 'when out of custom and in accordance to the rule we say "every-

---

33 *Ibid.* 17, 308.

34 *Ibid.* 12, 296: 'Vere in libre non sunt nec possunt esse virtutes, sed figure litterarum cum incausto protracte per quas potes legendo verba formare que sunt signa et note in anima.' Cf. Boethius' translation of *De interpretatione*: ' Sunt ergo ea quae sunt in voce earum quae sunt in anima passionum notae […]', *Aristoteles Latinus* II, 1–2, *De interpretatione vel Periermeneias*, ed. L. Minio-Paluello (Bruges/Paris, 1965), 5–38, at 5.

35 *Vita Siardi* 5, 270.

36 On the magpie and its imitation of human speech the author draws from the classical and medieval (encyclopaedic) tradition, see e.g. Ovid, *Metamorphoses* 5, 674–80; Isidore of Seville, *Etymologiae* 12.7.46, *Isidori Hispalensis Episcopi Etymologiarum sive originum libri XX*, ed. W. M. Lindsay (Oxford, 1911, repr. 1985) II.

thing is held in common", let us thus be like that inside in our soul before God'. Shifting to an Augustinian register he explains how 'from a good affect of the will, the word of truth fully proceeds without any ambiguity'.[37]

Leinsle has shown how the author in these philosophical digressions was out of touch with the really modern issues of his time.[38] Here, I should like to suggest how his rather poor grasp of linguistic matters serves as an argument for inwardness. Without the possession of books, one can concentrate on the inner virtues. (Besides, at the hour of death, others will, in their turn, not be distracted by their desire for your books to pray for you.) This inwardness is a recurring motif in the *Vita*. Siard's fasting habits provoke associations – he is imitating Eliah in the desert, and thus arrives at Mount Horeb, which means Raven – which then enable the author to explain that beneath the external blackness internal wisdom is hiding: the more contempt one meets, the less receptive one is to the arrows of pride.[39] Also, because of his fasting, 'the Lord Jesus entered his heart spiritually and celebrated the Easter meal' (cf. Matt. 26, 18) with his soul.[40] In later times, this text would become a symbol for mystical union and the object of pictorial representations.[41] The *Vita Siardi* almost immediately returns to a quiet note of anticipation implicit in the texts from Revelation, which the author associatively calls to mind: '[...] so that the pious father already made the transition from earthly to heavenly things, and still in the flesh received a foretaste of the fragrance of heavenly food on earth, which without interruption, beyond human experience, he would enjoy with the saints and God's chosen people in heaven'.[42]

There is nothing exuberant or emphatic about Siard's inwardness, therefore – rather it is woven into the flow of associations, which determine the general mode of the Life. His inwardness is qualified, moreover, by what might be considered a sort of literalism. Thus, not to be a liar when singing: 'In the middle of the night I woke up to sing your praises' (Ps. 118, 62), Siard always went to sing matins in church with the brothers, however tired

---

[37] *Vita Siardi* 5, 270–72. On Augustine's view of the will and its affects, see e.g. his *De ciuitate Dei*, XIV, 6, ed. B. Dombart and A. Kalb, Corpus Christianorum Series Latina 48 (Turnhout, 1955), 421.

[38] Leinsle, 'Aristoteles und die "Modeni" in der Vita Siardi', 224.

[39] *Vita Siardi* 2, 252.

[40] *Ibid.* 4, 264. See above, n. 19.

[41] For examples of such representations, see J. Hamburger, *Nuns as Artists. The Visual Culture of a Medieval Convent* (Berkeley and London, 1997).

[42] Vita Siardi 4, 264: '[...] ita videlicet ut iste pater transitum iam faceret a terrenis ad celestia, et adhuc in carne positus odorem celestis alimoniae pregustaret in terris, quo sine interruptione super experientiam humanam, fruiturus cum sanctis et electis Dei erat in celis.' For the preceding passage, see also above, n. 20.

he might be.[43] This is reminiscent of a similar discussion in the exchange between Abelard and Heloise, a century earlier. Heloise had worried about hymns whose words do not correspond with reality at the time of singing. Thus, for example, some hymns may refer to nighttime while being sung during the day or the other way round. For example, the traditional demand of the Rule of Benedict which stated that 'our mind may be in agreement with our voice' ('... et sic stemus ad psallendum, ut mens nostra concordet uoci nostrae') was translated by Heloise into the demand that 'liturgy should be truthful in its linguistic expression'.[44] This points to the ideal of mutual transparency of outer and inner. This transparency was what Hugh of Saint-Victor proposed to his readers in his *Institutio novitiorum*. In his discussion of *disciplina*, for example, Hugh explained how, although the root of our unrest is often interior, the *disciplina* of the outer man will set off a process which will restore not only the outer but also an inner rest: 'Slowly the same form of virtue will by custom be imprinted on the mind as is conserved by discipline in the bodily posture'.[45] In the Life of Saint Francis, the same concern can be seen. Here Francis' behaviour could even be considered an externalisation, an acting out of inner states in outer behaviour, for example, when he refused to accept alms beyond what was sufficient for one day, to obey the Gospel 'Take no thought for the morrow' (Matt. 6, 34).[46] This qualification of inwardness brings out its distinct qualities as compared with modern notions of interiority. Rather than being the domain of the markedly personal and private (however illusionary such a notion may be), what is at issue is a personal appropriation of a general ideal, valid for everyone.

---

[43] *Ibid.* 18, 298.

[44] *Regula Benedicti* 19,7, ed. R. Hanslik, Corpus Scriptorum Ecclesiasticorum Latinorum 75 (Vienna, 1960), 75. Abelard comments on this in one of his sermons for the Paraclete, *Sermo* XIV, I sermoni di Abelardo per le monache del Paracleto, ed. P. De Santis, Mediaevalia Lovanensia Series I, Studia 31 (Leuven, 2002), 207–18, at 208. See also Abelard's Letter on the monastic Life, *Epistola* VIII, T. P. McLaughlin, ed., 'Abelard's Rule for Religious Women', *Medieval Studies* 18 (1956), 241–92, at 286; C. J. Mews, 'Liturgy and Identity at the Paraclete: Heloise, Abelard and the Evolution of Cistercian Reform', *The Poetic and Musical Legacy of Heloise and Abelard. An Anthology of Essays by Various Authors*, ed. M. Stewart and D. Wulstan (Ottawa, 2003), 19–33, at 29.

[45] *De institutione novitiorum, L'Oeuvre de Hugues de Saint-Victor*, I. *De institutione novitiorum. De virtute orandi. De laude caritatis. De arrha animae*, ed. H. B. Feiss and P. Sicard, trans. D. Poirel, H. Rochais, P. Sicard, Introduction, notes et appendices par D. Poirel (Turnhout, 1997), 18–114, at 48: 'Sicut enim de inconstantia mentis nascitur inordinata motio corporis, ita quoque, dum corpus per disciplinam stringitur, animus ad constantiam solidatur. Et paulatim intrinsecus mens ad quietem componitur, cum per discipline custodiam mali motus eius foras fluere non sinuntur.'

[46] See *Scripta Leonis, Rufini et Angeli sociorum S. Francisci. The Writings of Leo, Rufino and Angelo, Companions of St. Francis*, 4, ed. and trans. R. B. Brooke, Oxford Medieval Texts, Corrected Reprint (Oxford, 1970), 94–95.

The suspicion of any *singularitas* is a case in point. For example, as the author of the *Vita Siardi* explains in a sort of inner monologue, the singular thought may occur to him that on Friday, out of respect for the Lord's sufferings, he might not want to eat eggs, because carnal birds come out of eggs. However, refraining from eating eggs may then either give rise to the thought that he should have some fish instead, or another brother might think that he wishes to be holier than the others.[47] It is thus best to keep to the common rule.

The topos of 'doing what you preach', and thus Siard's exemplarity, is made to fit in this context as well. If Siard refused to dress in short furcoats, which had become fashionable among the brothers, this soberness was rewarded with the inner stole of virtues. But transparency is not to be taken for granted: dressing appropriately simply does not automatically mean that one is inwardly virtuous; but neither is it the other way round. Refined cloths may cover inside virtues, and under a poor garment the soul may be sordid.[48] On the other hand, if a brother comes to the choir without the appropriate dress, there is no reason to blame him; just tell him gently afterwards what the rule is: a rule that aims at external conformity as a sign of conformity and equality of the inner men.[49]

Inwardness and community

As this last example has shown, the idea of inwardness is embedded within that of community. More than in the Life of the founder or than in the portrait of his successors in the collective *Vita* following the Life of Siard, Siard stands out as a centre of the community. Fretheric was the efficient founder, sometimes quite distant and vengeful in his behaviour. Siard's relation to his brothers and to the wider surroundings is of a more intimate nature, as he teaches them as their example and model, but even more, he participates in the life of the community. Thus, he refuses to have special dishes prepared for him: he once entered the kitchen to see how the food was prepared for everyone, and saw a little separate pot. When he asked what it was, the brother explained it was some parsley soup, which would be good for kidney stones from which Siard was suffering. Siard took the pot and threw the contents into the big pot, saying that if it was good for him, it was good for everyone: let all that is ours be common, in imitation of the rule of the Apostles.[50] This was the occasion where the author explains the need to inwardly say 'ours', as I have discussed earlier.

---

47 *Vita Siardi* 5, 272.

48 *Ibid.* 7, 278.

49 *Ibid.* 7, 278–80.

50 *Ibid.* 5, 268.

As we have seen, Siard insists in doing his fair share of manual labour, whether it be work on the land or in copying books. The books that he produces are for the common use of the community, which provokes the author to denounce the private possession of books.[51] Moreover, Siard combined humility within the community with his status as their father when admonishing them. He was 'kind and accommodating' to his brothers, exhorting them, in travelling together, that they 'should depart cheerfully, be together peacefully and return faithfully'.[52] In the broader community of the lay people of the neighbourhood he was a peaceworker – here the *Vita* reflects the political reality of the time, when abbots ofen played a role as judges in Frisia where a central authority was absent.[53] However, he would always wait for people to ask him for help, because he did not do this for the sake of glory. He also knew that it was often difficult to re-establish the peace without running into difficulties.[54]

Another example of Siard's moderateness and openness that strikes the reader is his behaviour during journeys. Once he took a detour to visit a relative. When he finds him blind, Siard cures him.[55] Such a deed is far from being a common hagiographical pattern, where saints usually refuse to acknowledge anybody as a carnal relative.

During another visit he and his companions heard singing and dancing in a village – probably at a wedding party.[56] One would more usually expect a condemnation of such worldly recreation in a saint's life.[57] Far from condemning it, however, Siard has his companions take some rest and starts to meditate, in accordance with the harmony of the songs:[58]

---

[51] *Ibid.* 12, 292–94.

[52] *Ibid.* 15, 302–04.

[53] A. Mulder-Bakker, 'De vrede van de abten', *Het Noorden in het midden*, ed. de Boer *et al.*, 3–17.

[54] *Vita Siardi*, 16, 304–06.

[55] *Ibid.* 21, 314–16.

[56] See Bremmer, *Hir es eskriven*, 120

[57] See, for example, in the twelfth-century *Liber restaurationis Sancti Martini Tornacensis*, written by Herman of Tournai, about the people in Tournai who have forgotten the origins of the yearly processions, meant to avert the plague, where one finds now 'more gaiety than religion and devotion', ed. M. G. Waitz, MGH Scriptores 14, 274–317, at 277 (Chapter Six) and Herman of Tournai, *The Restoration of the Monastery of Saint-Martin of Tournai*, trans. L. H. Nelson (Washington, 1996), 21.

[58] *Vita Siardi* 19, 310–12: 'Preterea iste bonus pater qui in tanta custodia sensus sui corporis ne mors aut mortis imago per fenestras illas intraret, ita fuit collectus in Deum et promptum spiritum habuit, ut cum dulcem audiret armoniam sepius in Dei amorem et contemplationem raperetur. Contigit itaque quodam tempore ut cum capellanis suis transiret prope villam que vocatur Ethelenge, in qua concordem cantum chorizantium equo insidens audivit. Dixitque fratribus: Divertamus a communi via in secretum locum, et paululum expectemus. Sicque factum est, et descenderunt de equis et in quadam sicca

> [...] Siard would be so concentrated on God and be prepared in his spirit, that, when he heard a sweet harmony, he would be rapt in love for God and contemplation. Thus it happened once that he and his chaplains passed by a village called Jellum, where, sitting on his horse, he heard the harmonious singing of some dancers. He said to his brothers: 'Let us turn from the common road to a remote spot and wait there a while'. So they did, and they got off their horses and paused in some dry and grass-covered ditch under the willows. The father himself, however, arms and breast leaning on the saddle, began through the harmony of the singing with sweet tears to meditate about the harmonious jubilation of the holy angels, and about the never-ending marriage supper of the Lamb (Rev. 19, 9) and of the Church triumphant, oblivious of the transitory harmony, absorbed in that one that is above. And none of the chaplains said: 'What are we waiting for here?' They were heeding what is read in the Canticle: 'I adjure you, daughters of Jerusalem, by the gazelles or the wild does, do not stir up or awaken the beloved until he wishes' (Cant. 2, 7; 3, 5). Finally, because he could not cross the boundary which the Lord had set him to be dissolved and be with Christ (Phil. 1, 23), the good father laid down the wings of contemplation and said to the brothers: 'Shall we go from here?' And they nodded, saying: 'Dearest father, why did you want to linger here?' He said to them: 'Truly, brothers, from the round dance that we heard coming from the other side of the village, the desire took me to stay a while and to meditate on how the Lord Jesus, the Bridegroom of the Church, surrounded by the round dances of the virgins and all the saints, forever makes them joyful, and on what feast it will be there, where the Bridegroom of the Church, the Lord Jesus himself, will go round and minister his beloved spouse. Hearing this, the brothers knew that such a joy was revealed to him by divine revelation.

---

et graminosa fossa sub salicibus moram fecerunt. Ipse autem bonus pater brachiis et pectore incumbens selle, ex concordia cantus cepit dulcibus lachrimis meditari de concordi iubilatione sanctorum angelorum, et perpetuis nuptiis agni (Rev. 19, 9) et ecclesie triumphantis, oblitus armonie transitorie, in illam que sursum est absorptus. Nec aliquis capellanorum dicebat: quid hic moramur? Servantes quod legitur in Canticis Canticorum: Adiuro vos filie Iherusalem per capreas cervosque camporum, ne suscitetis neque evigilare faciatis dilectum donec ipse velit (Cant. 2, 7; 3, 5). Denique bonus pater quia non potuit transgredi terminum quem posuit ei Dominus ut dissolveretur et esset cum Christo (cf. Philipp. 1, 23), deposuit alas contemplationis dicens fratribus: Volumus hinc abire? Et annuerunt illi dicentes: Carissime pater cur hic moram fecistis? Quibus ipse dixit: Vere fratres ex chorea quam audivimus ex alia parte ville, libuit michi moram facere et meditari qualiter Dominus Ihesus sponsus ecclesie, septus choreis virginum et sanctorum omnium, ipsos in perpetuum letificat (cf. Isaiah 56, 7), et qualis ibi sit solemnitas ubi ipse sponsus ecclesie Dominus Ihesus transiens ministrabit sue sponse dilecte. Hoc audientes fratres, cognoverunt tale gaudium ei divinitus revelatum.' For the author's admonition with which this passage concludes, see above, note 29.

The passage illustrates in a way that is typical for the whole Vita, namely how, literally in this case, the Frisian landscape encloses the life of the saint and the monks. It also exemplifies the associative knitting together of biblical associations that is found throughout the work. It shows especially how Siard's contemplation, however high it momentarily elevates him above the world, is at once less 'unworldly' – provoked as it is by presumably secular singing, taking place near a dry ditch under the willows – and less exclusively personal than one would maybe expect. If the account of Siard's contemplative moments is perhaps not yet suggesting the mystical union that became increasingly current in saints' lives during the thirteenth century, it certainly is profoundly indicative of Siard as the centre of his community.

Conclusion

Constance Brittain Bouchard has shown for twelfth-century Auxerre how in the succession of bishops more and less business oriented bishops often succeeded each other, and how this is reflected in their hagiographies or biographies.[59] Such a mechanism may have played a role in the life of Mariëngaarde and its abbots. In the Life of Fretheric we see a determined founder, well immersed in local affairs. Siard, according to other sources, looked after the interest of the community,[60] and the *Vita Siardi* implicitly acknowledges his role in this respect. However, the emphasis is on Siard as a spiritual leader. His successors, who are discussed in one Life, are shown once again as predominantly good administrators. Even within the series of these three Lives, however, a similar alternation is noticeable. After Sibrand, whose administrative efficiency is well elaborated in the Life, the aged and inevitably less efficient Iarich is chosen. He in his turn is succeeded as abbot by Ethelger, who may even have been too young then for this office, but who developed as an active player on the monastic scene in Frisia.

This pattern may help to account for the character of Siard as the anonymous author describes it. This does not exclude, rather it implies the possibility that the other element to which I alluded, the hagiographical self-perpetuation which Vauchez observed in later medieval hagiography, played a role as well.[61] From this point of view there is not necessarily a dilemma between a 'real person' and an idealised portrait.

---

[59] C. Brittain Bouchard, *Spirituality and Administration: The Role of Bishops in Twelfth-Century Auxerre*, Speculum Anniversary Monographs 5 (Cambridge, MA, 1979), 141–44.

[60] See, e.g., the *Vita Sibrandi, Iarici, Ethelgeri*, in *Vitae abbatum* 354; 358.

[61] See above, note 15.

It is, moreover, the hagiographical perspective, which raises the life of a modest prior and his community above the concerns of the local level and imparts an air of universality onto the Frisian background. The Siard of the *Vita* may not have embodied what were the most fashionable virtues for a saint in other parts of Europe in the thirteenth century. We find in his Life no intimate Marian devotion or Meditations on the Life of Jesus. However, he combines many elements that had long been part of the slowly moving world of hagiographical and monastic ideals which were still relevant. Maybe the *Vita Siardi* is less exciting than the Lives of Siard's predecessor and successors. Yet, in recommending to its readers the *vita apostolica* and care for the poor, the *vita angelica* and anticipation of apocalyptic joy, and through its combination of action and contemplation, and of inwardness and community, this work of an anonymous Frisian writer pays tribute to quiet unpretentiousness shot through with glimpses of heavenly bliss.

Her Bendix is wrbeck fonden. Die altfriesische Terminologie im Bereich des Zivilprozessrechtes

Oebele Vries

1. EINFÜHRUNG[1]

Am 28. Juli 1507 versammelten sich auf Befehl des sächsischen Statthalters in Westfriesland, Heinrich Graf von Stolberg und Wernigerode, in der Hauptstadt Leeuwarden sämtliche *grietmannen*, d.h. die Richter in den Landbezirken dieser Landschaft. Ziel der Versammlung war die Darlegung von 'mannigfachen Klagen seitens unserer gnädigen Herrn Untersassen' bezüglich Gerichtsbarkeit und Verwaltung, die beim Statthalter eingegangen wären, bzw. die Ermahnung der zusammengekommenen Richter, künftig in jeder Hinsicht gemäß der Ordonnanz des sächsischen Herzoges d.J. 1504, d.h. der sg. Sächsischen Ordonnanz, zu handeln.[2] Die uns hier interessierende Klage bezieht sich auf das Verfahren in den Zivilprozessen. Der einschlägige Abschnitt des in niederländischer Sprache abgefassten Rezesses der Versammlung beginnt so:

> An ons is oeck vaste claghes wyse ghelanghet, dat die Gherechts processen oenordentlyck gheholden worden ('An uns ist auch häufig die Klage gelangt, dass die Gerichtsprozesse unordentlich abgehalten werden').

Darauf folgt, neben anderen Punkten, bemerkenswerterweise auch eine Äußerung zur benutzten Terminologie:

> desghelyckx worden daer nae die ordelen ende sententien oenformelyck wuytghesproecken, *alzo ick wyse die man voert, ende den to beck &c.*, ('desgleichen werden danach die Urteile und Sentenzen nicht der Form gemäß ausgesprochen, *also ich weise diesen Mann fort und jenen zurück u.s.w.*).

[1] Ich danke Prof. Mr. P. Gerbenzon, Dr. B. S. Hempenius-van Dijk und Drs. A. T. Popkema für ihre wertvollen Hinweise.

[2] Text des Rezesses einschließlich der angehängten Artikel: GPCB II, 70–73. Vgl. auch P. Gerbenzon, 'Enkele nieuwe gegevens over de receptie van het Romeinse recht in Friesland', *TRG* 27 (1959), 133–57, hier 150–52 (versehentlich mit falscher Datierung: 18. statt 28. Juli).

Der Richter sollte stattdessen in seiner Sentenz klar aussprechen, *wat elcke part ghewonnen oft verloren heeft* ('was jede Partei gewonnen oder verloren hat'). In den angehängten 'Artikeln' wird der terminologische 'Missstand' noch einmal, allerdings mit etwas abweichendem Wortlaut, umschrieben, und zwar folgendermaßen:

> Naedeen oeck die Onderrechters in huer sententie ghewoentlyck pleeghen te schryuen, dat zie tot des enen parts profyt ende tot des anderen achterdeel een sententie weesen, ... ('Indem auch die Unterrichter [d.h. die *grietmannen*] in ihrer Sentenz üblicherweise zu schreiben pflegen, dass sie zum Vorteil der einen Partei und zum Nachteil der anderen Urteil sprachen, ...').

Der hier kurz skizzierte Vorgang d.J. 1507 macht einen Aspekt der anscheinend als typisch friesisch empfundenen, von den sächsischen Behörden jedoch als unklar und somit als überholt betrachteten Terminologie im Bereich des Zivilprozesses in Westfriesland sichtbar. Ziel des vorliegenden Aufsatzes ist die diachron-semantische Bearbeitung gerade dieses 'juristischen Wortfeldes' im Altfriesischen.[3] Ausgangspunkt der Untersuchung ist das Verfahren im Zivilprozess in den jüngeren, d.h. insbesondere aus dem 15. Jh. stammenden, aber noch nicht vom 'gelehrten', d.h. kanonischen und römischen Recht beeinflussten Rechtsquellen aus Westfriesland. Es wird allerdings ebenfalls Bezug genommen auf die älteren Rechtsquellen dieses Gebietes, und zwar insbesondere das Ältere und das Jüngere Schulzenrecht. Berücksichtigt wird, soweit möglich, auch die in den Quellen leider nur schwach vertretene Prozessterminologie im osterlauwersschen Teil Frieslands.

2. Der Zivilprozess im mittelalterlichen Friesland

Unter Zivilprozess versteht man das Gerichtsverfahren zwischen Privatpersonen, das in erster Linie dazu dient, den zwischen ihnen entstandenen Streit, insbesondere bezüglich vermögensrechtlicher Ansprüche seitens der einen Partei auf die andere, durch richterliches Urteil entscheiden zu lassen.[4] Ein komplizierender Faktor ist der Umstand, dass im 14. bis 16. Jh. eine Zäsur liegt, die einerseits durch die Aufnahme des weitgehend verschrifteten

---

[3] Vgl. O. Vries, 'The Importance of Legal History for Old Frisian Lexicography', *Dictionaries of Medieval Germanic Languages: A Survey of Current Lexicographical Projects*, K. H. van Dalen-Oskam u.a., Hg. (Turnhout, 1997), 135–47.

[4] HRG, s.v. *Zivilprozeß*.

romano-kanonischen Zivilprozesses und andererseits durch die Aufspaltung des Gerichtsverfahrens in einen Zivil- und einen Strafprozess bedingt ist.[5]

Die vorliegende Untersuchung beschränkt sich auf das traditionelle, noch nicht oder nur kaum verschriftete Verfahren germanischer Prägung, wie es im mittelalterlichen Friesland üblich war. Demnach ist die kanonistisch fundierte kirchliche Gerichtsbarkeit, die ihren Niederschlag im Sendverfahren fand, hier grundsätzlich ausgeklammert. Auch das romano-kanonische Gerichtsverfahren, das in Westfriesland ab 1504 in kurzer Zeit den traditionellen Prozess völlig verdrängte, bleibt hier außer Betracht. Auf die romano-kanonischen friesischen Texte (Rudolfsbuch, *Haet is riucht*, *Excerpta legum* und *Jurisprudentia Frisica*) sowie das romano-kanonische Prozesshandbuch *Processus Judicii* (Übersetzung der lateinischen 'Summa Antequam') wird somit nicht oder nur ausnahmsweise Bezug genommen. Der Strafprozess (die 'peinliche Klage'), der sich in den jüngeren friesischen Rechtsquellen bereits ziemlich deutlich vom Zivilprozess abhebt, wird ebenfalls nicht berücksichtigt.

Das mittelalterliche friesische Prozessrecht germanischer Prägung ist erstaunlicherweise bislang kaum erforscht worden. In seiner Studie über die ältere Phase des afr. Rechts beschreibt Algra beispielsweise lediglich den Prozessgang in der *Lex Frisionum* (um 800).[6] Dieses Verfahren unterscheidet sich allerdings nicht grundsätzlich von demjenigen gemäß den aus der sg. Grafenzeit (bis etwa 1250) stammenden Schulzenrechten, wenn auch in der *Lex Frisionum* weder Schulze noch Graf noch der für die Schulzenrechte charakteristische Rechtsvorsprecher (Asega) erwähnt werden. Die sg. 'höhere Klage' (die Schritte 9 und 10 in der nachstehenden Übersicht des Verfahrens gemäß den Schulzenrechten), eine verstärkte Form der Klage, wobei der Kläger durch sofort beigefügtes Beweisanerbieten die Verteidigung des Beklagten wesentlich erschwert,[7] stellt eine grundsätzliche Neuerung dar, die sich in den Schulzenrechten durchgesetzt hat.

Das Verfahren gemäß den Schulzenrechten lässt sich folgendermaßen zusammenfassen:[8]

1) Der Kläger (oder sein Vorsprecher)[9] erhebt in der Gerichtssitzung Klage und fordert Genugtuung.

---

5 HRG, s.v. *Gerichtsverfahren*.

6 N. E. Algra, *Oudfries recht 800–1256* (Leeuwarden, 2000), 113–14.

7 J. J. W. Planck, *Das Deutsche Gerichtsverfahren im Mittelalter*, 2 Bde. (Braunschweig, 1879) I, 369–72.

8 Dieses basiert insbesondere auf den Artikeln 36 und 37 des Älteren Schulzenrechts sowie den Artikeln 1 und 34 des Jüngeren Schulzenrechts.

9 Von der Erwähnung der Möglichkeit des Auftretens eines Vorsprechers als Vertreter des Klägers oder des Beklagten wird im weiteren abgesehen. Dieser Vorsprecher sollte nicht mit dem Rechtsvorsprecher (Asega) verwechselt werden.

2) Der Beklagte wird vom Schulzen vorgeladen.
3) In der einberufenen Gerichtssitzung erscheinen der Kläger und der Beklagte. Falls der Beklagte die Gerichtstermine versäumt, ist er überführt.
4) Der Kläger trägt seine Klage vor.
5) Der Schulze (oder der Graf) fordert den Beklagten auf, entweder zu gestehen oder zu leugnen. Nötigenfalls erkennt der Asega dieses Gebot.
6) Gesteht der Beklagte, so ist er überführt und soll er dem Kläger die vom Asega für die verübte Tat festgesetzte Genugtuung verschaffen.
7) Leugnet der Beklagte und bietet er an, sich eidlich, d.h. mit der erforderlichen Zahl von Eideshelfern, von der Klage zu reinigen, so hat sich, falls es ihm gelingt, die erforderliche Zahl beizubringen, die Klage erledigt. Falls er nicht imstande ist, sich zu reinigen, so ist er überführt und soll er dem Kläger die vom Asega für die verübte Tat festgesetzte Genugtuung verschaffen.
8) Falls der Kläger den Eid des Beklagten zurückweist, so erfolgt ein Gottesurteil (Zweikampf).
9) Falls der Kläger den Beklagten 'höher' angeklagt hat und der Beklagte leugnet und anbietet, sich eidlich zu reinigen, so hat der Kläger 'näheres' Recht, mit qualifizierten Zeugen des Beklagten Schuld zu beweisen als der Beklagte, sich zu reinigen.
10) Falls der Kläger bei der 'höheren Klage' mit qualifizierten Zeugen des Beklagten Schuld beweist, so ist der Beklagte überführt und soll er dem Kläger die vom Asega für die verübte Tat festgesetzte Genugtuung verschaffen.

Auch in den jüngeren, fast ausschließlich aus der Spätphase des 1498 abgeschlossenen Zeitalters der friesischen Freiheit stammenden westfriesischen Rechtsquellen begegnet immer noch ein durch strenge Förmlichkeit auffallendes mündliches Prozessverfahren. Der gräfliche Schulze, dessen Rolle im Grunde auf das Fragen des Rechts beschränkt war, hat allerdings dem nicht-herrschaftlichen, selbst urteilenden Richter Platz gemacht, und nicht nur der Graf, sondern auch der Asega ist von der Bildfläche verschwunden. Eine ins Auge fallende Neuerung ist die im Rahmen des Verfahrens stattfindende Pfandsetzung. Eine notwendigerweise modellhafte, auf die Wesenszüge beschränkte Darstellung des Verfahrens in den jüngeren westfriesischen Quellen (auch den städtischen) sieht so aus:[10]

1) Der Kläger (oder sein Vorsprecher)[11] erhebt am Gerichtstag Klage vor dem Gericht, wobei er sein Pfand anbietet (oder bereits übergibt).[12]

[10] Basiert insbesondere auf O II 82, IV 8 und SnR 197.
[11] Wie Anm. 9.
[12] Letzteres ist der Fall in O II 82.

2) Der Beklagte wird vom Richter vorgeladen.
3) Auf dem einberufenen Gerichtstag erscheinen der Kläger und der Beklagte. Falls der Beklagte die Gerichtstermine versäumt, ist er überführt.
4) Der Kläger übergibt sein Pfand (falls er das nicht bereits getan hat) und trägt seine Klage vor.
5) Der Richter fragt den Beklagten, nötigenfalls an mehreren Gerichtstagen, ob er ebenfalls ein Pfand übergeben und seine Unschuld bezeugen will.
6) Falls dies der Fall ist, so übergibt der Beklagte ebenfalls sein Pfand und bezeugt seine Unschuld.
7) Es erfolgen die Rede und die Gegenrede der Parteien.
8) Das Gericht fällt meistens mehrere Zwischenurteile, wobei beispielsweise eine der beiden Parteien aufgefordert wird, ihre Behauptungen mit Zeugen oder Schriftstücken zu beweisen.
9) In letzterem Fall fragt das Gericht den Prozessgegner, ob er dem angebotenen Beweis widersprechen will.
10) Falls der Prozessgegner dem angebotenen Beweis nicht widerspricht, hat er sein Recht verwirkt.
11) Das Gericht fällt ein Endurteil.
12) Die ins Unrecht gesetzte Partei kann das Urteil 'schelten', d.h. anfechten.
13) Falls die Parteien das Urteil annehmen, d.h. das Urteil nicht gescholten wird, erlangt es Rechtskraft.

Es handelt sich hier um das bloße Grundmuster des Verfahrens, das in den weiteren Einzelheiten zweifelsohne regional mehr oder weniger unterschiedlich ausgestaltet war. So fällt auf, dass in den Willküren von Wymbritseradeel d.J. 1404 (s. unten) Rede und Gegenrede, die sonst immer mündlich erfolgen, bereits wie im romano-kanonischen Verfahren in schriftlicher Form verlangt werden.[13]

Die jüngere Form des traditionellen Verfahrens begegnet hauptsächlich in folgenden Quellen:

1. den Willküren von Wymbritseradeel (*Papena ponten*), 1404;[14]
2. den Willküren von Utingeradeel (*Utendengeradelis riocht*), 1450;[15]

---

[13] P. Gerbenzon, *Excerpta legum. Onderzoekingen betreffende enkele Friese rechtsboeken uit de vijftiende eeuw* (Groningen und Djakarta, 1956), 373–74.

[14] *Westerlauwerssches Recht I, Jus Municipale Frisonum*, W. J. Buma und W. Ebel (unter Mitwirkung von M. Tragter-Schubert), Hg., AR 6 (Göttingen, 1977), 612–27; M. Oosterhout, 'De "Papena Ponten"', *Wymbritseradiel. Skiednis fan in greidgritenij*, G. Bakker, Hg. (Boalsert, 1974), 63–83 (mit neufriesischer Übersetzung).

[15] O II 29.

3. den Stadtrechten von Bolsward (1455, 1479) und Sneek (1456) (in ndl. Sprache);[16]
4. einigen Urkunden;[17]
5. der Stadttafel von Sneek, 1490–1497 (in deren Fortsetzung, dem teilweise niederländischsprachigen Rezessbuch von Sneek, 1506–1517, setzt sich das romano-kanonische Verfahren durch).[18]

3. Die untersuchten Begriffe

Es kann sich hier lediglich um eine Auswahl der im Prozessverfahren gängigen Termini handeln. Besprochen werden die Bezeichnungen der nachstehenden Begriffe, zunächst in den jüngeren und, gegebenenfalls, auch in den älteren Quellen. Letztere werden, falls sie nicht allgemeinfriesisch sind, wie die Siebzehn Küren und die Vierundzwanzig Landrechte, in westerlauwerssche (d.h. westfriesische) und osterlauwerssche (d.h. ommelandische und ostfriesische) differenziert.

Klagen und Klage (3.1.)
Kläger und Beklagter (3.2.)
Vorladen und Vorladung (3.3.)
Einsetzen von Pfändern (3.4.)
Rede und Gegenrede (3.5.)
Urteilen (3.6.)
Urteil (3.7.)
Schelten des Urteils (3.8.)

Die einschlägige Terminologie in den Nachbarsprachen des Altfriesischen, dem Mittelniederländischen und dem Mittelniederdeutschen, ist bislang noch weithin unerforscht. Parallelen aus diesen Sprachen werden ausnahmsweise berücksichtigt.

3.1. Klagen und Klage

Dieses Begriffsfeld wurde bereits von Freudenthal (1949) erforscht. Die von ihm aufgestellte Liste von afr. Bezeichnungen in diesem Bereich ist beein-

---

[16] *De Friesche Stadrechten*, A. Telting, Hg. ('s-Gravenhage, 1883), 9–180.

[17] Die wichtigsten sind: O I 42, II 82, IV 7, 8, 9. Vgl. zu O IV 7: E. H. Bary und M. P. van Buijtenen, 'Synode en seendrecht. Doorwerking in middeleeuws Friesland', *Kerk in beraad. Opstellen aangeboden aan prof. dr. J. C. P. A. van Laarhoven bij gelegenheid van zijn afscheid als hoogleraar aan de Katholieke Universiteit Nijmegen*, G. Ackermans, A. Davids und P. J. A. Nissen, Hg. (Nijmegen, 1991), 103–23, hier 112–14.

[18] SnR 1–2039 (Stadttafel) bzw. 2040–5290 (Rezessbuch).

druckend.[19] Dennoch ist sie ziemlich ungenau, indem sich der Autor kritiklos auf die damals verfügbaren Wörterbücher stützt, und erschöpfend ist sie noch keinesfalls, denn das reiche afr. Urkundenkorpus wird nicht einbezogen. Nicht alle von Freudenthal angeführten Begriffe im Bereich des Klagens werden im Nachfolgenden erörtert, weil dieser Abschnitt sonst den Rahmen dieses Aufsatzes sprengen würde.

Die im Verfahren ganz wesentliche Handlung des Klagens, mit welcher der Prozess eingeleitet wurde, wird in den jüngeren westfriesischen Quellen gewöhnlich mit der wörtlichen Entsprechung bezeichnet. Im Afr. begegnet sie daher in der Form *klagia*. Dieses Verb kann auch mit der Präposition *up-* ('auf') zusammengesetzt sein, wie in den Willküren von Wymbritseradeel und in den Willküren von Utingeradeel, jeweils mit einer Person als Objekt. Die genaue Bedeutung ist in diesem Fall somit '(jemand) anklagen, verklagen'. So heißt es in Art. 22 der Wymbritseradeeler Küren: *hwae soe en oerne opclaghet* ('wenn jemand einen anderen verklagt'). Die Mündlichkeit der Handlung wird durch die Bezeichnung *onspreka* (wörtlich 'ansprechen') betont, die in einigen Urkunden sowie in der Sneeker Stadttafel begegnet.[20] Dieses Verb kann ebenfalls mit einer Person als Objekt verbunden sein.

Als Substantive begegnen *klage* sowie *onspreke*. Daneben stoßen wir ausnahmsweise auf den Terminus *reppinge* (wörtlich: 'Berührung'). Das ist etwa der Fall in einer Urkunde d.J. 1474: *ner aec enich reppinghe jeff claghe toe mettyen* ('noch auch jegliche Klage [2x] zu erheben').[21] Ob die Begriffe *klage* und *reppinge* völlig synonym sind, lässt sich nicht feststellen. Der Begriff *reppinge* begegnet weiterhin lediglich in Schriftstücken d.J. 1488 und 1489.[22] Das Benennungsmotiv ist undeutlich.

Die Bezeichnung des Begriffes 'klagen' bzw. 'anklagen, verklagen' mit dem Verb *klagia* (einmal *upklagia*) ist auch in den Schulzenrechten belegt.[23]

[19] K. F. Freudenthal, *Arnulfingisch-karolingische Rechtswörter. Eine Studie in der juristischen Terminologie der ältesten germanischen Dialekte* (Göteborg, 1949), 141–46.

[20] Z.B. O I 42: SnR 42, 1854, 1991.

[21] O I 253.

[22] O II 161, 165. Vgl. auch L.-E. Ahlsson, *Die altfriesischen Abstraktbildungen* (Uppsala, 1960), 81, sowie O. Vries, 'Een communalistische voorloper van het Hof van Friesland: de colleges van recht en raad van Oostergo en Westergo', *500 jaar Hof van Friesland. Bijdragen aan het herdenkingssymposium, gehouden te Leeuwarden 24 september 1999*, D. P. de Vries und P. Nieuwland, Hg. (Hilversum und Leeuwarden, 2000), 25–40, hier 34.

[23] N. E. Algra, 'Rechtshistorische aspecten van het *Landrecht der Vriesne*', *Landrecht der Vriesne: tekstuitgave en commentaar*, Ph. H. Breuker, Hg. (Leeuwarden, 1996), 91–223, hier 125, 198, wählt für das im Älteren Schulzenrecht (Art. 57) einmal belegte Verb *upklagia* die spezifischere Übersetzung 'vor einem höheren Gericht anklagen', und zwar lediglich aufgrund der Tatsache, dass *up* 'nach oben, aufwärts' bedeuten kann. Dies kann jedoch nicht überzeugen, insbesondere nicht, weil sich das Verb *upklagia* in den Willküren von Wymbritseradeel und Utingeradeel keinesfalls auf die Klage vor einem

Am häufigsten stößt man in diesen älteren westfriesischen Quellen jedoch auf ein weniger durchsichtiges Verb, und zwar *greta* (wörtlich: 'grüßen'), das ebenfalls sowohl mit einer Person als Objekt wie auch ohne Objekt verwendet wird. Als Beispiel diene hier Art. 24 des Jüngeren Schulzenrechts (zitiert wird der Text der Handschrift Jus), der sich auf den Fall bezieht, dass ein bestohlener Mann sich mit dem Diebe aussöhnt, worauf der Schulze gegen den Bestohlenen Klage erhebt: *zoe wol di scelta greta ende sprect aldus: 'Jc bitighie ioe dis ...'* ('so will der Schulze Klage erheben und spricht wie folgt: "Ich beschuldige Sie dessen ..."').[24] Zur Bezeichnung der verstärkten Form der Klage (vgl. Abschnitt 2.) begegnet im Jüngeren Schulzenrecht (Art. 1a) der Ausdruck *hag(e)ra greta* (wörtlich: 'höher klagen').

Im westfriesischen Bereich hat sich auf der Basis der sich dort ergebenden semantischen Entwicklung des Verbs *greta* die Zusammensetzung *gretman* (wörtlich: 'Grussmann', d.h. Klagemann) herausgebildet, und zwar zur Bezeichnung des im Zeitabschnitt der Friesischen Freiheit in Westfriesland amtierenden nicht-herrschaftlichen Richters. Mit dieser Benennung wurde betont, dass die Anklage von Amts wegen ('ex officio') eine der Hauptaufgaben dieses Amtsträgers darstellte.[25] So wird es auch zum Ausdruck gebracht im Amtseid der *grietmannen* (*grietman* ist eine jüngere Form von *gretman*) von Wymbritseradeel: *dat yemme dat al riuchtelike grete ende riuchte* ('dass ihr das völlig rechtsgemäß anklagt und aburteilt').[26]

Der Begriff 'Klage' wird in den Schulzenrechten mit dem von *greta* abgeleiteten Substantiv *gretene* oder auch mit der Zusammensetzung *gretwerd* (wörtlich: 'Grusswort', d.h. Grussgebot) bezeichnet. Im Jüngeren Schulzenrecht ist auch einmal von *onspreke* die Rede (Art. 29), aber lediglich in einer vermutlich aus späterer Zeit stammenden Überschrift dieses Artikels in der Handschrift Jus.

In einem dem Alter nach mit den Schulzenrechten vergleichbaren Text, dem Marktrecht (*Merkedriucht*), begegnet das Verb *onthingia* (wörtlich: 'andingen') als Bezeichnung des Verklagens.[27] Mit dieser Umschreibung wird allerdings nicht die Handlung des Klagens, sondern das 'vor das Gericht (*thing*) bringen' der Streitsache hervorgehoben. Der Begriff *thingia*

höheren Gericht bezieht (s. oben).

24 *Westerlauwersches Recht I*, Buma und Ebel, Hg., 224.

25 M. S. van Oosten, *De ambtshalve vervolging naar Oud-Friesch recht* (Leiden, 1938), 36–37. Die Anklage seitens des *grietman* war allerdings wohl ersatzweise ('subsidiär'), d.h. für den Fall, dass ein Verbrechen nicht bestraft wurde, indem die verletzte Partei das Klagen unterließ.

26 *Westerlauwersches Recht I*, Buma und Ebel, Hg., 628.

27 *Ibid.* 244.

bezieht sich freilich nicht, wie Buma und Ebel meinen, auf die Handlung des Klagens, sondern auf das Prozessieren.[28]

Wenden wir uns jetzt den osterlauwersschen Quellen zu. Eine Fülle von Belegen begegnet hier im Brokmerbrief. Die übliche Bezeichnung für die Handlung des Klagens ist hier das Verb *baria*.[29] In § 124 heißt es beispielsweise: *Thet wellath Brocmen, thet ma thria barie* ('Dies wollen die Brokmer, dass man dreimal Klage erhebt').[30] Auch hier ist die Verbindung mit einer Person als Objekt möglich, wie in § 130: *Barath ma enne thiaf* ('Klagt man einen Dieb an'). Weiterhin begegnet das Verb *baria* in dieser Bedeutung im vom Brokmerbrief beeinflussten Emsinger Pfennigschuldbuch, und zwar in § 28 und 29 (letzterer scheint freilich § 130 des Brokmerbriefs entnommen zu sein). In § 28 fällt ein Unterschied zwischen den beiden Fassungen dieses Textes auf: in der Handschrift E2 heißt es: *Olrec monne mot baria hwane sa hi wel* ('Jeder Mann darf anklagen, wen er will'), in der Handschrift E3 hingegen: *Allermonnik mot ma baria, thet is wrklagie* ('Jeden Mann darf man anklagen, das ist verklagen').[31] Das Besondere hier ist die Erklärung des Wortes *baria* mit Hilfe des Synonyms *urklagia*. Offenbar wurde das Wort *baria* vom Abschreiber der Handschrift E3 oder bereits in deren Vorlage als nicht mehr einleuchtend betrachtet, weswegen ein besser verständliches Synonym hinzugefügt wurde. Das Wort *baria* war allerdings auch in den Ommelanden bekannt, wie einige Belege in lediglich in niederdeutscher Übersetzung überlieferten Willküren, insbesondere denen von Humsterland, beweisen.[32]

---

28 Vgl. W. J. Buma, *Vollständiges Wörterbuch zum westerlauwersschen Jus Municipale Frisonum* (Leeuwarden, 1996), s.v. *thingia*. Bedeutung I.3 ist hier zu streichen (die einschlägigen Verweise gehören unter Bedeutung I.2).

29 Die von Buma und Ebel verwendete Übersetzung 'Sühneklage erheben' wurde von Algra aus gutem Grund kritisiert (N. E. Algra, Besprechung von *Das Brokmer Recht*, W. J. Buma und W. Ebel, Hg., in *TRG* 36 [1968], 599–611, hier 609–11). Dessen eigene Übersetzung ('den Frieden kündigen') ist allerdings auch nicht präzise. Algra nimmt keine Rücksicht auf die Zusammensetzung *ienbare*, mit der dem Begriff 'Gegenklage, Gegenrede' bezeichnet wird (s. Abschnitt 3.5.), und er vernachlässigt die Übersetzungsgleichung in der Handschrift E3 (*baria, thet is wrklagie*) (s. Anm. 31). Vgl. auch Th. S. B. Johnston, *Codex Hummercensis (Groningen, UB, PEIP 12). An Old Frisian Legal Manuscript in Low Saxon Guise* (Leeuwarden, 1998), 189, 566 ('to file a charge').

30 Sämtliche Verweise auf den Brokmerbrief sind *Das Brokmer Recht*, W. J. Buma und W. Ebel, Hg., AR 2 (Göttingen, 1965), entnommen.

31 *Das Emsiger Recht*, W. J. Buma und W. Ebel, Hg., AR 3 (Göttingen, 1967), 158, 216.

32 Johnston, *Codex Hummercensis*, 566.

Das Simplex *bare* gehört, wie bereits Van Helten dargestellt hat, zu altem **bar*, 'offenbar'.[33] Die wörtliche Bedeutung des Verbs *baria* ist somit 'offenbaren'. Im westfriesischen Bereich hat sich diese Bedeutung augenscheinlich behauptet, z.B. in Art. 33 und 67 des Älteren Schulzenrechts, wie auch, und zwar in der Form *foerd ti barriane* ('weiter zu offenbaren', d.h. bekanntzumachen), im bereits erwähnten Amtseid der *grietmannen* von Wymbritseradeel.[34] Allerdings hat das Wort *bare* (jüngere Form: *baer*), und somit auch das Verb *baria*, in den späteren westfriesischen Quellen eine ganz neue Bedeutung erhalten, und zwar 'Schiedsspruch'.[35]

Es begegnen in den osterlauwersschen Quellen noch mehrere Bezeichnungen für die Begriffe '(an)klagen' und 'Klage'. Auch im Brokmerbrief stoßen wir beispielsweise auf das Verb *onspreka* sowie auf das Substantiv *onspreke* (vgl. § 19). Im sg. Asegarecht wird der Begriff 'anklagen' ebenfalls als *onspreka*, in den Hunsingoer Küren (Art. 18) hingegen als *biklagia* bezeichnet.[36] Bestimmt nicht synonym ist das jeweils mit Objekt vorkommende Verb *kema* (auch *bikema*), das als 'klagen über (etwas)' zu übersetzen ist. Schließlich sei hier noch auf die Umschreibungen *tichta* und *tichtega* (wörtlich: 'bezichtigen, beschuldigen' bzw. 'Bezichtigung, Beschuldigung') hingewiesen, die in mehreren osterlauwersschen Quellen, dabei auch in einigen Fassungen der Siebzehn Küren, begegnen.

*

Aus dem Vorhergehenden ergibt sich: die Umschreibung *baria* (mit Substantiv *bare*) ist beschränkt auf den osterlauwersschen, die Umschreibung *greta* (mit den Substantiven *gretene* und *gretwerd*) auf den westfriesischen Teil Frieslands. Weiterhin fällt auf, dass *greta* in den jüngeren westfriesischen Quellen als Rechtswort nicht mehr begegnet. Hier hat sich also deutlich eine Verschiebung im Wortfeld ergeben.

Bei einem Vergleich mit der Terminologie in den Nachbarsprachen des Altfriesischen zeigt sich, dass insbesondere die Bezeichnung *baria* (*bare*) eine eigenständige friesische Entwicklung darstellt.[37] Kein Einzelfall hin-

---

[33] W. L. van Helten, 'Zu den malbergischen glossen und den salfränkischen formeln und lehnwörtern in der lex salica', *BGdSL* 25 (1900), 225–542, hier 469–70; idem, *Zur lexicologie des altostfriesischen* (Amsterdam, 1907; Nachdruck: Vaduz, 1984), 25.

[34] *Westerlauwerssches Recht I*, Buma und Ebel, Hg., 630.

[35] O. Vries, 'Die Terminologie des schiedsgerichtlichen Verfahrens in der altfriesischen Urkundensprache', *Friesische Studien I. Beiträge des Föhrer Symposiums zur Friesischen Philologie vom 10.–11. Oktober 1991*, V. F. Faltings, A. G. H. Walker und O. Wilts, Hg., *NOWELE* Suppl. 8 (Odense, 1992), 29–52, hier 37.

[36] *Das Fivelgoer Recht*, W. J. Buma und W. Ebel, Hg., AR 5 (Göttingen, 1972), 176; *Das Hunsingoer Recht*, W. J. Buma und W. Ebel, Hg., AR 4 (Göttingen, 1969), 122.

[37] Vgl. DRW, s.v. *baren*.

gegen ist die Verwendung des Wortes *greta*. Der Gebrauch des Begriffes 'grüßen' (Grundbedeutung: 'laut rufen') zur Bezeichnung des Klagens begegnet auch im Sachsenspiegel, dem berühmten um 1225 schriftlich festgelegten sächsischen Land- und Lehnrecht. Nach Freudenthal hat sich die Bedeutung 'klagen' aus 'jmdn (vor Gericht) anreden, um anzuklagen' entwickelt.[38] Allerdings wird der Begriff 'grüßen' im Sachsenspiegel lediglich zur Bezeichnung der peinlichen Klage angewendet: *grot dat is of he'n pinlike beklaget*.[39] Für die nicht-peinliche Klage ist im Sachsenspiegel das Verb *klagen* gängig.[40] Inwieweit der teilweise entsprechende Gebrauch des Begriffes 'grüßen' in der friesischen und der sächsischen Rechtsterminologie das Ergebnis gegenseitiger Beeinflussung ist, ist schwierig zu entscheiden. Der Begriff *klagia* ist wohl jüngeren Datums, denn das Grundwort *klage* ist ein ursprünglich nur oberdeutsches Wort.[41]

3.2. Kläger und Beklagter

Für den Begriff 'Kläger' überwiegt die wörtliche afr. Entsprechung *klagere*, und zwar in den jüngeren wie auch in den älteren Quellen. In den jüngeren Quellen begegnet daneben auch *onspreker(e)*, Ableitung des Verbs *onspreka*. Auffälligerweise fehlt in der Sneeker Stadttafel jeglicher Beleg für den Begriff 'Kläger'; im Rezessbuch wie auch in den Stadtrechten von Bolsward und Sneek sind die beiden obenerwähnten Bezeichnungen jedoch belegt.[42] Eine Ableitung des Verbs *greta* zur Bezeichnung des Begriffs 'Kläger' sucht man vergebens. Das in Art. 45 des Älteren Schulzenrechts belegte nomen agentis *gretwerder* stellt nicht, wie doch offenkundig scheint, eine Ableitung von *gretwerd* (vgl. Abschnitt 3.1.) dar, sondern hängt mit mhd. *gruz* ('Grieß, Sand') zusammen.[43] Die Bedeutung des Wortes *gretwerder* ist demnach nicht 'Kläger', sondern 'Kampfrichter, Schiedsrichter'.

Im Älteren Schulzenrecht ist nebst *klagere* einige Male die Rede von *onthingere*. In den osterlauwersschen Quellen stoßen wird allerdings lediglich auf die Bezeichnung *klagere*.

Für den Begriff 'Beklagter' wird in den jüngeren westfriesischen Quellen fast ausnahmslos die Bezeichnung *sitter* (wörtlich 'Sitzer') angewendet. Das Benennungsmotiv ist in diesem Fall auf den ersten Blick unklar. Algras

[38] Freudenthal, *Arnulfingisch-karolingische Rechtswörter*, 159.

[39] DRW, s.v. *grüßen*. Vgl. auch AFW, s.v. *greta*.

[40] G. Köbler, 'Klage, klagen, Kläger', *Zeitschrift der Savigny-Stiftung für Rechtsgeschichte (Germanistische Abteilung)* 92 (1975), 1–20, hier 1–3.

[41] Freudenthal, *Arnulfingisch-karolingische Rechtswörter*, 161.

[42] Der Begriff *onspreker* ist im Rezessbuch allerdings nur einmal belegt: SnR 2180 (1512).

[43] Th. Siebs, 'Geschichte der friesischen Sprache', *Grundriss der germanischen Philologie*, H. Paul, Hg. (Strassburg, 1901), 1152–464, hier 1347; DRW, s.v. *Grieß'wart*.

Interpretation (der Kläger steht, der Beklagter sitzt) trifft nicht zu.[44] Es ist ja der Richter, der sitzen muss,[45] und nicht der Beklagter. Die Erklärung liegt auf der Hand: der 'Sitzer' ist derjenige, der auf dem strittigen Gut 'sitzt', es also 'in Besitz' hat. Man vergleiche den Wortlaut von Art. 29 des Jüngeren Schulzenrechts, der sich auf den Rechtsgang beim Streit um das Eigentum eines Grundstücks bezieht: *nv ist alle riocht, dat hi alsoe sitta schel, ief hi moet. Jef hi naet sitta ne moet, soe hwa soe him oenspraka wille, ...* ('nun ist es völlig rechtens, dass er so besitzen soll, wenn er kann. Wenn er nicht besitzen kann, so soll derjenige, der ihn verklagen will, ...').[46] Zu diesem Ergebnis gelangte bereits Van Helten, der auch die Möglichkeit sieht, dass der romano-kanonische Sprachgebrauch, in dem das Wort *possessor*, also 'Besitzer', mitunter auch für den Beklagten gilt, auf die friesische Rechtssprache eingewirkt hat.[47]

In den Willküren von Utingeradeel wird der Begriff *sitter* einmal neben dem gleichbedeutenden *werman* (wörtlich: 'Widermann', d.h. Widerpart) gestellt: *soe schel hi dae sitter ofta wermanne al sulke boet ende betringha dwaen* ('so soll er [der Kläger] dem Beklagten oder Widerpart derartige Buße und Entschädigung bezahlen').[48] Auch in sonstigen Quellen, wie den Willküren von Wymbritseradeel und einer Urkunde d.J. 1423,[49] ist der Begriff *werman* belegt. In den Stadtrechten von Sneek und Bolsward heißt der Beklagte hingegen *sitter*,[50] eine Bezeichnung, die im Sneeker Rezessbuch nicht mehr verwendet wird; der Beklagte wird hier konsequent *beclaegde* genannt.[51] Es nimmt nicht wunder, dass gerade diese Bezeichnung auch in der Sächsischen Ordonnanz d.J. 1504 verwendet wird.[52] Erstaunlicherweise hält das einige Jahre später (1509/1515) für den Gebrauch durch westfriesische Richter verfasste niederländischsprachige Prozesshandbuch *Dit is dat beginsel van de nieuwe Rechten* noch an den herkömmlichen Bezeichnungen *aenspraker* und *sitter* fest.[53]

---

44 Algra, *Oudfries recht*, 423 (s.v. *Sitter*).

45 E. Frhr. von Künßberg, *Rechtliche Volkskunde* (Halle/S., 1936), 97–99.

46 *Westerlauwerssches Recht I*, Buma und Ebel, Hg., 226.

47 W. L. van Helten, *Zur lexicologie des altwestfriesischen* (Amsterdam, 1896; Nachdruck: Vaduz, 1966), 52. Van Helten stützt sich auf H. E. Dirksen, *Manuale Latinitatis fontium juris civilis Romanorum. Thesauri Latin. epitome in usum tironum* (Berlin, 1837), s.v. *possessor* (Bedeutung 3: Reus in iudicio ['Beklagter im Prozess']).

48 O II 29i.

49 O IV 8.

50 Stadtrecht Sneek: Art. 17, 20, 24; Stadtrecht Bolsward (1479): Art. 10–13.

51 Erstes Beleg: SnR 4689 (1514).

52 Z.B. Art. 41 (GPCB II, 41).

53 GPCB II, 51–59. Siehe auch O. Vries, *'Naar ploeg en koestal vluchtte uw taal'. De verdringing van het Fries als schrijftaal door het Nederlands (tot 1580)* (Leeuwarden, 1993), 80.

In den älteren westfriesischen Quellen begegnet der Begriff 'Beklagter' nur äußerst selten. Im Älteren Schulzenrecht wird der Beklagte einmal als *hal(d)ere* (wörtlich: 'Hälter') bezeichnet (Art. 40), ein Wort, das auch im Rudolfsbuch verwendet wird.[54] Weiterhin begegnet es auch einmal in den niederdeutschen Küren von Humsterland.[55] Auch im 5. der Vierundzwanzig Landrechte ist von dem *haldere* die Rede, wenn auch lediglich in der Rüstringer Fassung dieses Textes.[56] In einer niederdeutschen Übersetzung dieser Fassung wird der *haldere* als *holder des landes* bezeichnet.[57] Aus dieser Formulierung lässt sich schließen, dass auch mit dem 'Hälter' der Besitzer des strittigen Gutes gemeint ist.[58]

Nach der Rüstringer Fassung handelt es sich im 5. Landrecht um folgenden Fall: wenn von jemandem ein von ihm erstandenes Gut oder Grundstück gerichtlich abgefordert wird, so hat der *haldere*, also der Beklagte, mit rechtmäßiger Gegenrede zu antworten. In den sonstigen Rezensionen der Vierundzwanzig Landrechte ist es auffälligerweise nicht der *haldere*, der antworten sollte, sondern *ther alder, ther anda huse heldest se* ('der Ältere, der im Hause der Älteste ist') (E1), bzw. *thi eldera erwa* ('der ältere Erbe') (H) bzw. *di aldera* ('der Älteste [im Hause]') (Jus).[59] Etwas vergleichbares ergibt sich im 21. Landrecht, mit der Maßgabe, dass in der Rüstringer Fassung derjenige zu antworten hat, 'von dem man es fordert'.[60] Algra, der die beiden Fälle ausführlich bespricht,[61] unterlässt es, auf diese Unstimmigkeit hinzuweisen. Es lässt sich allerdings nicht mit Sicherheit feststellen, welche Lesart die ursprüngliche ist, weil beide Formulierungen (Beklagter und Ältester) einen Sinn ergeben.

In den osterlauwersschen Quellen suchen wir den Begriff 'Beklagter' weiterhin vergebens. Zwar begegnet im Brokmerbrief ziemlich häufig das Wort *hana*, das nach Van Helten erstaunlicherweise sowohl den Beklagten

---

54 *Westerlauwerssches Recht I*, Buma und Ebel, Hg., 352. S. auch Anm. 134.

55 Johnston, *Codex Hummercensis*, 338.

56 *Das Rüstringer Recht*, W. J. Buma und W. Ebel, Hg., AR 1 (Göttingen, 1963), 46.

57 *Die niederdeutschen Rechtsquellen Ostfrieslands. Bd. I: Die Rechte der Einzel-Landschaften*, C. Borchling, Hg. (Aurich, 1908), 158.

58 Anders: AFW, s.v. *haldere* ("ich denke, weil er zu vertheidigen hat [to haldande hach])".

59 *Das Emsiger Recht*, Buma und Ebel, Hg., 32 (*alder* wird hier unrichtig als 'hervor', also als Adverb, interpretiert); *Das Hunsingoer Recht*, id., 34; *Westerlauwerssches Recht I*, id., 154. In F fehlt der einschlägige Satz.

60 *Das Rüstringer Recht*, Buma und Ebel, Hg., 54; *Das Emsiger Recht*, id., 54 (hier das 22. Landrecht); *Das Hunsingoer Recht*, id., 40 (auch hier das 22. Landrecht); *Westerlauwerssches Recht I*, id., 164.

61 N. E. Algra, *Ein. Enkele rechtshistorische aspecten van de grondeigendom in Westerlauwers Friesland* (Groningen, [1966]), 49–52. Vgl. auch id., *Zeventien Keuren en Vierentwintig Landrechten* (Doorn, 1992), 390 (Anm. 59) sowie Van Helten, *Zur lexicologie des altostfriesischen*, 11–12.

wie auch den Kläger bezeichnen kann.[62] In der Übersetzung des genannten Rechtsbuches von Buma und Ebel ergibt sich hierfür: zweimal 'Beklagter', einmal 'Angeschuldigter' (=Beklagter) und siebenmal 'Kläger'. Diese verwirrende Interpretation des schwachen maskulinen Substantivs *hana* (wörtlich: 'Gehöhnter') ist jedoch, wie Algra gezeigt hat, mangelhaft.[63] Die zutreffende juristische Übersetzung ist 'Verletzter' (ndl. 'gelaedeerde').[64] Algra hat ebenso schlüssig dargestellt, dass der Begriff *hauding* (wörtlich: 'Häuptling') an einigen Stellen im Brokmerbrief nicht als 'Kläger', sondern als 'Leiter einer Partei im Rechtsstreit' zu übersetzen ist.[65]

*

Aus dem Vergleich mit der Terminologie der Nachbarsprachen ergibt sich, dass die ältere Bezeichnung *haldere* auch in Holland gängig war.[66] Ganz eigenständig ist die jüngere Bezeichnung *sitter*, die im westfriesischen Bereich das Wort *haldere* verdrängt hat. Ebenfalls nicht in den Nachbarsprachen belegt ist die Bezeichnung *onthingere*.[67] Bemerkenswerterweise scheint im Sachsenspiegel zur Umschreibung des Beklagten das Abstraktionsvermögen noch nicht voll ausgebildet zu sein. Statt eines nomen agentis begegnen hier die Umschreibungen *de oppe den de klâge geit* ('derjenige, auf den die Klage geht') sowie *de oppe den man sprikt* ('derjenige, auf den man spricht').[68]

3.3. Vorladen und Vorladung

Die Handlung des Vorladens wird in den jüngeren Quellen gewöhnlich mit dem Verb *lathia* (*ladia*, *laia*) ('laden') bezeichnet.[69] Im Älteren Schulzenrecht stoßen wir zwar auch einmal auf dieses Verb, aber viel häufiger ist hier die Verwendung des Zeitworts *bodia*. Die Synonymie der beiden Bezeichnungen wird in Art. 58 dieses Rechtsbuches belegt, wo die Notwendigkeit

---

62 Van Helten, *Zur lexicologie des altostfriesischen*, 164. So auch bereits AFW, s.v. *hana*.

63 Algra, Besprechung von *Das Brokmer Recht*, 606–08. Die verfehlte Interpretation noch bei H. H. Munske, *Der germanische Rechtswortschatz im Bereich der Missetaten. Philologische und sprachgeographische Untersuchungen*, Bd. I (Berlin und New York, 1973), 149 (Anm. 230).

64 Vgl. auch MNHW, s.v. *hôn(e)* ('der Geschädigte, Beleidigte').

65 Algra, Besprechung von *Das Brokmer Recht*, 606–08.

66 MNW, s.v. *houdere* (4).

67 Vgl. DRW, s.v. *andinger*.

68 K. Hyldgaard-Jensen, 'Zur Erforschung der west- und nordmittelniederdeutschen Rechtssprache', *Niederdeutsche Mitteilungen* 22 (1966), 115–31, hier 121. Vgl. auch Planck, *Das Deutsche Gerichtsverfahren*, I, 168.

69 Vgl. zum Vorladen: M. J. Noordewier, *Nederduitsche regtsoudheden* (Utrecht, 1853), 390–95.

einer neuen Vorladung, und zwar vor das Grafengericht, besprochen wird: *aldeer di fria Fresa om clage toe hoeue ladeth wirt* [...]*; soe schel ma him al ieta nies bodia, als ief hi eer naet bodath ne were* ('wenn der freie Friese wegen einer Klage vor das Grafengericht geladen wird, ... dann soll man ihn wieder von neuem vorladen, wie wenn er zuvor nicht vorgeladen wäre').[70]

Auch im Jüngeren Schulzenrecht ist *bodia*, das als eine Ableitung von *bod* ('Gebot') zu betrachten ist,[71] gängig. In diesem Text begegnet überdies zweimal das Verb *upthingia* (wörtlich: 'aufdingen') zur Bezeichnung der Handlung des Vorladens,[72] und zwar in den folgenden Fällen. In Art. 5 bezieht das Vorladen sich auf den Hausmann, der die Haussteuer (*huuslaga, huslotha*) nicht bezahlt, in Art. 29 auf eine Vorladung nicht seitens des Gerichtes (*bannitio*), sondern seitens des Klägers (*mannitio*). In Art. 77 des Älteren Schulzenrechts schließlich ist einmal die Rede von der Vorladung eines Schulzen durch den Gerichtsboten, und zwar im Auftrag desjenigen, der etwas gegen den Schulzen vorzubringen hat.[73] In diesem Fall wird die Handlung des Vorladens mit dem Verb *askia* (wörtlich: 'heischen, fordern') bezeichnet (ebenso in Art. 80b). Im westfriesischen Sendrecht bezeichnet der Terminus *askia* allerdings nicht die Handlung des Vorladens, sondern die des Klagens, dem die Vorladung durch den Richter folgte, wie in Art. 19 belegt wird: *Jef en wyf hir aefta man aesketh oen dae bannede synnethe, so aegh him di decken mey ladenghum ti anderde ti brengane* ('Wenn eine Frau Klage gegen ihren Ehemann erhebt im gebotenen Sendgericht, so soll ihn der Dekan durch Vorladungen zur Verantwortung ziehen').[74]

Wir können feststellen, dass die Termini *lathia* und *bodia* – wie oben gezeigt – als Synonyme verwendet werden können. Ob eine semantische Differenzierung zwischen diesen beiden Verben und den Verben *upthingia* und *askia* möglich ist, muss dahingestellt bleiben.

Lediglich in den westfriesischen Quellen des 15. Jhs. begegnet das zusammengesetzte Verb *forthaskia* (wörtlich: 'fort-heischen', d.h. 'auffordern, vor dem Gericht zu erscheinen'), ein zweifelsohne der mnl. Rechtssprache

---

70 *Westerlauwerssches Recht I*, Buma und Ebel, Hg., 108, 110.

71 Vgl. MNW, s.v. *bodinge* sowie s.v. *bot*. Anders: DRW, s.v. *boten* ('durch Boten vorladen').

72 Algra, *Ein*, 83, entscheidet sich für die spezifischere Übersetzung 'vor ein höheres Gericht vorladen'. Dies überzeugt jedoch nicht, weil das Vorladen vor ein höheres Gericht, und zwar das Grafengericht, im Jüngeren Schulzenrecht ansonsten als *to houe bodia* (Art. 34c) und im Älteren Schulzenrecht ebenfalls als *to houe bodia* (Art. 57, 60, 61) sowie einmal als *to houe lathia* (Art. 58) bezeichnet wird.

73 *Westerlauwerssches Recht I*, Buma und Ebel, Hg., 124.

74 *Ibid.* 176. Buma und Ebel übersetzen das Verb *askia* weniger genau als 'vor das Gericht fordern'. In Art. 11 des westfriesischen Sendrechts passt allerdings, anders wie in Art. 19, die Übersetzung 'vorladen'.

entliehener Begriff,[75] der dem Vorladen nah verwandt zu sein scheint. In den Willküren von Utingeradeel wird das Wort im folgenden Kontext verwendet: falls ein Mensch misshandelt, beraubt oder bestohlen wird und er den Namen des Täters nicht nennen will oder nicht den Mut dazu hat, so hat das Gericht *den hana vort (to) aschiana* ('den Verletzten fortzuheischen') und soll dieser den Namen des Täters nennen.[76] Von Richthofen, dem lediglich diese eine Belegstelle bekannt war, übersetzt das Verb als 'vorfordern'.[77] Bei den weiteren Fundstellen geht es u.a. um das Aufrufen von Personen zum Zeugen[78] bzw. von Prozessparteien, die ihren Beweis oder Zeugen vorbringen sollten (in diesem Fall ist von einer dreimaligen Aufrufung die Rede),[79] oder von Parteien, denen das Gericht die Gelegenheit bietet, ihr Näherrecht in Anspruch zu nehmen.[80] Im Bolswarder sowie im Sneeker Stadtrecht finden wir eine Satzung, derzufolge die Schöffen einen Nicht-Bürger *voerteischen* können, und zwar *bi daghen* (wörtlich: 'bei Tagen'), d.h. in diesem Fall viermal.[81] In einer Urkunde d.J. 1438 bezieht das Verb sich auf Personen, denen ein Verbrechen zur Last gelegt wurde.[82] Der *grietman* ließ sie dreimal *laya* (also 'vorladen'), und, so fährt der Text fort, *ford aeschade in myne waerstal* ('heischte [sie] fort in meine Gerichtstätte'). Die Leute erschienen jedoch nicht, blieben also säumig. Insbesondere der letztere Fall macht deutlich, dass sich die Handlung des 'Fortheischens' nicht einfach mit der des Vorladens decken muss. Hier bezieht der Begriff sich offensichtlich auf das Aufrufen von vorher bereits vorgeladenen Personen. Wahrscheinlich sollte man sich das so vorstellen, dass der Richter zu Beginn der Gerichtssitzung einige Male, und zwar so oft wie bei dem betreffenden Gericht üblich, die Namen der vorgeladenen Personen ausrufen ließ.[83]

Besonders in der Sneeker Stadttafel[84] und viel öfter noch im Sneeker Rezessbuch begegnet der Begriff *witen* (wörtlich: 'Wissen'). Mit diesem Terminus ist nicht die Vorladung, sondern die Zustellung (ndl. 'betekening, insinuatie, gerechtelijke aanzegging') oder vielmehr der Zustellungsbrief ge-

---

75 MNW, s.v. *vorteischen*. Vgl. auch DRW, s.v. *fortheischen*.

76 O II 29g.

77 AFW, s.v. *forthaskia*.

78 *Codex Aysma. Die altfriesischen Texte*, W. J. Buma, P. Gerbenzon und M. Tragter-Schubert, Hg. (Assen und Maastricht, 1993), 124 (A60.1).

79 O II 89 (1479).

80 O I 404 (1493), IV 74, 76 (1487), 90 (1491). Man vergleiche auch noch den Wortlaut von O I 75 (1438) und II 26 (ca. 1440).

81 *De Friesche stadrechten*, Telting, Hg., 16 (Art. 23), 85 (Art. 66), 150 (Art. 27).

82 O II 23.

83 Vgl. S. Gratama, *Een bijdrage tot de rechtsgeschiedenis van Drenthe, meer bijzonder de rechters en de rechtspleging betreffende* (Assen, 1883), 144.

84 SnR 243, 306, 330, 660, 1184.

meint.[85] Der Begriff wird in letzterem Fall häufig mit dem Partizip Perfekt *seind* ('gesandt') oder auch mit *brocht* ('gebracht') oder *sigelet* ('besiegelt') verbunden. In einer Urkunde stoßen wir einmal auf die Schreibweise *hwijt*,[86] also mit hyperkorrektem *h*.

In osterlauwersschen Quellen ist der Begriff 'vorladen' ziemlich schwach vertreten. In § 144 des Brokmerbriefs stoßen wir auf die zweigliedrige stabreimende Paarformel *bonna ieftha baria*. Das Verb *bonna* (wörtlich 'bannen') bezeichnet hier nach Van Helten, wie auch in der Fivelgoer Fassung des 21. der Vierundzwanzig Landrechte, die Handlung des Vorladens.[87] Aller Wahrscheinlichkeit nach trifft diese Interpretation zu, obwohl der Gebrauch des Begriffs 'bannen' zur Bezeichnung des Vorladens nicht gerade geläufig ist.[88] Übrigens wird auch in osterlauwersschen Quellen einige Male die Bezeichnung *lathia* verwendet, beispielsweise in den Hunsingoer Küren (Art. 24).

Der Begriff 'Vorladung' wird in den jüngeren wie in den älteren Quellen, die osterlauwersschen eingeschlossen, nahezu ausnahmslos als *lathinge* (*ladinge, lainge*) bezeichnet.[89] Die entsprechende Ableitung des Verbs *bodia* ist ebenfalls belegt.[90] Im Älteren Schulzenrecht begegnet einmal (Art. 61) die Zusammensetzung *hofbodinge* ('Vorladung vor das Grafengericht') sowie im IJsbrechtumer Deichrecht d.J. 1473 das Simplex *bodinge*.[91] Im Sneeker Stadtrecht werden die Termini *ladinge* und *bodinge* ohne Unterschied verwendet.[92] Zu erwähnen ist hier weiterhin ein Abschnitt der friesischen Übersetzung des romano-kanonischen Prozesshandbuches Processus Judicii im Codex Unia: *Thio lainge is ene bodinge enes mensches thi tha riochte*.[93] Der lateinische Grundtext ist folgenden Wortlauts: *Citatio est vocatio alicuius ad iudicium* ('Die Vorladung ist die Ladung eines Menschen vor das Gericht').[94] Ob *lainge* hier wirklich semantisch von *bodinge* geschieden werden soll, ist allerdings zweifelhaft. Hervorzuheben

---

85 Siehe besonders SnR 3014 (1507). In dieser Eintragung ist allerdings auch von 'fortheischen' die Rede. Vgl. J. van Kuyk, *Rechtsingang en verstek in de middeleeuwsch-stedelijke procedure in verband met het recht der Republiek* ('s-Gravenhage, 1910), 42–43.

86 O III 27 (1498).

87 Van Helten, *Zur lexicologie des altostfriesischen*, 62.

88 DRW, s.v. *bannen*. Van Oosten, *De ambtshalve vervolging*, 55 (Anm. 1) bespricht freilich die Ausdrücke 'banne' und 'baren' in den Küren von Humsterland, aber das Wort *banne* bezieht sich hier auf ein Substantiv ganz anderer Provenienz.

89 Vgl. Ahlsson, *Die altfriesischen Abstraktbildungen*, 68.

90 Vgl. *ibid.* 42.

91 O II 76h. Der einschlägige Textabschnitt ist unklar.

92 *De Friesche stadrechten*, Telting, Hg., 70 (Art. 15, 16).

93 Oxford, Bodleian Library, Ms. Junius 49, f. 51r.

94 *Ein Kompendium De processu et ordine iudicii, aus den Handschriften der Ritter-Akademie zu Brandenburg a.H.*, E. Köpke, Hg. (Brandenburg a.H., 1882), 8.

ist schließlich noch eine Bestimmung in den Willküren von Wininge, nach der sich der Dorfrichter nicht öfter als einmal darauf berufen dürfe, dass er eine von ihm zu erledigende Vorladung vergessen habe. Solch eine versäumte Vorladung heißt dort *wanlathinge*.[95]

*

Eine bedeutsame Verschiebung innerhalb des Wortfeldes fällt auf: die Verdrängung des Verbs *bodia* durch das konkurrierende *lathia*, *ladia*. Beide Verben sind allerdings keinesfalls eigenständig friesisch.[96] Anders verhält es sich mit *upthingia*, das übrigens schwach belegt ist.[97]

3.4. Einsetzen von Pfändern

Der Sinn der verpflichteten Pfandsetzung seitens des Klägers ist wohl, ihn von leichtsinniger Klage abzuhalten.[98] Die Notwendigkeit eines Pfandeinsatzes seitens des Beklagten bezweckte wohl Ähnliches: auch der Beklagte sollte von unbegründeter Einrede zurückgehalten werden. Die Bedeutung der Pfandsetzung im Prozessverfahren, die bislang noch unerforscht geblieben ist, wird im vorliegenden Aufsatz allerdings nicht eingehend erörtert, weil es hier vor alles um die Terminologie geht. Es sei jedoch darauf hingewiesen, dass das Verfahren an die sg. *kenning* erinnert, eine insbesondere im holländischen Rijnland übliche Art von Prozessieren, bei der die eine Partei ein Pfand (*wedde*) bot, worauf die Gegenpartei verpflichtet war, ein Gegenpfand (*wederwedde*) zu bieten. Es handelte sich dabei um eine feste Summe, die bei den Schöffen zu hinterlegen war.[99]

Eine wichtige Belegstelle in den jüngeren westfriesischen Quellen findet sich in Art. 35 der Willküren von Wymbritseradeel d.J. 1404: *Ende comt di sitter to andert ende beseth ende meth des onsprekers pant* ('Und erscheint der Beklagte und 'besetzt' und begegnet er des Klägers Pfand').[100] Es handelt sich in diesem Textabschnitt darum, dass, nachdem der Kläger bereits sein Pfand übergeben hat, auch der Beklagte sein Pfand übergibt (oder lediglich anbietet?), womit er das seinige dem des Klägers 'gegenüberstellt'. Die Bedeutung dieses Gegenzuges des Beklagten ist, dass dadurch der Prozess rechtshängig wird. Charakteristisch bei der Formulierung dieser

95 *Fryske stikken út Codex Furmerius. In rige foarstúdzjes fan Grinzer en Uterter frizisten*. Estrikken 33–34, 2 Bde. (Groningen, [1963]) II, 74.

96 DRW, s.v. *boten* bzw. *laden*.

97 DRW, s.v. *aufdingen* (mit der auf von Richthofen zurückgehenden Interpretation 'anklagen').

98 Vgl. Noordewier, *Nederduitsche regtsoudheden*, 399.

99 A. Nortier, *Bijdrage tot de kennis van het burgerlijk proces in de 15e eeuw binnen de stad Leiden* (Leiden, 1874), 48–54.

100 *Westerlauwerssches Recht I*, Buma und Ebel, Hg., 624.

Handlung ist der Gebrauch der Verben *bisetta*, welches hier das Begegnen des Pfandes der Gegenpartei mittels der Übergabe eines eigenen Pfandes bedeutet,[101] und *meta*, das sich auf die gleiche Handlung seitens des Prozessgegners bezieht.

Genau dieselben Verben begegnen auch in einer Urkunde d.J. 1476, in der das Urteil des Gerichtes in Leeuwarderadeel in einem Streit zwischen den *thremdelen* (wörtlich 'Dritteln', hier den drei Unterbezirken) dieses Bezirkes festgelegt wurde.[102] Hier wird folgendermaßen formuliert: Walthia Kempa zin und Haija Heringha, die die klagende Partei (den mittleren und den südlichen Unterbezirk) vertreten, *bisetten mith panden op dat nordste thremdeel* ('besetzten mit Pfändern auf den nördlichen Unterbezirk', d.h. die beklagte Partei), sich nicht einer bestimmten Verpflichtung zu entziehen. Es handelt sich hier also um die Pfandsetzung seitens des Klägers. Die Vertreter der beklagten Partei sind nach Vorladung zur Gerichtssitzung erschienen (*kamen toe ande(r)th*), worauf der Gerichtsvorsitzende sie mehrere Male fragte, ob sie *Walthia ende Haija pand aeth mette wolden* ('dem Pfand von Walthia und Haija in einigerlei Weise begegnen wollten') *ende brenghet deer reden op* ('und ob sie Beweise dafür beibringen'), d.h. Beweise für die Unzulässigkeit der Klage.[103] Die beklagte Partei zeigte sich allerdings nicht bereit, dem Pfand des Klägers zu 'begegnen' und brachte auch keine Beweise bei, weder mit Urkunden noch mit dem Zeugnis alter Leute (*dat hijae Walthia ende Haija pand naet meta wolden toe nener tijt ende brochten aeck nen reden in ws riucht haer mith brieuen ner mith alda lijoedem*). In Abweichung von dem oben zitierten Art. 35 der Willküren von Wymbritseradeel, in denen die Handlung des 'Besetzens' wie auch die des 'Begegnens' dem Beklagten zugeschrieben werden, wird erstere hier vom Kläger und lediglich die zweite vom Beklagten vorgenommen. Die in der Urkunde des Leeuwarderadeeler Gerichtes skizzierte Vorgehensweise er-

---

[101] Diese Bedeutungsangabe fehlt im DRW, s.v. *besetzen*. Vgl. J. de Rhoer, *Aanteekeningen, ter opheldering van het Stadboek van Groningen* (Groningen, 1828), 117; W. L. van Helten, 'Zur lexicologie und grammatik des altwestfriesischen', *BGdSL* 19 (1894), 345–440, hier 382; O. Vries, '*Nijaer is sijd ende pliga allijnna in Freesland.* Die Terminologie bei der Ausübung des Näherrechts im Altfriesischen', *Approaches*, 335–37.

[102] O II 82. Weiterhin in einem Friedebannverfahren vor dem Gericht der Stadt Leeuwarden d.J. 1493 (O I 406). Zum Friedebannverfahren: s. Anm. 113.

[103] Dass mit *reed* 'Beweis der Unzulässigkeit einer Klage' gemeint sein kann, wurde bereits von W. L. van Helten, 'Zur lexicologie und grammatik des altostfriesischen', *BGdSL* 14 (1889), 232–87, hier 267–68, angesetzt. Im oben angeführten Zitat stellt *reden* also eine Pluralform dar; eine Kürzung von *redene* wäre sonst durchaus möglich, aber ist hier auf Grund der Semantik wohl auszuschließen. Die von F. Holthausen und D. Hofmann, *Altfriesisches Wörterbuch* (Heidelberg, 1985), s.v. *rēdene* aufgeführte Bedeutung 'Beweis' ist vielleicht nicht zutreffend.

scheint plausibler: die Gegenpartei 'begegnet', was wohl das 'Besetzen', d.h. den Pfandeinsatz seitens dieser Partei, also des Beklagten, mit einschließt. Übrigens geht auch in Art. 33 der Willküren von Wymbritseradeel die Handlung des 'Besetzens', wie in der Urkunde d.J. 1476, eindeutig von der Partei des Klägers und nicht, wie in Art. 35, des Beklagten aus.[104] In diesem Fall handelt es sich um die Klage gegen die Richter, wohl wegen eines ungerechten Urteils.

Aus terminologischer Sicht interessant ist auch eine Urkunde bezüglich eines Sneeker Prozesses d.J. 1492, die auf einem in der Sneeker Stadttafel eingelegten einzelnen Blättchen festgehalten ist.[105] Es handelt sich hier allem Anschein nach um ein Eilverfahren, d.h. um einen Prozess, der innerhalb eines Tages (afr. *dwers wr nacht*)[106] abgewickelt wurde. In diesem Fall erschien der Kläger vor dem Gericht *mey syn pand* ('mit seinem Pfand') um Klage zu erheben. Die nächste Handlung bestand darin, dass er *syn pand keerde in ws* ('sein Pfand an uns, d.h. die Richter, übergab') und seine Klage vortrug. Der Beklagte *meth syn pand* ('begegnete seinem Pfand') und bezeugte seine Unschuld (*ende seyde hy weer dat naet schildich*).

Im Sneeker Rezessbuch sind die Ausdrücke '(mit einem Pfand) besetzen' als Handlung des Klägers und 'dem Klägers Pfand begegnen' als Handlung des Beklagten immer noch geläufig.[107] Besonders aufschlussreich ist eine (niederländischsprachige) Eintragung d.J. 1507.[108] In dieser Aufzeichnung 'besetzt' der Vorsprecher des Klägers 'mit seinem Pfand', dass dem Vorsprecher der Gegenpartei, namens Bocka Claessoen, nicht gestattet werden könne, als Prozessbevollmächtigter vorzugehen, solange er nicht vereidigt worden sei. Es erfolgt dann die Mitteilung: *Doe seide bocka dat pand moete Jck* ('Da sagte Bocka: "dem Pfand begegne ich"'). In diesem Fall werden ausnahmsweise die seitens des Beklagten oder dessen Vorsprechers obligatorisch auszusprechenden Worte (der 'Prozessformel', ndl. *dingtaal*) wörtlich, und zwar in ndl. Lautung (*moete* statt *meete*), zitiert.

Die Pfandsetzung seitens des Klägers sowie des Beklagten wird in der Sneeker Stadttafel einmal folgenderweise umschrieben: Kläger und Beklagter *brochten* [...] *panden gaer* ('brachten Pfänder zusammen').[109] Mit diesem Wortlaut werden also die Handlungen beider Parteien zusammengefasst. Zu beachten ist auch noch Art. 14 der Willküren von Wininge: der

---

104 *Westerlauwerssches Recht I*, Buma und Ebel, Hg., 622.

105 SnR 197. Vgl. auch SnR 1167 (ebenfalls 1492).

106 Im einschlägigen Text fehlt dieser Wortlaut. Vgl. Van Kuyk, *Rechtsingang en verstek*, 170–75.

107 Z.B. SnR 3208 (1508).

108 SnR 2974.

109 SnR 208 (1494). Die gleiche Formulierung auch im Rezessbuch: SnR 3014 (1507), 4006 (1510).

Beklagte braucht keinen Beweis zu liefern *eer dy clager byset* is.[110] Die von Buma vorgeschlagene Übersetzung 'bevor ein Pfand gegen den Kläger gesetzt worden ist',[111] trifft nicht zu, weil sich die Handlung des Pfandsetzens auch in diesem Fall eindeutig auf den Kläger beziehen muss. Zu bevorzügen ist deswegen folgende Übersetzung: 'bevor dem Kläger auferlegt worden ist, ein Pfand zu setzen'.

In der oben bereits zitierten Urkunde des Gerichtes von Leeuwarderadeel d.J. 1476 wird festgestellt, dass die beklagte Partei, indem sie dem Pfand des Klägers nicht 'begegnet' und auch keine Beweise beigebracht hat, *relawich ende sethlawich* geworden ist. Diese Paarformel, die eine nähere Betrachtung verdient, begegnet im afr. Quellenmaterial weiterhin nur noch einmal, und zwar in einem vom Gericht der Stadt Leeuwarden ausgefertigten Friedebann d.J. 1433.[112] In dem in Westfriesland bei der Eigentumsübergabe von Liegenschaften obligatorischen Friedebannverfahren spielte der Widersprecher der Veräußerung der Liegenschaft die Rolle des Klägers, der Käufer der Liegenschaft die des Beklagten.[113] Im einschlägigen Text ist davon die Rede, dass der Widersprecher der Veräußerung, also der Kläger, *reed lauwech ende set lauwech* wurde.[114] Es stellt sich also heraus, was freilich auch durchaus logisch ist, dass sich der Ausdruck sowohl auf den Kläger als auf den Beklagten beziehen kann.

An anderer Stelle, und zwar in einer Sentenz des sg. Niogen-Gerichtes d.J. 1423, ist davon die Rede, dass Kläger und Beklagter im Gericht *to ree ende to setta ghinghen*.[115] Auffällig ist hier natürlich die Symmetrie mit dem Ausdruck '*ree(d)lawich ende setlawich* werden'. Mit *set* ist zweifelsohne das von den beiden Parteien anzubietende und zu übergebende Pfand gemeint. Dies wird bestätigt vom Wortlaut einer Sentenz des Gerichtes in Dongeradeel d.J. 1425,[116] in der ausgeführt wird, dass der Kläger nach Erhebung seiner Klage *syn seth al deer vp baed* ('sein Pfand darauf anbot')

---

110 *Fryske stikken út Codex Furmerius,* II, 74.

111 *Ibid.* 77 (s.v. *bisetta*).

112 O I 63.

113 Vgl. über dieses Verfahren: O. Vries, '*Also dat wy habbet ferdban kloppet.* Die Terminologie des Friedebannes bei der Eigentumsübergang von Immobilien in der altfriesischen Urkundensprache', *A Frisian and Germanic Miscellany, Published in Honour of Nils Århammar on his Sixty-Fifth Birthday, 7 August 1996* (Odense und Bredstedt, 1996) (= *NOWELE*, vol. 28/29), 251–71.

114 In seiner Edition dieser Urkunde liest Sipma irrtümlicherweise zweimal *lauweth* statt *lauwech*. Dieser Fehler wurde nicht korrigiert in O. Vries, *Correcties op P. Sipma, Oudfriesche Oorkonden I–III, aangevuld met een overzicht van schrijvershanden*. Estrikken 64 (Groningen, 1984).

115 O IV 8.

116 O I 42. Vgl. R. P. Cleveringa Pzn., *Het Oud-Friese 'kestigia'* (Amsterdam, 1959), 32–33.

und der Beklagte *syn seth al deer tho Ienst baed In lijka furma* ('sein Pfand dagegen anbot [begegnete] in gleicher Form'). Wenn auch das Suffix *lawich* unklar ist, so lässt sich doch vermuten, dass mit dem Adjektiv *setlawich* etwa 'pfandsäumig' gemeint ist. Die Begriffe *ree(d)* und *ree(d)lawich* werden unten besprochen (Abschnitt 3.5.).

Von der Klage gegen den (oder die) Richter, wie in Art. 33 der Willküren von Wymbritseradeel, ist auch die Rede im Brokmerbrief. In § 19 heißt es: *Vvel mar enne rediewa onspreca vmbe enne vndom, sa skel ma [...] wernia oppare stede* ('Will man einen *redjeva* [nicht-herrschaftlichen Richter] wegen eines ungerechten Urteils verklagen, so soll man [...] auf der Stelle Pfänder setzen'). Sind Pfänder gegen einen *redjeva* gesetzt, so ist er *biwernad* (wörtlich: 'bepfandet') (§ 20, 21).[117] Die Bezeichnung der Pfandsetzung mit dem Verb *wernia*, das von Richthofen mit ags. *warnian* (lat. *cavere*) in Zusammenhang bringt,[118] begegnet lediglich im Brokmerbrief.

Einen Hinweis auf Pfandeinsatz im Rechtsverfahren ergeben auch die Hunsingoer Küren. In Art. 24, der sich gerade auf den Prozessgang bezieht, stoßen wir auf den folgenden Satzteil, in dem der Begriff *bisetta* wiederum auftaucht: *and nenne thingath te herane, hi ne besette thene brecma.*[119] Ich übersetze diesen Passus, in Anschluss an Cleveringa,[120] folgendermaßen: der Richter braucht keine Einrede des Beklagten anzuhören, d.h. zu akzeptieren, wenn dieser kein Pfand für die Brüche gesetzt hat. In diesem Fall ist der Zweck der Pfandsetzung also nicht, den Beklagten von leichtsinniger Einrede abzuhalten, sondern ihn zur Leistung von Sicherheit für die Bezahlung der wegen Säumnis verschuldeten Brüche zu zwingen.

*

Soweit ersichtlich hat sich im Bereich des Pfandeinsatzes eine ganz eigenständige friesische Terminologie entwickelt.

3.5. Rede und Gegenrede

In der Urkunde bezüglich des schon öfter erwähnten Sneeker Prozesses d.J. 1492[121] wird ausgeführt, dass – nach den Pfandsetzungen sowie den Schuld- bzw. Unschuldbezeugungen der beiden Parteien – der Kläger sein *riocht*

---

117 *Das Brokmer Recht*, Buma und Ebel, Hg., 33, übersetzen hier unrichtig: 'durch (Urteils)pfand gesichert'.

118 AFW, s.v. *wernia*.

119 *Das Hunsingoer Recht*, Buma und Ebel, Hg., 124. Von *bisetta* ist auch die Rede in einem Text aus der Fivelgoer Handschrift (*Das Fivelgoer Recht*, Buma und Ebel, Hg, 162).

120 Cleveringa, *Het Oud-Friese 'kestigia'*, 69 (Anm. 13).

121 SnR 197.

(wörtlich: 'Recht') aussprach sowie seinen Beweis beibrachte, worauf der Beklagte seine *andert deer toe Jenst* (wörtlich: 'Antwort dagegen') aussprach. Das Gericht fällte dann sein Urteil *twiska tael ende andert.* Mit letzterem Ausdruck wird zweifellos gemeint: entschied, d.h. machte seine Wahl, zwischen der Rede (*tael*) und der Gegenrede (*andert*, wörtlich: 'Antwort') der Parteien. Der Begriff 'Rede' wird hier also einmal als *riocht* und einmal als *tael* bezeichnet, die 'Gegenrede' jeweils als *andert.* Allerdings wird häufig auch die Gegenrede mit dem Wort *tael(e)* oder *tele* umschrieben. Sowohl im Sneeker Schöffeneid wie im Amtseid der *grietmannen* in Wymbritseradeel heißt es beispielsweise, dass das Urteil *twijscha twyra tael / twiska twira tale* (wörtlich: 'zwischen zweier Rede', d.h. zwischen der Rede und der Gegenrede der zwei Parteien) gefällt werden sollte,[122] wobei mit *tael* also eindeutig auch die Gegenrede gemeint ist. Im Franeker Bürgerbrief d.J. 1417 wird etwas abweichend formuliert: *tuisscha der igna tale* ('zwischen der Rede der Parteien').[123]

Der Ausdruck *twira tale* begegnet einmal auch im Älteren Schulzenrecht. In Art. 65 heißt es, dass jemand gegen einen anderen prozessieren sollte *mey twira taele.* In einigen osterlauwersschen Rechtsquellen ist der Ausdruck *twira tale* ebenfalls belegt. Im erbrechtlichen Rätsel von den drei Brüdern (E1 sowie H) ist sogar zweimal die Rede von *bi tuira tele.*[124] Auffälligerweise folgen dem Syntagma *mey* bzw. *bi twira t(a)ele* in den älteren Quellen jeweils die Worte *and bi asega dome* ('und nach dem Urteil des Asegas'). Aus diesem Wortlaut lässt sich schließen, dass der einschlägige Rechtsstreit nach Rede und Gegenrede der Parteien durch das Urteil des Asegas entschieden wurde. Hervorzuheben ist weiterhin noch die Möglichkeit der Verbindung mit semantisch unterschiedlichen Präpositionen: 'zwischen' in den jüngeren, 'mit' und 'bei' in den älteren Quellen.

Nicht unwichtig ist, dass die Begriffe 'Rede' und 'Gegenrede' bereits in den Siebzehn Küren und den Vierundzwanzig Landrechten, dem zentralen Teil des afr. Rechts, begegnen. Von großer Bedeutsamkeit ist besonders die Verwendung in der 17. Kür, in der König Karl das Privileg erteilt, dass alle Friesen *bi twira taele ende bi aesga dome* (Jus; auch in den sonstigen Handschriften jeweils mit der Präposition *bi*) prozessieren sollen, was dem Wortlaut in den oben erwähnten älteren Quellen genau entspricht. In der lat.

---

122 *De Friesche stadrechten*, Telting, Hg. 138; *Westerlauwerssches Recht I*, Buma und Ebel, Hg., 630. Buma und Ebel übersetzen 'nach Anhörung der beiderseitigen Verhandlungen'. Der Begriff 'Verhandlung' ist hier verfehlt.

123 O II 10.

124 *Das Emsiger Recht*, Buma und Ebel, Hg., 48; *Das Hunsingoer Recht*, id., 46. Der Ausdruck begegnet auch im Wortlaut der Lösung des Rätsels im westfriesischen Rechtsbuch Jurisprudentia Frisica (*Jurisprudentia Frisica of Friesche regtkennis*, M. Hettema, Hg., 3 Bde. [Leeuwarden, 1834–1835)] II, 130).

Fassung der Siebzehn Küren wird dies folgendermaßen ausgedrückt: *per duorum allegationes et secundum asega iudicium.*[125] Wir können den Schluss ziehen, dass der noch i.J. 1492 verwendete Ausdruck *bi twira tale* zweifelsohne auf die berühmte 17. Kür zurückgeht und somit langlebig war. Weiterhin wird deutlich, dass die Verbindung mit der Präposition *bi*, allerdings im hier besprochenen Ausdruck, die ursprüngliche ist.

Beachtenswert ist nicht nur die 17., sondern auch auch die 3. der Siebzehn Küren, in der das Privileg festgelegt wurde, dass jedermann ungestört auf seinem Gut 'sitzen' konnte, *hit ne se thet [ma] hine mith tele and mith rethe end mith riuchte thingathe urwinne* ('es sei denn, dass man ihn mit Rede und mit Gegenrede und in einem rechtmäßigen Verfahren überführe') (H).[126] In dieser Kür wird der Begriff 'Rede' also mit dem üblichen Wort *tele* und die 'Gegenrede' mit dem weniger gebraüchlichen Wort *rethe*, übrigens der genauen Entsprechung des Wortes 'Rede', bezeichnet. Wir können jetzt feststellen, dass *rethe* (jüngere Formen: *rede, reed, ree*) Bestandteil der oben (Abschnitt 3.4.) zitierten Ausdrücke *to ree ende to setta* sowie *ree(d)-lawich ende sethlawich* ist, und zwar mit der Bedeutung 'Rede' (oder auch 'Gegenrede'). Das Wortpaar *ree(d)lawich ende sethlawich* kann somit als 'redesäumig und pfandsäumig' übersetzt werden. Dass in der Urkunde von Leeuwarderadeel d.J. 1476 das Wort *rede*, wie eindeutig aus dem Kontext hervorgeht, die Bedeutung 'Beweis' aufweist, ist vielleicht eine semantische Entgleisung, die nur möglich war, indem die ursprüngliche Bedeutung von *rethe, rede* nicht mehr verstanden wurde.

Im 1. der Vierundzwanzig Landrechte, das im Grunde genommen eine Wiederholung der 3. Kür darstellt, wird die gleiche Formulierung wie in dieser Kür angewendet: *hit ne se thet ma hine mith tele, mith rede and mith riuchta thingade ther ofbrenge* (Jus).[127] In der 7. Kür wird wahrscheinlich dasselbe gemeint, aber mit abweichender Formulierung: dass alle Friesen *fria spreka and fri ondwarde* (wörtlich: 'freie Klage und freie Antwort') haben.[128] Leider fehlt dieser Passus in der lat. Fassung der Siebzehn Küren. Allerdings geht aus diesen Worten eindeutig hervor, dass man im afr. Recht großen Wert auf das freie Prozessieren legte.

---

125 *De eerste en de tweede Hunsinger Codex*, J. Hoekstra, Hg., OTR 6 ('s-Gravenhage, 1950), 89.

126 Lat. Übersetzung: *nisi ratione et iusta allegatione conuincantur* (*De eerste en de tweede Hunsinger Codex*, Hoekstra, Hg., 86). Lat. *ratione* entspricht hier wohl afr. *rethe* und lat. *allegatione*, wie auch oben, afr. *tele/taele*. Die Bedeutung von lat. *ratio* ist 'Vernunft', nicht 'Rede'. Offenbar wurde afr. *rethe* unrichtig übersetzt. Dieses Beispiel spricht dafür, dass die afr., nicht die lat. Fassung die ursprüngliche ist.

127 Lat. Übersetzung: *nisi sit quod ter neget rectas allegationes* (*De eerste en de tweede Hunsinger Codex*, Hoekstra, Hg., 90). Diese Übersetzung entspricht dem afr. Text auffälligerweise überhaupt nicht.

128 *Das Rüstringer Recht*, Buma und Ebel, Hg., 36.

Weiterhin ist noch hervorzuheben, dass in einigen osterlauwersschen Fassungen der 16. Kür von einem Mann die Rede ist, der *mith riuchtere tele and mith asega dome* überführt wird.[129] Wir stoßen also im Text der Siebzehn Küren nochmals auf das Wort *tele* zur Bezeichnung des Begriffes 'Rede (und Gegenrede)' sowie auf die Verbindung mit dem Begriff *asega dom*.

Abschließend kann noch festgestellt werden, dass im Brokmerbrief jeglicher Hinweis auf die hier besprochenen Bezeichnungen der Begriffe 'Rede' und 'Gegenrede' fehlt. In diesem Rechtsbuch stoßen wir zwar auf den Begriff 'Gegenrede', der hier jedoch als *ienbare*, also als Gegenklage (vgl. Abschnitt 3.1.), bezeichnet wird (§ 126, 127).

*

Der Ausdruck 'zwischen zweier (Männer, Menschen, Parteien) Rede' begegnet häufig, sowohl im Sachsenspiegel wie auch in den holländisch-utrechtischen Quellen.[130] Soweit ersichtlich lediglich in friesischen Quellen belegt ist das Wortpaar *tele and rethe*, das mnl. *tale ende wedertale* entspricht. Der Begriff *ienbare* ist, wie *bare*, eigenständig osterlauwerssch.

3.6. Urteilen

Um das Jahr 1440 (das genaue Datum steht nicht fest) wurde angeordnet, dass im westfriesischen Rechtsbezirk Baarderadeel hinfort an zwei Orten, und zwar in Baard wie auch in Jorwert, gerichtet werden sollte.[131] Betont wurde, dass den in Jorwert und in Baard gefällten Urteilen gleiche Bedeutung zugemessen werden sollte. In diesem Zusammenhang werden nacheinander mehrere Bezeichnungen des Begriffes 'urteilen' aufgelistet: *hoth soma tho Jorwert jefta tho Bauwert wijsd dometh eynt ende deelt* ('was man zu Jorwert oder zu Baard urteilt [4x]'). Es handelt sich hier also um die Verben *wisa*, *domia*, *enda* und *dela*.

Gibt es möglicherweise Bedeutungsnuancen zwischen den genannten Verben? Eines, und zwar *enda* ('enden, beenden, zum Abschluss bringen'), hat in diesem Zusammenhang zweifelsohne die spezifische Bedeutung: ein Endurteil sprechen, womit es sich deutlich von den übrigen abhebt. Das Besondere des Verbs *domia*, Ableitung von *dom*, ist wohl seine Seltenheit in den jüngeren Quellen. Es begegnet allerdings auch in der oben (Abschnitt 3.4.) bereits ausführlicher zitierten Urkunde d.J. 1476, in der das Gericht

---

129 *Ibid*. 40.

130 Planck, *Das Deutsche Gerichtsverfahren*, I, 250; MNW, s.v. *tale*. Siehe auch J. A. Feith, *Het gericht van Selwerd. Bijdrage tot de vaderlandsche rechtsgeschiedenis* (Groningen, 1885), 110.

131 O II 26.

von Leeuwarderadeel den Rechtsstreit zwischen den Unterbezirken dieses Rechtsbezirks entschied. Das Sprechen des Urteils wird hier mit folgenden Worten umschrieben: *ende mosten wij [...] bij Walthia ende Haija panden domija ende habbet al deer bij dompet* ('und mussten wir ... bei Walthias und Haijas Pfändern urteilen und haben dabei geurteilt'). Interessant ist hier die Verbindung des Begriffes *domia* mit den Pfändern der Partei, zu deren Gunsten geurteilt wurde.

Die gängigen Bezeichnungen des Begriffes 'urteilen' in den jüngeren westfriesischen Quellen sind die Verben *dela, finda* (das in obiger Auflistung fehlt) und *wisa* (wörtlich: '(er)teilen, finden, weisen'), zwischen denen offensichtlich keine Bedeutungsnuancen bestehen. Eine Gemeinsamkeit dieser drei Verben ist, dass jedes davon mit dem Präfix *forth-* verbunden werden kann, wodurch sie die Bedeutung 'urteilen zugunsten von' erhalten,[132] sowie mit den Präfixen *tobek-* und *urbek-*, was die Bedeutung 'urteilen zuungunsten von' ergibt. Es folgt hier jeweils ein Beispiel:

ende aylko ende wylko [...] furth deelth waerthen myth hiara ryuchte ('und es wurde zugunsten von Aylko und Wylko mit ihrem Rechtsanspruch geurteilt')[133]

dat ma dine haldere aegh foerd ti fijndane ('dass man zugunsten des Beklagten urteilen soll')[134]

dat wy wyset Fraenkera [...] mit hiara riocht foerd ('dass wir zugunsten der Franekerer mit ihrem Rechtsanspruch urteilen')[135]

Dy riuchter di is scildich, den oenspreker al tyda to becke to delen ... ('Der Richter ist verpflichtet, zu allen Zeiten zuungunsten des Klägers zu urteilen ...')[136]

Hier op hebben wy pater voert vonden ende lywert toe beck ('Hierauf haben wir zugunsten des Paters und zuungunsten von Lywert geurteilt')[137]

---

132 Vgl. Van Helten, 'Zur lexicologie und grammatik des altwestfriesischen', 381–84. Dessen Übersetzung 'ein gerichtliches urteil fällen, gerichtlich erkennen' ist allerdings nicht ganz präzise.

133 O IV 5.

134 *Westerlauwerssches Recht I*, Buma und Ebel, Hg., 352 (Rudolfsbuch).

135 O II 71. Der Begriff begegnet auch in den ndl. Stadtrechten von Sneek und Bolsward, woraus es in das MNW gelangte (s.v. *vortwisen*). Die dort angegebene Bedeutung 'in rechte verder gaan met iem. recht te doen' ist allerdings verfehlt.

136 *Codex Aysma*, Buma, Gerbenzon und Tragter-Schubert, Hg., 146 (A69.2). Die dort aufgeführte Übersetzung 'abweisen' ist weniger genau.

137 SnR 2299 (ndl. Eintragung) (1512).

ende wijse Attija meij sijn paert foerd ende liuue van sijn paerts weijna toe beck ('und urteilen zugunsten von Attija mit seiner Partei und zuungunsten von Liuue wegen seiner Partei')[138]

And Ayelika vorscreuen myt sin endum ford deeld warden [...] And Sirk vorscreuen myt sine riocht vr beck ('Und es wurde zugunsten von obengenanntem Ayelika mit seinen [??] und zuungunsten von vorgenanntem Sirk mit seinem Rechtsanspruch geurteilt')[139]

dat her Bendix is wrbeck fonden ('dass zuungunsten von Herrn Bendix geurteilt wurde')[140]

dat wy wyset [...] Harnsera buren wrbeck ('dass wir zuungunsten der Harlinger Bürger geurteilt haben')[141]

Die am 28. Juli 1507 vom Statthalter kritisierte Terminologie (*ick wyse die man voert, ende den to beck*, Abschnitt 1.) wurde doch nicht sofort abgestellt, jedenfalls nicht im Sneeker Rezessbuch. Es finden sich in dieser Quelle nach dem genannten Zeitpunkt etwa noch nachfolgende Varianten: *bocka is foerd fonden ende melys contrari* (22. November 1507); *tot profyt van Euert ende contrary heer gerbren mey syn parten* (1510); *tot profyt van symon ende Joest ende tot achterdeel* ['Nachteil'] *van watthia* (1512).[142] Im Jahre 1512 heißt es sogar wieder: *voert ... toe beck.*[143]

In den afr. Urkunden begegnen noch einige andere Bezeichnungen des Begriffes 'urteilen zu(un)gunsten von': *tojenisfinda* (wörtlich: 'entgegenfinden'), und *ene wonnene seke towisa* (wörtlich: 'eine gewonnene Sache zuerweisen'):

then fynd ther syric [...] to jenys fonden warth ende aylka forth fonden warth ('das Urteil, das zuungunsten von Syric und zugunsten von Aylka gefällt wurde')[144]

Ende wi wiset eesk ende siin broer toe ene wonnenne seke ('Und wir urteilen zugunsten von Eesk und seinem Bruder')[145]

Die afr. Quellen zeigen somit eine Fülle von Ausdrücken zur Bezeichnung des Begriffes 'urteilen zu(un)gunsten von'.

---

138 SnR 4867 (1515). Attija und Liuue sind die Prozessbevollmächtigten der beiden Parteien.

139 O IV 7 (1418). Die genaue Bedeutung des Wortes *endum* ist hier unklar.

140 O II 139 (1486).

141 O II 71 (1472).

142 SnR 4595, 2454, 2194 (ndl. Eintragung).

143 Siehe Anm. 137. Vgl. auch Anm. 138.

144 O IV 6 (1418).

145 O IV 9 (1436). Im gleichen Text begegnet die Umschreibung *foerd fonden*, die sich offenbar auf ein Zwischenurteil bezieht.

Kehren wir zum Begriff 'urteilen' zurück. Neben den vier oben bereits erwähnten Bezeichnungen (*wisa*, *domia*, *enda* und *dela*), begegnen weiterhin noch *ordelia* und *sentencieria*. Ersteres Verb erscheint in Art. 7 der Willküren von Wymbritseradeel (*di gretman scel ordelia*, 'der *grietman* soll urteilen'), letzteres in einer Urkunde d.J. 1483 (*vysd of sentencierid*).[146] Ebenfalls eine Bezeichnung des einschlägigen Begriffs ist das besonders im Sneeker Rezessbuch frequente Verb *kenna* (wörtlich: 'kennen'). In diesem Fall wäre eine eingehende Untersuchung erforderlich, insofern das Wort, wie auch in der mnl. Rechtssprache,[147] eine Reihe von Bedeutungsnuancen aufzuzeigen scheint. Hier kann nur vorläufig festgestellt werden, dass sich der Begriff *kenna*, auch wenn es sich um eine Handlung seitens der Schöffen handelt, doch nicht auf die eigentliche Urteilsfällung bezieht. Dies zeigt sich etwa darin, dass die Schöffen (oder auch der Rat) der Stadt Sneek mehrfach in bereits durch ein Urteil oder einen Schiedsspruch geschlichteten Differenzen 'kennen'. In solchen Fällen handelt es sich augenscheinlich um einen Beschluss in Nebensachen, beispielsweise über die Vollstreckung des Urteils oder des Schiedsspruches. Die zutreffende Übersetzung ist hier somit wohl 'entscheiden' (ndl. 'beschikken').

Zur Illustration diene folgendes Beispiel aus dem Rezessbuch. Am 24. November d.J. 1509 wurde von den Schöffen ein Endurteil in einer Streitsache zwischen Broer Goythiazin und Marten Tijernazin gefällt, und zwar zuungunsten von Marten, der Broer die strittige Geldsumme entrichten sollte. Am 12. April des nächsten Jahres *kennen* die Schöffen, dass Broer die genannte Summe gemäß dem am 24. November gefällten Urteil erhalten soll, und zwar nach Säumnis der Appellation seitens seines Prozessgegners.[148] Demzufolge würde ich den Satz *Alsoe dat wy sceppnen kennen ende wysen foer een sentencie*, in dem m.E. die beiden Verben nicht synonymisch verwendet werden, sondern semantisch unterschiedlich, folgendermaßen übersetzen: 'sodass wir, Schöffen, entscheiden und als Urteil aussprechen'.[149]

Jetzt zu den älteren Rechtsquellen. Im Brokmerbrief wird der Begriff 'Urteil fällen' als *dom dela* bezeichnet (daneben begegnet: *undom dela,* 'ein ungerechtes Urteil fällen'). Diese Bezeichnung hat sich noch bis in das 16. Jh. behauptet im inoffiziellen Titel des Landrichters im Dienste der Häuptlinge aus dem Haus Cirksena (ab 1464 Grafen in Ostfriesland): *domdeler*.[150]

---

146 O I 328.

147 S. Muller Fz., *De Middeleeuwsche rechtsbronnen der stad Utrecht. Glossarium* ('s-Gravenhage, 1885), 40–42.

148 SnR 3982, 2422, 2423.

149 SnR 3483.

150 J. König, *Verwaltungsgeschichte Ostfrieslands bis zum Aussterben seines Fürstenhauses* (Göttingen, 1955), 285; MNDW, s.v. *dômdeler*.

Von *dom dela* ist ebenfalls die Rede in den Siebzehn Küren und den Vierundzwanzig Landrechten. Hier bezieht sich der Ausdruck allerdings nicht, wie im Brokmerbrief, auf die Urteilsfällung des Richters (*redjeva*), sondern auf die Haupttätigkeit des Asegas, die Erteilung eines Vorschlages bezüglich des einschlägigen Rechtsverfahrens. Letztere Bedeutung ist in den afr. Quellen zweifelsohne die ursprüngliche. Die genannte Tätigkeit des Asegas kann übrigens auch kurz als *domia* (daneben auch, durch Einwirkung des i-Umlauts, *dema*)[151] oder als *dela* erscheinen: *alsa him sin asyga dome and dele* ('was ihm sein Asega erteile [2x]').[152] Im Rüstringer Sendrecht ist allerdings belegt, dass die Tätigkeit des Asegas auch mit dem Verb *finda* bezeichnet werden kann (*riucht urdel to findande*).[153] In den Schulzenrechten wird die Tätigkeit des Asegas üblicherweise mit dem Verb *dela* bezeichnet. Ausnahmsweise begegnet hier aber auch *wisa* (Jüngeres Schulzenrecht, Art. 34c). Aus dem Vorhergehenden ergibt sich also, dass einige der zur Bezeichnung des hier untersuchten Begriffes belegten Verben, und zwar *dela*, *domia* (bzw. *dema*), *finda* und *wisa*, aus der Tätigkeitssphäre des Asegas hervorgehen.

*

Bezüglich des Begriffes 'urteilen' lassen sich keine wirklichen diachronen Verschiebungen und auch keine auffälligen Unterschiede zwischen dem westfriesischen und dem osterlauwersschen Bereich feststellen. Es lässt sich der Schluss ziehen, dass das Verschwinden des mit dem 'Urteilen' beauftragten Asegas nicht zu einer Erneuerung des Vokabulars geführt hat. Allerdings scheint die afr. Terminologie auch nicht eigenständig friesisch zu sein. Eine interessante Neuerung ohne Entsprechungen in den Nachbarsprachen ist hingegen das Aufkommen einer vielfältigen eigenen Terminologie zur Bezeichnung der Begriffe 'urteilen zugunsten von' bzw. 'urteilen zuungunsten von'. Vergleichbar sind, soweit ersichtlich, lediglich die nachstehenden Bezeichnungen in den Utrechter Küren: *enen in den onrechten vinden* bzw. *enen in den onrechten wisen* ('urteilen zuungunsten von einem').[154] In den *kenningen* der Stadt Leiden (vgl. zu diesem Verfahren Abschnitt 3.4.) wird folgendermaßen formuliert: die Schöffen *geven A. die*

---

151 Siebs, 'Geschichte der friesischen Sprache', 1325; D. Boutkan and S. M. Siebinga, *Old Frisian Etymological Dictionary* (Leiden und Boston, 2005), 70. Im Deichrecht der Hemmen (O II 33) werden die (Deich)richter als *demeren* bezeichnet.

152 Buma und Ebel, *Das Rüstringer Recht*, 42 (1. der Vierundzwanzig Landrechte).

153 *Ibid.* 112. Vgl. auch *ibid.*, 104 (Art. 10).

154 MNW, s.v. *vinden* c.q. s.v. *wisen*. Vgl. auch Muller, *Rechtsbronnen Utrecht*, glossarium s.v.

kennijnge gewonnen ende B. verloren.[155] Dieser Wortlaut entspricht auffälligerweise genau der i.J. 1507 vom sächsischen Statthalter gewünschten Terminologie (vgl. Abschnitt 1.).

3.7. Urteil

In den jüngeren westfriesischen Quellen ist das dem Lateinischen entnommene Wort *sentencie* die gängigste Bezeichnung des Begriffes 'Urteil'. In Art. 35 der Willküren von Wymbritseradeel, der frühesten Fundstelle, heißt es beispielsweise: *dae jeen, deer dae sententia wysa scellet* ('diejenigen, die das Urteil fällen sollen'). Mitunter begegnet jedoch auch *dom*, das Grundwort des Verbs *domia*. Die Synonymie der beiden Wörter wird belegt im folgenden, einer Urkunde d.J. 1456 entnommenen Zitat: *alle [...] secka [...] deer nyn sentencie ner doem oen wysd ner deeld is* ('alle Sachen, in denen kein Urteil [2x] gefällt [2x] worden ist').[156] Im Franeker Bürgerbrief sowie in den Küren von Utingeradeel, in denen der Begriff 'Urteil' jeweils einmal begegnet, wird er mit dem Wort *dom* bezeichnet.[157] Im Amtseid der *grietmannen* von Wymbritseradeel finden wir ebenfalls einen Beleg: *dat iemma twiska twira tale ene riuchte doem dele* ('dass ihr nach der Rede der zwei Parteien ein gerechtes Urteil fällt').[158] Die Bedeutung des Ausdrucks *to dom koma*, der einige Male in den Urkunden auftaucht[159] und ebenfalls in Art. 11 des Jüngeren Schulzenrechts begegnet, ist am besten zu umschreiben mit 'sich dem Gericht stellen'.

In den Willküren von Wininge ist ausnahmslos von *find* die Rede, ein Terminus, der auch in den Willküren von Wymbritseradeel benutzt wird. Mit der Rechtssatzung *nene claghe in dene fynd tho slane wytha breeff* (wörtlich: 'keine Klage in das Urteil zu schlagen gegen den Brief') wird in den Küren von Wininge (Art. 6) angezeigt, dass kein Richter in irgendeinem Rechtsverfahren ein mit dem Rechtsbrief von Wininge strittiges Urteil sprechen darf. In diesen Küren (Art. 8) begegnet auch die figura etymologica *een fynd fynda* ('ein Urteil finden'; wörtlich: 'einen Fund finden').[160]

In der Sneeker Stadttafel ist wiederholt von *ordel* ('Urteil') die Rede, nahezu ausschließlich ohne weiteren oder höchstens mit sehr beschränktem Kontext (z.B. *om j ordel*).[161] Viel häufiger noch begegnet die Zusammen-

---

155 P. J. Blok, *Leidsche rechtsbronnen uit de Middeleeuwen* ('s-Gravenhage, 1884), 89–367 (passim).

156 O II 41.

157 O II 10 (Art. 9), 29k.

158 *Westerlauwerssches Recht I*, Buma und Ebel, Hg., 630.

159 O II 76, 117, 161, III 25.

160 Auch in *Codex Aysma*, Buma, Gerbenzon und Tragter-Schubert, Hg., 48 (A24.1), 64 (A32.1).

161 Z.B. SnR 318.

setzung *mandordel* ('gemeinsames Urteil'), öfter mit dem gleichen Kontext (*om j mandordel*).[162] Eine einzige Eintragung, die nicht – wie sonst üblich – vom Stadtschreiber, sondern von einem Unbekannten geschrieben wurde, zeigt etwas mehr Kontext auf: *lythia henrick ordel van andert van claes symen zin claeg*.[163] An anderer Stelle hat der Stadtschreiber selbst eine sich offensichtlich auf die gleiche Angelegenheit beziehende Notiz gemacht: *lijttija henrick om j wanandert [...] claes symon claegh*.[164] Aus diesen Worten lässt sich schließen, dass 'kleiner' Heinrich in einem Verfahren einen Gerichtstermin versäumte, worauf das Gericht auf die Klage seines Prozessgegners ein *ordel* fällte, in dem er der Säumnis für schuldig befunden wurde. Es handelt sich in diesem Fall also eindeutig nicht um ein End-, sondern um ein Zwischenurteil.

Wir stoßen auch auf Fälle, dass in einem Verfahren mehrere *ordelen* gefällt wurden: *om iiij ordelen, om ij ordelen*.[165] In diesem Zusammenhang ist darauf hinzuweisen, dass im Prozess germanischer Prägung das Verfahren sich von Urteil zu Urteil bewegte. Aus der Rechtsliteratur des 14. und 15. Jhs. sind Gerichtsformulare überliefert mit über 20 Urteilsfragen von seiten des Klägers, ebenso vielen des Beklagten und mehr als 25 im anschließenden Beweisverfahren.[166] Unter solchen Umständen ist die Fällung eines Endurteils die Ausnahme, des Zwischenurteils die Regel.

Was ist ein *mandordel*? Aller Wahrscheinlichkeit nach bezeichnet diese Umschreibung dasselbe wie die Kollokation *menen fijnd* (Akkusativ) in Art. 7 der Willküren von Wymbritseradeel, und zwar ein von sämtlichen Richtern gefälltes Urteil.[167] Wenn dies zutrifft, würde das darauf hinweisen, dass auch in Sneek die Urteilsfrage zunächst an einen aus der Gruppe der Schöffen gerichtet wurde. Konnte dieser das Urteil nicht 'finden', so sollte gemeinsam ein Urteil gefällt werden.[168] Auffällig ist allerdings, dass im Sneeker Rezessbuch, anders als in der Stadttafel, der Begriff nur noch einmal erwähnt wird.[169] Im Stadtrecht fehlt der Begriff vollends.

Abschließend noch einige Bemerkungen zum Begriff 'Urteil' in den Sneeker Quellen. Im Stadtrecht werden die Wörter *oerdel* und *sentencie*

162 Z.B. SnR 310–17.

163 SnR 204 (terminus a quo: 1–3–1494; terminus ante quem: 25–4–1494).

164 SnR 1676 (14–4–1494).

165 SnR 890, 894.

166 G. Landwehr, '"Urteilfragen" und "Urteilfinden" nach spätmittelalterlichen, insbesondere sächsischen Rechtsquellen', *Zeitschrift der Savigny-Stiftung für Rechtsgeschichte (Germanistische Abteilung)* 96 (1979), 1–37, hier 3–5.

167 Oosterhout, 'De "Papena Ponten"', 67, übersetzt diesen Begriff folgendermaßen: 'fûnis, dêr't allegearre, to witten (ek) de meirjochters oan meidogge' ('Urteil, an dem sich alle, nämlich (auch) die Mitrichter, beteiligen').

168 Vgl. Landwehr, '"Urteilfragen"', 5.

169 SnR 3022 (1507, Überschrift).

ohne Unterschied verwendet.[170] In der bereits öfter zitierten Urkunde bezüglich des Prozesses d.J. 1492 wird die Umschreibung *sentencie* angewendet. Ein Zwischenurteil heißt im Rezessbuch auch *interlocutorie sentencia, sentencia interlocutorie* oder kurzweg *interlocutorie*,[171] Bezeichnungen, die der romano-kanonischen Terminologie angehören.

Wird ein Urteil nicht gescholten oder, wie im jüngeren Prozessverfahren üblich, wird bezüglich eines Urteils nicht Berufung eingelegt, dann wird es zu einem 'Endurteil'. Für diesen Begriff begegnen im Rezessbuch mehrere Bezeichnungen, die ebenfalls als von romano-kanonischer Herkunft zu charakterisieren sind: *diffinityff ordel*,[172] *diffinityff sentencie*[173] sowie *sentencie diffinityff*.[174] Die in der Stadttafel belegten Kollokationen *fol sentencie* und *volcommen sentencie*[175] ('voll prozediertes Urteil') sollten nicht mit dem Begriff 'Endurteil' in Verbindung gebracht werden.

Die 'klassische' Bezeichnung des Begriffes 'Endurteil' ist *ende* (wörtlich: 'Ende, Schluss'). In den Willküren von Wininge (Art. 7) heißt es beispielsweise: *een mene jnsegel tho makyane, derma alle enden mithe byschrewen inseglye* ('Es soll ein gemeinsames Siegel angefertigt werden, mit dem man alle geschriebenen Endurteile versiegeln soll'). Wir begegnen dem Begriff auch einmal im Brokmerbrief (§ 27). In den Hunsingoer Küren (Art. 20) stoßen wir auf die als Kontamination anmutende Umschreibung *endadne ende* (wörtlich: 'beendetes Endurteil').[176] Eine ausgesprochen klare Formulierung, in der die gleiche Umschreibung verwendet wird, finden wir im Rechtsbuch Excerpta legum: *Dit js riucht, dat en aynt eeynde aech to staene, dar en man nat van biroept haith bynna tyen degum* ('Dies ist Recht, dass ein Endurteil, gegen das man nicht innerhalb von zehn Tagen Berufung eingelegt hat, Bestand haben soll').[177]

Interessant ist auch die Umschreibung in der bereits öfter zitierten Urkunde d.J. 1476: die ins Unrecht gesetzte Prozesspartei hat das Urteil nicht gescholten (*dae sentencie naet bij leckit*) (vgl. für diesen Ausdruck Abschnitt 3.8.), sondern *bij ghroija ende in her macht gaen leten* (wörtlich: 'bewachsen und in ihre Macht ergehen lassen').[178] Mit dem Partizip Perfekt des Verbes *bigroia* (ndl. *begroeien*) wurde nicht nur in Westfriesland,

---

[170] *De Friesche stadrechten*, Telting, Hg., 71–72 (Art. 20, 21).

[171] Z.B. SnR 2454, 2460 (1510), 4371 (1507).

[172] Z.B. SnR 2107, 2192 (1512).

[173] Z.B. SnR 2448, 2451 (1510).

[174] SnR 3728 (1509).

[175] SnR 197 (1492), 218 (1494).

[176] *Das Hunsingoer Recht*, Buma und Ebel, Hg., 125, übersetzen den Begriff wohl fehlerhaft: 'eine *[durch Vergleich]* beendete Sache'. Vgl. auch die Ausführung von Van Helten, *Zur lexicologie des altostfriesischen*, 95–96.

[177] *Codex Aysma*, Buma, Gerbenzon und Tragter-Schubert, Hg., 12 (A5.4).

[178] O II 82.

sondern auch in Groningen und Drenthe noch im 18. Jh. bezeichnet, dass ein Urteil Rechtskraft erlangt hatte (ndl. 'in kracht van gewijsde gaan').[179]

Die übliche Bezeichnung des Begriffes 'Urteil' im Brokmerbrief sowie in den Hunsingoer Küren ist *dom*. Wenn in den Schulzenrechten von *dom* die Rede ist, was häufig der Fall ist, handelt es sich ausnahmslos um die Rechtsweisung des Asegas. Wir beobachten hier, wie das Verfahren sich vom einen *dom* des Asegas zum anderen bewegte, vergleichbar mit dem oben geschilderten Ablauf, in welchem das eine *ordel* dem anderen folgte. Art. 64 des Älteren Schulzenrechts bezieht sich auf den Fall, dass der Asega durch seinen *dom* eine Streitsache beendete (*dae di aesga ... mey syne doeme dae secke endegade*). Bei alledem ist eindeutig, dass der Begriff *dom*, ebenso wie das davon abgeleitete Verb *domia*, aus dem Tätigkeitsfeld des Asegas hervorgeht.

Der Terminus *ordel* hat in den älteren Quellen, wie im 23. der Vierundzwanzig Landrechte, im Älteren Schulzenrecht und auch in dem westfriesischen Sendrecht, die prägnante Bedeutung 'Gottesurteil'.[180]

*

Die älteren Quellen, sowohl die westfriesischen wie die osterlauwersschen, weisen eine einzige Bezeichnung des Begriffes 'Urteil' auf, und zwar *dom*. Es handelt sich hier um einen gemeingermanischen Terminus.[181] In den jüngeren westfriesischen Quellen hat das Wort zwar noch nicht völlig das Feld geräumt, aber es ist doch größtenteils von den neuen Begriffen *find*, *ordel* und insbesondere dem ganz modernen Wort *sentencie* verdrängt worden.[182] Dass der Begriff *ordel* in der friesischen Rechtssprache erst später auftaucht, ist keineswegs eine Überraschung, weil es sich, wie Freudenthal gezeigt hat, um ein Rechtswort fränkischen Ursprungs handelt.[183] Auch im Angelsächsischen bezieht sich das Wort *ordál*, wie *ordel* in den älteren friesischen Quellen, lediglich auf die Gottesurteile.[184] Allerdings blieb im Englischen, anders als im Afr., diese Bedeutung die einzige.

---

179 WNT, s.v. *begroeien* (hier auch ein Beispiel d.J. 1884); S. J. Fockema Andreae, *Proeve van een woordenlijst der aan Friesland (onder de Republiek) eigene bestuurs- en rechtstermen* (Leeuwarden, 1967), s.v. *begroeid*.

180 AFW, s.v. *ordel* und Buma, *Vollständiges Wörterbuch*, s.v. *ordêl, ordil* entschließen sich bezüglich der hier genannten Quellen in einigen Fällen, m.E. zu Unrecht, für die Bedeutung 'urtheil, richterspruch, rechtsentscheidung'.

181 Freudenthal, *Arnulfingisch-karolingische Rechtswörter*, 71.

182 Vgl. für letzteres Wort: *ibid.* 98, sowie P. Gerbenzon, *Friese rechtstaal en vreemd recht* (Groningen, 1958), 12.

183 Freudenthal, *Arnulfingisch-karolingische Rechtswörter*, 75, 200 (Karte).

184 *Ibid.* 124–25.

Eigenständig friesisch ist schließlich noch die Umschreibung des Endurteils als 'beendetes Ende'.

3.8. Schelten des Urteils

Das Anfechten ('schelten' oder 'strafen') des Urteils (lat. *sententiam blasphemare*)[185] seitens der vom Richter ins Unrecht gesetzten Partei, womit der Weg zu einem neuen Prozess vor einem höheren Gericht eröffnet wurde, wird in den jüngeren Quellen nahezu ausnahmslos mit dem Verb *bilekkia* (wörtlich: 'bemängeln', mnl. *belaken*) bezeichnet.[186] In der wiederholt zitierten Sneeker Urkunde d.J. 1492 wird das Unterbleiben der Urteilsschelte beispielsweise folgendermaßen formuliert: *welke sententie dae iggen habbet consenteret ende naet fan bylecket* ('welches Urteil die Parteien angenommen haben und nicht [von] angefochten').[187] Auch in Art. 33 der Willküren von Wymbritseradeeel ist von *bilekkia* die Rede, während im Franeker Marktrecht d.J. 1402 sowie im Franeker Bürgerbrief die Form *lakia*, also ohne Präfix und Tonerhöhung des Vokals, begegnet.[188]

In den Willküren von Utingeradeel finden wir einen möglichen Hinweis auf die Handlung des Scheltens: *off enich man enen doem weder spreeck danne naet ferra toe bi seken dan omda presteren wssis deels* ('falls irgendein Mann einem Urteil widerspricht, dann soll man ihm nicht weiter widersprechen als bei den Priestern unseres Bezirks').[189] Wenn diese Interpretation zutrifft, wird die Urteilsschelte in dieser Quelle also mit zwei Verben bezeichnet: *wederspreka* und *biseka* ('widersprechen, leugnen, bestreiten').

In den Schulzenrechten fehlt jegliche, in den osterlauwersschen Quellen nahezu jede Spur des Scheltens. Im Emsinger Pfennigschuldbuch ist zwar einmal die Rede von *straffia* (wörtlich: 'strafen'), aber das Verb bedeutet hier lediglich 'widersprechen'.[190] Ein einziges Mal ist der Begriff in den älteren Quellen belegt, und zwar in Art. 20 der Hunsingoer Küren. Es handelt sich hier um den Fall, dass ein Mann das Endurteil nach einem Jahr noch anfechten will: *thes letera ieres welle wlemma*.[191] Van Helten hat bereits nachgewiesen, dass das denominative Verb *wlemma*, Ableitung des Substantivs **wlame* ('Mangel'), semantisch genau dem Verb *lekkia* ('mängeln') entspricht.[192]

---

185 De Rhoer, *Aanteekeningen*, 28.

186 Vries, 'Een communalistische voorloper', 28–31.

187 SnR 197.

188 O II 7, 10j.

189 O II 29k.

190 *Das Emsiger Recht*, Buma und Ebel, Hg., 224, 225 (Übersetzung).

191 *Das Hunsingoer Recht*, Buma und Ebel, Hg., 124.

192 Van Helten, *Zur lexicologie des altostfriesischen*, 95–96; G. Walter, *Der Wortschatz des Altfriesischen. Eine wortgeographische Untersuchung* (Leipzig, 1911), 59.

Im Brokmerbrief wird zwar auch das Anfechten eines Urteils erwähnt, aber die Formulierung weicht hier stark ab. So heißt es, wie in Abschnitt 3.4. bereits zitiert wurde, in § 19: *Vvel mar enne rediewa onspreca vmbe enne vndom* ('Will man einen *redjeva* wegen eines ungerechten Urteils verklagen'). In diesem Fall wird also nicht das Urteil als ungerecht 'gescholten', sondern der Richter, der das als ungerecht empfundene Urteil gefällt hat, verklagt. In der Praxis macht das allerdings keinen wirklichen Unterschied.

*

Die Terminologie in den jüngeren westfriesischen wie in den älteren osterlauwersschen Quellen (*bilekkia* bzw. das lediglich einmal belegte Verb *wlemma*) entspricht nicht derjenigen der Nachbarsprachen. Sie ist somit eigenständig friesisch.

4. Schlussbetrachtung

Der vom sächsischen Statthalter i.J. 1507 als unklar abgelehnte Wortlaut des Richterspruchs in Westfriesland ('ich weise diesen Mann fort und jenen zurück') war keinesfalls untauglich. Er war nur eigenständig friesisch, genauer gesagt: westfriesisch, und aus diesem Grund für Fremde ungewöhnlich. Die vorliegende Untersuchung zeigt, dass sich gerade zur Bezeichnung des Begriffes 'urteilen zu(un)gunsten von' in Westfriesland eine vielfältige eigentümliche Terminologie entwickelt hat. Die afr. Terminologie im Bereich des Zivilprozessrechts zeigte manches Eigenständige; allerdings war sie teilweise auch ganz 'normal', d.h. nicht abweichend von den Nachbarsprachen des Altfriesischen, dem Mittelniederländischen und dem Mittelniederdeutschen.

Ein konservativer Zug der afr. Terminologie im Vergleich mit derjenigen der Nachbarsprachen ist das lange Festhalten am Wort *dom* zur Bezeichnung des Begriffes 'Urteil'. Die in den Nachbarsprachen bereits länger gängige Umschreibung *ordel* hat sich hier erst sehr spät und überdies lediglich in begrenztem Umfang durchgesetzt, vielleicht weil der Begriff *ordel* in Friesland noch lange die Erinnerung an das Gottesurteil aufrief. Interessant ist dabei, dass das Substantiv *dom* wie auch das denominative Verb *domia* nicht mit dem Verschwinden des ursprünglich mit dem 'Urteilen' beauftragten Asegas aufgegeben wurden, sondern seither das Urteil bzw. das Urteilen des neuen genossenschaftlichen Richters bezeichneten. In dieser Hinsicht gab es überdies, anders als in vielen anderen Fällen, zwischen Westfriesland und dem osterlauwersschen Teil Frieslands keinerlei Unterschied.

Es fallen im untersuchten Wortfeld nicht nur regionale, sondern auch diachronische Unterschiede auf, wenn sich letztere auch, aufgrund des Verschwindens der afr. Schreibsprache östlich der Lauwsers, sich lediglich im westfr. Bereich beobachten lassen. Besonders der Brokmerbrief weist mit Termini wie *bare* und *ienbare* ('Klage' bzw. 'Gegenklage') und dem davon abgeleiteten Verb *baria* sowie *bonna* ('vorladen') eine eigenständige Terminologie auf. Eine ins Auge fallende Verschiebung im westfriesischen Wortgebrauch stellt die Verdrängung der Umschreibung *greta* ('klagen') durch die Worte *klagia* und *upspreka*, eine andere die von *haldere* ('Beklagter') durch *sitter*. Bei letzterem Wort, das auf den ersten Blick kaum auffällt, handelt es sich tatsächlich um eine der charakteristischsten Neubildungen der afr. Prozessterminologie. Möglicherweise haben wir es hierbei mit einer Lehnübersetzung aus der romano-kanonischen Prozessterminologie zu tun. Das einzige Beispiel für den Gebrauch eines dem Lateinischen und somit dem romano-kanonischen Recht entnommenen Wortes ist *sentencie*.

Besonders charakteristisch ist noch die Bezeichnung des Begriffs 'schelten', sowohl im wester- wie auch im osterlauwersschen Bereich (*bilekkia* bzw. *wlemma*). Der im friesischen Gerichtsverfahren übliche Pfandeinsatz ergab eine reiche Terminologie, die auch völlig eigenständig erscheint. Ob der nicht-eigenständige Teil der afr. Prozessterminologie stärker vom Ndl. als vom Nd. beeinflusst wurde, ist allerdings schwer zu entscheiden.

Abkürzungen

AFW — K. von Richthofen, *Altfriesisches Wörterbuch* (Göttingen, 1840; Nachdruck: Aalen, 1970).

DRW — *Deutsches Rechtswörterbuch (Wörterbuch der älteren deutschen Rechtssprache)*, I–... (Weimar, 1914–...).

GPCB — *Groot Placaat en Charter-boek van Vriesland*, G. F. thoe Schwartzenberg en Hohenlansberg, Hg., 6 Bde. (Leeuwarden, 1768–1795).

HRG — *Handwörterbuch zur deutschen Rechtsgeschichte*, A. Erler, E. Kaufmann und D. Werkmüller, Hg., 5 Bde. (Berlin, 1964–1998).

MNDW — K. Schiller und A. Lübben, *Mittelniederdeutsches Wörterbuch*, 5 Bde. (Bremen, 1875–1880).

MNHW — A. Lasch und C. Borchling, *Mittelniederdeutsches Handwörterbuch*, I–... (Neumünster, 1956–...).

MNW — E. Verwijs und J. Verdam, *Middelnederlandsch Woordenboek*, 9 Bde. ('s-Gravenhage, 1885–1929).

O — *Oudfriesche Oorkonden*, P. Sipma, Hg., Bd. 1–3. OTR 1–3 ('s-Gravenhage, 1927–1941); *Oudfriese Oorkonden*, O. Vries, Hg., Bd. 4. OTR 14 ('s-Gravenhage, 1977).

SnR — *Snitser Recesboeken 1490–1517*, M. Oosterhout, Hg. (Assen, 1960).

WNT — *Woordenboek der Nederlandsche Taal*, 29 Bde. (Leiden und 's-Gravenhage, 1882–1998).

Early Christian Loans in Old Frisian: The Linguistic Evidence

David Yeandle

The purpose of this essay is to examine the linguistic evidence in Old Frisian which relates to the earliest Christian loans from Latin and Greek to the Germanic languages. This cannot be done in isolation, but must be undertaken in the wider Germanic context, especially in relation to Old High German, but also with reference to Old Low German and Old Low Franconian. Our primary point of enquiry will therefore be: What, if any, light does an investigation of the Old Frisian evidence – which has hitherto largely been ignored or at best treated in a cursory manner – shed on the wider Germanic picture with regard to dating and point of entry, etymology, meaning, usage, distribution and frequency of the earliest Christian loan words?

We are comparatively well informed about the origins of Christianity in Frisia. Willibrord,[1] an Anglo-Saxon missionary, the Apostle to the Frisians, was given *citerior Fresia*[2] (which had recently been conquered) by Pippin II as his area of activity in 690. He was made Archbishop of the Frisians five years later by the Pope, and in 719, after having been forced to withdraw from Utrecht, after it had been reconquered by the pagan Frisians under Redbad, he was able to return, aided this time by Boniface, who, a few years later would turn his attention to Hesse and Thuringia and become the Apostle to the Germans.[3] An easy assumption might be that all Christian vocabulary entered Old Frisian via these two missionary sources. However, the earliest loans to the Germanic languages from the Roman Empire predate this period of missionary activity by several centuries.

---

1 Willibrord was born ca. 658 and died in 739.

2 Frisia to the south-west of the Old Rhine.

3 See O. Vries, 'Geschichte der Friesen im Mittelalter: West und Ostfriesland', *Handbuch / Handbook*, 535–50, at 540. In detail, see H. Halbertsma, *Frieslands oudheid: Het rijk van de Friese koningen, opkomst en ondergang*, ed. E. H. P. Cordfunke and H. Sarfatij (Utrecht, 2000); L. E. von Padberg, *Mission und Christianisierung: Formen und Folgen bei Angelsachsen und Franken im 7. und 8. Jahrhundert* (Stuttgart, 1995), 49–50.

The dating of loan words is a notoriously difficult procedure. If there is no firm historical evidence in the form of words attested shortly after their introduction to the recipient language for the first time in contemporary (reliably datable) manuscripts, something that for much of Germanic is sorely lacking, then we are dependent upon phonological and cultural-historical criteria.[4] The Christianization of the Germanic tribes is a tangled skein, with many uncertainties, suppositions, and assumptions. The accuracy of some of attributions of provenance is not only questionable but indeed unverifiable. In the case of Old Frisian, the problems are even greater, since the corpus of Old Frisian texts dates from such a late period, relative to the topic under consideration.[5] It is reckoned that the majority of Christian terms were transmitted to the Germanic tribes in the earliest phases of Christianization, which for the Anglo-Saxons means the late sixth and early seventh century, and for the Frisians the Carolingian period during the seventh and eighth centuries.[6] Nevertheless, it is thought that some basic words of Christian vocabulary were borrowed at a very early stage before the (widespread) conversion of individual tribes through contact with Roman civilization in the late imperial period, dating back to the fourth century.[7] Frisia was situated on the borders of the Roman Empire together with other Germanic dialects, which existed together in a Germanic linguistic continuum, and there is ample evidence for direct borrowings from Latin in the (late) Imperial period, even though historically not much is heard of the Frisians in the period between the beginning of the fourth century and the reign of Clovis (481–511),[8] we may assume that there were trading and military links and that the Frisians did not remain enclosed within an isolated community.[9] The Rhine and Moselle served as important trade routes which

[4] See A. Wollmann, 'Zu den frühesten lateinischen Lehnwörtern im Altfriesischen', *Aspects*, 506–36, at 511; K. Dekker, 'Between Rome and Rüstringen: Latin Loan Words in Old Frisian', *Philologia Frisica anno 1999* (Leeuwarden, 2000), 27–56.

[5] Wollmann, 'Zu den frühesten lateinischen Lehnwörtern', 507.

[6] *Ibid.* 511. The West Frisians were converted at the end of the seventh century, the East Frisians in the course of the eighth century.

[7] Cf., amongst others, *ibid.* 511: 'ein Teil des christlichen Grundwortschatzes wie die Bezeichnungen für "Teufel" (afries. *diōvel*, *dīvel*; ae. *dēofol*), "Kirche" (afries. *kerke*, *karke*, *zerke*, *ziruke* [sic, read *ziurke*]; ae. *cirice*), "Bischof" (afries./ae. *biscop*) oder "Engel" (afries. *engel*, *angel*; ae. *engel*) [dürfte] schon vor der Christianisierung als "Fremdwörter" bekannt gewesen sein'.

[8] Cf. Halbertsma, *Frieslands oudheid*, 49.

[9] Cf. Dekker, 'Between Rome and Rüstringen', 31–32: 'The earlier contacts between Frisians and speakers of Latin and Romance took place in a spoken linguistic environment. Frisians traded with Romans and Romanized Franks, served as legionaries, or were captured as slaves. In the resulting linguistic interaction the loan words were completely adapted to the Germanic accent system, and developed along the lines of Germanic phonology'.

also carried loan traffic northwards. Although the Roman Empire's official boundary was the west bank of the Rhine, many loans spread out beyond this limit.[10] Wollmann summarizes the linguistic situation thus:[11]

> Der Einfluß des Lt. hörte jedoch nicht mit dem Zusammenbruch des römischen Reiches auf, sondern das Rom. wirkte weiter auf die in der Entstehung begriffenen westgerm. Einzelsprachen. Dies ist daran erkennbar, daß die kontinentalwestgerm. Sprachen zahlreiche lt. Lehnwörter aufweisen, die das Ae. – bedingt durch die Einwanderung der angelsächsischen Stämme nach Britannien im Laufe des 5. Jhs. – nicht mehr aufgenommen hatte. Wir wollen diese Wörter als 'spätere Lehnwörter' bezeichnen.

Our earliest Frisian texts date from the late thirteenth century. Many are attested much later, some as late as 1600, even though some texts show archaic features which indicate a linguistic form that predates the manuscript evidence. Thus, half a millennium separates the coming of Christianity to Frisia from the attestation of most of the vocabulary and almost a whole millennium has elapsed since the earliest Roman contacts. Given these circumstances, we clearly cannot rely primarily on the dating of the Old Frisian texts when making comparisons with other Germanic languages, which were almost all – in particular Gothic, Old English, Old High German, and Old Saxon – attested much earlier, the most obvious points of comparison – Old English and Old High German – being attested from the eighth/ninth centuries. In view of this situation, it is necessary to heed phonological criteria[12] and the evidence of dialect geography.[13] It is a well-known facet of the north-west area of the Lower Rhine that this is a linguistically conservative area as regards borrowing, which by and large rejects the overlayering of old loan words with new, as witness the preservation of conservative (pagan Roman) days of the week, the Old Frisian forms of which are: *sunnandei, mōnandei, tīesdei, wedenesdei, thunresdei, frīadei, sāterdei.*[14] Frings has referred to this area in this respect as a 'Beharrungsgebiet'.[15]

We are fortunate to possess, through the good offices of the Fryske Akademy and the Frisian Institute of the University of Groningen, a sub-

[10] See T. Frings, *Germania Romana*, Mitteldeutsche Studien 19/1, 2nd ed. G. Müller, 1. Teil (Halle/S., 1966), *passim.*

[11] Wollmann, 'Zu den frühesten lateinischen Lehnwörtern', 535–36.

[12] *Ibid.*, passim.

[13] See Frings, *Germania Romana*.

[14] The form is, of course, under Anglo-Saxon influence; *thunresdei* shows the original Germanic translation, which in English was later changed under Norse influence to *Thursday*.

[15] See Frings, *Germania Romana*, 45.

stantial collection of the most important Old Frisian texts in digital format.[16] These permit a full analysis of the Christian vocabulary of Old Frisian. Only such an approach will do justice to the multiplicity of variant orthographic forms and the complexity of the lexemes. It would be impossible, in the confines of this essay, to list and comment on the whole Christian vocabulary in Old Frisian or even the loan vocabulary.

Holthausen drew up a list of loan words in 1921.[17] In Köbler's online dictionary, based on Holthausen, the loan vocabulary is individually marked.[18] A large proportion of these loans are Christian or have Christian associations, as is immediately apparent from the not unrepresentative letter 'A', which contains a variety of loan words, both secular and religious, from a variety of periods; some, earlier loans, being more fully assimilated than others:[19]

abba, abbet(e), abbit, ebbete abt: l. *abbas*, gen. *abbatis* (gr. syr.) (s. v. H., Aofr. 8.389).
absolvēria absolvieren: l. *absolvere*.
advent m. advent: l. *adventus*.
agripīnisk kölnisch: l. *Agrippina*.
altare, alter m. n. altar: l. *altāre*, *altar*.
*amīe f. geliebte: frz. *amie* < l. *amica*.
apostol, -el m. apostel: l. *apostolus* (gr.).
*aventūre f. zufall, ereignis: afrz. ~ < l. *adventūra*

Our investigation will necessarily – for reasons of space – be restrictive, singling out a handful of words for scrutiny which previous scholarship has identified as belonging to the earliest stratum of Christian loan vocabulary. Scholars have differed in the words assigned to this earliest group. While Wollmann has selected *Teufel*, *Kirche*, *Bischof*, and *Engel* as belonging to this earliest group for Old Frisian,[20] Bremmer has additionally selected

---

[16] I should like to express my thanks to Han Nijdam of the Fryske Akademy for providing me with the Academy's electronic corpus of Old Frisian texts, to Oebele Vries of the Frisian Institute, University of Groningen, for supplying me with digital versions of the Old Frisian Letters, the Charters, and the *Snitser Recesboeken*, and to Rolf Bremmer, University of Leiden, for advice on the texts and filling in some gaps.

[17] F. Holthausen, 'Nordfriesische Studien 5. Die fremd- und lehnwörter', *BGdSL* 45 (1921), 34–39.

[18] F. Holthausen, *Altfriesisches Wörterbuch* (Heidelberg, 1925), 2nd ed. D. Hofmann (Heidelberg, 1985); Gerhard Köbler, *Altfriesisches Wörterbuch*, 2nd ed. (2003), <http://www.koeblergerhard.de/afrieswbhinw.html>. The entries are marked *Lw.* 'Lehnwort', *Lüs.* 'Lehnübersetzung', *Lüt.* 'Lehnübertragung'.

[19] The variety of forms shown by *abba*, *abbet(e)*, *abbit*, *ebbete* signals widespread dissemination and a natural assimilation into the spoken language, suggesting an earlier dating. Cf. also Wollmann, 'Zu den frühesten lateinischen Lehnwörtern', 536.

[20] Cf. fn. 7, above.

kersten.[21] Frings, in his pioneering work on contacts between the Roman Empire and Germania, has singled out the following as belonging to this period, which he calls a 'vorfränkische Schicht': *Kirche*, *Bischof*, *opfern* ('*offerre*'–'*operari*'), *Almosen*.[22] For all these words, then, we pose the question: Is a date of borrowing into Frisian between the fourth to sixth centuries, before mainscale conversion, a probability or possibility, even though in view of the dating of the texts no ultimate certainty can be achieved? It is often assumed that the early loans to the Germanic languages from Latin were merely fortuitously picked up as constituent elements of Roman civilization, without any process of conversion of the Germanic speakers. Although there was no full-scale missionary activity and mass conversion, there is evidence of missionary activity in Trier and Cologne, and hence not far removed from the Old Frisian area, as for example by Bishop Maternus,[23] first Bishop of Cologne and possibly third of Trier: 'Vieles spricht dafür, daß er am Niederrhein bzw. im Raum Köln-Tongern als erster bischöflicher Amtsträger (und Missionar) zu gelten hat'.[24] Nevertheless, in looking at this earliest period of influence, it may be helpful to think of a relationship between Christianity and Roman society akin to that which exists, say, between Islam and contemporary European society. Just as the average European citizen knows probably very little of the tenets of the Islamic faith, he or she is acquainted with the physical presence of mosques, knows of the existence of imams and mullahs, would be hard pressed to define these exactly, and has some conception of Ramadan as a sacred time, involving a fast. Such would no doubt have been the kind of acquaintance of the unconverted populace within the Roman Empire – here specifically the Gaulish and Germanic provinces – in the first three or four centuries of the Christian era. There is evidence, for example, from Latin texts, which shows

---

[21] Cf. R. H. Bremmer Jr, *An Introduction to Old Frisian* (forthcoming), § 172: 'The conversion to Christianity brought a new wave of Latin loans. To the earliest of these words, dating back to perhaps even before the conversion, belong *biskop* 'bishop' (< *episcopus*), *diōvel* 'devil' (< *diabolus*), *kersten* 'Christian' (< *c(h)rīstiānus*). Other loans related to the conversion include *engel/angel* 'angel' (< *angelus*), *skrīva* 'to write; impose penance' (< *scrībere*; the native word was *wrīta* 'write'), *fīre* 'liturgical feast' (< *fēria*), *kersoma* 'chrism' (< *c(h)rīsma*), *degma/dek(e)ma* 'tithe' (< *decima*), *spīse* 'food' (< ML *spēsa* < *expensa (pecūnia)* 'expenses for food'), *lēka*, *leia* 'lay(man)' (< *laicus*).'

[22] See Frings, *Germania Romana*, I, 47–48, 51 and passim. Following Frings, see D. H. Green, *Language and History in the Early Germanic World* (Cambridge, 1998), ch. 16 'The Influence of Provincial Roman Christianity', 291–307.

[23] 'ein Vertrauensmann Constantins', according to Frings, *Germania Romana*, 49.

[24] S. Ristow, 'Maternus', *Biographisch-Bibliographisches Kirchenlexikon*, vol. XX (2002), cols. 994–97 <http://www.bautz.de/bbkl/m/maternus_v_k.shtml>. See also E. Dassmann, *Die Anfänge der Kirche in Deutschland: von der Spätantike bis zur frühfränkischen Zeit*, Urban-Taschenbücher 444 (Stuttgart, 1993), 69–70 and passim; Frings, *Germania Romana*, 45; Green, *Language and History*, 292–96.

an acquaintance with things Christian amongst the pagan Romans, extending even to knowledge of specifically Christian words.

1.1 *Tzerke*

We begin our investigation with one of the most salient features of Christianity, obvious and recognizable to all, whether Christian or pagan, the church building or 'house of the Lord', a word which is ultimately derived from Gk *κυριακόν*.[25] It is attested in Old High German, Old Saxon, Old Frisian, and Old English (late 7th c.), and thence later transmitted to Old Norse.[26] Its provenance has been variously explained: the older view of von Raumer and Kluge and others was to regard it as a loan from Gothic,[27] but this has been challenged by more recent scholarship.[28] Not only is there no evidence for a Gothic word to correspond to the forms attested in the other Germanic languages, but the earliest attestations are in place names scattered over a wide area, encompassing, besides Bavaria (where we would expect Gothic influence first to be felt), Alsace, Francia, and Frisia.[29] The revised view of scholars is that the term originated in the West, either through contact with Greek traders, with a base in Marseilles and links to Trier and the Rhineland,[30] or as objects of booty and plunder, in whatever part of the Empire, by pagan Germanic tribes.[31] It is known that Constantine, who, as Augustus of the West, had his headquarters in Trier (306–312), built

---

[25] *το κυριακῴν* is a substantive formed from the adjective *κυριακός* 'lordly, of the lord', hence its literal meaning is 'that belonging to the lord'. In detail, see A. Masser, *Die Bezeichnungen für das christliche Gotteshaus in der deutschen Sprache des Mittelalters. Mit einem Anhang: Die Bezeichnungen für die Sakristei*, Philologische Studien und Quellen 33 (Berlin, 1966), 17–25. According to Masser, the earliest attestation of the word is from Origen (*PG* 17,132,34): *Excerpta in Psalmos* (A.D. 2–3) *Eἰ δὲ μὴ, κρεῖττόν ἐστι τὴν ἀρχὴν μὴ δανείσασθαι, μάλιστα τὰ τοῦ ταμείου τοῦ Κυριακοῦ, ἢ ἀπολέσαι τὰ τοῦ βασιλέως χρήματα* (quoted from *Thesaurus Linguae Graecae* [TLG] online <http:// www. tlg.uci.edu/>).

[26] Cf. Green, *Language and History in the Early Germanic World*, 298.

[27] See R. von Raumer, 'Über den geschichtlichen Zusammenhang des gotischen Christenthums mit dem althochdeutschen', *ZfdA* 6 (1848), 401–12; Friedrich Kluge, 'Gotische Lehnworte im Althochdeutschen', *BGdSL* 35 (1909), 124–60.

[28] The first to suggest provenance from the Roman Empire was Ulrich Stutz, 'Arianismus und Germanismus. Eine kritische Studie', *Internationale Wochenschrift für Wissenschaft Kunst und Technik* 3 (1909), cols. 1561–82, 1615–22, 1634–048 (1640f.); see also Green, *Language and History*, 298f.

[29] See Masser, *Die Bezeichnungen für das christliche Gotteshaus*.

[30] On this, see Green, *Language and History*, 296–301.

[31] See *Oxford English Dictionary* (*OED*), electronic online edition, s.v. *church*.

churches which were designated by the term *κυριακόν*, pl. *κυριακά*.[32] It was a temporally restricted term which was known from the early third century and throughout the fourth in the Greek-speaking world, which temporarily challenged *βασίλικα* and *εκκλησία*. It was not primarily a literary word and failed to find a lasting place in Greek vocabulary. During the first half of the fourth century, Greek must have been almost as important as Latin in imperial and ecclesiastical affairs in and around Trier[33] and Cologne,[34] so that basic Greek words of ecclesiastical organization were bound to become known to speakers of the vernacular languages (Romance and Germanic) at a time when churches were establishing themselves in German(ic)-speaking territories. As we have seen, there is evidence of native Greek-speaking bishops in Trier and Cologne, and Greek inscriptions are found in Trier besides Latin, so Greek was bound to have an influence on the nascent church organization in Germania and to be passed on beyond the congregations of Christians to the wider population.

It is generally assumed that *κυριακόν*, in whatever form, was loaned directly from Greek into German(ic), not via the medium of Latin. One of the problems of a direct loan from *κυριακόν* is that of the word's gender, neuter in Greek, feminine in Germanic, to which we shall return below. Although there is no early evidence for an equivalent Latin term, by the time

---

32 Eusebius in *De laudibus Constantini,* 17,4,9 refers to them specifically, drawing attention to the meaning 'house of the Lord': *ὁ δὲ τρόπαια νικητήρια παραχρῆμα πανταχοῦ γῆς ἀνίστη, ναοῖς τε ἁγίοις καὶ προσευκτηρίων σεμνοῖς ἀφιερώμασι τὴν σύμπασαν οἰκουμένην αὖθις ἐξ ὑπαρχῆς κοσμήσας, κατὰ πόλεις τε καὶ κώμας χώρας τε πάσας καὶ τὰς τῶν βαρβάρων ἐρήμους ἱερὰ καὶ τεμένη ἑνὶ τῷ πάντων βασιλεῖ θεῷ, τῷ δὴ καὶ τῶν ὅλων δεσπότῃ, καθιερώσας, ἔνθεν καὶ τῆς τοῦ δεσπότου προσηγορίας ἠξίωται τὰ αθιερωμένα, οὐκ ἐξ ἀνθρώπων τυχόντα τῆς ἐπικλήσεως, ἐξ αὐτοῦ δὲ τοῦ τῶν ὅλων κυρίου, παρὸ καὶ κυριακῶν ἠξίωνται τῶν ἐπωνυμιῶν* (TLG). ['Our Saviour, therefore, without delay erected trophies of this victory everywhere, and once more adorned the world with holy temples and consecrated houses of prayer; in every city and village, nay, throughout all countries, and even in barbaric wilds, ordaining the erection of churches and sacred buildings to the honor of the Supreme God and Lord of all. Hence it is that these hallowed edifices are deemed worthy to bear his name, and receive not their appellation from men, but from the Lord himself, from which circumstances they are called churches (or houses of the Lord)' — translation from <http://www.newadvent.org/fathers/2504.htm>.

33 Saint Agritius (c. 260– c. 329/333/335) was the first bishop of Trier. He may have been a patriarch of Antioch before being called to Trier by Pope Silvester I, on the bidding of Empress Helena. Athanasius was exiled to Trier from 335–337, and was full of praise of the missionary work done there. A further Greek-speaking bishop, exiled to Trier, was Paul of Constantinople (338–340).

34 S. Ristow, 'Euphrates', in *Biographisch-Bibliographisches Kirchenlexikon* XX (2002), cols. 472–75: 'Euphrates, zweiter bekannter Bischof von Köln, stammte dem Namen nach aus dem griechischen Sprachraum, war also wohl östlicher Herkunft', <www.bautz.de/bbkl/e/euphrates.shtml>.

a Latin form is first attested in the first half of the ninth century, it has already adopted the feminine gender and appears as *kyriaca* in the writings of Walahfrid Strabo, in a chapter entitled *Quomodo Theotisce domus Dei dicatur* ['How the house of the Lord is referred to in German'] where he explains: 'Sicut itaque domus Dei, basilica, id est regia, a rege: sic etiam Kyriaca, id est Dominica, a Domino nuncupatur, quia Domino dominantium, et Regi regum in illa servitur' ['Thus just as the house of the Lord is called *basilica* [house of the King], that is *regia* [house of the King], from *rege* [king]: in the same way it is called *Kyriaca* [house of the Lord] that is *Dominica* [house of the Lord], from *Domino* [Lord], for in it is served the Lord of lords and King of kings.'] (PL 114, 927B),[35] and Peter Lombard (c. 1100–c. 1164) in his Commentary on the Psalms of David writes: 'Quasi dicat: Ad tuam misericordiam confugio, ut gravibus vulneribus ciriacam remissionis infundas' ['It is as if he says: I flee to your mercy, so that you fill the church with remission for its grave wounds'] (PL 191, 484B–85A). Sicardus Cremonensis (12th c.) in *De nominibus ecclesiae*, provides some speculative etymologizing amongst the more sober detail:

> Dicitur et basilica, ut in Paralipomenon invenitur; id est regalis, quia ibi Regi regum ministratur, basileus namque *rex* interpretatur, quasi basis. Kasa, id est *columna*, et sustentamentum populi, unde et basiliscus rex serpentum dicitur. Dicitur et Kyriaca, id est *Dominicalis*, quia ibi Domino dominorum servitur. Kyrios enim *Dominus* interpretatur. Unde Kyrie eleyson. *Domine, miserere*. (PL 213, 26A–27B)
> ['It is also called *basilica* (house of the king), as is found in Chronicles; that is *regalis* (royal), for there the King of kings is served, for *basileus* (king) is interepreted as *rex* (king), as it were basis. *Kasa*, that is *column*, and the support of the people, whence the basilisk is called the king of the serpents. It is also called *Kyriaca* (house of the Lord), that is *Dominicalis* (lordly), for there the Lord of lords is served. For *Kyrios* is interpreted as *Dominus* (lord). Whence *Kyrie eleison*. Lord, have mercy.']

Like *dominicum*,[36] a calque of the Greek original, *kyriaca* is not commonly attested in written documents, and its existence may well point to a much

---

[35] All quotations from the *Patrologia Latina* are taken from the online version http://pld.chadwyck.com/, an electronic version of the first edition of J.-P. Migne's *Patrologia Latina*, published between 1844 and 1855, and the four volumes of indexes published between 1862 and 1865.

[36] Cf. Augustinus Hipponensis Sermo XXXII in Psalmum CXLIII. *De Golia et David, ac de contemptu mundi*. Caput XXV: 'Audiant ergo, velint, nolint, et discant venire ad Dominicum, non in superbia Goliae, sed in humilitate David.' ['Let them hear therefore, let them want, not want, and learn to come to the House of the Lord, not in the pride of Goliath, but in the humility of David.'] For further examples of *Dominicum* = *kyriakon* 'house of the Lord', see PL, *ibid*., footnote (b).

later latinization of the established German word.[37] But might its use in Vulgar oral Latin possibly be assumed in the fourth century? If it could, it would explain the entry of the term into Germanic, moreover with the feminine gender.

It is normally assumed that *basilica* gave rise to the feminine gender in Germanic, assuming that the word borrowed was based on the original Greek *το κυριακόν* rather than a variant Vulgar Greek form.[38] That is to say that *κυριακόν* assumed the feminine gender from the preceding term *basilica*.[39] Such a process would normally assume that a Germanic word had existed which was superseded and would pass on its gender to the new word, as happened with OHG *uuant* (f.) – Lat. *mūrus* (m.) > OHG *mūra* (f.), the change taking place on or shortly after transference into the Germanic languages.[40] This was clearly not the case with *κυριακόν*, since *basilica* was not used in Old High German.[41] There are numerous examples in Greek of *κυριακη*, especially in the context of the 'day of the Lord' (*κυριακῇ ἡμὲρᾳ*) and of *κυριακα*, both in the plural and as an adjective in the 'Lord's supper': *δεῖπνα κυριακὰ*. Despite the assertions of some scholars, I have not been able to find any attestations of *κυριακη οικια* 'house of the Lord', which has been advanced as an explanation of the feminine gender. Pogatscher has suggested that the Greek plural form gave rise to the feminine gender.[42] A solution which does not have to rely on linguistic hypothesis is that the Germanic weak feminine **kirika*, from which the historical forms are derived, could be a backwards formation from Gk *κυριακόν*, which could have been perceived as the oblique forms of a weak feminine noun in Germanic languages. If we imagine German(ic) speakers faced with *κυριακόν* for the first time, and then attempting to assimilate it

---

37 See Masser, *Die Bezeichnungen für das christliche Gotteshaus*, 26–27.

38 Kluge, *Etymologisches Wörterbuch der deutschen Sprache*, 23rd ed. E. Seebold [Berlin and New York 1995], 443) supposes a derivation from Vulgar Greek: 'entlehnt aus vulgär-gr. **kyrikē* (nur in ntl.-gr. *kȳriakē* "Sonntag"), eigentlich ntl.-gr. *kȳriakós* "zum Herrn gehörig" ... . Das Wort ist wohl zunächst ins Fränkische entlehnt und dann mit der fränkischen Kirchensprache verbreitet worden.' To base the etymology on an unattested Greek form seems a very bold step!

39 Cf. Frings, *Germania Romana*, 41: 'das weibliche Geschlecht des neuen Modewortes mag durch das untergehende *basilica* bestimmt sein'.

40 See R. Froschauer, *Genus im Althochdeutschen: eine funktionale Analyse des Mehrfachgenus althochdeutscher Substantive*, mit einem Vorwort von R. Bergmann und E. Leiss, Germanistische Bibliothek 16 (Heidelberg, 2003).

41 K. Schäferdiek ('*Kirihha - *cyrica - kyriakon*: Zum geschichtlichen Hintergrund einer Etymologie', *BGdSL* [T] 106 [1984], 46–50) suggests that *basilica* came into vogue after *κυριακόν* and retrospectively imposed the feminine gender on the latter term in Trier.

42 A. Pogatscher, *Zur Lautlehre der griechischen, lateinischen und romanischen Lehnworte im Altenglischen*, QF 64 (Strassburg, 1888), § 284.

to the phonological and morphological patterns of their own language, we should find that the *-on*[43] of Gmc **kyriakon* would produce a nominative *kyriaka*, with the Germanic initial stress leading to a loss of the first *a* and a consequent form **kirika*.[44]

All this is of course far removed from Old Frisian in its attested forms in the thirteenth century. However, it is not to be ruled out that the Frisians, along with the Anglo-Saxons, acquired the word for church as early as the fourth century, simply as an object of contact with the Roman Empire.[45] From Frisia to Trier is a distance of only some 150 miles. The Old Frisian forms of the word are as just about as multifarious orthographically as one might imagine. In the following list of 468 attestations from our digital corpus I cannot guarantee to have tracked down the last possible variant form:

czstercka	1	stherecon	1	sziurka	2
kerc	2	stherek	6	szurka	4
kerck	16	sthereka	7	szurke	1
kercke	11	sthereke	1	szurk[a]	1
kercken	12	stherekon	3	tserka	3
kerec	1			tsiurc	2
kerk	1	stiercka	1	tsiurca	2
kerka	10	stierka	2	tsiurk	3
kerke	5	stzerck	8	tsiurka	4
kerken	14	stzerka	1	tsiurke	2
serk	2	stzercks	1	tsyureka	1
serke	4	szerka	2	tsyurika	2
stercka	1	sziurcha	2	tsyurka	2

[43] The ending *-on* occurs beside *-un* in the historically attested dialects, e.g. Old High German and Old Saxon. See W. Braune, *Althochdeutsche Grammatik*, 12th ed. W. Mitzka (Tübingen, 1967), §§ 221–25. On the complexities of the derivation from *κυριακόν*, assuming possible Gothic transmission, see *OED*, s.v. *church*.

[44] On the multiplicity of forms in Old High German, see E. Karg-Gasterstädt, T. Frings, E. von Steinmeyer, *Althochdeutsches Wörterbuch* (Berlin, 1952ff.) V, 195–98, s.v. *kirihha*; on the etymology G. Müller und T. Frings, *Germania Romana II. Dreißig Jahre Forschung. Romanische Wörter*, Mitteldeutsche Studien 19/1, 2 (Halle/S., 1968), 116–18.

[45] 'But it is by no means necessary that there should have been a single *kirika* in Germany itself; from 313 onward, Christian churches with their sacred vessels and ornaments were well-known objects of pillage to the German invaders of the Empire: if the first with which these made acquaintance, wherever situated, were called *κυριακά*, it would be quite sufficient to account for their familiarity with the word. The Angles and Saxons had seen and sacked Roman and British churches in Gaul and Britain for centuries before they had them of their own, and, we have every reason to believe, had known and spoken of them as *cirican* during the whole of that period' (*OED*, s.v. *church*).

tszaerka	1	tzercke	25	tzierke	1
tszerka	2	tzercken	6	tzierken	2
tszierka	1	tzerk	1	tziurk	1
tsziureka	1	tzerka	63	tziurka	6
tszurke	1	tzerke	27	tzurc	4
tzarka	1	tzerken	6	tzurka	11
tzarken	1	tzerkie	1	tzurke	1
tzeerck	1	tzerkum	1	tzurkum	1
tzeercke	1	tzherka	2	tzyarke	2
tzeerke	1	tzierc	4	ziurka	2
tzeerkha	1	tzierck	2	ztercka	11
tzerca	1	tziercka	4	ztercke	1
tzerck	24	tziercken	1	zterka	1
tzercka	92	tzierka	8	*Total*	*468*

The very wide level of spread in the manuscripts – [E] and [W] indicating provenance from East or West of the River Lauwers, and hence their dialect[46] – and the number of attestations confirm this word's universal acceptance and are further evidence in favour of an early loan.

[E] First Brokmer MS	8
[E] First Emsingo Codex	3
[E] First Hunsingo Codex	5
[E] First Riustring Codex ('Asegabuch')	18
[E] Fivelgo MS	18
[E] Foerdgung this Riuchtis	1
[E] Second Brokmer MS	9
[E] Second Emsingo Codex	21
[E] Second Emsingo Codex – Appendix	7
[E] Second Hunsingo Codex	6
[E] Summa Agrorum in Slochtra	2
[E] Third Emsingo Codex	4
[W] Codex Aysma – Gesta Fresonum	19
[W] Codex Aysma – I Excerpta legum	37
[W] Codex Aysma – III Processus judicii	4
[W] Codex Furmerius – III Hunsinger Keuren	1
[W] Codex Furmerius – V Gesta Fresonum	3
[W] Codex Furmerius – XIX Oorkonde	1
[W] Codex Furmerius – XX Zeendrecht van Leeuwarden	1
[W] Codex Parisiensis	2
[W] Freske Riim	7

[46] See R. H. Bremmer Jr, 'The Geographical Division and Periodization of Old Frisian', *Handbuch / Handbook*, 602–06.

[W] Friese Brieven	9
[W] Oudfriesche Oorkonden	126
[W] Gerbenzon Kleine Oudfriese Kronieken – Kroniekencompilatie	2
[W] Jus municipale Frisonum – Landrechten	8
[W] Jus municipale Frisonum – Middeleeuws register	4
[W] Jus municipale Frisonum – Oudere Schoutenrecht	1
[W] Jus municipale Frisonum – XV Over schandelijke misdaden	1
[W] Jus municipale Frisonum – XVI Over schaakroof	1
[W] Jus municipale Frisonum – XXXIII Bolswarder Seendrecht	12
[W] Minor OWFris texts – Âldfryske Oarkonde út Gint	1
[W] Oudfriese Kronieken – Bisschoppen van Utrecht/Graven van Holland	1
[W] Oudfriese Kronieken – De Vriesche Aenteyckeninge c.a.	1
[W] Oudfriese Kronieken – Vroegste geschiedenis van de Friezen	16
[W] Snitser Recesboeken	78
Total	*468*

From the extensive list of 79 variants (including inflected forms), it will be apparent that there are two basic spelling variants: those in *sth-* / *tz-* (etc.) and those in *k-*. The earliest attested forms (ca. 1300) are the first group from the First Riustring Manuscript (R1). Boutkan and Siebinga explain: ‘The spelling (R) *sth-*, *ts-*, *sz-* indicate palatalisation and assibilation of the initial **k-*. The absence of this process in *kerke* suggests that we are dealing with a recent loan.’[47] It is not altogether clear whether we are dealing with palatalization /tʃ/ or assibilation /ts/ or perhaps a combination of both /stʃ/ (cf. R1 spellings).[48] However, these different forms have led scholars to assume possibly different points of borrowing for the terms. Wollmann suggests: ‘Auch bei einigen zu Anfang der Christianisierung entlehnten Wörtern lassen sich “volkstümliche Einflüsse” feststellen. Das Wort “Kirche” wurde wahrscheinlich nicht direkt aus dem volkssprachlichen gr. *kyriké* entlehnt, sondern gelangte über asächs. und ae. Vermittlung (asächs. *kirika*, ae. *cyrice*) zu den Friesen. Im Afries. haben wir die auf das asächs. Wort zurückgehenden *tsirike*, *tserike*, während *tsiurike* aus dem ae. *cyrice* entlehnt wurde.’[49] It is perhaps worth reminding ourselves that the earliest Old English form was *cirice* which would have been pronounced /'kirikə/. Only later was the /k/ palatalized and the *i* changed to *y* before *r*.[50] The Old Frisian forms seem uniformly to exclude the palatalization of the second /k/, which, however, occurred in later Old English /tʃy:ritʃə/. This would suggest that the Frisian forms were derived from the Old English form prior to

47 D. F. H. Boutkan and S. M. Siebinga, *Old Frisian Etymological Dictionary*, Leiden Indo-European Etymological Dictionary Series 1 (Leiden, 2005), 374–75.

48 Cf. B. Sjölin, *Einführung in das Friesische* (Stuttgart, 1969), 26f.

49 Wollmann, ‘Zu den frühesten lateinischen Lehnwörtern’, 534.

50 *OED*, s.v. *church*.

palatalization in that language and that the palatalization would have taken place in Old Frisian.[51] The forms in *k-* have been regarded as examples of a later borrowing (from Old Saxon); the absence of palatalization and assibilation is thought to explain this.[52] The form *kerikon* (dat.sg.) is found attested in Old Saxon, otherwise the Saxon forms have an *i*.[53] Middle Low Franconian / Middle Dutch *kerke* provide a possible further source of borrowing.[54] The spread of the *kerk* forms is as follows:[55]

[E]	First Brokmer MS	4
[E]	First Emsingo MS	1
[E]	First Hunsingo MS	1
[E]	Fivelgo MS	2
[E]	Second Emsingo MS	12
[E]	Second Hunsingo MS	1
[E]	Summa Agrorum in Slochtra	2
[W]	Freske Riim	7
[W]	Friese Brieven	2
[W]	Oudfriesche Oorkonden	6
[W]	Snitser Recesboeken	31
	Total	*69*

Ultimately, we may wish to entertain the possibility of this being an 'early form' or a word that was borrowed before conversion at the same time as the word was loaned into Old English. There is little doubt that it was also influenced by Old English during the conversion of the Frisians. The word in Frisian encompasses the primary meaning 'house of the Lord' (*κυριακόν*),[56]

---

51 Cf. 'Die fries. Assibilierung nach vorangegangenem Palatisierungsprozess ist eine sehr alte Erscheinung, die vor dem i-Umlaut anzusetzen ist…', Wollmann, 'Zu den frühesten lateinischen Lehnwörtern', 514.

52 Boutkan and Siebinga, *Old Frisian Etymological Dictionary*.

53 See G. Köbler, *Altsächsisches Wörterbuch*, 3rd edn. (2000.), <http://www.koeblergerhard.de/aswbhinw.html>.

54 Cf. also Wollmann, 'Zu den frühesten lateinischen Lehnwörtern', 525, fn. 56: 'Steller Alfriesische Grammatik, § 9, Anm. 2 stellt eine allgemeine Regel auf: "*i* steht häufig im Wechsel mit *e*, besonders unter dem Einfluß eines folgenden *r*." Dem entsprechen auch die Formen *kerke*, **kirke*, *ziurke*, "Kirche"; s. hierzu Siebs, ibid. S. 150, 153'.

55 The relatively high incidence of *kerk*-forms in the Second Emsingo Manuscript and the *Snitser Recesboeken* is due to the presence of Low German texts in these two sources.

56 E.g. 'Andreas Aerndsen in voertyden prebendarius in sinte Vits tzercka' ['Andreas Aerndsen, in former times prebendary in St. Vitus' Church'], *Oudfriesche Oorkonden*, ed. P. Sipma, OTR 1 (The Hague, 1927) I, no. 363.

as well as the meaning, derived from *ecclesia*, 'congregation of the faithful', 'collection or Christians' and associated usages.[57]

1.2 *Biscop*

The ultimate origins of WG **biskop* go back to a Romanic form **biscopo* or vulgar L. *(e)biscopus* (*OED*) < Gk. *ἐπίσκοπος*.[58] *Biscop* is one of the earliest Christian loans to Old English, where the attested forms are *biscop*, *-sceop*, *-scep*; the Old Saxon form is *biscop*.[59] Green reckons, as opposed to Frings,[60] with a provenance from Frankish, rather than Gallo-Roman.[61] As with *kerk*, there is no ultimate proof of Old English transmission. It is not inconceivable that this word found its way northwards along the Moselle and Rhine from Trier and Cologne, where it would have been well known and frequently used at some time in the fourth century.[62]

With 285 occurrences, the word is not so widely attested as *tzerke*, nor does it show so many variant forms (27). That this word is not so widespread as *tzerke* is not surprising, as there would be fewer occasions to refer to bishops than churches. However, it shows a good spread geographically and in terms of orthography, again indicating an early loan, possibly direct from Latin speakers. The following list shows the variant forms:

bischoep	1	biscopa	2	biscopie	1
bischop	6	biscopar	3	biscopis	8
bischope	3	biscope	26	biscopon	1
bischopes	1	biscopen	9	biscoppe	4
bischops	6	biscopes	18	biscoppen	1
biscoep	1	biscoph	1	biscops	18
biscop	161	biscopia	1	biscopum	1

[57] E.g. 'Sommighe liode sinter, darma hiara offer nat ach to ontfaen om openbere zaka als om manslachta ende der arme liodena onriucht deth, der rawera, der wokera, dar da tzerka byfyochte' ['There are some people whose offering one may not receive because of manifest cases such as murderers and those who inflict injustice to poor people, robbers, usurers and those that fight the Church'], Codex Aysma – *Excerpta legum*, 376.

[58] See in detail A. Waag, 'Die Bezeichnungen des Geistlichen im Althoch- und Altniederdeutschen. Eine wortgeschichtliche und wortgeographische Untersuchung', *Teuthonista. Zeitschrift für deutsche Dialektforschung und Sprachgeschichte* 8 (1931–32), 1–54, at 20–31; Frings, *Germania Romana*, I, 40, 47; Müller and Frings *Germania Romana*, II, 235–38; also Green, *Language and History*, 302–04.

[59] See *OED*, s.v. *bishop*.

[60] Frings, *Germania Romana*, I, 40, 47

[61] Green, *Language and History*, 304.

[62] See Wollmann, 'Zu den frühesten lateinischen Lehnwörtern', 521: 'Abgesehen von afries. *biscop* < lt. *episcopus* mit sonorisiertem /b/ < /p/ bietet das Fries. nur *kede(n)* … dürfte es sich um eine sehr alte Entlehnung ab dem ausgehenden 4. Jh. handeln.' See also above, the discussion of *tzercka* and its possible provenance from Gallo-Roman.

bisschop	2	bisscop	5	*Total*	*285*
bisschopp	1	bisscops	2		
bisschops	1	byscopis	1		

The list contains a few instances of the personal name 'biscop' (e.g. 'dirc reynties ende peter biscop' – *Snitser Recesboeken*) as well as numerous attestations of the earliest sense of *biscop* in the Germanic languages which was 'A clergyman consecrated for the spiritual government and direction of a "diocese", ranking beneath an archbishop (where these exist) and above the priests or presbyters, and deacons' (*OED*, s.v. *bishop*). This is thus the most widespread sense in Old Frisian. The following passage from *Excerpta legum* (Aysma) shows all the various ecclesiastical ranks in order:

> Dyo viij seck is: dar biscop, prester, dyaken, subdiaken daet slacht ende vader ende moder slacht daet iefta mit foeten stat, den mey nemma absoluerya oers so dy paus. (575)
> ['The eighth matter is: where a bishop, priest, deacon, sub-deacon kills someone and kills his father and mother or kicks with his feet, no-one may absolve him other than the Pope.']

In the table that follows, all the attestations in the various Old Frisian monuments are shown: these indicate a wide spread in both East and West Frisian, pointing to an early borrowing.

[E] Third Emsingo Codex	1
[E] First Brookmer MS	2
[E] First Emsingo Codex	4
[E] First Hunsingo Codex	4
[E] First Riustring Codex	26
[E] Fivelinger Codex	8
[E] Foerdgung this Riuchtis	2
[E] Second Brookmer Codex	2
[E] Second Emsingo Codex	13
[E] Second Hunsingo Codex	4
[E] Second Riustring Codex	2
[W] Aysma – Gesta Fresonum	32
[W] Aysma – I Excerpta legum	21
[W] Aysma – III Processus judicii	7
[W] Codex Furmerius – V Gesta Fresonum	5
[W] Codex Furmerius – VIII Willekeuren van de Opstalsboom	1
[W] Codex Furmerius – XX Zeendrecht van Leeuwarden	7
[W] Codex Furmerius – XXII Fragm. Alg. Westerlauwerse Zeendrecht	1
[W] Freske Riim}	2
[W] Friese Brieven	3

[W] Friesche Oorkonden}	14
[W] Jus municipale Frisionum – 17 Keuren	2
[W] Jus municipale Frisionum – 24 Landrechten	18
[W] Jus municipale Frisionum – Magnuskeuren	1
[W] Jus municipale Frisionum – Middeleeuws register	3
[W] Jus municipale Frisionum – XXX Kleine Oudfriese Kroniek	9
[W] Jus municipale Frisionum – XXXI Friese Kroniek	10
[W] Jus municipale Frisionum – XXXIII Bolswarder Seendrecht van 1404	3
[W] Jus municipale Frisionum – XXXV Ambtseed Wymbritseradeel	1
[W] Jus municipale Frisionum – XXXVI Ambtseed Zuidwestfr. kustgebied	1
[W] Minor OWFris texts – Als wy lesset in cronicis	7
[W] Oudfriese Kronieken – Bisschoppen van Utrecht/Graven van Holland	12
[W] Oudfriese Kronieken – De Vriesche Aenteyckeninge c.a.	3
[W] Oudfriese Kronieken – Vroegste geschiedenis van de Friezen	18
[W] Snitser Recesboeken	4
[W] Gerbenzon Kleine Oudfriese Kronieken – Kroniekencompilatie	16
Total	*285*

1.3 *Offeria*

In Old High German there exists a pair of similar-sounding loan words for the sense of 'make a religious offering, perform sacrifice': *offrôn* and *opharôn/ opfarôn*.[63] Although the former might at first sight seem to show the Second Sound Shift, it is usually taken to be a loan from Lat. *offerre* and hence had no opportunity to be shifted. The latter is thought to be borrowed from *operari* (though not all agree)[64] and to show the shift of *p* > *pf*.[65] Some early attested forms in Old High German have the double fricative rather than the affricate: *Abrogans* MS Ra (Cod. Aug. CXI Bl. 76r–90r = 'Abrogans deutsch', Karlsruhe): *offaronti*, *offaron*; Pa: *offoronne* (MS. lat. 7640 Bl. 124r–132v =

63 See Frings, *Germania Romana*, I, 42–43, 53, 105–07; Müller and Frings, *Germania Romana*, II, 340–46; also Green, *Language and History*, 305.

64 Cf. DWB (electronic edition on CD-ROM: *Der digitale Grimm: Deutsches Wörterbuch von Jacob u. Wilhelm Grimm*, ed. T. Burch, K. Gärtner, *et al.* [Frankfurt, 2004], s.v. *opfern* [vol. 13,7]: '*verb. sacrificare, immolare, libare. ahd.* opfâron, opphorôn, opferôn *und* offarôn, offorôn; *mhd.* opfern, ophern, *md.* offern *und* oppern; *alts.* offrôn, *ags.* offrjan, *entlehnt aus lat.* offerre, *wie schon* AVENTIN. *bemerkt hat:* kains opfers hat er (*könig Tuitscho*) gar nit gedacht ... darumb wir dannoch kain teutsch wort haben, das solchs, unsern vätern unbekant, hiesz opferen; ist vom lateinischen "offerre" gezogen. 4, 77, 28, s. RAUMER *einwirkung* 318. GRIMM *myth.*[4] 29. *der alte germ. ausdruck dafür war goth. ags.* blôtan, *altn.* blôta, *ahd.* pluazan, plôzan, *eigentlich wol (opfer) anzünden, verbrennen, griech.* φλοιδουν myth.[4] 30 anm. 3. SCHADE *altd. wb.*2 1, 78b. opfern *bedeutet etwas als opfer oder wie ein opfer darbringen.*'

65 For attestations of the various forms, see Müller and Frings, *Germania Romana*, II, 341–44.

'Abrogans deutsch', Paris BN).[66] Others have *ph* – *opharondi*. The circumstances surrounding the introduction of these words into the Germanic dialects are indeed a tangled skein, which is most fully illustrated and discussed by Müller and Frings (*ibid.*). The basic thesis of Frings and Müller/Frings is that *offeren* and related words belong to the Gallo-Roman influence in an area stretching from Trier north-eastwards whereas *opfern* belongs to the south (Upper German). In addition to the ecclesiastical meaning, a secular meaning of *opper-* is found in the sense of 'perform physical work', seen in the opposition *oppermann* 'Handlanger' and *offermann* 'Küster', both of which occur together in the Rhineland.[67]

Green's investigation of the circumstances establishes, in agreement with others, primarily a geographic contrast: 'whereas the second German form [sc. *opharôn*] was at home in the south (SRhFr., Alemannic, Bavarian) the first [sc. *offrôn*] was concentrated in the north-west (OS, Low Franconian, Middle Franconian, *Isidor*).'[68] This reference only to dialect areas, however, distorts the picture, for when one looks at numbers and forms of attestations, one finds that there are often few or no examples of particular words. This is particularly true of the first group.

Looking at the *offrôn* group first,[69] there is no Old Saxon attestation of the verb, but the noun *offar* is attested in the *Westfälisches Taufgelöbnis*, and two compounds occur in other texts, viz. *offarman* 'sexton, verger' Gloss (Oxford, Bodleian Library, Junius 83), *offarmelo* (Gloss Trier) 'offering flour'. Low Franconian provides four attestations of *offron* in the *Altmittelfränkische und altniederfränkische Psalmen*. The *Isidor* translation (Lotharingian / Rhenish Franconian) renders *sacrificium* twice in the same way with *offerunc ghelstar*,[70]

66 On the significance of these forms, see *ibid.* 344–45.

67 See Frings, *Germania Romana*, I, 106.

68 Green, *Language and History*, 305.

69 The attestations are listed in Müller and Frings, *Germania Romana*, II, 341, without context.

70 *offerunc* may have been intended as a gloss, originally: <http://www.cis. uni-muenchen.de /cgi-bin/ahdeutsch/lex.pl?lemma=offarung>: 'Huuanda so selp so im noh ein tempel ni bileiph noh einich altari noh einich offerunc ghelstar, so sama ni bileiph im einich chuninc noh einich sacerdos iudęoliudim. Noh einich lughin ni mac uuesan osee propheta, dher quhad heilegu gheistu: ›Sitzent israheles suni ano chuninc ano herrun ano offerunc ghelstar ano altari ano bisscofheit ano araucnissa' (35,14.21). Rather than posit a gloss that was 'left behind' in the translation, one might suppose an uncertainty with the terminology, the Christian *offarunc* perhaps being not quite appropriate for the Jewish sacrifice, whereas the pagan *ghelstar* might have been felt to have too many pagan connotations. It might be a question of hedging ones bets as for example, Johann Dietenberger, a Roman Catholic rival translator of the Bible, wishing to preserve the popular form of Luther and still remain faithful to the Vulgate: 'DEr Her regirt oder weidet mich', *Bibell. Das ist/ Alle bucher Alts vnd News Testaments/ nach alter in christlicher kyrche gehabter Translation/ mit Auslegung etlicher dunckeler ort/ vnd*

using a potentially Christian *offerunc*, combined with a pagan Germanic term. However, the verb is not attested. It will be readily appreciated that the linguistic evidence in favour of the verb, assumed to be the form that was earliest loaned and on which other parts of speech are based, is but scant. It must therefore be stated that the verb **offrôn* is not attested in Old High German or Old Saxon;[71] it occurs only in Low German, Old English, and Old Frisian (which will be investigated further). One attestation that should receive our attention is that of *kaoffarot* < *offarôn* in the *Murbacher Hymnen*.[72] On the face of it, this form with *-ff-* might seem to be derived from *offerre*,[73] but it is most likely a loan from *operari*, especially in view of its Alemannic provenance (Reichenau). The *Isidor* form *offerunc* is assumed to be derived from *offeren/offrôn*, but there are High German and Central German forms in Middle High German: *opferunge* (Beheim, *Evangelienbuch*[74] 286a), *offerunge* (Janota, *Psalmen*[75] 41), which leave open the question of a back formation from *opharôn*.[76]

Commenting on the state of affairs surrounding *opharôn*, Green writes: 'From the geographical spread of another word in Germany it is assumed that *operari* also entered this same region from northern Gaul, not in the religious sense which underlies *opharôn* in Upper German, but in the secular sense "to work" (cf. OFr. *ovrer* and such north-west German dialect forms as *oppermann* "workman, handyman").' Green considers that the north-western form (operari) was brought to Germany by the Romans 'as part of their building programme?', whereas 'the southern import was reinterpreted as an ecclesiastical term ("work, service" > "religious service")'.[77]

---

besserung vieler verruckter wort vnd sprueche/ Durch Doctor Johan Dietenberger/ fleissig/ trewlich vnd christlich corrigiert vnd gebessert in seinem leben (Cöln, 1556 – reprint of Mainz edn., 1534).

71 *oppraiu* is attested in Old Saxon, on which see Müller and Frings, *Germania Romana*, II, 343.

72 *Die Murbacher Hymnen*: Nach der Handschrift herausgegeben von E. Sievers, (Halle/S., 1874) [available in facsimile online <http://www.literature.at/webinterface/library/ALO-BOOK_V01?objid=10798>] 21,4,1: *giu ostrun unsar Christ ist/ der kasc[l]actot lamp ist/ dera lutri derpaz/ lihamo sin kaoffarot ist*; cf. R. Schützeichel, *Althochdeutsches Wörterbuch* (Tübingen, 1969), s.v.

73 Cf. Boutkan and Siebinga, *Old Frisian Etymological Dictionary*, 298.

74 *Des Matthias von Beheim Evangelienbuch in mitteldeutscher Sprache. 1343* ed. R. Bechstein, Mittheilungen der Dt. Gesellschaft zur Erforschung vaterländischer Sprache und Alterthümer in Leipzig 3 (Leipzig 1867).

75 [Lower Rhenish] *Übersetzung von Psalmen, Hymnen und Kirchengebeten aus dem 14. Jh.*, ed. E. Janota, Jahresber. des k. k. vollst. Gymnasiums in Krakau (Vienna, 1855).

76 Cf. also 'opferunge, offerunge, opperunge: immolatio, libatio, oblamen', *Mittellateinisch–hochdeutsch–böhmisches Wörterbuch, nach einer Hs. vom Jahre 1470*, ed. L. Diefenbach (Frankfurt, 1846), 287c, 326b, 387b.

77 Green, *Language and History*, 305.

It might be appropriate, at this stage, to review the meanings of the Latin words: *offerre* was used in ecclesiastical Latin only to mean:[78]

> (a). *To offer to God, to consecrate, dedicate*, e.g. Exodus 38,24 *omne aurum quod expensum est in opere sanctuarii et quod oblatum in donariis viginti novem talentorum fuit.* (b). *To offer up, sacrifice*, Gen. 4, 3f. *factum est autem post multos dies ut offerret Cain de fructibus terrae munera Domino. Abel quoque obtulit de primogenitis gregis sui et de adipibus eorum et respexit Dominus ad Abel et ad munera eius.*

On the other hand, *operari* had, besides its secular meaning of 'work', already a long history in classical Latin of 'perform pagan sacrifices to the gods':[79]

> In partic., in relig. lang., *to serve the gods, perform sacred rites, to honor or celebrate by sacrifices* ... e.g. *operari est deos religiose et cum summā veneratione sacrificiis litare*, Non. 523, 9

The earliest attestations of *opharôn* are to be found in the South-West Alemannic region of St Gall (Abrogans Gloss), where the occurrences have no religious connotations. Since *offerre* cannot mean 'to perform work', the derivation from *operari* rather than *offerre* would appear certain. The following correspondences are found: *functus. opharondi* 'Arbeit verrichten'[80] (Gl I: 146, 13); *seruitium. opparoht* (Gl I: 202, 1) 'service';[81] *obsequitur. opfarod* (Gl I: 148, 36) 'ausführen';[82] *ad officium. za opfron* 'verrichten, eine Arbeit ausführen'[83] (Gl I: 34, 19). These are all secular meanings reflecting the original secular sense of the Latin *operari*, without a connexion with L *offerre*.

---

78 Lewis and Short online <http://www.perseus.tufts.edu/cgi-bin/resolveform?lang=la>, s.v. (*A Latin Dictionary, Founded on Andrews' Edition of Freund's Latin Dictionary*, rev. ed. C. T. Lewis and Charles Short [Oxford, 1879]).

79 *Ibid.*, s.v. *operari*.

80 The modern German equivalents are from the excellent online Old High German dictionary: *Lexikon des Althochdeutschen (8. Jahrhundert)*, ed. E. Seebold *et al.* <http://www.cis.uni-muenchen.de/ahdeutsch/lexikon.html>. A printed version is available as *Chronologisches Wörterbuch des deutschen Wortschatzes : der Wortschatz des 8. Jahrhunderts (und früherer Quellen)* ed. E. Seebold, with B. Bulitta *et al.* (Berlin, New York, 2001).

81 'Zugrunde liegt eine Verkürzung der [sic] Abba-Glossar lat. *liminum* : *seruitium*, *terminus* "Verbannung : Knechtschaft, Ende"' (*ibid.*, s.v. *opfarôn*).

82 'Zugrunde liegt die unvollständig überlieferte Glossengruppe lat. *fungitur* : *agitur* (für: *agit*), *obsequitur* "er verwaltet : er betreibt, er verfolgt"' (*ibid.*).

83 'Zugrunde liegt die Glossengruppe lat. *ad officium* : *ad obsequium*, *ad ministerium* (Glossar AA) "zu einem Dienst : zu einer Aufgabe, zu einem Amt". Wiedergabe eines Substantivs durch einen substantivierten Infinitiv.' (*ibid.*).

Looking next at the evidence for *opfarôn*, we find, in addition to the example from the *Murbacher Hymnen* (*kaoffarot*), four occurrences of the verb in Otfrid, where the affricate pronunciation is confirmed by the spelling: *ópphoron*,[84] *ópphorotin*,[85] *oppherota*,[86] *ópphoroti*.[87] The first refers to the offering of incense by Zacharias, symbolic of the prayers of Israel being heard by God, and is the equivalent of an offering/giving of something to God, rather than a sacrifice involving killing. The other three refer to ritual sacrifice: of two turtle doves or two young pigeons by Mary at her purification, of a ram by Abraham, in place of his son Isaac, of the Passover lamb. The remaining four nouns *óp(p)her* refer once to the offering of incense by Zacharias (I,4,81), twice to Abraham's sacrifice (II,9,34.59) and once relating to the washing of animals before sacrifice in the pool of Bethesda (III,4,6). One occurrence of the substantive, a translation of the Latin *hostia* ('sacrificial animal'), is found in Tatian 7,3, relating to Mary's purification, as above:[88]

> Inti thaz sie gabin obphar after thiu giquetan ist in euuu truhtines, zua gimachun turtilitubun edo zuei tubiclin.
> ['And that they should offer a sacrifice according to that which is said in the law of the Lord, A pair of turtledoves, or two young pigeons.']

Notker's works contain a plethora of attestations (67), of verb, noun, and compounds.[89] These show a similar distribution of senses among them, viz. (i) offering an object, money, incense, etc. to God (ii) performing sacrifice (of animals) (for God):

opfer	3	opfero	2	ópferota	1
ópfer	6	opferôen	1	ópferotôn	1
ópfere	2	opferon	1	ópfer-uuîzegungo	1
ópferfrískingen	1	ópferon	1	opher	10
ópfer-frískingo	1	ópferôn	1	ópher	10

[84] *Otfrids Evangelienbuch*, ed. O. Erdmann, 6th ed. L. Wolff, Altdeutsche Textbibliothek 49 (Tübingen, 1973), I,4,12 'ópphoron er scólta bi thie síno suntan' (Zacharias).

[85] Otfrid I,14,23 'Thaz síu ouh furi thaz kínd sar ópphorotin góte thar' (Mary and Joseph).

[86] Otfrid II,9,61 'Thaz gifíang er tho sár inti oppherota iz góte thar' (Abraham sacrifices the ram 'scaf').

[87] Otfrid IV,9,1f. 'Gistúant thera zíti guati thaz man ópphoroti,/ joh man zi thíu gisazi, thaz lamp thes náhtes azi' (Jews offering Passover).

[88] *Tatian: Lateinisch und altdeutsch mit ausführlichem Glossar*, ed. E. Sievers, 2nd rev. ed., Bibliothek der ältesten deutschen Literatur-Denkmäler V ([1892], repr. Paderborn, 1966), 7,3 = Luke 2,24 'Et ut darent hostiam, secundum quod dictum est in lege domini, par turturum aut duos pullos columbarum'.

[89] These include glosses by the St. Gall glossator.

ópherbluôte	1	ópheron	5	ópheruuîn	2
óphere	3	ópheront	2	ophir	2
ópherfriskinga	2	opherota	1	*Total*	*67*
ópherfrúnscing	1	opheroton	1		
opheron	2	ópheroton	3		

The likelihood is that the sense of *opfarôn* (ii) in addition to its meaning of 'perform work' took on the senses of *offeren* 'to offer to God, to consecrate, dedicate'. Indeed, we should assume cross-fertilization of the two and a gradual merging of the forms phonologically and semantically. We might bear in mind also that *offerre* in Latin was originally from *obferre*, a form that still had some currency, and that this bears a remarkable similarity to *opferôn* – cf. especially the form in Tatian (above) *obphar*. However, as we have seen from the examples, there is an almost exclusive attestation of *opfarôn* in High German at the expense of *offeren*.

Coming now to the Old Frisian evidence, we confirm the findings in respect of Old High German. In the West Frisian Aysma – *Excerpta legum* precisely the religious sense for *offrian* which we had seen as the first of *offerre* is attested: 'to offer to God, to consecrate, dedicate', more specifically now in the ecclesiastical context 'to make an offering/gift' [to the church]. The transitive verb is combined with the object, 'half a penny', to be offered at 'Easter, Whitsun, Midwinter, and on Our Patron Saint's day': 'Ende da frowa agen da pappan to offriane enen haluen pennich to paeschen, to pinxteren, to midwintera ende to vses patroens dey' (376) ['And the women are to offer to the parson a halfpenny at Easter, Pentecost, Midwinter and on our Patron's day.'] A similar sense is found in the [W] *Oudfriesche Oorkonden*:

> Item, compt dyr eenich haehtijd yn dae jongerpresters wyka, der man ende frouwe tolike schildich sint toe offerien ney syd en pliga yn Kornyem [gap in MS] stacie toe biwarrien; Item hat offerjilde dan compt to wss liaewe frouwe aulter up wtleden tritighedeij ende jeertyden in Kornijem dy jongerprester allinna toe habben.
> ['Likewise, if there is some feast in the chaplain's week (to celebrate mass), when a man and woman are obliged to offer (a charitable gift) according to custom and tradition, in Cornjum [gap in MS]. Likewise, whatever offer money is put on Our Lady's altar at a funeral, at the thirtiest day after a funeral (when a mass for the dead is celebrated) and at the annual memorial mass in Cornjum, only the chaplain shall have it.]

The *Friese Brieven* refer also to the practice of making an offering to the parson:

> Erbare wyse here ende guede vriond mij comt claegh dat dy persona to aulda tzercka hat dae meent forclaget dat hya hem op alre hilgena dey naet habbet offerit ... [W] Friese Brieven (15)
> ['Honourable wise lord and good friend, I have received a complaint that the parson of Aldtsjerk has accused the community of not having made him an offering on All Saints' Day ...']

In the [E] Fivelinger Codex, the intransitive verb is used with an understood object in the context of contracting a marriage, where it amounts to little more than 'pay one's dues':

> ... to tzurka geng, tzurcstal stod, alter erade, tha prestere offerade. thet afte bigeng, alsa thi freia Fresa mither freia Fresinna scold. ([E] Fivelinger Codex 6:3).
> ['... went to the church, attended the service, honoured the altar, offered to the priest, entered matrimony, just as a free Frisian man should do with a free Frisian woman'.]

A similar sense is found in the [W] *Oudfriesche Oorkonden* with reference to paying one's dues in full and being no longer responsible for them:

> Ick Wyrd Wyrdissma gameich tho Ferwert dwe kuth ende vppenbeir myth disse brewe dat dyo schyling der was tuischen my ende den convent fan Claercamp vm sauwen pundameta der ic da conuent myt myn brower Syppa der God nedich se offert habbe ende der hya twyra fan wandelet habbeth fan my ende een kapet ende wol bytallet (0001 10130)
> ['I, Wyrd Wyrdissma, parishioner in Ferwert, make known and public with this document that the dispute that was between me and Claercamp Abbey concerning seven measures of land which I and my brother Syppa (may God have mercy on him) had offered and of which they [the monks] have exchanged two with me and bought and paid well one.']

It will be clear from these examples that the usual sense of *offria* in Old Frisian is 'to offer or present (something) to God/the Church as an act of devotion, a freewill offering, or as one's due' (cf. *OED*, s.v. *offer*). There are no overt senses of 'to sacrifice' here.

The noun *offer* (18 attestations) shows the sense of '(freewill) offering, tithe, due', as we have seen with *offria*, but additionally there is a rare mention of the sense of animal sacrifice in the sacrifice of Noah: [W] Freske Riim 250: 'Her Noe him sijn offer brochte' ['Noah presented his sacrifice to Him']. *offerhande tyden* in the *Oudfriesche Oorkonden* (I, no. 342) refers to the 'times of offering', i.e. the various set days in the year when ecclesiastical monies were due.

An attestation of *offerman* 'sacristan, verger'[90] in the Fivelinger Codex will lead us to the alternative form *oppermon* and related forms with the double stop *-pp-*: *oppermon* occurs twice in R1 with the same specific ecclesiastical meaning.[91] This goes contrary to Frings' assertion of the opposition of *oppermann* 'Handlanger (labourer)' and *offermann* 'Küster (verger)'. Although there are numerous attestations of the graphic form *opper*, all but two are variant forms of *uppa* 'on, upon' and hence not relevant. The *Oudfriese Kronieken* attest *opper clerck*, the meaning of which is not immediately clear. It is used to describe (Saint) Ricfrid (806–815?),[92] Bishop of Utrecht: 'ritfridus een freesa een opper clerck' in the list of bishops of Utrecht.[93] *opper clerck* might mean 'cleric responsible for the collection of offerings and dues', but it appears to be a rather lowly occupation to have had, prior to becoming Bishop of Utrecht. Alternatively, if *opper* were to refer to the (sacrifice) of the Mass,[94] then it might mean a cleric[95] in minor orders who assists at the Mass in some capacity, as reader, or a 'sacristan' in minor orders etc. Alternatively, and more likely, *opper* could be used, as in Dutch, as the comparative form of *uppa*, equivalent to E *upper*, HG *ober*, meaning 'superior, chief, high' (cf. Du *opperhoofd* 'chieftain', *opperpriester* 'high/chief priest'). In which case *opper clerck* might indicate a high ecclesiastical rank, such as an archdeacon. Another attestation of *opper* is found in the same manuscript in the section *Vroegste geschiedenis van de Friezen*: 'een lits eylant hiet opper bant' ['a little island called Opperbant']. There is no suggestion of *opper* meaning 'sacrifice' here. Thus the Frisian forms show a mixture of *-ff-* and *-pp-* without distinction of meaning. The

---

90 'and mitha offer manne ther tha klocca hlette' ['and with the verger who rang the bell'], Fivelinger Codex 6:3.

91 13:3 'Sa hwersa en mon anda ende leith . and wili ologad wertha . and thi oppermon nawet rede nis mith tha sletelon . sa hachma thet godis hus to brekande . and godi tha selua sele to winnande.' ['Wenn jemand im Sterben liegt und die letzte Ölung haben will, und der Küster nicht zur Hand ist mit den Schlüsseln, so soll man die Kirche aufbrechen und diese Seele für Gott gewinnen.']; 15:7 'Thi prestere and thi oppermon tha willath binna there withume wesa . mith hiara weruon . and thet nis nen riucht . umbe thet . Sa hwasa to breue and to bonne cumth . sa leith ma hini buta there withume . and buta tha helich drachta.' ['Der Priester und der Küster wollen mit ihren Hofräumen innerhalb des geweihten Kirchplatzes liegen, aber es gibt kein Recht in dieser Beziehung. Wenn jemand mit dem Kirchenbann belegt wird, so begräbt man ihn außerhalb des geweihten Platzes um die Kirche und jenseits des Prozessionspfades.']

92 The usual form of his name, not *Ritfridus*. Very little seems to be known about him.

93 In Meijering, Co-Frisica IA/IB (A.8).

94 An interesting insight into the huge range of vocabulary based on *offer* in an ecclesiastical context is seen in the poem by Joost van den Vondel, *Altaer-Geheimenissen Ontvouwen in drie boecken door I.V.V.*, Te Keulen In de Nieuwe Druckerye. (1645), online <http://www.dbnl.org/tekst/vond001dewe04/vond001dewe040138. htm>.

95 'A person who has been legitimately received into the ranks of the clergy', *Catholic Encyclopedia*, <http://www.newadvent.org/cathen/04049b.htm>.

origins of the *-ff-*forms would seem to be securely Gallo-Roman *offerre*. The *-pp-* forms might have been influenced by the Southern Christian *operari* or they could show an extension of the secular *operare* 'handlangern' to the religious sphere by analogy with the *-ff-* forms.[96]

1.4 *Elmisse*

Elmisse is thought also to be one of the earliest Christian loans to Germanic and to have been loaned before widespread conversion had taken place, at a time when pagan speakers of the Germanic dialects would have been able to observe the charitable practices of Christians.[97] The Greek word was a technical term which went beyond the literal giving of alms and encompassed compassion and mercy, indeed the so-called 'corporal works of mercy'.[98] The loan into Ger manic is unproblematic, since the Greek word became well established in Latin as *eleemosyna* and, it is assumed, thence passed into Germanic.[99]

There are eight occurrences in our corpus, with considerable variance in the spelling.[100] These reflect a wide range of meaning which is consonant with the above sense of almsgiving and compassion. The earliest attestations are from the *Oudfriesche Oorkonden* (1327) in the senses 'alms, offerings (for the repose of a soul)' and 'tithes, offerings, dues' (owed by Friars) [twice]. The next occurrence, from the *Excerpta legum* of the Codex Aysma (ca. 1500) refers to 'works of mercy' in the wider sense, distinguishing carefully between three types: corporal, spiritual, correctional:

> Jtem. Thrira handa ielmisse sinter: dyo arste is lichaemlic, yennum to yane dar hy byhoef is hoth zo hi byhowet; dio oer gastlijc, yennum to vryane, dar yens dy misdeen had; dat tredde dine to biriuchtane, der dwaleth ende to bringhen inder wey der wirde. (379)

---

96 See Frings, *Germania Romana*, I, 106–007, and Müller and Frings, *Germania Romana*, II, 88–89.

97 Green, *Language and History*, 275.

98 Cf. *Catholic Encyclopedia* <http://www.newadvent.org/cathen/01328f.htm>, quoting Aquinas: 'I answer that, External acts belong to that virtue which regards the motive for doing those acts. Now the motive for giving alms is to relieve one who is in need. Wherefore some have defined alms as being "a deed whereby something is given to the needy, out of compassion and for God's sake," which motive belongs to mercy, as stated above (*Summa theologica* II.ii., Question 30, Articles 1,2). Hence it is clear that almsgiving is, properly speaking, an act of mercy. This appears in its very name, for in Greek *eleemosyne* it is derived from having mercy *eleein* even as the Latin "miseratio" is. And since mercy is an effect of charity, as shown above (Question 30, Article 2, Article 3, Objection 3), it follows that almsgiving is an act of charity through the medium of mercy.'

99 Cf. Green, *Language and History*, 306.

100 *Ielmissen*, *jelmisse*, *jelmissen*, *aelmissen*, *ielmisse*, *elmeze*, *elmase*, *aelmisse*.

['There are three kinds of alms: the first is corporal, to give someone who is in need whatever he needs; the second is spiritual, to forgive someone who has tresspassed against you; the third is to correct one who errs and to bring him back on the road of truth.']

Here the word has the basic meaning 'good works, acts of charity'. A further attestation from the same portion of the same manuscript explains that neither with fasting nor with vigils nor with abstinence can one overcome the Devil, only with *elmeze* 'mercy' and *mildicheit* 'generosity':

> Jtem. Hwer is dyo were wysheit? Mer inder leringhe Gods; der omme so fintmar nenne wys, der sint lerende fander leringhe Godes. Cortlike seit dio dicht, datma mit festiaen ner mit wakyane ner mit onhaldicheide ne meyma den dyowel nat vorwynna, mer allenna mit elmeze ende mildicheit. (383)
> ['Where is true wisdom? Only in God's teaching. Therefore take no- one for wise who is teaching away from God's teaching. The treatise [viz. *Autentica Riocht*] concisely says that the Devil cannot be overcome by vigils or abstinence, but only by alms and generosity.']

Finally, two attestations from the Codex Furmerius (ca. 1600) in the phrase *elmase bidda* occur with the sense of 'beg for alms' with reference to mendicant friars:

> Thyo xxj secke is Dat tha Jacopinen and tha minra broderum and tha Staringhera broderum thera alra ekem orlef elmase tho biddane alzo fyr hya beschelyke broderen wtsende sonder her Folperte fan Staren thy is allenna wt nymen and elckers fan alle oorden ne moeten nene broderen aelmisse bidden eer disse thryne broderen beden habbet. (VIII. Willekeuren van de Opstalboom).
> ['The 21st article is: That the Dominicans and Franciscans and the (Benedictine) brethren in Staveren, inasfar as they want to send out certain brothers, have been given permission to beg for alms, but Dom Folpert of Staveren, he alone is to be excluded; and otherwise from all orders no brethren are allowed to beg for alms before these three fraternities have begged.']

Wollmann assumes that OE *ælmesse* is derived from Vulgar L **al(i)mosina*, itself being a loan from Gk *ελεημοσυνη*. The /æ/ of OE is explained as a substitution for Latin /a/ as in many Old English loans, e.g. *cæster* < L *castra*; *mægester* < L *magister*. He considers that it was originally a learned word that became popular. The Old Frisian form could have been loaned direct from Latin or via Old English, or Old English could have exerted a later influence on an earlier borrowing.[101]

Conclusions

Having surveyed the evidence for some of the early Christian loans to Frisian, we can draw the following conclusions:

1. The preconditions for influence on the earliest stages of the Frisian language direct from Gallo-Roman sources, particularly in the West in the context of traffic along the Lower Rhine and beyond its eastern bank from Trier and Cologne are positive and make such contact likely.
2. Although mainly secular vocabulary is expected in this early period, there is evidence that religious vocabulary was transferred along with the secular, in particular some basic facets of a mainly external nature, pertaining to church organization.
3. The addition of Frisian to an investigation of these earliest origins adds a dimension which had hitherto largely been ignored by previous scholarship.
4. However, owing to the dating of the Old Frisian texts and their late attestation, it is impossible to be certain of a direct influence from Gallo-Roman sources.
5. Any such influence must be consonant with phonological criteria.
6. *tzerke* and *biscop* show a wide variety of forms and wide geographical spread. These factors point to an early date of borrowing. Both words admit the possibility of direct borrowing from Gallo-Roman and also possible later influence from Anglo-Saxon.
7. *offeria* is by no means as widely attested, but here we find parallels with the forms in *-ff-* in other Germanic dialects, borrowed from *offerre*, whilst forms in *-pp-* indicate either a borrowing from the secular *operare* and its subsequent integration, by analogy with the religious *offeria*, or influence from Dutch forms and disprove the assertion that in the north-west there was a distinction between the secular *oppermann* 'labourer' and religious *offermann* 'verger'. It is likely that confusion and conflation of form and meanings of the variants in *-ff-* (from *offerre*) and *-pp-* / *-pf-* (from *operari*) took place.
8. Whilst *elmisse* 'alms' would also be a candidate for a direct loan from Gallo-Roman, phonological criteria suggest later influence from Old English.
9. Ultimately, it is frustrating not to be able to be more precise about the earliest Old Frisian Christian loan words. Whilst we can be fairly certain, for

[101] A. Wollmann, *Untersuchungen zu den frühen lateinischen Lehnwörtern im Altenglischen. Phonologie und Datierung*, Texte und Untersuchungen zur Englischen Philologie 15 (Munich, 1990), 172–73.

historical and phonological reasons, of Old English influence on these words during the course of the centuries, we can also state with some certainty that nothing stands in the way of the assumption of an early borrowing from Gallo-Roman and that the Old Frisian words help to complete a picture in this area which is otherwise only partial.

Contributors

Alderik H. Blom (1978) studied Mediaeval History, Celtic, and Germanic Philology at the Universities of Utrecht and Amsterdam, and at the National University of Ireland, Galway. He obtained his Ph.D. at Peterhouse, University of Cambridge, in 2007. During 2006–2007, he was Sir John Rhys Scholar in Celtic Studies at Jesus College, Oxford. Since October 2007 he is Katherine Jex-Blake Research Fellow in Celtic Sudies at Girton College, Cambridge.

Rolf H. Bremmer Jr (1950) is Professor (by special appointment) of Frisian Language and Literature at Leiden University besides holding a lectureship in English Philology. He has published widely, including *'Hir is eskriven'. Lezen en schrijven in de Friese landen rond 1300* (2004). He has co-edited a number of volumes, most recently *Signs on the Edge. Space, Text and Margin in Medieval Manuscripts* (2007) and *Foundations of Learning. The Transfer of Encyclopaedic Knowledge in the Early Middle Ages* (2007).

Kees Dekker (1964) teaches English and Old Germanic Studies at Groningen University. His interests include the historiography of Germanic studies as witnessed by his *The Origins of Old Germanic Studies in the Low Countries* (1999). He is co-author, with Rolf Bremmer, of *Manuscripts in the Low Countries* (vol. 13 of Anglo-Saxon Manuscripts in Microfiche Facsimile, 2006) and has co-edited a number of volumes, including *Rome and the North: the Early Reception of Gregory the Great in Germanic Europe* (2001) and *Rhetoric, Royalty, and Reality: Essays on the Literary Culture of Medieval and Early Modern Scotland* (2005).

Siebren Dyk (1953) is a fellow of the Fryske Akademy, Leeuwarden, where he worked for many years on the *Wurdboek fan de Fryske Taal*. Gradually he became more involved in grammatical studies, as witnessed by his *Noun Incorporation in Frisian* (1997). He is also active in the study of Frisian dialects, notably the almost extinct dialect of the island of Schiermonnikoog, and in the historical linguistics of Frisian. At present he is preparing a comprehensive descriptive grammar of Modern West Frisian, together with Willem Visser.

Concetta Giliberto (1965) is Associate Professor in Germanic Philology at the Università degli Studi di Palermo. She wrote a study on the Frisian runic inscriptions, *Le iscrizioni runiche sullo sfondo della cultura Frisone alto-medievale* (2000), and, for example, articles on the Old English and Old High German traditions of the Fifteen Signs before Doomsday.

Eric Hoekstra (1960) is a fellow of the Fryske Akademy, Leeuwarden, and was trained as a linguist at the University of Groningen. He is especially involved in research into the grammar of Frisian dialects, often in comparative perspectives. He has also been working on a translation into Frisian of the works of Friedrich Nietzsche, such as *Dat sei Zarathustra* en *Oarekant goed en kwea*, for which he received the Obe Postma Award in 2002.

Stephen Laker (1976) holds an MA degree in German linguistics, Semitic languages and English philology from the University of Munich. He is now completing a dissertation on the early linguistic contacts between Anglo-Saxon and British Celtic at Leiden University. He has published a number of articles based on his doctoral research and on other linguistic topics.

Erika Langbroek (1951) teaches German at the Vossius Gymnasium, Amsterdam. She has published on Old High German glosses, notably *Zwischen den Zeilen: Untersuchungen zu den lateinischen Kommentaren und den deutschen Glossen der Edinburgher Handschrift Adv. Ms. 18.5.10* (1995). Together with Annelies Roeleveld she has edited *Valentin und Namelos: Mittelniederdeutsch und Neuhochdeutsch* (1997) and *Het Hartebok: Hs. Hamburg, Staats- und Universitätsbibliothek, 102c in scrinio* (2001).

Rosemarie Lühr (1946) is Professor of Indo-European Studies at the Friedrich-Schiller-Universität Jena. Her interests concern both literature and linguistics, exemplified by such books as *Studien zur Sprache des Hildebrandliedes. Teil I: Herkunft und Sprache. Teil II: Kommentar* (1982), *Expressivität und Lautgesetz im Germanischen* (1988) and *Gedichte des Skalden Egill* (2000). She is co-editor of the multi-volume *Etymologisches Wörterbuch des Althochdeutschen* (1988–..).

Henk D. Meijering (1936) is Professor Emeritus of Frisian and German at the Vrije Universiteit Amsterdam. He has written extensively on Old Frisian, including a monograph on *De Willekeuren van de Opstalsboom (1323). Een filologisch-historische monografie* (1974) and an edition of late-medieval Frisian chronicles: *Oudfriese kronieken uit het handschrift Leeuwarden RA Schw. 3992* (1986). Another interest of his is Yiddish: he has co-authored *Hebreeuwse en Jiddische woorden in het Nederlands (2002).*

Johannes (Hans) A. Mol (1954) is Director of the Department of History, Literature and Onomastics at the Fryske Akademy, Leeuwarden, and Professor of Medieval Frisian History at the University of Leiden by special appointment. In additions to many articles on medieval Frisian history, he has authored a book on the Teutonic Order in the western part of Frisia, *De Friese huizen van de Duitse orde : Nes, Steenkerk en Schoten en hun plaats in het middeleeuwse*

Friese kloosterlandschap. He is co-editor of *Military Orders and the Reformation. Choices, State Building and the Weight of Tradition* (2004).

Robert Nedoma (1961) teaches Scandinavian and Germanic Philology at the University of Vienna. His research interests range from saga literature to runic inscriptions. He is one of the co-editors of the authoritative *Reallexikon der Germanischen Altertumskunde* and author of, for example, *Kleine Grammatik des Altisländischen* ([2]2006) and *Personennamen in südgermanischen Runeninschriften* (2004).

Anne Tjerk Popkema (1975) studied Frisian Language and Literature at Groningen University, specializing in Old Frisian and lexicography. After working on an edition of the Old Frisian incunabulum at the Fryske Akademy, Leeuwarden, he was employed by the Frisian Department of Kiel University in 2004. Besides teaching Old Frisian, he is completing and editing the unfinished *Altfriesisches Handwörterbuch* by the late Dietrich Hofmann. His publications include studies on the Old Frisian incunabulum, on Old Frisian lexicology and on the history of Old Frisian texts.

Irmengard Rauch (1933) is Professor of German linguistics, both historical and modern, at the University of California, Berkeley. Since her first book on Old High German diphthongization, she has published, besides numerous articles, *The Old Saxon Language: Grammar, Epic Narrative, Linguistic Interference* (1992); *Semiotic Insights: The Data Do the Talking* (1999); *The Gothic Language. Grammar, Genetic Provenance and Typology, Readings* (2003). She has also been very active in editorial work, including the five volumes of *(New) Insights in Germanic Linguisitics* (1995–2002). Her latest book is *The Phonology / Paraphonology Interface and the Sounds of German across Time* (2008).

Joseph C. Salmons (1956) is Professor of German at the University of Wisconsin-Madison. He has published widely on modern and historical aspects of the German language and on general, comparative and variation linguistics. He is co-author of the *Cambridge History of the Germanic Languages* [in press] and is executive editor of *Diachronica. International Journal of Historical Linguistics*.

Sjoerd M. Siebinga (1977) studied English and Old Germanic Studies at the University of Amsterdam. He has held appointments at the Fryske Akademy, Leeuwarden, and the Instituut voor Nederlandse Lexicologie, Leiden. At present, he is a technical developer of the European Library, a project to provide access to the forty-seven national libraries of Europe, housed in the Koninklijke

Bibliotheek, The Hague. He finalized and edited *An Old Frisian Etymological Dictionary* (2005) by the late Dirk Boutkan.

Laura Catharine Smith (1971) is Assistant Professor in Germanic Linguistics at the Brigham Young University, Provo (Utah). She received her PhD from the University of Wisconsin-Madison in 2004 and has several articles recently published and about to be published, such as 'The Resilience of Prosodic Templates in the History of West Germanic' and, together with Joseph Salmons and David Holsinger, 'The Mediation of Perceptual Cues: Evidence from Cluster Reduction and Vowel Loss'.

Ineke van 't Spijker (1954) is an independent scholar in Cambridge, where she is a Life member of Clare Hall, Cambridge. As a historian, she has specialized in the religious thought of the High Middle Ages, with an emphasis on the Victorines. In addition to many articles, she has written *Als door een speciaal stempel. Traditie en vernieuwing in Heiligenlevens uit Noordwest-Frankrijk (1050–1150)* (1990) and *Fictions of the Inner Life: Religious Literature and Formation of the Self in the Eleventh and Twelfth Centuries* (2004).

Oebele Vries (1947) teaches Old Frisian and Frisian History at the University of Groningen and has published frequently in these two fields of study. His most recent publication is a trilingual edition of a voluminous anthology of Old Frisian texts, provided with an introduction and Dutch and Modern Frisian translations: *Asega is het dingtijd? De hoogtepunten van de Oudfriese tekst-overlevering* (2007). He was co-editor of *Aspects of Old Frisian Philology* (1990) and *Advances in Old Frisian Philology* (1998).

David Yeandle (1955) is Professor of German at King's College, University of London. His research interests include both the modern and the historical side of German. His publications include a *Commentary on the Soltane and Jeschute Episodes in Book III of Wolfram von Eschenbach's PARZIVAL* (1984) and a semantic study of the medieval German vocabulary of 'shame', *Schame im Alt- und Mittelhochdeutschen bis um 1210: eine sprach- und literatur-geschichtliche Untersuchung unter besonderer Berücksichtigung der Heraus-bildung einer ethischen Bedeutung* (2001).